Banking Strategy, Credit Appraisal, and Lending Decisions

A Risk–Return Framework

Second Edition

Hrishikes Bhattacharya

OXFORD

UNIVERSITY PRESS

OXFORD
UNIVERSITY PRESS

Oxford University Press is a department of the University of Oxford.
It furthers the University's objective of excellence in research, scholarship,
and education by publishing worldwide. Oxford is a registered trademark of
Oxford University Press in the UK and in certain other countries

Published in India by
Oxford University Press
22 workspace, 2nd Floor, 1/22 Asaf Ali Road, New Delhi 110002

First Edition published in 1997
Second Edition published in 2011

ISBN-13 (print edition): 978-0-19-807410-6
ISBN-10 (print edition): 0-19-807410-7

ISBN-13 (eBook): 978-0-19-908856-0
ISBN-10 (eBook): 0-19-908856-X

Typeset in Amo Pro 11/13.2
by Excellent Laser Typesett ers, Pitampura, Delhi 110 034
Printed in India by Repro India Limited

Banking Strategy, Credit Appraisal, and Lending Decisions

Dedicated to
Hena Chandra
under whose wings I continue to fly

Contents

Appendices

Annexures

For you O princely friend, Incomparable lover, the stintless, boundless gift. That which you gave
I give, and am debtor still.

—Rabindranath Tagore

Preface to the Second Edition

The first edition of the book came out in 1997. Since then it has seen 12 reprints, which indicate that it has been well-received by students and the banking community.

I had refrained myself from writing a second edition for a long time because so many changes were taking place around the globe changing the very notion of banking. The system was in a fluid state.

Now that the system has stabilised largely, I thought it was time to come out with a second edition.

I have written three new chapters for the book, which are the products of my considerable research during the past two years. In the first section of Chapter 1, I have dealt with the impact of capital regulation on the risk attitude and profitability of banks. In the second section, I have provided alternative strategies to protect banks from a liquidity crisis.

Chapter 2 discusses the liquidity strategies of banks. Assets–liabilities strategies, which are part of liquidity management, follow thereafter.

Lending strategies are discussed at length in Chapter 4. I have adopted a portfolio approach in developing models for credit exposure and loan management within a risk–return framework. These should be part of a loan policy document of a bank.

Most of other chapters are virtually rewritten to accommodate overwhelming changes that have taken place during the past many years.

The book will continue to be useful to students pursuing post-graduate programme in management, aspiring chartered accountants, cost accountants, lenders, bankers, and credit analysts of rating agencies.

hbcharya@iimcal.ac.in
November 2010

HRISHIKES BHATTACHARYA

Acknowledgements

Besides my students and participants of various management development programmes who have enriched my knowledge about the 'real thing' in business, I have benefitted from the cooperation of a number of banking and non-banking organisations which have allowed me to use their data under the condition of anonymity. I thank all of them.

My wife Gouri and children Orphi and Saraswat ensure that I am the least disturbed during the preparation of the manuscript. I am grateful to them for bearing with me.

For the first edition of the book, Subal Mukherjee, Asit Kumar Manna, Amiya Adhikary, and Dibyendu Das, amongst themselves, produced the typescript in the shortest possible time, in spite of much other work that I usually gave them. Akshoy Singha and Bijay Bikash Chandra helped me in the statistical analysis and drawing diagrams. Mehboob Alam, Md. Ilias, Patras Singh, and Sudhakar Khan xeroxed and arranged the manuscript in the form of chapters. I continue to thank them all.

Bijay K. Datta, former Executive Director of UCO Bank and a very close friend of mine has helped me in updating various chapters of the book. He has also read the first chapter of the new edition and offered constructive suggestions. If I even try to thank him, he will reprimand me. So, I stop short of it.

I have benefitted from long discussion with Jay Prokash Chandra, Chartered Accountant, on the current accounting practices relating to profit and loss account and balance sheet.

Debanjan Bhattacharya (my little master) who is now doing his PhD in the United States has helped me solve many mathematical and statistical problems. Indrajit Bhattacharya has drawn several graphs for the book. They are so young that I cannot thank them; I can only bless them with a prosperous life.

The first edition of the book came out when Nitasha Devasar was Senior Commissioning Editor at Oxford University Press. Now as the Academic Director of the Press, she continues to be as enthusiastic as ever. I always like her constant but respectful prodding but for which the manuscript of the present edition would not have been ready even by the extended time that she kindly allowed.

HRISHIKES BHATTACHARYA

Acknowledgements

Light, my light, the world-filling light, the eye-kissing light, heart-sweetening light!
—Rabindranath Tagore

Introduction

The classical economic functions of banks and other financial intermediaries all over the world have remained virtually unchanged in modern times. What has changed is the institutional structure, the instruments, and the techniques used in performing these functions.

The pace of structural and technological changes depends upon the intensity of competition, and also ironically, regulatory restrictions (which need not necessarily mean governmental controls); these can as well emanate from the market in a competitive environment. For nearly half a decade, the Indian financial system has been experiencing these two apparently conflicting phenomena. On the one hand, we find interest rate deregulation, and on the other, capital adequacy requirement and prudential norms. In a situation like this, institutions are compelled to work out a strategic framework with well-defined objectives.

Although profit has all along been *the* motive force of bankers all over the world, it has never been accepted as such by economic planners; rather, attempts are always made to suppress it. Only during the past 15 years or so has profit come to be accepted as legitimate. The power of this motive force was demonstrated in India during the first four years of liberalisation, when a number of major commercial banks in the nationalised sector registered a turnaround, shedding a legacy of 25 years of accumulated bad debts.

Since profit is now the major focus of the Indian banking industry, in spite of the continuance of directed lending, the strategic plan must evolve around a profit objective, which demands the building up of quality loan-assets portfolios and adequate capital growth to ensure continuity of the banking organisation. Section I of the first chapter[1] deals with this. We have used the case study of a nationalised bank that had a staggering level of accumulated losses, and intended to turn around. The data sets are so designed as to maintain the bank's anonymity. In Section II the importance of loan policy documents in protecting banks against over exposure and maladministration of the credit department, and in arresting further creation of non-performing assets, is highlighted.[2]

[1] Now Chapter 3.
[2] Now Chapter 4.

In Chapter 2 through Chapter 8,[3] the reader is first familiarised with various financial and operating variables of a borrowing unit, and then asked to take a critical look at each such variable from a lender's point of view. In doing this, I have highlighted the differences in approach between a corporate finance manager and a credit manager of a lending organisation. Chapter 3 is primarily engaged in dispelling doubts and controversies subsisting between a borrower and the banker for a correct understanding of the borrower's working capital requirement. We have shown that the need for working capital emanates from the techno-financial structure of a business.

Chapter 9[4] introduces the new technology of lending, beginning with the Tandon Committee's and Chore Group's recommendations as are relevant today. Each aspect of the modern techniques of lending is covered in a separate chapter, in which actual examples from the business and financial world are worked out in great detail to enable a lender to use this book as a reference for his day-to-day operations. Evaluation of business forecasting—an area of weakness for most lenders—is dealt with in Chapter 10[5] with the help of statistical tools made simpler to facilitate easy understanding. In the following chapter[6] and in Chapter 13,[7] besides discussing the funds-flow approach to credit appraisal, the importance of cash flow analysis as a modern day tool of appraisal and monitoring is highlighted.

As banks and financial institutions are expected to move in a big way towards project financing in the years to come, I have, in Chapters 14 and 15,[8] covered the major aspects of project appraisal and financing—beginning with product identification and evaluation, to feasibility studies, and ending with the lending decision. In doing so, I have drawn the attention of the banker to the fact that all financially viable projects are not always bankable, though the obverse is always true. This last point is vindicated at the end of the ensuing chapter, where I have evaluated an actual project. The concerned bank received this proposal for composite financing—both term loan and working capital.

Chapter 16[9] is written in the belief that techniques of credit appraisal and lending decisions are universal in character and neutral to the size of the loan. I have attempted to prove this point by taking up the case of a small business loan proposal from the files of a bank.

The final chapter[10] is devoted to a full-scale credit risk analysis of a lending decision and pricing of a particular risk category of a borrower. The approach is kept simple and practical and demonstrated with real-life examples, so that the system proposed can be easily implemented by lending organisations in India.

The book is the natural outcome of an evolutionary process that began 15 years ago when I first wrote a book titled *Comprehensive Credit Appraisal*. This was followed by another, *Bank Lending*, written in 1990. The present one is the product of my experience of nearly three decades first as a practising banker, then as a teacher offering courses to MBA students of the institute where I am

[3] Now Chapters 5–11.
[4] Now Chapter 12.
[5] Now Chapter 13.
[6] Now Chapter 14.
[7] Now Chapter 16.
[8] Now Chapters 17 and 18.
[9] Now Chapter 19.
[10] Now Chapter 20.

presently engaged, and of other institutes and universities to which I am attached, and finally, as a trainer and consultant to a number of banking organisations and a cross-section of a wide range of industries.

The book will benefit post-graduate students in management and those pursuing courses in chartered accountancy, cost accountancy, and secretarial practice.

This book will be of immense help to bankers, lenders, and credit analysts of rating agencies, who can use it as a reference book.

HRISHIKES BHATTACHARYA

Indian Institute of Management Calcutta
September 1996

Critics never worry me unless they are right—but that does not often occur.

—Noel Coward

1 Capital Regulation and Risk Management Strategy

INTRODUCTION

Banking is the most regulated among all industrial sectors of the economy. More than 25 years ago Buser et al.[1] remarked that a bank has traditionally been conceived as more than just another business firm; it operates under unusual regulatory restrictions. The regulatory environment has not changed much since then, except that the focus has now shifted towards stringent capital regulation.[2] Banking is now the only industry which is subject to international capital regulation supervised through the Basle Capital Accords.

There are arguments for and against capital regulation, which are summarised below. Some of the papers referred to here have featured in both sets of arguments. This is either due to their being review articles or the author(s) is (are) referring to an argument which may not be the main theme of the paper. Our intention is to divide the arguments between two groups, not the authors.

Arguments for Capital Regulation

1. Banks are more risky than any other business firm; capital reduces bank risk-taking and provides risk-mitigating incentive for bank managers.[3]

2. Banks are vulnerable to runs due to provision of liquidity services; the depositors suffer from an asymmetry of information about a bank's assets which may cause runs; an all deposit structure could lead to runs when the value of real assets falls;

[1] Buser, Stephen A., Andrew H. Chen and Edward J. Kane, 'Federal Deposit Insurance, Regulatory Policy, and Optimal Bank Capital', *Journal of Finance*, March 1981, 35(1): 51–60.

[2] Matten, Chris, *Managing Bank Capital: Capital Allocation and Performance Measurement* (2nd edition), John Wiley & Sons Ltd., West Sussex, UK, 2001.

[3] Ross, Stephen, 'The Determination of Financial Structure: The Incentive Signaling Approach', *Bell Journal of Economics*, 1977, 8: 23–40; Harris, Milton and Artur Raviv, 'Capital Structure and the Informational Role of Debt', *Journal of Finance*, June 1990, 65(2): 321–49; Cebenoyan, Sinan A. and Philip E. Strahan, 'Risk Management, Capital Structure and Lending at Banks', *Journal of Banking & Finance*, 2004, 28: 19–43.

a bank's capital, therefore, forms a kind of cushion against losses for depositors.[4]

3. Increase in leverage increases the cost of financial distress; cost of financial distress rises with the decline of the capital ratio.[5]

4. Banks are prone to take extraordinary risks; high risk-taking has almost become part of banking culture—a protective equity cushion should vary directly with a bank's risk exposure.[6]

5. Capital regulation is necessary for long-term solvency and public credibility—capital acting as buffer against insolvency; maintenance of a sufficient capital cushion can solve the financial fragility problem and prevent a liquidity crisis from occurring.[7]

6. In the absence of sufficient equity 'at stake' banks may make investment decisions which could be sub-optimal for the society, though optimal for the shareholders; banks are motivated to reduce assets risk in the face of higher capital requirement; it induces the banks to choose safer assets, thereby mitigating the 'moral hazard' problem which the depositors face.[8]

7. Capital regulation has the desirable effect of discouraging unsound and

[4] Diamond, Douglas W. and Philip H. Dybvig, 'Bank Runs, Deposit Insurance and Liquidity', *Journal of Political Economy*, 1983, 91(3): 401–19; Charles J. Jacklin and Sudipto Bhattacharya, 'Distinguishing Panics and Information-based Bank-runs: Welfare and Policy Implications', *Journal of Political Economy*, 1988, 96: 568–92; Bhattacharya, Sudipto and Anjan V. Thakor, 'Contemporary Banking Theory', *Journal of Financial Intermediation*, 1993, 3: 2–50; Diamond, Douglas W. and Raghuram G. Rajan 'A Theory of Bank Capital', *Journal of Finance*, 2000, 55 (6): 2431–65; Kashyap, Anil K., Raghuram G. Rajan and J.C. Stein, 'Banks as Liquidity Providers: An Explanation for the Coexistence of Lending and Deposit Taking', *Journal of Finance*, 2002, 57(1): 33–73; Morrison, Allan D. and Lucy White, 'Crisis and Capital Requirements in Banking', *American Economic Review*, 2005, 95(5): 1548–72.

[5] Cooke, Peter, 'International Convergence of Capital Adequacy Measurement and Standards', in Edward, P.M. Gardener (ed.), *The Future of Financial Systems and Services*, The Macmillan Press Ltd., London, 1990, pp. 296–310; Berger, Allen N., Richard J. Herring and Giorgio P. Szego, 'The Role of Capital in Financial Institutions', *Journal of Banking & Finance*, 1995,19: 393–430.

[6] Kerkhof, Joroen and Bertrand Melenberg, 'Back-testing for Risk-based Regulatory Capital', *Journal of Banking & Finance*, 2004, 28: 1845–65; Lindquist, Kjersti-Gro, 'Banks' Buffer Capital: How Important is Risk', *Journal of International Money and Finance*, 2004, 23: 495–513; Kopecky, Kenneth J. and David VanHoose, 'A Model of the Monetary Sector with and without Binding Capital Requirements', *Journal of Banking & Finance*, 2004, 28: 633–46; Kashyap, Anil K., Raghuram G. Rajan and J.C. Stein, 'Banks as Liquidity Providers: An Explanation for the Co-existence of Lending and Deposit Taking', *Journal of Finance*, 2002, 57(1): 33–73.

[7] Dowd, Kevin, 'Bank Capital Adequacy versus Deposit Insurance', *Journal of Financial Services Research*, 2000, 17: 7–15; Kashyap, Rajan, and Stein, 'Banks as Liquidity Providers', 2002; Barrios, Victor E. and Juan M. Blanco, 'The Effectiveness of Bank Capital Adequacy Regulation: A Theoretical and Empirical Approach', *Journal of Banking & Finance*, 2003, 27: 1935–58.

[8] Furlong, F.T. and M.C. Keeley, 'Capital Regulation and Bank Risk Taking: A Note', *Journal of Banking & Finance*, 1989, 13: 883–91; and Furlong, F.T. and M.C. Keeley, 'Reexamination of the Mean-variance Analysis of Bank Capital Regulation', *Journal of Banking & Finance*, 1990,14: 69–84; Cooper, Russel and Thomas Ross, 'Bank Runs, Deposit Insurance, and Capital Requirements', *International Economic Review*, 2002, 43: 55–71.

undesirable institutions from setting up operations.[9]

8. Increasing the capital standards results in a contract adjustment that mitigates between the higher cost of required capital and the cost of probable bankruptcy resulting in lower risk of insolvency.[10]

9. When monitoring costs are above a critical level, regulators are able to increase efficiency by imposing a higher capital adequacy requirement.[11]

10. In a real world, only a small fraction of the banking system is typically constrained by capital requirements.[12]

11. Capital regulation is necessary but, in a dynamic environment, it is not sufficient to protect banks from high risk-taking; it should be combined with deposit-rate controls.[13]

Arguments against Capital Regulation

1. Higher capital ratio does not always predict a lower probability of bank failure—

the relationship between the capital ratio and bank safety is often weak.[14]

2. Capital regulation decreases loan supply, dampens entrepreneurial activity, reduces the size of the banking industry, and the quantity of intermediation; it may also exacerbate the business cycle and even accentuate systemic risk.[15]

3. If it is too costly for a bank to raise equity to meet higher capital standards tomorrow, an alternative is to increase the risk today.[16]

4. The counter-cyclical regulatory capital requirements are inconsistent with 'market capital requirements' prompting banks to escape stricter regulatory norms in good times by regulatory arbitrage, while providing little relief in bad times as banks are held to higher market norms.[17]

5. A higher capital requirement acts as a tax on depositors by discouraging the risk-

[9] Morrison, Allan D. and Lucy White, 'Crisis and Capital Requirements in Banking', *American Economic Review*, 2005, 95(5): 1548–72.

[10] Santos, João, 'Bank Capital and Equity Investment Regulations', *Journal of Banking & Finance*, 1999, 23: 1095–1120.

[11] Morrison and White, 'Crisis and Capital Requirements in Banking', 2005.

[12] VanHoose, David, 'Theories of Bank Behavior under Capital Regulation', *Journal of Banking & Finance*, 2007, 31: 3680–97.

[13] Hellman, Thomas, Kevin C. Murdock and Joseph E. Stiglitz, 'Liberalization, Moral Hazard in Banking and Prudential Regulation: Are Capital Requirements Enough?', *American Economic Review*, 2000, 90: 147–65.

[14] Thomson, J.B., 'Predicting Bank Failures in 1980s', *Federal Reserve Bank of Cleveland Economic Review*, 1991, 27(1): 9–20.

[15] Santomero, Anthony M. and Ronald D. Watson, 'Determining an Optimal Capital Standard for the Banking Industry', *Journal of Finance*, September 1977, 32(4): 1267–82; Crockett, A. 'Marrying the Micro-and Macro-Prudential Dimensions of Financial Stability', Speech Delivered at the Eleventh International Conference of Banking Supervisors, Basel, 2000; Kopecky and VanHoose, 'A Model of the Monetary Sector', 2004; Estrella, Arturo, 'The Cyclical Behaviour of Optimal Bank Capital', *Journal of Banking and Finance*, 2004, 28: 1469–98.

[16] Blum Jürg, 'Do Capital Adequacy Requirements Reduce Risks in Banking?', *Journal of Banking and Finance*, 1999, 23: 755–77.

[17] Diamond, Douglas W. and Raghuram G. Rajan, 'The Credit Crisis: Conjectures about Causes and Remedies', *American Economic Review*, 2009, 99(2): 606–10.

taking behaviour of banks, which reduces inter-bank competition for deposits to the disadvantage of the depositors.[18]

6. When banks are forced to increase the capital ratio that lowers the expected return they may respond by choosing an assets portfolio with a higher risk; higher capital requirement might induce banks to seek higher returns in areas that are high risk or outside their core business.[19]

7. Capital regulation, if not based on any consistent economic soundness standards, results in regulatory tax which drives the market to seek alternative ways to reach equilibrium like regulatory capital arbitrage, innovative and often risky financial instruments and so on.[20]

8. Supervisory capital restrictions have become effectively irrelevant to the largest US banks since about 1992 as they have chosen their own (market valued) capital ratios in response to market pressure.[21]

During recent times, advocates of capital regulation have marched over those against it. The current belief is that bank capital has special purposes not amenable to market laws; when risk goes up, banks should increase capital, because they need a bigger buffer. To echo a sarcastic Miller: when it comes to banking the market cannot be left to their own devices.[22] In fact, bank capital regulation is based on this premise. Capital regulation is now taken for granted. The question now is not about the efficacy or otherwise of capital regulation but about the arithmetic of calculating capital–assets ratio and the algebra of risk models to determine what should be the appropriate ratio. None of the financial liberalisation indexes developed by various researchers considers bank capital regulation as an indicator of financial repression,[23] though capital regulation has the effect of reducing the size of financial intermediation. The Board of Governors of the Federal Reserve System[24]

[18] Bhattacharya and Thakor, 'Contemporary Banking Theory', 1993.

[19] Kim, D. and A.M. Santomero, 'Risk in Banking and Capital Regulation', *Journal of Finance*, 1988, 43: 1219–33; Rochet, Jean-Charles, 'Capital Requirements and Behavior of Banks', *European Economic Review*, 1992, 36(5): 1137–78; Gennotte, G. and D. Pyle, 'Capital Controls and Bank Risk', *Journal of Banking & Finance*, 1991, 15: 805–24.

[20] Kane, Edward J., 'Good Intensions and Unintended Evil: The Case Against Selective Credit Allocation', *Journal of Money, Credit and Banking*, February 1977, 9: 55–69; Gardener, E.P.M., 'Innovation and New Structural Frontiers in Banking', in Philip Arêtes, (ed.), *Contemporary Issues in Money and Banking: Essays in Honour of Stephen Frowen*, The Macmillan Press Ltd., London, 1988, pp. 7–27; Donahoo, K.K. and S. Shaffer, 'Capital Requirements and the Securitization Decision', *Quarterly Review of Economics and Business*, 1991, 31(4): 12–23; Merton, R.C., 'Financial Innovation and the Management and Regulation of Financial Institutions', *Journal of Banking & Finance*, 1995, 19: 461–81; Jones, David, 'Emerging Problems with the Basel Capital Accord: Regulatory Capital Arbitrage and Related Issues', *Journal of Banking & Finance*, 2000, 24: 35–58; Pauls, Calem and Michael

Lacour-Little, 'Risk-based Capital Requirements for Mortgage Loans', *Journal of Banking & Finance*, 2004, 28: 647–72.

[21] Flannery, Mark. J. and Kasturi P. Rangan, 'What Caused the Bank Capital Build-up of the 1990?', FDIC Center for Financial Research, Working Paper, 2004–03, 2004.

[22] Miller, Merton H., 'Do the M&M Propositions Apply to Banks?', *Journal of Banking & Finance*, 1995, 19: 483–89.

[23] Abiad, Abdul and Ashoka Mody, 'Financial Reform: What Shakes It? What Shapes It?', *American Economic Review*, March 2005, 95(1): 66–88.

[24] Federal Reserve System, Board of Governors, 'The Supervisory Capital Assessment Program:

while presenting 'The Supervisory Capital Assessment Program (SCAP): An Overview of Results' (2009) aptly captured the essence of the current mood in the introduction to the report:

A banking organisation holds capital to guard against uncertainty. Capital reassures institution's depositors, creditors and counter parties—and the institution itself—that an event such as an unexpected surge in losses or an unanticipated deterioration in earnings will not impair its ability to engage in lending to creditworthy borrowers and protect the savings of its depositors.

The report goes on to determine the amount of additional capital that the 19 largest bank-holding companies (BHCs) are required to bring in. Although at year-end 2008 all the 19 BHCs exceeded minimum regulatory-capital ratios, the report advocates increase of capital for about half of these BHCs. Banks holding capital buffers stem from the fear of costly regulatory actions, including loss of charter if there is a violation of the minimum capital standards in future for reasons beyond the control of banks.

Literature published in the aftermath of the recent financial and banking crisis have highlighted the existence of a culture of excessive risk-taking due to high performance pressure on the CEOs of banks resulting in huge investments of short-term funds in exotic mortgage backed securities and other risky loans. Fahlenbrach and Stultz have found that CEOs took exposures that they felt were profitable for their shareholders *ex-ante*, but these exposures performed very poorly *ex-post*.[25]

The first point that is missed in the debate is why there is a change in banks' risk-taking behaviour. Bankers are known to be conservative people. Why have they crossed boundaries and reached for high-risk-assets during the past two decades—obviously for high returns—but what is the immanent cause behind such a high 'return pressure' on CEOs of banks?

The second point is the virtual unconcern about servicing the capital that banks hold, or are required to bring in, to conform to capital standards. While it is said that the banks should be subjected to market discipline, equity holders are often not considered as constituents of the 'market'. For example, Flannery and Rangan define the market as bank counter parties, which comprises 'depositors, guarantee beneficiaries, FX and derivative traders' but not equity investors.[26]

Banks could be 'special institutions' but they are primarily business organisations whose ultimate aim is to generate enough profit to satisfy a market determined Return on Equity (ROE). Capital structure (mix of equity and debt) of any business is an endogenous variable geared towards generating a required level of sales (which is also an endogenous variable) with a certain return from which to earn the required profit to satisfy the ROE requirement of the shareholders. For banks, sales are analogous to generating banking assets; everything else is

---

Overview of Results', 2009. Available at http://www.federalreserve.govt.

[25] See, for example, Douglas W. Diamond and Raghuram G. Rajan, 2009; and Fahlenbrach, Rüdigar and René M. Stulz, 'Bank CEO Incentives and the Credit Crisis', National Bureau of Economic Research,

---

Working Paper 15212, July 2009. Available at http://www.nber.org/papers/w15212.

[26] Flannery and Rangan, 'What Caused the Bank Capital Build-up of the 1990?', 2004. However some writers, while dealing with 'moral hazard' problem in a market discipline framework, do include shareholders along with depositors and other debt holders (see, for example, Park, Sangkyun and Stavros Peristiani, 'Are Bank Shareholders Enemies of Regulators or a Potential Source of Market Discipline?', *Journal of Banking & Finance*, 2007, 31: 2493–2515.

the same. As capital regulation is administered through the capital–assets ratio, an increase in the ratio lowers down the sales (banking assets) generating capacity of banks. Thus, regulatory intervention seeking to alter the capital structure of banks, transforms the character of some of the endogenous variables (like leverage and assets-capacity) to exogenous variables. Such intervention may defeat the very purpose of capital regulation. With fewer assets available, banks may be forced to cross boundaries and reach for high-return-high-risk assets, which have the potential of endangering the system as a whole.

In particular, we seek to establish the following:

1. Bank capital regulation has reduced the growth of assets of US banks substantially over the pre-regulation period. The reduced level of assets has forced the banks to make investments in assets with higher rate of return in order to earn enough to satisfy a certain market determined ROE.

2. As higher rate of return on assets is associated with higher risk; capital regulation has ultimately resulted in increasing the level of losses, thereby increasing the risk of the banking industry.

Some of the literature cited above has focused on financial deregulation, competition, financial market developments, impact of information technology, and return to scale while explaining the performance of banks, particularly during the capital regulation period. We have instead put forward a single variable (capital regulation) explanation for the rising risk of the banking industry.

This study is based on data of US insured banks for the period, 1950–2004 as available from the Historical Statistics on Banking published by the Federal Deposit Insurance Corporation.[27] We have chosen US as the country of study, because of the consistency of the time series data, a transparent reporting system, and more particularly, because the recent financial and banking crisis originated in this country.

Prior to 1980 bank supervisors in the US did not impose specific numerical capital adequacy standards. Instead, the supervisors applied informal and subjective measures tailored to the circumstances of individual institutions. Since 1980, bank supervisors have placed much more emphasis on precisely defined numerical minimum capital standards. This was later firmed up with the passage of the Institutional Lending and Supervision Act of 1983, which adopted a leverage ratio of primary capital (consisting mainly of Equity and Loan Loss Reserves), to average total assets.[28] The first Basle Capital Accord, which was introduced in 1988, expanded the idea and brought in international convergence of capital standards. The data period for the study is, therefore, divided into two parts: (1) The pre-regulation period (1950–79), and (2) the post-regulation period (1980–2004).

Unlike Saunders and Flannery and Rangan who prefer market-value accounting, we have followed book-value accounting (nominal values) as in Kopecky and VanHoose.[29] This approach

---

[27]   Available at http://www2.fdic.gov/hsob/hsobrpt.asp. Accessed on 26 February 2009.

[28]   Besanko, David and George Kanatas, 'The Regulation of Bank Capital: Do Capital Standards Promote Safety?', Journal of Financial Intermediation, 1996, 5: 160–83; Federal Deposit Insurance Corporation (FDIC), 'Basel and the Evolution of Capital Regulation: Moving Forward, Looking Back', Federal Deposit Insurance Corporation, 2003. Available at http://www.fdic.gov/bank/analytical/fyi/2003.

[29] Saunders, A., Financial Institutions Management, McGraw-Hill, New York, 2000; Flannery and Rangan, 'What Caused the Bank Capital Build-up of the

appears to be more appropriate while presenting a critique of bank capital regulation, which itself is based on book-value accounting. Definitions of the variables are given in Appendix 1.1.

The study is diagnostic in nature. Statistical models presented in the text are based on the ordinary least square (OLS) linear regression.[30] These are not meant for forecasting. However, in a time series model, the presence of serial correlation though does not cause bias in the estimate of the regression coefficients, it may result in underestimation of standard errors (and overestimation of 't' values), questioning the validity of the model. We have, therefore, used autoregressive models as prescribed in the Ochrane-Orcutt estimation procedure wherever serial correlation is found to be present at $\alpha = 0.01$. These are given in Appendix 1.2. It may be seen that though the 't' values of the regression models have fallen as expected, they mostly remain significant (or otherwise) as in the OLS estimations presented in the text.

We have not also de-trended the data in the text, as our purpose is to capture the trends. However, in order to bring out the correct trends it may be necessary to eliminate any obscuring cyclical or random (irregular) fluctuations. To partially minimise the impact we have excluded unusual years from our data set, wherever found appropriate, following Demirgüc-Kund and Detragiache.[31] Additionally, we have

taken a three-year moving average of the data. Regressions run on moving average of variables are reported in Appendix 1.3. The findings are similar to those in the text.

General Assumptions

1. Cash flows from securitised assets are continuously invested in either balance sheet assets or other securitised assets. Income (loss) derived from such transactions is ultimately reflected in the return on (balance sheet) assets.
2. Risk is defined as the probability of loss of assets. As losses are the materialisation of risks, increase in assets loss is considered as an indicator of an increase of risk in the banking industry.
3. While calculating capital ratios subordinated debt is excluded; only Tier I capital (equity) is considered. This is in line with major studies cited earlier. For 1980–2004 average subordinated debt is found to be only 11.5 per cent of the total 'regulatory capital' of US banks.
4. Statistical models used throughout this study are based on ordinary least square linear regressions.

INTER-RELATIONSHIP AMONG CAPITAL, ASSETS, ROA, AND ROE

The basic equation that captures the relationship among equity capital (C), return on assets (ROA), and return on equity (ROE) is given by:

$$ROE = E/C \tag{1.1}$$

where E, is earnings

$$Or, E = ROE * C \tag{1.2}$$

1990?', 2004; Kopecky and VanHoose, 'A Model of the Monetary Sector', 2006.

[30] The technique of least square regression analysis is discussed in Chapter 2 under 'Determining Core Liabilities and Assets'. It is discussed more fully in Chapter 13. (For further insights see, Norman R. Draper and Harry Smith, *Applied Regression Analysis* (2nd edition), John Wiley & Sons Inc., New York, 1981.

[31] Demirgüc-Kund, Asli and Enrica Detragiache, 'Cross-country Empirical Studies of Systemic Bank

Distress: A Survey', International Monetary Fund, Washington DC , IMF Working Paper, 05/96, 2005.

E is further defined as A * ROA, where A is assets. Equation 1.1 can now be re-arranged as:

$$C = (A * ROA)/ROE$$
$$\text{Or, } C/A = ROA/ROE \tag{1.3}$$

$$\text{Or, } ROA = (C/A)* (E/C)$$
$$\text{Or, } ROA = E/A \tag{1.4}$$

Equation 1.3 is an identity, the LHS of which is the Capital–Assets Ratio (CAR).

ROE of an industry is market determined in a risk–return framework. Average ROE should remain fixed or change slowly over a long period. When there is a substantial shift in the required ROE, it can be presumed that the market has altered the risk–return characteristics of the industry.[32] In fact, growth rate of ROE (CAGR) of US banks was a mere 0.46 per cent for 1950–2004. The null hypothesis that mean ROE of 1950–79 has remained the same during 1980–2004 $[H_0: \mu_1 - \mu_2 = 0]$ cannot be rejected ($Z < 1.96$) at $\alpha = 0.05$.

ROE is also not dependent on the amount of capital but on the risk characteristics of the business. It is, therefore, not advisable to establish a functional relationship between ROE and capital.

Since income and assets strategies of a bank are determined *ex-ante* (as explained later) henceforth, we will be taking the income and assets variables at before income/assets loss like assets before loss (ABL), earnings before loss (EBL), return on assets before loss [ROA (B)], and return on equity before loss [ROE (B)]. These are more fully defined in Appendix 1.1.

Variation in ROE (B) can be measured indirectly by establishing a functional relation derived

from Equation 1 such as, EBL = f (Capital). The regression results are shown in Table 1.1.

TABLE 1.1   Results of Regression Analysis: EBL vs Capital

Period	Constant	Coefficient of Capital
1950–79	−1484.16 (−0.405)	0.179**** (56.91)
1980–2004	−5529.67 (−1.782)	0.177**** (22.07)
1950–2004	−414.63 (−0.405)	0.189**** (48.69)

Note: ****significant at $\alpha < 0.001$.

Table 1.1 shows that the coefficient of capital, which is virtually the ROE (B) of the industry in terms of Equation 1.2, remained almost constant at around 18 per cent during both pre- and post-regulation periods.

Income Strategy of Banks

With the ROE thus fixed (and it is risky for a bank to alter the market determined ROE as capital may move out or move in to the disadvantage of the bank), the earnings of a bank should rise or fall in response to the rise or fall in capital.

The income strategy of a bank in the absence of capital regulation will be:

Required		To be achieved
C * ROE (B)	= EBL =	ROA (B) * ABL

where, ROE (B) is fixed and there is no restriction to assets growth.

When there is no restriction on assets growth, and assuming that there are enough investment opportunities available in the market at a given risk-tolerance rate, the required earnings can be achieved by increasing assets proportionately without altering the standard ROA.

When the regulatory CAR restricts the growth in assets by a certain capital multiplier (M),

[32] Even during the new ROE period, the average ROE shall remain constant.

(which is the reciprocal of CAR), a bank has to increase earnings (EBL) by contracting assets with higher returns (which may fall beyond the existing risk-tolerance level of the bank). The income strategy of the bank, therefore, changes during the regulation period as shown below:

Required   *To be achieved*
C * ROE (B)   = EBL =   ROA (B) * C * M

where, *ROE (B)* is fixed but there is restriction to assets growth.

These two propositions are graphically represented in Figure 1.1.

In Period I (pre-regulation), Assets (I) grow freely with the rise in capital at a given ROA (I). During Period II (post-regulation), growth of assets is lower than in Period I as it is restricted by the capital-multiplier (M). When capital increases in Period II earnings shall increase to ROE * C', ROE remaining constant, but assets could be increased only to C' * M which is less than Assets I. Consequently, return on assets increases to level II.

Hence, ROA (II) = E'/(C' * M) or, (ROE * C')/ (C' * M) or, ROE/M.

We can now rewrite the pre- and post-regulation strategies of banks in terms of capital-multiplier (M) as follows:

PRE-REGULATION

Required   *To be achieved*
C * ROE (B)   = EBL =   ROA (B) * C * M_U

POST-REGULATION

Required   *To be achieved*
C * ROE (B)   = EBL =   ROA (B) * C * M_R

Subscripts $_U$ and $_R$ denote unrestricted and restricted level respectively.

The following two propositions follow from this:

1. Proposition I: When $M_U/M_R \gtreqless 1$, ROA_R will increase (decrease) by the same ratio, that is

   $$ROA_R = ROA_U * (M_U/M_R).$$

2. Proposition II: It follows from Proposition I that when $M_R = M_U$ there is no change in *ROA*. Banks have no incentive to go beyond their risk-tolerance level

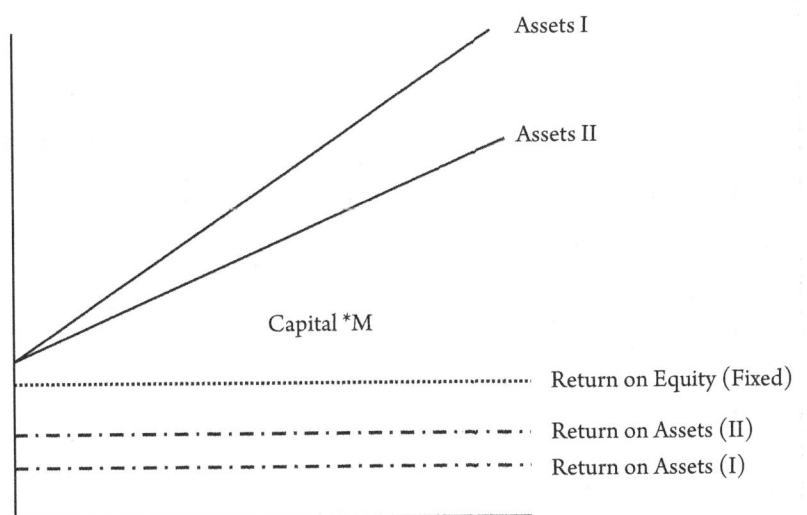

FIGURE 1.1   Movement of Assets and Return on Assets during Pre- and Post-regulation Periods

and contract assets with higher return and higher risk, but are still able to meet the required ROI.

Fall in Assets Growth

In Figures 1.2 and 1.3 we have shown movement of gross assets (ABL) against capital of US banks for 1950–79 and 1980–2004 respectively.

These two Figures show that the rate of growth in gross assets (ABL) against capital of US banks during 1980–2004 is substantially lower than it was in 1950–79. The results of

regression analysis are shown in Table 1.2 also support this view.

TABLE **1.2** Results of Regression Analysis: Gross Assets (ABL) vs Capital

Period	Constant	Coefficient of Capital
1950–79	–95102**** (–6.85)	18.01**** (55.84)
1980–2004	1225491**** (16.29)	9.11**** (46.88)

Note: **** Significant at $\alpha < 0.001$.

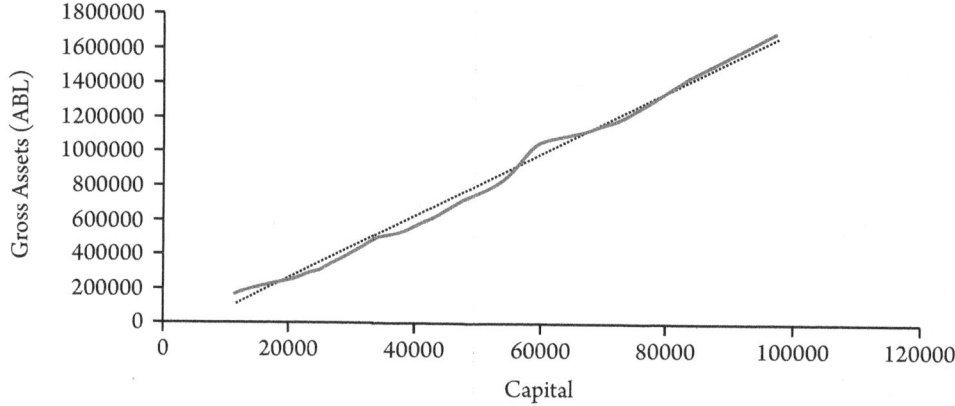

FIGURE **1.2** Movement of Gross Assets (ABL) Against Capital: 1950–79

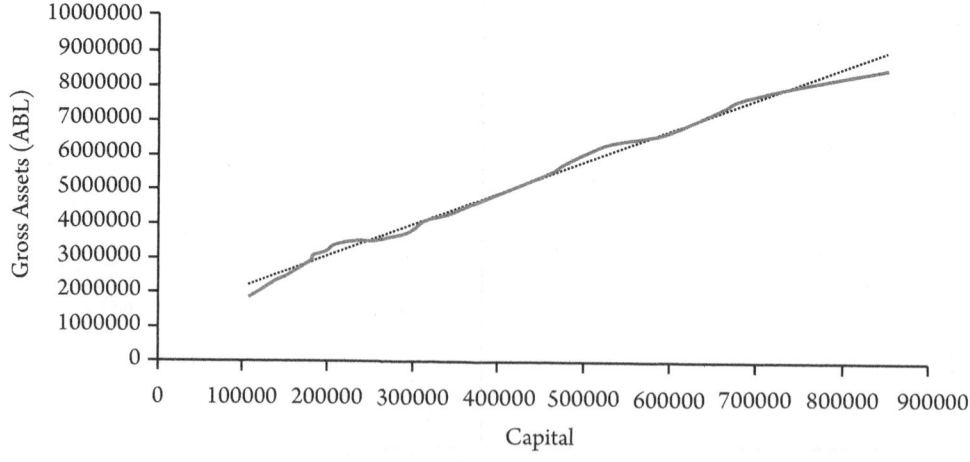

FIGURE **1.3** Movement of Gross Assets (ABL) Against Capital: 1980–2004

The coefficient of capital [which is the capital-multiplier (M)] has almost been halved during the post-regulation period, which means lowering down the assts expansion capacity of banks to almost half of what it was during the pre-regulation period. A lower (M) also indicates that banks are required to bring in additional capital to meet regulatory requirements. In fact, during the regulation period, the mean percentage growth of capital increased to 9.1 as compared to 7.7 during the pre-regulation period. This additional capital needs to be serviced at the current ROE, which puts pressure on the profitability of bank assets. With fewer assets available for every increase in the capital base there should be an upward pressure on ROA (B) during the post-regulation period.

Increase in Return on Assets

In Figures 1.4 and 1.5 we have shown the movement of return on gross assets [ROA (B)] against gross assets (ABL) of US banks for 1950–79 and 1980–2004 respectively. We notice that there is an increase in ROA (B) during 1980–2004 as compared to the previous period.

Similar to ROE (B), it is not justifiable to establish a direct functional relationship between ROA (B) and ABL, because a bank *ex-ante* decides the level of earnings (EBL) based on capital expansion and fixed ROE (B); it then decides a volume and a class of assets, the average return of which generates earnings enough to reach the targeted EBL. ROA (B) has, therefore, a chain relationship with all these variables. However, it is possible to determine the movement of ROA (B) indirectly by establishing a functional relationship between EBL and ABL as in Table 1.3.

The coefficient of ABL, which can be considered as ROA(B) of the US banking industry, increased by almost 100 per cent during the post-regulation period as compared to the pre-regulation period. However, ROA (B) derived

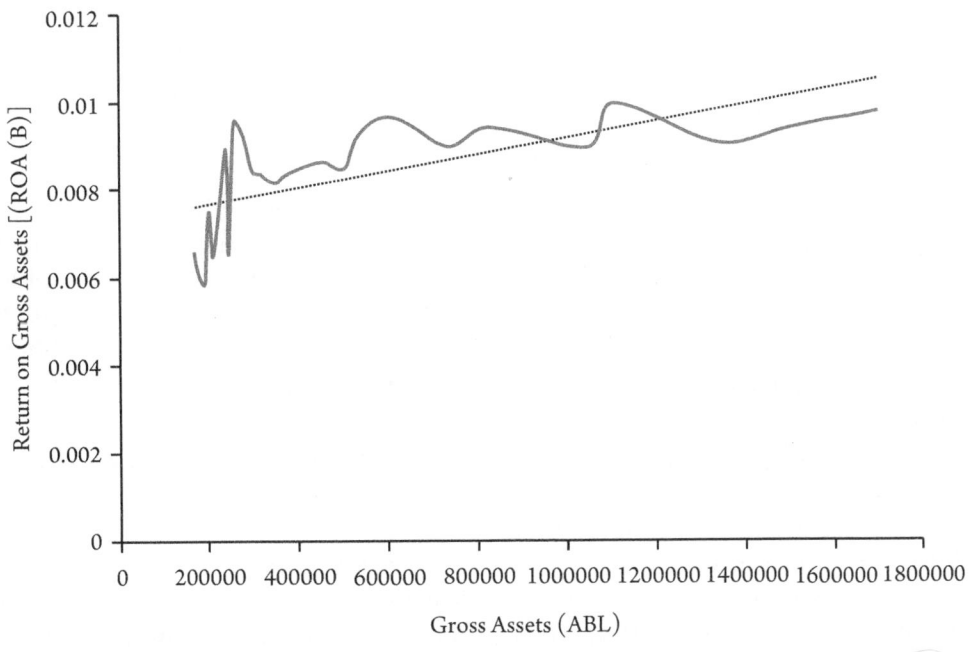

FIGURE **1.4**   Movement of Return on Gross Assets (ROA [B]) vs Gross Assets (ABL): 1950–79

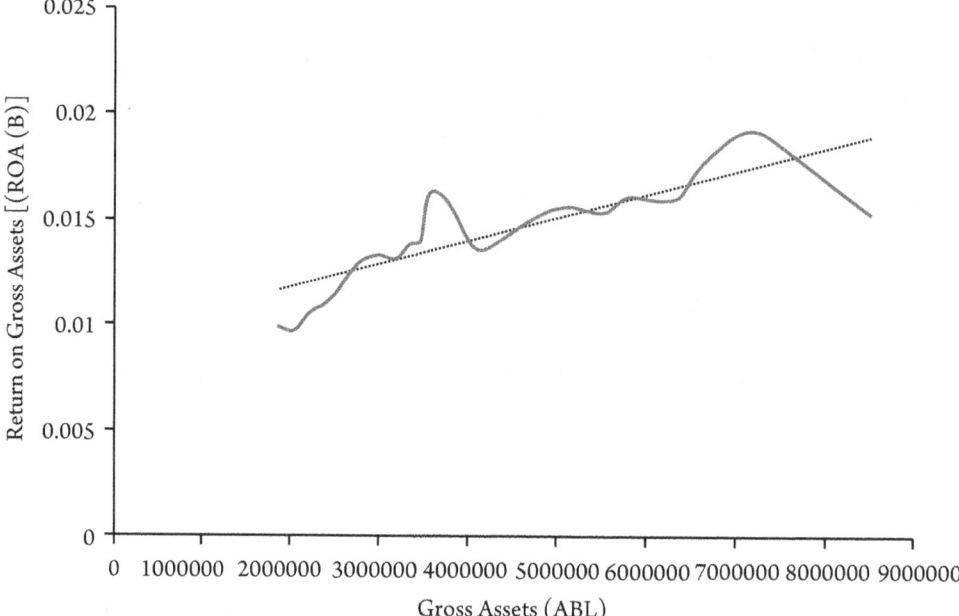

FIGURE **1.5**   Movement of Return on Gross Assets (ROA [B]) vs Gross Assets (ABL): 1980–2004

TABLE **1.3**   Results of Regression Analysis: EBL vs ABL

Period	Constant	Coefficient of ABL
1950–79	–527.69**** (–6.52)	0.010**** (85.60)
1980–2004	–18644.4**** (–6.08)	0.019**** (29.44)
1950–2004	–5962.23**** (–5.35)	0.017**** (48.06)

Note: **** Significant at $\alpha < 0.001$.

TABLE **1.4**   Results of Regression Analysis: ΔEBL vs ΔABL (Excluding years: 1951, 1955, 1959, 1962, 1994, 2003, and 2004)

Period	Constant	Coefficient of ΔABL
1950–79	170.74 (1.55)	0.008**** (6.20)
1980–2004	–114.78 (–0.076)	0.025**** (4.46)
1950–2004	–484.20 (–0.908)	0.025**** (9.06)

Note: **** Significant at $\alpha < 0.001$.

from Table 1.3 indicates only the average of return on assets; it does not indicate the average returns on incremental assets. In Table 1.4, we have regressed incremental earnings (ΔEBL) against incremental assets (ΔABL) to find out ΔROA (B) as a coefficient of ΔABL. For this analysis, we have excluded seven years from the data set (1951, 1955, 1959, 1962, 1994, 2003, and 2004) where ΔEBL is negative.

Table 1.4 shows that coefficient of ΔABL or ΔROA (B) for 1980–2004 is about three times the coefficient of the earlier period, and 30 per cent higher than the ROA (B) of the same period. When the same number of years are excluded from the calculation of regression coefficients as in Table 1.3, the coefficient of ABL—ROA (B) is found to be 0.021 for 1980–2004 (coefficients for other periods remain the same). On this basis, ΔROA (B) of 1980–2004 is 2.5 times the coefficient of the earlier period, and 19 per cent higher than ROA (B) of the same period.

We have indicated earlier that the decision of a bank to target a particular average rate of return on assets [ROA(B)] depends upon the target level of earnings (EBL), which in turn depends upon return on equity [ROE(B)] and the regulatory capital–assets ratio [CAR(B)]. Hence, there should exist a causal relationship between ROA (B) and CAR (B), which we have tested in Table 1.5.[33] Henceforth, wherever appropriate, we will be excluding data of some unusual years marked by major banking crisis namely, 1976 and 1987–91 following Kund and Detragiache, as referred to in Schaeck, et al.[34]

The regression parameters shown in Table 1.5 corroborate our earlier observation. Coefficient of CAR (B) and R^2 (0.05) of the pre-regulation period are found to be insignificant, meaning thereby, that it has little influence on the determination of ROA (B) during the period. However, they are highly significant

TABLE 1.5   Results of Regression Analysis: ROA (B) vs CAR (B)

Period	Constant	Coefficient of CAR(B)	R^2
1950–79 (Ex. 1976)	0.011**** (4.79)	–0.04 (–1.22)	0.05
1980–2004 (Ex. 1987–91)	–0.001 (–0.45)	0.18**** (7.40)	0.75
1950–2004 (Ex. 1976 and 1987–91)	–0.003 (–0.82)	0.18**** (4.29)	0.28

Note: **** Significant at α < 0.001.

during the post-regulation period suggesting a strong influence of the regulated capital ratio on the ROA (B) of this period.

A general conclusion that can be reached from these findings is that other things remaining the same, the regulatory capital–assets ratio has contributed significantly to the high growth of ROA (B) during the post-regulation period.

We can now recall Propositions I and II prove them empirically:

Proposition I: When $M_U/M_R \gtrless 1$, ROA_R will increase by the same ratio, that is

$$ROA_R = ROA_U * (M_U/M_R).$$

$M_U = 18.01$; $M_R = 9.11$ (refer to Table 1.2); $ROA_U = 0.01$; (refer to Table 1.3). Hence, $ROA_R = 0.01 * (18.01/9.11) = 0.019$, which is same as derived in Table 1.3.

Proposition II: The system will be stabilised when, $M_R = M_U$.

That is, $\Delta C_{T(1)} * M_U * ROA (B)_U = EBL' = \Delta C_{T(1)} * ROE (B) = EBL''$, where $\Delta C_{T(1)}$ is the average incremental capital of the post-regulation period, which is 30945.

Putting other appropriate figures from Tables 1.1, 1.2, and 1.3 in this equation, we get: $30905 * 18.01 * 0.01 = 5573 = 30945 * 0.18 = 5570$. The small difference is due to approximation.

[33] As defined in Appendix 1.1, ROA (B) is calculated by dividing net income before charge-offs by gross total assets before charge-offs. An alternative idea is to take gross income before all expenses and losses as the numerator variable. It has been tried, but in most of the cases where the alternative ROA is taken as a variable instead of the original ROA (B), regressions are not found to be statistically significant.

[34] In fact, during the post-World War II period through the early 1970s bank failures were few in number and the banking industry was generally considered strong (FDIC, 'Basel and the Evolution of Capital Regulation', 2003). Also see, Schaeck, Kalus, Cihak Martin and Simon Wolfe, 'Are Competitive Banking Systems More Stable?', *Journal of Money, Credit and Banking*, 2009, 41(4): 711–34.

These findings together with that in Table 1.2 suggest that but for capital regulation, average assets of US banks would have been higher by 100 per cent. In that case, banks could have achieved the required ROE (B) without seeking higher returns in areas that are high risk.

COMPETITION FOR FUNDS

Hellman et al. have argued that bank capital regulation should be combined with deposit-rate controls, because with freely determined deposit rates and increased competition, banks have excessive incentives to compete for funds by offering higher rates, which in turn lowers the incentives for making good loans.[35]

Although mean interest expenses as percentage of mean interest paying funds (deposit + borrowed funds + subordinated debts) increased to 4.22 per cent during 1980–2004 from 2.88 per cent of the earlier period, it may not be due to increased competition unleashed by financial sector liberalisation as argued by Hellman et al. With the average ROE (B) remaining fixed (as shown earlier) and operating expenses as percentage of total income exhibiting a rising trend (about 1.5 per cent during the regulation period), apparently there should be no incentives for banks to enter into a rate war for contracting required funds, save other exogenous factors like inflation, FED's interest rate policy, and the savings rate of the economy. The rate war also did not cause any extraordinary growth of deposits of the banking industry during the regulation period. On the contrary, mean percentage growth of deposits during the regulation period came down to 5.8 per cent from 7.9 per cent in the earlier period (percentages are 6.3 and 8.3 respectively for the total interest paying funds). As against this, mean percentage growth of capital increased to 9.1 per cent during the regulation period as compared to 7.7 per cent in the earlier period. These two together pushed up the (interest paying) funds multiplier of assets during the regulation period as may be observed from Table 1.6. It may be noted that when capital multiplier decreases, the funds multiplier increases.[36] Hence, there should be a scramble for capital and high return assets to service such capital rather than a scramble for deposits.

TABLE 1.6   Results of Regression Analysis: ΔABL vs ΔFund

Period	Constant	Coefficient of ΔFund
1950–79	304.96	1.11****
	(0.25)	(64.44)
1980–2004	–5610.65	1.26****
	(–0.45)	(26.22)
1950–2004	–4955	1.25****
	(–1.14)	(52.92)

Note: ****Significant at $\alpha < 0.001$.

During the post-regulation period, the traditional association between funds and interest expenses was also disturbed as shown in Table 1.7. Coefficient of correlation between funds and interest expenses was as high as 0.97 ($R^2 = 0.94$)

[35] However, having examined publicly held bank-holding companies during the crisis of 1986–92 Park and Peristiani (2007) have observed that risk-taking incentives were confined only to a small fraction of highly risky institutions. Also see Hellman, Thomas, Kevin C. Murdock and Joseph E. Stiglitz, 'Liberalization, Moral Hazard in Banking and Prudential Regulation: Are Capital Requirements Enough?', *American Economic Review*, 2000, 90: 147–65.

[36] Funds multiplier is given by (Capital*M)/ [(Capital*M) – Capital], where Capital*M =Assets. When M is increased to M′ capital requirement increases for both the existing as well as incremental assets, that is Capital′ = (Capital*M)/M′. As C′ > C, capital funding of assets will increase resulting in rise of funds multiplier.

in 1950–79, which came down to –0.18 (R^2 = 0.03) during 1980–2004. Regression shows that only the constant term, 167941 (mean, 153695) is significant in 1980–2004. This suggests that interest expenses no longer rise or fall with the rise or fall of funds.

TABLE 1.7   Results of Regression Analysis: Interest Expenses vs Funds

Period	Constant	Coefficient of Funds	R^2
1950–79	–11266**** (–7.26)	0.048**** (20.77)	0.94
1980–2004	167941**** (9.44)	–0.004 (–0.87)	0.03

Note: **** Significant at $\alpha < 0.001$.

We do not want to investigate further into the causes behind the independency of interest expenses during the period of regulation, as it is not the focus of this chapter.

RISE IN LOSSES

In the previous section, we showed that during the capital regulation period, the rate of return on assets, particularly the incremental rate of return, increased substantially over the pre-regulation period. This is in conformity with established economic principles: when regulation lowers down the lending capacity of banks they tend to raise the equilibrium return on financing until the required return on equity is achieved. But this does not explain fully why it should lead to banks taking riskier positions. We are aware that higher expected returns are associated with higher risk. When rate of return increases the probability of losses also increases.[37]

[37] Fama, Eugene F. and James D. Macbeth, 'Risk, Return and Equilibrium: Empirical Tests', *Journal of Political Economy*, 1973, (81): 607–36.

Assume now that before capital regulation, when there was no restriction on assets growth, the equilibrium level of net earnings to satisfy the required ROE could be achieved by contracting an assets portfolio with a certain ROA and risk probability of say, $\sigma 1$. During the regulation period, when assets growth is limited by CAR, banks would attempt to raise the equilibrium return by rearranging their portfolios with a higher ROA and risk probability of say, $\sigma 2$. Assuming further that all risks mature *ex-post* at the estimated σ, assets loss will be higher in the latter case. Although banks can still meet the required ROE, the banking system moves to a higher risk level. Observing a rising trend in charge-offs, FDIC noted that rising loan losses reflect a gradual shift to higher (credit) risk in US banking. The ultimate source of the rising risk of the banking industry can, therefore, be traced to the regulated capital–assets ratio. We are going to show this in the following sub-sections.

Rise in Capital Ratio, Fall in Assets Growth, Rise in ROA, and Increase in Loss on Assets

Although volatility of loss on assets (LOA) is high, the rise of mean LOA from 0.095 per cent in 1950–79 to 0.48 per cent in 1980–2004 gives us some indication about the steep rise of assets loss during the post-regulation period. In Figure 1.6 we have shown comparative movement of return on assets [ROA (B)] and loss on assets (LOA) during 1950–2004.

The trend lines shown in Figure 1.6 indicate a rising trend in both ROA (B) and LOA. However, the trend lines are not parallel, which indicates that the rate of growth of LOA is lower than that of ROA(B). The LOA started rising fast from 1981 reaching its peak in 1992, reflecting the banking crisis during the period (for some of the years during this period LOA increased against a fall in ROA (B)]. In the following two years,

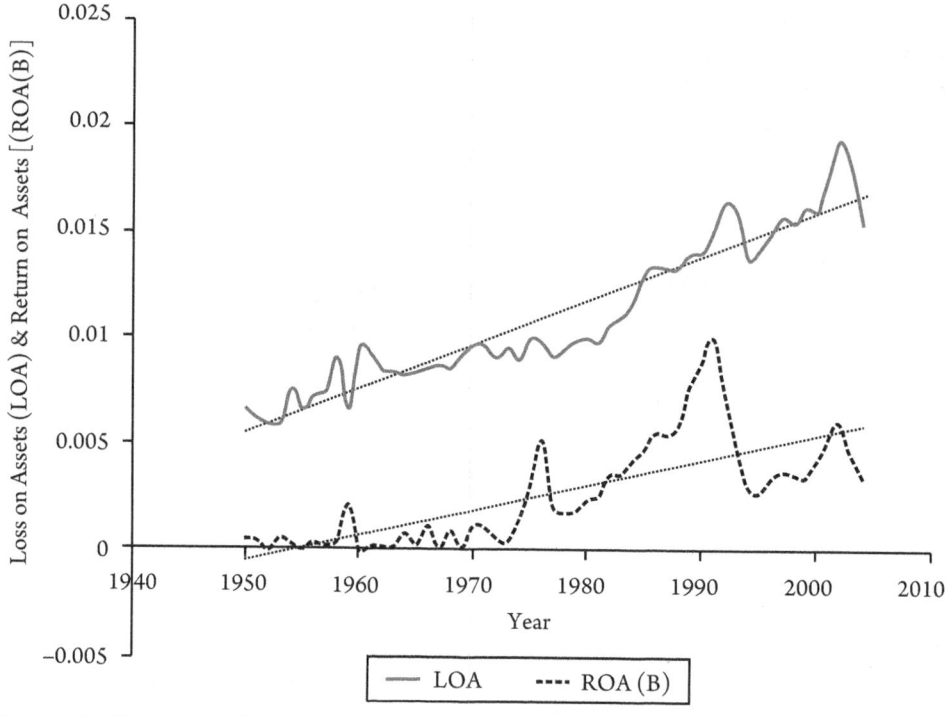

FIGURE **1.6**   Movement of Return on Assets [ROA (B)] and Loss on Assets (LOA) during 1950–2004

LOA fell but again started showing an upward trend until 2002. During 2003–04, there was also a decline in LOA with the fall in ROA (B). These observations are reflected in the regression results shown in Table 1.8.

TABLE **1.8**   Results of Regression Analysis: LOA vs ROA (B)

Period	Constant	Coefficient of ROA(B)	R^2
1950–79 (Ex. 1976)	−0.002 (−1.62)	0.29* (2.15)	0.15
1980–2004 (Ex. 1987–91)	0.000 (0.296)	0.26** (2.88)	0.32
1950–2004 (Ex. 1976 and 1987–91)	0.003**** (−6.56)	0.49**** (11.21)	0.73

Note: ****Significant at $\alpha < 0.001$, **significant at $\alpha < 0.01$, and *significant at $\alpha < 0.05$.

Test statistics of regressions for 1950–79 and 1980–2004 are not as strong as for the entire period, 1950–2004. However, they do suggest that LOA of US banks rises with an increase in ROA (B).

LOA can be derived indirectly from the assets loss function. Results of the regression analysis for the two periods (excluding the crisis years) are shown in Table 1. 9.

Capital coefficient of assets loss is derived in Table 1.10. A comparison of Table 1.9 and Table 1.10 reveals that though the loss coefficient of capital remained constant during pre- and post-regulation period, loss coefficient of assets, which can be taken as LOA, increased by 2.5 times during the post-regulation period. To get further insight, regression equations from Table 1.9 and Table 1.10 are written below ignoring the constant terms.

TABLE 1.9   Results of Regression Analysis: ALOSS vs ABL

Period	Constant	Coefficient of ABL	R^2
1950–79 (Ex. 1976)	−617.15**** (−4.86)	0.002**** (12.10)	0.84
1980–2004 (Ex.1987–91)	−1527.70 (−0.49)	0.005**** (7.23)	0.74
1950–2004 (Ex. 1976 and 1987–91)	−1733.68* (−2.51)	0.005**** (21.11)	0.91

Note: ****Significant at $\alpha < 0.001$, and *significant at $\alpha < 0.05$.

TABLE 1.10   Results of Regression Analysis: ALOSS vs Capital

Period	Constant	Coefficient of Capital	R^2
1950–79 (Ex. 1976)	−807.20**** (−5.06)	0.04**** (10.50)	0.80
1980–2004 (Ex.1987–91)	3751.21 (1.45)	0.042**** (6.82)	0.72
1950–2004 (Ex. 1976 and 1987–91)	−367.97 (−0.51)	0.05**** (18.96)	0.88

Note: ****Significant at $\alpha < 0.001$.

1950–79	1980–2004
1. ALOSS = 0.002 ABL	1. ALOSS = 0.005 ABL
2. ALOSS = 0.04 Capital	2. ALOSS = 0.042 Capital

Rearranging and dividing (1) and (2) we get:

ABL/Capital or, M = 20   ABL/Capital or, M = 8.4

Thus, it can be said that, other things remaining same, higher assets loss during the post-regulation period is related to the lower assets expansion capacity of banks as denoted by a lower (M).

A direct regression of ALOSS on CAR (B) shows the following results (Table 1.11).

TABLE 1.11   Results of Regression Analysis: ALOSS vs CAR (B)

Period	Constant	Coefficient of CAR(B)	R^2
1950–79 (Ex. 1976)	8628**** (6.87)	−115105**** (−6.44)	0.61
Beta		−0.78	
1980–2004 (Ex.1987–91)	−30661*** (−3.58)	657509 **** (5.89)	0.66
Beta		0.81	
1950–2004 (Ex. 1976 and 1987–91)	−37813*** (−3.95)	636117**** (4.85)	0.33
Beta		0.58	

Note: ****Significant at $\alpha < 0.001$ and ***significant at $\alpha < 0.005$.

Table 1.11 shows that the loss coefficient of CAR (B), which was negative during 1950–79, turned out to be positive with a large value during the regulation period signifying its positive association with the assets loss of US banks in this period.

It should be clear by now that there exists a causal relationship between the capital–assets ratio, return on assets, and assets loss. We, therefore, intend to test a functional relationship by including both ROA (B) and CAR (B) in the model such as, LOA = f [ROA (B), CAR (B)]. Results of the regression are shown in Table 1.12.

Regression statistics for 1950–79 are not as strong as for 1980–2004 or for the entire period, 1950–2004. Coefficient of partial determination (R^2_p) for 1950–79 indicates a very low explanatory power of ROA (B). It can be surmised that as during the pre-regulation period assets could grow freely with capital, there was no pressure on ROA (B), which remained within the risk-

TABLE 1.12   Results of Regression Analysis: LOA vs ROA (B) and CAR (B)

Period	Constant	Coefficient of ROA(B)	Coefficient of CAR(B)	R^2
1950–79	0.004	0.20	−0.072***	0.41
(Ex. 1976)	(2.03)	(1.69)	(−3.44)	
Beta		0.26	−0.53	
VIF		1.08	1.08	
R^2 (partial)		0.10	0.32	
1980–2004	0.002*	0.77****	−0.121 ****	0.71
(Ex. 1987–91)	(2.29)	(6.27)	(−4.78)	
Beta		1.65	−1.26	
VIF		4.04	4.04	
R^2 (partial)		0.70	0.57	
1950–2004	0.001	0.61****	−0.077****	0.83
(Ex. 1976 and 1987–91)	(1.13)	(14.84)	(−5.37)	
Beta		1.06	−0.38	
VIF		1.39	1.39	
R^2 (partial)		0.83	0.39	

Note: ****Significant at $\alpha < 0.001$, **significant at $\alpha < 0.005$, and *significant at $\alpha < 0.05$.

tolerance level of banks. Assets loss was, therefore, a normal business loss (say, 0.2 per cent as shown in Table 1. 9), not dependent so much on ROA (B).

The situation changed considerably during the post-regulation period. ROA (B) is found to have the highest explanatory power ($R^2_p = 0.70$). Coefficient of partial determination for CAR (B) also increased to 0.57 during the post-regulation period. This finding suggests increased influence of both the variables on the LOA of US banks during the post-regulation period.

Regression results show that CAR (B) has a negative sign, which tells us that if ROA (B) is held constant LOA will increase (decrease) with the decrease (increase) in CAR (B). Let us examine whether this holds true during the capital regulation period. As explained earlier, any increase in the capital–assets ratio will decrease the asset creation capacity of banks and consequently, increase return on assets. Hence, ROA (B) cannot be held constant when CAR (B) increases. This causal relationship has resulted

in some degree of collinearity between CAR (B) and ROA (B), which is more pronounced in the post-regulation period. In fact, presence of collinearity itself suggests that when CAR (B) (which has become an exogenous variable during the regulation period) changes, ROA (B) shall also change. The correlation analysis shown in Table 1.13 also supports this conclusion: the coefficient of correlation between ROA (B) and CAR (B), which was insignificant during the pre-regulation period, became highly significant during the post-regulation period.

In this section, we have analysed the impact of capital regulation on assets return and loss of assets of US banks from various angles. Our findings suggest that capital regulation has contributed to banks seeking higher return on assets, which in turn has increased asset losses. Higher assets return and higher assets loss suggest that the US banking system has moved to a higher risk level during the regulation period. Capital regulation has, therefore, not served the purpose for which it was intended.

TABLE 1.13   Correlation Analysis between
ROA (B) and CAR (B)

Period	Pearson's 'r'	Level of Significance (two tailed)
1950–79 (Ex. 1976)	−0.23	Not significant
1980–2004 (Ex. 1987–91)	0.87	Significant at 0.01
1950–2004 (Ex. 1976 and 1987–91)	0.53	Significant at 0.01

RISK MANAGEMENT: A STRATEGIC ISSUE

Capital forms a small part of a bank's total funds. In fact, banks do not need capital to fund their assets; bank deposits can do this with easier covenants and at a much lower cost than capital in general, and debt of other non-banking firms, in particular. First Goldsmith bankers did banking only with deposits. However, the free flowing nature of deposits can be maintained so long as the value of bank assets does not fall below the value of deposits. This is the domain of strategic management of bank assets.

Most of the literature on capital adequacy requirements for banks have taken a 'gone concern' approach. That is, what is 'left' if the bank goes bankrupt. Hence, the analysis has mostly proceeded from the liability side of the balance sheet to locate the 'cushion' available in the form of net worth (equity) to protect the interests of the depositors. For example, Barrios and Blanco proceeded with the definition of balance sheet as assets = net worth + debt and concluded that after calculating final net worth as the difference between the value of assets and liabilities if it is found that the net worth < 0 then, the bank would default. While this approach may be correct from an accountant's 'gone concern' approach, it draws attention away from the assets side of the balance sheet where the risk lies.

The value of a business depends upon the earning capacity of the assets. This value is independent of its funding structure, though ultimately the value is shared by equity and debt; any tax advantage due to existence of debt accrues to equity. This is also substantiated by the fact that the age-old net present value (NPV) method of valuation of a project takes into account only the future earning capacity of its assets. The liability structure does not enter into the valuation exercise. So long as the market value of assets is greater than or equal to the market value of its liabilities, a business can be said to be 'safe' for liability holders. In other words, when the market value of a bank's assets falls short of its liabilities the bank is insolvent.[38] Hence, risk management essentially boils down to management of assets and the risk thereof in such a way that the value does not fall below the risk–return equilibrium level. From the strategic point of view, capital is irrelevant; it has no role in the risk management of assets of a firm. From a bank's point of view, it is just another source of funding its assets, and from the bank shareholders' point of view, it is a means by which to reward themselves for the risk taken.

Strategic Model for Risk Management

The critical parameters to be considered for protecting a bank against the risk of bankruptcy are only two—net return from assets and cost of deposits. At the end of the day all decisions of a bank would ultimately be reflected in these two parameters. So long as the return from assets exceeds or equal to the cost of deposits, the value on both sides will be maintained, and thus the

---

[38] Kane, Edward, J., 'Three Paradigms for the Role of Capitalization Requirements in Insured Financial Institutions', *Journal of Banking & Finance*, 1995, (19): 431–59.

bank cannot go bankrupt. In the analysis that follows, we have ignored capital and assumed that the assets of the bank are entirely funded from deposits and other interest paying liabilities.

Broadly speaking, a bank holds two kinds of assets—risky assets, primarily composed of loan assets and non-risky assets comprising predominantly of government securities held partly for liquidity management and cash balances. Earning from risk assets is taken to be net of bad debt and loss provisions, which is the prevalent practice. Return from government securities is taken to be the average rate of return on the portfolio of these securities. For ease of calculation, deposits include all interest paying borrowings and subordinated debts, and cost of deposits include, besides the average interest payable on these funds, the intermediation costs as well.

Our proposition is that a bank remains solvent as long as the market value of its assets is equal to the market value of its deposits, which may be written as below:

$$\frac{A_R\,(1+R_R)}{1+M_R}+\frac{A_F\,(1+C_R)}{1+M_R}\geq\frac{D\,(1+D_R)}{1+M_R} \quad (1.5)$$

Where: A_R = Risky assets

$\quad\quad A_F$ = Risk-free assets

$\quad\quad D$ = Deposits

$\quad\quad R_R$ = Net return on risky assets

$\quad\quad C_R$ = Rate of return on risk-free assets

$\quad\quad D_R$ = Gross rate payable on deposits inclusive of intermediation costs

$\quad\quad M_R$ = A benchmark market rate applied uniformly

The left hand side of the model represents the market value of total assets (A_V) and the right hand side represents the market value of deposits (D_V). Algebraic manipulation of this inequality gives rise to:

$A_R R_R + A_F C_R \geq A_R D_R + A_F D_R$, because

$A_R + A_F = D$ $\quad\quad\quad\quad\quad\quad\quad\quad\quad\quad (1.6)$

Or, $A_R\,(R_R - D_R) \geq A_F\,(D_R - C_R)$ $\quad\quad (1.7)$

Or, $\dfrac{A_R}{A_F} \overset{\leq}{\underset{>}{}}\ \dfrac{D_R - C_R}{R_R - D_R};$ $\quad\quad\quad\quad (1.8)$

depending upon the sign of numerator and denominator.

At the first, the above proposition leads to the following general conclusion:

If, LHS = RHS, then $A_V = D_V$ $\quad\quad\quad (1.9)$

Where, A_V = Market value of assets

$\quad\quad\quad D_V$ = Market value of deposits

In Table 1.14, nine combinations of the variables along with their effects on the market value of bank assets and deposits are considered.

Strategic Options

It may be seen that LHS is the ratio between risk assets (A_R) and risk-free assets (A_F) and RHS is the ratio between the differential of their earning rates. Risk management in banks ultimately boils down to maintaining these two ratios. Of the nine combinations presented in Table 1.14, combinations (3), (6), and (7) are not acceptable on the face of them, because A_V is less than D_V. We take up these special cases later.

The best combination among the remaining is (2), where A_V shall always be greater than D_V, no matter what the ratio between risk assets and risk-free assets. Required condition for this is, $D_R < C_R$ and $R_R > D_R$.

This leads us to interesting strategic options. If the objective of the bank is to reach combination (2), which is always value increasing, it should proceed towards ensuring that the average rate payable on deposits (D_R) is always less than the rate (C_R) available from risk-free investments. This will make the numerator of RHS negative.

TABLE 1.14   Parameter Combinations and their Effect on Value

Sl. No.	Combinations	Effects
1.	$D_R > C_R$ and $R_R > D_R$	(a) Both the numerator and denominator of RHS are <u>positive</u> resulting in a positive ratio. (b) LHS = RHS = $A_V = D_V$ (c) LHS > RHS; $A_V > D_V$ (d) LHS < RHS; $A_V > D_V$
2.	$D_R < C_R$ and $R_R > D_R$	(a) Numerator of RHS is <u>negative</u> while the denominator is <u>positive</u> resulting in a <u>negative</u> ratio. (b) A_V shall always be more than D_V, whatever the LHS.
3.	$D_R < C_R$ and $R_R > D_R$	(a) Denominator of RHS is <u>negative</u> while the numerator is <u>positive</u> resulting in a <u>negative</u> ratio. (b) A_V shall always be less than D_V whatever the LHS.
4.	$D_R < C_R$ and $R_R > D_R$	(a) Both the denominator and numerator are <u>negative</u> resulting in a <u>positive ratio.</u> (b) LHS = RHS = $A_V > D_V$ (c) LHS < RHS; $A_V > D_V$ (d) LHS > RHS; $A_V > D_V$
5.	$D_R = C_R$ $R_R > D_R$	$A_V > D_V$
6.	$D_R = C_R$ $R_R > D_R$	$A_V < D_V$
7.	$D_R = C_R$ $R_R > D_R$	$A_V < D_V$
8.	$D_R = C_R$ $R_R > D_R$	$A_V > D_V$
9.	$D_R = C_R = R_R$	$A_V = D_V$

Note: Effects of combinations (5) and (6) are determined by setting $D_R = C_R$ and that for combinations (7) and (8) by setting $R_R = C_R$ in Equation 1.6.

If along with this, the rate payable on deposits is also less than the net return on risk assets, then the denominator will be positive. Combination (2) will thus be achieved. If, however, D_R cannot be reduced below R_R then the denominator becomes negative leading us to combination (4). The attention of the bank may now be focussed on LHS, that is, the ratio of risk assets and risk-free assets. The bank should move towards reducing this ratio below that of RHS, which will have the same effect as in combination (2). The other option is to make it at least equal to the ratio in RHS which will make $A_V = D_V$. In case of combination (1) where $R_R > D_R > C_R$ the attention of the bank should similarly be shifted to LHS with a view to changing the ratio equal to or greater than RHS.

Strategy for Critical Situations

Combinations (5)–(9) have low probability of occurrence in real life situation. Even then, combinations (5), (8), and (9) are acceptable as $A_V \geq D_V$. In combinations (3), (6), and (7) average rate payable on deposits is either equal to or greater than the rate of return from risk-free assets. On the face of it, there appears to be a scramble for deposits leading perhaps to a rate war, which may be the cause behind the rise in the deposit rate to an uneconomic level. Such a situation may occur when demand for loans is rising fast causing a hike in the loan rate much beyond the deposit rate or the risk-free rate. But when we look at the other part of these combinations we find that the loan rate remains either less than (combination [3] and [6]) or equal to deposit rate (combination [7]), which cannot be the case when demand for loan is rising. Hence, from a macroeconomic point of view none of the combinations hold. However, the situations could be bank-specific due to loan losses (reducing the R_R) or wrong interest rate policies pursued so far by an individual bank or a disproportionate rise in intermediation costs which increase D_R, that is, gross rate payable on deposit. In case of combination (6), R_R has fallen below D_R but C_R is equal to D_R. A bank will thus have no further motivation to make loans; the tendency will be to gradually shift towards risk-free assets, which will increase A_V and also change the LHS ratio. At the same time, the bank would attempt towards reducing intermediation costs to bring down D_R below either R_R or C_R, which will lead the bank to a viable combination. Combination (7) is rather peculiar. Here, return from risk assets is equal to the rate payable on deposits, which however, is greater than the rate of return on risk-free assets. Hence, the bank will have no further motivation to invest in risk-free assets; it will rather shift towards building up risk assets by selling risk-free assets. The situation now is analogous to what has been outlined for combination (6). Once the process is complete the equality, $A_V = D_V$ will be reached in both cases. However, the process of conversion is faster in combination (7) than in combination (6), because liquidation of loan assets could be slower than the liquidation of

risk-free investments, despite the development of market for securitised assets.

In case of combination (3), where D_R is higher than both C_R and R_R, the strategy will be to reduce D_R primarily by focussing on intermediation costs. An individual bank cannot vary the rate payable on deposits, except marginally whether it is a controlled or market-driven economy. Hence, if D_R is rising for an individual bank it must be due to a disproportionate rise in intermediation costs. Appropriate strategies would now be to reduce the intermediation costs to the market level in order to bring down D_R, and at the same time, increase/reduce investments in risk assets or risk-free assets depending on whether $R_R > C_R$ or $C_R > R_R$ which will have the effect of increasing A_V. The bank may be neutral between the two assets-class if $R_R = C_R$. In this process once D_R becomes equal to or goes down below either R_R or C_R, even marginally, and A_V is also increased with a change in the LHS ratio, the bank would have more than one combination to choose from to make $A_V \geq D_V$. In combination (9) the bank can be said to be just maintaining its value. Nothing additional is being created. The situation may not be sustained in the long run. Attention should, therefore, be drawn towards reducing D_R below either C_R or R_R. Alternatively, the bank can also try to increase R_R beyond D_R by making appropriate changes in loan policies. It may not be possible to change C_R because it is exogenously determined. A summary of strategies to be followed by an individual bank when its initial income and cost parameters have the immediate effect of making $A_V < D_V$ are presented in Table 1.15.

An examination of Tables 1.14 and 1.15 and the analysis done would point out that the critical factors for protecting the interest of depositors are D_R and C_R, more particularly D_R. If D_R is less than either C_R or R_R, the bank can always avert a crisis.

TABLE 1.15   Strategy for Critical Situations

SL	Combinations	Immediate Effect	Strategy
1(d)	$D_R > C_R$; $R_R > D_R$ and LHS < RHS	$A_V < D_V$	Gradually change the proportion between risk assets and risk-free assets so that LHS ratio becomes equal to or greater than the RHS ratio.
3	$D_R > C_R$; $R_R < D_R$	$A_V < D_V$	(i) Reduce intermediation costs to bring down D_R at least equal to or less than either C_R or R_R. (ii) If necessary, change the proportions between risk assets and risk-free assets depending upon whether $R_R \geq C_R$ or $C_R \geq R_R$. (iii) Once the objective in (ii) is achieved follow the combination(s) from Table 1.14 appropriate to the evolved relationship.
4(d)	$D_R < C_R$; $R_R < D_R$ and LHS>RHS	$A_V < D_V$	Strategy similar to the one prescribed for combination 1(d) above should be followed.
6	$D_R = C_R$; $R_R < D_R$	$A_V < D_V$	(i) Gradually shift the assets portfolio to risk-free assets preferably through securitisation of risk assets. (ii) Reduce the intermediation costs to bring down D_R below either C_R or R_R. (iii) Once the objective in (ii) is achieved follow the combination(s) from Table 1.14 appropriate to the evolved relationship.
7	$D_R > C_R$; $R_R = D_R$	$A_V < D_V$	(i) Shift the assets portfolio to risk assets by selling risk-free assets. (ii) Reduce intermediation costs to bring D_R below either C_R or R_R. (iii) Once the objective in (ii) is achieved follow the combination(s) from Table 1.14 appropriate to the evolved relationship.

The analysis done so far in this section does not consider equity capital as a means to protect the bank against bankruptcy or in other words, to protect the interests of depositors; it is strictly a capital structure issue internal to the bank management. Risk management in a bank is typically a strategic issue while movement of equity capital and its appropriate level in a firm are grounded in economic laws. The two should not be confused and mixed up. Only by allowing capital full freedom to optimise its risk–return potential, can the interest of depositors be protected. Both the bank and the regulators should, therefore, focus on 'value maintenance', because so long as the market value of assets is equal to or greater than the market value of outside liabilities a bank continues to be a viable organisation. For this, they need only to specify that at any time the D_R should be less than either R_R or C_R.

CONCLUDING REMARKS

Bank capital, like any other business capital, needs to be serviced by a certain ROE, which is determined by the market within a risk–return framework; the leverage structure of a bank is determined accordingly. Mean ROE remains more or less fixed over a long period. The required ROE is satisfied by making investments in assets with rate of returns determined within the risk tolerance limits of banks. When the assets generation capacity of banks is restricted by the regulatory–capital ratio (which also alters the leverage structure of banks), banks are induced to go beyond their risk tolerance levels to seek assets or businesses that provide higher rates of return. As higher risk is associated with higher returns, the risk of the banking industry is increased.

In this chapter, we have shown that during the post-regulation period the assets generation capacity of US banks was halved while return on assets doubled and loss on assets increased by 2.5 times over the pre-regulation period. Capital regulation has, therefore, resulted in higher risk of the banking industry. It is necessary, therefore, to seek alternative strategies to protect the interests of the banks as well as their depositors. Towards this end, we have laid down alternative strategies based on the concept of 'value maintenance', which upholds that a bank remains solvent as long as the market value of its assets is equal to the market value of its deposits.

Appendix 1.1

DEFINITION OF VARIABLES

1. Assets loss (ALOSS)
    This item is composed of credit/loan/lease losses and securities losses
(a) Credit/Loan/Lease losses
    This figure is not available directly from the published accounts of banks. Instead, we get the following two items:
    i.   *Loan and lease loss allowances:* This item is available from balance sheet. It is also called 'loan loss reserves', which exist in recognition that some loans will not be paid. The reserve increases with the growth in problem loans and decreases with net loan charge-offs.
    ii. *Provision for loan and lease losses:* This item is available from income statement. It is a deduction from income representing a bank's periodic allocation to its loan loss reserves. Conceptually, the management is allocating a portion of income to reserves to protect against potential loan losses. Provision for loan and lease losses differs from actual losses (charge-offs). The latter indicates loans and leases that a bank formally recognises as uncollectable and charges-off against loan and lease loss allowances. Consequently, assets are reduced to the extent of such write-offs.[39]

These two definitions can be reduced to the following arithmetical calculation to determine:
(a) *Credit losses:* Credit/loan/lease losses (net of recoveries) or simply net credit losses = (loan and lease loss allowances at the end of last year + provision for loan and lease losses and other adjustments of the current year) − (loan and lease loss allowances at the end of the current year).
(b) *Securities Losses:* This item is available from published income statements.

Assets Loss (ALOSS) is then given by: net credit losses + securities losses.
2. Assets before loss (ABL): net assets + loan and lease loss allowances.
3. Earnings before losses (EBL): net income + provision for loan and lease losses.
4. Return on equity (ROE): net income (E)/total equity capital (C).
5. Return on equity before losses [ROE (B)]: EBL/total equity capital.
6. Return on assets (ROA): net income (E)/net assets (A).
7. Return on assets before losses [ROA (B)]: EBL/ABL.
8. Loss on assets (LOA): ALOSS/ABL.
9. Capital–assets ratio (CAR): total equity capital (C)/net assets.
10. Capital–assets ratio before assets losses [CAR (B)]: C/ABL.

[39] Koch, Timothy W. and Scott S. Macdonald, *Bank Management*, Thomson Asia Pvt. Ltd., Singapore, 2004.

Appendix 1.2

AUTOREGRESSIVE MODELS (COCHRANE-ORCUTT ESTIMATION METHOD)

TABLE 1(AR)   Results of Autoregression Analysis: EBL vs Capital

Period	Constant	Coefficient of Capital	Rho (AR1)	D-W Statistic
1950–79	−1682.16**** (−6.81)	0.184**** (35.77)	0.533	1.65
1980–2004	22040* (2.37)	0.133**** (13.01)	0.704	0.94
1950–2004	705.26 (0.43)	0.181**** (31.66)	0.40	1.01

Note: ****Significant at $\alpha < 0.001$ and *significant at $\alpha < 0.05$.

TABLE 2(AR)   Results of Autoregression Analysis: EBL vs ABL

Period	Constant	Coefficient of Capital	Rho (AR1)	D-W Statistic
1950–79	−130093*** (−3.67)	18.70**** (29.28)	0.75	1.85
1980–2004	3826872**** (5.61)	6.05**** (10.06)	0.95	1.08

Note: ****Significant at $\alpha < 0.001$ and ***significant at $\alpha < 0.005$.

TABLE 3(AR)   Results of Autoregression Analysis: EBL vs ABL

Period	Constant	Coefficient of ABL	Rho (AR1)	D-W Statistic
1950–79	−527.69**** (−6.52)	0.010**** (85.60)	No serial correlation	2.11
1980–2004	−18644.4**** (−6.08)	0.019**** (29.44)	No serial correlation	1.23
1950–2004	−4935 (−1.58)	0.016**** (20.10)	0.75	1.11

Note: ****Significant at $\alpha < 0.001$.

TABLE 4(AR)   Results of Autoregression Analysis: Δ EBL vs ΔABL
(Excluding years: 1951, 1955, 1959, 1962, 1994, 2003, and 2004)

Period	Constant	Coefficient of ΔABL	Rho (AR1)	D-W Statistic
1950–79	170.74 (1.55)	0.008**** (6.20)	No serial correlation	2.16
1980–2004	−114.78 (−0.076)	0.025**** (4.46)	No serial correlation	1.67
1950–2004	−484.20 (−0.908)	0.025**** (9.06)	No serial correlation	1.61

Note: ****Significant at $\alpha < 0.001$.

TABLE 5(AR)   Results of Autoregression Analysis: ROA (B) vs CAR (B)

Period	Constant	Coefficient of CAR(B)	Rho (AR1)	D-W Statistic
1950–79 (Ex. 1976)	0.010* (2.70)	–0.019 (–0.37)	0.65	2.4
1980–2004 (Ex. 1987–91)	0.005 (1.53)	0.119* (2.68)	0.56	1.04
1950–2004 (Ex. 1976 and 1987–91)	0.007 (1.45)	0.083 (1.73)	0.93	1.98

Note: *Significant at $\alpha < 0.05$.

TABLE 6(AR)   Results of Autoregression Analysis: Δ ABL vs Δ Fund

Period	Constant	Coefficient of ΔFund	Rho (AR1)	D-W Statistic
1950–79	304.96 (0.25)	1.11**** (64.44)	No serial correlation	1.44
1980–2004	–5610.65 (–0.45)	1.26**** (26.22)	No serial correlation	1.80
1950–2004	–4955 (–1.14)	1.25**** (52.92)	No serial correlation	1.72

Note: ****Significant at $\alpha < 0.001$.

TABLE 7(AR)   Results of Autoregression Analysis:
Interest Expenses vs Funds

Period	Constant	Coefficient of Funds	Rho (AR1)	D-W Statistic
1950–79	–23398** (–2.89)	0.071**** (9.11)	0.85	1.12
1980–2004	196417**** (5.32)	–0.011 (–1.25)	0.59	1.39

Note: ****Significant at $\alpha < 0.001$ and **significant at $\alpha < 0.01$.

TABLE 8(AR)   Results of Autoregression Analysis: LOA vs ROA (B)

Period	Constant	Coefficient of ROA(B)	Rho (AR1)	D-W Statistic
1950–79 (Ex. 1976)	–0.002 (–1.62)	0.29* (2.15)	No serial correlation	1.56
1980–2004 (Ex. 1987–91)	–0.007* (–2.35)	0.67**** (4.97)	0.90	1.71
1950–2004 (Ex. 1976 and 1987–91)	–0.002* (–2.25)	0.39**** (4.86)	0.58	2.23

Note: ****Significant at $\alpha < 0.001$ and *significant at $\alpha < 0.05$.

TABLE 9(AR) Results of Autoregression Analysis: ALOSS vs ABL

Period	Constant	Coefficient of ABL	Rho (AR1)	D-W Statistic
1950–79 (Ex. 1976)	−617.15**** (−4.86)	0.002**** (12.10)	No serial correlation	1.47
1980–2004 (Ex. 1987–91)	1700.03 (0.27)	0.004*** (3.33)	0.53	1.23
1950–2004 (Ex. 1976 and 1987–91)	−1499 (−1.16)	0.004**** (11.83)	0.53	1.23

Note: ****Significant at $\alpha < 0.0001$ and ***significant at $\alpha < 0.005$.

TABLE 10(AR) Results of Autoregression Analysis: ALOSS vs Capital

Period	Constant	Coefficient of Capital	Rho (AR1)	D-W Statistic
1950–79 (Ex. 1976)	−807.20**** (−5.06)	0.04**** (10.50)	No serial correlation	1.21
1980–2004 (Ex. 1987–91)	8070.51 (1.44)	0.03* (2.79)	0.58	1.16
1950–2004 (Ex. 1976 and 1987–91)	529.15 (0.34)	0.04**** (8.96)	0.61	1.10

Note: ****Significant at $\alpha < 0.001$ and *significant at $\alpha < 0.05$.

TABLE 11(AR) Results of Autoregression Analysis: ALOSS vs CAR (B)

Period	Constant	Coefficient of CAR(B)	Rho (AR1)	D-W Statistic
1950–79 (Ex. 1976)	8190**** (4.25)	−106585**** (−3.87)	0.61	1.68
1980–2004 (Ex. 1987–91)	−13849 (−0.74)	449454* (2.08)	0.70	1.13
1950–2004 (Ex. 1976 and 1987–91)	−949.27 (−0.054)	264991 (1.76)	0.96	1.30

Note: ****Significant at $\alpha < 0.0001$ and *significant at $\alpha < 0.05$.

TABLE 12(AR) Results of Autoregression Analysis: LOA vs ROA (B) and CAR (B)

Period	Constant	Coefficient of ROA (B)	Coefficient of CAR(B)	Rho (AR1)	D-W Statistic
1950–79 (Ex. 1976)	0.004 (2.03)	0.20 (1.69)	−0.072*** (−3.44)	No serial correlation	2.13
1980–2004 (Ex. 1987–91)	0.002* (2.29)	0.77**** (6.27)	−0.121 **** (−4.78)	No serial correlation	1.39
1950–2004 (Ex. 1976 and 1987–91)	0.001 (1.13)	0.61**** (14.84)	−0.077**** (−5.37)	No serial correlation	1.80

Note: ****Significant at $\alpha < 0.001$, ***significant at $\alpha < 0.005$, and *significant at $\alpha < 0.0$.

Appendix 1.3

RESULTS OF REGRESSION ANALYSIS (MOVING AVERAGE DATA)

TABLE 1(MA)   Results of Regression Analysis: EBL vs Capital

Period	Constant	Coefficient of Capital
1950–79	−1528.87****	0.18****
	(−14.21)	(73.24)
1980–2004	2272.86	0.19****
	(1.32)	(39.27)
1950–2004	−1356.38*	0.19****
	(−2.4)	(85.07)

Note: ****Significant at α < 0.001 and *significant at α < 0.05.

TABLE 2(MA)   Results of Regression Analysis: Gross Assets (ABL) vs Capital

Period	Constant	Coefficient of Capital
1950–79	−99581****	18.07****
	(−8.02)	(63.76)
1980–2004	3826872****	9.35****
	(5.61)	(54.73)

Note: ****Significant at α < 0.001.

TABLE 3(MA)   Results of Regression Analysis: EBL vs ABL

Period	Constant	Coefficient of ABL
1950–79	−531.12****	0.010****
	(−12.26)	(163.05)
1980–2004	−21102****	0.020****
	(−12.38)	(52.16)
1950–2004	−6205****	0.017****
	(−6.19)	(51.18)

Note: ****Significant at α < 0.001.

TABLE 4(MA)   Results of Regression Analysis: ΔEBL vs ΔABL

Period	Constant	Coefficient of ΔABL
1950–79	7.92	0.010****
	(0.21)	(19.73)
1980–2004	645.02	0.017****
	(0.55)	(4.16)
1950–2004	−187.66	0.019****
	(−0.493)	(10.14)

Note: ****Significant at α < 0.001.

TABLE 5(MA)   Results of regression Analysis: ROA (B) vs CAR (B)

Period	Constant	Coefficient of CAR (B)
1950–79	0.012****	−0.057*
	(6.37)	(−2.05)
1980–2004	0.002	0.17****
	(1.29)	(8.99)
1950–2004	0.001	0.14***
	(0.36)	(3.10)

Note: ****Significant at α < 0.001, ***significant at α < 0.005, and *significant at α < 0.05.

TABLE 6(MA)   Results of Regression Analysis: ΔABL vs Δ Interest paying Funds

Period	Constant	Coefficient of ΔFund
1950–79	407.55	1.11****
	(0.50)	(91.88)
1980–2004	−5269	1.26****
	(−0.60)	(33.87)
1950–2004	−4888	1.25****
	(−1.68)	(71.17)

Note: ****Significant at α < 0.001.

TABLE 7(MA)   Results of Regression Analysis: Interest Expenses vs
Interest paying Funds

Period	Constant	Coefficient of Funds	R^2
1950–79	−11761****	0.053****	0.94
	(−7.35)	(21.10)	
1980–2004	155054****	−0.000	0
	(10.35)	(−0.04)	

Note: ****Significant at α < 0.001.

TABLE 8(MA)   Results of Regression Analysis: LOA vs ROA (B)

Period	Constant	Coefficient of ROA(B)	R^2
1950–79	−0.004***	0.59****	0.40
	(−3.54)	(4.22)	
1980–2004	0.002	0.23	0.09
	(0.72)	(1.48)	
1950–2004	−0.004****	0.60****	0.67
	(−5.82)	(10.10)	

Note: ****Significant at α < 0.001 and ***significant at α < 0.005.

TABLE 9(MA)   Results of Regression Analysis: ALOSS vs ABL

Period	Constant	Coefficient of ABL
1950–79	−791.77**** (−4.70)	0.003**** (12.01)
1980–2004	2061.20 (0.59)	0.004**** (5.45)
1950–2004	−1471 (−1.70)	0.005**** (17.51)

Note: ****Significant at α < 0.001.

TABLE 10(MA)   Results of Regression Analysis: ALOSS vs Capital

Period	Constant	Coefficient of Capital
1950–79	−1045.63**** (−5.06)	0.051**** (10.72)
1980–2004	7607.95* (2.70)	0.039**** (4.97)
1950–2004	351.16 (0.37)	0.056**** (14.20)

Note: ****Significant at α < 0.001 and *significant at α < 0.05.

TABLE 11(MA)   Results of Regression Analysis: ALOSS vs CAR (B)

Period	Constant	Coefficient of CAR (B)
1950–79	11593**** (7.88)	−154867**** (−7.63)
1980–2004	−16727 (−1.75)	507067 **** (3.87)
1950–2004	−20812 (−1.87)	427476** (2.75)

Note: ****Significant at α < 0.001 and **significant at α < 0.01.

TABLE 12(MA)   Results of Regression Analysis: LOA vs ROA (B) and CAR (B)

Period	Constant	Coefficient of ROA (B)	Coefficient of CAR (B)
1950–79	0.004* (2.59)	0.373**** (3.76)	−0.093**** (−6.04)
1980–2004	0.004**** (3.87)	1.51**** (10.96)	−0.28 **** (−10.48)
1950–2004	0.003*** (3.38)	0.74**** (17.66)	−0.124**** (−8.46)

Note: ****Significant at α < 0.001, ***significant at α < 0.005, and *significant at α < 0.05.

She was a sinking ship firing upon her rescuers.

—Alexander Woollcott

2 Liquidity Management and Assets-Liabilities Strategy

INTRODUCTION

Liquidity is the ability to pay in time. The last two words are important, because an individual, firm. or a bank may pay given some more time. Many a times they may be correct but the signal that a non-payment gives to the market may often be construed as 'distress', which could be a self-fulfilling prophecy that has the potential of bringing down the organisation much faster than what was originally anticipated by the payees. This happens in two ways: first, the market stops supplying further liquidity to the business, be it materials or cash and then, on top of it , demands back all the dues whether matured or not. The action snowballs across the market; the organisation stands garroted for want of liquidity. Liquidity is the oxygen of an economic unit; in absence of it, an individual or a business goes bankrupt.

'Ability to pay' depends upon the income generation capacity of a salaried individual or the assets of a business. A bank giving a loan to either an individual (consumer loan, housing loan etc.) or to a business has to depend upon this income generation capacity of a borrower whose future income behaviour is external to the bank, but on this depends the ability of the bank to pay on time the suppliers of fund (predominantly depositors). This is what makes a bank different from other businesses. Any impairment of the income generation capacity of borrowers impairs the liquidity of a bank.

Liquidity management in banks is more crucial, because depositors, who constitute nearly 85 per cent of the fund sources of a bank, have the option of withdrawing their fund before the contracted period, though banks are not legally bound to break a term deposit before the expiry of the term (embedded option). As against this, banks cannot recall a performing loan before the due date, though they can often do so legally by virtue of a covenant to that effect.

However, the very business of the bank is to make loans without which it cannot service the depositors, and every loan has the potential of becoming illiquid.

LIQUIDITY MANAGEMENT THEORIES

Theories of liquidity management have evolved over a long period of time. Since the early days of commercial banking to the present day, liquidity continues to be of prime concern for bank management. Different theories have emerged during different periods to accommodate changing characteristics of banking but complete replacement of one theory by a new one has not been possible as the basic tenets of liquidity continue to be the same. All the theories have tried to balance between the bank's concern for liquidity and the deployment need of the society in a particular period. We will now summarise the major theories of liquidity management and some aspects of each of which have stood the test of time.

Commercial Loan Theory

This theory is as old as banking. It evolved primarily from English banking practices of the eighteenth century. This theory underlines that a bank's liquidity can be assured so long as the assets of the bank remain self-liquidating. This is possible only when the bank restricts itself to financing movements of goods through successive stages of production and consumption. The focus is on financing inventories held in the production process namely, raw materials, work-in-process, and finished goods, and in the final sale of goods namely, debtors. In other words, it is working capital finance as we understand today, which continues to be the major part of bank finance. In those days, banks were virtually forbidden to lend on a long term, and against shares and debentures other than sovereign securities. In fact, throughout much of the history of banking, and more particularly till the Great Depression of 1930s banks did not favour long-term agricultural loans, real estate financing, and lending for purchase of shares and consumer goods. They restricted themselves to short-term production finance, because a bank's primary source of funds (deposits) was also short-term in nature. Although this was considered as 'prudent banking' during that time (even presently, many bankers deep in their mind continue to believe this; they are more comfortable in working capital financing than long-term financing of capital

assets), it was not serving the broader economic purposes; banks had failed to take into account the credit needs of a growing economy. Adherence to this theory discouraged banks to lend long-term for financing plants and machinery, land development, housing, infrastructure and so on. As an economy cannot stay in vacuum for long when a need is created, other specialised institutions come up to finance the gap, or political intervention forces the banks to accommodate the growing needs of the economy, as happened in India during the 1970s.

Bankers subscribing to the commercial loan theory failed to see beyond the nomenclature of deposits—savings deposits, current accounts, term deposits—and notice the inherent stability of a significant part of such deposits, which could as well be deployed long-term.

This theory is also found to be pro-cyclical in nature, which comes to the surface during recessionary periods when the working capital cycle gets lengthened due to unsold inventories and unpaid debtors. As a result, borrowers are unable to repay on time. The rigid bankers would call up the loan 'on default', which aggravates the recessionary cycle. Assets of the defaulting borrowers are foreclosed but these cannot be sold owing to non-availability of buyers that in turn leads to a liquidity crisis in banks.

Shiftable Theory

The weaknesses of the commercial loan theory led to the emergence of shiftable theory. This theory holds that as long as banks hold assets that could be 'shifted', that is, transferred or sold for cash, banks would continue to be liquid. Under this theory, banks would insist on borrowers to put in readily saleable collaterals in addition to principal assets like inventories and debtors so that when the loan or loan assets become sticky, the banks can sell the collaterals. In addition to this, it puts emphasis on banks holding liquid government securities, which could be sold or transferred to the central bank for quick realisation of cash in times of liquidity shortages. Under this theory, the role of the central bank is enlarged. It is held that so long as the central bank stands ready to discount assets offered by the banks, the system would continue to be liquid.

This theory has also enlarged the very notion of liquidity. Quick access to liquidity rather than liquidity *per se*, as envisaged in the commercial loan theory, has become the theme of liquidity management. This has led to the growth of the wholesale funds market in both breadth and depth aided by the emergence of innovative financial instruments; a bank need not hold too many liquid assets, because the funds market can be accessed as and when necessary.

Anticipated Income Theory

The shiftable theory gave rise to a security oriented approach in lending. It does not support entrepreneurial ventures where collaterals are not available though the venture has the potential to generate enough cash flows to repay the debt. The security orientation of banks had hindered the post-Second World War reconstruction of devastated economies of Europe. Banks have not also been helpful in financing entrepreneurial ventures in emerging economies, which has resulted in the emergence of venture capitalists.

The anticipated income theory, though not denying the basic tenets of the commercial loan and shiftable theories, has drawn the attention of bankers to base their liquidity management by linking loan repayment on future income (cash flow) of a borrower. Over a period this theory has helped in the emergence of purpose oriented lending, though not jettisoning the security aspects of a loan. This theory upholds that a bank's liquidity is assured as long as a business remains well-functioning, which itself

is the biggest security of a loan. Hence, banks should lay more emphasis on assessing the viability of a business than the collaterals it can offer; if a business fails, no amount of security would be able to cover the loan under a distress sale. It is necessary, therefore, to install proper monitoring and follow-up systems as a part of credit management of banks.

The cash flow approach embedded in the anticipated income theory has focused the attention of banks towards sanctioning of loans which could be amortised, that is, the loan is repayable by monthly or quarterly instalments linked to the generation of cash flows at the borrower's business. The growth of business term loans, consumer instalment loans, and housing loans during the post-Second World War era is due to the understanding of the importance of cash flows in the liquidity management of banks. On the investment front, banks are similarly encouraged to stagger maturities of the portfolio so that redemptions occur on a regular and predictable basis to match the liquidity needs of a bank. This has come to be known as the 'ladder effect'. For the first time in the history of banking, this theory recognises that so long as the maturity pattern of loan and investment assets is matched with the maturity pattern of liabilities, banks will not be facing a liquidity crisis. This laid the foundation of the assets–liabilities strategy that emerged during the later part of the 1980s.

FLUCTUATIONS IN THE ECONOMY

When economic activity increases, demand for loans also increases. If there is a deposit withdrawal at the same time or deposits do not grow commensurately a liquidity gap is created, the funding of which may often be difficult and costly. In fact, most of the liquidity problems in a bank emanate from fluctuations in the economy, the broad classifications of which we will now discuss.

Seasonal Fluctuations

As the name suggests, seasonal fluctuations relate to seasons, which in turn relate to climate, weather, and religious and other social festivities; all these change over time so also the seasonal impact on commercial activities. Moreover, new seasons are added like father's day and lover's day while old seasons like the 'Amon' festival die out gradually.

In a vast country like India, the monsoon varies from region to region, so also agricultural activities. During the sowing time, demand for loan increases while deposits fall. Hence, a bank having large exposure in rural areas would experience a liquidity shortage. During the harvesting season, the opposite happens. Similar is the case with construction activity, which increases during the spring and winter seasons and virtually comes to a halt during the rainy season. Spring and winter seasons are also marked for marriage ceremonies. Banks experience heavy withdrawals during this period, particularly in rural India.

Religious and social customs play an important role in determining liquidity needs. Christmas is now a pan-India affair, not confined to Christians alone. Id, Durga Puja, Ganesh Chaturthi, Diwali, Pongal among others are the other major religious festivals observed in different parts of India. During these festivities consumer demands increase, making retailers hold higher levels of inventories of various consumer goods, both durables and non-durables. This in turn increases inventories at all points along the backward linkage ending with the manufacturers. Consequently, loan demand shoots up so also the draw down of deposits causing widening of the liquidity gap.

Besides demand seasonality, we also observe input seasonality where demand of the final product is generally uniform throughout a year but the inputs required to produce the final product are seasonal. This is mostly observed in agro-based products. For example, while demand for sugar is not so seasonal, sugarcane production is very much seasonal. Sugar producers have to procure as much sugarcane as is necessary, process it as fast as possible to obtain the best yield, and store it for the year's sale. Hence, demand for loans from sugar manufacturers rise during the sowing season (advances) and also during the processing period when the inventory of sugar goes up unmatched with the current demand.[1]

Seasonal fluctuations affect small banks, which operate in a local or regional market, because of lack of diversity. In India, this is mostly the case with cooperative banks and regional rural banks.

Although seasonal fluctuations do have an impact on the liquidity position of banks, it is possible to predict the variations in demand and supply of funds, as seasons are mostly recurrent in nature.

Cyclical Fluctuations

Trade cycles are not as easily predictable as seasonal fluctuations, though in an open and deregulated economy these are bound to occur. Earlier, business cycles were of a longer duration and were few in number, but during the post-Second World War era, business cycles have increased in number though these are of smaller durations. Researchers have identified various causes of business cycles, which could be broadly classified with respect to their origin, under external and domestic shocks. As the economies in the present day world are more integrated, shocks are quickly transmitted from one country to the other. The shocks could be financial (the Asian crisis of 1998, the banking crisis of United States during 2007–08, and the debt crisis of Dubai and

---

[1] As is the custom of the trade, sugarcane manufacturers have to pay advance to the farmers during the sowing season that gets adjusted from the contracted price of harvested sugarcanes.

Greece during 2009–10), monetary fiscal (like currency devaluations, interest rate policy of central banks, budgetary or fiscal surpluses, taxation policy and so on), technological innovation and discoveries (the dot.com boom, discovery of oil fields like North-sea oil, and life saving drugs), and wars and invasions (world wars and the invasion of Iraq).

All the shocks, whether they result in a boom or recession, influence the liquidity of an economy and change the inventory behaviour of firms. During the expansion phase large-scale production reduces the marginal cost of production (economies of scale) that provides incentive to further increase production. Although movement of the inventory is faster during the boom, the sales–inventory ratio (SI) increases, because firms bunch production more than is necessary to match the fluctuations in sales ('buyers-not-to be returned' syndrome). Increase in production followed by capacity expansion (and vice-versa) and a larger SI ratio demand very high liquidity stretching the capacity of the banking system. Overproduction in anticipation of increasing demand during the boom time ultimately leads to contraction or crash followed by recession due to mismatch between production and real demand for goods and services; the sales–inventory ratio starts falling sharply, which forces the firm to cut back production, reduce employment, and hold a minimum level of inventory thereby ushering in recession. In fact, the behaviour of firms in a competitive economy is pro-cyclical in nature, which is often accentuated by banks by providing excess liquidity during a boom and withholding liquidity during a recession when it is most needed. Without going into the merit of such behaviour of firms and financial institutions, the operational aspects of liquidity management over business cycles could be analysed.

During the expansion phase loan demand outstrips growth in deposits (individual deposi-

tors draw down deposits to support their growing demand of consumer goods). As a result, the liquidity gap widens forcing banks to either resort to bulk loans (certificates of deposits) or loans from inter-bank-inter-corporate markets at high costs or sell securities below its opportunity costs. During contraction, though loan demand falls, deposits may also shrink (because depositors might withdraw deposits to support their consumption expenditure on the face of falling income), which, however is less than the rate of fall in demand. The problem during recession is, therefore, to find avenues for investing excess liquidity. In the absence of loan demand, the excess liquidity generally finds place in government securities.

Banks should anticipate monetary policy intervention by the central bank. During the expansion phase, demand for goods and services increases faster than the productive capacity of the economy (as many expansion projects are yet to commence production). As a result, there is a possibility of runaway inflation. In order to prevent such a situation from occurring, monetary authorities may pursue restrictive policies to contain the excess liquidity in the system by adopting several measures like raising the cash reserve ratio/statutory liquidity ratio (CRR/SLR) (discussed later), increasing policy rates, and engaging in open market operations. While demand for loans increases, such measures by the central bank may affect the ability of banks to make additional loans, which may push up interest rates to a very high level. Banks that have high liquidity (net of CRR/SLR) will profit from such high rates while banks with low levels of net liquidity will lose out not only on profitability but also on loan-customers.

Although it is difficult to predict the date and duration of business cycles, bankers may adopt a proactive approach by studying the liquidity behaviour in similar cycles in the past and put in place contingent plans for various scenarios that might emerge during such a cycle and get themselves ready without being surprised by the event (knee-jerk reactions).

Secular Movements

These are changes that mostly occur over a long period of time and may encompass several business cycles during which life style changes occur due to accumulation of experiences in the changing socioeconomic framework and advancement of technology that alters the approach to life and living and the risk-taking behaviour of a society. Sensitive business managers would locate these changes at the time of their initial occurrences as primary trends, some of which may finally qualify for being considered as long-term secular trends. In India until the 1970s, bank and post office deposits were perhaps the only mode of institutional savings by individuals; these were no-risk safe deposits. But from the 1980s onwards, a distinct change was observable in the risk-taking behaviour of households. They gradually started moving a part of their savings to mutual funds and also a small amount directly to the stock market. By the 1990s, the secular trend had stabilised. Banks initially reacted against erosion of their deposit bases but have finally come around and started selling mutual fund products and depository services coupled with providing a platform for share trading by individuals.

These economic fluctuations impact on loan demand and deposit flow which make liquidity planning imperative for a bank. In the absence of proper plans drawn in anticipation of different scenarios in the short- and medium-term, a bank may be taken unaware in the face of a sudden liquidity shortage or surplus. The former may lead to a crisis of confidence and the latter may seriously affect the profitability of a bank.

While planning for liquidity a bank has to keep in mind the statutory reserve requirements.

In India, there are two kinds of such reserves expressed in ratio form as percentage of demand and time liabilities: Cash Reserve Ratio (CRR) and Statutory Liquidity Ratio (SLR). Any movement in the level of deposits proportionately changes the level of these two reserves.

LIQUIDITY PLANNING

All these discussions can be summarised in a planning format as changes in liquidity:

1. Increase or decrease in funds due to increase or decrease in deposits.
2. Increase or decrease in funds due to decrease or increase in loans and investments.
3. Increase or decrease in funds due to decrease or increase in statutory reserves as a consequence of decrease or increase in deposits.

Table 2.1 gives an example of liquidity planning of a bank. It is based on the incremental funds flow approach that is easily understandable by bank managers.

The periods shown in the second column onwards in Table 2.1 could be a week, a month, or a quarter depending upon the planning horizon of a bank or on the exigency of a situation. The period can also be broken down to one day to take care of the intra-day liquidity position of a bank.

Period 1 appears to be a busy period when demand for loan is high; there is also an erosion of deposits. Loan demand reaches its peak in period 3 when the bank is required to resort to borrowings as growth in loan demand exceeds growth in deposits. Seasonal fluctuations in loan demand or in deposits are normal to the banking system; what is important is to examine how the bank has planned to take care of such fluctuations, and where it is leading. In Table 2.2 the bank's strategy is analysed.

TABLE 2.1   Liquidity Planning of a Commercial Bank (Funds Flow Approach)

Uses of Funds (Incremental)	Period			
	1	2	3	4
Government & Approved Securities (SLR–25%)	–525	550	300	–125
Balance with RBI (CRR–14.5%)	–300	320	175	–75
Cash & Bank Balances	–50	25	25	–30
Loans and Advances	2600	3000	3900	3010
Other Market Securities	775	105	1300	1520
Total	2500	4000	5700	4300
Sources of Funds (Incremental)				
Demand Deposits	–700	1300	1000	–1200
Certificate of Deposits	–2500	200	–1400	–500
Time Deposits	1100	700	1600	1200
A. Sub-total	–2100	2200	1200	–500
Borrowings				
Reserve Bank of India	500	200	500	0
Institutional Borrowings & Refinance	1300	300	500	1800
Money Market Borrowings	800	1300	2500	2000
B. Sub-total	2600	1800	3500	3800
Maturity of Securities	1000	0	0	0
Sale of Securities	1000	0	0	1000
Sale & Repurchase of Securities (REPOS)	0	0	1000	0
C. Sub-total	2000	0	1000	1000
Total (A+B+C)	2500	4000	5700	4300

The funds flow analysis done in Table 2.2 reveal heavy dependence of the bank on external borrowings to support liquidity demand in periods II–III. This is clearly observable from the summary given at the bottom of the table. While in period I an internal source is funding the net demand almost fully (92.73 per cent), its contribution turned out to be negative in the following three periods, the highest being in period III. The reason behind this is that the growth in expected demand of loan has outstripped the projected growth in deposits leaving a huge gap which the bank proposes to fund by raising market loans and from sale of securities, both of which being high cost sources may affect the profitability of the bank.

Except refinance, borrowings through CDs, repos, and other money market instruments are short-term in nature and of fixed tenor and may not always be renewable while loans are generally long-term in nature. Hence, heavy dependence on market borrowings makes a bank vulnerable to liquidity risk; the problem is aggravated when there are maturity mismatches between assets and liabilities.

TABLE 2.2   Incremental Funds Analysis of the Bank

Period I

Demand

Commercial		Regulatory		Net Demand
Increase in Loans & Advances	2600	Decrease in SLR	−525	
Increase in Net Deposits	−400	Decrease in CRR	−300	2200−825 = 1375
Total	2200		−825	1375

Fund Sources

Internal		External Market		Net Sources
Decrease in Cash & Bank Balances	50	Increase in Borrowings	2600	1275+100 = 1375
Decrease in Net Securities	1225	Decrease in CDs	−2500	
Total	1275		100	1375
Ratio of Net Sources on Net Demand (%)	92.73		7.27	100

Period II

Demand

Commercial		Regulatory		Net Demand
Increase in Loans & Advances	3000	Increase in SLR	550	
Increase in Net Deposits	−2000	Increase in CRR	320	1000+870 = 1870
Total	1000		870	1870

Fund Sources

Internal		External Market		Net Sources
Increase in Cash & Bank Balances	−25	Increase in Borrowings	1800	2000−130 = 1870
Increase in Net Securities	−105	Increase in CDs	200	
Total	−130		2000	1870
Ratio of Net Sources on Net Demand (%)	−6.95		106.95	100

Period III

Demand

Commercial		Regulatory		Net Demand
Increase in Loans & Advances	3900	Increase in SLR	300	
Increase in Net Deposits	−2600	Increase in CRR	175	1300+475 = 1775
Total	1300		475	1775

Fund Sources

Internal		External Market		Net Sources
Increase in Cash & Bank Balances	−25	Increase in Borrowings	3500	
Increase in Net Securities	−1300	Decrease in CDs	−1400	3100−1325 = 1775
		Increase in REPOS	1000	
Total	−1325		3100	1775
Ratio of Net Sources on Net Demand (%)	−74.65		174.65	100

(contd.)

Table 2.2 (*contd.*)

Commercial		Period IV Demand				Net Demand
		Regulatory				
Increase in Loans & Advances	3010	Decrease in SLR		−125		
Increase in Net Deposits	0	Decrease in CRR		−75		3010−200 = 2810
Total	3010			−200		2810
Internal		Fund Sources				
		External Market		Net Sources		
Decrease in Cash & Bank Balances	30	Increase in Borrowings		3800		
Increase in Net Securities	−520	Decrease in CDs		−500		3300−490 = 2810
Total	−490			3300		2810
Ratio of Net Sources on Net Demand (%)	−17.44			117.44		100

	Summary of Ratios of Net Sources on Net Demand			
	Period I	Period II	Period III	Period IV
Internal (%)	92.73	−6.95	−74.65	−17.44
External (%)	7.27	106.95	174.65	117.44
Total	100	100	100	100

Notes: 1. Certificates of deposit (CDs) are not to be considered as part of other deposits. These are wholesale funds raised from the market; major suppliers of this fund are banks, corporate and financial institutions having surplus funds for a short period. CDs have a fixed term and may not be renewed on maturity. Banks cannot redeem CDs before maturity. As such, it is desirable to consider them as part of market borrowings.
2. Securities are marketables, held as 'available for sale'.

It appears that the bank is highly aggressive in the loan market; the incremental credit–deposit ratio is very high in all the periods. The bank would do well to rein in the galloping horse before it reaches the brink.

LIQUIDITY RATIOS

It is necessary now to discuss certain ratios pertinent to this analysis. Before we do so it is important to lay down a few basic principles of ratio analysis. Ratio for a single period is meaningless except for statutory ratios like CRR and SLR. A ratio has to be taken over a period to discern the trend; whether it is decreasing or increasing. Often a firm's ratio is compared with the industry average. While such a comparison may be useful at it tells us the behaviour of the firm vis-à-vis the competition, it is more important to know

whether a particular ratio is deviating from its normative behaviour. For example, the normal behaviour of the gross profit ratio (GP ratio) of a manufacturing firm is that it should remain stable during a given technology period; it may increase marginally during the initial period of technology absorption but thereafter the ratio should be flat. Any downward movement of the GP ratio may signal a failure of the cost control mechanism of the manufacturing management in the sense that important cost items, for example, labour are becoming sticky.[2] These two basic rules apply to all

[2] For an elaborate discussion see, Bhattacharya, Hrishikes, *Total Management by Ratios: An Analytic Approach to Management Control and Stock Market valuation* (2nd edition), Sage Publications, New Delhi, 2007.

ratio analyses for management control across all industries, be it manufacturing or banking.

CRR and SLR

These two regulatory ratios originally evolved to ensure the ultimate liquidity of a bank. However, over a period they have become important tools—to the point of being blunt—at the hands of the Reserve Bank of India (RBI) for liquidity control of the economy as a whole. By increasing or decreasing CRR (calculated on demand and time liabilities) RBI can suck out liquidity or inject liquidity from or into the system, the ultimate effect being discouraging or encouraging granting of credit by commercial banks. Since the purpose of CRR is immobilisation of liquidity, the fund cannot be invested by the central bank (which will defeat its very purpose) and hence, no interest could be earned and as such no interest is payable to banks on CRR balances.[3] Therefore, CRR not only takes away a part of the available fund, it also imposes a cost on the bank, which should be factored in while determining the base lending rate, which is discussed in Chapter 4.

The next claimant on a bank's fund is another statutory ratio—SLR. Similar to CRR this ratio is also prescribed by the monetary authorities from time to time. As the name suggests, this ratio along with CRR intends to provide for the ultimate liquidity of a bank. Similar to CRR this is also calculated on the demand and time

[3] However, the Reserve Bank of India had been paying interest on CRR balances beyond the required statutory minimum of 3 per cent of demand and time liabilities. The rate of interest was as high as 10.5. per cent per annum as on 26 October 1985, which was gradually reduced over a period ending with 3.5 per cent per annum as on September 2004. RBI must have been paying this interest from its other income, as banks' CRR balances cannot be invested. RBI has since stopped paying any interest on CRR balances.

liabilities of a bank. The statute requires that the funds under SLR have to be invested primarily in government securities. Although the original objective of this ratio was to ensure the liquidity of the banking system, over a period this is predominantly being used for supporting government's borrowing programmes—banks are used as a captive market for this purpose.

For a long time the general belief was that sovereign securities do not default but the experience of the past three decades shows that sovereigns do default (Nigeria, Dubai, and Greece are some examples). Besides, all government securities may not have ready marketability at certain times—securities of certain duration may become sticky. Such a situation may exacerbate a liquidity crisis unless the central bank quickly provides a repurchase window. Although CRR and SLR can be bracketed as long-term liquidity ratios of a bank, their immediate effect is erosion of liquidity. At the operational level funds available from deposit sources are limited by, $(1-CRR-SLR)$.

Loan to Deposit Ratio or Credit–Deposit Ratio

The ratio is given by:

$$\frac{Loan\ (Credit)}{Deposits}$$

This is a policy ratio, which has an impact on the long-term liquidity of a bank. In India, it is popularly known as the C–D ratio. For the bank as a whole, the C–D ratio should not be more than

$$\frac{Credit}{Deposits\ (1-CRR-SLR)\ +\ Capital\ Fund}$$

except when a bank resorts to market borrowings. Credit should include loans advanced by way of subscription to the bonds issued by the borrowing companies but shall not include those bonds picked up from the market for investment purposes.

The modified C–D ratio is a superior ratio for management control of liquidity. The denominator of this ratio indicates the available funds for credit deployment, hence a ratio more than one may indicate that the bank is over expanding that may create liquidity problems. The conventional C–D ratio has a politico-economic overtone, particularly in a country like India, which suffers from uneven economic development across states/regions.[4]

It is observed that large banks with an international presence have higher C–D ratios than smaller banks. The reasons behind this are a higher risk appetite, superior appraisal and monitoring systems, market dominance in the big ticket loan market (which also requires making available large funds at short notice), superior technology, and access to the wholesale funds market.

Large banks also enjoy (or, suffer from) the aura of 'too big to fail'. While on the one hand bank customers and the public in general are led to believe that such a huge bank just cannot fail,

on the other, the bank executives believe that even if the bank fails, the government would ultimately bail it out for political reasons as it cannot afford to see a large bank going bankrupt (the credibility of the government or the country is often synonymous to the credibility of its large banks). These two together lead to the irresponsible lending behaviour of large banks in a spree to expand market shares. Such behaviour is reflected in an unusual increase in the C–D ratio. This is often overlooked by bank regulators (as many of the recent banking crises would reveal); banks are allowed to operate with a thin liquidity margin. When some of the big ticket loans (including securitised loan assets) fail and the sources of market borrowings dry up the liquidity crisis would have a cascading effect on the financial system of a country.

However, the C–D ratio does not tell anything about the quality of the loan portfolio; one bank may have a higher growth in non-performing assets (NPAs) than another bank but both may have the same C–D ratio. As NPAs are a source of illiquidity (and a major one in times of financial crisis), the C–D ratio as a measure of liquidity should be considered together with the NPA ratio of a bank. Although the C–D ratio per se does not indicate the quality of the loan portfolio, the movement of this ratio over a period would generally indicate quality migration of the loan portfolio. When the C–D ratio is lower than the policy standard, or competition, or the 'advisory' standard of the central bank there would be pressure on the operational management to increase lending quickly. This is done mostly by increasing the discretionary powers of managers at the operational level. This pressure leads to dilution of the credit standard, resulting in a fall in the overall quality of the loan portfolio. As against this, a bank having a higher C–D ratio than the standard would try to contain credit expansion by increasing the level of the credit

---

[4] This is also observed in the developed world. For example, in the US, Section 109 of Riegle-Neal Interstate Banking and Branching Efficiency Act, 1994, prohibits a bank from establishing or acquiring a branch or branches outside of its home state or branches of banks controlled by out-of-state bank holding companies primarily for the purpose of deposit production. The first step in the process involves a loan-to-deposit ratio screen that compares a bank's state-wide loan-to-deposit ratio to the host state ratio for banks in a particular state. If a bank's state-wide loan-to-deposit ratio is less than one-half of the published ratio for that state, the regulating agency is to determine whether the bank is reasonably helping to meet the credit needs of the communities served by the bank's inter-state branches, if not the violating bank will be subject to sanctions by the regulator.

standard and a stricter monitoring of it, which will have the effect of improving the quality of lending.

The C–D ratio also does not tell anything about the periodic cash flows of a loan or the stability of deposits, that is., the liquidity content of a loan and the true liquidity demand of deposits. A bank having a C–D ratio of say 70 per cent may be more liquid than a bank with a ratio of 50 per cent, because a major part of the loan portfolio of the former may constitute short-term or amortised loans with shorter term periodic repayments, say monthly (cash inflows), while the loan portfolio of the latter bank may predominantly contain cash credit type of loans (virtually, no repayment) or term loans having single or longer term repayments (say yearly). It may also be that the stable part of the deposits of the first bank may be more than that of the second bank. We will see later that the assets-liabilities strategy of banks is based on these considerations.

In conclusion, it can be said that the C–D ratio has its limitations in capturing the true liquidity position of a bank but a careful watch on the movement of this ratio would tell us whether a bank is moving towards a liquidity crisis by 'overtrading'.

Cash Ratio

Unlike the C–D ratio, this ratio measures the liquidity position of a bank directly. There are two variations of this ratio:

$$\text{(a)} \quad \frac{\text{Total Deposits}}{\substack{\text{Cash and Balances with Other Banks +} \\ \text{Government \& Approved Securities +} \\ \text{Other Marketable Securities}}}$$

The denominator of this ratio represents the aggregate of cash assets. This is a long-term liquidity ratio of a bank. While discussing CRR and SLR we mentioned that in India a major part

of these cash assets constitute statutory reserves, which are not available for the short-term liquidity need of a bank; on the contrary, they demand liquidity. This limitation gives rise to the next ratio.

$$\text{(b)} \quad \frac{\text{Total Deposits}}{\text{Net Cash Assets}}$$

Net cash assets are calculated by excluding CRR and SLR assets from the total cash assets. This is a superior short-term liquidity ratio of a bank, though it ignores the ability of a bank to raise funds from other sources like market borrowings, refinancing, bills rediscounting, repo financing, and so on. However, one should remember that when a bank faces a liquidity problem (and the market comes to know about it) then most of the other sources dry up except perhaps the repo financing window of the central bank.

In both the cash ratios the variable—total deposits—is taken to the numerator suggesting that these should be considered as turnover ratios, that is, how fast or how slow the cash assets are being turned over the deposits. While some analysts may like to compare these bank ratios with the industry average, some others may contend that the deposit profile of a particular bank has to be taken into account while making such a comparison. A bank with a higher level of fixed deposits in its portfolio will require lesser amount of cash assets, and as such, its turnover will be higher than a bank with a lower level of fixed deposits in its portfolio. A bank may, therefore, be tempted to augment its turnover by contracting more long-term deposits. This was the case in India until even the early 1990s when deposit mobilisation was geared towards garnering more fixed deposits; even savings bank account holders were persuaded to transfer a part of their balances to term deposits. Such a strategy though lowered the liquidity requirement of

Indian banks (in fact, liquidity management was not much of a problem then), it resulted in a substantial increase in the cost of funds, which made the banks vulnerable to competition that came to light when banking in India was being deregulated. A change in strategy followed but it had to contend with the fact that every bank has a regional orientation—no matter how large it is—and every region has peculiar behavioural formations towards savings that ultimately shape the deposit profiles of banks.

Liquidity Model

It is necessary now to find out the optimal cash assets holding of a bank. We intend to present here a model, which is less mathematical, and easily implementable by bank managers. This is a modified version of the cash management model generally used for working capital management.[5]

We first determine the cost of maintaining cash (liquid) assets (CML) which is given by:

$$CML = LR * C$$

where, C is the opportunity cost per rupee of liquid resources (LR). Now, not all cash assets are non-earning. Funds invested in marketable securities do earn a return. Opportunity cost should, therefore, be the average rate of return on loan assets (ROLA) minus the rate of return on marketable securities (RMS). That is:

$$C = ROLA - RMS.[6]$$

[5] See, Bhattacharya, Hrishikes, *Working Capital Management: Strategies and Techniques* (2nd edition), PHI Learning (P) Limited, New Delhi, 2009.

[6] One may notice that we have not taken return on assets (ROA) in this equation because ROA is the return on total assets of a bank, which include non-earning assets also (say, buildings).

The expected cost of not maintaining sufficient liquid resources depends upon the probability (p) of being out of liquidity and the cost that a bank may incur in restoring such liquidity. Unlike other businesses, the cost of being illiquid is very high in banking. If timely action is not taken, the situation may snowball into a banking crisis. The cost is determined by the demand and supply situation in the money and inter-bank market, and the declared repo rate of the central bank.

The penal cost of arranging cash on an urgent basis is given by the total cost of raising such funds reduced by the available liquid resources. That is:

$$\text{Penal Cost (PC)} = Lcf * i - LR * m[7]$$

where, Lcf is the lowest level of cash flow during a period, (i) is the average percentage cost of raising such a fund and (m) is the rate of opportunity savings for having the existing liquid resources (LR).

Therefore, the expected cost of liquidity (COL) will be:

$$COL = \frac{|\ LR - Lcf\ |}{Lcf + Lmf} * PC$$

where, (Lmf) is the highest level of cash flow during a period.

The total expected cost of maintaining liquidity (TCML) will finally be:

$$TCML = CML + \frac{|\ LR - Lcf\ |}{Lcf + Lmf} * PC$$

[7] Generally, (m) should be greater than (i) because the existing (LR) not only saves on (i), it also earns some return as indicated in the discussion. Therefore, (m) can be taken as, i + RMS.

The obvious assumption behind this model is that a bank is presumed to be illiquid when the cash flow is negative, that is., the bank is unable to meet the demand of its depositors as well as its borrowers to whom commitments have already been made or have to be made in accordance with the business plan of the bank. Hence, (Lcf) in the above model will always be negative. When (LR) is equal to or greater than the Lcf in the numerator of the model then the probability of the bank not being able to meet the liquidity gap should be considered zero.

An Example

The assets–liabilities management (ALM) department of a bank finds that the net cash flow of the bank during a period would vary between a negative of Rs 157 crore and a positive of Rs 385 crore following a uniform distribution pattern.

Average rate of return on loans and advances is 9 per cent while that on marketable securities is 6 per cent. The department finds that when net cash flow becomes negative and the bank would have to arrange for liquidity on an urgent basis the average rate may go up to 20 per cent.

The top management of the bank wants to know what should be the optimal level of liquid resources that the bank must hold.

Solution

The following steps are to be followed:

1. Cost of maintaining liquidity (CML)

$$CML = LR * C,$$

where   C = ROLA – RMS.

or, C = 0.09 – 0.06 = 0.03

Hence, CML = LR * 0.03

2. Expected cost of liquidity (COL)

(a)

$$p = \frac{|LR - Lcf|}{Lcf + Lmf} = \frac{|LR - 157|}{157 + 385} = \frac{|LR - 157|}{542}$$

(b) Penal cost (PC) = Lcf * i – LR * m = 157 * 0.20 – LR (0.20 + 0.06) = 31.40 – LR * 0.26.

Hence,

(c) Expected cost of liquidity (COL)

$$COL = \frac{|LR - 157|}{542} * (31.40 - LR * 0.26)$$

3. Total expected cost of maintaining liquidity (TCML)

$$TCML = CML + \frac{|LR - Lcf|}{Lcf + Lmf} * (PC)$$

or, $0.03\,LR + \dfrac{|LR - 157|}{542} * (31.40 - 0.26\,LR)$

In Table 2.3 we have shown calculations to derive the total expected cost of maintaining liquidity (TCML) assuming different levels of LR.

In column 1 of Table 2.3 we have first assumed different levels of (LR). The rest of the columns are calculated against each level of such (LR) in accordance with the formulae shown above. A scrutiny of the entries in Table 2.3 will reveal that for an (LR) level of Rs 110 crore (column 1), the total expected cost of maintaining liquidity (column 5) is at its minimum (Rs 3.54 crore), against a 9 per cent probability of being out of liquidity (column 2).

Although Table 2.3 provides the least cost solution at a 9 per cent probability of being out of liquidity, it may not be acceptable to another bank, because of its different risk-profile (which in turn depends on size, capital, market access, system efficiency, managerial skills among others). A bank with a superior risk-profile may settle for a higher probability, say 15 per cent, while a bank with a lower risk-profile would not like to go beyond a 5 per cent probability of being out of liquidity. Thus, a bank, which does not agree with the least cost solution, may first choose its level of tolerance (p) from column 2 of

TABLE **2.3**   Total Expected Cost of Maintaining Liquidity

(Rupees in Crore)

Level of Liquid Resources (LR) 1	Probability (p) 2	Cost of Maintaining Liquid Resources (CML) 3	Expected Cost of Liquidity (COL) 4	Total Expected Cost of Maintaining Liquidity (TCML) (Col. 3+4) 5
90	0.1236	2.7	0.99	3.69
80	0.1421	2.4	1.51	3.91
70	0.1605	2.1	2.12	4.22
60	0.179	1.8	2.83	5.13
50	0.1974	1.5	3.63	5.73
40	0.2158	1.2	4.53	6.43
30	0.2343	0.9	5.53	
100	0.1052	3	0.57	3.57
110	0.867	3.3	0.24	3.54
120	0.0682	3.6	0.014	3.61
130	0.0498	3.9	−0.12	3.78
150	0.013	4.5	−0.01	4.5

Table 2.3 and then locate the level of liquid resources required against it from the corresponding row in column 1 and the required total cost (TCML) from column 5.

BALANCE SHEET APPROACH

We have so far discussed certain individual liquidity ratios. Now, we will take a balance sheet view of the liquidity position of two banks with the help of several other ratios and make a comparative analysis of the liquidity strategies of these two banks (Table 2.4).

The comparative analysis done in Table 2.4 reveals that the liquidity position of bank 'B' is significantly better than that of bank 'A'. It is unlikely that bank 'B' with a quick liquid assets ratio of 30 per cent and net liquid assets ratio of 47 per cent would face any liquidity problem under normal circumstances if the current liquidity and loan policies are maintained. It appears that bank 'B' is a deposit oriented conservative

bank; it prefers putting a sizeable part of its funds in secured assets—balances with RBI and investment in government securities is more (14.83 per cent) than the statutory minimum. This bank is less aggressive in the loan market as indicated by a comparatively small C–D ratio. This conservative approach may lower the profitability of the bank. But this could be a deliberate policy of a trade-off between risk and profitability, more so because the equity capital of the bank as a percentage of assets is comparatively lower than bank 'A', thus requiring a lesser level of profit to service its capital.

Bank 'A' has a quick liquid assets ratio of 9 per cent; its net liquidity assets ratio is marginally higher than this. As on the date of the balance sheet, aggregate of CRR and SLR balances of the bank, as percentage of total assets, is in the negative. There could be nothing wrong about this if the bank's policy is to maximise returns by deploying its funds in more profitable loan

TABLE 2.4   Comparative Liquidity Ratios of Two Banks

	A' Bank	B' Bank
Asset–Liquidity Ratios		
A. Percentage of Total Assets		
1. Cash in hand and with banks in current accounts	5.41	6.37
2. Inter-bank loans	0.36	0
3. Reverse repurchase agreements	1.75	14.82
4. Treasury bills (unencumbered)	1.54	8.47
Quick Liquid Assets	9.06	29.66
5. Debentures & bonds (unencumbered and less than one year maturity)	5.31	2.98
6. Balances with RBI (CRR) + SLR securities	−2.75	14.83
Net Liquid Assets	11.62	47.47
B. Credit–Deposit Ratio	118.48	64.18
Liability–Liquidity Ratios		
A. Percentage of Total Assets		
1. Demand deposits	15.37	33.22
2. Savings bank deposits	23.64	22.06
3. Time deposits	22.73	29.8
4. Other deposits (including Bills payables)	4.31	6.6
Total Deposits	66.05	91.68
5. Call deposits and Certificate of Deposits (CD)	17.02	0
6. Refinance and REPOS	4.47	0
Total Outside Liabilities	87.54	91.68
7. Share capital, Reserves & Surpluses	12.46	8.32
Total Liabilities	100	100
B. Non-performing Assets to Loans & Advances	1.03	0.78
C. Provision for Bad Debts (NET) to Loans & Advances	0.59	1
D. Reserve for Loan Losses to Loans & Advances	1.76	1.05

assets; a C–D ratio of more than 100 per cent supports this view. This also suggests that unlike bank 'B', this bank is highly aggressive in the loan market. Bank 'A''s reliance on deposits to fund assets is much lower than bank 'B''s. Bank 'A' is a large bank with a significantly higher level of equity capital that allows access to the wholesale funds market—more than 20 per cent of the assets of the bank are funded by market borrowings including refinances. These borrowings, particularly CDs and inter-bank loans, are of fixed tenure and renewable only at the option of lenders. The wholesale funds market constitutes mostly short-term surplus funds of corporate and banks, the term varying between one day and less than a year. The market is also highly volatile. If a part of this fund, say 50 per cent is not renewed then the bank with a liquid assets ratio of 9 per cent will be on the borderline of a liquidity crisis. A high capital–assets ratio may give easy access to the wholesale funds market but when the market dries up it ceases to be of much help. There will be some solace if a sizeable part of the loan portfolio is short-term in nature—which closely matches the characteristics of the wholesale funds market—and/or cash flow based (which makes it eligible for securitisation). It is advisable for a bank to match, as closely as possible, the characteristics of a fund source with that of the deployment, the trade-off being profitability.

DEPLOYMENT STRATEGIES

POOL OF FUNDS STRATEGY

Originally, the deployment strategies of banks rested on the pool of funds concept.[8] The idea was that though funds flow into a bank from different sources, once they enter the pool they lose the characteristics of the sources from which they have come. Funds are then deployed from the pool to different assets in accordance with a rather vague understanding of the trade-off between liquidity and profitability. Figure 2.1 explains this strategy.

The strategy depicted in Figure 2.1 is partly influenced by the shiftable theory discussed earlier. The uniform light arrows shown on the left hand side of Figure 2.1 signify that no special importance or priority is attached to any of the fund sources (though at the operational level more importance is still attached to the time deposit for liquidity consideration which is discussed later). However, on the right hand side, priorities are attached to investments in different assets. For example, the thickest line for primary reserves (CRR assets) shows that the highest importance is given to it, followed

by secondary reserves (SLR assets). Loans and advances are third in order of importance as these are considered less liquid. In this model, investments in 'other securities' do not flow from the liquidity strategy of a bank but from pure commercial considerations.

The pool of funds strategy lays down only a broad set of rules for allocating funds to various assets; it does not explicitly provide for means to determine the proportion to be allocated to different assets, neither does it suggest a solution to the dilemma between liquidity and profitability, though always emphasising the former without providing any methodology for determining the liquidity requirements of different liabilities and assets. This has resulted in placing greater emphasis on time deposits, which are believed to have a lesser liquidity demand. Bankers are thus found to mobilise larger amounts of time deposits than savings and current account deposits, even encouraging depositors to move balances from the latter two accounts to time deposits. This has increased the cost of funds. It has been found that during the period 1950–70 cost of funds of US banks increased rapidly. In India, the same thing was observed until the early 1990s. All through, the general understanding was that since loan assets are mostly illiquid they should be funded by time deposits that have longer maturity and lesser demand for liquidity.

The pool of funds strategy, coupled with an accrual system of income booking (whereby interest income is booked simply by debiting the loan account irrespective of its actual realisation), has resulted in losses or a substantial erosion of the profitability of commercial banks throughout the world. With the opening up of the economy and the gradual deregulation of the banking industry, bankers are forced to have a relook at the pool of funds strategy and the existing accounting system. The latter has been replaced by a cash-based system under 'prudential norms'

---

[8] The basic idea can be found in Crosse, Howard D., *Management Policies for Commercial Banks*, Prentice-Hall, Englewood Cliffs, New Jersey, 1962.

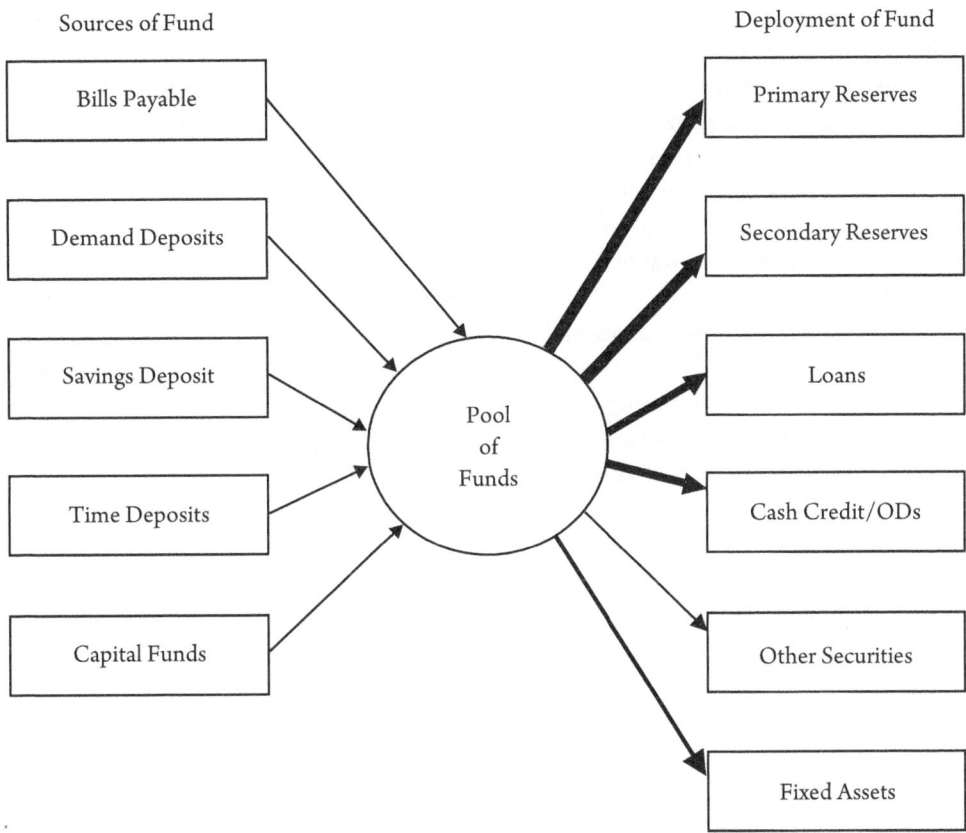

FIGURE 2.1   Pool of Funds Strategy

and the deployment strategy has been modified to address the changing notion of liquidity and profitability. The modified strategy has come to be known as the asset allocation strategy.

Asset Allocation Strategy

The underlying principle behind this strategy is that the liquidity demands of different liabilities and assets vary and hence, there should be some matching between the liquidity demand of a particular group of assets with that of liabilities. The basis of this principle is the legal requirements of reserves and the observed liquidity behaviour of liabilities and assets. For example, demand deposits have higher liquidity requirements (though this group of liabilities enjoys a

dynamic stability, which is discussed later). This group of deposits does not have any interest cost though its cost of operation is the highest among all liability groups. But taken together, the overall cost of demand deposits is lower than all other deposits particularly when we factor in the minimum balance requirement for current and saving accounts. These factors have to be considered while matching demand deposits with assets.

The asset allocation strategy adopts a liquidity-profitability approach in the allocation of funds. Liquidity demand and profitability/cost of each group of liabilities are first determined and then matched with assets having similar characteristics (though exact group-by-group matching may not be possible). Each group of liabilities and assets is considered as a separate liquidity-profitability centre as if these are mini banks within a bank. Conceptually, it is an internal financial market where fund managers and asset managers compete to obtain the best terms. At a higher level of understanding, managers of these centres are allowed to move to external financial markets if they do not get a suitable matching term internally.

This strategy is more fully explained in Figure 2.2.

Figure 2.2 depicts an ideal strategy for the deployment of funds. The thick arrow lines indicate which group of liabilities should first fund a particular group of assets; the remaining surplus may move to other asset groups which are next in order of liquidity-profitability as indicated by the thin arrow lines. For example, demand deposits are least in cost but high in liquidity

demand. They should, therefore, be funding primary reserves fully, because the velocity of both the demand deposits and the primary reserves is very high, though both enjoy dynamic stability. Besides, primary reserve assets, which do not earn any income, cannot carry a high cost fund; they look for fund which has the least cost.

Savings deposits have an interest cost (though small) besides the cost of management, which is next to demand deposits (but the aggregate cost would not be more than one-third of other fund sources). The liquidity demand of savings deposits is also much below that of demand deposits. It is, therefore, likely that savings deposits would fund secondary reserves comprising primarily of government securities with comparatively lower returns and lesser liquidity demands. Any surplus left in savings deposits after funding secondary reserves should first go to fund that

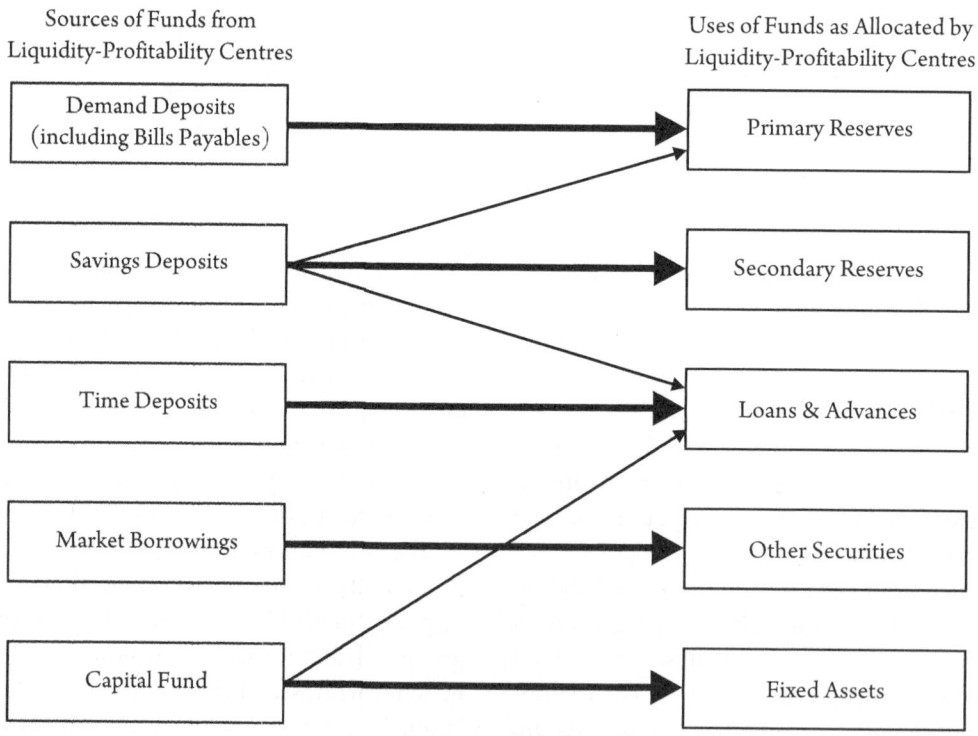

FIGURE 2.2   Asset Allocation Strategy

portion of primary reserves, which could not be funded by demand deposits, and then to loans and advances.

Although time (fixed) deposits are not as fixed as the name suggests, because of the embedded option of breaking them before maturity, they have lower liquidity demand than demand and savings deposits; their management cost is also lower. But the interest cost of time deposits is the highest among all the interest bearing deposits. Hence, it is appropriate that they should fund loans and advances, which are mostly of longer term (even the cash credit type of advances, though termed as short-term loans, are in fact long-term in nature because of renewals). Return on loan assets is also the highest among all banking assets, except perhaps marketable securities comprising company shares.

Market borrowing (except institutional refinances) is short-term in nature, highly volatile, and costly. Ideally, it should finance investments in marketable securities, which exhibit similar characteristics. Unfortunately, in India, banks are found to resort to market borrowings like certificates of deposits, inter-bank loans and so on to meet the shortfall in CRR and SLR requirements on the reporting Friday. This practice not only affects profitability but also results in an asset-liability mismatch.

Bank capital, like any other corporate equity, is costliest among all funds sources. For example,

even for public sector banks in India, the government desires at least a 20 per cent dividend. Equity capital is also the least volatile. Therefore, capital is expected to fund fixed assets comprising banking infrastructure, including technology platforms, returns of which may not be visible but without which earning is not possible. The amount available after funding fixed assets should go towards long-term loans (prudence demands that fixed assets should not be more than 20 per cent of the capital fund).

These analyses suggest that at the operational level the deposit mobilisation strategies of banks should be such that demand deposits and savings deposits together should not only fund primary and secondary reserves fully but also leave a surplus to fund loans and advances.

Assuming that the CRR and SLR requirements are 5 per cent and 25 per cent respectively the assets allocation strategy discussed earlier should result in the balance sheet given in Table 2.5.

It may be seen from Table 2.5 that demand and savings deposits together have contributed Rs 2,500 to loans and advances (13.16 per cent) after fully funding both primary and secondary reserves. The remaining amount of loans and advances is financed first by time deposits (78.94 per cent) and then by the capital after it has fully funded the fixed assets. The balance sheet aims to maintain a balance between the liquidity and

TABLE 2.5 Strategic Asssets Allocation Balance Sheet of a Bank

Liabilities	Amount	% of Total	Assets	Amount	% of Total
Demand deposits	2000	7.14	Primary reserves	1250	4.46
Savings bank deposits	8000	28.57	Secondary reserves	6250	22.32
Time deposits	15000	53.57	Loans & Advances	19000	67.86
Market borrowings	1000	3.57	Marketable securities	1000	3.57
Capital & reserves	2000	7.15	Fixed assets	500	1.79
Total	28000	100	Total	28000	100

profitability of a bank. However, a bank's profit-ability can be increased without disturbing the balance sheet by increasing the demand-savings deposit component of the total deposits and reducing the high cost time deposits. But this depends largely upon the population concentration of a particular bank that influences the behaviour of depositors. For example, the demand-savings component will be higher for a bank which is concentrated in metropolitan and urban areas while a bank having a larger rural concentration will have a much higher level of time deposits. Besides, in the former case, the stable component of demand-savings deposits will also be high which can very well finance a larger part of loans and advances at a lower cost, more so because more often loan demands originate from current deposits which are mostly business accounts.

In Table 2.6, the liquidity-profitability attributes of individual liabilities and assets are presented by way of illustration.

Liquidity-profitability attributes of different liabilities and assets will help sharpen the decision making process in a bank in matters of picking up an appropriate set of liabilities when it is expecting an increase in demand for a particular type of loans. Or, when and which type of other assets to invest in when there is a surplus fund. For example, if a bank is expecting an increase in demand in cash credit, particularly during the onset of a busy season, then its deposit mobilisation strategy should gear towards raising fixed and savings deposits. Or, if there is a demand for bridge loans, which are for a short period, the bank would do well to issue certificates of deposit for an appropriate maturity rather than

TABLE 2.6   Liquidity-Profitability Attributes of Liabilities and Assets of a Bank

High	Medium	Low
A. Liquidity Attributes of Liabilities		
Demand deposits	Savings deposits	Time deposits
Bills payables	Certificate of deposits	Share capital & reserves
Interest accrued & payables	Refinance/Borrowings	Bonds
B. Liquidity Attributes of Assets		
Cash in hand	Cash credit & overdrafts	CRR with RBI
Balance with other banks	Bills purchased & discounted	Term loans
Marketable securities	Certificate of deposits of other banks	Investment in subsidiaries
		SLR with RBI
C. Profitability Attributes of Assets		
Cash credit & overdraft	Certificate of deposits of other banks	Cash in hand
Marketable securities	SLR securities	Balances with other banks
Bills purchased & discounted	Priority sector loans	Balances with RBI over CRR
Loans		Fixed assets
Investment in subsidiaries		
D. Cost Attributes of Liabilities		
Share capital & reserves	Savings bank deposits	Demand deposits
Time deposits	Refinance	Bills payables
Bonds		Interest accrued & payables
Certificate of deposits		
Other borrowings		

picking on other fund sources, except when the bank already has surplus funds waiting for investment.

MATURITY MATCHING STRATEGY

So far, we have discussed a matching strategy between broad groups of liabilities and assets within a liquidity-profitability framework. When this framework is installed and monitored, a bank is not likely to face any major liquidity problems. Another approach that came up during the 1980s focuses on a time-bucket analysis to locate emerging liquidity problems due to an asset-liability mismatch. In this approach, assets and liabilities are classified under uniform time-buckets ranging from one day to 365 days and more. When liabilities exceed the assets in a particular time-bucket it is concluded that the bank faces a liquidity shortage in that bucket meaning thereby that when all the liabilities and assets mature in that bucket there would not be sufficient cash to pay for all the maturing liabilities. The bank may have to either sell-off a part of the excess assets (primarily marketable securities) in other time-buckets or call back loan assets (which may not always be possible because of existing terms and conditions between the borrowers and the bank; it also gives a distress signal to the market). Securitising assets followed by a sale can mask the situation. But all banking assets are not amenable to securitisation; this also has its own dangers. From the 1990s, exotic derivative instruments flooded the market, which virtually robbed off the security aspect of securitisation. How much it is for bending the capital regulation or masking a deep-rooted structural liquidity problem or simply greed is not known but the financial and banking crisis of 2008–09 is ample proof that things have gone too far.

It is, however, possible that all the liabilities or a major part of it in the given time-bucket may be renewed, thus creating no serious liquidity problem. This depends on the behaviour of liabilities in the time-bucket meaning thereby that the bank enjoys a dynamic stability of liabilities in that time-bucket. The stable part of short-term liabilities can be used to fund long-term assets. When this happens, a liquidity shortage may appear under that bucket but it is not likely to cause any liquidity problem under normal circumstances. It is necessary, therefore, to estimate the stable part of liabilities as well as assets before putting them in time-buckets. When this is done the matching exercise is amenable to a cash flow format.

When liquidity shortage in a time-bucket is real and no feasible solution is available, banks are often found to exhibit knee-jerk reactions by contracting further liabilities, which may provide immediate liquidity, but if the situation persists or it is recurring in nature, there is a chance that the bank has entered into a liquidity trap. In such a situation, the bank has to recognise that there exists a structural problem in the balance sheet which needs to be corrected first; persistent knee-jerk reactions may ultimately break the knee.

In Table 2.7(A and B) we have presented a time-bucket analysis of liability and asset flows of a bank in India. Let us call it ABC Bank. The format is as prescribed by RBI. We have, however, converted all flows as percentages of total flows for a better understanding of the problem.

Before we analyse the structural assets-liabilities profile of ABC Bank given in Table 2.7, we should point out that a fully matched assets–liabilities position is one where for every liability maturing on a certain date there is an asset of equal amount maturing on the same day; there is no mismatch and hence there is no liquidity problem. But such a situation may not be possible because the objectives of depositors and borrowers are often at variance with the objectives of the ALM department, nor is it desirable, because banks would like to increase

TABLE 2.7(A)   ABC Bank Statement of Structural Liquidity (Projected)
As on ————

Particulars	Day 1	2 to 7 Days	8 to 14 Days	15 to 28 Days	29 Days and up to 3 Months	Over 3 Months and up to 6 Months	Over 6 Months and up to 1 Year	Over 1 Year and up to 3 Years	Over 3 Years and up to 5 Years	Over 5 Years	Total
Items in Cash Outflow											
1. Capital	—	—	—	—	—	—	—	—	—	2.00	2.00
2. Reserves and Surplus	—	—	—	—	—	—	—	—	—	5.00	5.00
3. Deposits											
i. Current Deposits			0.51					2.89			3.40
ii. Savings Bank Deposits			1.20					10.80			12.00
iii. Term Deposits		0.90	2.00	5.10	6.90	0.80	1.00	1.60	0.85	0.45	19.60
Normal Deposits											
Bulk Deposits										—	—
iv. Certificates of Deposit				1.20	8.59	7.72	1.18				18.69
4. Borrowings											
i. Call and Short Notice	0.20	2.80	1.95								4.95
ii. Inter-Bank (Term)					2.75	8.55	1.10				12.40
iii. Refinances		1.25			1.25	4.22					6.72
iv. Other Borrowings— Subordinated Bonds									2.85		2.85
5. Other Liabilities & Provisions											
i. Bills Payable			0.35					0.05			0.40
ii. Inter-Office Adjustment			0.01							0.02	0.03
iii. Provisions										0.01	0.01
iv. Others											—
6. Lines of Credit committed to											
i. Institutions			1.23								1.23
ii. Customers			2.51		0.99						3.50
7. Unavailed portion of Cash Credit/Overdraft/Demand Loan component of Working Capital					0.06	0.05	2.30				2.41

Particulars	Day 1	2 to 7 Days	8 to 14 Days	15 to 28 Days	29 Days and up to 3 Months	Over 3 Months and up to 6 Months	Over 6 Months and up to 1 Year	Over 1 Year and up to 3 Years	Over 3 Years and up to 5 Years	Over 5 Years	Total
8. Letters of Credit / Guarantees						0.07	0.09	0.02			0.18
9. Repos					1.11						1.11
10. Bills Rediscounted (DUPN)					1.77						1.77
11. Swaps (Buy/Sell)/Maturing forwards			0.03	0.06				0.04			0.13
12. Interest Payable CFD Interest						0.16	0.12	0.56	0.64		1.48
13. Others (specify) Interest Payable		0.14									0.14
A. Total Outflows	0.20	5.13	9.79	6.36	23.42	21.57	5.79	15.92	4.34	7.48	100.00
B. Cumulative Outflows	0.20	5.33	15.12	21.48	44.90	66.47	72.26	88.18	92.52	100.00	100.00

TABLE 2.7(B) ABC Bank Statement of Structural Liquidity (Projected)

As on ————

Particulars	Day 1	2 to 7 Days	8 to 14 Days	15 to 28 Days	29 Days and up to 3 Months	Over 3 Months and up to 6 Months	Over 6 Months and up to 1 Year	Over 1 Year and up to 3 Years	Over 3 Years and up to 5 Years	Over 5 Years	Total
Items in Cash Inflow											
1. Cash	0.56										0.56
2. Balances with RBI	0.08	0.05	0.19	0.32	0.77	0.43	0.11	0.76	0.04	0.02	2.77
3. Balances with Other Banks											
i. Current Account	0.62							0.20			0.82
ii. Money at Call and Short Notice, Term Deposits and Other Placements			0.30	0.80							1.10
4. Investments (including those under Repos but excluding Reverse Repos)			0.85	1.81	2.30	2.20	2.55	2.70	3.25	6.20	21.86

(contd.)

Table 2.7(B) (contd.)

Particulars	Day 1	2 to 7 Days	8 to 14 Days	15 to 28 Days	29 Days and up to 3 Months	Over 3 Months and up to 6 Months	Over 6 Months and up to 1 Year	Over 1 Year and up to 3 Years	Over 3 Years and up to 5 Years	Over 5 Years	Total
5. Advances (Performing)											
i. Bills Purchased				0.86	5.56	1.20					7.62
ii. Cash Credits, Overdrafts and Demand Loans			3.52	10.66				20.14			34.32
iii. Term Loans				0.80	1.54	1.32	1.01	5.03	3.11	0.92	13.73
6. NPAs									0.65	0.15	0.80
7. Fixed Assets										1.44	1.44
8. Other Assets											
i. Inter-Office Adjustment											—
ii. Leased Assets											—
iii. Others										0.22	0.22
9. Reverse Repos	1.69	2.20									3.89
10. Swaps (Sell/Buy)/ Maturing forwards	0.04		0.03	0.06							0.13
11. Bills Rediscounted (DUPN)					1.77						1.77
12. Interest Receivable			0.74	1.00							1.74
13. Committed Lines of Credit			3.74		0.99						4.73
14. Export Refinance from RBI		1.25			1.25						2.50
15. Others specify											—
16. Net Foreign Exchange Exposures— On Balance Sheet											—
17. Accumulated Loss											—
C. Total Inflows	1.26	3.03	11.57	16.31	14.18	5.15	3.67	28.83	7.05	8.95	100.00
D. Mismatch (C–A)	1.06	(2.10)	1.78	9.95	(9.24)	(16.42)	(2.12)	12.91	2.71	1.47	—

E. Mismatch as % of Outflows (D as % to A)	-40.94%				-31.45%	-76.12%	-36.61%			
F. Cumulative Mismatch	1.06	(1.04)	0.74	10.69	1.45	(14.97)	(17.09)	(4.18)	(1.47)	—
G. Cumulative Mismatch as % to Cumulative Outflows (F as % to B)	530.00%	-19.52%	4.89%	49.77%	3.23%	-22.52%	-23.65%	-4.74%	1.59%	0.00%
Prudential Limits										

Notes:

Assets Flows (Inflows)

1. Balances with RBI: While the excess balance over CRR/SLR requirements may be shown in the near term, the statutory balances should be distributed amongst various time-buckets corresponding to the maturity profile of demand and time liabilities (DTL).

2. Current account deposits with other banks: Required minimum balances may be shown under the 'over 1–3 years' bucket and the remaining under the near term bucket.

3. Investments: These are to be taken as net of provisions.

(a) Approved securities, corporate bonds, certificates of deposit, commercial papers, redeemable preference shares, close-ended units of mutual funds etc. should be shown under respective maturity buckets.

(b) Company shares, open-ended units of mutual funds, and investments in subsidiaries and joint ventures are to be shown under the 'over 5 years bucket'.

(c) Securities in the trading book: Respective time buckets according to the defeasance period.

4. Advances (performing): These are to be shown as net of provisions.

(a) Bills purchased and discounted: Respective maturity buckets of the bills.

(b) Cash credit, overdraft, and demand loan: Banks should make a study of the behavioural/seasonal pattern to identify the core (stable) and volatile portions. The former may be shown under the 'over 1–3 years' bucket while the latter may be placed under the near term bucket.

(c) Term loans and leased assets: Interim cash flows should be shown under respective maturity buckets.

5. Non-performing assets:

(a) Sub-standard assets: Over 3–5 years bucket.

(b) Doubtful and loss assets: Over 5 years bucket.

6. Fixed assets: Over 5 years bucket.

7. Other assets:

(a) Interest receivables: All accrued interest as on reporting date should be placed under the respective maturity buckets.

(b) Inter-office adjustments: The net debit balance should be shown under the near term bucket.

(c) Intangible assets and asses not representing cash receivables may be shown under the 'over 5 years' bucket.

Liability Flows (Outflows)

1. Capital, reserves, and surpluses: Over 5 years bucket.

(*contd.*)

Table 2.7(B) (*contd.*)

2. Subordinated debts: Residual maturity bucket.

3. Current and savings deposits: Behavioural study of these deposits should be made to identify the core and volatile portions of these deposits. The former should be placed under the 'over 1–3 years bucket' and the latter under the near term bucket. In absence of such a behavioural study, RBI has suggested a benchmark of 10 per cent of savings deposits and 15 per cent of current deposits as volatile.

4. Time deposits: These should be placed under respective time-buckets. However, banks should recognise that in spite of contracted maturity terms there always exists the embedded option of breaking the deposits before maturity. Hence, similar to savings and current deposits, banks should make a study of the behavioural pattern of this deposit source to identify core and volatile portions and accordingly place them under appropriate time-buckets. But if a bank has contracted wholesale deposits for given terms these should be placed under the respective maturity buckets.

5. Certificates of deposit, borrowings etc.: These should be placed under the respective maturity buckets. However, when an issue has call/put option the call/put dates should be reckoned for determining the maturity buckets.

6. Other liabilities and provisions:

(a) Bills payable: The core portion as observed from the behavioural study should be placed under the 'over 1–3 years' bucket and the balance amount under the near term bucket.

(b) Interest payable: All accrued interest should be placed under the respective maturity buckets.

(c) Inter-office adjustment: The net credit balance should be placed under the near term bucket.

(d) Provisions and other liabilities: These should not include provisions for loan losses and depreciation on investments. Maturity buckets should be chosen considering the purpose for which a particular provision is created. However, items not representing cash payables, for example, income received in advance, may be placed under the 'over 5 years bucket.

7. Export refinance: The availed portion of eligible refinance should be placed under the respective maturity buckets of the underlying assets and the unavailed portion may be placed under the near term bucket.

8. Contingent liabilities:

(a) Lines of credit committed to/from: Under the near term bucket.

(b) Unavailed portion of cash credit/overdraft etc.: Maturity buckets should be determined in accordance with the findings of behavioural and seasonal patterns of potential availments.

(c) Letters of credit/guarantees: Pattern of devolvement of letters of credit and guarantees is to be determined from a historical trend analysis. Assets created due to devolvement may be shown under respective maturity buckets based on probable recovery dates.

(d) Repos/bills rediscounted/swaps/forex forward contracts: Respective maturity buckets.

9. All maturity buckets are to be based on residual maturity. However, all overdue liabilities are to be placed under the near term bucket.

10. For further details, refer to RBI's website at www.rbi.org.in.

their profits by contracting assets with somewhat longer maturity than liabilities as yield increases with time.

The projected structural liquidity profile as presented in Table 2.7(A and B) is in effect a cash flow analysis. A maturing liability is cash outflow while a maturing asset is cash inflow. All cash inflows and outflows are put along a maturity ladder in accordance with the timing of the cash flows. No distinction is made between balance sheet items and off-balance sheet items (contingent liabilities/assets), including lines of credit committed at a future date and the unavailed portion of cash credit type of loans.

The liquidity profile of ABC Bank has been drawn by converting absolute figures as percentage of total liabilities flows/assets flows. This gives a total view of the liquidity position of the bank. For example, mismatch in the '2–7 days' bucket is about 41 per cent of the outflows meaning thereby that 41 per cent of the outflows are not covered by appropriate assets inflow during the period, which far exceeds the 20 per cent prudential limit suggested by RBI. But if we expand our view to the '15–28 days' bucket we find that as against liabilities of 21.48 maturing up to this bucket the assets inflow is 32.17 leaving a positive gap of 10.69.

The liquidity position of the bank worsens during the next three time buckets (covering '29 days and up to 3 months' period to 'over 6 months and up to one year' period). The aggregate mismatch is a negative of 27.78, which as a percentage of outflows is 45.29. Cumulative mismatch has never been positive beginning the period, '29 days and up to 3 months'. The negative mismatch up to this period is 27.78 – 10.69 = 17.09, which is funded from long-term assets flows of the next three buckets. In other words, the long-term assets of the bank are more than long-term liabilities meaning thereby that the gap can only be funded by short-term liabilities.

There may not be anything wrong about this—a moderate level of mismatch is desirable from the profitability point of view—so long as the core portion of the short-term liabilities can take care of the gap, and the mismatch in any bucket is within a reasonable limit. However, if this is not the case then there could be serious liquidity problems during the short term.

Matching the Mismatches

There are several means of financing a negative mismatch: which ones to adopt depends on the time-bucket where the mismatch has occurred. In the case of ABC Bank the first mismatch occurs in the near term time bucket namely, '2–7 days'. For such a short-term mismatch, banks generally go for call loan or repos, particularly when the next near term bucket has a positive gap (as is the case with this bank), which can take care of the newly contracted loan when it falls due for payment, as otherwise the bank may enter into a debt trap.

For longer term mismatches, say in 3–6 months bucket to one year (after adjusting for the core portion of liabilities and assets) the bank has to recognise that there exists a structural problem which needs a long-term solution. The bank has to delve into its pool of 'reserve assets' comprising redeployable assets like bills which can be rediscounted, refinances—except export refinance the unavailed portion of which has already been taken into account in the liquidity statement (item no. 14 in Table 2.7[B])—securitisable assets, and foreign currency resources that could be converted in rupees. For example, ABC Bank has a bill portfolio of 7.62 of which 1.77 has already been rediscounted leaving a balance of 5.85 for further rediscounting. But this may not be sufficient to meet the gap. It may be necessary to explore the possibility of securitising eligible loan assets as part of the strategy of the bank's long-term liquidity management.

Another approach would be to reorient the lending policy of the bank more towards cash flow-based loans than cash credit types, which in effect does not have any repayment programme. A part of the core portion of the projected cash credit could be sanctioned/converted as working capital term loans repayable in say quarterly instalments. This will unlock the fund tied in the core portion of this loan asset. We have mentioned in Chapter 11 that RBI desires that 80 per cent of working capital limits should be sanctioned by banks by way of loans to borrowers having working capital limits of Rs 10 crore and above from the banking system. Banks should also persuade borrowers having working capital limit of less than Rs 10 crore to follow this arrangement by offering them an incentive in the form of lower interest rates for the loan component.

Maturity mismatch is more pronounced in infrastructure financing by banks, because of the long-term nature of the loan and rather short-term liabilities of banks. Banks can circumvent this mismatch to a large extent by resorting to take-out financing. This is an arrangement designed to enable banks to avoid asset-liability mismatches that may arise out of extending long tenor loans to infrastructure projects. Under this scheme, banks financing infrastructure projects would have an arrangement with the Infrastructure Development and Finance Company (IDFC) or any other financial institution for transferring to the latter the outstanding in their books on a pre-determined basis. IDFC and State Bank of India (SBI) have devised different take-out financing structures to suit the requirements of various banks, such as liquidity, asset-liability mismatches, limited availability of project appraisal skills and so on. They have also developed a model agreement that can be considered for use as a document for specific projects in conjunction with other project loan documents. The agreement between SBI and IDFC could

provide a reference point for other banks to enter into somewhat similar arrangements with IDFC or other financial institutions.

As an alternative to take-out financing, IDFC and SBI have devised a product providing liquidity support to banks. Under this scheme, IDFC would commit at the point of sanction, to refinance the entire outstanding loan (principal plus unrecovered interest) or part of the loan to the bank after an agreed period, say five years. The credit risk on the project would remain with the bank. The bank will repay the amount to IDFC with interest as per the agreed terms. Since IDFC would be taking a credit risk on the bank, the interest rate to be charged by it on the amount refinanced would depend on its risk perception of the bank. The refinance support from IDFC would particularly benefit those banks which have the requisite appraisal skills and the initial liquidity to fund the project.[9]

The liquidity strategy of a bank should be geared towards maximising the core portion of short-term liabilities and minimising the core portion of short-term assets.

Determining Core Liabilities and Assets

This task forms the basis of the assets–liabilities management of a bank.

The 'core' can be defined as the *de facto* maturity or the length of time for which balances are actually kept, which is more than the contractual maturity. The 'core' is more relevant in deposits like demand deposits, savings deposit, short-term deposits, including even call money and certificates of deposits, and loan assets like cash credit, overdrafts, and other demand loans.

In demand and savings deposits the 'core' gets evolved principally due to the transaction motive of the depositors, their motive for targeted

[9] Available at www.rbi.org.in/SCRIPTs/Notification, accessed on 12 August 2010.

savings, say for children's education or marriages or simply for a 'rainy day'. It also depends on the income and demographic characteristics—age, other life cycle correlates, and loyalty. These characteristics do not change rapidly and hence the deposit behaviour reflects stability.

A large customer base comprising small denomination depositors is a major source of core deposits.

A bank can increase core deposits by establishing meaningful customer relationships, by providing safety and convenience, by increasing the efficiency of delivery of financial services, and providing innovative value added services. The package should be so designed as to encourage customers to withdraw less at a time. Core depositors are also a source of significant fee income for the services provided.

Interest rates paid on core deposits are among the lowest, though the transaction costs are high (unless these can be passed on to the customers). Core depositors mostly have a non-investment orientation and are hence relatively less rate sensitive. Repricing should be infrequent to maintain the basic characteristics of the core deposit. In a normal rate environment repricing should be a slow process as otherwise it might give a jolt to the customers who may suddenly migrate to other modes of savings. However, in a rising rate environment a slow or small increase in the rate on interest bearing core deposits may cause an outflow to comparatively high yielding instruments as, for example, debt oriented mutual funds or money market mutual funds.

We have mentioned earlier that the behaviour of major liabilities and assets should be studied to determine the core and volatile portions to enable a bank to place them under appropriate time-bucket(s). A large number of statistical models—some are highly sophisticated—have been and are being developed since the ALM fully emerged as a discipline. Many of these models are not easily understandable or implementable at the operational level except at high costs. In what follows we present a simple model based on the highly popular least square regression analysis of the following type:

$$y = a + bx$$

where 'y' is the dependent variable, say savings deposit, 'a' is the intercept, and 'b' is the coefficient (slope) of independent variable (x), say the time period. In this exercise, our focus of attention is the intercept (a) as will be evident from Figure 2.3.

The intercept (a) can be considered as the core portion of the variable (similar to a break-even chart) because in the above equation when 'b' is zero, that is, there is no growth, the second term also equals zero; what remains is the intercept.

Coefficient 'b' and the intercept 'a' are given by:

$$b = \frac{n\Sigma x_i y_i - \Sigma x_i \Sigma y_i}{n\Sigma x_i^2 - (\Sigma x_i)^2}$$

$$a = \overline{y} - b\overline{x}$$

This is explained with an example of the savings deposit of a bank in Table 2.8 A.

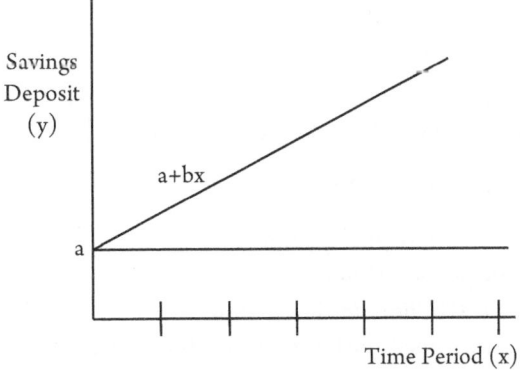

FIGURE 2.3 Movement of Savings Deposit over a Period

TABLE 2.8(A)   Regression Analysis of Savings Bank Deposits of a Bank

(In Billion Rupees)

Period (x_i)	Savings deposit (y_i)	x_i^2	$x_i y_i$	y_i^2	$(y_i-y_c)^2$
1	150	1	150	22500	21.84
2	140	4	280	19600	97.1
3	160	9	480	25600	31.57
4	170	16	680	28900	123.03
5	150	25	750	22500	180.5
6	162	36	972	26244	35.55
7	185	49	1295	34225	156.53
8	165	64	1320	27225	144.38
9	190	81	1710	36100	71.52
10	185	100	1850	34225	1.15
Total (Σ) 55	1657	385	9487	277119	863.17
Mean 5.5	165.7				

The first column of Table 2.8(A), that is, the period could be a month, a quarter, or a year, which should be coded as, 1, 2, 3, ... It is preferable to take quarterly data for 10 or 15 quarters as they capture the recent behaviour of the variable. In our example, however, we have taken data for 10 quarters.

The value of 'b' and 'a' can be determined by putting appropriate figures from this table:

$$b = \frac{10 * 9487 - 55 * 1657}{10 * 385 - (55)^2} = 4.527$$

$$a = 165.7 - 4.527 * 5.5 = 140.80$$

We can now write the trend equation:

$$y_c = 140.80 + 4.527x$$

The derived equation (y_c) indicates that the core portion (intercept) of savings deposits is Rs 140.80 billion. In this analysis, we have assumed a linear relationship between the two variables, which is likely to be the case under normal circumstances. This can be tested by calculating

correlation coefficient (r) between the two variables. The following formula may be used:

$$r = \frac{n\Sigma x_i y_i - (\Sigma x_i)(\Sigma y_i)}{\sqrt{n\Sigma x_i^2 - (\Sigma x_i)^2}\sqrt{n\Sigma y_i^2 - (\Sigma y_i)^2}}$$

Putting respective values in the above formula from Table 2.8(A) we obtain:

$$r = \frac{10 * 9487 - 55 * 1657}{\sqrt{10 * 385 - (55)^2}\sqrt{10 * 277119 - (1657)^2}}$$

or, $r = 0.81$

A correlation coefficient (r) of 1 signifies a perfect linear correlation, which is unlikely to be observed among business variables. A coefficient of 0.65 and above is acceptable.

When 'r' is positive, 'b' will also be positive. This means that when 'x' increases by one unit 'y' also increases, that is, there is a directly linear relationship between 'x' and 'y'. On the other hand, when 'b' is negative (so also 'r') a unit increase in 'x' will cause a decrease in 'y', that is, the relationship is inverse. In the present example, 'b' is found to be positive, which tells us that when time period (x) increases savings deposit (y) also increases. In other words, the trend is positive.

This trend equation can also be used to predict the volume of savings deposits for the next period. But for this we need to understand certain basic properties of the regression analysis. Regression line or values at different points deviate from the observed values. In order to estimate the deviation we first take the square of all the deviations and add them together as, $\Sigma (y_i - y_c)^2$. The total will be smaller than any other straight line that could be drawn through the original points. This is the reason why the estimation method is called the least square regression.

The calculations are shown in column 6 of Table 2.8A. Summation of the squared deviations is 863.17. To determine the average deviation, known as standard error of estimate (SE) we take the square root of this figure that is:

$$SE = \sqrt{863.17} = 29.38$$

It tells us that the estimate of the dependent variable (y_c) may vary by $\pm$ 29.38. We can now factor in the SE in our derived equation for predictive purpose as:

$$y_c = a + bx \pm SE$$

Or, as in our example, we can write:

$$y_c = 140.80 + 4.527x \pm 29.38.$$

With the help of this equation, we can now predict the volume of savings deposits of the bank for the eleventh quarter as:

$$140 + 4.527 * 11 \pm 29.38 = 190.60 \pm 29.38.$$

That is, the expected savings deposit of the bank for the eleventh quarter will vary between a high of Rs 219.98 billion and a low of Rs 161.22 billion. As the trend is upward, we can settle for the higher of the range. There is a caution: the predictive equation so derived should not be used for more than 1–2 future periods.

When new data is available for the eleventh quarter, we should incorporate it for the tenth period deleting the first period data (so that the data set is always for 10 periods) and work out a new equation. This is done in Table 2.8(B) by incorporating the actual savings deposits of Rs 215 billion of the eleventh quarter in the tenth period.

The derived equation from Table 2.8(B) is:

$$y_c = 138.26 + 6.17x.$$

One may notice that the intercept (a), that is, the core savings deposit has changed to Rs 138.26 billion as against Rs 140.80 billion observed earlier (so also the coefficient).

Determination of core deposits/assets during a period marked by seasonal fluctuations can also be done within this framework by changing the data period to a week instead of a quarter.

The beauty of the methodology prescribed here is that it always tries to capture recent changes in the behavioural pattern of the variable. The core portion of a particular group of liabilities/assets is not fixed but changes with the change in its behavioural pattern.[10]

[10] For further understanding of the regression analysis the reader may consult any standard text books on business statistics. For example, Wayne W. Daniel and James C. Terrel, *Business Statistics for Management and Economics*, Miffin Company, Boston, MA, 1992.

TABLE 2.8(B)   Regression Analysis of Savings Bank Deposits of a Bank

(In Billion Rupees)

Period (x_i)	Savings Deposit (y_i)	x_i^2	$x_i y_i$	y_i^2
1	140	1	140	19600
2	160	4	320	25600
3	170	9	510	28900
4	150	16	600	22500
5	162	25	810	26244
6	185	36	1110	34225
7	165	49	1155	27225
8	190	64	1520	36100
9	185	81	1665	34225
10	215	100	2150	46225
Total (Σ) 55	1722	385	9980	300844
Mean 5.5	172.2			

CONCLUDING REMARKS

Liquidity management in a bank is closely linked with its assets–liabilities strategy. This linkage came into sharp focus during the banking crisis of 1979–80 marked by widespread bank failures in the US and Europe. Bank of America was on the brink of bankruptcy primarily due to a structural assets–liabilities mismatch.

A fully matched position is ideal—a self-liquidating balance sheet—but this is not observable in real life, because of the conflicting objectives of a bank and its borrowers, nor is it desirable due to its negative impact on profitability; a reasonable level of mismatch enhances profitability.

Although statutory reserves are designed to ensure the long-term liquidity of a bank, they are a drain on liquidity at the operational level of liquidity management. There is also an opportunity cost, because return on primary reserve assets (CRR and SLR balances) is very low. These two factors have to be taken into account while developing an optimal liquidity management model of a bank.

All liabilities and assets have a core portion that does not leave the system whatever might be their nomenclatures like current account deposits and savings deposits and short-term loans like cash credit and overdrafts. One important task of liquidity management is to determine the core and volatile portion of such liabilities and assets. The more the core portion of the liabilities of a bank the more it is equipped to lend on a long-term and the more the profitability as yields increase with time. However, on the assets side it is desirable to bring down the core portion as it blocks liquidity. The assets–liabilities strategy of a bank should be geared towards maximising core liabilities and minimising core assets.

With regard to excellence, it is not enough to know but we must try to have and use it.

—Aristotle

3   Banking Strategy

INTRODUCTION

The last four decades have seen unprecedented changes in the banking and financial systems all over the world. While England, the historical seat of banking, witnessed a process of deregulation of the financial system at the beginning of the 1970s (which was soon to cross the Atlantic to the US), India moved in the opposite direction, tightening controls over the financial system by nationalising the major commercial banks of the country. This was done at a time when the Indian banking system, having established itself domestically in strength and stability, was about to move towards global integration. For that, it had to wait for a quarter of a century.

In India, the decade beginning 1990 saw the culmination of the crisis of the regulated regime with a worsening of the external balance of payments, a low foreign exchange reserve, raging inflation, and a dwindling gross national product (GNP). It was felt that a major restructuring of the Indian economy was needed. On the external front, the signing of the General Agreement on Tariffs and Trade (GATT), followed by membership of the World Trade Organisation (WTO), paved the way for global integration. Financial sector reforms were set into motion.

FINANCIAL SECTOR REFORMS

While the gradual loosening of controls was liberating the real sectors of the economy, financial sector reforms were to move in tandem to support the restructuring process. The Narasimham Committee, appointed for this purpose, recommended sweeping changes that came to be regarded as landmarks in the history of banking in India.[1]

The objectives of the reform packages were three-fold:

1. Liberalisation of all markets by quickening the process of deregulation.
2. Increasing competitiveness in all spheres of economic activity.
3. Ensuring financial/fiscal discipline in all economic agents, be it the public or private sector.[2]

These objectives are so interlinked that failure in realising any one of them would lead to the

[1] Reserve Bank of India, *Report of the Committee on the Financial System*, November, 1991.

[2] Sengupta, Arjun, 'Financial Sector and Economic Reforms in India', *Economic and Political Weekly*, 7 January 1995, pp. 39–44.

failure of others resulting in a total collapse of the reform process. The third objective is the most crucial responsibility of the financial system, because by its lending activities it extends the budgets of the economic agents beyond current inflows. In doing so, it has to make an intelligent assessment of the economic performance of others (borrowers) in matching current borrowings with the future stream of income flows. The RBI is expected to do it for the government; banks and financial institutions for others. A mismatch may result in either inflation or recession, leading to a failure of the economic process. It is this task and the onerousness of it that distinguishes banks and financial institutions from other sectors of the economy. The performance of no such sector is as contingent upon the future performance of other enterprises as that of the financial sector. This contingency is so high that it has always been difficult for the banking industry to pursue the objective of profit maximisation as zealously as any other industry. It is this difference which explains precisely why lenders cannot simply lend to those who are willing to offer the highest price (interest rate).[3] This is not to say that profit is not among the important objectives of the banking industry: it is, as we will see later, but profit cannot be earned at the cost of stagnating credit flows through the economy by building up assets which do not perform.

DECLINE OF TRADITIONAL BANKING

The 'unfortunate' part of the liberalisation of the financial market is that the importance of banks and financial institutions, as intermediary institutions starts declining, because of the livening up of the capital market due to the shifting preferences of the savers to directly invest in the capital market and the emergence of market institutions, like mutual funds, to cater to these changing preferences. Corporates with high credit worthiness, who had hitherto obtained funds from banking organisations, now have the opportunity to approach the capital market directly to access funds at a lower cost and with less conditionality hazards. Access of the creditworthy corporate sector to the growing bond, commercial paper, derivative financial products, and fixed deposit markets is opening a new vista for corporate finance. This accessibility itself creates a competitive edge for them to bargain for funds from banks and financial institutions at a cheaper cost—more often at a rate lower than the prime lending rate (PLR). This exerts pressure on the spread of banking organisations.

Spread also comes under pressure from the liability side of the balance sheet of a bank. As indicated before, liberalisation of the financial system has a tremendous influence on the expanse and depth of the market. A number of savings and investment institutions have come up, with a large range of financial instruments as alternatives to bank deposits. This is happening in India at a pace which is often dubbed as 'mushroom growth'. Banks are no longer the only institutions for savers. As the depth of the financial market is also increasing, banks will lose their importance as the sole providers of liquidity to savers. In this emerging scenario, we find banks competing for funds in the market place. The interest rate ceiling having been almost removed as part of the reform process,[4] it is being aligned to other rates in the market.

---

[3] Greenworld, Bruce and Joseph Stiglitz, 'Information, Finance and Markets: The Architecture of Allocative Mechanism', Working Paper No. 3652, National Bureau of Economic Research, Cambridge, Mass, 1992.

[4] With the recent removal of interest rate ceilings for non-banking financial companies (NBFCs), the interest rates of a economy are virtually deregulated.

Importance of Off-Balance Sheet Business

Banks all over the world are facing competitive challenges and pressure to enhance earnings. The traditional 'bread and butter' market is no longer in a position to sustain the banking structure in an era of deregulation and globalisation. The dismantling of cartels for interest rate determination or withdrawal of the administered rate regime, which provided an umbrella to the banks for long, is no longer there. Interest rate risk has emerged as one of the dominant risk elements with such a force that a number of well-known international banks suffered heavily, because of mismanagement of this risk. Due to all these factors commercial banking (lending and retail deposit taking) is now moving down to the third position with investment banking and asset management moving up to the number one and number two activities respectively. The accent is now on the off-balance sheet business, or 'sweeteners' as is the current terminology in the banking market. Now the volume of 'sweeteners' is often regarded as a condition precedent for granting a loan. The present age of financial innovation is concentrating heavily on developing financial instruments which may not find a place in the main body of the balance sheets of banking organisations. The total volume of off-balance sheet transactions is many times more than the balance sheet assets of major international banks. While the reward is high in this expanding business segment, it would be wrong to consider these as risk-free. The Basle Committee drew the attention of bankers and regulators to the risk-proneness of these instruments and brought them within the framework of capital adequacy norms. It is being increasingly felt that decision parameters for direct lending decisions should be the same for off-balance sheet items as well, because of similar types of risk-exposure, though the *structure* of the risk attached to different kinds of off-balance sheet businesses may appear to be low.[5]

CHANGING SAVINGS AND INVESTMENT BEHAVIOUR

The Keynesian theory of investment states that investment would be larger, the lower the rate of interest. This theory came under fire following empirical investigations during the pre-Second World War period, and the decades beginning the 1970s. It has been observed that investment is interest-inelastic; the rate of interest is not uppermost in the minds of entrepreneurs making investments.[6] However, this can be explained within the Keynesian framework of investment behaviour where marginal efficiency of investment is determined by long-term profit expectations, while the rate of interest is determined exogenously by the desire for liquidity and supply of money. It follows, therefore, that when the economy is in a growth phase, particularly when the market forces are liberalised, the long-term profit expectations of entrepreneurs, both domestic and foreign, will be high, especially in sectors where value addition is showing an increasing trend. On the supply side, while corporate savings will rise (due particularly to finance expansion), the household sector's absolute savings will fall during the initial

---

[5] Bank for International Settlements, *The Management of Banks' Off-balance Sheet Exposures: A Supervisory Perspective*, Basle, March 1986.

[6] Chick, Victoria, 'Sources of Finance, Recent Changes in Bank Behaviour and the Theory of Investment and Interest', in Philip Arestis (ed.), *Contemporary Issues in Money and Banking*, Macmillan Press, London, 1988.

This has resulted in banks facing stiff competition for funds from the NBFCs.

periods (due to a rise in consumption expenditure), and then rise as the country moves from low-income (as is the case with India) to low-middle-income status, then to upper-middle-income and finally to high-income status.

The relationship between the level of income and personal savings appears to be non-linear in nature, with the largest increase in the savings *rate* occurring in the transition from low-income status to low-middle-income status. The *rate of increase* falls in the subsequent transition to upper-middle-income status and tapers off in the transition to high-income status, by which time, of course, the absolute percentage would have become close to double, providing a large savings base for the economy.[7]

Attempts to induce savings by raising domestic interest rates has not been very successful in developing countries like India, where income distribution is skewed—though India, among the other developing nations of Asia, has a more equitable income distribution than Latin American countries—and a large proportion of the population lives at a near-subsistence level. It has been found that a 1 percentage point increase in the real interest rate would elicit an increase in the savings rate of only about 2/10th of 1 percentage point for low-income countries.[8] For the wealthiest countries, by contrast, the rise in the savings rate in response to a similar change in the real interest rate would be about 2/3rd of 1 percentage point.[9] This aspect is often missed by

banks of newly liberalised developing countries, where the interest rate ceiling has been removed, as in India. Pushed by the increasing demand for funds, competing banks may raise the real rate of interest to attract deposits,[10] which unfortunately may not increase the level of deposits very significantly for the reasons mentioned earlier, though it may increase the total cost of lendable funds. Shortage of money supply, due primarily to rising government expenditure, also contributes to this mad rush.

In a low-income country where people of the poorer strata, who do not have much access to credit, would ordinarily tend to save the most, propelled by the precautionary motive. People belonging to the upper-income bracket would also save, driven both by investment and liquidity motives, as long as banks provide a reasonable return with high access to liquidity. As the market for financial instruments becomes broad-based and deep, competition intensifies around liquidity.

LIQUIDITY NEWLY DEFINED

The need for liquidity has now broadened to include, besides the precautionary motive, the investment motive as well, defined nowadays as the motive for quickly shifting the portfolio to alternative investment opportunities.

The term 'liquidity' itself has undergone an outlook change. Traditional means of satisfaction of liquidity claim a cost in the form of idle balances, and constrain economic allocation of resources. It is now access to liquidity that matters more than liquidity per se. A credit card, for example, provides access to liquidity. One can enjoy multiple access to liquidity at any time without much of a cost. For corporates, a well developed short-term funds market with an array of

---

[7] IMF, *World Economic Outlook*, Washington, *and Adjustment Policy Research Report*, World Bank, Oxford University Press, New York, 1994.

[8] Real interest rate = ([1 + nominal interest rate]/[1 + inflation rate]) − 1. The inflation rate can be on WPI or CPI. In most of the analyses, however, CPI is used.

[9] Ostry, J.D., and C.M. Reinhart, 'Savings and Real Interest Rate in Developing Countries', *Finance & Development*, December 1995, pp. 16–19.

[10] Real interest rate on deposit = [(1 + nominal interest rate on deposit) (1 + CPI growth rate)] − 1.

instruments—both spot and forward—provide access to liquidity.

With the liquidity need mostly taken care of by providing access to it, every economic agent—be it a household or a corporate—now has the opportunity to become an investment manager. This change is more perceptible among well-managed corporate entities. Instead of continuing to remain passive players in the financial market, they have become highly active, and often more proactive than the banking institutions. Every company worth the name now has a full-fledged treasury department organised as a profit centre. It operates in almost all the banking fields, be it deposits, credit, foreign exchange, or the derivative markets. Companies, which were hitherto buyers in the financial market are now becoming sellers as well, and in the process competing against the banks themselves.

When corporates are thus 'becoming banks', banks themselves are becoming 'corporates'. The motive force once again is the changing concept of liquidity. Liberalisation has helped the emergence of increasingly active wholesale fund markets—both the call money and certificates of deposit markets are almost completely deregulated and broadened to include new players. This active wholesale fund market provides tremendous access to liquidity. More often than not 'liability selling' gains precedence over deposit mobilisation. It is being increasingly used as an effective means to manage the interest rate risk.

SECURITISATION

On the assets side of the balance sheet, banks are attempting to liquefy their loan portfolios through a process now universally known as 'securitisation'. This concept is revolutionising loan banking in all important financial markets of the world. In the years to come, the loan market may look like any other securities market: traded, rated, liquid, and standardised. In the

US, important rating agencies like Moody's and Standard & Poor's are rating bank loans to pave the way for the emergence of an effective loan market. Banks are now selling their loan holdings aggressively.

In India, non-banking financial companies first started the process of securitisation.[11] Rangarajan has correctly observed that the trends that have shaped commercial banking worldwide have come into play in India as well.[12]

Till recently (and dominantly even today), unlike bonds and equities, loans generally have not been traded, except to a limited extent, through participation certificates and syndication. The age-old concept of relationship banking that demands a bank to hold the loan on its books is being replaced gradually by fee-based banking, because of the sheer pressure of competition and the need to keep the balance sheet in liquid form in an uncertain financial environment. Securitisation is essentially the process of removing the hitherto non-traded loan assets from a bank's balance sheet, packaging them in a convenient form, and selling the packaged securities in a financial market.[13]

---

[11] During recent times, micro-finance companies have started securitising their loan assets by bundling up good quality micro-loans and converting them into pass through certificates (PTCs) or non-cumulative debentures (NCDs). These securities are rated and traded in the market like any other instruments. See the portal of Institute for Financial Management and Research at www.ifmr.ac.in. However the RBI cautioned that in their spree to raise money through securitisation micro-finance companies might misuse the opportunity by including low quality loans in a bundle.

[12] 'Indian Financial System: The Emerging Horizon', *RBI Bulletin*, May 1994.

[13] See, Kuhn, R.L. (ed.), *Mortgage and Asset Securitisation*, Dow-Jones, Irwin, Homewood, Illinois, 1990, for a detailed discussion on securitisation.

The RBI defines securitisation as a process by which assets are sold to a bankruptcy remote special purpose vehicle (SPV)[14] in return for an immediate cash payment. The cash flow from the underlying pool of assets is used to service the securities issued by the SPV. Securitisation thus follows a two-stage process. In the first stage, there is the sale of a single asset or pooling and the sale of a pool of assets to a 'bankruptcy remote' SPV in return for an immediate cash payment, and in the second stage there is repackaging and selling of security interests representing claims on incoming cash flows from the asset or pool of assets to third party investors by issuance of tradable debt-securities.[15]

Securitisation is widespread in mortgage loans, automobile loans, credit card receivables, and leasing transactions in the US and major parts of Europe. A secondary loan market, which had been almost unheard of even a decade ago, has already become a reality in mature financial markets. The emerging markets of Asia have not lagged behind with the speeding up of the process of liberalisation and global integration. Commercial bank lending is moving towards adopting a portfolio approach.

However, central to the development of a healthy securitised loan market is the creditworthiness of both the original borrower and the lender. Although there are methods available for upgrading the 'credit worthiness' of a loan, the importance of installing a proper appraisal system cannot be overstated, as otherwise the loan market will downgrade itself to a trading centre for distressed loans. The signs were

already evident in the US in 1995: about half the loans traded were distressed, sold in the market at a heavy discount as a way of realising losses on poorly performing or non-performing assets but this could not stave off the crisis.[16] But no lessons were learnt. The banks continued to do the same. The main reason behind the global banking and financial crisis of 2008–09 that originated in the US is once again ascribed to the securitisation of mostly bad loans through esoteric instruments, and palming them off to unsuspecting buyers by large banks.

The RBI, being aware of the dangers in dealing with securitised securities, has issued the following directives to banks:

1. A bank must, on an ongoing basis, have a comprehensive understanding of the risk characteristics of its individual securitisation exposures, whether on balance sheet or off-balance sheet, as well as the risk characteristics of the pools underlying its securitisation exposures.

2. Banks must be able to access performance information on the underlying pools on an ongoing basis in a timely manner. Such information may include as appropriate: exposure type; percentage of loans 30, 60 and 90 days for default rates; pre-payment rates; loans in foreclosure; property type; occupancy; average credit score or other measures of creditworthiness; average loan–to–value ratio; and industry and geographic diversification.

3. A bank must have a thorough understanding of all structural features of a securitisation transaction that would materially impact the performance of the bank's exposures to the transaction. For

---

[14] 'Bankruptcy remote' means the unlikelihood of an entity being subjected to voluntary or involuntary bankruptcy proceedings, including by the originator or its creditors.

[15] Refer to RBI circular DBOD. No. BP. BC. 15/21.06.00/2010/11 dated 1 July 2010, available at www.rbi.org.in.

[16] Edwards, Ben, 'Let's Shuffle Those Loans', Euromoney, August 1995, pp. 22–6.

example, contractual waterfall and waterfall-related triggers, credit enhancements, liquidity enhancements, market value triggers, and deal specific definitions of default.[17]

Securitisation is intended to make the balance sheet liquid by bringing the loan assets to the market place. It is not to be used to palm-off bad loans. Greater transparency and easy understanding of the risk and return of a securitised instrument can only prevent the misuse of such an innovative process.

STRATEGIC PLANNING

Strategies of a banking organisation must undergo radical changes in order to attain the following broad objectives:

1. Maximising profits both in the short- and long-terms.
2. Maintaining an adequate capital base for growth and regulatory requirements.
3. Conducting the lending function within a managed risk framework.

Profit maximisation had always remained, and continues to remain, at the back of the mind of all bankers, all over the world. The history of banking, at least in the US and Great Britain, has seen large shifts between assets in response to movements in differentials among rates of return. These shifts suggest a fairly regular pattern of bank behaviour based on profit maximisation and extrapolative expectations.[18] Unfortunately, as we have seen in Chapter 1, the profit motive of a banking organisation is berated by economists, who claim that the standard theory of the

firm is not applicable to banks, because of the peculiarities of their business, and by politicians and other social scientists who warn that it is too dangerous to allow the profit motive to take control of banks, because it has the potential to destroy the socioeconomic fabric of a nation. The 'villain' is the tremendous power of credit (money) creation *ad infinitum* by the banking system. The history of banking shows that banking organisations are regarded as something more than a necessary evil; they are always ready to substitute profit for sound banking, which brings to naught all measures of monetary and fiscal controls. Hence, the prescription: banks need to be restrained, and their fundamental motive force—profit maximisation—must be suppressed at all costs! But the profit motive has been so strong among banking organisations, that in spite of a growing assemblage of laws and regulations, bankers have pursued it, though not always overtly, by bypassing the regulations! The large-scale spurt in financial innovations during the 1970s and 1980s was largely to circumvent regulations. Empirical studies on the monetary history of nations have revealed that monetary expansion and consequent inflation have largely been due *not* to the credit creation capacity of the banks, but to the unbridled power of the government to print money for ill-conceived and often wasteful public expenditure. We have pointed out in Chapter 1 that even today the mindset of the policy makers has not changed to treat the banking organisation like any other firm whose predominant motive is profit maximisation. The paradigm that banking services are nothing but products, which are sold for making profit, may still take a long time to be established.

Return of the Profit Motive

In India, for more than two decades since 1969 when major banks were nationalised, profit

---

[17] Refer to footnote 15.

[18] Wood, J.H., *Commercial Bank Loan and Investment Behaviour*, John Wiley & Sons Ltd., London, 1975.

was relegated to a low position of importance. Attention was shifted so much to the directed sectoral deployment of credit that profit as the ultimate sustaining mechanism of commercial banks was almost forgotten. In almost all the policy directives issued by RBI during this period, the word 'profit' was hardly mentioned, except in passing. When 'profit' is removed from the first chapter of commercial banking, 'loss' occupies its place with such a force that the capital base of the banks gets wiped out. This is precisely what happened to Indian banks. It was not the bankers who did it; it was the government, as the owner, that desired them to do it. The recapitalisation of major nationalised banks is to recompensate a part of the 'sin' committed on the banking system. In 1993–5 Rs 10,987.12 crore of recapitalisation funds were pumped into the nationalised banking sector. Since then there has been intermittent infusion of funds to individual banks on a selective basis. This time the finance minister of the country has declared that Rs 16,500 crore as recapitalisation funds would be infused into the banks during 2010–11 ostensibly to help them maintain 6 per cent Tier-I capital. All these attempts towards recapitalisation are indicative of the extent of capital erosion in nationalised banks, due mainly to the directed lending and regulated interest rate regime.

Financial sector reforms with the laudable objectives of deregulation of interest rates, dismantling of directed credit, reforming the banking system, and improving the functioning of the capital market, were introduced in mid-1991 to usher in a second 'banking revolution'. This was aimed at making the banking system viable and efficient. The message is now clear: in order for a bank to remain viable it has to bring back profit as the prime motive force, and quality of assets as the necessary condition for sustaining such a motive. Bankers have reacted quickly to the unshackling (though still partial) of the

basic motive force. Within a short period, quite a few large nationalised banks have brought themselves back on the rails and are moving fast; others are following the path zealously despite the constraints of directed lending that still exists.

Profit now being the central focus of the banking organisations, and 'liquidity' being newly defined as 'access to liquidity', as discussed earlier, strategic planning for a bank has almost taken an about turn. Hitherto, the approach was to move from the deposit side of the balance sheet, that is, Deposits $\longrightarrow$ Assets $\longrightarrow$ Profit; now the move is from the opposite side:. Profit $\longrightarrow$ Assets $\longrightarrow$ Deposits. It is profit planning from which other policy sub goals like targeted deposit growth, credit–deposit ratio, and portfolio mix will follow. One should remember that in the case of a banking business, market share as a strategic goal is not as important as it is in a manufacturing business.

Strategic planning in banks now being essentially proactive in nature (it is no longer reactive to the level of deposits), a bank having decided a particular profit target would next move to planning of assets under three broad categories—statutory (CRR and SLR investments), directed (priority sector and exports), and discretionary (commercial, industry and trade, and market investments). In the final stage, funds planning would essentially be a matching process both in terms of maturity to take care of the liquidity demand, and average cost to ensure a net return that satisfies the profit target.

Targeted profit, both in the short- and medium-term of a modern banking organisation should be the outcome of capital planning and a dividend policy. The most important component of profit planning is loan pricing, which operationalises the profit target of a bank. The strategic planning so prepared will then give rise to the formulation of a loan policy document.

Capital Planning

The function of capital in banks and other financial institutions is claimed to be substantially different from that in most other business enterprises. For example, in a manufacturing concern, the capital fund is used primarily for acquisition of fixed assets, while in a banking organisation the function of capital is primarily to provide a guarantee fund. Its usage in the acquisition of fixed assets is hardly more than 15 per cent (and it should never be more than 20 per cent). Capital performs a guarantee function in other enterprises too, but not so predominantly. The capital of a manufacturing concern is something of a cushion for long- and short-term creditors to fall back on, but this is only one of its purposes. As shown in Chapter 1, votaries of capital regulation hold that bank capital has almost no other purpose.

The Basle Committee holds that besides depositors, a bank has to have the *confidence* of the supervisory authorities about the general health of the bank to withstand shocks; of the borrowers that the bank would be in a position to meet their credit needs in both bad times and good; and of the general public, that the most important institution of the economy is functioning well. The confidence is ascribed to the capital funds of banks and financial institutions. With a debt–equity ratio of more than 10 how much confidence capital can provide is doubtful.

Notwithstanding capital adequacy norms, the capital plan of a banking organisation is a bridge between its strategic plan and profit plan. The reason behind this is that though there are quite a few ways to increase capital, such as selling additional shares or reducing the growth (to which we come later), the most effective and desirable long-term solution is by internal accruals in the form of earnings retained in various reserves. This is more so because the history of world banking in the past 60 years has shown that capital in the

form of additional equity is hard to come by, maybe because of low earning per share (EPS) and capital appreciation of bank shares in the stock market as compared to the shares of other companies. There are no signs that the situation will improve in the foreseeable future, and banks will have to depend increasingly on internal accruals for growth. The relationship between profit, dividend pay–out, and growth of a banking organisation is examined in the next section.

The first question is what should be the adequate amount of capital, and its measurement criteria. In order to answer this question, the first problem that one encounters is the inverse relationship between a bank's capital and its earning capacity given by the earnings leverage (EL). This is calculated as:

$$EL = \frac{Assets\ of\ the\ Bank}{Amount\ of\ Capital}$$

For example, suppose a bank has a capital-to-asset ratio of 6 per cent at present, which it seeks to raise to 8 per cent by issue of shares, its earning leverage will immediately fall by 23.52 per cent, as can be seen from Table 3.1.

The problem is compounded, because unlike a manufacturing company, capital does not ordinarily increase the earning power of a bank by, say investing in plant and machinery as in the case of the former. Capital adequacy norms

Table 3.1   Effect of New Capital Issues on Earning Capacity

Capital Issues	Before New Issues	After Capital Change	Percentage Change
Assets	100	102	+2
Deposits	94	94	0
Capital	6	8	+33.33
Earning leverage	16.67	12.75	– 23.52

prescribed by the Basle Committee are arbitrary as they do not pay much attention to the earning leverage. When capital is raised from the market, let the market determine the adequacy of capital in banking organisations within its risk–return framework.

Capital Growth and Dividend Policy

There are only two ways to increase the level of Tier I capital of a banking organisation: by issue of new shares and by retained earnings. In India, public sector banks are now allowed to raise capital from the market. Except a few almost all banks have gone public, though the government still holds the majority shares. But boosting up of the capital by new issues is not always a viable proposition due to the reasons mentioned earlier. Attention is, therefore, drawn more towards retained earnings as a means to increase the core capital base of a bank. The history of banks is indicative of the fact that bank capital has been built mainly by the retention of earnings. Internally funded capital is always superior to selling shares, since existing shareholders are not forced to invest their after-tax income to maintain their percentage holdings. But at the same time, a banking organisation must ready itself for access to the capital market in an environment of market-propelled growth and competition. The choice will, therefore, lie between retention of earnings and dividend policy that will maintain the market price of a bank's shares and its attractiveness as an investment by the general public, so that additional capital, when needed, can be readily raised from the market.

From the viewpoint of the shareholders, it is just as important not to have too much capital, as it is essential, from the viewpoint of safety and growth, to have enough. If the policy is to keep the bank under tight control, minimum dividend and maximum retention could be the possible choice. But this also helps perpetuate the merger trend, as is being observed internationally. On the other hand, a policy of the widest possible distribution of a bank's shares would call for both a reasonable level of cash dividend, and stock dividend in the form of bonus shares. In India, a middle-of-the-road policy is being advocated for ownership of banks' shares. The distribution is wide, but not wide enough to dilute control. This has also been the general trend in major international banks. For a banking company, a dividend pay–out ratio of 50 per cent was advocated during the early part of the 1980s. But with the shifting of attention towards capital growth after the Basle Accord, a lower pay–out ratio of 30–40 per cent, with a minimum benchmark of 20 per cent, is being thought to be reasonable. This is advocated to increase retained earnings. It is important to remember here, as some observers have noted, that a desirable dividend policy for banks is one that makes it possible for them to raise funds from any source—retained earnings, debt, or equity—when it is needed for sustenance and growth.[19]

GROWTH MODEL

By now it should be clear that the growth of a banking organisation is conditioned essentially by the required capital, which in turn depends primarily upon internal accruals. We can now develop a simple mathematical model to establish relationships between profits, dividend pay-outs, and growth with a given capital adequacy norm.

Growth (G) of a banking organisation depends upon the following relation:[20]

---

[19] Reed, W. Edward and Edward K. Gill, *Commercial Banking*, (4th edition), Prentice-Hall International, Englewood Cliffs, New Jersey, 1989.

[20] This part of the model is taken from *The Bank Director's Handbook*, Bank Administration Institute, Chicago, 1981, p. 100.

$$G = \frac{Average\ Assets}{Average\ Capital} \times \frac{Net\ Income}{Average\ Assets} \times (1 - Dividend\ pay\text{-}out\ ratio) \qquad (3.1)$$

Although the model can ordinarily be reduced to:

$$\frac{Net\ Income}{Average\ Capital} \times (1 - Dividend\ pay\text{-}out\ ratio),$$

the purpose of showing it in the extended form is to draw attention to the three ratios separately for the purpose of evaluating their properties.

The first ratio on the right hand side of the equation lays down the capital requirement for assets growth. The numerator and denominator of this ratio are so inter-related that manoeuvrability of this ratio is very difficult.[21] In this particular case it is virtually acting as a constraint. The next two ratios have greater scope of manoeuvrability, because the variables that have gone into making these ratios are capable of being handled independently of each other. That is, managerial discretion can play a great role in improving upon these two ratios. For example, net income for the same amount of assets can be increased by placing the lendable assets in an appropriately higher risk–return category and funding the same by low-cost deposits. Managerial discretion is larger in case of dividend pay–out ratios.

Let us now work out the model with an illustration. Assume the following figures of a bank as at the end of a given year:

Growth Variables of a Bank	(Rs in crore)
Assets	= Rs 11250
Capital	= Rs 900 (or 8 per cent)
Net income (profit after-tax)	= Rs 100
Dividend pay-out	= 35 per cent

The bank can grow at the following rate:

$$G = \frac{11250}{900} \times \frac{100}{11250} \times (1 - 0.35)$$

or, 0.0722
or, 7.22%

In other words, given a capital adequacy norm of 8 per cent, a return on assets of $100/11250 = 0.89$ per cent, and a dividend pay–out ratio of 35 per cent, the bank can grow only at 7.22 per cent annually.

Assume that in the next year:

Assets grow by 7.22 per cent to Rs 12,062 crore

Net income @ 0.89 per cent on assets = Rs 107.22 crore

Dividend pay–out ratio remains at 35 per cent

Hence:

$$0.0722 = \frac{107.22}{Capital} \times 0.65$$

or, 0.0722 × Capital	=	69.693
or, Required Capital	=	69.693/0.0722
	=	Rs 965 crore, which is 8 per cent of projected assets of the next year

It may be seen that the first ratio on the right hand side of Equation (3.1) is nothing but the reciprocal of the capital–assets ratio (C). The next ratio is simply the return on assets (R).

[21] For a detailed discussion of this particular property of the ratio see, Bhattacharya, Hrishikes, *Total Management by Ratios—An Analytic Approach to Management Control and Stock Market Valuations*, (2nd edition), Sage Publications, New Delhi, 2007, pp. 49–52.

Denoting dividend pay–out ratio as 'D', Equation (3.1) can be re-written in the following form:

$$G = \frac{1}{C} \times R \times (1-D)$$

$$\text{or, } G = \frac{R}{C} \times (1-D) \qquad (3.2)$$

If our bank in question desires to grow not at 7.22 per cent but at a rate equal to the required capital growth, that is 8 per cent, then either it has to increase 'R', or reduce 'D', or adjust by a trade-off. Setting the growth rate (G) at 8 per cent, and keeping 'D' constant, the required 'R' should be as follows:

$$0.08 = \frac{R}{0.08} \times (1-0.35)$$

or, $0.65\,R = 0.08 \times 0.08$
or, $R \quad = 0.00985 \text{ or } 0.985\%$

Now, keeping 'R' constant and setting the growth rate at 8 per cent as before, the required change in 'D' will be:

$$0.08 = \frac{0.0089}{0.08} \times (1-D)$$

or, $0.0089\,(1-D) = 0.08 \times 0.08$
or, $(1-D) \qquad = 0.72$
or, $D \qquad = 0.28$

That is, as against the 35 per cent dividend pay–out ratio proposed earlier, the bank now has to reduce it to 28 per cent to achieve a growth rate of 8 per cent.

Finally, multiplying R with $(1-D)$ gives rise to a new ratio, namely retained earnings as percentage of assets, which we denote as 'E'. In its shortest form, Equation (3.2) will now look like:

$$G = \frac{E}{C} \qquad (3.3)$$

E can be derived as:

$$E = \frac{Net\ Income}{Average\ Assets} \times (1-D)$$

$$\text{or, } E = \frac{100}{11250} \times (1-0.35)$$

or, E = 0.005777
or, E = 0.578%

Now, 'C' remaining the same at 8 per cent, the growth rate (G) will be:

$$G = \frac{0.005777}{0.08} = 0.0722 \text{ or } 7.22\% \dots Q.E.D.$$

BANKING STRATEGY: THE CASE OF ABC BANK

The growth model and its two variations discussed earlier have made it abundantly clear that the future growth of a bank ultimately depends on the return on assets (ROA). ROA, in turn, depends upon the quality of loan assets under the appropriate risk–return parameters and their funding operations. Banking strategies must essentially be formulated along these lines. In illustrating these strategies, we make use of the annual accounts of a nationalised bank with suitable assumptions to make it amenable for analysis. For purposes of anonymity, let us call this bank ABC Bank.[22]

ABC Bank's banking strategy should emanate from its overall corporate objectives. In a com-

---

[22] The example is drawn from a consultancy assignment undertaken by the author some years back. Some of the variables like capital adequacy norm, interest rates both on deposits and advances, yield on government securities, and exposure norms have changed since then. Although these changes do not affect the framework presented here, we have indicated the recent changes wherever applicable by way of footnotes.

petitive environment, the strategy formulation should be dominantly proactive. Having first decided on a key variable, its growth (or decrease) is projected for short and medium/long-term and then interventionist strategies in both the internal and external environments are formulated so that all inter-related variables are aligned in such a manner as to subserve the attainment of the projected growth/deceleration of the key variable.

We have already indicated that profit is now the principle objective (key variable) of a banking organisation. Unfortunately, ABC Bank has suffered most on the performance of this variable. Last year ('O' year), it made a loss of Rs 103.92 crore and its accumulated loss was Rs 1478.70 crore. The bank has, however, made an 'operating profit' of Rs 45.43 crore, that is, before making a loss provision of Rs 149.35 crore.[23] At present the capital risk–assets ratio (CRAR) of the bank is 8.44 per cent, that is, 0.44 per cent over the minimum prescribed, or Rs 27.44 crore, which entitles the bank to do additional risk-attached business of Rs 343 crore only.[24] However, assets formation could be planned in such a manner as to ensure simultaneous formation of capital not only to take care of the minimum prescribed norm, but also to leave adequate additional capital for future expansion and growth. In this section, we engage ourselves in drawing up such a strategic plan for ABC Bank. The first task towards this direction is to examine carefully the present state of the important variables of the bank and their parameters. The status of

the important variables can be seen in Tables 3.2 to 3.4.

Critical Observations and Resultant Assumptions for Strategic Planning

Table 3.2 reveals that the deposit growth of ABC Bank has been erratic. The bank has never been able to touch the growth rate of the industry, except in the 5th year, preceding 'O' year. With the present level of the savings rate of the economy and general deceleration in deposit growth owing to the emergence of alternative financial instruments and competitive pressures from other financial institutions, it is likely that deposits of the banking industry will grow at a slower pace. The trend in ABC Bank suggests that in the short- and medium-term, its deposits will grow at around 12 per cent per annum, on a conservative basis.

Table 3.3 indicates a good deposit profile. The average interest paid on deposits, including bills payable, is 6.47 per cent, which is among the lowest in Indian banks. Presently, the average rate paid on term deposits is about 9.75 per cent per annum.[25] We have assumed it to be 10.75 per cent per annum, for the reasons explained later.

Though borrowings constitute only 2.20 per cent of the total outside funds, the cost is very high. It is desirable for the bank to concentrate on low-cost deposit funds, and repay the borrowings at the first opportunity. It is likely that borrowings had to be resorted to due to a funding mismatch.

Table 3.4 indicates that the average interest earned on government and other approved securities is 10.15 per cent. With the general hike in the coupon rate of government papers,

---

[23] Here the term 'operating profit' is a misnomer, because loss provisions are operating in nature. But it has found its place in Indian banking terminology during recent years, though it does not have sanction in the pedagogy of financial accounting.

[24] Capital–to–risk-assets ratio is presently 9 per cent.

[25] Presently, the rate varies between 7.5 and 8 per cent (August 2010).

TABLE 3.2   Percentage Growth of Deposits of ABC Bank

	5th Year	4th Year	3rd Year	2nd Year	1st Year	'O' Year
Global deposits	17.77	(–) 2.77	15.12	4.10	(–) 7.03	11.08
Indian deposits	18.03	5.03	3.67	14.38	3.15	9.85

TABLE 3.3   Global Liabilities of ABC Bank and Cost of Fund

(Rs in crore)

Items (1)	Amount (2)	% of Total (3)	Interest Paid (4)	Average Interest Paid as % of Deposits (5)	Remarks (6)
Demand deposits	1897.53	14.50	—	—	Figure against Sub-total and Total under column 5 are average interest paid as percentage of sub-total and total respectively
Bills payable	277.98	2.12	—	—	
Saving Bank deposits	3220.79	24.62	98.72	3.07	
Term Deposits	7688.82	58.76	748.45	9.73	
A. Sub-total	13085.12	100.00	847.17	6.47	
B. Borrowings	291.49	—	77.75	26.40	
Total (A+B)	13376.61	—	924.92	6.91	

Note: 'Interest Accrued & Payable' and 'Provisions' are not included in this table, as these are considered to be transient liabilities.

the average return is likely to increase to 12 per cent.[26]

In fact, the coupon rate could be more considering the government's concern for keeping the inflation rate low on the one hand, and its public expenditure imperatives on the other. But we have taken a lower average rate to take care of depreciation of government stocks, which is rising with the increase in coupon rates, and RBI asking banks to mark 75 per cent of holdings to the market. RBI desires that it should increase to 100 per cent in the near future.[27] Elsewhere

we have provided a normal depreciation for risk adjustment. SLR is 25 per cent of incremental net demand and time liabilities (NDTL). It is unlikely to come down further in the near future, owing to the reasons mentioned earlier.

The CRR has been moving between 15 per cent and 6 per cent during the past five years in response to inflationary pressures in the economy. Although lately inflation has been somewhat under control, the pressure on price levels is being felt. It is likely that during the strategic plan

[26] During August 2010 the average yield on government bonds varied between 8.3 and 8.5 per cent.

[27] Although RBI desires banks to mark-to-market 100 per cent of their investment portfolios, it is not

a feasible proposition because banks do not have much freedom to get in or get out of investments in government securities because of SLR requirement; banks are treated as a captive market for placement of government securities.

TABLE **3.4** Assets of ABC Bank, Interest Earned, and Other Income

(Rs in crore)

Items (1)	Amount (2)	% of Total (3)	Interest Earned (4)	Average Interest Earned as % of Assets (5)	Remarks (6)
Government and other approved securities	5354.92	93.72	543.62	10.15	Interest earned on other investments includes Rs 35.55 crore as profit on sale of investments
Other investments	358.54	6.28	45.64	12.73	Figures against Sub-total and
A. Sub-total	5713.46	100.00	589.26	10.31	Total under column 5 are average
Bills discounted and purchased	965.09	15.96	98.49	10.20	interest earned as percentage of Sub-total and Total respectively
Cash credit, overdrafts etc.	2710.60	44.83	300.77	11.10	
Term loans	2370.71	39.21	217.81	9.19	
B. Sub-total	6046.40	100.00	617.07	10.20	
Total (A+B)	11759.86	100.00	1206.33	10.25	

Other information:

Paid-up capital, reserves, and surpluses	:	Rs 1927.18 crore
Credit–deposit ratio	:	46.20%
Priority sector as percentage of total domestic advances	:	35.50%
Exchange and commission earned	:	Rs 93.78 crore
Profit on forex transactions	:	Rs 16.79 crore
Miscellaneous income (Rentals, recovery of charges etc.)	:	Rs 23.65 crore (increasing at an annual rate of 3%)

period there shall be intermittent increase and fall in the inflationary level of the economy due to lags between investment and output so peculiar to the early growth phase of an economy under a liberalised regime. CRR is also likely to move in tandem with such increases and falls in price levels. An average CRR of 12 per cent is expected to exhibit its impact on banks' deposit resources during the plan period.[28] We may point out here that even without changing the CRR percentage its impact is often increased by bringing certain hitherto excluded liabilities within the purview of CRR.

[28] Presently the CRR is 6 per cent.

Banks are now allowed to invest in market instruments like shares and debentures subject to certain restrictions. The risk–return profile of these investments is high, hence the restriction. This is, however, beyond the scope of this book.

The advances profile of ABC Bank leaves much to be desired. Its major concentration is in the cash credit segment, which reflects the general profile of the industry. This is likely to change substantially, as cash credits are replaced by loans. RBI has desired that 80 per cent of the working capital finance of Rs 10 crore and above from the banking system should be in the form of term loans. For advances below Rs 10 crore, banks should persuade a borrower to accept the same arrangement by offering an incentive in the form of a lower interest rate on the loan component.[29] The management cost of cash credit advances is very high as compared to the other forms of financing, as we will see later. Therefore, it is desirable that this component of the advances portfolio is brought down gradually (in which the performance of ABC Bank is not encouraging), and replaced by loans and bills.

The credit–deposit ratio is well below the industry average, while that of the priority sector advances is close to it. Although the Narasimham Committee recommended a lowering of the priority sector's commitment to 10 per cent of total credit, such a drastic reduction is unlikely to occur because of political imperatives.[30] In the present case, considering that the bank is in a turnaround phase, we have assumed priority sector advances at 30 per cent of net bank credit during the plan period. One good sign is that interest rates on advances beyond Rs 2 lakh has been freed.[31] But it will be difficult for banks to charge full commercial rates on all priority sector advances beyond Rs 2 lakh, because many borrowers will not be able to bear this except at

the cost of sickness. Since banks have to be on constant vigil against further increase in NPAs, they have to see that NPAs are not created by high interest costs, which ultimately may not be realised. Considering these, the average interest on priority sector advances should be around 16.5 per cent per annum.[32] Once this is decided as a strategic sub-goal, it becomes incumbent upon credit managers to be so selective in the priority sector credit portfolio as to earn an average rate of 16.5 per cent per annum, without creating additional NPAs in the system.

During the past four years, interest rates on commercial advances moved on an average between 16.5 per cent per annum and 24 per cent per annum. Although the concept of PLR was introduced in between, the actual rates charged by the banks virtually had no relevance to PLR. RBI asked banks not only to declare their individual PLRs, but also a band within which interest could be charged to borrowers of different credit ratings. But it did not help much. Over a period, PLR lost its relevance as banks were found to lend below PLR to retain highly creditworthy customers. During 2010, banks were asked to move to the base rate regime and declare their base rates, which should be the minimum rate that a bank must charge.

High interest rates were primarily due to a high rate of inflation. While the rate of growth in price levels has come down presently to a single digit, with a consequent fall in interest rates, inflationary expectation in the economy is still high, which may push up interest rates further as the demand for credit grows. However, it is unlikely to go up as high as the previous level of 24 per cent per annum. Instead, it is expected to

[29] See RBI circular DBOD. No. Dir. BC. 13/13.03.00/2010-11 dated 1 July 2010. Available at www.rbi.org.in.

[30] In fact, target for priority sector advances has been enlarged for domestic Indian banks. While the 40 per cent target remains, the deployment will be larger because unlike before when the percentage was calculated on net bank credit it would now be calculated on adjusted net bank credit (ANBC), which besides the net bank credit, includes the bank's investment in non-SLR bonds held in held-to-maturity category.

[31] Previously, the maximum interest rate chargeable on advances up to Rs 2 lakh was the benchmark prime lending rate (BPLR) of the bank. With the introduction of the base rate during 2010 BPLR has been withdrawn. Since the base rate is the minimum rate of a bank, it is expected that banks would apply the base rate only for such loans.

[32] During August 2010, interest rate on priority sector advances varied between 4 to 6 per cent over the base rate of banks which varied between 7.25 and 8.5 per cent among banks.

hover around 20 per cent during the strategic plan period.[33]

It is also incumbent upon ABC Bank, which is seeking a turnaround, to target such an average level of interest on commercial loans by shifting its preference to such segments of the loan market which are high yielding but less risky, for example, housing loans, advances to the small and medium enterprise (SME) sectors, and lease financing.

It may be noted here that even if there is a general fall in interest rates, its impact on the income spread is mitigated to a large extent by a simultaneous fall in the cost of deposits. Further, by careful asset-liability management the negative impact can not only be minimised further, but it can also turn out to be positive due to an 'endowment effect'. Hence, our strategic plan is not expected to be affected significantly by such a turn of events.

At present, off-balance sheet items constitute about 132 per cent of total advances, which is not very encouraging. The percentage should be at least 150 (as will be explained later). We have taken the following average rates of return on various off-balance sheet items as recommended by the Indian Banks Association.

(a) Financial guarantees   : 1.55%
(b) Performance guarantees,
    bid bonds etc.   : 1.05%
(c) Letters of credit   : 1.00%
(d) Foreign exchange transactions   : 1.25%
(e) Bills/cheques collection charges : 0.40%
(f) Demand drafts/telegraphic
    transfers   : 0.20%

[33] In fact, the average rate remained at 20 per cent during this period. Presently, interest rate varies between 5 per cent over the base rate for A++ borrowers and 8.5 per cent over the base rate for C category borrowers.

ABC Bank will not be required to pay any income tax on its profits during the forthcoming years due to carry forward of huge accumulated losses. The government may also waive payment of dividends to help the bank in capital formation. However, all these do not entitle the bank to escape proper servicing of capital, whether tax and dividends are paid or not. The bank must go by the book. As a matter of policy, the bank should endeavour to ensure a 15 per cent per annum after-tax return on incremental capital invested, and a statutory reserve of 20 per cent on profit after-tax (considering notionally that the dividend is paid). Assuming a 50 per cent tax on profit, the bank should target a before-tax return of 37.5 per cent on incremental capital invested, as calculated below:

$$\frac{15}{80} \times 100 \times \frac{100}{50} = 37.5\%$$

STRATEGIC PLANNING EXERCISE OF ABC BANK

Based on the observations and assumptions made earlier, we are now set to formulate a strategic plan for ABC Bank. As has already been indicated, in modern day banking, as in any other enterprise, the planning exercise must begin with a profit objective. The bank made an 'operating profit' of Rs 45.43 crore in 'O' year, which, however, is reduced to a net loss of Rs 103.92 crore owing to provisioning requirements that are made gradually stricter to become at par with global prudential norms. It is, therefore, likely that a substantial part of the backlog has been provided for during the past five years, and the bank can now start with a clean slate with normal loss provisions, provided it is careful in investing only in quality loan assets by careful appraisal and monitoring of credit.

The goal setting process in any organisation should be participative in nature involving all levels of the organisation, particularly the operational management. The process should settle on a goal which has the following attributes:

(a) It is expressed numerically; mere statements like 'bringing back the bank to its past glory' may not help.
(b) It is achievable; too high a goal leads to inaction.
(c) It should be challenging; too low a goal also leads to inaction.
(d) Progress towards achievement of the goal should be measurable and capable of monitoring.

Considering all these attributes the bank has finally settled the following medium-term strategic goal:

The bank intends to wipe out its entire accumulated losses of Rs 1,478.70 crore within five years from its *banking business*.

Short-term objectives will necessarily emanate from a medium-term goal, once it is translated into actionable strategies. It may be seen that the goal statement emphasises on *banking business* only, which means that it intends to ignore income from non-banking businesses like rentals, as clubbed together under the head 'Miscellaneous Incomes' in the profit and loss account. The purpose behind this is that the bank must turnaround on its *core* banking business, and not on the peripherals, though the latter's contribution to the profit of the bank is not minimised.

COST ALLOCATION

Any profit planning exercise should be preceded by a cost analysis and cost projection. While the costs of various sources of funds is reasonably well-known, much easily targeted, and allocated to different earning assets, the problem arises in estimating operating costs (henceforth called management costs of various products and services of a bank.

In the mid-1960s, attempts were made by a few progressive banks to estimate costs of various banking services by the scientific application of a time and motion study, but these ended with failure due to stiff resistance from trade unions. Later, the Institute of Cost and Works Accountants of India attempted to cost various banking services by an indirect method. RBI and various management services cells of commercial banks followed this up. The dominant criterion used in these studies is the number of vouchers passed in delivering a service to the customer. But with the increasing computerisation of banks, the 'voucher method' is fast losing its relevance. Besides, even the costs arrived at by the existing methodology are hardly taken into consideration while fixing the prices of different products and services. In a competitive market, costing is peculiar to an individual bank, because it provides a competitive edge and a strategic cost leadership in the market. Management costs not only differ from bank to bank, but also from one zone/region to another zone/region of the same bank.

Management Cost Factor (MCF)

For the purpose at hand, we can follow a variation of the transaction method of costing to allocate management costs to various banking products and services. The principle behind this methodology is that all activities performed for selling a banking product or service are ultimately captured in the general ledger of the respective account head as either a debit or a credit transaction. The volume of these transactions, being the aggregate of debit and credit summations, attracts costs. For example, suppose a branch of a bank has only three deposit heads—current, savings, and term and one loan head—cash credit. The operational details pertaining to a year given in Table 3.5.

In this example we have ignored other assets like cash and balances with other banks and with the head office for ease of understanding. It may be seen that the transaction volume in the cash credit account is the highest, followed by the current account. It is the lowest in term deposit accounts, whose average balance (incidentally) is the same as that of the cash credit account. If one looks at the size of these four departments, with respect to both allotted space and workforce in any branch of a bank, one will notice a similar pattern. The cash credit department occupies the largest space and manpower, and the term deposit department occupies the least. It is, therefore, not the size of the balance in an account, but the nature of the account, as reflected by the volumes transacted through that account, that attracts management (operational) costs. In other words, management time, attention, and hence costs, are attracted in terms of the nature and complexities of the account as reflected by its transactional characteristics.

We have taken the rupee value of the volume transacted, and not volume by units, for example, the number of vouchers passed through an account. A question may be raised that this does not reflect the workload in the management of an account head. For example, the rupee value of the volume transacted in the savings bank account head could be just Rs 10 crore in a given year, while the same could be the volume transacted in a cash credit or current account head for a fortnight. But the number of (small) cheques handled under the savings bank account head could be as high as Rs 25 lakh, while that for the latter could just be Rs 10 lakh. Hence, it may be argued that the workload in a savings bank account is much higher than it is in a cash credit or current account. An officer in the branch management would, however, quickly agree that a single cheque of Rs 1 crore coming in a cash credit or current account draws greater management attention and time, and hence cost, due to more complexity and risk associated with it than 1 lakh cheques of Rs 100 each aggregating Rs 1 crore coming in the savings bank account. In the current or cash credit accounts, cheques of smaller denominations are unlikely to come by as also small credits or debits through the electronic clearing system (ECS), while the nature of the savings bank account is such that ordinarily transactions are done in smaller denominations. Moreover, a large section of savings bank account holders transact through ECS, and automated teller machines (ATMs) spread across the country. This is not the case with current or cash credit accounts. A large fund transfer through electronic means also draws higher management

TABLE 3.5   Operational Characteristics of Account Heads

(Rs in crore)

Account Head (1)	Average Balance (2)	Debit Summations (3)	Credit Summations (4)	Total Volume Transacted (5)
Current deposit	20	400	400	800
Savings bank deposit	30	225	225	450
Term deposit	50	100	100	200
Cash credit	50	1375	1375	2750
Total	150	2100	2100	4200

attention and cost. Similar arguments are extendable in allocating management costs incurred in administrative offices, including the head office of a bank.

For our illustrative branch, let us assume now that its operational expenditure or management cost of the given year is Rs 3 crore. Dividing this by the total volume transacted will give us the management cost factor (MCF) per Rs 1 crore of volume transacted. That is:

$$\frac{3}{4200} = Rs\ 0.0007143$$

or, Rs 7,143 per Re 1 crore of volume transacted.

MCF can now be multiplied with the volume transacted under each account head to arrive at the cost of managing an account head. One should remember, however, that MCF is valid for a given year. It should be adjusted with the projected level of operating expenditure for the planning period. For example, if the operating expenditure is to increase by 10 per cent in the following year, the present MCF of the branch will also increase by the same percentage, that is, $0.0007143 \times 1.10 = 0.0007857$.

MCF at the bank level can be used as a strategic tool for holding down costs. It may also be used at the industry level for inter-bank comparisons on cost efficiency.

Transaction Velocity

From Table 3.5 we can also calculate the transaction velocity (TV) or turnover of each account head by dividing the figures in column 5 with those in column 2 for each account head. This transaction velocity reflects the general nature of the account and its characteristics obtainable in a given branch/region/zone, and hence it will remain constant for a reasonably long period. Since a bank as a whole is the conglomerate of all

its branches/regions/zones, the TV of an account will reflect the average characteristics obtainable in all its branches/regions/zones, though there may be inter-spatial variations amongst them. For corporate strategic planning, TVs are to be calculated at the bank level by calling from the branches the general ledger summations of all account heads, while for other lower operational units, for example, zones or branches, the same exercise is to be done at those unit levels. For a bank with a very large network of branches, a stratified sample procedure can be adopted. In the past, it was imperative to draw debit and credit summations of all account heads in a general ledger as soon as the balance was carried forward to the next ledger folio. Unfortunately, this excellent practice has long been stopped. Still, it has been found that it takes about two days for a single clerk with a calculator to do the entire job for a medium-sized branch. For computerised branches, it can be done by just pressing a few keys. As, once calculated, TVs for account heads will remain constant for at least three years, this is not going to be a terrible workload on the employees of a bank. For any projected level of individual asset or liability, what remains, therefore, is just to multiply it with the appropriate TV to arrive at the projected transaction volume. Multiplying it further with MCF, one gets the cost of managing a particular asset or liability.

Necessary figures for calculating TVs and MCF for ABC Bank are given in Table 3.6.

The operating expenditure of ABC Bank for 'O' year was Rs 489.67 crore. The management cost factor is now calculated as below:

$$MCF\ for\ \text{`O' year} = \frac{489.67}{628997} = 0.0007785$$

or, Rs 7,785 per Rs 1 crore of volume transacted.

TABLE 3.6   Balance Outstanding, Aggregate Summations, and TVs of ABC Bank for 'O' Year Ending 31 March

(Rs in crore)

Account Head (1)	Outstanding Balance (2)	Aggregate Summations or Volume Transacted (3)	Transaction Velocity (col. 3 ÷ col.2) (4)	Allocated Cost (col. 3 × MCF) (5)
Demand deposit	1898	75148	40	58.50
Savings bank	3221	47122	15	36.68
Term deposit	7689	28285	4	22.02
Bills payable	278	6694	24	5.21
Interest accrued & payable	741	2904	4	2.26
Interest accrued & receivable	300	6648	22	5.17
Borrowings	292	10702	36	8.33
Cash credit etc.	2711	135550	50	105.52
Bills purchased and discounted	965	19003	20	14.79
Term loans	2371	23820	10	18.54
Cash in hand	117	5845	50	4.55
Balances with RBI	1635	31905	20	24.84
Balances with other banks	612	18363	30	14.30
Investments	5729	112403	20	87.51
Other assets	589	22604	38	17.60
Bills for collection	937	10830	12	8.43
Guarantees, underwriting & repos	2616	14955	6	11.65
Letters of credit, acceptance & endorsements	894	6838	8	5.33
Foreign exchange contracts	3527	49378	14	38.44
Total		628997		489.67

By way of example, MCF of 0.0007785 is used to allocate management costs to different account heads in column 5 of Table 3.6.

For the strategic planning exercise, we have assumed that the management of ABC Bank would like to hold its MCF at the present level. This assumption is reasonable because ABC Bank is already smarting under a high operating expenditure. It is under pressure from the government to hold on to its cost line.

RISK COMPONENT

Any credit or investment decision involves considering the risk of bad debt, or depreciation of the market value of investments even in case of gilt-edged securities like government papers. While a detailed risk analysis of a borrowing customer is the subject matter of a separate chapter, we are concerned here about the risk component of various assets in general for estimating true returns from risk assets.

Sectoral estimation of the risk of bad debt or depreciation of the market value of investments can be done by studying the performance of various asset segments over a period. For a bank, this can be done by taking the percentage of NPAs on aggregate advances made in a particular sector. One should, however, remember that the sectoral risk profile changes with changes in the external environment (both economic and physical, for example, the monsoons for agriculture) directly affecting the performance of a sector. This risk profile is also affected by the quality of lending decisions. During recent years, closer attention is being paid to this aspect to guard against creation of more than normal NPAs in the system.

Risk Coverage

In major developed countries, almost all kinds of lending risks are insurable. There are specialised agencies who undertake this risk. In India, risk insurance is available for housing loans, trade receivables, portfolio risks, and short-term credit risks. The major providers of credit insurance are ICICI Lombard and The New India Assurance Company.

In the agricultural sector, crop insurance is available under national agricultural insurance schemes administered by the Agriculture Insurance Company of India Limited. The company was sponsored by the General Insurance Company of India Limited, the National Bank for Agriculture and Rural Development, and four public sector general insurance companies. Although the company commenced operations in 2003, it has extended its operations in all the states. As of February 2010 the company had covered 13.46 crore farmers. Besides providing general crop insurance for all food products, oil seeds, and horticulture produces, the company offers specialised insurance products like weather based crop insurance (against adverse weather incidences) and rainfall insurance for coffee. Special insurance packages are also available for rubber plantation, cardamom, and coconut.

Two public sector organisations provide a risk cover for select sectors. The Credit Guarantee Fund Trust for Micro and Small Enterprises (CGTMSE) offers risk coverage for MSE advances,[34] and the Export Credit Guarantee Corporation (ECGC) does the same for export credit.

A derivative instrument, credit default swap (CDS) emerged in 1997, which acts as a sort of hedge or credit insurance policy against the default risk of a bond or loan. It is now widely used in global financial markets. A buyer of a CDS contract passes on the risk of default to another institution for a fee. Like any other derivative instrument, the CDS contract is not actually tied to the loan or the bond, but instead references it, which is called a 'reference obligation'. Though the CDS concept emerged to protect a lender against default risk, it soon moved to the speculative market. One of the reasons behind the financial crisis of 2008–09 is ascribed to the speculative misuse of CDS contracts. For example, the American Insurance Group (AIG) sold enormous amount of CDSs against sub-prime loans most of which turned bad. For this reason, RBI has been slow in introducing CDS instruments in the Indian financial market. However, recently RBI has shown its willingness to introduce CDS in India by floating a discussion paper seeking opinion of prospective users and issuers.[35] As credit derivatives are expected to make an entry in the Indian market soon, we

[34] The CGTMSE was formed by the Government of India in collaboration with the Small Industries Development Bank of India (SIDBI). The guarantee schemes became operational from 1 January 2000. The guarantee is available for loans up to Rs 100 lakh per borrowing unit sanctioned by banks/FIs without any collaterals and third party guarantees. In general, the maximum coverage is 75 per cent of the sanctioned limit. However, the coverage is 80 per cent for loans up to Rs 5 lakh, for enterprises operated by women, and all loans sanctioned in the northeast region (available at www.cgtsi.org.in).

[35] See RBI's press release dated 4 August 2010.

have provided a short introduction to these instruments in Appendix 3.1.

The actual exposure of a bank to advances in the sectors mentioned earlier is, therefore, limited by the coverage available from these guarantee/insurance organisations. Table 3.7 gives the risk component of various assets of ABC Bank, and its net exposure considering the availability of guarantee/insurance cover.

ASSET ALLOCATION

We begin with the decision to make an additional Rs 100 crore commercial loan and analyse its impact on the profitability of the bank. (This need not be one single loan but an aggregate of several loans of varied amounts.) The priority sector commitment being 30 per cent of the aggregate bank credit, the total additional advances of the bank come to be $100/70 \times 100 = $ Rs 142.86 crore, of which Rs 42.86 crore will go towards the priority sector. These additional assets will attract capital adequacy norms as:

Capital requirement	(Rs in crore)
(a) Commercial loan @ 8% on Rs 100 crore	= Rs 8.00
(b) Priority sector @ 8% on 50 % of Rs 42.86 crore (assuming guarantee cover is taken)	= Rs 1.71
Total	Rs 9.71

TABLE 3.7 Risk Exposure of Sectoral Advances of ABC Bank

Item (a)	Risk Component (b)	Guarantee Coverage* (c)	Actual Exposure b(1–c) (d)	Risk-adjusted Assets Factor (1–d) (e)
Priority Sector				
Direct agriculture	0.25	0.50	0.125	0.875
Indirect agriculture	0.15	0.50	0.075	0.925
Small-scale industries	0.20	0.50	0.10	0.90
Transport	0.10	0.50	0.05	0.95
Retail trade	0.20	0.50	0.10	0.90
Professional, Education Loans, and others	0.30	0.50	0.15	0.85
Other Sectors				
Export	0.05	0.80	0.01	0.99
Public sector	0.02	0	0.02	0.98
Trade (including consumer loans)	0.05	0	0.05	0.95
Industry	0.015	0	0.015	0.985
Investments				
Government and approved securities	0.01	0	0.01	0.99
Other market securities	0.15	0	0.15	0.85

Note: Interest income will be booked only on risk-adjusted assets as appearing in column (e) of this table.

  * Although available guarantees are higher than this under various credit guarantee schemes, the experience of the bank is that in reality they get a much lower amount than the guarantee coverage as credit guarantee organisations deduct several items from the claimed amount for one reason or the other.

This capital of Rs 9.71 crore is also available to fund a part of the total assets of Rs 142.86 crore. Additional deposits required to fund the assets will, therefore, be Rs 142.86 – 9.71 = Rs 133.15 crore. Any additional deposit will attract CRR and SLR requirements of 12 per cent and 25 per cent respectively. Hence, in order to make available a free deposit of Rs 133.15 crore, the total deposit requirement will be $[133.15/(100-12-25)]$ × 100 = Rs 211.35 crore, from which Rs 25.36 crore and Rs 52.84 crore will go towards meeting CRR and SLR requirements respectively. We can now summarise the formation of domestic assets and liabilities consequent upon the decision to make a Rs 100 crore commercial loan.

Partial Balance Sheet of ABC Bank

(Rs in crore)

Liabilities		Assets	
Capital	9.71	Balance with RBI (CRR)	25.36
Deposits	211.35	Investments (SLR)	52.84
		Loans	
		Priority sector	42.86
		Commercial sector	100.00
Total	221.06	Total	221.06

We now analyse the cost and profitability of various assets so generated from these operations.

CRR and SLR Assets

1. *Balance with the Reserve Bank of India (CRR):* Rs 25.36 crore. No interest is paid by RBI on CRR balances. But the bank will incur the following management cost.

Balance with RBI × Transactional Velocity (TV) × Management Cost Factor (MCF)

or, Rs 25.36 × 20 × 0.0007785

or, Rs 0.40 crore.

2. *SLR Investments: Rs 52.84 crore.* These investments earn interest and incur management costs. Costs and returns calculations are shown in Table 3.8.

Portfolio of Priority Sector Advances

The portfolio of priority sector advances should be arranged in such a manner as to minimise the total risk exposure as shown in Table 3.9. This is done with the help of the risk exposure of various assets given in Table 3.7.

In Table 3.10, we calculate management costs and returns on these advances. It may be observed

TABLE 3.8   Bifurcation of SLR Investments, Costs, and Returns

(Rs in crore)

	Amount (1)	Risk Exposure (2)	Risk Adjusted Assets (3)	Trans-action Velocity (4)	Volume Trans-acted (5)	Manage-ment Cost (6)	Loss Pro-vision (7)	Return (8)	Net income/ cost (9)
Cash in hand (being 0.5% of deposits)	1.06	0	1.06	50	53	0.04	0	0	(0.04)
Balances with other banks in current account being 1% of deposits	2.11	0	2.11	30	63	0.05	0	0	(0.05)
Government & other approved securities	49.67	0.01	49.17	20	993	0.77	0.50	5.90	4.63
Total	52.84		52.34			0.86	0.50	5.90	4.54

Note: Cash in hand and balances with other banks are eligible for inclusion in SLR assets.

TABLE 3.9   Risk Exposure, Portfolio Allocation, and Risk-Adjusted Assets of Priority Sector Advances

(Rs in crore)

Sub-Sectors (1)	Risk Exposure (2)	Earning Assets (1−col. 2) (3)	Allocated Portfolio (see note) (4)	Amount (Rs 42.86 × col. 4) (5)	Risk Adjusted Factor (6)	Risk Adjusted Assets (7)	Provision for Bad Debts (8)
Direct agriculture	0.25	0.75	0.156	6.69	0.875	5.85	0.84
Indirect agriculture	0.15	0.85	0.177	7.59	0.925	7.02	0.57
Small-scale industries	0.20	0.80	0.167	7.16	0.900	6.44	0.72
Transport	0.10	0.90	0.187	8.00	0.950	7.60	0.40
Retail trade	0.20	0.80	0.167	7.16	0.900	6.44	0.72
Professional & others	0.30	0.70	0.146	6.26	0.850	5.32	0.94
Total	—	4.80	1.000	42.86	—	38.67	4.19

Note: Portfolio allocation amongst various sub-sectors of the priority sector is done in such a way as to minimise the risk of the total portfolio. By setting the total of column 3 to 1, percentage distribution among various sub-sectors has been done as follows:

Say, for direct agriculture: $(1/4.80) \times 0.75 = 0.156$ or 15.6%.

TABLE 3.10   Management Cost of Priority Sector Advances

(Rs in crore)

Form of Credit (1)	Percentage Allocation (2)	Amount (Rs 42.86 × col. 2) (3)	Transaction Velocity (4)	Volume Transacted (col. 3 × col. 4) (5)	Management Cost (col. 5 × 0.0007785) (6)
Cash credit etc.	0.50	21.43	50	1072	0.83
Bills purchased and discounted	0.15	6.43	20	129	0.10
Term loans	0.35	15.00	10	150	0.12
Total	1.00	42.86	—	1351	1.05

that the forms of credit to all these priority sector advances are moderately changed from the existing pattern.

Interest income @ 16.5 per cent on the net credit (after risk adjustment), that is, Rs 38.67 crore = Rs 6.38 crore. Net income from priority sector advances (before cost of fund) is finally calculated as below:

Net Income from Priority Sector Advances	(Rs in crore)	
Income		Rs 6.38
Less: Management cost	Rs 1.05	
Provision for bad debts	Rs 4.19	Rs 5.24
Total		Rs 1.14

Commercial Advances

In the case of priority sector advances, we have more or less followed the existing distribution among different forms of credit, because in the short-term it is difficult to alter the arrangement for priority sector borrowers who are predominantly small. For example, a major shift towards bills financing may not be feasible for many of them. But such is not the case with large borrowers. RBI has been emphasising for quite some time that a good part of permissible bank finance should be made available to the borrowers only in bill form. This not only makes the advance self-liquidating, it is cost-saving as well. On a broader scale, it helps develop a healthy bill market, which adds liquidity to the financial system. A bill system of financing is also more transparent. The present forms of financing commercial borrowers at ABC Bank are, therefore, altered moderately in Table 3.11. In Table 3.11, we also calculate the cost of, and return from, Rs 100 crore commercial credit assuming an average interest rate of 20 per cent per annum, and a loss provision of 1.5 per cent as indicated before.

In Table 3.12 we present a summary of costs of and returns from various assets, before the cost

of funding, to determine precisely at what cost of funds can these assets be carried by the bank.

Loss Provision and Calculation of Net Income

It may be seen in Table 3.8 to Table 3.12 (and elsewhere also) that income from assets is first calculated on risk adjusted assets, that is, after adjusting estimated bad debts or loss provisions, and then from this income the amount of estimated bad debts or loss provisions is again deducted to arrive at the net income from an asset. This is so, because a lost asset not only does

TABLE 3.11   Cost and Income Analysis of Rs 100 Crore Commercial Advance

(Rs in crore)

Form of Credit (1)	Amount (2)	Risk Adjusted Assets @ 98.5% (3)	Loss Provision (4)	Return @ 20% pa (on col. 3) (5)	Trans-action Velocity (6)	Volume Transacted (col. 2 × col. 6) (7)	Management Cost (col. 7 × MCF) (8)	Net Income (col. 5 – col. 4 – col. 8) (9)
Cash credit etc.	40	39.40	0.60	7.88	50	2000	1.56	5.72
Bill purchased and discounted	25	24.63	0.37	4.93	20	500	0.39	4.17
Term loans	35	34.47	0.53	6.89	10	350	0.27	6.09
Total	100	98.50	1.50	19.70	—	2850	2.22	15.98

TABLE 3.12   Costs of and Returns from Assets

(Rs in crore)

Asset Type (1)	Amount (2)	Return (3)	Management Cost (4)	Loss Provisions (5)	Net Return (6)
1. Cash in hand	1.06	—	0.04	—	(–) 0.04
2. Balances with RBI (CRR)	25.36	—	0.40	—	(–) 0.40
3. Balances with other banks	2.11	—	0.05	—	(–) 0.05
4. Government & other approved securities	49.67	5.90	0.77	0.50	4.63
Advances					
5. Priority sector	42.86	6.38	1.05	4.19	1.14
6. Commercial sector	100.00	19.70	2.22	1.50	15.98
Total	221.06	31.98	4.53	6.19	21.26

not earn any interest income; it also eats into the earned income of other good assets. For example, suppose a bank has lent Rs 100 lakh at an interest rate of 20 per cent, of which Rs 10 lakh have either gone bad, or are expected to. The bank, therefore, earns interest @ 20 per cent only on Rs 90 lakh, that is, Rs 18 lakh. At the same time, the bank has also lost the entire amount of Rs 10 lakh. Hence, the net income receivable by the bank would be Rs 18–10 = Rs 8 lakh. In other words, the net income is the closing balance of the asset plus interest earned minus the opening balance of the asset. The treatment is somewhat different when compared with other business enterprises, where sales include the element of profit and bad debt, or its provision is debited to the profit and loss account in full sales value. The resultant effect will, however, be the same in both the cases.

COST OF FUNDS

Cost of Capital

Capital requirement has already been assessed as Rs 9.71 crore, which is to be serviced @ 37.5 per cent. The cost of capital will, therefore, be Rs 9.71 crore × 0.375 = Rs 3.64 crore, which includes, besides notional dividend, provision for statutory reserves also.

Expected Cost of Deposit Fund	(Rs in crore)
Net return from assets (as shown in Table 3.12)	Rs 21.26
Less: cost of capital	3.64
Maximum cost payable on deposits	Rs 17.62

We have shown earlier that the cost of borrowing for ABC Bank has been very high, and hence we have decided not to take recourse to borrowing further, but repay the existing outstandings at the earliest. Besides capital, deposit should be the only source for funding its working assets during the plan period.

The maximum average rate (inclusive of management cost) payable on deposits should, therefore, be [17.62/211.35] × 100 = 8.34 per cent.

We have already shown in Table 3.3 that the existing deposit profile of ABC Bank is good, with average interest paid being 6.47 per cent (exclusive of management costs). We intend to alter this profile only moderately, not only to make it a little more cost-effective, but also to sustain the challenge for keeping its deposit cost at a competitive minimum. In Table 3.13 the projected deposit profile of ABC Bank along with its costs are tabulated.

The profitability of the entire funded operation can now be summarised as:

Profit Summary of Funded Business	(Rs in crore)
Income from assets	21.26
Less: Total cost of deposits fund	16.60
Net income	4.66
Less: Cost of capital	3.64
Net return:	1.02

It is evident now that the incremental funded business is just able to meet the full cost of capital. There is a small surplus of Rs 1.02 crore. Let us now see whether the position can be improved from off-balance sheet businesses.

Off-balance Sheet Business

At present, the aggregate outstanding of the off-balance sheet business is Rs 7974 crore (including bills for collection), which is about 132 per cent of the total credit. The performance of ABC Bank under this head is not very encouraging. It is no use comparing this with international standards, but even for Indian nationalised banks which are performing well, the average is about two times the total credit. With the globalisation of Indian banking, and newer instruments coming up, this business is going to develop at a faster rate. As indicated earlier, the future of banking lies more in the 'sweeteners'

TABLE 3.13   Projected Deposit Profile and Cost

(Rs in crore)

Type (1)	Amount (2)	Percentage of Total (3)	Transaction Velocity (4)	Volume Transacted (col. 2 × col. 4) (5)	Management Cost (col. 5 × MCF) (6)	Interest Cost/ Return (7)	Total Cost (8)	Remarks (9)
1. Demand deposits	29.41	13.91	40	1176	0.915	—	0.915	
2. Bills payable	4.41	2.09	24	106	0.082	(−) 0.106	(−) 0.024	Cols 7 and 8 represent commission earned on remittances (see note 2).
3. Savings bank	57.06	27.00	15	856	0.667	1.712	2.379	Interest at an effective rate of 3% p.a.
4. Term deposits	120.47	57.00	4	482	0.375	12.950	13.325	Interest at an effective rate of 10.75% that is, 1% increase from the existing average.
Total	211.35	100.00	—	2620	2.039	14.556	16.595	

Notes: 1. The deposit profile shown in this table is arrived at through a process of iteration, that is by developing various possible profiles, and picking one among them which is the most feasible.

2. Bills payable are assumed to include predominately remittance instruments like demand drafts and telegraphic transfers, which are sold but yet to be presented for payment at the drawee branch. Banks normally enjoy this float fund. The outstanding in the bills payable account is assumed to be 15 per cent of demand deposits.

The transaction velocity of bills payable is 24, which is the aggregate of both debit and credit summations, but the actual business done under this head is represented by credit summations only. Therefore, half of the volume transacted is to be taken to determine the actual business which, in the present case, is 106/2 = 53. Multiplying this with the rate of commission charged, we obtain the gross income under this head as 0.002 × 53 = Rs 0.106 crore.

This argument holds good for selling of any off-balance sheet instruments where only credit entries (summations) represent the actual volume of business done. For calculating the cost we take the total 'volume transacted'; for calculation of income we take only half of it.

than in hardcore lending, though the relationship between the two is unlikely to snap. It is expected, therefore, that ABC Bank would also gear up its machinery to have a reasonable share in this growing business segment. At the same time, the bank has to move cautiously, because as the Basle Committee has warned, off-balance sheet businesses are fraught with risks which are often new and not visible. The collapse of the 223-year-old Barings Bank in February 1995 is a pointer to the danger of uncontrolled expansion of off-balance sheet businesses.

Considering all this, we suggest that ABC Bank should try to achieve and maintain a level of outstanding balance in off-balance sheet businesses equal to 1.5 times the average level of credit, which is both cautious and challenging. Under this assumption, the total off-balance sheet business comes to Rs 142.86 × 1.50 = Rs 214.30 crore. The existing percentage distribution amongst various off-balance sheet businesses has, however, been maintained with a little challenge thrown in some sectors. In Table 3.14 we have calculated the capital requirement, costs, and profitability of these businesses.

Gross surplus or incremental capital formation from the entire operation is shown in Table 3.15.

Table 3.15 clearly reveals the importance of non-funded business in a bank. This is also supported by the fact that as on date, income from ABC Bank's non-funded business is close to 47 per cent of its net interest margin, excluding interest on pre-1992 CRR balances.

OPERATIONAL PLAN FOR FIVE YEARS

We are now ready to draw up the operational plan of ABC Bank for the next five years, keeping the profit objective in view. As dividend and tax are taken notionally because none is really payable, the gross surplus should be considered as the retained profit of the bank.

Now, by using a simple unitary method, the projected profit objective of ABC Bank can be arithmetically related to its other objectives by calculating relative profit factors (RPF) for surplus, assets, and other liabilities as in Table 3.16.

All the assets and liabilities are now so related through RPF, that any of the assets and liabilities can be projected by multiplying or dividing them with the relative factor. For example, for a given level of profit of Rs 84.77 crore, the deposit requirement will be Rs 84.77 × 18.52 = Rs 15 70 crore. Similarly, for a given level of deposits of Rs 1,570 crore, the profit will be Rs 1570/18.52 = Rs 84.77 crore.

Earlier, we had assumed a 12 per cent per annum cumulative growth of deposits for ABC Bank. On this basis, the projections for the next five years are given in Table 3.17.

In Table 3.18, projected surpluses (profit) for the next five years are calculated by dividing the annual incremental deposits with RPF of 18.52 appearing in column 2 of Table 3.17.

The staircase pattern of profit projections as shown in Table 3.18 is due to the fact that unlike other business organisations where sales are always new sales year-by-year, in the case of banks a given level of funds once sold as assets will generate a continuous stream of income on the assumption that all repayments are simultaneously invested under the same terms.

Let us now recall that the present exercise started with the goal that ABC Bank would wipe out its entire loss of Rs 1,478.70 crore in five years. The aggregate surplus figure of Rs 1,494.28 at the end of the fifth year, as shown in Table 3.18, appears to be fulfilling the objective.

Projection of Assets and Liabilities

With the projected profit (surplus) figure now available, our next job is to make projections of various assets and liabilities of the bank for the next five years. This is done by multiplying the

TABLE 3.14 Capital Requirement, Costs, and Profitability of Off-Balance Sheet Business

(Rs in crore)

Items (1)	Amount (2)	Capital Requirement (3)	Cost of Capital @ 37.5% (4)	Transaction Velocity (5)	Volume Transacted (6)	Management Cost (col. 6 × MCF) (7)	Rate of Return (%) (8)	Gross Return (9)	Net Income (col. 9 – col. 4 – col. 7) (10)
Bills for collection	32.14 (15)	—	—	12	386	0.30	0.40	0.77	0.47
Guarantees: Financial	40.72 (19)	3.26	1.22	6	244	0.20	1.55	1.89	0.47
Others	40.72 (19)	1.63	0.61	6	244	0.20	1.05	1.28	0.47
Letters of credit	25.72 (12)	0.41	0.15	8	206	0.16	1.00	1.03	0.72
Foreign exchange	75.00 (35)	0.12	0.05	14	1050	0.82	1.25	6.56	5.69
Total	214.30 (100)	5.42	2.03	—	2130	1.68	—	11.53	7.82

Notes: 1. Capital requirements under column 3 are calculated in terms of capital adequacy norms as Basel I, ignoring any collateralisation by cash or deposit margin.

2. For rate of return under column 8, page 81.

3. Gross returns under column 9 are calculated as half of 'volumes transacted' in column 6.

4. A general loss provision of 1.7 per cent is made on the outstanding balance appearing in column 2, after deducting the amount outstanding against bills for collection, which carries virtually no risk. That is, 0.017 (214.30–32.14) = Rs 3.10 crore (approximately). The net income from non-funded business after providing for probable counter-party risk, therefore, comes to Rs 7.82 crore – Rs 3.10 crore = Rs 4.72 crore. The loss provision by ABC Bank is not expected to be highly risk-prone with adequate caution. In fact, one of the strategies of the bank in the planned restructuring and consolidation period should be to move cautiously, and not to chart itself out to unknown and high-risk-prone areas.

TABLE 3.15   Incremental Capital Formation

Nature of Business (1)	Net Return (2)	Capital Servicing (3)	Gross Surplus or Capital Formation (col. 2 + col. 3) (4)
Funded business	1.02	3.64	4.66
Non-funded business	4.72	2.03	6.75
Total	5.74	5.67	11.41

TABLE 3.16   Relative Profit Factor for Surplus, Assets, and Liabilities

(Rs in crore)

	Surplus (1)	Funded Assets (2)	Deposits (3)	Non-funded Assets (4)	Capital Requirement Funded Assets (5)	Capital Requirement Non-funded Assets (6)	Capital Requirement Total (Cols 5 + 6) (7)
Amount	11.41	221.06	211.35	214.30	9.71	5.42	15.13
Relative profit factor	1	19.37	18.52	18.78	0.85	0.47	1.32

TABLE 3.17   Five Years' Projections of Deposit Growth

(Rs in crore)

Year (1)	Incremental Deposit (2)	Total Deposits (3)	Remarks (4)
'O'	—	13085	Deposits include
1	1570	14655	Bills payable
2	1758	16413	
3	1970	18383	
4	2206	20589	
5	2471	23060	

relative profit factors for individual assets and liabilities as given in Table 3.16 with the annual projected profit (surplus) figure given in Table 3.18. For example, the projected incremental profit (surplus) in year 2 is Rs 94.92 crore (see column 2 of Table 3.18). The RPF for funded assets is 19.37 crore (see Table 3.16). Hence, the projected incremental funded assets in year 2 will be Rs 94.92 × 19.37 = Rs 1,839 crore. The final projections are given in Table 3.19. Similar calculations are made by taking cumulative surplus figures as appearing in the total column of Table 3.18. These are shown in Table 3.20.

TABLE 3.18   Five Years' Projections of Surpluses (Profit)

(Rs in crore)

Year	1	2	3	4	5	Total
1	84.77	—	—	—	—	84.77
2	84.77	94.92	—	—	—	179.69
3	84.77	94.92	106.37	—	—	286.06
4	84.77	94.92	106.37	119.11	—	405.17
5	84.77	94.92	106.37	119.11	133.42	538.59
Total	423.85	379.68	319.11	238.22	133.42	1494.28

TABLE 3.19   Projected Incremental Assets and Liabilities

(Rs in crore)

| Year | Deposits (1) | Funded Assets (2) | Non-funded Assets (3) | Capital Requirement | | | Surplus (7) |
				Funded Assets (4)	Non-funded Assets (5)	Total (Cols 4 + 5) (6)	
1	1570	1642	1592	72.05	39.84	111.89	84.77
2	1758	1839	1783	80.68	44.61	125.29	94.92
3	1970	2060	1998	90.41	49.99	140.40	106.37
4	2206	2307	2237	101.24	55.98	157.22	119.11
5	2471	2584	2506	113.41	62.71	176.12	133.42
Total	9975	10432	10116	457.79	253.13	710.92	538.59

TABLE 3.20   Projected Assets and Liabilities Incremental Cumulative

(Rs in crore)

| Year | Deposits (1) | Funded Assets (2) | Non-funded Assets (3) | Capital Requirement | | | Cumulative Surplus (7) |
				Funded Assets (4)	Non-funded Assets (5)	Total (Cols 4 + 5) (6)	
1	1570	1642	1592	72.05	39.84	111.89	84.77
2	3328	3481	3375	152.73	84.45	237.18	264.46
3	5298	5541	5373	243.14	134.44	377.58	550.52
4	7504	7848	7610	344.38	190.42	534.80	955.69
5	9975	10432	10116	457.79	253.13	710.92	1494.28

Note: Cumulative surpluses in column 7 are calculated from the 'Total' column of Table 3.18.

The surpluses appearing in column 7 of Table 3.19 not being taxed and distributed as dividends, will go towards the formation of ABC Bank's Tier-I capital after loss adjustments. It may be seen, however, that in the first year, the projections reveal a shortage of required capital to the tune of 111.89 – 84.77 = Rs 27.12 crore. This will not create any problem, because the bank already has excess capital of 0.44 per cent, or Rs 27.44 crore over and above the required minimum, with which the shortage could be met.

Table 3.20 reveals that, on the face of it, the cumulative surplus of Rs 1,494.28 crore at the end of the fifth year is more than adequate to wipe out the accumulated loss of Rs 1,478.70 crore. But this is not all. In the absence of tax and dividend payment, the surplus created every year contains an amount of free cash, which a prudent banker is not expected to keep idle; he would invest it continuously. He can do it either by making further loans and advances, or by investing in government securities, which are credit risk-free. The former will attract capital adequacy norms, while the latter will not. As the bank is in need of building up its capital base, it is preferable that the free surplus cash is invested in government securities continuously for five years, so that at the end of five years it will have a sizeable capital base after wiping out its backlog of accumulated losses.

A part of the surplus appearing in column 7 of Table 3.19 already stands invested in funded assets generated for the year; the remaining part is only available for further investment. For example, in the second year, out of an incremental surplus (column 7) of Rs 94.92 crore an amount of Rs 80.68 crore (column 4) is already invested in funded assets, leaving an amount of Rs 14.24 crore as additional investible resources. In Table 3.21 we have calculated the annual accretion of additional resources.

As mentioned earlier, the additional investible resources from annual surpluses appearing in Table 3.21 will be invested continuously at 12 per cent per annum in government securities. The annual sums available being constant for every year, we can use the following standard formula for calculating the five-year-end compounded value of the annual sum invested:

$$S_t = A_t \left[\{(1+r)^n - 1\}/r \right]$$

where

1. 'S_t' is the amount of funds available at the end of period 't', which are 5, 4, 3, 2, 1 in the present case.

2. 'A_t' is the amount of incremental additional resources available for year 't', which are 1, 2, 3, 4, 5 in the present case.
3. 'r' is the rate of interest, which is 0.12 in the present case.
4. 'n' is number of years.

For example, A_t for the first year's operation being Rs 12.72 crore, the amount available at the end of the fifth year (S_t), will be 12.72 $[\{(1+0.12)^5 - 1\}/0.12]$ = 12.72 × 6.352847 = Rs 80.81 crore.

The pre-calculated compounding factors representing $\{(1+r)^n - 1\}/r$ are also available from any standard table. These are given in the penultimate line of Table 3.21. The amounts thus available at the end of the period are shown at the bottom of Table 3.21. The final amount that the bank will get at the end of five years is, therefore, Rs 260.02 crore, by continuously investing the annual available surpluses aggregating Rs 224.19 crore over a 5-year period. The net amount accruing to the bank will, therefore, be 260.02 – 224.19 = Rs 35.83 crore. The management cost of these investments will be 224.19 × 20 × 0.0007785 = Rs 3.49 crore. The net amount available to the bank will, therefore, be 35.83 – 3.49 = Rs 32.34 crore (ignoring loss

TABLE 3.21 Additional Investible Resources Available from Surplus

(Rs in crore)

Year	1	2	3	4	5	Total
1	12.72	—	—	—	—	12.72
2	12.72	14.24	—	—	—	26.96
3	12.72	14.24	15.96	—	—	42.92
4	12.72	14.24	15.96	17.87	—	60.79
5	12.72	14.24	15.96	17.87	20.01	80.80
Total	63.60	56.96	47.88	35.74	20.01	224.19
Compounding factors	6.3528	4.7793	3.3374	2.1200	1.0000	—
Amount at the end of the period	80.81	68.06	53.26	37.88	20.01	260.02

provisions), which is now added to the cumulative surplus of Rs 1,494.28 crore to determine the final surplus available to the bank at the end of the fifth year, that is 1494.28 + 32.34 = Rs 1,526.62 crore.

It may be recalled that ABC Bank has a Tier I capital of Rs 1,927.18 crore before adjustment of accumulated losses of Rs 1,478.70 crore at the beginning of the plan period. Tier I capital at the end of the 5-year period will, therefore, be 1927.18 + 1526.62 − 1478.70 = Rs 1,975.10 crore, net of all losses and provisions.

Concluding Remarks

Financial sector reforms and the transparency requirement have brought forth the weaknesses of Indian banks, particularly the nationalised ones. The government desires that the banks should evolve their own turnaround strategies. Simultaneously, attempts are made to recapitalise these banks by infusion of capital, so that they fulfil the capital adequacy requirement within a time-bound programme.

The profit motive has come back to the centre stage of Indian banking. As against the earlier strategic plan of Deposit ⟶ Assets ⟶ Profit, the new strategy has made an about turn along the Profit ⟶ Assets ⟶ Deposit path.

A case study of a real-life commercial bank in the public sector, which desired to evolve a turnaround strategy was analysed. Management accounting techniques were employed first to allocate costs to the various products and services offered by the bank, and then relative profit factors were derived for every asset and liability that the bank could contract, including quasi-assets like off-balance sheet instruments. These profit factors provide a linkage among all balance sheet and off-balance sheet businesses of the bank in such a manner that given a particular volume of any such item, all others are determined automatically. Some of the assumptions made in this case study are peculiar to ABC Bank, which may not hold good for other banks, for whom separate assumptions may have to be made. But once the techniques for evolving the strategic plan of a commercial bank are understood properly, it will be found that the system can not only work under different assumptions, it can also generate alternative plans to enable a bank to undertake sensitivity analyses and to keep alternative action plans ready under each such assumption.

Appendix 3.1

AN INTRODUCTION TO CREDIT DERIVATIVES

As the name suggests, derivative instruments are derived from the value of underlying assets. A currency note is, perhaps, the first derivative instrument issued by note issuing authorities against the value of assets like gold, silver, bullions, coins etc. Share of a limited company is another example of derivative instrument. The value of currency notes changes with the value of the economy while the value of a share changes with the value of the company issuing it.

The beauty of a derivative instrument is that it can be so designed as to protect adverse changes in the underlying assets. For example, possible adverse movement of the external value of a currency can be protected by entering a forward contract.

A derivative instrument contains a contingent claim. For example, Option is a kind of derivative instrument, which is based on the happening or non-happening of an event that changes the value of an underlying asset.

Market for derivative instrument exists because of diverse needs and different estimation of economic agents about the future value of an underlying asset. For example, one may desire to limit exposure to certain loans whose risk has increased while another may desire to increase the risk exposure. Or, one economic agent estimates that the future value of or cash flows from an asset may decline while another thinks that these will increase. The derivatives market brings together these parties with diverse interest to strike a deal to protect and/or profit from the movement of the underlying asset.

Credit derivatives are special instruments which separate the elements of other risks like market risk or operational risk. These instruments are increasingly being used by banks for credit risk management of its portfolio of advances. These are also used as hedge against adverse changes in the credit quality of a borrower or the liability instruments issued by a borrowing entity (e.g. bonds, commercial papers etc.).

Credit Risk

Credit risk is composed of the following three risk elements.

1. Credit Default Risk: This is defined as the risk of non-payment of services due from a loan in time. Default risk is analysed in detail in chapter 20.
2. Credit Spread Risk: Credit spread is defined as the difference between the risks weighted interest rate on a loan asset and the rate on risk-free assets (e.g. treasury bills). In fact, the spread is so designed as to compensate the lender for the risk taken.

    When the credit spread increases (or widens) the market price of the loan asset declines (assuming no change in the rate on risk-free assets). The risk may increase for a particular industry or sector or for the economy as a whole. For example, during recession cash flows to service debt obligations may decrease causing an increase in the spread and a decline in the value of the underlying asset (though actual default may not have occurred).

    In theory, credit spread should increase in line with increasing default risk and maturity. However, it is observed in practice that credit spread increases with maturity only for higher credit quality loan assets and decreases for lower quality issues. It is also found that while marginal default risk for lower quality firms is higher in absolute terms, it decreases with maturity for lower rated firms. As against this, the marginal default risk of higher rated firms increases with maturity. This finding is also consistent with the mean reversion process in rating outlook where performance of lower rated firms improve, middle rated ones remain the same and higher rated firms tend to decline on average.[36]

3. Credit Quality Downgrade Risk: This emanates from credit spread risk as it is related to changes in the rating of an enterprise or the loans issued by it. Rating agencies not only rate the borrower or the loan asset they also monitor the credit quality of the asset and, if necessary, downgrade or upgrade the rating based on the performance of a loan obligation or on the general economic outlook. A downgrading of rating increases the credit spread and decreases the price of the loan issue. This is the credit quality downgrade risk.

The International Swaps and Derivatives Association (ISDA) has standardised credit derivative instruments and also defined various terminologies that are used in designing such instruments. Some major terms as defined by ISDA are noted below.

(a) *Reference entity:* The entity against which credit protection is sought. Pricing of credit derivative depends upon the credit profile of the reference entity.
(b) *Reference obligation:* The obligation of the reference entity like servicing of loan or a bond as per terms of issue.
(c) *Credit event:* An event affecting the reference entity or reference obligation (like default, downgrade of credit quality etc.) that triggers settlement between protection buyer and protection seller.

Major credit derivative instruments can be divided under three broad heads: credit swaps, credit options and credit forward contracts.

Credit Swaps

Credit swaps are principally of the following types

1. Total Return Swap (TRS)

Under this swap, a lending bank enters an agreement with another bank or investor to pass on the risk exposure and benefits of a loan without shifting it from its books. This may happen when, for example, the lending bank wants to reduce its exposure to a borrower, a group, an industry or a segment of the market which is crossing or about to cross the risk-limit of the bank while there is another bank which is inclined to increase its risk exposure in those areas. TRS creates a synthetic long (purchase) position for the latter bank whereby it takes over the risk and in return enjoys the economic benefits of a loan without actually funding the loan asset that remains in the books of account of the lending bank. In effect, the latter bank is guaranteeing the performance of the loan. This bank is therefore, regarded as protection seller while the lending bank is the protection buyer.

The beneficiary bank or the protection buyer agrees to pass on to the protection seller the total return from the loan asset which comprises interest and any appreciation in the value of the loan asset plus a fee for providing the protection. The fee or the risk premium is based on the perceived risk of the reference asset. The higher the risk, the higher the premium. A TRS can be executed without any knowledge of the borrower (reference entity).

The loan (reference obligation) is marked to the market on the appointed date(s). The return is usually based on a reference rate (RR). On the maturity date of the swap or on the occurrence of an event like loan default

---

[36] Choudhry, Morad, *The Bond and Money Markets: Strategy, Trading, Analysis*, Butterworth-Heinemann, Burlington, M.A., 2003.

the lending bank receives the RR plus a spread over the RR and the amount of depreciation in the value of the reference asset. Thus the protection seller is not only providing guarantee against the default of the borrower but also against any deterioration in the value of loan asset even when there is no default.

Transactions under a TRS are illustrated in Figure 3.1.

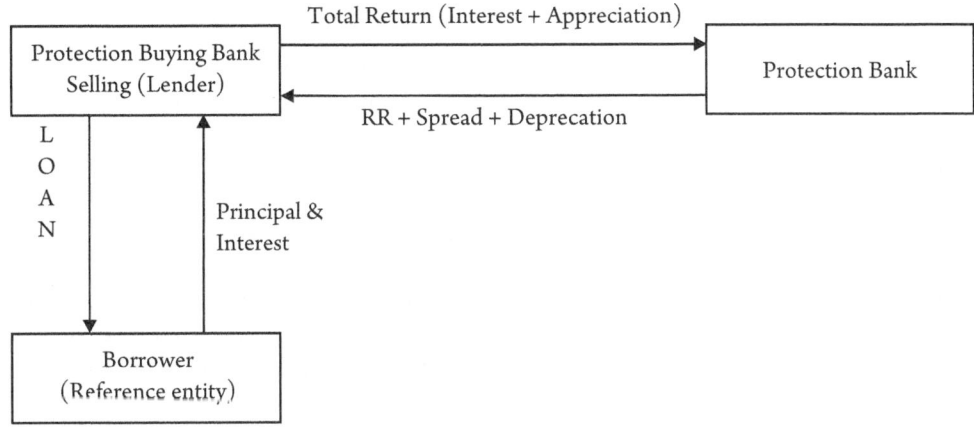

FIGURE 3.1   Total Return Swaps (TRS)

It may be noted that when the loan is also priced with reference to the RR, the RR is cancelled out as one party pays the RR while the other party receives it.

2. Credit Linked Note (CLN)

Under this swap, a bank transfers both the funding for loan(s) and also the default risk to a special purpose vehicle (SPV) which is usually a trust company.

The SPV issues securities (CLNs) against the underlying loan asset(s) to investors who tend to believe that they are participating in a certain quality loan and are, therefore, willing to bear the risk of default.

Every tranche of CLNs contains loan(s) of a particular credit rating. The bank can substitute one set of loans by another so long as the average rating of a tranche remains the same.

The SPV pays investors a steady stream of income as long as the reference entity or entities service the loan. The total return of the CLNs is linked to the market value of the reference loan or an underlying pool of securities.

The CLNs are redeemable at par on specified date if there is no default. When default occurs the CLNs are redeemed early and the investors are paid the post-default price of the referenced loan(s).

Banks often use CLNs to reduce the regulatory capital requirement as loans move from the balance sheet of the bank so also the risk.

A typical CLN structure is shown in Figure 3.2.

The Citigroup used a somewhat modified form of CLNs totaling US$ 1.4 billion during August 2000 to May 2001 through several paper trusts to hedge its exposure to Enron Corporation. The CLNs were of 5-year term during which time the investors would receive a steady stream of fixed payments that included a premium over the market rate. However, if Enron did not pay the service obligations, payment to investors would be stopped. The Citigroup invested the funds received from the investors in government securities and

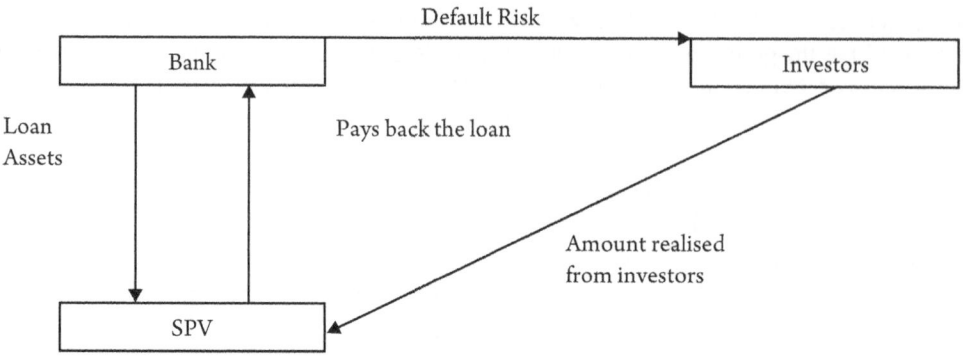

FIGURE 3.2   Credit Linked Note (CLN)

highly rated corporate bonds. On maturity of the CLNs these investments would be realised to pay back the principal amount of CLNs provided there was no default. If, however, Enron failed to repay its loan or files for bankruptcy, the Citigroup would stop repayment to the investors, transfer the debts to the investors and encash the securities to liquidate the Enron loan. When Enron went bankrupt in December 2001, the investors were left with worthless Enron debt papers.

3. Credit Default Swap (CDS)

This is the most popular credit derivative. Under a CDS contract, the lending bank (beneficiary) transfers the credit risk of the reference asset (loan) to the protection seller. The beneficiary bank (swap purchaser) pays to the protection seller fixed periodic payment(s) calculated as percentage of the par value of the reference asset during the life of the contract. The price of the CDS is linked to the perceived riskiness of the reference asset. In return, the protection seller agrees to pay the beneficiary bank an agreed sum when default occurs before maturity of the contract (which may be based on the market value of the reference asset or a fixed percentage of the reference asset). In effect, when a default occurs the protection seller pays the CDS buyer the difference between the principal amount of the reference asset and the actual market value of the asset in default. If no default occurs during the life of the CDS no amount is payable by the protection seller.

In a CDS contract, it is necessary to clearly define the default, which could be insolvency, bankruptcy or simple payment default. The contract should also provide the methodology of determining the post-default value of the reference asset.

A bank that has exceeded the maximum risk tolerance level can buy CDS for some of the high risk loans to lower down the average risk exposure without actually shifting the loan assets.

In addition to credit protection, CDS contracts can also be used by a bank to correct maturity mismatches.

Credit default swap is similar to non-life insurance product where the insured pays a certain premium to the insurance provider who agrees to indemnify the insured for any loss occurring to him due to certain specified events like fire, burglary etc. For a CDS the specified event is the default of the reference loan asset, all other things are almost same.

Credit default swap is also similar to total return swap (TRS) discussed earlier except that in the former case protection is available against credit default while in the latter case protection is provided against loss of value of the reference asset irrespective of the default like widening of credit spreads, rating downgrade etc.

A typical CDS framework is illustrated in Figure 3.3.

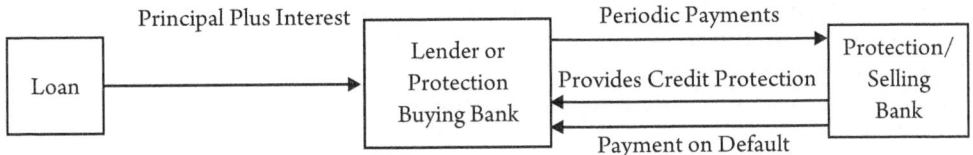

FIGURE 3.3   Credit Default Swap (CDS)

Speculation

Seeds of speculation are embedded in the structure of credit swaps discussed above. A speculator can bet on the credit quality of a reference entity and sell or buy a credit derivative depending upon his view on the upgrade or downgrade of the credit quality of the reference entity or asset. If he holds a positive view, he may sell a CDS and collect payments without actually investing in the loan. Another may view a downgrade of the credit quality and buys a CDS with small periodic payments only. If default occurs, he is in for a big payoff. Although a swap purchaser can always protect himself by selling a swap under same terms on the other sided of the market, speculators prefer to maintain an open position with the hope of reaping windfall profit.

Credit swap is an over the counter (OTC) product. As such, it requires intricate knowledge of the market and the type and value of the underlying assets. Otherwise, there is a chance of swap users falling prey to speculators. This is the reason why the Reserve Bank of India is moving cautiously in introducing credit swaps in Indian financial market.

Credit Option

Credit option contract is an extension of stock options introduced in stock exchanges during the early part of 1970s. Option gives the buyer a right but no obligation. In other words, an option seller (writer) grants the option buyer against payment of a fee (option price) something at a predetermined price of the underlying asset (strike price) within the life of the option.

There are two types of options:

(a) *American option:* It can be exercised at any time up to the date of the expiration of the contract.
(b) *European option:* It can be exercised only on the expiration date of the option.

The names indicate only the nature of the option not a geographical boundary. For example, an American option can be traded in any European exchange or anywhere in the world. The same is the case with a European option.

Although an option holder has the right to strike, he does not have to exercise that right. He may walk out if things are not favourable to him. His loss is limited to the option price paid by him.

Generally, two types of credit options are traded in the market. In the first type, the pay–out is determined on the default of the underlying asset (the value of which could be actual or notional. The amount of pay–out is a fixed amount determined at the time of writing the option. If there is no default, there is no pay–out.

The second type of credit option is much broader in scope as it can be related to any other credit events besides default. It can be a credit quality downgrade, a fall in net worth, decrease in current ratio, increase in debt–equity ratio or any other financial measure. However, most of this type of option is related to credit downgrade or widening of the credit spread.

The pay–out in the first type of credit option is straightforward. If default occurs, the option buyer exercises the right to strike and receives from the option seller the predetermined amount.

Under the second type where the option is related to say, credit downgrade the exercise price is based on the difference between the actual credit spread and the strike spread multiplied by a risk factor and the (notional) amount of the underlying asset. That is,

Pay–out = (Credit spread at the date of expiration—Strike spread) × Risk factor × Notional amount.

An example will make it clear.

Example

The following are the elements of a credit option contract:

    i.   Notional amount : Rs 10 crore
    ii.   Risk factor : 4
    iii. Strike spread : 200 basis points, that is, 2 per cent.

If at the strike (expiration) date the credit spread widens to 250 basis points the amount payable to option purchaser will be as below.

Pay–out = (0.025 – 0.020) × 4 × Rs 10 crore

Or, Pay–out = Rs 20 lakh.

However, if at the strike or expiration date, the spread is equal to or below the strike spread no amount is payable by the option seller.

Credit Forward Contract (CFC)

Although credit swaps and credit options are most popular forms of credit protection, a lender may also opt for a credit forward contract. The formula for determining the pay–out is shown below.

Pay–out = (Credit spread on settlement day—Credit spread on the contract date) × Risk factor × Notional amount.

The formula may appear to be similar to that of credit option but it differs from it in the sense that pay–out occurs on both sides. For example, suppose that the lending bank having advanced a loan of Rs 10 crore with a risk factor of 4 and a spread of 250 basis points feels that the spread might increase beyond 250 basis points and hence, enters a credit forward contract to protect itself against widening of spread. Depending on the event, the pay–out will be determined as follows.

Event I

Credit spread on settlement day increases to 300 basis points. The pay–out for the lending bank will be,

Pay–out = (0.030 – 0.025) × 4 × Rs 10 crore

Or, Pay–out = Rs 20 lakh.

Event II

Credit spread on the settlement day decreases to 220 basis points. The lending bank would be required to pay the following amount to the counterparty (indicated by the negative sign).

Pay–out = (0.022 – 0.025) × 4 × Rs 10 crore

Or, Pay–out = (–) Rs 12 lakh.

A lender can protect himself from the downside risk by simultaneously entering a forward purchase contract and a forward sell contract.

Never invest your money in anything that eats or needs repairing.

—Billy Rose

4 Lending Strategy and Loan Policy

INTRODUCTION

Elements of lending strategy are primarily drawn from the strategic plan of a banking organisation. Various assumptions made in drawing up the strategic plan in Chapter 3, ultimately become targets while implementing the plan. Although it is true that assumptions about the performance of the external environment may not always hold true in spite of the best predictions, and it is difficult for a single organisation to influence the external environment except by concerted action at the industry level through trade associations, the internal targets set forth in a strategic plan enable the organisation to adjust quickly to environmental changes in order to hold on to the principal strategic goal. The principal objectives of the lending strategy are:

1. to attain a targeted credit–deposit ratio both at the bank level and also in states/ regions.
2. to optimise yield on advances without scarifying the quality of loans.
3. to maintain sector-wise balance in the credit portfolio so as to avoid concentration of credit in any particular industry/ sector and group.
4. to keep in mind the national objective of financial inclusion in matters of disbursement of loans.

5. to minimise assets–liabilities mismatches keeping in view the maturity profile of fund sources.

The loan policy articulates the lending strategy of a bank.

NEED FOR A LOAN POLICY

The principal objective of a loan policy is to arrive at a trade-off between returns and risks within the broader framework of the strategic plan of the bank. In fact, loan policies should be such as to maximise returns while minimising risks. We shall, therefore, discuss the agenda for the formulation of loan policies centred on the risk–return criteria.

The growing complexity of banking, with deregulation and movement towards global integration, and imposition of prudential norms like capital adequacy and stricter provisioning requirements as market-safeguards, demands a carefully drawn up policy framework for the lending activities of banks and financial institutions. It is not that the need is newly felt. In the late 1950s, the need for a loan policy for commercial banks was felt at the level of bank regulators of the US and a major part of Europe, perhaps due to the publication of a seminal paper by

Gurley and Shaw[1] which redirected the attention of policymakers towards the overall interaction between the financial structure and the real activity, particularly the important role of banking intermediaries in the credit supply process as opposed to the money supply process, which was hitherto the dominant focus of banking regulation. It was also during the 1960s that competitive pressure was intensified in the banking sector all over the world, including in India, through the entry of foreign banks in the domestic field. The peculiarity of this decade was that competition co-existed with control. In order to withstand competition in the face of control, attempts were made to circumvent it by cartelisation and subsidiarisation on the one hand, and dilution of credit standards on the other. The latter was possible because in most of the banks, whether they were global giants or country banks, a well-documented loan policy did not exist. The next decade of banking beginning 1970 had to suffer from the follies of the past.

When banks were small and predominantly regional in nature, banking was a relatively simple operation with a well-charted boundary, and when official controls regulated a large part of the lending activity, banks could afford to do without a written lending policy. This situation prevailed in the major part of the banking world until the mid-1960s, and in India for two and a half decades beginning 1969, when banks entered into an era of directed lending with the nationalisation of major banks.

For a long time, a loan policy as a written document did not find favour with a large number of bankers on the ground that it created inflexibility in lending decisions. There was also an unspoken reason: absence of a written loan policy came in handy while dealing with the regulatory authority. The debate continued for a long time amidst an environment of large-scale expansion of banks marked occasionally by a few bank failures. The bankers gradually came to realise that too much discretion in lending decisions enlarges the 'grey area' by such an expanse that it might ultimately whiten up the entire structure.

Liberalisation creates a competitive environment in the financial market. Traditional boundaries between different players in the financial market break down, both locally and globally, making it difficult to define a neatly segmented banking or financial market. In such an environment formulating a lending policy becomes the order of the day. It enables a banking organisation to position itself correctly in the market and impose self-regulation. The policy provides a blueprint for lending decisions and monitoring in order for it to hold its position in the market, which now often enters turbulence, close to chaos. It is unlikely that the turbulence among financial variables is going to subside in the distant future. This makes the banking business more risky today, but at the same time it becomes more challenging than ever before.

Dangers in the Absence of a Loan Policy

As early as 1962, Howard D. Crosse, the then Vice President of the Federal Reserve Bank of New York, and an ardent votary of a documented loan policy, emphasised that the very act of formulating a policy and expressing it in words that all agree with will sharpen the issues and make the end product more effective.[2] But unfortunately over the years, this spirit behind formulating a loan policy document has been lost. It is painful to observe today that written

[1] Gurley, John and Edward Shaw, 'Financial Aspects of Economic Development', *American Economic Review*, September 1955, pp. 515–38.

[2] Crosse, Howard D., *Management Policies for Commercial Banks*, Prentice-Hall, Englewood, New Jersey, 1962.

loan policies, wherever they do exist, are often written only to satisfy regulatory requirements rather than to reflect the current thinking of the board and the management. Consequently, such policies are unworkable and ignored by loan officers.[3]

The casual approach to a loan policy has led to many banking disasters during recent times of the deregulation of banking. The turbulence in the Bank of America in the 1980s is one such example. Until 1979, the Bank of America, the world's largest bank, had no strategic planning and no loan policy worth the name, while at the same time, lending decisions were highly decentralised with the loan authority shifting increasingly from the headquarters to line organisations. At one stroke the loan authority of field managers was increased from US$ 5 million to US$ 20 million with a continued push for profit engineered by A.W. (Tom) Clausen,[4] the then President of the Bank of America. The credit–deposit ratio of the bank began growing at a very fast rate. Under Clausen, Bank of America 'shoveled' money so fast that it could not keep track of it. Under the pressure to build the loan portfolio, bank officers had started disbursing loans before all the financial analysis and documentation was complete. 'This resulted in a raft of loans that should never have been made. Writing loans was more important than collecting them'.[5] The virtual absence of a well-

documented loan policy and pressure of growth under a highly decentralised credit organisation produced billions of dollars of risky loans which ultimately shot at the backbone of the world's largest bank when charge-offs jumped to 61 per cent in 1983 and continued to rise thereafter, making it a loss-making sick bank by 1986 with its rating plummeting to a horrendous C/D.[6] Attention was then drawn to restructure the entire credit organisation with the installation of a formal credit policy committee which was to lay down a new and very tough credit appraisal system as an attempt towards a turnaround of the Bank of America.[7]

The crisis of the Bank of America is just an example of what might happen to a bank if it did not have a well laid down loan policy, particularly at a time when the financial market was being deregulated. The irony of fate is that only after a disaster do bankers sit together and pay attention to the importance of formulating a loan policy. In the present era of intense competition, unleashed by the very fast deregulation of financial markets and their global integration, the importance of a documented loan policy cannot be denied. It provides checks and balances not only for internal management but also for the regulatory authority.

As changes in the financial and banking structure are in response to changes in the real sectors of the economy, it is imperative that the formulation of a loan policy must precede an analysis of the changing sources of finance and pattern of financial management of the borrowing customers, who primarily belong to the real sectors. In order for a loan policy to remain dynamic it

[3] *The Bank Director's Hand Book*, Bank Administration Institute Foundation, Chicago, 1981.

[4] Tom Clausen left the Bank of America in 1980 to become president of the World Bank. He came back once again in October 1986 and announced an ambitious agenda for revival and growth. In 1987 the bank posted the highest losses, which threw the bank close to bankruptcy.

[5] Hector Gary, *Breaking the Bank: The Decline of Bank of America*, Little Brown & Company, New York, 1988.

[6] Vietor, R.H.K., 'Bank of America and Deregulation: The Great Turnaround', in S.L. Hayes, III (ed.), *Financial Services*, Harvard Business School Press, Boston, Massachusetts, 1993, pp. 1–34.

[7] Ibid.

has be responsive to the changing scenarios of the financial markets around the world. There should be a built-in review mechanism linked to the banking strategy of a bank. Otherwise, it becomes 'dead wood' that makes the entire organisation drift towards bureaucratic complacency.

CREDIT–DEPOSIT RATIO

The credit–deposit (C–D) ratio of banks is normally be given by, total credit/deposits. Assuming that credit is funded only from deposits, the amount available for credit dispensing out of say Rs 88 deposits would be Rs 60.72 considering the present level of CRR (6 per cent) and SLR (25 per cent).[8] The C–D ratio would, therefore, be 69 per cent. However, besides deposits a part of the capital fund also goes towards funding credit deployment. Assuming further that the net worth of a bank is Rs 6 and an equal amount is available from subordinated debts, and 10 per cent of net worth is invested in fixed assets and 5 per cent of deposits goes for non-SLR investments, the amount available for credit disbursement would be Rs 12 – 0.60 – 4.40 = Rs 7.[9] Assuming this fund goes entirely for credit disbursements, total credit goes up to Rs 60.72 + Rs 7 = Rs 67.72. The C–D ratio would now be 67.72/88 = 76.95 per cent.

The C–D ratio is one of the indicators of the state of the economy. During recession when the demand for credit is low the ratio falls; banks park the non-deployable fund to investments, particularly in SLR securities. When the economy is in the process of recovery, the ratio may go up to the maximum level shown above, provided there is no intervention by the central bank by way of raising the CRR and/or SLR. During 2009 when the Indian economy was smarting under global recession the C–D ratio of Indian banks fell to around 70 per cent from 75 per cent a year ago. As the economy is recovering and once again moving on the growth path, the C–D ratio is also increasing. As of July 2010, it had gone up to 73.50 per cent.

However, within the overall C–D ratio at the bank level the C–D ratio varies among region and states. For some states/regions the C–D ratio could be as high as 100 per cent or more (say Chandigarh and Tamil Nadu), while for others it could be as low as less than 30 per cent (Bihar, Jharkhand, Tripura, Sikkim, and Goa).[10] This is due primarily to the uneven economic development of Indian states. Bankers are aware of the political problems it creates. They are caught in a 'chicken or egg' problem. The tendency of finance capital is to move towards regions with higher economic development, due not only to higher productivity of capital, but also to higher demands for funds from these regions. It is also observed that in an area experiencing high economic growth, or in a period of rising economic activity, loan demand outstrips deposit growth. Due to the operation of these two phenomena, the C–D ratio of these regions or of that period also rises fast. This rising C–D ratio has to be supported by an inflow of deposit funds from other regions where loan demand is not so high, due to a lower level of economic growth. In addition to these, banks feel shy of investing in regions of lower economic growth because the incidence of bad debt is higher in these regions. Due to the interplay of all these forces, the underdeveloped regions are deprived of funds, which retards their economic development even further, and the bankers are blamed for this! One thing that

---

[8] As of August 2010.

[9] Presently, this structure is observable in moderately progressive banks in India.

[10] See Report of the Expert Group on Credit–Deposit Ratio of Banks, 2005. Available at www.rbidocs.org.in. The author was a member of the group.

must be clearly stated is that banks do banking business only by reacting to the demand made by the real sector of the economy. They cannot by themselves engage in setting up industrial units in a region short of economic development, and thereby minimise unevenness between regions. This has to be done by someone else, be it the state, by providing various incentives for setting up units in backward areas, or entrepreneurs themselves who may do it with or without such incentives. Banks can only support their activity by providing finance. If these important points are missed by the planners both at the state and the bank levels, then the principle of the competitive allocation of funds, which is so important for a liberalised market regime, will be defeated.

Notwithstanding this, the RBI desires that for regions/state/district where the C–D ratio is below 60 per cent inclusive of banks' investments in NABARD's Rural Infrastructure Development Fund, banks should take steps to increase the ratio to the prescribed level.[11]

Nevertheless, it is necessary for a bank to lay down specific C–D ratios for individual states, and within a state for specific regions, depending upon the present state of economic development and future prospects. In fact, this should form part of the loan policy document. However, this calls for developing investment grades for different states. One such attempt was made by the 'Business Standard'. They used variables like infrastructural availability in different states, namely economic, social, and administrative, the fiscal balance, the growth of the state's domestic product, and also the fiscal dependence of a particular state relative to the rest, and developed an overall index, which was named the Investment Rating and Credit Assessment

Index (IRCA).[12] Since then specialised agencies have engaged themselves in this rating job. Banks can also develop in-house rating procedures. In conclusion, it can be said that it is the banks that compete for suitable investment opportunities, and it is the states or regions that must compete for banks' funds by providing such investment opportunities.

Traditionally, the C–D ratio is found to have an inverse relationship with the investment–deposit ratio, because loans and investments are the two claimants of the deposit funds of a commercial bank. In the developed world, the investment–deposit ratio of commercial banks is already on the ascent, due firstly to the increasing pressure on the spread, which motivates banks to shift a part of their lendable deposit funds to market investments. Secondly, with the development of the wholesale liability market the reliance of banks on deposit funds for making loans is on the decline. In India, this situation does not prevail, because of limited opportunities available to commercial banks for investment in market instruments, and the lack of depth and spread in the wholesale liability market. However, the investment–deposit ratio for a number of commercial banks has gone up during the recent period. This is due to the increase in investments in government and approved securities beyond the prescribed minimum, because of banks' tendency to play safe against the backdrop of burgeoning NPAs, and their anxiety to maintain the capital adequacy norm by investing in the zero-risk category of assets. This tendency should pass out with banks gaining strength, because in the absence of opportunities to increase investment in market instruments, the return on risk-free assets, which is the minimum rate in the economy, cannot sustain banks for long.

[11] Refer RBI circular RPCD.LBS.BC.No.47/ 02.13.03/2005–06 dated 9 November 2005.

[12] Drabu, Haseeb, 'State Secrets', in *The Money Manager*, Business Standard, 6 May 1996.

While the credit–deposit ratio of a bank should follow the economic and financing principles mentioned earlier, any unusual growth in the ratio is a concern for the banking community as it might be happening at the cost of dilution of the quality of loans. When it happens to one bank it soon affects the other banks in a competitive economy. The crisis of Bank of America, as recounted earlier, soon affected the entire US banking industry.

THE THREAT OF DILUTION IN THE QUALITY OF LOANS

The two-pronged pressure on the traditional spread of banking organisations is forcing them to dilute the quality of borrowers, particularly at a time when by virtue of prudential norms imposed on them, including provisioning requirements and capital adequacy ratios, nationalised banks are already smarting under the heavy load of NPAs. The problem is more accentuated in a rising interest rate regime. In their seminal paper, Stiglitz and Weiss have shown that an increase in the rate of interest on riskless assets, for example, treasury bills, forces up the loan rate, and the average quality of borrowers falls.[13] This is so because with a rise in the interest rate, entrepreneurs with relatively safe projects would be the first to drop out from the loan market. Thus, after a point, further increases in the interest rate may lower lenders' expected returns and hence, exert pressure on the spread. In an environment of rising rates, borrowers with lower creditworthiness and projects with higher risk would flock around the banks due to their having very little access to the capital market, and the banks having investable funds but fewer first class borrowers left, would tend to be drawn towards this flock. Besides this,

driven by the profit motive banks have an incentive to make riskier loans in expectation of premium returns against the same marginal cost of funds. This perpetuates the 'lemons problem' in the market as propounded by Akerlof.[14] Jacoby and Saulnier's classical hypothesis that contrary to popular belief, banks do not get their business from premier business concerns but rather from a distinctly second-rate group who cannot secure funds from the investment market, still holds ground in all the major empirical researches cited here.[15] Due to these reasons, for the past many years a belief has been gaining ground that commercial banking, defined as an intermediation activity between savers (deposits) and investors (loans), is declining. Globally, the return on assets (ROA) for major international banks in Europe, America, and Asia is falling.

POLICY EMPHASIS ON NON-FUND BUSINESS

We have seen in Chapter 3 that a lending business by itself can just about meet the cost of capital. In order to ensure capital *growth*, the bank has to rely substantially on its non-funded business, which happens to have a relationship with the lending activity. The overall target set in the strategic plan is that the outstanding balance in non-funded business should not be less than 150 per cent of the total lending business, including priority sector advances. While we

[14] Akerlof, George, 'The Market for Lemons: Qualitative Uncertainty and the Market Mechanism', *Quarterly Journal of Economics*, 1970, 84: 488–500. The 'Lemons problem' is defined as follows: As the market price reflects buyers' perceptions of the average quality of the product being sold, sellers of low-quality goods—lemons—enjoy a premium at the expense of those selling high-quality products. As a result, high-quality sellers will stay out of the market.

[15] Jacoby, N.H. and R.J. Saulnier, *Business Finance and Banking*, National Bureau of Economic Research Study, Princeton University Press, Princeton, 1947.

[13] Stiglitz, Joseph and Andrew Weiss, 'Credit Rationing in Markets with Imperfect Information', *American Economic Review*, June 1981, pp. 393–410.

have apportioned the total credit between the commercial and the priority sectors as 70:30, it is not expected that the two sectors will be able to offer off-balance sheet business in the same proportions, simply because the nature of business and size of individual enterprises in the latter sector do not have equal need of non-fund based services. The major part of this business does, and must, come from the commercial sector. Non-funded business is, therefore, allocated between the two sectors as follows:

Commercial Sector: 185 per cent of credit granted

Priority Sector: 66 per cent of credit granted

This guideline means that as a matter of policy, a credit proposal will be treated as bankable only when it can generate enough off-balance sheet business equal to at least 185 per cent of credit outstanding at any point of time for the commercial sector, and 66 per cent for the priority sector. There is, however, no straitjacketing of the policy within a sector. Since it is ultimately a sectoral policy guideline, a credit manager has scope for manoeuvrability among different credit proposals within a given sector, as long as the overall target for the sector is achieved.

Interest Rate Policy

While laying down the banking strategy of ABC Bank in Chapter 3 we assumed a commercial lending rate of 20 per cent, and a priority sector leading rate of 16.5 per cent per annum.[16] These are averages for the sector, and not necessarily for individual loans within a sector. As a matter of policy, it is preferable for the bank to link the

rates to a 'floor rate' (FR) or the base rate (BR) as introduced by the RBI in 2010. In fact, the RBI has directed that even the rate on the interest-rate-directed priority sector lending should be linked to the BR of a bank. Since the floor or base rate depends, among other things, on the cost of funds, including management costs, it provides flexibility to the bank in rate determination, keeping the overall profit objective in view. The methodology of determining the floor or base rate is discussed later in this section.

It is true that in a market economy, the general level of rates is determined by the demand for, and supply of, funds in the market. While demand for funds rises with the rise in business activity, and falls during a slack period, supply of funds is largely determined by the credit policy of the central banking authority. When funds available in the market are plentiful, rates will not only get lowered, but in their bid to find investible opportunities banks will also bring a large number of marginal borrowers into their fold. This increases the overall risk of the loan portfolio, and hence lowers the profit from the expected level due to bad debts. *A banker should remember that most bad loans are contracted during a period not of rising demand for loans, but of a slackening of the demand.* When there is a shortage of funds and the demand is high, a bank is doubly cautious as to whom it is giving loans. The opposite is true when the supply of funds is high, but the demand is low.

There is a tendency amongst bankers to add a high-risk premium to the floor or base rate for a low credit-worthy borrower, and feel content that the risk is adequately matched by the premium charged. Two important points are missed here. First, the risk premium added is not the kind of insurance premium paid to an insurance company to cover the risk of default. When the default arises, the risk squarely falls on a bank itself, and the premium charged remains on

---

[16] As of August 2010, average interest rate on priority sector advances is about 13 per cent. On commercial loans, the rate varies between 13 per cent and 16.5 per cent depending up on the risk rating of a borrower.

paper only. Secondly, a borrower who is not so creditworthy has either a cash flow, or a capital adequacy problem. A high rate of interest will more often aggravate the problem rather than solving it. Banks are expected to take moderate risks. The risk premiums are chargeable along the moderate risk scale only. Beyond this, it becomes meaningless. There should, therefore, be a benchmark risk-level below which a loan proposal is just not acceptable for consideration.

Floor Rate

While the level of rates depends on the interplay of demand for and supply of funds in the market, the costs of lending constitute a 'floor' which must lie well below the market determined rate for the bank to survive in competition. These costs, as we have analysed before, include (1) cost of funds, (2) management costs, (3) cost of bad-debts, and (4) a minimum margin of profit to service the capital. We have also seen that the aggregate cost of making a loan varies amongst different forms of loans—cash credit, bills, and term loans. While it is true that the form of a loan is often dictated by the need of the customer, the loan policy document must provide a general guideline about the combination of various forms of loans, which besides conforming to the general pattern of customer need and regulatory directive, must also remain cost effective. One such model has been worked out while developing the strategic plan of ABC Bank, which must now form a part of the lending policies, and is therefore repeated in Table 4.1.

Credit managers must be made aware of the floor cost of different forms of loans, not only to motivate them to achieve the above allocative arrangement, but also to negotiate competitive rates with prospective borrowers. This leads us to the formulation of an optimum pricing policy for various combinations of loan forms. In what follows, we lay down the methodology for

TABLE **4.1**   Percentage Allocation of Credit

	Percentage Allocation	
Forms of Credit	Priority Sector	Commercial Sector
Cash credit etc.	50	40
Bills purchased and discounted	15	25
Term loans	35	35
Total	100	100

determining the pricing policy for a Rs 100 crore commercial loan.

From Chapter 3 we bring in the following cost figures for a Rs 100 crore commercial loan.

		(Rs in crore)
1. Total cost of deposit (including management cost)		16.60(5.93)
2. Cost of capital		3.64(3.64)
3. Management cost of:		
(a) Cash in hand	0.04	
(b) Balance with RBI (CRR)	0.40	
(c) Balances with other banks	0.05	0.49(0.49)
Total Cost		20.73(10.06)
Less: Net income from:		
(a) Priority sectors	1.14(1.14)	
(b) Government & approved securities	4.63(3.09)	5.77(4.23)
Net Cost		14.96(5.83)

Note: Figures in brackets denote cost and income calculations as per current rates as on 31.3.2009.

We will now determine the floor cost for various combinations of loan forms with the MCF of 0.0007785 and TVs of 10, 50, and 20 for term loans, cash credit, and bills purchased and discounted respectively (Table 4.2).

Out of the six combinations that we have presented in Table 4.2 (there could be many other combinations), the first one—'all term loans'—is the least costly, and 'all cash credit' is the

TABLE **4.2**   Calculation of Floor Cost

(Rs in crore)

Combinations			Cost Calculations	Floor Cost
1.	All term loans		14.96 + (100 × 10 × 0.0007785) (5.83)	= 15.74% (6.61%)
2.	All cash credit		14.96 + (100 × 50 × 0.0007785) (5.83)	= 18.85% (9.72%)
3.	All bills purchased and discounted		14.96 + (100 × 20 × 0.0007785) (5.83)	= 16.52% (7.39%)
4.	Term loans Bills Cash credit	35} 25} 40} 100	14.96 + [{(35 × 10) + (25×20) (5.83) + (40 × 50)}] × 0.0007785]	= 17.18% (8.05%)
5.	Term loans Bills Cash credit	25} 30} 45} 100	14.96 + [{(25 × 10) + (30×20) (5.83) + (45 × 50)}] × 0.0007785]	= 17.37% (8.24%)
6.	Term loans Bills Cash credit	45} 35} 20} 100	14.96 + [{(45 × 10) + (35×20) (5.83) + (20 × 50)}] × 0.0007785]	= 16.63% (7.50%)

Notes: 1. Figures in bracket are based on current rates as of 31.3.2009.

2. It may be seen that in the ultimate analysis, commercial loan subsidises the priority sector advances that are formed as a result of a commercial loan. This is so because though the lending rate has been freed, directed lending to priority sectors continues. Priority sector borrowers cannot carry the commercial rate.

costliest. Among 4, 5, and 6, though 6 is the least, this may not always be feasible considering the need and condition of a borrower. However, banks should persuade the borrower to accept this combination as desired by the RBI. The most feasible combination that we have chosen for our loan policy is the fourth combination, with a floor cost of 17.18 (8.05) per cent.

The pricing of each combination of loan forms can now be done by loading the rates with a profitability factor of 3 per cent, which goes towards capital formation.[17] Accordingly, prices of

different combinations of loan forms are finally determined in percentage forms (Table 4.3).

It should be remembered that income from off-balance sheet (non-fund) business up to the minimum stipulated is a profitability-condition precedent to granting the loan. This cannot go towards reducing the rate. However, if a borrower could give additional business beyond the stipulated minimum (here it is 150 per cent of the credit), then the rate can be reduced up to a maximum of the additional income accruing due to the incremental off-balance sheet business beyond the stipulated minimum.

While in Chapter 20 we will go into the details of risk analysis of a borrowing customer, as broad guidelines the following classifications

[17] The floor cost includes cost of servicing the capital by maintaining a pay–out ratio. Profit load is meant to ensure the sustainable growth of a bank.

TABLE 4.3   Determination of Floor Rate

Combination	Floor Cost	Profit Load	Floor Rate
1.	15.75 (6.61)	3.00	18.75 (9.61)
2.	18.85 (9.72)	3.00	21.85 (12.72)
3.	16.50 (7.39)	3.00	19.50 (10.39)
4.	17.20 (8.05)	3.00	20.20 (11.05)
5.	17.40 (8.24)	3.00	20.40 (11.24)
6.	16.60 (7.50)	3.00	19.60 (10.50)

Note: 1. Figures in bracket denote the current position.

2. We have added a profit load of 300 basis points to the floor cost to determine the floor rate. An individual bank may decide to increase or decrease the profit load in accordance with its profitability requirement, which includes inter alia the expected earning per share (EPS) and generation of incremental NPA.

of borrowers are made, and interest rates are indicated along the risk-continuum assuming a floor rate of 11 per cent (Table 4.4). The methodology of linking interest rates with the risk category of the borrowers is also discussed in Chapter 20.

The methodology for determining the floor cost and the floor rate in replacement of PLR was suggested by us as early as 1998.[18] Only recently, the RBI issued instructions to banks to replace PLR by a 'base rate'.[19] The methodology suggested by RBI is given in Annexure 4.1. While the RBI methodology has taken the costs and incomes on the aggregate (for example, the entire overhead cost is loaded on deployable deposits), we have gone into the details of income and cost of each segment of the business to enable a bank to take a strategic position in the various business segments of the bank. One should remember that the floor rate is not simply

[18] See the first edition of this book published in 1998.

[19] See RBI circular DBOD.No.Dir.BC.9/13.03.00/ 2010–11 dated 1 July 2010.

a method for interest rate determination; it is a strategic tool for optimising the profitability of a bank.

The price relatives calculated in Table 4.4 also enable a bank to practice rate differentials to which we are coming now.

Rate Differentials

Although by the theory of economics, competitive market forces ultimately tend to bring a parity amongst the rates charged by different banks, in actual practice there always remains scope for fine differentials. This is possible only when the costs of different forms of loans as discussed earlier are known by the credit manager. Rate differentials can be maintained to the advantage of a borrowing customer when part of the loan is collateralised by deposits, because the capital requirement for such a loan is proportionately reduced. Besides, it is almost a general practice now to offer a better rate to a borrowing customer when the scope for obtaining non-fund business from him is substantially larger than the required minimum. As discussed earlier, the rate can be proportionately reduced up to a maximum of the additional profit that can be earned from non-fund based business beyond the minimum prescribed.

Rate differential is also an effective tool for credit rationing. It can be deliberately maintained to encourage a borrower to seek credit elsewhere when he is no longer a desirable customer, or when a bank decides to minimise its exposure to a particular industry to which a borrower belongs. On the other hand, it can also be used to encourage some groups of customers to seek loans from banks rather than from finance companies. One such example is consumer loans. Banks can afford to offer lower rates than finance companies because the total cost of making term loans by a bank may be lower than that of finance companies.

TABLE 4.4   Risk Classification of Borrowers and Lending Rates

	Excellent (0)	Very Good (1)	Risk Category Good (2)	Fair (3)	Doubtful (4)	Poor (5)
Lending Rate	FR (say 11% p.a.)	12.30%	14.00%	16.00%	19.00% Reject	23.10% Reject

Note: It may be seen that the increase in interest rate is more than proportional to the increase in risk category. This is because the increase in risk is also more than proportional to the increase in risk category (see Chapter 20 for a detailed discussion).

LOAN PORTFOLIO AND EXPOSURE POLICY

Although portfolio management concepts have been in use for a long time in the bond and equity market, it is only recently that modern international banks are moving towards introducing portfolio management techniques in the lending business. The reason behind this delay is that unlike bonds and equities, loans are generally not traded, and relationship banking still has a sway over the decision making process in a bank. However, there are indications that more aggressive banks are reorienting relationship banking towards fee-based banking by treating a loan like any other product which is sold in the market place at a price.[20] The portfolio orientation of lending decisions is possible now, because of the securitisation of debts and its growing market in the developed world. The process of introducing debt-securitisation has already begun in India, though at a slower pace. The future of lending operations for Indian banks lies in 'securitisation'. Once a market for debt-securities evolves in India, it would be possible to shuffle loans amongst its portfolio to attain the best risk–return objective. Till that time, perhaps Indian credit managers will have to wait for a full-fledged application of portfolio management concepts. However, a beginning can be made now.

[20] Edwards, Ben, 'Let's Shuffle Those Loans', *Euromoney*, August 1995, pp. 22–6.

Although experienced credit managers always have some hands-on understanding of the present performance of various industries from their day-to-day handling of advances to different industrial units, it is difficult for them to estimate the future performance of an industry consequent upon changes in environmental variables, both domestic and global. Besides, signals of decline in a particular industry often are not understood clearly by a very busy credit manager, except at a time when nothing can be done to retrace the position. Banks, particularly in the nationalised sector, face the problem of walking out or otherwise of an industry during its cyclical downturn because of socioeconomic problems. However, banks should understand that this is the time when the industry needs most support. But historically, bankers are known for their conservatism and one of the planks of such conservatism is pure self-centeredness. A bank's reluctance to support borrowers during the cyclical downturn aggravates the crisis. One way of overcoming a part of the problem is to provide a general exposure norm for industries that shall remain more or less fixed during the upswing as well as downswing in cycles. If this policy is upheld conscientiously—both against the temptation of making larger commitments in a fast growing industry, and the tendency to walk out from downswing industries—then it becomes easier to convince the borrowers and the regulators about the objectivity of a bank's lending decisions. The policy can be made both rigid and flexible by first providing a general exposure norm across industries—say not more than 5 per cent of the total commercial credit of a bank can be invested in a particular industry—and then within this maximum limit, annual exposure is fixed depending upon the condition, need, and demand of an industry, and a bank's own liquidity and income needs.

An alternative policy, which is regarded by some bankers as more pragmatic than the one discussed earlier, is to lay down specific industry-wise exposure with periodical review, instead of a blanket percentage as in the former case. The principal argument behind this policy is that the industry-exposure policy of a bank should remain dynamic to capture an increasing share of business from a fast growing or sunrise industry. While there is nothing wrong in this policy both from the point of view of revenue considerations and making a bank's presence felt in such industries, a banker should guard himself well against overexposure.

A prudent banker should always remember that whenever a bank out steps its limit of exposure in an industry or sector which is fast growing and in consequence deprives other industries hitherto belonging to its existing loan portfolio, it commits a sin which has to be consummated later by huge losses when that industry suffers a downswing in the market. Over commitment of large banks in the western world and in Japan in the real estate and computer industries (the dot. com boom) during the latter part of the 1980 had rebounded terribly with the downturn of these two industries during the next decade. Many banks having suffered huge losses were thrown to the brink of bankruptcy.

The third alternative could be the policy of developing industry-wise specialisation by concentrating on a few industries only, so that a bank's name gets identified with a particular industry. Some banks in India already have some amount of industry-specialisation. In fact, before nationalisation quite a few banks were directly identified with a specific industry. One of the reasons behind this could be that a majority of these banks were also controlled by a specific industrial group(s). This policy is, however, fraught with certain risks. The first is that if a bank concentrates too much on a particular industry, then a bank's fortune becomes directly linked with the fortunes of that industry. The second risk is that once a bank gets identified with one industry, other industrial borrowers may shy away from that bank for fear of inexperienced handling of their financial problems. So even when such a bank desires to stretch out to other industries, may be due to a recession in its specialised industry, it may find that the others are not too willing to do business with it.

Considering all these, we may suggest that a bank should fix limits for aggregate commitments to specific sectors/industries having regard to the performance of different sectors/industries within a risk–return framework.

The second set of norms should concern itself with a bank's exposure to an individual borrowing unit within a given industry. Such norms should first prescribe an outer limit related to the paid-up capital and reserves of an enterprise, and within that a bank should fix a limit of maximum exposure (related to its own net worth) to a particular enterprise or group of enterprises belonging to a particular house, popularly known as 'group industries'.[21] The idea behind this is not to deprive an individual borrower of his genuine credit need, but to safeguard an individual bank against overexposure. Consortium lending or

---

[21] The guiding principle behind defining a 'group' is controlling shareholding, commonality of management, and effective control of the affairs of a company.

syndication of loans can satisfy both the objectives by sharing the total exposure of a borrowing unit by a number of banks within their own exposure limits. The RBI has desired that a bank's exposure to a single borrower should be restricted to 15 per cent of its net worth, while for a 'group' the percentage could go up to 40 per cent. According to the RBI's, guidelines on risk management, banks are required to introduce a 'substantial exposure limit' according to which the sum total of exposures in all the single borrowers enjoying credit facilities in excess of threshold limit, say 10 per cent or 15 per cent of a bank's capital fund, should not exceed 6 to 8 times respectively a bank's capital fund. This means that if a bank sets its threshold limit at 10 per cent of its net worth, the 'substantial exposure limit' for all such individual borrowers will be 6 times the net worth. RBI's prudential norms are fair from the point of view of credit risk management.

Hitherto, activities like hire purchase, equipment leasing, and factoring services were the domain of specialised institutions. Banks were content with financing such institutions against book debts. But in the process, banks have also gained a fair understanding of these businesses and have also realised the profitability of such operations. Hence, they have expressed their desire to enter into such segments directly. The RBI has not objected to banks' entry into these fields but has desired that they move slowly as many banks may not have developed necessary skills. Overexposure driven by a profit motive may affect banks' health. Hence, the RBI has specified certain limits of exposure to hire purchase, equipment leasing, and factoring services. Banks' exposure to each of these activities should not exceed 10 per cent of the total advances.[22]

The RBI also does not want banks to be overexposed in capital markets. In has specified that a bank's total exposure to capital markets, including fund and not-fund based credit lines to capital market borrowers, shall not exceed 40 per cent of its net worth. Within this outer limit a bank's own investment in shares, debentures, equity-oriented mutual funds and so on shall not exceed 20 per cent of its net worth. In a bid to stop financing speculative activities (like cornering of shares) in capital markets the RBI has directed that loans to individuals against security of shares, convertible bonds and debentures, and units of equity oriented mutual funds shall not exceed Rs 20 lakh from the *banking system* as a whole. It is desirable that within this overall ceiling a bank should formulate a loan policy that limits its exposure to each of these capital market segments including venture capital funds.[23]

Loan Portfolio of a Bank

In Chapter 3, we showed how to develop a loan portfolio for priority sector advances by inverting the risk parameters of various sub-sectors. In this section, we develop a total loan portfolio of a bank keeping in mind the points discussed earlier. Let us call this bank XYZ Bank. We have adopted the same methodology with some minor modifications. The portfolio is presented in Table 4.5.

It may be seen that in Table 4.5 we have included a new factor, current slippage to modify the RAF originally obtained. Although RAF is given by 1-NPA percentage, it does not capture the current risk behaviour of a particular industry/sector. The behaviour is captured by the downward movement of standard assets to NPAs in a particular industry/sector. We have denoted this downward movement as current

---

[22] For further details of RBI exposure norms see, RBI circular DBOD. No. DIR. BC. 14/13.03.00/2010/11 dated 1 July 2010. Available at www.rbi.org.in

[23] Ibid.

Table 4.5   XYZ Bank's Exposure to Industries/Sectors and Recommended Exposure Norms and Proposed Loan Portfolio

(Rs in crore)

Industry/Sector	Present Exposure	NPA(%)	RAF	Current Slippage (%)	Modified RAF	Mod. RAF for Selected Sectors	Portfolio Allocation (%)	Present Position (%)
FOOD & FOOD PRODUCTS								
Agriculture	304	51	0.49	11.2	0.44	0.44	2	3.93
Tea	249	22	0.78	2.4	0.76	0.76	3.46	5.08
Rice/Pulses/Flour Mills	39	51	0.49	9	0.45	Not selected		0.5
Other food processing	23	57	0.43	0.8	0.43	Not selected		0.26
Sub-total [A]	615	N/A	N/A	N/A	N/A	N/A	5.46	9.77
INDUSTRIES								
Tobacco and Beverage	8	50	0.5	0.8	0.5	0.5	2.27	0.1
Mining and Quarrying	106	8	0.92	0.1	0.92	0.92	4.18	2.54
Textile	154	75	0.25	31.7	0.17	Not selected		0.99
Paper	32	59	0.41	2.1	0.4	Not selected		0.34
Newspapers	62	39	0.61	7.8	0.56	0.56	2.55	0.99
Leather products	24	38	0.62	0.3	0.62	0.62	2.82	0.39
Rubber products	19	74	0.26	2	0.25	Not selected		0.13
Fertilisers	121	1	0.99	0	0.99	0.99	4.5	3.14
Pharmaceuticals	41	44	0.56	0.3	0.56	0.56	2.55	0.6
Plastics	17	65	0.35	49.8	0.18	Not selected		0.16
Other chemicals	71	41	0.59	18.6	0.48	Not selected		1.1
Petroleum	478	8	0.92	0	0.92	0.92	4.18	11.57
Cement	44	23	0.77	0.8	0.76	0.76	3.46	0.89
Iron and Steel	384	14	0.86	4.8	0.82	0.82	3.73	8.61
Other metals	93	47	0.53	7.2	0.49	Not selected		1.28
Engineering	274	37	0.63	7.9	0.58	0.58	2.64	3.14
Wood products	72	81	0.19	48.2	0.1	Not selected		0.37
Glass and ceramics	8	75	0.25	0.2	0.25	Not selected		0.05
Other industries	77	62	0.38	6.9	0.35	Not selected		0.76
Sub-total [B]	2085	N/A	N/A	N/A	N/A	N/A	32.88	37.15

SERVICES, TRADE, HOUSING

Power	80	15	0.85	1.9	0.83	0.83	3.77	1.78
Construction	62	73	0.27	0.3	0.27	Not selected		0.44
Wholesale trades	168	67	0.33	2.8	0.32	Not selected		1.47
Retail trades	395	50	0.5	10.5	0.45	0.45	2.05	5.13
Land/Water transport	84	67	0.33	13.3	0.29	0.29	1.32	0.73
Air transport	279	0	1	0	1	1	4.55	7.3
NBFC/HP/Leasing	71	9	0.91	5	0.86	0.86	3.91	1.28
Finance companies	168	0	1	0	1	1	4.55	4.4
Cold storage	45	9	0.91	0.9	0.9	0.9	4.09	2.32
Public utilities	2	50	0.5	0.4	0.5	0.5	2.27	0.03
Hotels	143	20	0.8	14.6	0.68	0.68	3.09	3.01
Artisans	25	72	0.28	17.6	0.23	0.23	1.05	0.18
Consumer durables	18	6	0.94	1.6	0.92	0.92	4.18	0.44
Housing	32	4	0.96	0.4	0.96	0.96	4.37	0.81
Housing Boards	293	0	1	0	1	1	4.55	7.67
Education	2	0	1	1	0.99	0.99	4.5	0.05
Personal loans	121	7	0.93	1.3	0.92	0.92	4.18	2.96
Professionals and self-employed	13	46	0.54	23.7	0.41	0.41	1.86	0.18
Other services	73	19	0.81	2.5	0.79	0.79	3.59	1.54
Miscellaneous	518	16	0.84	1.6	0.83	0.83	3.78	11.36
Sub-total [C]	2592	N/A	N/A	N/A	N/A	N/A	61.66	53.08
TOTAL [A+B+C] (excludes Food credit)	5292	N/A	N/A	N/A	26.13	21.99	100	100

Notes: 1. Risk Adjusted Assets (RAF) = (100–NPA percentage)/100

2. Current slippage = Migration of standard assets to NPA during the current year percentage migration of standard assets to NPA during the current year

3. Modified RAF = [RAF × (100–Current slippage in percentage)]/100. For example, for Agriculture sector the Modified RAF will be : [0.49 (100 – 11.20) /100 = 0.44

4. Portfolio allocation = (Individual Modified RAF/Total Modified RAF for selected sectors) × 100
For example, portfolio allocation for Hotels = (0.68/21.99) × 100 = 3.09.

slippage. If there is a slippage, the modified RAF will be higher than the original RAF. This makes the risk-based asset allocation dynamic. We have ignored any guarantee coverage to estimate the actual default risk of an industry/sector.

Any industry/sector that has modified RAF of less than 0.50 is not considered for further exposure except for priority sectors like agriculture, retail trade, land and water transport, artisans, professionals, and self-employed. However, in all such cases the strategy of a bank should be to take effective steps to reduce its exposure in a time-bound basis. Sectors like 'other chemicals' and 'other metals' are on the borderline, modified RAF being 0.48 and 0.49 respectively. While a bank could consider inclusion of 'other metals' it should not do so for 'other chemicals', because the current slippage at 18.6 per cent is very high. The current exposure of a bank in this sector is Rs 71 crore. It is necessary for a bank to inquire into the causes of such high slippage and if necessary to take steps in recalling the advances or securing them by collaterals.

However, when a particular industry/sector is in a recessionary phase or it is facing problems that are peculiar to it, it may be necessary to direct special attention to that industry/sector and take steps to help revive borrowing units in that industry/sector, including restructuring of loans and providing additional credit lines to carry unsold inventories.

In sectors like tea, petroleum, iron and steel, engineering, air transport, and housing boards, a bank's exposure is higher than the allocation. A bank should not only stop further advances in these sectors but also chalk out a plan to reduce the present exposure to the allocated levels. Funds should be redirected to sectors where the current exposure is much below the allocated level, for example, beverage and tobacco, leather, cement, cold storage, public utility, and consumer durables.

The objective of the lending strategy of a bank is to develop a portfolio of loans as diversified as to spread risk evenly to ensure a targeted return on assets (ROA).

LOAN–TO–VALUE RATIO

The third set of norms would aim at limiting a bank's exposure to the assets it finances. This is done by setting a maximum limit of a loan–to–value ratio. A minimum current ratio norm across borrowers has been set with the implementation of the Tandon and Chore Committees' recommendations, some of which though forming a part of the loan policy documents, are discussed in Chapter 12. While the minimum current ratio norm prescribed for the three methods of lending suggested by the Tandon Committee aims at ensuring partly a borrower's own stake in current assets financing, and partly at providing a cushion against a maturity mismatch between current inflows and outflows, the loan–to–value ratio aims at ensuring the safety of bank loans made to a borrowing unit.[24] Within a given current ratio, the loan–to–value ratio may vary, and so also the safety of a bank's funds. The following example, based on the second method of lending suggested by the Tandon Committee, will make the position clear.

	Case I	Case II	Case III	Case IV
Current assets Rs 100	100	100	100	
Less: Current liabilities 10	20	30	50	
Working capital gap 90	80	70	50	
Less: Margin being 25% of current assets 25	25	25	25	
Permissible bank credit 65	55	45	25	
Current ratio 1.33	1.33	1.33	1.33	
Loan–to–value ratio 72.22%	68.75%	64.28%	50%	

[24] Loan–to–value ratio is calculated as loan/(current assets—supply creditors).

It may be seen that though the current ratio remains the same in all the four cases, the loan-to-value ratio, which is calculated on chargeable (free) current assets, varies amongst the four cases. It is as high as 72.22 per cent in Case I, and as low as 50 per cent in Case IV. It is important, therefore, for a bank to prescribe the minimum loan–to–value ratio in the loan policy document to ensure reasonable safety of its funds. A safer limit will be 60–70 per cent.

In the case of term loans, lending decisions are based primarily on the debt–equity ratio. This always forms an important part of the loan policy of a banking organisation. The general average market norm for debt–equity has already come down to 1.5, and it is moving towards 1. However, it still remains, and will continue to remain, industry-specific, where it may vary anywhere between 3 and less than 1, depending on the need and specific conditions of a particular industry and the available and projected level of lendable resources of a bank. Since most large-term loans are made under a consortium or syndication, banks and financial institutions join in prescribing a particular debt–equity ratio norm for a particular industry. One such recent example is the telecom industry, where financial institutions have jointly decided to insist on a debt–equity norm of 1:1.

Similar to the current ratio, the debt–equity ratio also attempts to ensure a borrower's own stake in financing a project. Unlike the debt–equity ratio the loan–to–value ratio norm for term loans need not always be industry-specific, but general in nature across all term loans. In the industrialised world, the norm is 30–40 per cent. Though such a norm cannot be made applicable to developing countries like India, it should not exceed 15 per cent of the international norm. Although, once determined, the loan–to–value ratio should not be varied as a matter of policy, bankers cannot always ignore the specific need and financial conditions of a particular borrower who is not able to satisfy the prescribed loan-to-value ratio norm. In that case, the up gradation can be done by obtaining other collateral securities. But such up gradation should be limited to 25 per cent of the prescribed norm.

REPAYMENT POLICY

The loan policy document should provide for repayment norms for loans made by a bank. As a general rule, all loans must be repaid and a definite repayment programme should be established for every loan, no matter how well-secured it is. Robert G. Rodkey emphasised as early as 1944 that, 'even with loans secured by stock market collaterals having clearly adequate margins, it is desirable to have some orderly plan of repayment for the benefit both of a borrower and a bank'.[25] The principle behind this is the old adage that a good loan must also be a collectable loan.

From the point of view of a bank as well as a borrower, the repayment programme should be such as to enable a borrower to repay it out of the net revenue generated from the project for which the loan has been taken, and not from another loan. When this type of 'ever greening' is allowed, a borrower is pushed to a debt trap. Repayment programmes for term loans are project-specific, and hence it is difficult to lay down a general policy norm for a definite repayment period. But the loan policy document must contain the following rules to be observed with regard to the repayment of term loans:

1. While the repayment period is always project-specific, it must not unreasonably exceed industry practices.

[25] Rodkey, Robert G., *Sound Policies for Bank Management*, The Ronald Press Company, New York, 1944, p. 98.

2. A borrowing unit is not allowed to declare a dividend unless annual repayment obligations are fully met.
3. As a matter of policy, any loan beyond a certain term, say five years, should be supported by collaterals.

Repayment programmes for demand type of loans are more difficult to handle. Any practical banker will agree that demand loans are often the slowest and longest in repayment: some may also go further to suggest that a demand loan, like cash credit, is the most permanent type of loan. The demand promissory note taken from a borrower stays on records only, and can hardly be invoked as long as a borrower is a going concern. Both the Tandon and Chore Committees had gone into the problems of the cash credit system of financing but neither thought that the time was appropriate for replacing it by a repayable loan system. We have mentioned in Chapter 3 that RBI has desired a phased replacement of the cash credit system of financing working capital by the loan system. It is expected that in the near future the entire cash credit system would be completely replaced. While the attempt is laudable, there is always the chance that the entire loan system might ultimately be reverted to a cash credit system only, though by a new name. Repayment might soon become synonymous with renewals. For long, bankers had been allowing themselves a self-delusion in repayment policies. A study by the Federal Reserve Bank of Cleveland, USA, revealed that the practice of allowing credit that is normally short-term to become prolonged by repeated renewals is deeply entrenched in American banking practice. A borrower is hardly subjected to anything more compelling than the vague threat of a loan maturity that will *probably* be renewed if everything goes alright, and that will *certainly* be renewed if his affairs

deteriorate to the point that repayment is impossible.[26] Since Indian banks are breaking away from a century old practice of the cash credit system, the pull of reversion will be there. Bankers and regulators would do well to guard against such reversion.

The threat of reversion will remain as long as working capital loans are made repayable annually, and the timing matches the annual review or renewal of the loan. The prudent policy should, therefore, be to lay down a quarterly repayment programme. At the same time, there is nothing wrong in treating a working capital loan as any other term loan, the repayment of which might extend over a period much longer than one year, going even beyond that of a term loan, because in reality a working capital loan is often more permanent than the term loan, except when the business is seasonal in nature.

Concluding Remarks

In this chapter, we laid down the principles behind the formulation of the lending strategy and loan policy of a bank in a competitive environment. Lending strategies should emanate from the banking strategy. In this sense this is an extension of Chapter 3 where the banking strategy of a real-life bank was formulated. The assumptions made here are to a large extent realistic for this bank, but they may not be so for other banks, for whom separate sets of assumptions have to be made.

A loan policy document should be written and well-communicated at all levels of a bank's management. It should be simple, straightforward, and quantitative in nature. The success of a loan policy document lies, however, not in its drafting, but in its zealous implementation.

[26] Federal Reserve Bank of Cleveland, *Monthly Business Review*, US, September 1956.

Lending strategies are operationalised by developing a system of credit appraisal and lending decisions. This requires a clear understanding of the different operating and financial variables of a business. Chapters 5–11 are devoted to this purpose. In the remaining nine chapters, attempts are made to develop a system of credit appraisal and lending decisions.

Annexure 4.1

RBI's Illustrative Methodology for Computation of the Base Rate

Base rate = a + b + c + d

(a) Cost of deposits/Funds = D_{cost}
   (benchmark)

(b) Negative Carry on CRR and SLR = $\left[\left[\dfrac{\{D_{cost} - \{SLR \times T_r\}\}}{\{1 - (CRR + SLR)\}} \right] * 100 \right] - D_{cost}$

(c) Unallocatable Overhead Cost = $\left(\dfrac{U_c}{D_{ply}} \right) * 100$

(d) Average Return on Net Worth = $\left[\left(\dfrac{NP}{NW} \right) * \left(\dfrac{NW}{D_{ply}} \right) \right] * 100$

where:

D_{cost} = Cost of deposits/Funds

D : Total Deposits = Time deposits + Current deposits + Saving deposits

D_{ply} : Deployable deposits = Total deposits less share of deposits locked as CRR and SLR balances that is, = D * [1 − (CRR + SLR)]

CRR : Cash Reserve Ratio

SLR : Statutory Liquidity Ratio

T_r : 364 T-Bill rate

U_c : Unallocatable overhead costs

NP : Net profit

NW : Net worth = Capital + Free reserves

Negative carry on CRR and SLR

Negative carry on CRR and SLR balances arises, because the return on CRR balances is nil, while the return on SLR balances (proxied using the 364-day Treasury bill rate) is lower than the cost of deposits. Negative carry on CRR and SLR is arrived at in three steps. In the first step, return on SLR investment is calculated using 364-day Treasury bills. In the second step, effective cost is calculated by taking the ratio (expressed as a percentage) of cost of deposits (adjusted for return on SLR investment) and deployable deposits (total deposits less the deposits locked as CRR and SLR balances). In the third step, negative carry cost on SLR and CRR is arrived at by taking the difference between the effective cost and the cost of deposits.

Reference: RBI circular DBOD.No.Dir.BC.9/13.03.00/2010–11 dated 1 July 2010.

Consider the postage stamp: its usefulness consists in the ability to stick to one thing till it gets there.

—Josh Billings

5 Fixed Assets

INTRODUCTION

An economic unit trades in wealth—the *purpose* being to increase it. And in the process it contracts liabilities, acquires assets, and finally makes a profit or incurs a loss. When it makes a profit, its wealth is increased; when there is a loss the wealth is reduced. The global evolution of the accounting system has standardised the nomenclature of the results of this operation, the broad categories being assets and liabilities: expenses and incomes. A convention has also developed by which operating objects, namely expenses and incomes, are revealed in profit and loss accounts, and financial objects, namely assets and liabilities, are reported in balance sheets. These two statements together indicate the level of operational efficiency and condition of the financial health of a unit. A modern banker who lays down his depositors' money to such an economic unit should, therefore, know what goes into these statements.

In this chapter we deal with fixed assets. A manufacturing unit is said to be set up only when it has acquired all the fixed assets needed. When these fixed assets are put to use for generating wealth, the unit needs working capital/current assets (discussed in the next two chapters). Liabilities, which fund all these assets, and the profit and loss account, which shows the result of operations, will then be taken up, before we draw up a balance sheet in Chapter 11.

As we go on unfolding the nature of each item of fixed assets, we try to indicate what a lender should look for in each such item: how he should value it and where he is likely to be fooled or led to misinterpretation and hence, a wrong judgement on the viability of the proposal. This chapter is also the foundation work for the appraisal of a term loan proposal by a banker, which is taken up in Chapter 17.

DEFINITION

Fixed assets are those assets which are not normally disposed of within a short period, but are carried over to the following years for productive use while a fraction of them, that is, their annual usage, is charged to expenses every year as depreciation. A piece of a fixed asset, say machinery, has a total capacity of goods and services stored in it, a portion of which is realised every moment it is put to use. Generally, the total capacity is divided by the number of years of expected life of the machinery, which is called the annual capacity. This is further sub-divided into a month, a day, and an hour to determine monthly, daily, and hourly capacities. Naturally, when this capacity is realised in the form of goods and services, the machinery loses its value to that extent, which is charged to depreciation, and deducted from the value of the machinery, while the remaining portion is carried over to the next period.

LAND AND BUILDINGS

The type of ownership of land determines its status and treatment in business. Ownership may be freehold or leasehold. Freeholding is tantamount to absolute ownership. The owner is within his rights to dispose of the land in any manner he likes—by sale, mortgage, or otherwise. *Mortgage of land is the best tangible security for a banker*, because unlike machinery, the value of land normally goes on increasing because of increasing pressure on land. The capacity of land is limited only by its size, which makes the law of diminishing returns operate on it in the case of agricultural production. It is, therefore, not necessary to charge depreciation on land and reduce its value. On the contrary, there is a case for appreciation of its value. But there is nothing wrong for a business unit to charge depreciation on land, though by a nominal percentage, say 1–2 per cent, because it might be intended to create a fund by setting aside a portion of profit for purchase of additional land for future expansion.

The position is, however, very different in the case of leasehold land, where ownership is not absolute, but for a given period only. Leasehold interest in the property can be disposed of by way of mortgage or sale, if the terms of lease so permit, but the beneficiary's rights continue only up to the expiry date of the lease period, after which it goes back to the absolute owner. Hence, the property has to be written off on the expiry of the lease. The price paid for it divided by the number of years of lease is treated as depreciation, and deducted from the value of the leasehold land every year.

In case of large companies, land is generally held in the company's name, and a lender does not find much difficulty in getting it mortgaged. In case of a partnership or a proprietary concern, it is often found that the land is either standing in the name of a partner or the proprietor, or even in the name of close relatives. *A banker would do well to insist upon such land to be transferred to the firm before making an advance.* A well-meaning borrower would normally agree to this proposal. If he does not, then at the first instance the banker may doubt the seriousness of the borrower. A serious borrower who is out to make a living in business would not mind staking his personal property, particularly when the bank is staking its depositors' money in his business. The borrower may sometimes offer sentimental reasons for not transferring the property to the firm, but these should not hold ground before an objective banker. If the borrower refuses to transfer the land to the firm, then a banker also has a right to refuse considering the credit proposal further.

Land may not, however, be kept vacant by the business unit, unless trading in landed property is itself the business of the unit. It may be used either for the factory shed or office premises. While the land may appreciate in value and may not suffer any wear and tear, a factory or building does suffer wear and tear, which must be provided for as depreciation. The rate of depreciation may be low for an office building, but it will be more for a factory shed because of faster wear and tear.

FACTORY SHED LOCATION

While appraising a credit proposal, the appraiser should focus his attention on the factory because that is the place where capital spins and pays for itself. Location is not only important for any manufacturing unit, but also for a trading unit, which primarily does retail sales. Nearness to sources of raw materials or stocks-in-trade could be of advantage because this saves transport costs. When it is not possible to set up the factory near the source of raw materials, then it should at least be near the major markets for goods. Barring the first starter, it is always advantageous to set up a factory at a place where external economies like proximity of skilled labour, sources of power, developed roads, and ancillary industries are available. However, as industries generally move towards a place where external economies are available, underdeveloped regions remain backward. In order to remove these regional imbalances, the government often allows various financial and fiscal incentives to entrepreneurs for setting up industries in backward areas. A lender is well-advised to examine whether the borrower really intends to set up an industrial unit in a backward area, or he just wants to put up a fake company to merely get the loan and enjoy the incentives.

Location has a direct bearing on the follow-up of advances. A factory should be situated within a manageable distance from the branch. The command area concept, which came up in the 1970s has since been diluted to a great extent, and now, except in rural areas and for agricultural advances, it has lost much of its meaning. In large towns or cities where the transport system is fairly developed, a manageable distance for an advance may even go beyond 10 kilometres. Different banks have framed different policies in this respect, but one thing common in all these policies is that *the branch manager should be in a position to supervise the working of the factory intermittently.*

Physical Condition

Inside the factory, a banker should examine its physical condition, particularly the state of repairs. It is often found that even when the unit is running at a profit, this aspect is neglected, resulting in fast ageing of the factory. Repairs are undertaken only when it becomes unavoidable. At that point, however, because of long neglect, small repairs might have multiplied to such a staggering level that they now necessitate a large sum of money, which the unit may not be able to arrange. As a result, only immediate repairs are made on an ad hoc basis until a further crisis occurs. *Unfortunately, a banker hardly looks at this aspect when appraising the business of a borrower.* It is essential that the banker keeps this aspect in mind while sanctioning a credit proposal, and follows it up with the borrower for keeping the factory under constant repairs. This is particularly important for a wasting type of manufacturing process, like a chemical industry where wear and tear of the factory is very high. We should point out that consistently rising expenditure on repairs and maintenance is often an indication of a sound operating management. We elaborate on this in a subsequent chapter.

Manoeuvrability

Another aspect of a factory that needs to be considered is the manoeuvrability of its design and layout. This is very important from a banker's point of view. If with suitable but less costly modifications, a factory is able to accommodate another product line of the same range, then, at the time of falling demand of a particular product, the unit can easily switch over to another product whose demand is rising, and thus save itself from a catastrophe. A banker is well-advised to discuss this aspect in detail with a borrower, and *keep notes of the range of products that the factory is able to produce, with or without modifications, so that if the unit falls sick at any time, both a borrower and a banker can explore the possibility of changing the product line.*

PLANT AND MACHINERY

The established accounting convention treats plant and machinery in one group, which besides machinery includes layout installations and equipments. We have dealt with factory in the preceding paragraphs. In this section, we propose to take up machinery, equipment, and installations which are directly engaged in production. In deciding whether an item of assets will be included under the head 'plant and machinery', we have to consider the nature of the business. A ship will be a piece of fixed assets for a shipping company, but not so in the case of a ship manufacturer. In the latter case, it is a stock of finished goods bracketed under current assets.

DEPRECIATION

Plant and machinery depreciate faster than land and buildings. One school of accountants holds that by charging depreciation to the profit and loss account, a depreciation fund is created, which is used to replace the machinery when it is fully used up. Another school of accountants, however, regards depreciation as the cost of usage of the machinery, which should be charged to the profit and loss account. This latter school argues that as the fund set aside by way of depreciation is hardly invested outside the business, but is drawn into the total pool of funds of the business itself, the concept of a depreciation fund no longer holds good. This school holds that a piece of machinery is never replaced, but a new and more advanced machine is bought from the funds of the business. This is more so at a time of fast technological advances, when a piece of machinery may become obsolete within a few years of purchase, and a new, more advanced type has to be purchased at a time when the accumulation of depreciation is only negligible. In such a situation, the business has to arrange for funds from various sources, including internal

generation of funds, of which depreciation can only be a small part.

Whatever may be the arguments of these two schools, a banker should see that adequate depreciation is charged to these assets. The Indian Companies Act has mandatory provisions for charging depreciation, but no such compulsion is there for partnership or proprietary concerns. A credit appraiser should, therefore, see that in the latter cases, adequate depreciation is charged and the value of assets written down accordingly before distribution of profits. Otherwise, these firms will not only eat up a portion of the profits which they have not earned, but also show the assets at inflated value making all financial assessments wrong.[1]

APPRECIATION

Borrowers may often claim that the value of their plants and machinery is more than what is shown in the balance sheets. Their argument is more

---

[1] On the other hand, it is likely that proprietary or partnership firms may charge depreciation at the rates provided in the Income Tax Act and present the same profit and loss account and balance sheet to a bank as has been given to the tax authorities. Although the Indian Companies Act has delinked the provisions for depreciation charge from that of the Income Tax Act, proprietary or partnership firms remain outside its purview. As such, under the accelerated depreciation allowance presently provided in the Income Tax Act, many of the fixed assets of such firms will be wiped out from their books of accounts much earlier than their actual working life. Such a balance sheet drawn according to the Income Tax Act may not, therefore, give a true and fair view of the assets. A banker should, therefore, ask for an alternative balance sheet from such firms where depreciation is charged in regard to accounting and financial principles. It is always advisable to follow, even in the case of proprietary or partnership firms, the provisions of depreciation as scheduled in the Indian Companies Act for presenting a true and fair view of the business.

pronounced in the case of imported machines. *A banker is well-advised to take this argument with a pinch of salt, because as has been said earlier, fast technological advances make machines obsolete in quick succession.* Hence, the machines that the customer claims to be of high value may not have any market at all. Besides, if a banker has to sell the plant and machinery to recover his advance when the unit has failed, there is every likelihood of a general depression of the product of the unit in the market, hence that of the machines producing it. Again, when a unit is under strain, it is the repair of machines which is first shelved. As a result, when the unit is finally liquidated, plant and machinery are found to be in the worst possible condition for want of repairs. Their market value is often reduced to the level of scrap. So long as the business is in running condition and making a profit, the plant and machinery are valuable; the moment it fails, the value of this once-valuable asset may come to naught.

While appraising a credit proposal, a banker must consider the following features of the plant and machinery which have a direct bearing on the financial requirements of a borrower and the viability of the proposal.[2]

Age

An assessment of the residual productive life of the plant and machinery is necessary to know whether an advance is going to be self-liquidating during the lifetime of the machines, or some machines or equipment need to be replaced during the currency of the advance. In the latter case, one should examine whether the unit is in a position to generate enough funds for necessary replacements. If not, then how is this going to be financed: from additional equity capital, a long-term loan from financial institutions, or from banks. These questions should weigh in the mind

[2] For details see Chapter 17.

of a credit appraiser when sanctioning the initial credit lines. The project must contain provisions to meet this eventuality, or a banker would look foolish when he is left with a set of dead machines and a non-working 'working' capital advance. Threatened with a total loss of his advance, he may be tricked by a borrower to sanction additional funds for buying new machines, which in the ordinary course of business, should have come either from a borrower's own resources, or from other financial institutions.

A banker is not an expert in determining the residual productive life of a plant. The services of a chartered industrial valuer may be used for this purpose.

The Supplier

The reputation of suppliers of plant and machinery, fabricators or industrial consultants, who supervise the project is important not only to determine the quality of performance, but also to ensure the smooth working of the plant. Generally, a guarantee for satisfactory performance is available from the supplier or consultant. This needs proper scrutiny. If a banker is financing the plant and machinery as well as working capital requirements, he must insist on such a guarantee before sanctioning the proposal. It is needless to mention that the advance should be released in stages only, depending upon the progress of installation as certified by an independent, qualified engineer.

In a case where the plant and machinery are imported, a banker has to examine certain additional points. A service contract is an important aspect. Generally, the foreign supplier arranges it with an agent stationed in the importing country. This contract is to be examined to see whether it includes the supply of components and parts, and whether these can be imported under open general licence. If there are restrictions on their import, and the components are also not available locally, then it is not advisable to finance such a project.

Capacity

Generally, suppliers of machines quote the built-in capacity of a machine. This is the maximum capacity under the best working conditions, which are not obtainable in actual commercial run. A 10 to 15 per cent discount may be allowed to determine the normal working capacity. It is generally not possible even to reach *this* normal capacity within one or two years of the commencement of production. The capacity utilisation increases only gradually. *A credit appraiser has to settle the proposed utilisation of capacity on a year-to-year basis with a borrower.* Capacity utilisation goes on increasing as the workers become familiar and experienced in handling the machines. Both the borrower and the lender should allow the time needed for gaining experience. Sometimes, a borrower may be overenthusiastic in claiming that he would be able to reach the maximum capacity within a year, or as soon as the production starts, if only a bank provides necessary finance! A banker should advise him properly, and provide only that much finance which is necessary to reach a reasonably possible level of capacity utilisation.

Production Process

As far as possible, the hourly capacity of each machine should be determined by referring to the supplier. Necessary allowances, as mentioned earlier, should then be made. A banker then examines the production process to determine the number of stages involved. It may be seen that at each stage at least one machine is involved. For example, in a simple chemical industry, at least three stages are involved—reaction, drying, and grinding. Three machines are needed to perform these three functions. The capacities of all the three machines should be so synchronised that

no imbalance occurs. A lower capacity in an intermediate stage would jeopardise the entire production process. Any excess capacity will tie up capital unproductively.

A thorough understanding of the time taken to complete every stage of the production process is very important to decide on the working capital necessary for the project. In fact, any appraisal of credit proposals for working capital finance should begin with this. We take up this aspect in greater detail in the next chapter. At this stage, it will be sufficient to bear in mind that the level of capacity utilisation determines the level of working capital.

Companies publish figures for installed capacity, licensed capacity, and utilised capacity of their products in their annual reports. Installed capacity is the maximum capacity obtainable from the existing plant and machinery as discussed earlier. Licensed capacity is the capacity utilisation permitted by the government in some restricted industries. A comparative study of these figures for the past three to five years gives a better indication of the performance of the unit than a comparison of annual sales, because *any inflationary price rise of products may cover up a fall in capacity utilisation.*

CAPITAL WORK-IN-PROGRESS

This generally includes construction of buildings or plants in progress, for which part payment has been made. Any advance payment made to the contractor or supplier before the commencement of construction would, however, not come under this head, but be treated as an advance paid to the supplier and included in the current assets as per standard accounting practice (we show later that a credit appraiser should exclude this type of item while evaluating current assets for purpose of assessing the working capital requirement). It is obvious that whatever payment is made to the contractor or supplier for capital construction cannot be accounted for as capital work-in-progress. Only that portion of the job that has been certified as completed will come under this head. Normally, in this type of work the contractor's bill is not fully paid, but a certain agreed percentage is held back as retention money, which is released only after the job is completed and a trial run is done to the satisfaction of the purchaser. Information regarding the total value of the contract(s) and outstanding liabilities are available from the published balance sheet of companies under the head 'contingent liability'. *A banker is advised to enquire into this matter to know, in particular, (a) the phased programme of payment, (b) how the company proposes to pay, and (c) when the project is to be completed.* He should ensure that payment for capital expenditure is made from out of the long-term funds of the company, without affecting the working capital. On the assets side, any payment made for capital projects immediately affects the level of current assets, because payment is made either out of cash or bank balances, which are part of current assets.

Furniture and Fixtures

Furniture is like the ornaments of an institution. Taste, culture, and the general business approach of a borrower are reflected in the furnishing style of the office. A banker meets his customer first in his office, and obviously the furnishing style of the office creates an impression on him. *Although it is a fair indication of the general business condition of a borrower, a banker is warned against too gaudy and flashy a set-up, because behind this a borrower may be covering up his shabby business.* A disproportionate investment in furniture and fixtures, except in retail stores of luxury goods, is indicative of a lack of seriousness of a borrower in the business venture. He is more prone to showing off, than to doing real business. It is also indicative of over financing of the unit.

Excess finance, which cannot be used for productive purposes, finds its way to gaudy furnishings in offices.

Fixtures which are attached to the wall and are specially designed for a particular office room have little value in the market. Moveable furniture, if maintained in a proper condition, however, has good market value.

Furniture and fixtures normally have a longer life than the plant and machinery. The rate of depreciation should, therefore, be lower in ordinary circumstances.

Motor Vehicles

Unless the business of the unit is manufacturing of or trading in motor vehicles, this item is grouped under fixed assets. Besides the personal conveyance provided to executives, this item primarily comprises transport vehicles for carriage of goods. A banker providing working capital finance is often approached to finance transport vehicles. A banker will, of course, make a cost-benefit analysis to determine whether hiring transport services from established transport operators is more advantageous than owning a transport fleet. The same analysis should also be made if it is found that a substantial investment has already been made under this head. This analysis may often reveal that the total per kilometre cost of the transport owned by the company is substantially higher than the hiring charges in the market. This may be due to high overheads by way of wages for drivers, and high cost of capital. In these days of high costs of motor vehicles, it is often not advisable to have a large fleet of transport vehicles. Instead of blocking a considerable part of the capital in motor vehicles, it may be advisable to hire services from the market by paying only hire charges. *An in-depth study may also reveal that at a time of tight money conditions, disposing of a large fleet may solve many a financial worries of a firm by providing immediate liquid cash, without increasing the overall cost of carriage.*

Motor vehicles depreciate faster than any other fixed assets discussed earlier.

CONCLUDING REMARKS

Fixed assets are the only assets which contribute to the profitability of a business. All other assets have negative contributions. It is only by the turn of wheels that outputs are produced, part of which gets blocked along the distribution channels creating 'unwanted' assets in the system. These have to be carried at a cost. The importance of fixed assets lies here. They provide the lifeline of the business. A lender, whether he is financing fixed assets or not, must, therefore, make a thorough analysis of the fixed assets of an enterprise, because it is only on proper functioning of fixed assets the ultimate repayment capacity of a borrower lies.

I cannot spare the luxury of believing that all things beautiful are what they seem.

—Halleck

6   Working Capital
A Techno-Financial Approach

INTRODUCTION

One of the important activities of a commercial bank is financing the working capital requirements of firms. In fact, working capital advance forms the major part of the advances portfolio of a commercial bank. But the nature of working capital and its relationship with current assets and current liabilities is often not clearly understood. In this chapter, we develop a proper understanding of working capital and its various components.

SHOULD WE HATE CURRENT ASSETS?

We know that assets denote wealth, but an entrepreneur may not like to hold many of the assets appearing on the balance sheet. While he may like to hold fixed assets like plant and machinery, which generate goods and services (the sale of which gives him a profit), he would hate to hold 'current assets' like debtors, stock, or even cash. He would like to imagine himself in a situation where his production process takes very little time to convert inputs into finished products, which get sold immediately and in cash the moment they roll out of the process; and the input market is so perfect that any amount of raw material is available at any time at a fixed price. But the entrepreneur's dream is hardly realised. He finds, instead, that his production process takes quite some time; the finished products are not sold so quickly (a quantity of stocks remain in the godown); and the sales are not always in cash (some amount of credit has to be given, and the input market is so uncertain that he has to keep a certain amount of safety stock all the time). The 'non-ideal' technology and imperfect market thus generate all these assets, which we call current assets. The entrepreneur does not like them, because, in effect, these current assets block his funds which should otherwise have been available to him for meeting working expenses. In other words, we can say that each and every current asset of a firm is nothing but a blockage of working expense funds. A business is a continuous process; every cycle of operation generates these current assets which demand to be funded for immediate financing of working expenses. This funding of current assets for release of money needed for payment of working expenses is done by, what we popularly call, working capital.

CURRENTNESS CONCEPT AND OPERATING CYCLE THEORY

In defining the 'currentness' of current assets and current liabilities, there are controversies, which in turn create problems for determining working capital. For many years, the most popular definition of current assets has been 'cash, bank balances, and other resources that are reasonably expected to be realised or consumed within one year from the date of the balance sheet', and that of current liabilities has been 'those obligations of the enterprise that are reasonably expected to be liquidated within one year from the date of the balance sheet, either through the use of resources classed as current assets or through the creation of other current liabilities'. These two definitions came under attack immediately after the publication of the International Accounting Standard Committee (IASC) monograph on the subject. It was contended that in the case of both current liabilities and current assets, there may be firms where the maturity period of any of the items may be more than a year. The most glaring example, besides trade liabilities, is bank finance for working capital. Many such bank overdrafts have, in recent years, been regarded as medium-term finance, although in theory they are repayable on demand. This is more so in India in the cash credit system of financing the working capital requirements of a firm. Although bankers would raise serious objections to any firm's attempts to delete this item from current liabilities, in reality the cash credit liability of a firm had lost its currentness a long time back.

NATURAL BUSINESS YEAR

Park and Gladson[1] held that the one-year temporal standard to determine the currentness was arbitrary and not universally valid. What was current or non-current depended on the nature of the core business activity, marked by technological requirements and trading practices. They used the term natural business year within which an activity cycle is completed. The yardstick for judging the 'currentness' of an item, both of assets and liabilities, would be this natural business year. It could be three months for a fruit processing unit, or two to three years for a ship building firm. The natural business year concept was developed later into the operating cycle (OC) theory of working capital. The Accounting Principles Board of the American Institute of Certified Public Accountants, while defining working capital, used this operating cycle concept. Numerous attempts were made later to find a more satisfactory definition of working capital, usually linked to the length of the operational cycle of a business, but none of these has come to be generally accepted.

In India, perhaps the first attempt to capture the essence of the natural business year and translate it into an OC was made by Chakraborty.[2] He defined 'currentness' on the basis of the OC, and stated that any item liquidating itself or getting converted into cash within the OC period is a 'current' item, the rest are 'non-current'. It is necessary to go at length into the calculation of the OC proposed by Chakraborty to understand its meaning as well as limitation.

Chakraborty identified four current assets: raw materials in store, work-in-progress, finished goods in store, and receivables, and only one item of current liabilities, namely trade creditors, to calculate the OC of a business. He calculated the OC of a company in numbers of days from its published accounts in the following manner:

[1] Park, C. and J.W. Gladson, *Working Capital*, The Macmillan Co., New York, 1963.

[2] Chakraborty, S.K., 'Management of Working Capital and Working Capital Concept', *Economic and Political Weekly*, 25 August 1973.

Item	Formula Used	No. of Days
1. Raw materials in store	*Average stock of raw materials × 365/ consumption of raw materials*	105
2. Work-in-progress (conversion process)	*Average stock of work-in-progress × 365/ cost of finished goods produced*	14
3. Finished goods in store	*Average stock of finished goods × 365/ cost of goods sold*	23
4. Receivables sales during the year	*Average receivables × 365/sales during the year*	16
	Total	158

Chakraborty assumed that the company was able to secure 55 days credit from suppliers of raw materials (although it is not clear why he made this assumption, and also whether these 55 days represent consumption days or purchase days of raw materials). Deducting this from the days of raw materials in store, he finally calculated the OC of the company as 103 days.

NEGATIVE OPERATING CYCLE

The methodology adopted by Chakraborty in calculating the OC contradicts the conceptual framework presented by him. The 103 days OC is, in fact, the net OC of the company, which is more or less equivalent to the net working capital, as we will see later. This cannot be equated with the natural business year of the company, within which all the current items mature. Suppose, for example, the company could obtain credit from its suppliers equal to or more than 158 days (such a situation need not be imaginary, particularly in India where many firms manage to obtain such long credit by exploiting numerous small suppliers; it may also happen when a unit has become financially sick and is unable to pay the creditors), then according to the methodology adopted by Chakraborty, the company would have a zero or a negative OC. A situation like this, though very probable, betrays the concept of the OC presented by him because in such cases all the current items would either mature on zero or 'negative days'. In fact, *Ramamurthy found it odd enough to have a negative OC for the rubber plantation industry.*[3] He could not explain it, except by saying that this was due to suppliers' credit being for nearly a year. Chakraborty, perhaps, mixed up the OC of a business with the financing of it, and finally landed up with what we call net working capital. If we conform to the definition of OC as it emanates from the concept of a natural business year, then the OC of the company should be 158 days and not 103 days, or if the credit available from the market is for more than 158 days, say 160 days, then the OC should be 160 days, and neither 158 days nor (−) 2 days. If, therefore, we follow the logic of a natural business year as interpreted by Chakraborty, then the true OC of a business should be either the days of current assets or current liabilities (trade creditors under this concept), whichever is higher. Only in such an OC will all current items, as considered by Chakraborty, mature.

LIMITATIONS OF OPERATING CYCLE THEORY

While there could be some justification in following the OC theory for judging the currentness or otherwise of assets and liabilities, Chakraborty went a little further. He calculated the working capital (net) turnover of the company as 3.5 (365/103) and computed projected working capital (net) requirement of the company for a projected sale by dividing the projected operating expenses (treated with an inflationary price rise of 6 per cent) with the working capital turnover

[3] Ramamurthy, V.E., *Working Capital Management,* Institute for Financial Management and Research, Chennai, 1976.

(3.5). The implicit assumption here is that projected operating expenses and the working capital turnover as derived by him from his OC are divisible. That they are not can be proved by the following analysis.

MATHEMATICAL FALLACY

Let us first put the OC proposed by Chakraborty in algebraic form as some writers have:

$$OC = (R_t - C_t) + W_t + F_t + D_t$$

This form of presentation (which is correct in terms of the OC concept laid down by Chakraborty) may lead us to a mathematical fallacy, because we are led to assume that all the 't's representing days are similar, universal, and comparable. If we refer back to the calculation of OC days shown earlier, we will find that R_t of 105 refers to raw material consumption days; W_t or 14 refers to days of cost of production; F_t of 23 means days of cost of goods sold; and D_t of 16 represents days of sales. All these 'days' are not similar, because these are not derived from a common denominator. These are distinct 'days'. As the variables come successively, as in a chain, we can know the blockage of funds at each stage in terms of the number of days, and by adding them together we may at best try to find out only the total number of days the funds get blocked in the system (but that too is incorrect as we will see later). The exercise on OC theory with all its shortcomings should have stopped here. Extending it to the forecasting of the working capital requirement of a firm creates even more problems.

The 3.5 times turnover of OC capital may mean simply that the 'funds blocked in net current assets got released 3.5 times in a year'. While agreeing with Chakraborty that working capital is needed to meet all operating expenses of a firm, dividing the projected operating expenses

with the turnover of the OC will be wrong, because each component of the OC was derived with different numerators and denominators, and none of them was the *operating expense* of the firm. If the numerator was common all through, then it could be so divisible because only in such a case would the model have satisfied the reversibility condition. But as this condition was violated, we could not go back to the net working capital level prevalent in the company during the given year. Let us prove this point from the following analysis of the example given by Chakraborty.

REVERSIBILITY TEST

The total operating expenses of the company in the given year were Rs 39.35 crore; dividing this with a 3.5 turnover rate, the net working capital of the company, according to Chakraborty should have been Rs 11.2 crore. Let us now calculate the actual net working capital for the same period on the basis adopted by him.

	(Rs in crore)
Average stock of raw materials	5.46
Average work-in-progress	1.40
Average stock of finished goods	2.62
Average receivables	2.10
Average gross current assets	11.58
Less: Average sundry creditors (converting 55 days credit to consumption of raw materials as in the example)	2.86
Average net current assets or net working capital level	8.72

Note: All the above current assets and current liabilities are taken as averages of opening and closing balances, because the OC has been calculated on this basis only.

Now if the methodology proposed by Chakraborty was correct, we should get back to the above figure of net working capital, but instead, we got an entirely different figure. This is so because different denominators were used for calculating the days of holding in each case. If the same denominator, namely operating expenses, was used throughout, we should have obtained the same figure in both forward and backward calculations. The turnover of net working capital so derived from the OC cannot, therefore, be used to project the net working capital requirement of a firm. While elaborating on the OC concept, Chakraborty stated that the meaning of the OC is that each rupee put into the business [sic] on the first day of the year starts again in the cycle of operations immediately after the passage of OC days. As pointed out earlier, each component of the OC represents funds blocked in it in terms of a particular expense item. This may not have anything to do with the actual number of days for which the fund is blocked. A particular problem is created here by the work-in-progress, the holding of which has been derived in terms of days of cost of production. These 'days' may be totally different from the actual days taken by a particular process. A certain number of days of cost of production may be held in the process for a different number of actual days, and the fund will be released from the process only after the passage of these technical days. Hence, a rupee put in the process gets released not after the cost of production days, but after the process or technical days. Any calculation of the OC of the natural business year of a firm should, therefore, be based on the actual days of holding of the current assets, and not on their financial days.

An Alternative Theory of Working Capital

In earlier sections we have argued that the natural business year or the OC theory has only limited use in judging currentness or otherwise of some of the balance sheet items, provided we take into account the actual days of blockage of funds in a current asset, and not the financial days. Further, we cannot use this concept in its present form for the projection and management of the working capital of a firm.

Other Working Current Assets

During the operations of its business, a firm generates quite a few 'other' assets besides what have been taken into consideration in calculating the OC. Some of the examples are, advances made to suppliers and employees (not of a long-term nature), security deposits with suppliers or various statutory authorities, current account balances with customs, port trusts, excise department etc., advance received against sales, advance income tax, and minimum cash balances. The OC theory does not capture these items. Any of these assets and liabilities may fall outside the OC days, and hence should be taken out of the 'current' list according to that theory. If these items are not current items, then how do we define them? The RBI invented a term 'non-current asset', which, however, was not defined clearly, except by way of examples that include some of the items mentioned here, though not all. From an analysis of the examples given by the RBI, we are led to believe that non-current assets are halfway between fixed assets and current assets. Their convertibility into cash is restricted or doubtful due to the passage of time (as in the case of debtors more than six months old). Banks had been asked not to take these items into account while calculating the working capital requirements of a firm. Obviously the RBI wanted the firm to finance these non-current assets from its long-term resources. This was more in the nature of a policy decision of the RBI to gradually reduce the level of short-term lending to the commercial sector rather than making an attempt to properly define the nature of these assets.

The items mentioned earlier are almost compulsorily generated out of the operations of the business. Whatever name one can ascribe to them, there is no denying the fact that the current funds of a firm get blocked (or released) in these assets (or liabilities). Like all other 'current liabilities or assets' these groups of items also have a dynamic stability. And hence, a finance manager's or banker's worry is not solved by simply taking them out of the 'current list'. They, therefore, need a theory and tool by which they can estimate the true working capital requirements of a firm. In this section, we lay down the foundation for developing an alternative theory and tool of working capital management which can take care of these problems.

We start with the basic premise that once a firm has installed the plant and machinery, it needs capital to finance the working expenses required to generate sales. This capital, which is needed to pay for working expenses, is what we call working capital. Instead of making disputable distinctions between 'current' and 'noncurrent' assets (and hence liabilities), we simply concentrate on items which are generated out of operations where funds, otherwise available for meeting working expenses, get blocked (and on liabilities where they get released).

Systems Approach: Pipeline Inventories

First we adopt a systems approach in analysing the production and distribution processes of a manufacturing firm, and then examine their financial implications to evolve a theory of working capital. This theory is then applied to forecast the working capital requirements of a firm, and to indicate a methodology for its control and management.

A productive system can be defined as the means by which resource-inputs are transformed into products or services while a distributive system is defined as the means by which such products are distributed to consumers. The process by which inputs are transformed into output is popularly called the conversion process, which is determined by the technology adopted by a particular firm. This is central to the productive-distributive system of a firm (linked backwardly to the input market, and forwardly to the output market). The technology, economic conditions, customs, and practices determine the levels of holding of assets at various points of the total system. A finance manager has to take an integrated view of the whole system for a proper management of the working capital. In the present study we take up each sub-system individually, and then link them together to evolve an integrated system of working capital management.

The Conversion Process

Let us assume that the conversion process of a productive system has three sequential stages: S_1, S_2, and S_3, taking 6 hours, 4 hours, and 8 hours respectively. The technology being given, an operations manager will find that there will be idle time and consequent overheads between stages. He will, therefore, have to balance the line in such a way that there is minimum idle time. Although sophisticated computerised procedures are available to solve complex line-balancing problems, a straightforward way to solve a somewhat simple problem like this is to take the lowest common multiple of the designated hours of each stage, and increase the number of work places under each stage accordingly. In the present case the lowest common factor being two, S_1 will have three work places, and S_2 and S_3 will have two and four work places respectively. Assuming that there is sufficient demand in the market and the process is continuous, the balanced conversion line will generate 12 units a day—the determining factor being the highest hourly time amongst the three stages. Hence, the production cycle time is 2 hours. We present this balanced conversion process in Figure 6.1.

Except the first operation of the conversion process given in Figure 6.1, the line will run

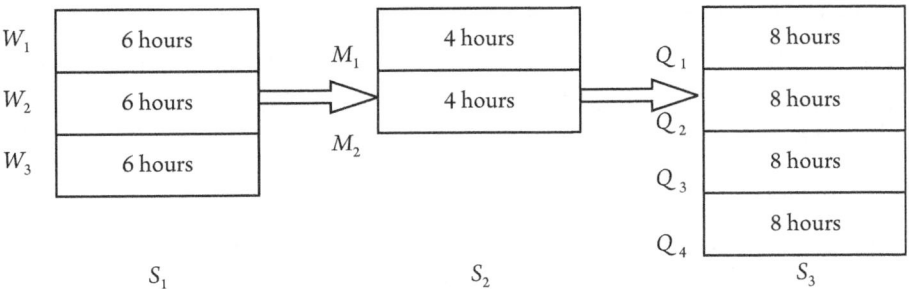

FIGURE **6.1** Conversion Process

Note: W, M, and *Q* are workplaces for stages S_1, S_2, and S_3, respectively.

continuously with no stage remaining idle at any time, and produce one unit every two hours. But an examination of the conversion process will reveal that in order to enable the process to produce one unit every two hours, all work places of each stage must always be full. That is, in all, nine units of inputs will always be in the pipeline.

The Distributive Process

Let us now design an elaborate distribution system of the outputs produced in this firm. As the process is continuous, the flow of finished goods from the conversion process is 12 units per day. The finished goods inventory passes through various stages of the distribution system before it reaches the final consumer. With this passage of goods, there is always some passage of time that holds up some amount of inventory all the time along the pipeline. Let us make the following reasonable assumptions to devise a distribution system:

1. Goods produced from the process are immediately transferred to the factory storage, and then the day's production is transferred to a warehouse on the following day (it takes one day to transfer the goods from the factory to a warehouse).
2. The warehouse takes five days to handle the goods and process orders from dis-

tributors, and it takes five days to transport goods from the warehouse to the distributors.

3. Distributors take two days for handling and processing orders. The transportation time from distributors to retailers is three days.
4. The retailer takes one day for handling and processing, and sells the goods to final consumers on 30 days credit (the transportation time is one day).

On the basis of these assumptions, the average holding along the distribution pipeline is given in Table 6.1.

We can now present a flow chart for the entire distribution system of the firm with the help of Table 6.1, adding to it the selling sub-system, assuming that a day's production of 12 units gets sold every day on 30 days credit (Figure 6.2).

The pipeline inventory of the distribution system as a whole is, therefore, 588 units of which the finished goods inventory is 228 units and debtors 360 units. Assuming now that one unit of input is producing one unit of output, the entire pipeline of the productive-distributive system will contain $588 + 9 = 597$ units. In order to enable the system to produce one unit of output every two hours, and sell 12 units a day under the given technology and distributive practices,

TABLE 6.1   Pipeline Inventory of Finished Goods (Average Flow of Goods: 12 units per day)

Sequence		Average Time in Days	Average Pipeline Inventory (12 × No. of days)
1.	Factory storage	1	12
2.	Factory to warehouse	1	12
3.	Handling and processing delay at warehouse	5	60
4.	Warehouse to distributor	5	60
5.	Handling and processing delay with distributor	2	24
6.	Distributor to retailer	3	36
7.	Handling and processing delay at the retailer	1	12
8.	Retailer to consumer	1	12
	Total:	19 days	228 units

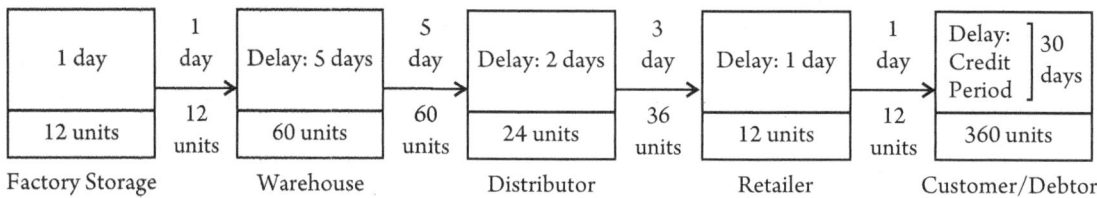

FIGURE 6.2   Distribution Process

the pipeline inventory of 597 units cannot be reduced. It may also be observed that the pipeline inventory is proportional to the system's flow rate and physical flow time. If the system's flow rate increases, the inventory in the pipeline will also increase proportionately, and vice versa. It also holds true for physical flow time.

The Pipeline Must be Full

Once every stage of the pipeline is full and the system is operating continuously, every day it will not only produce 12 units, but will also give a back value of 12 units to the production process, making the system self-sustaining. No additional inventory of raw materials or other inputs should normally be necessary. Before we proceed further on the subject, let us combine all the three segments of the pipeline in both physical and financial terms for easy understanding. For this purpose the following monetary values

are assigned to units at different transformation stages:

			(In Rs) Amount
Conversion Process			
Stage one (S_1)	:	Raw materials	10.00
		Other manufacturing expenses	2.00
		Total	12.00
Stage two (S_2)	:	Value received from S_1	12.00
		Other manufacturing expenses	4.00
		Total	16.00
Stage three (S_3)	:	Value received from S_2	16.00
		Other manufacturing expenses	8.00
		Total	24.00
Distribution Process	:	Value received from conversion process	24.00
		Average administrative and distribution costs per unit	1.00
		Total	25.00

We have not added profit to the cost of sales because our purpose is to find out the quantum of operating funds blocked in the system. We have also excluded depreciation and interest costs from our calculation because the former is not a cash expense, and the latter is a finance cost. The flow chart of the entire productive-distributive system is given in Figure 6.3.

DISCRETE OPERATING INVENTORIES

It may be clear from Figure 6.3 that the productive-distributive process becomes self-sustaining once the pipeline is full. But independent of this pipeline, inventories are also built up or funds blocked in some other forms in response to:

1. broader corporate objectives of optimising the cost and usage of funds, ensuring a reasonable liquidity, maintaining customers' goodwill and shareholders' confidence, and
2. the demand and regulation of public authorities, and the customs of the trade.

Let us explain this by way of some examples.

Cycle Inventory

Each of the operators in the productive-distributive process, like a factory, warehouse, and distributor does not order an inventory as and when necessary, but follows a cyclical replenishment method based on the review of demand and inventory status, transmission time, etc. However, once an ordering cycle is decided and the order is placed, the physical flow cycle follows as shown in Figure 6.3. Suppose that the distributor has decided to have an ordering cycle of two weeks, that is, when he places an order it must be for a two-week supply to meet the average demand. In the example given earlier, the distributor sells 84 units per week, or 168 units during a two-week ordering cycle.

That is, no less than 168 units must be in his hand to service sales during the replenishment period. The average inventory holding in this case will be half this amount, or 84 unit.[4] While other operators along the integrated process like warehouses and retailers will have similar cycle inventories for finished goods, the factory will hold the same for raw materials. A statement of the cycle inventory requirement in the present example based on an imaginary ordering cycle is given in Table 6.2.

Buffer Inventory

Besides cycle inventories, a firm is also required to hold additional inventories to absorb random fluctuations in consumer demand so that no consumer returns from the shop for want of the product. This inventory is called buffer inventory. Several models based on probabilistic distribution are available to estimate the buffer stock necessary to cushion the effects of greater-than-expected demand, and also the average demand during the supply lead time. Let us assume that based on one such model, the firm has decided to hold buffer stock as in Table 6.3.

A summary of the total inventory blocked up in the system as a whole is given in Table 6.4.

It will be clear from Table 6.4 that the productive-distributive system of the firm as a whole would demand 1161 units of inputs/outputs, and hence block a fund of Rs 25724 all the time under the assumed structure of the system, ordering rules and the service levels used. This is the minimum possible amount necessary to operate the system. Inventories might be larger than this minimum if controls are not effective,

---

[4] For further details, refer to any standard textbooks, for example, Levin, R.I., C.A. Kirkpatric, and D.S. Rubin, *Quantitative Approaches to Management*, (5th edition), McGraw-Hill International, Tokyo, 1982, Chapters 7 and 8.

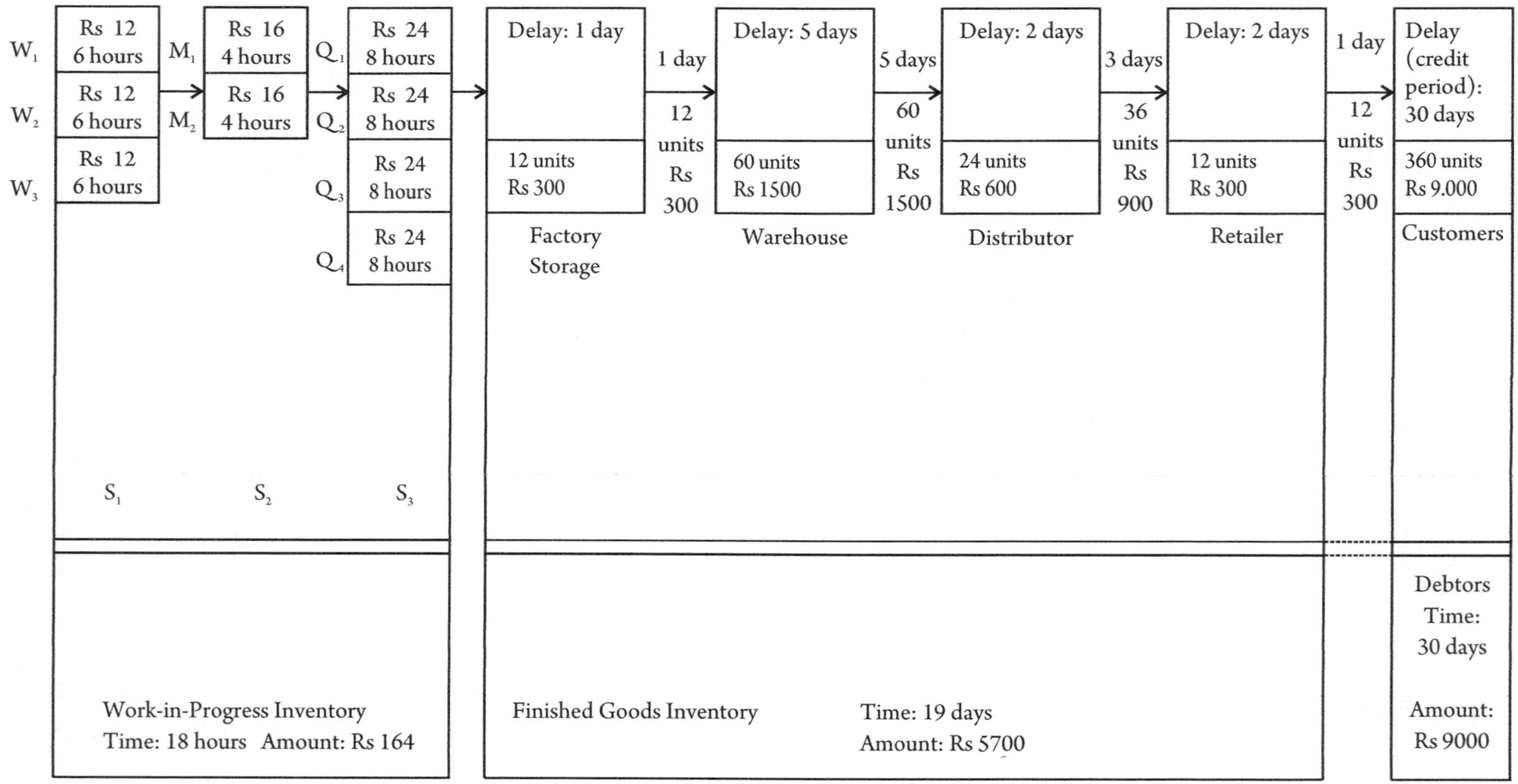

FIGURE 6.3 Production and Distribution Process and Pipeline Inventory

Delay: 1 day — Factory Storage — 12 units Rs 300

1 day — 12 units Rs 300

Delay: 5 days — Warehouse — 60 units Rs 1500

5 days — 60 units Rs 1500

Delay: 2 days — Distributor — 24 units Rs 600

3 days — 36 units Rs 900

Delay: 2 days — Retailer — 12 units Rs 300

1 day — 12 units Rs 300

Delay (credit period): 30 days — 360 units Rs 9.000 — Customers

W₁: Rs 12 6 hours | M₁ | Rs 16 4 hours | Q₁ | Rs 24 8 hours
W₂: Rs 12 6 hours | M₂ | Rs 16 4 hours | Q₂ | Rs 24 8 hours
W₃: Rs 12 6 hours | Q₃ | Rs 24 8 hours
Q₄ | Rs 24 8 hours

S₁   S₂   S₃

Work-in-Progress Inventory
Time: 18 hours   Amount: Rs 164

Finished Goods Inventory
Time: 19 days   Amount: Rs 5700

Debtors
Time: 30 days
Amount: Rs 9000

Notes:
Annual production/sales : 4320 units
Total Cost of Production : Rs 103680
Total Cost of Sales : Rs 108000
Year : 360 days

TABLE **6.2**   Cycle Inventory Requirements

Operators	Ordering Cycle (Weeks)	Type	Average Cycle Inventory (in units)	Monetary Value of Average Holding (in Rs)
Factory	3	Raw materials	126	1260
Warehouse	1	Finished goods	42	1050
Distributor	2	Finished goods	84	2100
Retailer	1	Finished goods	42	1050
		Total	294	5460

TABLE **6.3**   Buffer Inventory Requirements

Operators	Type	Average Cycle Inventory (in units)	Monetary Value of Average Holding (in Rs)
Factory	Raw materials	90	900
Warehouse	Finished goods	14	350
Distributor	Finished goods	80	2000
Retailer	Finished goods	86	2150
	Total	270	5400

or if seasonal inventories get accumulated in the system.

TABLE **6.4**   System's Total Inventory

Type	Units	Amount (Rs)	Remarks
Pipeline inventories	597	14864	Refer to Figure 6.3
Cycle inventories*	294	5460	Refer to Table 6.2
Buffer inventories	270	5400	Refer to Table 6.3
Total	1161	25,724	

Note: *Under the just-in-time manufacturing system, cycle inventories can be reduced to zero by staggering the order placements with properly developed vendors.

Where Does the Pipeline Stop?

A finance manager must have a clear idea of the physical and financial implications of the system dynamics discussed earlier because a small rise or fall in demand at the tail end of the pipeline may have a severe impact on the system as a whole making it totally unbalanced and creating strain on the firm's resources. But it may not be necessary for him to fund the entire system unless the firm owns the system as a whole. If the firm sells all its products to distributors, then the firm-system ends at the warehouse stage, but the inventory will include the goods-in-transit to distributors. In such a case a distributor will not be satisfied with 30 days of credit. He will calculate the system's flow in days/units commencing from his stage to the end of the pipeline. Instead of 30 days' credit he may demand a minimum of 37 days' credit from the firm. The same rule will apply in case the firm-system stops short of the retailer stage. In our subsequent analysis, however, we take the entire productive-distributive system as given in Figure 6.3.

OTHER DISCRETE CURRENT ASSETS

We have indicated earlier that besides the funds blocked in physical inventories, the productive-distributive system of a firm may generate other discrete assets, independent of the pipeline, where also funds get blocked. The first example is cash, per se. A firm may have to hold a certain level of liquid cash, like buffer inventory, as a cushion against a sudden lengthening of the pipeline, or a rise in its intensity caused by a demand push. Some other examples are security deposits with statutory authorities like excise and customs departments and/or, in some cases, with the suppliers of raw materials, advance payment of income tax, or even advances paid to suppliers and employees. These assets capture a sizeable amount of funds of the business for some firms. But the OC theory is unable to capture these important items excepting perhaps to some extent cash, by days of working expenses. We now propose an alternative theory of working capital by incorporating all the assets generated from operations into the integrated operational system of the firm. For this purpose a summary of the pipeline, cycle, buffer inventory, and other discrete assets (value assumed) is presented in Figure 6.4.

TECHNO-FINANCIAL APPROACH

Figure 6.4 gives an analytical presentation of the generation of various assets due to the operation of the business. While the amounts shown in the bottom row are aggregate of these assets that we see in a balance sheet under the head 'current assets', columns under each head show how these have been generated and their distinct nature. Under the OC method—which stops at the block of debtors—a rupee put into the system will recycle back in 96.57 days as calculated below:

Assets	Amount Rs	OC Days
Raw materials inventory	2160	18.00 days of consumption
Work-in-progress inventory	164	0.57 days of COP
Finished goods inventory	14400	48.00 days of COP
Debtors	9000	30.00 days of COP
Total	25724	96.57 days

But the flow chart of the entire production and distribution system given in Figure 6.3 reveals that a rupee put into the system recycles back in 49.75 days (0.75 + 19 + 30) only. This is the actual cycle time of the business, which is independent of the funds blocked in discrete assets elsewhere in the system. Another point that emerges from this comparative analysis is that though the OC or work-in-process is 0.57 days, in reality the production process takes 0.75 days to complete a product. It would have been all right to say that 0.57 days of cost of production is blocked for 0.75 days, but the OC theory, by implication, equalises the two. That is, it mixes financial days with technical days as we have indicated earlier.

We have shown in Figure 6.4 that many of the assets have different components independent of each other in origin and nature. While the OC theory can, to some extent, capture the pipeline component of the assets, it is unable to capture other discrete assets in terms of number of days, because these are not in the pipeline. In fact, any attempt to express working capital in terms of days will create not only definitional problems, but beat the cycle concept itself. In our subsequent analysis, therefore, we abandon the 'days', and try to develop some other dimension-free criterion.

CORE WORKING CAPITAL

We have said earlier that working capital is required to meet working (operating) expenses.

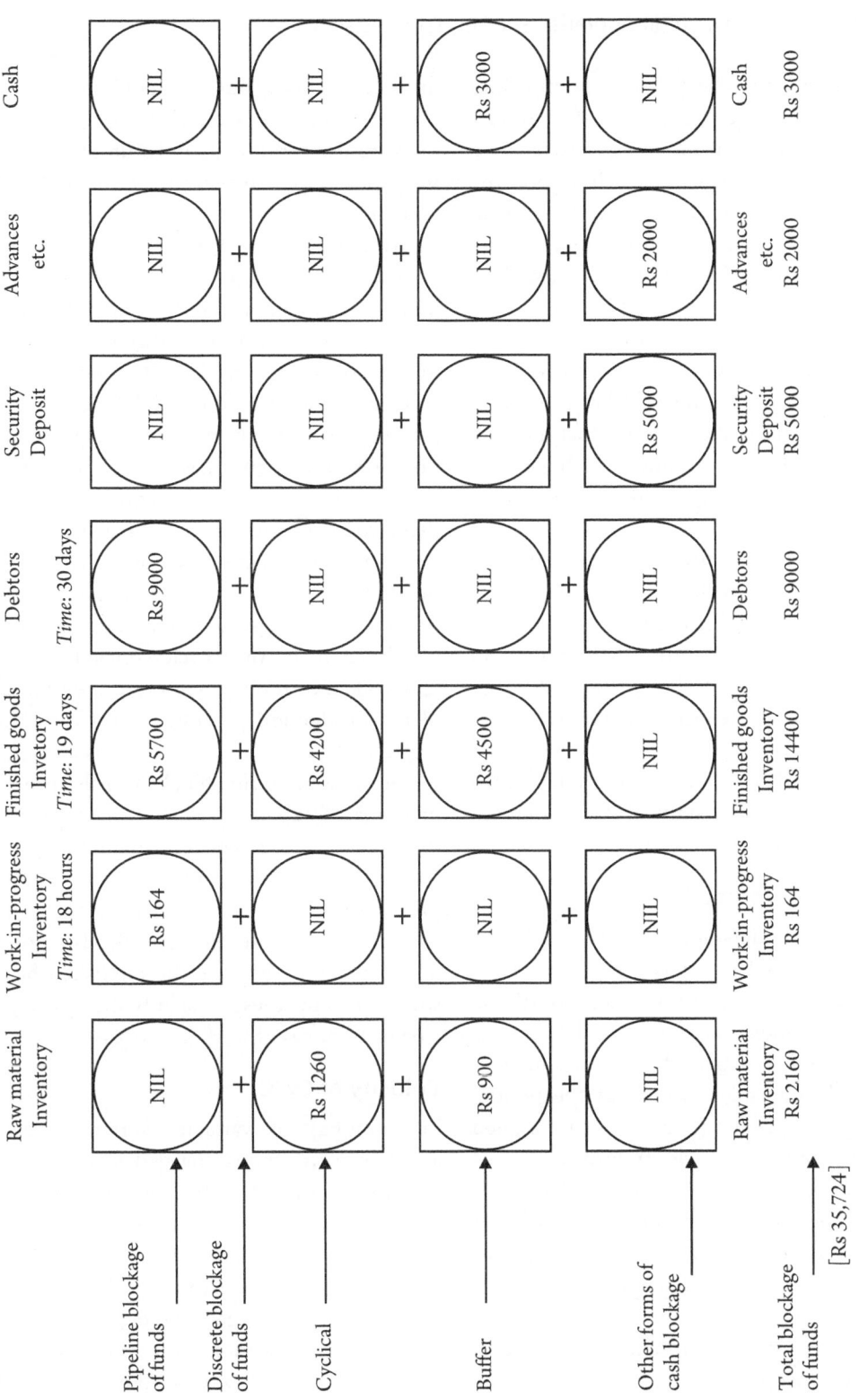

FIGURE 6.4 Pipeline and Discrete Blockage of Funds

Figures 6.1 and 6.3 reveal that if the pipelines were to stop at the conclusion of the production process, that is, if all the goods released by each production cycle (which is not the same as the conversion cycle) were to get sold immediately and in cash, the firm would require working capital only for meeting the first dose of all operating expenses that get blocked in the conversion process. We may call this the core working capital (CWC). All other assets can then be expressed in terms of CWC, implying thereby, as we have already said, that all such assets block an amount of funds which is otherwise available for meeting the operating expenses of a firm.

In our example, the firm has produced 4320 units in a year (360 days), the cost of production and cost of sales of which are Rs 1,03,680 and Rs 1,08,000 respectively, the distribution and administrative overheads being Rs 4,320. The conversion cycle of the firm takes off every time from the entry of inputs into stage S_1 of the process, and ends at the point of rolling out of finished products from stage S_3. Operating expenses are incurred on these cycles.

Allocation of Overheads

As is generally understood, operating expenses are broadly divided under two heads: variable and fixed expenses. The former is proportional to the volume under conversion in the process, while the latter is a period cost presumed to be incurred uniformly throughout the period. Extending this presumption, it can be argued that every conversion cycle uniformly absorbs overheads. That is, every finished product coming out of the process per conversion cycle not only absorbs variable input costs but also proportional fixed overheads. If a portion of the selling cost is found to be variable with the volume of sales, there is no harm in allocating this cost also to the conversion cycle and thereby to the

finished products coming out of it, because if the system is continuous, it can be presumed that the sales are also continuous and uniform, and hence selling costs are also being incurred continuously and uniformly.

We have seen in Figure 6.1 that the actual (physical) conversion cycle of the firm is 18 hours. An attempt can be made to allocate fixed overhead costs in terms of hours spent in the conversion process. It is possible for a finance manager to do this job product- and process-wise if the firm is producing only a few products, but when it has multiple products he may face difficulties in calculating and allocating these costs. An outside analyst will face bigger problems because he may not be aware of the different processes and the time spent on them. A solution to these problems can be found if we abandon the time cycle concept altogether and instead turn our attention to the fund cycle of the production process. A firm may have a single, or multiple products, but it is not difficult to calculate the funds blocked in the processes in terms of expenses, which are variable with the volume under conversion in the process. In fact, the coefficients of the inputs are almost pre-determined at the installation stage of the project. An outside analyst will also not face much difficulty, because the published balance sheets of companies reveal both the opening and closing balances of work-in-process.

Velocity of CWC

The amount of variable working expenses, and hence the funds engaged in a conversion process are thus nothing but the value of the work-in-process as we commonly understand it in accounting terminology. The velocity of the conversion fund-cycle can now be determined by dividing the aggregate cost of production with the value of the work-in-process at any point of time. In our present example, the cost of production is Rs 1,03,680, whereas the funds engaged in work-in-process are Rs 164. Dividing the former by the latter, we obtain 632.2 conversion fund-cycles in a year. In other words, the velocity of the conversion fund is 632.2 times a year. We now take the reciprocal of this figure and obtain the unit velocity (UV) of the conversion fund (this can also be calculated straightaway by dividing the work-in-process fund with the cost of production). The unit velocity (UV) of the conversion fund so calculated is 0.00158179 (it is always preferable to take the figure to at least five decimal places because of the sensitivity of UV).

We can now allocate the fixed overheads to the conversion fund cycle. The fixed overheads of the firm are Rs 4,320 (presently allocated at Re 1 per unit). Multiplying this with UV, we obtain Rs 6.83, which is allocated to each cycle of the conversion fund. The total funds blocked in the conversion cycle are, therefore, Rs 164 + 6.83 = Rs 170.83. This is the minimum quantum of funds the enterprise requires, which we have termed as the core working capital (CWC).

PROJECTION OF WORKING CAPITAL

While CWC is the aggregate of conversion expenses (plus selling expenses, if these are variable [see note]) and fixed overheads per conversion fund cycle, its UV will obviously be the same as that of the conversion fund cycle. Suppose in our example the volume is doubled from 4320 units to 8640 units, the cost of production, and the funds engaged in the conversion process, being composed of variable expenses, will also double to Rs 2,07,360 and Rs 328 respectively. Assuming now that fixed overheads remain fixed at Rs 4,320, the cost of sales for the increased volume will be Rs 2,11,680. Multiplying appropriate figures with the pre-determined UV, we get the following values:

Conversion fund cycle	:	Rs 328.00
(0.00158179 × 207360)		
Fixed overheads per cycle	:	Rs 6.83
(0.00158179 × 4320)		
Core Working Capital*	:	Rs 334.83

Note: *Suppose that the firm also spends variable selling expenses at Re 0.25 per unit, that is, Rs 2160 for 8640 units sold. It will be charged to the CWC by multiplying the aggregate sum with the UV. That is, 2160 × 0.00158179, or Rs 3.42. The value of CWC will then become Rs 328 + 3.42 + 6.83 = Rs 338.25, against the total cost of sales of Rs 2,11,680 + 2160 = Rs 2,13,840.

The CWC figure thus calculated will be the same as that derived by multiplying the new cost of sales with the same UV (0.00158179 × 211680). It can be seen that fixed overheads per cycle remain at Rs 6.83 irrespective of the increase in volume. This is in conformity with the principles of cost accounting, because when volume increases per fund cycle, the same amount of overheads get distributed over a larger quantity of outputs, thus reducing the per unit full cost.

CWC Multipliers

We have already said that assets, both pipeline and discrete, generated out of operations block funds for operating expenses. In other words, if these assets were not generated, the conversion cycle would have proceeded smoothly with the first dose of funds, equivalent to the operating expenses engaged in the process. It can be said, therefore, that each such asset blocks a certain number of the fund cycle, or in our terminology, CWC cycle. All such assets can, therefore, be expressed in terms of the number of cycles that they block. In Table 6.5 we have transformed all such assets generated from operations of our imaginary firm into CWC cycles.

It can now be said that the entire productive-distributive system of the firm requires 209.12 CWC cycles or multipliers divided between various operating assets to keep the system

TABLE 6.5   Blockage of CWC Cycles

Name of Asset	Amount	No. of CWC Cycles/Multipliers	Remarks
Work-in-process inventory	164	0.96	*Notes:*
Raw materials inventory	2160	12.64	1. Core working
Finished goods inventory	14400	84.29	capital =
Debtors	9000	52.68	Rs 170.83
Security deposits	5000	29.27	2. No. of CWC
Advances etc.	2000	11.72	cycles/multipliers
Cash	3000	17.56	Operating asset
			$= \dfrac{\text{Operating asset}}{\text{CWC}}$
Gross current assets:	35724	209.12	

continually operating. Gross operating assets (or gross current assets as they are popularly called) of the firm are thus represented by the aggregate of these CWC cycles. In other words, the firm now has to find a capital of Rs 35,724 to fund 209.12 CWC cycles, which is the gross working capital (GWC) requirement of the firm.

The way the CWC cycles are blocked in various operating assets, some of these also get released by operating liabilities like trade and expense creditors and advances and deposits from customers. That is, these liabilities supply some of the CWC cycles to the enterprise. This is the first step towards funding GCA. These liabilities are dependent primarily on the volume of production, ordering cycle, and risk-taking capacity of the firm (buffer stock) for a given period and hence they also enjoy the dynamic stability similar to operating assets. Assuming now that trade and expense creditors of the firm aggregate to Rs 10,000 and the total of other operating liabilities is Rs 5,000, then they must have supplied 58.54 and 29.27 CWC cycles respectively, or in aggregate 88 cycles approximately (calculated by dividing the amount of liabilities with CWC, that is, Rs 170.83). Deducting these cycles from the total CWC cycles of gross current assets, we obtain 121 net CWC cycles, which will be equal to the net working capital

of the business, assuming that the firm has not taken any short-term finance from banks.[5]

Projections

Let us assume now that the firm has projected a 20 per cent increase in sales in the ensuing year. Assuming that the fixed costs will remain at the same level, we can project the working capital level of the firm through the following steps:

Step 1: Projected core working capital

		Rupees
(a) Projected cost of production (20 per cent rise)	:	124416
(b) Projected cost of sales (Rs 124416 + 4320)	:	128736
(c) Projected conversion fund cycle (0.00158179 × 124416)	:	196.80
(d) Projected fixed overheads per CF cycle (0.00158179 × 4320)	:	6.83
(e) Projected core working capital (0.0158179 × 128736 or [c] + [d])	:	203.63

[5] Truly speaking, this is the working capital gap (WCG), as we shall see in Chapter 11. If this entire gap is funded by a firm from its long-term sources, then NWC equals WCG. If bank finance (BF) is availed of to fund a part of it, then NWC = WCG – BF.

Step 2: Projection of current assets/liabilities and working capital

Based on the projected CWC as above and the CWC multipliers derived in Table 6.5 we have calculated the projected working capital of the unit in Table 6.6.

TABLE 6.6 Projected Working Capital

Name of Operating Assets/Liabilities (1)	CWC Multiplier (2)	Level (Rs) (3)
Work-in-process inventory	0.96	195.48
Raw material inventory	12.64	2573.88
Finished goods inventory	84.29	17163.97
Debtors	52.68	10727.24
Security deposit	29.27	5960.25
Advances etc.	11.72	2386.55
Cash	17.56	3575.74
Sub-total (A)	209.12	42583.11
Less:		
Trade and expense creditors	58.54	11920.50
Other operating liabilities	29.27	5960.25
Sub-total (B)	87.81	17880.75
Net CWC cycles or Net working capital (A–B)	121.31	24702.36

CHARACTERISTICS OF CORE WORKING CAPITAL

The UV of CWC is dependent upon a given technology and operating conditions. Hence, it should remain stable for a reasonably long period. When there is a change in technology or operating conditions, or a substantial increase in fixed overheads, UV should be calculated afresh. This new UV will then be valid for another technology period.

Single Measurement Unit

The CWC multipliers are homogeneous quantities which describe the operating-financial structure of a firm in one unit of measurement. These multipliers for various operating assets of a firm are also found to be more or less fixed for a reasonably long period under standard operating conditions. But that does not mean that, in general, these multipliers shall have to remain fixed for any operating asset of any firm even within that period (except, perhaps work-in-process inventory). The firm might be operating below the standard. While it may not be possible to do much about the work-in-process, there is scope for a finance manager to reduce the number of multipliers along the firm's distribution pipeline by reducing delays at various stages, and also of discrete components of the operating assets, even under the same head, by realigning the ordering cycle through staggering, and making fresh risk-adjustments for buffer holdings of a particular asset. It should be pointed out that *reducing one multiplier means release of one cycle fund or a unit of CWC.*

Independent of Capacity Utilisation

The UV of CWC, which is nothing but the UV of the conversion fund, is independent of capacity utilisation. It can be calculated under any given level of capacity utilisation. Increased capacity utilisation increases operating expenses, which when multiplied by the calculated UV, will indicate the level of CWC for the increased volume of business.

Independent of Price Level Changes

The UV of CWC is also independent of changes in the price level. Suppose the price level is expected to increase by a certain percentage point in the projected year, the UV will capture this inflationary expectation via an increased level of operating expenses, and indicate an appropriate level of CWC for the projected year.

Assumption

The assumption behind the theory of working capital presented here is that production is continuous and uniform with regard to volume throughout the year. Hence, funds held in the conversion process will also be uniform at any point of time throughout the year. The year-end value of work-in-process as appearing in the balance sheet of a firm as on a particular date can, therefore, be regarded as being held at any point of time during the previous year with regard to that year's volume of production, and hence be taken as the basis for calculating the UV of conversion funds (or CWC). However, in a real business situation when this uniformity cannot be maintained because the volume of production per conversion cycle could be stepped up only gradually, or there has been some other bottleneck, then it would be preferable to take weekly or monthly averages of work-in-process funds. However, an outside analyst may not have access to this inside information. In that case, it is advisable for him to take the average of the opening and closing balances of work-in-process from the published balance sheets. Unless the previous year had been very unusual, the UV of CWC calculated by an outside financial analyst will not be much different from that calculated by the finance manager of the enterprise. The same rule applies to the calculation of CWC multipliers for other operating assets and liabilities. However, whatever method is adopted, it must be uniform for calculating both the UV of CWC and its multipliers for operating assets and liabilities.

Control Mechanisms

The techno-financial theory of working capital has the unique advantage of enabling an analyst to monitor and control the entire operating system of the business in terms of a single unit of measurement—the CWC multiplier. Even for calculating the projected working capital he need not have to use different criteria for different types of operating assets, as in the OC theory.

The CWC multiplier can also be used for control of working capital. Any reduction or increase of cost or delay (which includes the credit period allowed to debtors) along the productive-distributive pipeline or anywhere in the system presented in Figure 6.4 will be reflected in an item-wise and/or aggregate variance analysis done in terms of CWC multipliers.

The UV or CWC determines the inter-firm technical efficiency within an industry. A highly efficient firm with respect to both modern technology and operating conditions would have a smaller UV than a less efficient firm. It also enables an investor to determine the techno-financial viability of competing projects.

Concluding Remarks

In this chapter, an attempt is made to enable the banker to take a total view of the business, and from that perspective, understand the nature of current assets, how these are compulsorily generated from out of the operations of a business, and finally find their place in the balance sheet after being funded by working capital. He is now in a better position to understand the nature of working capital and establish a clear communication with the finance manager of a company that requires working capital finance.

In a subsequent chapter where we deal with indicative norms of current assets holding originally suggested by the Tandon Committee for the purpose of working capital finance by banks, we will find that the committee abandoned the OC theory, and followed a kind of transaction cycle method where each item of current assets was represented individually in terms of days of particular costs blocked in it. But it must be pointed out that unless changes in cost levels and corresponding changes in current asset levels (where these costs get accumulated) due to the fixed nature of some of the costs are clearly understood, the application of norms to arrive at the projected level of a current asset can be arbitrary.

Besides, it will be observed that norms were applicable only for certain items of gross current assets (GCA), namely work-in-process, inventories of raw materials, and finished goods and receivables, leaving other items of GCA outside the purview. It will also be found that no norm had been developed for any item of current liabilities, for example, trade creditors, which is an important source of working capital finance. The approach remained partial. This is perhaps one of the reasons why the RBI ultimately freed banks from the bondage of these norms. As against this, we adopted a total systems approach in determining the entire working capital structure of a firm, a proper understanding of which will enable a banker to assess the correct working capital requirement of a business, free from arbitrariness.

He wears his faith but as the fashion of his hat; it ever changes with the next block.

—Shakespeare

7   Current Assets and Fictitious Assets

INTRODUCTION

In the last chapter, we saw how current assets are generated along the productive-distributive line of a manufacturing organisation. One of the principal objectives of a finance manager is to maintain the dynamic stability of current assets in response to the level of capacity utilisation. The dynamism can be maintained only when the quality of current assets is such as to ensure their fast movement by continuous replacement, so that they remain current. With this objective in mind, we critically examine major items of current assets.

CASH AND BANK BALANCES

The most liquid forms of current assets are cash and bank balances. An accountant would be a happy person if the company maintains large cash or bank balances. But a finance manager might feel the opposite, and so also a banker. For them it is a sign of bad financial management and/or an indication of the slackening of business.

A banker, like a finance manager, would definitely like the cash balance to be invested in production as soon as it is generated, because idle cash does not earn anything. As long as working capital is financed through a cash credit account, any cash received by the business is first deposited in that account pending further investment

or disbursement. A cash credit account is the best instrument for a short-term investment of excess cash. No other instrument can give a better return (through savings of interest payment) with as much liquidity as a cash credit system. This has been one of the principal reasons why the industry and trade resisted conversion of the cash credit system to the loan system for long. The situation changed during the last decade, with the RBI directing that a major part of the working capital financed by banks should be in the form of loans and bills.

In India, because of the prevalent cash credit system raw cash holding by firms was negligible. Even under a partial cash credit system, the situation has not changed much. However, one may find that some companies, at times, do maintain large cash balances for some impending payments like dividend or capital expenditure. If this is so, it should be excluded from current assets to arrive at their normal level. But here again, truly speaking, this cash-in-waiting should also be deposited in a cash credit account (still available as a part of total finance) to save on the interest for the period for which it is not needed. Even the buffer requirement of cash can be held in the cash credit account, because the drawing power available in that account is nothing but ready cash, which can be withdrawn at any time by issuing a cheque.

Under a full loan system of working capital finance, cash credit as a tool of cash management is not available to borrowers. Firms have to devise their own cash management systems to make profitable use of their occasional excess cash (resulting from the loan system of financing) by investing it in liquid short-term securities. A number of well-managed companies have geared up their treasury departments towards this objective.

SUNDRY DEBTORS/RECEIVABLES

These are next in liquidity. Unless sales are entirely for cash, these items will appear in the books of accounts of all businesses. Ordinarily, debtors are treated as near equivalent to cash, but their real value depends upon the ability of customers to meet their commitments in due time. The length of the credit period given to customers depends primarily upon the market command of the sellers. In case of a monopoly seller, not only will the volume of credit sales be less as compared to total sales, but also the credit period. In case of competitive firms, the period as well as the volume will be higher. From another viewpoint, if the buyer is monopsonic, the credit demanded by him will be longer. The market share of the firm is an indication of the degree of monopoly, which, among other things, determines the length of credit.

A good indication is the debtors' turnover ratio determined by comparing or dividing total sales with the level of sundry debtors. The resultant number, which is called the rate of turnover of debtors, may again be divided by 12 to determine the average length of credit allowed. The formula for calculating this ratio is given in the last chapter. This is taken up later in much more detail in this chapter. For the time being, it will be sufficient to remember that the

faster the turnover of debtors, or the shorter the credit period, the better it is for the liquidity of the company.

Recession

Receivables are often the largest of all the current assets of a company. There is nothing wrong in this. But if in any year, they are more than the average rate of holding vis-à-vis sales, a banker should normally smell an impending liquidity crisis. He may be approached for ad hoc working capital finance to tide over the 'temporary crisis', which, alas, is often not temporary, because there might be a structural retrogression already setting in.

An increasing volume of debtors without a matching increase in sales is an indication of the slowing down of debtors' realisation, which if not tackled immediately, may drive the unit towards sickness by choking the inflow of cash. This may be due to external economic conditions like general or sectoral recession in the market, which cannot be tackled by any single unit individually—one has to wait until the economy is revived. During this intervening period, banks are expected to come forward to help the units hit by recession to carry the increasing volume of debtors so that production is not cut back drastically. This is important because during recession, a seller's market is converted into a buyer's market; the customers demand longer credit which, if not allowed, affects the demand immediately, resulting in a cut-back in production, precipitating further crisis.

Competition

Slowing down of debtors' collection may also be due to the coming up of competitors in the field offering better products at a cheaper price. Frantic efforts to save the existing market are then made, first by offering a price discount, and then by longer credit. If the competitors' threat is real, then financing an increasing level of debtors will not solve the problem. Bankers who do it join hands with a borrower in a losing game. Their attention should now shift towards the technological aspect of the unit. What the unit needs now is long-term finance for technological renovation. Any further increase in working capital finance without technological renovation would be sheer wastage of a bank's resources.

An age-wise analysis of debtors will definitely reveal the phenomena mentioned here. If debtors are increasingly moving to higher age brackets (say, six months and above), it is time to take steps to prevent the impending sickness of the unit.

Seasonality

In case of seasonal industries, particularly those depending upon agriculture, there will be seasonal variations in the level of debtors. Hence, both peak level and average level of debtors' holdings should be taken into account while considering a credit proposal.

Composition of Debtors

The composition of debtors is also an important aspect. A borrower may prefer to deal with a single (or a few large) customer/s than with an array of small customers, because that saves a lot of trouble and avoidable expenditure in the administration of sales. But dependence on one or a few large customers is fraught with risk, because if for any reason there is a delay in payment, the unit comes to a halt immediately for want of cash. Besides, if any of these few customers goes into liquidation, he also takes with him the unit which sold the bulk of its production to him. It is preferable, therefore, to have the risk spread out amongst a fairly large number of debtors, so that failure of one or even a few customers may not jolt the unit beyond tolerance. Except those units that face monopsony buyers, it is desirable

that *not more than 5 per cent of credit sales be made to a single buyer*. This may be treated as the outer limit. As the units grow big, they should try to reduce this limit progressively to about 2–3 per cent.

Delayed Payment

A banker should call for a percentage-wise breakup of debtors as mentioned earlier to assess the spread of credit risk, and counsel a borrower accordingly. Particular attention should be given to those debtors who individually comprise 5 per cent or more of credit sales. It is often found that these are the customers who make the most delay. Small units are often helpless in the face of dilatory tactics of these big units. They turn to their bankers for carrying on these debtors for an unduly long period. Bankers are put in a dilemma, because withholding of additional finance at this stage would make the unit sick, but allowing finance for long-overdue debtors is also against the established principles of lending. Besides being risky, such finance to small units, in fact, means double financing the large customers.

In order to avoid this type of a frustrating situation a banker should make up his mind at the very outset of appraising the credit proposal. The names of big, established companies in the order book of a borrower may often make a banker complacent. No doubt, these names add weight to the credit proposal, but unfortunately these are the names which weigh heavily in the mind of a borrower, particularly of average means, when payment for goods sold is delayed beyond a tolerable period. He cannot stop making further supplies to these large customers for fear of losing 'valuable orders'. Debtors, therefore, pile up, needing more and more working capital. Experience tells us that this type of situation is going to stay in spite of occasional exhortations made by the government and the RBI to large companies for quicker payments to small units.[1] Hence, in order to be of real help to these units, banks should come down to reality and shed the conventional norm of financing, say, three months' debtors. They should extend the financing to the period of credit demanded by the big buyers, while at the same time urging a borrower to broad base credit sales and thereby shorten the average period of credit. Since small units are generally not within the purview of the Tandon Committee's norms of current asset holdings, and since, in any case, these norms are no longer mandatory but only indicative (as we shall see in Chapter 12), there is no reason why a banker should not take a realistic view.

Doubtful Debts

Experience also tells us that some of the debtors do not pay at all: some are willful defaulters, while some are unable to pay. For small debtors, recovery of dues through legal processes is often uneconomical. These are straightway written-off as bad debts and charged to the profit and loss account. Where suits are filed, but the enterprise is doubtful of full realisation, a provision to that effect is made and the amount is kept reserved from the profit to meet the eventuality. Besides these, firms generally make provisions for doubtful debts as a percentage of credit sales based on their past experience. A banker, while appraising a credit proposal, should compare the figures for bad debts and see whether their percentage of sales is rising or falling. If it is rising considerably over the years, it indicates either over enthusiasm of the marketing department, or inefficiency of the collection department. In their bid to sell, the marketing people often lose sight of the necessary precautions to be taken in the matter of choosing customers. A bad choice may ultimately lead to bad debt. If the percentage of

bad debt is high and is increasing, a banker may decide not to finance debtors at all, or may ask for a higher margin. The margin requirement on debtors' financing should have a direct bearing on the percentage of bad debt.

Government Buyers

In our country, both the central and state governments are often the largest buyers through their various departments and undertakings. They are good buyers but bad pay masters. The chances of bad debt are few, but delays in payments are almost inevitable. In such cases, banks should be prepared to extend larger credit.

In case of contractors, debtors often include retention money kept by the customers for successful execution of the contract. This is quite a vulnerable item, because any dispute with customers may make this sum fully or partially unavailable. A banker is well-advised to exclude this item (except in case of exports) while evaluating debtors, or take only a portion of it, depending upon the experience of a borrower in this respect.[2]

Bills Receivables

Debtors take this form when the seller draws bills on the buyers which are payable on the expiry of the credit period allowed. When bills are thus drawn and accepted by the buyer as a drawee, then an additional protection against default is available to the seller under the Negotiable Instruments Act. But the main purpose behind drawing such bills is to get them discounted with a bank where a bills purchase limit is available. Bills receivables will receive the same treatment at the hands of a banker as if they are a part of debtors. Bill purchase is a better form of financing debtors. Banks get double enforcement rights:

---

[1] The drawee bill system as discussed in Chapter 12 is meant to reduce the hardship of small suppliers.

[2] In case of export, special provision is made to extend credit against retention money.

first against the drawer, that is, a borrower, and then against the drawee in case of non-payment of the bill. However, banks do not generally purchase bills unless these are drawn on first class parties. Ironically, these are the parties who often make most of the delay in payment. Borrowers are pestered by the banks for delay in receiving payments of the bills purchased by them, but still they would not purchase bills drawn on small parties where payments are not so delayed. If the time extended to large buyers is also allowed to small parties and the banks decide to come in by purchasing the bills drawn on the latter, then both the borrowers and the small parties will get the advantage of extended credit. We will see in Chapter 12 that some steps have been taken to ease this problem by introducing the Drawee Bills Scheme as originally recommended by the Chore Group.

INVENTORY

This is the most crucial item of consideration in any credit proposal, because the bulk of the working capital finance is given against stocks only.

We have seen in the last chapter that the holding of stocks is dependent upon capacity utilisation, the production process, and sales turnover. Capacity utilisation determines the quantity of goods to be produced. The production process decides the quantity of raw materials needed, and the time taken for producing these goods, implying thereby, the blockage of stock during the production process, which is called work-in-progress. If the sales are in cash, the stock is replenished immediately, but if the sales are on credit, then during the credit period further stock is necessary to continue production. All these taken together determine the base level of stock at any point of time. Added to this is the minimum safety level of the stock to meet eventualities like unpredictable delay in debtors'

realisation, sudden shortage of raw materials, unforeseen wastage, and breakdown in the production process. Some analysts hold the view that this core stock is never available for production. It is that minimum level of chemical solution in an electroplating vat, which if consumed, will dry up the vat.[3] Whatever it is, no purchase manager or works manager would allow the last piece of raw material to be drawn out before ordering for further supplies. The concept of economic order quantity (EOQ) was developed to take care of, among other things, this eventuality.

The EOQ is a mathematical model, somewhat complicated because it has to take care of various eventualities and objectives which are often conflicting with each other. Without going into the detailed analysis of this model, we may generally discuss the factors to be taken into consideration by the banker to determine the economic level of the stock holding.[4]

Seasonal Variations

Seasonal variations may occur both in the demand and supply sides. A toy manufacturer will find demand for his product suddenly picking up before Christmas, which may compel him to order a very high level of raw materials at least three months before Christmas. For him, the average monthly holding of stocks during the first nine months of the year will have no bearing on the holding for the remaining three months.

On the other side, a manufacturer of jute goods may have to buy almost the entire annual requirement of raw jute immediately on its harvest when the price is low and there is no shortage. His stock holding will go down progressively as the stock of raw jute is used up in production.

---

[3] For details, see the Tandon Committee's recommendations in Chapter 12.

[4] See footnote 4 in Chapter 6.

It will almost reach the core level before the next season starts.

In the first case, a banker should assess the peak level requirement of stock. The stock level shoots up by the demand pull of the product of a borrower, which comes down to the average level almost immediately after the season is over. In the second case, the peak level of stock necessitated by a supply push will diminish gradually throughout the year.

Competitive Edge

Most retail goods and also major industrial intermediary goods are carried to stock to ensure prompt delivery. This is more important for retail stores. They have to keep a reasonable quantity of all brands of a particular item in order to cater to the demand of varied customers. This is necessary to maintain a competitive edge over others in the field by catering to the demand of 'every' customer. If a firm gains a bad reputation for being constantly out of stock, it may lose in competition and soon be out of the market.

Advantage of Producing and Buying in Large Quantities

It is almost market tautology that bulk buying is cheaper. Bulk production is also cheaper, particularly when machine set-up time between two batch cycles is significant. Overheads incurred in idle time are compensated for when large quantities are produced in each cycle.

There is, however, a danger involved in bulk buying. In their enthusiasm to obtain larger discounts, purchase managers often buy in large quantities quite disproportionate to actual requirements, resulting in blockage of working capital. A banker should always guard against such disproportionate building up of stock for his own interest, because he will soon be asked to provide additional working capital.

Continuity of Production

If the lead time between ordering and receiving goods is high and uncertain, firms buy in bulk so that production is not interrupted. This happens in case of controlled items, or those in short supply, or which are to be imported from a distant country. Firms may have to buy at least three to six months' requirements at a time.

VALUATION OF INVENTORIES

An enterprise may buy stocks continuously throughout the year at different prices. In case of small firms, buying only a few items of stocks, it is possible to keep track of the issue prices of materials released for production irrespective of their dates and prices of purchase. But for large units, buying huge quantities of stocks comprising a number of items at varied prices, some methods have to be devised to determine the prices at which these are to be issued to production, and subsequently valued at the end of the year. Two such methods which are adopted by most of the firms are now discussed.

First in First out (FIFO)

Under this method, it is presumed that materials are issued to production in order of their receipts in stocks. This method is easy to operate, and at times of stable prices the cost of production is correctly valued, and so also the stock. However, when prices are falling, the FIFO method overvalues production, while the cost of replacement is low. Conversely, when prices are increasing, production is undervalued, but the cost of replacement is high. A security-oriented banker will prefer the FIFO method of valuation of stocks when prices are increasing, because inventories at hand will command more value in the market, but he will not like it when prices are falling, because stocks at hand will fetch less value in the market.

Last in, First out (LIFO)

The presumption here is that materials are issued to production in the reverse order of FIFO, that is, the latest receipt being the first issue. A great advantage of this method is that the charge to production is closely related to current price levels. Since the assumption is that the latest purchases of materials are issued for production, what remain in stocks are valued at the old prices.

There are also other methods of valuing stocks like simple average, weighted average, and base stock and their variations. However, whichever method is used for valuation of inventories, a banker must see that the valuation of stock is closest to reality; if not, he must obtain full explanations for the deviations made. We should mention here that auditors do not 'take stock' or verify its value. They take it as certified by the directors, partners, or proprietor. This is rather ticklish, because a banker has to rely solely on the integrity of the director, partners, or proprietor. There is no independent check unless a banker takes it upon himself to cause an inspection. It is no wonder that banks lay so much importance on periodical inspection of inventories.

Changing Method of Valuation

In the profit and loss account, opening stock is shown on the expenses side (Dr.) and closing stock on the income side (Cr.). A firm can, by changing the method of valuation, overvalue its stock at the end of the year to show a larger amount of profit. A sizeable portion of the profit may, therefore, remain unrealisable. Hence, any payment of dividend out of this 'paper' profit will not only make an inroad into the net worth of the company, but also create an immediate working capital crisis. Banks are often approached to provide additional credit for payment of dividend. If the reasons for such requests are due to the overvaluation of closing stock, banks should not encourage such requests. Besides, profit attracts incidence of tax, which has to be paid from the real resources of the company, resulting in further erosion of working capital. Bankers should *always guard against any change in the method of valuation of inventories that result in overvaluation.*

All the valuation concepts and rules discussed here are applicable to finished goods and other inventories as well. Different kinds of inventories and their special features are discussed in the next section.

Similar to debtors, turnover of inventories is calculated by comparing it with the cost of consumption of materials, cost of production, or cost of goods sold for inventories of materials, and work-in-progress and finished goods respectively. Any slowing down of turnover as compared with the past year's average will indicate a fall in sales, or overproduction, or both. This is a dangerous situation, because if it persists then the unit will soon fall sick, with a huge quantity of unsold stock. A cutback in production or a change in technology may be the only solution.

A fast running down of stock below the average level is equally dangerous, because it indicates that the unit is not in a position to replenish stock as soon as it is consumed or sold. Production may soon be stopped. The most plausible reason is shortage of cash due to fall in debtors' realisation. The dangers involved in such a situation have been discussed earlier while discussing sundry debtors.

Various Types of Stocks/Inventories

A trader deals in finished stocks only, but stocks of a manufacturer comprise raw materials, work-in-progress, and finished goods. We have so far made a general treatment of stocks. It is necessary now to bring out certain special features of these three components of inventories which are of importance to bankers.

Raw Materials

A banker is expected to gather some knowledge of the goods manufactured by a borrower and the process of manufacture, at least to the extent of the absorbability of raw materials in production, and the time taken for their absorption. The faster the rate of absorption, the quicker is their conversion to finished goods, and the lesser is the holding of inventory. In the case of small units, basic materials, bought-in-components, materials for packaging, oil, fuel, and loose tools are grouped in one, but in larger units, these are shown separately. Where several types of raw materials are used conjunctly in production, shortage of one item may be crucial, because for a time it may freeze the production itself and leave the other items of stock, may be of high value, temporarily immobilised.

From the point of view of security, raw materials generally have good market realisability, unless there is a general recession in the market.

Work-in-progress/Process

Raw materials gain value as they are absorbed in the production process and take on this nomenclature. In case of liquidation, it is the most difficult item to sell, because there is hardly any buyer for semi-finished goods. Bankers must, therefore, keep a close watch on this item in inventories. If it is large in relation to other current assets, and does not compare favourably with the previous year's ratio, there is every likelihood that some manufacturing bottleneck has developed which needs immediate probing. We have already pointed out in the last chapter that work-in-progress is central to the assessment of the working capital requirements of a manufacturing firm. A correct valuation of this item is, therefore, entremely important.

A banker can make a fair estimate of the value of the work-in-progress by adding up the values of raw materials, wages, and other operating expenses spent on the normal conversion cycle. Under normal situations, the value of work-in-progress at any point of time should not be more than this estimate. This conversion cycle may be of a few days for a chemical unit, but may extend beyond one or two years in the case of ship builders, or units engaged in infrastructural projects.

In case of a large contract or turnkey job, part payment may be received as progress payment, which is treated as an advance received from the customer and included in the current liability, while on the assets side, cash or bank balance is increased to the extent of payment received. This treatment inflates both the current liabilities and current assets, because work-in-progress continues to be shown at full value in spite of part payment received against it. This accounting practice may confuse a banker. It is, therefore, necessary for a banker to enquire into the accounting practices of these units to arrive at the real value of current assets and current liabilities.[5]

Finished Stocks

We have already discussed the importance of turnover of stocks but some additional points need to be mentioned here. A banker must see that in case of fashionable goods, the turnover ratio is high, so that at any point of time the stockholding is not large. Fashions change fast. This may render the entire stock unsaleable at any time, and often without any notice.

In case of goods whose price elasticity is high, for example, luxury goods catering primarily to the need of the middle class, it is very difficult to raise the price in spite of an escalation in costs. Generally, the unit value of these goods is high, but their turnover is low. Overstocking of these goods keeps working capital blocked for

[5] See 'Classifications of Current Assets and Liabilities' in Chapter 12 for its treatment.

a long period. The cost of carrying this stock is, therefore, high which may eat up a substantial part of the profit. Both a borrower and a banker often miss this important point.

While concluding our discussion on finished stock, we want to emphasise once again that any excessive accumulation of stock is a danger signal, because it may be that while demand for the goods has fallen, profit on the unsaleable stock has already been taken and spent. This is nothing but eating out of the capital of the business.

Stores and Spares

These two items are either combined and included in raw materials, or shown separately. Although essential for any production process, these items are often the smallest of all the current assets. These are also the most uncontrollable of all the assets. Stores and spares are normally available locally, and purchased as and when the need arises. Hence, there is no necessity of building up a large stock. But in the case of some spare parts, which are crucial for the running of the machines, one or two additional spares always have to be kept in stock. Some of the spares may have to be imported. A reasonable quantity of these spares has to be kept in stock because of the lead time involved in importing them.

Since these are the most uncontrollable items of assets, the possibility of leakage of income through wastage is high. However, as these items are directly related to production, their consumption bears a definite relationship with the volume of production. A standard percentage is easily calculated by comparing their consumption in the total production over the preceding three years, either of the unit under appraisal, or of a few similar units in the field. Any upward deviation from the standard will indicate a mismanagement of stores and spares, and consequent leakage of income.

Banks are often reluctant to finance these items, because of their uncontrollable nature. But in case of spares, which are essential for continuous running of plants and machinery, there is no reason why banks should feel shy to finance them selectively. But they have to see that stores and spares do not exceed 5 per cent of the total inventory at any time.

LOANS AND ADVANCES

Under this head are included pre-paid expenses, loans and advances, and various deposits, both statutory and trade, which are not always directly related to production, but incidental to the running of the business. All of these, however, come under the broad head of current assets. But there is a distinction between all other current assets like debtors and stock as discussed earlier, and loans and advances. In the former case there is a future cash inflow, but in the latter case there is no such inflow of cash, except loans which are to be repaid at a future date. This point is explored further as we discuss some of the items that come under this head.

Pre-paid Expenses

At times, expenses are incurred for promises to be fulfilled over a period of time extending beyond the accounting year, but not for a very long period. For example a fire insurance premium for one year paid during the middle of the year, the benefit of which will be spread over the next year also. In such a case, it is not desirable to account for these expenses in one year. The expenses are, therefore, spread over—which however, should not exceed one or two years—for which benefits are to be received. Only that portion of the expense for which benefits or services have already been received during the accounting year is taken into account for that year, and the remaining portion is carried over as an asset to the following year/s as pre-paid expenses or unexpired benefits.

Although these items are treated as current assets, there is virtually no liquidity, because even if the unit is liquidated, it is unlikely that any refund will be received, for example, from the insurance company.

Loans and Advances

Advances are often made to employees against their future wages as festival advances or in terms of a settlement reached, particularly after a strike. Advances are also made to suppliers of plant and machinery or raw materials. Except advances made to suppliers of fixed assets, all other advances are in the nature of pre-paid expenses. In the former case, banker is well-advised to exclude it from a consideration of current assets, because it is a capital expenditure which would soon be transferred to fixed assets. This should be bracketed under non-current assets, as we shall see in a subsequent chapter.

Loans are generally made to employees for house building purposes or for buying conveyances etc. which are repayable over a period. In such cases, there is no reason to include these loans under current assets. They are purely long-term in nature.

Where loans are made to directors or partners, a banker should probe into the matter. Normally, there is no reason why any loans should be given to them. If special circumstances exist, they should be probed thoroughly. A banker should ensure that no such loans are given when the unit is not making any profit. It should also be seen that the repayment of the loan is made according to the terms. If the directors or partners do not repay the loans taken from the business, they have no right to ask a bank for loan. In fact, if such loans appear in the books of accounts of a borrower, a banker should require them to be repaid in full before considering the credit proposal.

Deposits

Deposits made with various statutory authorities like port trusts, customs, and excise or earnest/tender deposits which are more or less permanent in nature, should be excluded by a banker from evaluation of current assets.[6]

Investments

These assets are not engaged in the production directly. Funds invested in them are employed outside the business (for conversion into cash outside the trading cycle when the need arises). Some prefer to call them quasi-fixed assets. Investments are made for various purposes which determine their nature.

Investment for Replacement of Fixed Assets

Sometimes a fund is created for replacement of an asset from out of depreciation charged to the profit and loss account. This fund may be invested in good marketable securities like shares in other companies or government securities, so that at the time of replacement of the asset, money is readily available. This practice is now not very much in vogue. The depreciation fund is generally invested in the business itself. If such investments appear in the books of accounts of a borrower, a banker should ask him to realise them and invest the fund in the business where the expected return is higher than these securities.

---

[6] For purposes of credit appraisal some of these assets are regarded as non-current assets and are grouped separately, away from current assets. Please see 'Classifications of Current Assets and Liabilities' in Chapter 12.

Investment in Subsidiary Companies

Investments in subsidiary companies are quite fixed, and very difficult to realise. Shares in subsidiary companies may not be quoted in the market; hence, individual balance sheets of these subsidiary companies are to be analysed to determine the present value of the investment. It is always better, however, to assess the entire holding company than studying the subsidiaries individually. If the link between all these companies is very close, the failure of one company may result in the failure of the whole group. It is preferable, therefore, to finance the group as a whole in order to have a firm control over its affairs. However, if the holding company is an investment company only, it is advisable to finance 'individual' companies rather than the group.[7]

Besides these, investments are also made in outside securities for engaging surplus cash for a temporary period. This has been explained earlier while discussing cash.

Two more points need to be discussed before we conclude this section. If any company is found to be investing substantially in shares of a number of unrelated companies, it is likely that the company has engaged in speculative activities. This should act as a danger signal to a banker, because the working capital of the company, which the bank has financed, might have already been diverted to speculative activities.

The second point which a banker should like to see is whether the investments are in quoted securities or not. Unquoted securities are not only difficult to evaluate, but also difficult to realise. It is better to exclude them from consideration. On the other hand, quoted securities can be treated as current assets because of ready realisability.

INTANGIBLE AND FICTITIOUS ASSETS

We have so far discussed tangible assets whose existence is real, and the benefits derived from which can be fairly estimated. Besides these, there are other assets which are intangible in nature like goodwill and copyrights which are now discussed.

Goodwill

Goodwill is a very old concept. Nearly two centuries ago, goodwill was defined as 'the probability that old customers will resort to the old place'. In other words, it is the value attached to the reputation of a business, which is a real factor responsible for the sale of its goods and services. In this respect it may well be a real asset. Many a times, this is perhaps the single asset, the very strength of which enables its proud possessor to enjoy extensive facilities from banks. The names Tatas and Birlas weigh distinctly in the mind of a banker, which may outweigh all other assets of the business. This is the value of the business reputation and entrepreneurial acumen built up by these houses over a long period.

Why Bring Goodwill into the Books of Accounts?

Goodwill is an asset which can only be sensed from the experience of the customer, and is not to be valued in money terms and brought into the books of accounts. Any attempt to value reputation is a futile exercise. However, there may still be special occasions where it becomes necessary to measure goodwill. Some, for instance, do it by 'so many years' purchase of net profit of the business. Tax authorities in our country value it by this method for determining the value of the estate of a retiring or dead partner.

In fact, under normal circumstances when the firm is a growing concern, there is no necessity of raising goodwill in the books of accounts, because even without doing it, the firm is deriv-

---

[7] Ibid.

ing its benefit. When the firm becomes a losing concern, it is the goodwill which is wiped out first, and on liquidation one cannot get even a paisa out of it. But when a new partner joins in a profit-making concern, there arises the necessity of raising the goodwill, because the new partner has to pay for the reputation built by the existing partners over the years by their ardent labour. Goodwill is then raised either by 'so many years' purchase of profit as discussed earlier, or as the difference between the existing book value of the business and its probable market value, if it is sold as a going concern. The amount of goodwill thus raised is credited to the capital accounts of existing partners, and the new entrant is asked to pay for his share in proportion to the restructured capital base of the firm.

Write It Off

However, it is an established convention and sound business practice to write-off the goodwill within a few years from out of profits. If it is not done, a banker may well presume that the firm is losing goodwill.

Companies limited by shares have long stopped raising goodwill of their own businesses in their books of accounts. But when a compan purchases a new business (by acquisition or merger), goodwill may appear in its books of accounts representing the difference between the price paid for the business, and the actual estimated value of the net assets. This type of goodwill bears a direct relation to the super profit made by the acquired business over normal profit made by similar units in the market. Hence, it is desirable that the goodwill so raised should be written-off in the same manner from the super profit made by the newly acquired business.

Patents and Copyrights

These are instruments to protect a newly developed product or production process from being copied or pirated by others. These are registered with a statutory authority at a fee for a given number of years. The fee so paid, including the expenditure related to it, is for all practical purposes, an expense, which should be debited to the profit and loss account straightaway. But if the expense is quite substantial, and since the patent rights are available for a fixed number of years, it is written off annually, just like depreciation on other fixed assets.

Unlike goodwill, patents and copyrights have real value in the market even when a company is being wound up. Hence, it is difficult to ignore them while estimating the assets of a business. Though there are problems in the valuation of these assets, the cost of acquiring patents and copyrights may be included as part of assets.

Trade Mark

A trademark is either a symbol of the unit, or of the goods produced by it. Like a patent, it can also be registered with a statutory authority to protect its infringement by others. The registration is available for a fixed period against a fee. It is renewable for a further period. The trademark of a product being a brand equity has value in the market, and hence its cost of acquisition as appearing in the balance sheet should be treated at par with patents and copyrights.

FICTITIOUS ASSETS

Debit Balance in Profit and Loss Account

When a profit is made, a credit balance appears in the profit and loss account, which is transferred to the capital account in case of firms and to the general reserve (after appropriation is made for payment of dividend) in case of companies. But when there is a loss, the profit and loss account shows a debit balance, which may not be transferred to the capital account, but shown separately along with the other assets of the unit. The net effect of this loss, however, is to reduce the intrinsic value of the business, or net worth as it is generally called. It is ironic that while profit increases the liability of the enterprise to its owners, losses and dividends are means to discharge that liability.

Needless to mention that the existence of a debit balance in the profit and loss account in the balance sheet of a unit is a sure sign of weakness, except perhaps during the first one or two years of commencement of production when the unit may be suffering from teething troubles. Worse, however, is the situation when accumulated losses grow over the years. Something must have gone terribly wrong—it may be management, production, finance, marketing, or all of them taken together. The unit either may be overdue for liquidation, or may need intensive nursing.

A limited company is forbidden to declare a dividend when there is a loss. But in case of partnership firms or proprietary concerns, a banker should see that there is no unreasonable drawing by the partners or proprietor. If there is any such excess drawing, it would mean that the partners or proprietor must have been eating up the capital of the business; therefore, their intention cannot be treated as honest.

Other Fictitious Assets

There are other fictitious assets like preliminary expenses incurred during the formation of a company, expenses incurred in connection with the issue of shares of a company, large promotional expenditure, or other debit balances appearing in the books of accounts, which could not be written off during the accounting year. As these debit balances have no other place to go, they appear under the head 'assets' (as all assets also have debit balances) and hang on as undesirable appendages to the balance sheet until the unit's financial position permits these to be written-off.

Depending upon the volume, these expenditure may be amortised, that is, a part—generally, a pre-determined percentage—is charged to the profit and loss account every year. However, the existence of fictitious assts in the balance sheet of a company for a long time may suggest that the company is not making enough profit to write them off.

CONCLUDING REMARKS

Current assets are constraints to a business. Given a choice, no entrepreneur would like to hold current assets, because his valuable funds get blocked in these assets, and hence make an inroad into the profitability of the business. The modern approach to financial management, therefore, calls for reducing the level of current assets vis-à-vis sales, which, in other words, means increasing the turnover of current assets. This fits into the modern approach of a banker who desires a decreasing level of dependence by firms on banks for working capital finance. An enterprise with the least possible level of current assets enjoys a distinct competitive advantage over others in the market. A disproportionate increase in current assets is often a pointer to an impending liquidity crisis, unless it is deliberately designed and properly funded to make an entry into the market or to capture a larger share of the market.

Intangible assets are not always fictitious; some of them have real value in the market like patents, copyrights, and brand names and they have all the right to be treated at least at par with other assets, though their evaluation is often difficult.

We know accurately only when we know little: with knowledge doubt increases.

—Goethe

8   Long-Term Liabilities

INTRODUCTION

In the last three chapters, we have analysed various assets of a business unit. But we have not gone into the question of how such assets come into being. In this chapter we begin with the statement: *liabilities create assets*. To a common man this may appear perplexing, because he is accustomed only to own assets and to him liabilities are burdens which need to be paid off as quickly as possible. But for a business, and to a financial analyst, *liabilities constitute funds from which to acquire assets*.

DEFINITION

Liabilities are promises given against which assets are received. Standard accounting practice regards any object given as credit, and any object received as debit. The primary object that a business receives is cash against the promise given to the owner to repay it at some indefinite time in the future. This transaction can be recorded as:

Object received : Cash   *Debit*
Object given   : Promise to repay owner   *Credit*

The object given, that is, the promise to repay the owner, is the first liability of the business, which in accounting terminology is called promoter's capital or equity.

Cash is also received from non-owners against similar promises given to them, but here the promises to repay are more definite. For example, cash may be received from a bank against a promise given in the form of execution of a promissory note. This transaction is similarly recorded as:

Object received : Cash   *Debit*
Object given   : Promise to repay   *Credit*
                    bank loan

The object given in this case, that is, the promise to repay a bank a loan, is called a loan or an advance.

Suppliers of raw materials or stocks-in-trade may also supply them against a definite promise to be paid after a short period of time. This transaction is recorded as:

Object received : Goods   *Debit*
Object given   : Promise to pay   *Credit*
                    the suppliers

Suppliers to whom promises are made for repayment are grouped under the head 'trade creditors'.

All credit items discussed so far are simply promises given either in the form of share certificates (capital), or promissory notes (loan), or acceptance of the bills of suppliers (creditors). These promises are obligations (liabilities), as any promise is. Funds flow from the promises made, or in other words, promises are the sources of funds.

The fund is then utilised to acquire, convert, and reconvert various assets in the process of business. The matching concept of debit and credit in accounting tells us further that every liability must, therefore, find a matching asset somewhere in the business; and at any point of time, the total liabilities and assets of the business must match.

In this chapter and the next, we discuss long-term and current liabilities respectively. We go deep into each item of liability to enable a lender to have a proper understanding of its origin, nature, and intricacies. This detailed discussion is necessary because the author in his experience as a teacher and consultant has found that many bank officers, particularly from a non-commerce background, are unable to take a total view of the funding operations of a business, because they do not have a proper understanding of every item of liability that a business may contract. These two chapters will also lay the foundation for the funds and cash flow analysis that is discussed in Chapter 14.

EQUITY OR SHARE CAPITAL

In plain language, this is the fund supplied by the shareholders in the case of limited companies, and partners or proprietor in the case of firms. This is the primary source of funds for any business.

Technically speaking, a business being a distinct entity, it undertakes to repay this fund to the owners at some indefinite period of time, that is, on liquidation after all outside liabilities are paid off in full. When a business is under liquidation, the owners get the residual amount only, if there

is any after satisfaction of outside liabilities, and therefore there is a breach of promise by the business. But owners cannot sue the business for this breach of promise because *they* are the people who could not keep their promises in managing the business profitably.

The Cohen Committee of London[1] defined equity share capital as that part of the share capital, which confers a right either to the whole or part of any residue of any profits or to the whole or part of any residue of any assets remaining for distribution after satisfying the claims of any other shareholder whose right to participate therein is limited.

Shareholders owning this capital do not have any preference with regard to the payment of dividend or capital, but they are the real owners of the company. If there is no profit available after satisfaction of the claim of preference shareholders, they are left high and dry. The dividend payable to ordinary shareholders does not accumulate, and in case of liquidation, they wait until the end, often without any hope. Hence, they are the people who venture and take risks, and obviously, they will have the biggest say in the management of a company.

CONTRIBUTION OF PROMOTERS

Capital is the initial fund contributed by the proprietor/shareholders, the main purpose of which is to finance the acquisition of assets needed to do business. When an entrepreneur comes to a bank with his business proposal, it is obvious that he does not have all the capital to finance his project. The immediate question that comes to the mind of a banker is what should be the minimum amount that should be brought in by an entrepreneur as capital so that he has an adequate stake in the business and a bank is

[1] Report of the Committee on Company Law Amendment, London, June 1945.

not called upon to extend its finance to such an extent that it becomes an owner of the business rather than its financier.

This question has also been addressed by the SEBI, which requires that for any public issue of equity capital whether of a listed or unlisted company, the promoter(s) contribution should not be less than 20 per cent of the total issue of equity capital. A stake between 20 and 30 per cent is fair considering also the fact that it ensures representation on the board. Exceptions to this SEBI rule are the IPO of a government company, statutory authority or a corporation or any special purpose vehicle set up by them which is engaged in infrastructure projects. In the case of an existing company, the lock-in period for the minimum promoters' contribution is three years from the date of allotment. For a new company, the lock-in period is three years from the date of allotment or from the commencement of production, whichever is later. When promoters' contribution is more than the required minimum the lock-in period for such excess subscription is one year. Locked-in shares can be pledged with banks/financial institutions as collateral security for loans granted to the *company*. No other purpose is permitted.

It is obvious that banks should not finance a promoter's equity. Also banks should not grant advance for acquiring promoters' stake in other companies except in those existing companies engaged in implementing or operating infrastructure projects under certain conditions. Even in such cases, financing by banks should not exceed 50 per cent of the finance required for acquiring promoters' stake in the company being acquired.[2]

[2] See, RBI circular DBOD. No. Dir. BC.13/13.03.00/2010–11 dated 1.7.2010, available at www.rbi.org.in.

Sound banking principles demand that capital or long-term funds should not only finance the acquisition of long-term or fixed assets, but also a portion of the working capital requirements. Long-term funds may come, in addition to capital, from debentures, or term loans from financial institutions, or banks. But funds available from term loans have to be utilised primarily for acquisition of long-term assets. Financial institutions may not allow any portion of term loans to be utilised for financing current assets, unless the margin of working capital forms a part of project financing. Banks and financial institutions have developed certain norms about margin requirements, which we take up at appropriate places. However, at this stage we may recall that for the purpose of financing capital cost of a project by raising share capital from the market, the now defunct Controller of Capital Issues had fixed a 2:1 debt–equity ratio as a fair standard. This should give a cue to the financing bank.

In the case of a company limited by shares, only two types of share capital can be issued: preference and ordinary. A private company limited by shares can raise capital only by private placement, while a public company can do so both by private placement (closely held company) and by a direct offer to the public (listed company). This rule applies to all classes of capital, including debentures.

AUTHORISED CAPITAL

In the case of proprietary or partnership firms, capital appearing in the balance sheets is deemed to have been fully paid-up. But in the case of limited companies this may not be so. A limited company has authorised capital declared as such in its Memorandum and Articles of Association, which cannot be increased except by a special resolution of the shareholders, and in some cases, with the approval of the Company Law

Board.[3] To a banker, authorised capital does not have much meaning, except that in case a bank wants the company to augment its capital base, it may know to what extent the company may issue fresh capital without going through the formalities mentioned earlier. It may also be pointed out here that authorised capital, though appearing in the balance sheet, does not form a part of it, and is not included in the calculation of the net worth of a company.

ISSUED AND PAID-UP CAPITAL

When shares are issued to the public for subscription, from out of authorised capital, the nominal value of the shares is generally recovered from the subscribers in stages: on application, on allotment, and in subsequent calls. Issued share capital when subscribed is allotted against allotment money received from the subscribers who then become shareholders of the company. The remaining amount of the nominal value of the share is then called up, if not already received at the time of allotment. But a company may decide not to call up the entire capital, because it may not need all the money now. The uncalled capital is then treated as reserve capital, which can be called up whenever the company desires to augment its resources. This looks good on the face of it, and a banker may often feel complacent about it. But, although shareholders are liable to pay up the uncalled portion on demand under pain of forfeiture of shares (and their liability is absolute to outside creditors to the extent of the unpaid portion of the shares in the event of winding up of the company), the 'realisability' of uncalled capital is dependent upon the ability and

---

[3] Company Law Board (CLB) was dissolved by Companies (Amendment) Act, 2002. National Company Law Tribunal was formed in 2002 to take over the major functions of CLB; it started functioning from 2003.

willingness of the shareholders. This is more so in the case of a private limited company, where it may often be found that the shareholders are not in a position to pay up the shareholding.

Forfeiture of Shares

In case of a public limited company, shareholders may not be willing to respond to call notices if the company's performance is persistently bad and the market value of shares has come down well below its nominal value. They may decide to have their shares forfeited, lose only partly, rather than pouring in more money, and lose that too. A banker should, therefore, probe into the matter to find out the realisability of the uncalled capital. A good indication of the unrealisability of uncalled capital is the existence of a share forfeiture account in the books of accounts of a company for more than three months. If the amount is increasing, then the situation is even worse. Normally, if the company is performing well, forfeited shares would soon be sold out and the account adjusted. Hence, if uncalled share capital appears in the balance sheet simultaneously with the share forfeiture account, then the former has to be discounted heavily. It is doubtful whether it can any longer be called reserve capital.

Voting Right

For a public limited company, a voting right is proportional to the equity shareholding. But this rule is applicable only to resolutions put forward in the general meeting of the shareholders. In case of resolutions taken up in meetings of the board of directors, only a simple majority is required. However, for private limited companies, even voting rights of members need not be proportional to the shareholding. They may decide to have different voting rights, irrespective of shareholding. Banks dealing with a private limited company should, therefore, find out voting rights of the shareholders from the Articles of Association, and should not be carried away by the preconceived idea of 'one share, one vote', as in the case of a public limited company.

FEAR OF TAKEOVER

Although, on the face of it a public limited company with wide dispersal of shares amongst the general public is designed to be managed democratically, in effect the management is concentrated in the hands of an individual entrepreneur, or a group, or groups who command 51 per cent of the total equity shares. This has been the general rule of the book, but it has gone into further evolution. An entrepreneur or a group of entrepreneurs can now control a company by holding much less than 51 per cent of the equity share capital as long as the rest of the shareholders can be kept so dispersed that they cannot come together to stage a showdown. This is, however, possible as long as the dispersed shareholders are kept content and passive by providing a steady rate of dividend and ensuring growth of capital. The controlling group also keeps a close watch on the share markets to foil moves of interested groups to take over control by cornering shares. A company has a right to refuse registration of any transfer of shares. The central government may also direct prohibition of registration of shares if the acquisition is 10 per cent or more of the equity shares on the ground that it is not desirable in the interest of the company. However, SEBI intends to provide a level playing field as it believes that takeovers are normal in a market economy. A bank financing a company where the management is held by minority shareholders always runs the risk of the company being taken over by an undesirable group of people who may not see eye to eye with the bank. SEBI has now issued detailed guidelines to ensure transparency in takeover bids providing an option to the shareholders to sell their shares if they do not

have confidence in the likely new management.[4] Issue of non-voting share can also allay the fear of a takeover.

Non-voting Equity Share Capital

Until recently, public limited companies in India could not issue any other type of share capital besides ordinary (equity) and preference share capital, though this restriction was not applicable to private limited companies. A new class of equity shares, called non-voting shares, has recently been introduced in India.

This is a new class of equity capital that came up in the western world during the early part of the 1980s. It is very popular in countries like the US, the United Kingdom, France, Sweden, Germany, Switzerland, Italy, Indonesia, South Korea, and Singapore. During recent times, one of the largest issues of non-voting shares was made by BNP Paribus. On 31 March 2009 the company issued 5.1 billion euros as part of the plan of the Government of France to support the French economy.

As these shareholders will not have any say in the management, it is likely that they will enjoy a higher rate of dividend than the ordinary shareholders. Unlike preference shareholders, non-voting shareholders will have all the risks of ordinary shareholders, but no control over the management. This is designed to enable domestic entrepreneurs to retain control of the management, and at the same time obtain resources from the capital market by designing the issue attractively. The fear is that it could reduce the earning per share of the voting stock. Unless adequate care is taken while launching the issue, particularly with regard to its pricing, it may have a negative impact in the share market. Warren

[4] For details, see the Securities and Exchange Board of India, Substantial Acquisition of Shares and Takeovers Regulations.

Buffett, the doyen of American investors, experimented with a hybrid of non-voting shares. The 'B' shares in his company Berkshire Hathaway Inc. were valued at 1/30th of the 'A' shares, but had only 1/200th of the voting power. The issue was a tremendous success, because investors wanted to have a share in the growing investment venture of Warren Buffett. This gives us a cue that non-voting shares can be successful for strong companies which want to remain tightly controlled, but at the same time desire to expand the base of their risk capital.

In India, the idea was first mooted in 1989. The Working Group on the Development of Capital Market set up by Planning Commission in 1989 under the chairmanship of Abid Hussain recommended the introduction of non-voting equity shares. The study group constituted by the Government of India on 27 March 1991 under the chairmanship of M. J. Pherwani also strongly recommended the concept of non-voting shares. But only in 1994 did the finance ministry issue certain broad guidelines in this regard. Finally, with the passage of the Companies (Amendment) Act, 2000 and subsequent Rules made thereunder in 2001[5] the deck was cleared for companies to issue equity shares with differential voting rights. If the Articles of Association permits, a company limited by shares can issue equity shares with differential rights as to dividend, voting, or otherwise under the following terms and conditions:

1. A company issuing shares with differential voting rights must obtain approval of the shareholders in a general meeting. In case of listed companies, the approval can be obtained through postal ballot.

[5] Companies (Issue of Share capital with Differential Voting Rights) Rules, 2001.

2. The company has distributable profits for three years preceding the year in which it has decided to issue such shares and has duly filed annual accounts and annual returns for the same period.
3. The company has not failed to repay its deposits or interest thereon on the due date or redeem its debentures on the due date, or pay dividend.
4. The company has not been convicted of any offence under SEBI Act, 1992, Securities Contracts (Regulations) Act, 1956, and the Foreign Exchange Management Act, 1999.
5. The company has not defaulted in meeting investors' grievances.
6. The shares with differential voting rights shall not exceed 25 per cent of the total issued capital of the company.

A company is not permitted to convert its equity capital with voting rights into equity capital with differential voting rights and vice versa.

REDUCTION OF CAPITAL

Reduction of capital is permitted in exceptional cases and for limited purposes only. If there is excess capital or the accumulated losses are so high that they have eroded the capital base of the company substantially, then reduction of capital of a limited company is permitted in order to present a true and fair view of the business. This can be done in the following manner:

(a) Extinguishing or reducing the liability of any of its shares with respect to shares not fully paid-up. For example, if face value of a share is Rs 10 and only Rs 7.50 is paid-up, the share may be treated as fully paid-up for Rs 7.50.
(b) Either with or without extinguishing or reducing the liability on any of its shares,

cancel any paid-up capital, which is lost or is unrepresented by assets.

(c) Either with or without reducing the liability of any of its fully paid-up shares return a part of capital, which is in excess of the present need of the company. For example, out of a paid-up share of Rs 10 an amount of Rs 2.50 may be returned. However, the amount so returned may be called up again.

Buy-Back

Reduction of capital through a legal process is rarely resorted to, except when a company is re-constituted so that it can start afresh with a clean slate. The cumbersome procedure is avoidable by an enabling provision introduced in 1998 by which a company can buy-back its own shares with a view to:

(a) Increasing the underlying value of its shares as earning per share increases after the buy-back.

(b) Adjusting the capital base when it is over-capitalised.

(c) Returning surplus cash to shareholders (without paying dividend distribution tax) when reasonable investment opportunities are not visible in the near future.

(d) Preventing hostile takeovers as share price increases substantially after the buy-back.

A creditor of a company need not feel alarmed as both the Companies Act and SEBI provide for adequate protections, which include:

1. The company must file a declaration of solvency with the Registrar of Companies and with SEBI.
2. Buy-back in any financial year shall not be more than 25 per cent of its paid-up capital.

3. The debt–equity ratio of the company shall not be more than 2 after the buy-back.
4. Buy-back is only from out of free reserves, share premium account, or from proceeds of any shares or securities other than from the same kind of shares or securities. However, if the buy-back is less than 10 per cent of the paid-up capital and free reserves this requirement is not applicable.
5. Buy-back for treasury operations or trading in own shares is prohibited.
6. Buy-back with a view to delisting a listed company is not permitted.

Buy-back reflects a management's confidence, which generates positive sentiments in the market.

There is no question of banks financing buy-back as the fund for this purpose has to come from a company's own sources as mentioned in item No. 4 above.[6]

LIMITED LIABILITY: BANKER'S PROBLEM

Companies limited by shares and also limited liability partnership (LLP)[7] are regarded as distinct

[6] See, RBI circular DBOD. No. Dir. BC.13.03.00/2010–11 dated 1 July 2010.

[7] With the passage of Limited Liability Partnership Act, 2008, a new legal entity has come into being, which is separate from its partners. Any change in the partners for any reason whatsoever shall not affect the existence, rights and liabilities of LLP. Except in case of fraud, no partner is personally liable to the liabilities of LLP. Every partner is an agent of LLP but not of other partners. The act provides great flexibility in management and operations of the business. In most of the cases, provisions as contained in the partnership agreement prevail. At least two partners are required to form a LLP; there is no upper limit to membership.

entities in the eyes of the law. Outside creditors cannot proceed against the shareholders beyond the face value of the shares held by them, that is, to the extent of the unpaid portion of the share capital. This creates problems for banks and financial institutions, who are perhaps the biggest creditors of a business unit. This problem is circumvented to some extent by taking the guarantee of the directors of the company, who amongst themselves generally hold a controlling share in the business. But in the case of professionalised boards, professional directors hold only nominal shares and independent directors may not hold any shares at all. They are obviously reluctant to give guarantees for repayment of loans taken by the company. The RBI rose to this reality some years back, and advised that 'professionals who do not have a significant stake in a company may not be able to take upon themselves the onus of guaranteeing the unit's health and meeting its indebtedness to the banking system and/or financial institutions if the advances were to be recalled'. It is not necessary, therefore, for banks to insist on personal guarantees from such professional directors/managers, except in cases where they have a significant shareholding in the business. A banker is, however, well-advised to obtain guarantees from the controlling shareholders. Major shareholders of the company can be identified from the register of shareholders available for inspection at the registered office of the company. However, in some companies shares are held by particular business groups in the names of relatives or nominees, hence the register may not reveal the true picture. In such a situation, a banker should make necessary enquiries in the market to know the actual persons or group(s) behind the company. A definite source of information is the share market, particularly brokers who can give detailed information regarding the group or individuals having effective control of a particular company and also their interest in other companies.

PREFERENCE SHARE CAPITAL

Shareholders owning this type of capital have a preference with regard to the payment of dividend, and capital in the case of liquidation, over other types of shareholders. The rate of dividend is fixed or floating with a reference rate. In some companies preference shareholders have a right to share any residual profit left after the satisfaction of all other shareholders. This is called participating preference share. Preference shareholders have no say in the management of the company, except when their interests are directly affected.

They have a right to vote only on resolutions which directly affect their rights. Reduction of share capital or winding up directly affects the rights of preference shareholders.

If there is no profit in a year, the terms of issue may permit the dividend payable to be carried over to the following year(s), and accumulated dividend paid from out of the profits made in subsequent years. Such shares are called cumulative preference shares. Under no circumstances, however, dividend can be paid except out of profit.

Although preference share capital is treated as a part of share capital, for all practical purposes it is nothing but one of the various modes of financing the operations of a company to the maximum advantage of equity shareholders. Preference share capital issued by Indian banks is directly treated as borrowing.

In certain circumstances, preference share capital is treated as a part of the net worth. One such case is that of Compulsorily Convertible Preference Shares (CCPS) introduced in 1985. This class of shares can be issued for setting up new projects particularly infrastructural projects, expansion and diversification, modernisation, and for working capital. The amount of CCPS cannot exceed that of the total equity shares offered to the public, and it would be deemed to be equity issue for purpose of calculating the debt–equity ratio. The entire issue of CCPS must be converted into equity shares as may be decided by the company and approved by SEBI. Companies are now free to offer any rate of dividend on CCPS. The guidelines with respect to preference shares regarding the ratio of 1:3 as between preference shares and equity shares would not be applicable to CCPS.

During recent times, CCPS has gained wide acceptance among companies engaged in infrastructure development and finance. The Infrastructure Development Finance Company (IDFC) is the leader in the field. The company announced during July 2010 that it would issue CCPS to Khazanah, the investment arm of the Malaysian government and private equity firm Actis. The proposed CCPS would be converted to equity in 18 months.

Preference share capital is a good source of funding for infrastructure projects or companies engaged in infrastructure financing.

The ratio between preference share capital and equity share capital should not exceed 1:3 at any point of time, except CCPS or other convertible preference shares.

Redeemables and Irredeemables

Preference shares are further divided into redeemable and irredeemable shares. Earlier, if the articles of a company permitted, preference shares could be redeemed and paid out. If there was no such provision, these could not be redeemed except on liquidation. But the situation changed substantially, first, by the passage of the Companies (Amendment) Act, 1988. According to this amendment all irredeemable preference

shares were to be redeemed by a company within a period of five years from the commencement of the Act, and such preference shares standing in the books of the company which were redeemable beyond 10 years according to the terms of issue, should be redeemed by the company on the date on which these are due for redemption, or within a period of 10 years from the commencement of this Act, whichever was earlier. However, by a further amendment to the Companies Act in 1996, companies are allowed to issue redeemable preference shares for a maximum period of 20 years from the date of issue.[8]

A company is forbidden to declare equity dividend if it fails to redeem preference shares which have fallen due for redemption in any particular year. Preference shares can be redeemed only out of profit, or from the proceeds of a fresh issue of shares specifically made for this purpose. Any premium paid on such redemption must also come from profit or from fresh issue of shares.

On or before redemption, an amount equal to the value of shares being redeemed should be transferred to the capital redemption reserve

---

[8] In India, banking companies are allowed to issue perpetual non-cumulative preference shares (PNCPS), perpetual cumulative preference shares (PCPS), redeemable non-cumulative preference shares (RNCPS), and redeemable cumulative preference shares (RCPS) to boost their capital bases. PCPS shall be cumulative. RNCPS and RCPS could be cumulative or non-cumulative with a fixed maturity of 15 years. The instruments shall not be issued with put option. Call option is permitted after the instrument has run for at least 10 years. These instruments shall be classified as borrowings in the balance sheet of the issuing bank. While PNCPS are eligible for Tier-I capital, others are considered as part of Upper Tier-II capital. Refer RBI circular DBOD.No. BP.BC.15/21.06.001/2010–11 dated 1 July 2010.

fund. Repayment is then made by debiting the preference share capital account, and crediting cash. After full repayment of preference shares, the reserve fund forms a part of the paid-up share capital belonging to the ordinary shareholders. It can be used for issuing bonus shares.

Since redemption means immediate paying out of cash, a banker while appraising the future financial position of a company should enquire about the date of redemption, and the arrangement of cash made by the company for this purpose. Redemption when made from out of a fresh shares issue does not destabilise the existing financial position of the company. But it is dependent upon the ability of the company to attract buyers in the capital market, which again is dependent upon the consistently good performance of the company.

Financing the Redemption

When a company is unable to raise fresh capital in the market to pay for redemption, or has built up sufficient reserves from out of profits but is unable to arrange for cash, it may approach a bank for financing redemption. In such a situation a banker is often put in a dilemma, because in principle he is not expected to lay down funds for redemption of capital, but if he does not, then the disgruntled preference shareholders may bring the company to liquidation. In order to avoid such an unenviable situation, a banker should closely follow the performance of the company and not only ensure that a portion of the profits is transferred each year to the reserve fund to take care of future redemption, but also see that sufficient liquid resources are built up to ultimately pay for the redemption.

If the company is unable to raise sufficient cash resources from internal generation, and raising of capital from the market is also not possible, then a banker is well-advised to take a pragmatic view of the whole situation. The decision situation is similar to whether to call back the advance, or pour in further money to stave off the impending disaster, and thus save a bank's advance already made from being completely lost in the event of a forced liquidation. If an analysis of the present performance and future projections reveals that the company will be able to come around the present difficulty and generate sufficient cash in the future, there is no reason why a pragmatic banker should hold on to the 'golden principle' and withdraw himself from the problem. By doing so he would serve no purpose other than bringing about the total disaster to the company and consequent loss of a bank's funds.[9]

Share Premium

The next important item of capital funds is the share premium account. Companies are now free to decide the price at which the shares could be issued. The company and the lead managers to the issue decide the pricing of the shares. They can decide any price which they feel the market can bear. However, justification of such a price has to be provided in the offer document. Any amount received in excess of the face value of shares is credited to the share premium account. This is in fact a new class of paid-up capital. This item is peculiar to limited companies only. It is not observable in the books of accounts of firms. The amount of premium may be paid either in cash or in kind, or otherwise.

The amount of premium once received by the company cannot be distributed as dividend to shareholders. However, it can be used for reduction of capital in exceptional circumstances.

The existence of a share premium account in the balance sheet of a company is a good indication that the company is doing so well that its

---

[9] The decision situation is akin to that of bonus loans, which have since been permitted by the Reserve Bank of India.

shares are in high demand in the market, enabling the company to increase its price.

As this item is not part of divisible profits, a banker need not be very much concerned about its disposal. This almost forms part of the paid-up capital of the company. However, it can be disposed of in the following manner:

1. For making a fully paid bonus issue of shares when it is received in cash only.
2. For writing-off preliminary expenses, commission paid, or discount given earlier on issue of shares or debentures.
3. For providing any premium payable on redemption of preference shares or of debentures of the company.

A banker would obviously demand that the second course of action be taken first, because it is not desirable for a company to increase its share capital, and thus pay dividend on it when it has fictitious assets in its books waiting to be written-off.

The share premium account is considered as a special category capital reserve under the Companies Act.

DIVIDEND VERSUS RESERVES

A business can prosper when it accumulates capital, and this accumulation is possible only when it saves a portion of its profits every year. It is always a ticklish problem of balancing between the demand of partners/shareholders for higher dividends and the firm's need for growth through accumulation of capital.

In case of partnership or proprietorship firms, capital may get reduced by drawings when the partners/proprietor are making drawings in spite of losses or drawing more than the profit. When a lender finds this, he may get alarmed and doubt their integrity. But the matter should be looked at from the reality angle. An entrepreneur, who has invested all his money in the business, has to make a living as well, and if he has no other place to go, he will definitely turn to his business. During the initial period, the business may not make a profit from which to draw, but an entrepreneur has to survive, and the future of the business depends on his survival. Therefore, if the drawing is reasonable and the business has a future, a lender need not feel alarmed. There is nothing wrong in financing even the drawings, because partners or proprietors are even otherwise entitled to draw salaries. It is always advisable to include the salary of the entrepreneur in the project cost while assessing a credit proposal.

In case of a limited company, no dividend is payable except out of profit. Hence, the question of drawing out capital through drawings does not arise. The power to declare dividends rests with the board of directors, which is subsequently ratified by shareholders at a general meeting. Shareholders may make deliberations on the rate of dividend and recommend a higher rate but the decision of the board is final in this respect. They may, however, decide to accept a lower rate of dividend.

Before any dividend is declared (or the partners or proprietor are allowed to make drawings), a lender must see that adequate provision for depreciation is made. In the case of companies it is mandatory under law, but in the case of other firms it is only optional. Hence, a banker should be more particular in the latter case. From a bank's point of view, provision for depreciation is more important, because it not only provides for replacement of assets in the future, but also acts as a source of funds during the intervening period.

While a company should maintain a stable and reasonably rising rate of dividend to keep the shareholders satisfied and ensure market stability of its shares, it should also consistently build-up its capital base by transferring a portion of its profits each year to the reserve. This is necessary not only to finance future expansion, but also to enable the company to declare a dividend in a lean year (when it is unable to make sufficient profits) by transferring back a portion of the reserve. The Companies Act has also recognised this important aspect of sound management of companies. Section 205 of the Act (and the Rules made thereunder), make it incumbent upon a company to transfer a portion of the profits each year to its reserve in the following manner:

Rate of Dividend (%) (on paid-up capital)	Minimum Amount to be Transferred to Reserve from Profit (%)
Exceeds 10% but does not exceed 12.5%	2.5%
Exceeds 12.5% but does not exceed 15%	5.0%
Exceeds 15% but does not exceed 20%	7.5%
Exceeds 20%	10.0%

Where, however, profit is made but no dividend is declared in a year, then the amount transferred to the reserve shall be less than the average dividends declared by the company during the last three financial years.

We may notice from the above figures that the rate of transfer to the reserves has been made progressive with the rate of dividend. Although the minimum amount is set at a maximum of 10 per cent, the nature of the relationship between the rate of dividend and the percentage of transfer from profit to reserve, as given earlier, suggests that a company declaring a dividend of more than 20 per cent of its paid-up capital should follow the same progressive rate of transfer to the reserve. This is a sound principle decided after a lot of deliberation, and a banker can extend the same principle to firms also to establish a relationship between partners' or proprietor's drawings and profit.

Higher Transfer to Reserves

The above provisions of the Companies Act and Rules do not prohibit a company from voluntarily transferring a higher percentage of profit to the reserves, as long it leaves enough amount in profit to pay a dividend equal to the average rate of dividend paid to the shareholders during the last three financial years; or, if a bonus share is issued either in the same year or within the three preceding financial years, an amount equal to the average amount (quantum) of dividend declared during the three preceding years. But if the net profit (after-tax) in that year is lower than 20 per cent or more of the average net profit made during the last two years, then for purposes of transferring to reserve, no such minimum payment of dividend need be ensured, because when a company is losing, it is necessary to conserve whatever profit it is making rather than to fritter it away in dividend payment. This last point is very important to a lender because in order to maintain a stable rate of dividend to avoid the wrath of shareholders, companies may continue to declare dividends at the old rate in spite of the fact that net profit has reduced substantially in a given year. If the company has substantial reserves, or if the fall in profit in a particular year is only a temporary phenomenon, which does not reflect any sign of incipient sickness, there is nothing wrong in declaring dividend at the old rate to keep the shareholders satisfied and maintain stability of its shares in the market. If it is otherwise, it is necessary to conserve the strength by increasing the reserve rather than declaring a dividend. This is in the interest of the lender as well as the shareholders because if a company's financial position is not consolidated when signs of sickness are visible, the payment of dividend that year may ultimately lead to a total stoppage of dividend payment in the future.

FREE RESERVES: THE PROBLEM

Reserves created out of revenue (profit) that we have discussed so far, are also called free reserves. If they are not created or set apart for any special purpose, they are freely available to the shareholders. As indicated earlier, a company can pay dividend out of these reserves in lean year, but while doing so it has to provide for both accumulated and the current year's depreciation, which has not been charged to the profit and loss account for want of profit. The free availability of these free reserves to the shareholders creates problems for the bank. While calculating the net worth of the company, the lender takes into account the free reserves and considers them as indicating the financial strength of the company. That is, the lender includes them in the capital structure of the company. But all his calculations of the financial viability of the company may go astray if the company declares a dividend out of the reserves immediately after getting the loan. There is no law which prohibits a company from doing so if the rate of dividend so declared (i) does not exceed the average of the rates during the last five years, or 10 per cent of its paid-up capital, whichever is less; and (ii) the amount drawn from the reserves does not exceed one-tenth of the paid-up capital and free reserves and the balance of reserves after such a drawal does not fall below 15 per cent of its paid-up capital. A lender may look foolish in the face of such an about-turn by unethical directors.

Besides, under the Companies Act, a company cannot borrow more than its paid-up capital and free reserves (except temporary loans) unless this is approved by the shareholders at a general meeting. That is, contracting of loans by the board of directors beyond the aggregate amount of paid-up capital and free reserves is void not only to the company, but also to the lender, unless it is approved at the general meeting. Directors may hold up a dividend payment to show an increase in the reserves to augment borrowing power. Once the loan is availed of, they may subsequently declare a dividend (which may be readily approved by the shareholders). In order to prevent such an awkward situation, a bank or financial institution may require the company to give an undertaking to the effect that during the currency of the loan it will not declare dividend except out of current profits only. How far such an undertaking has the force of law is doubtful. It is advisable, therefore, to ask the company to capitalise a portion of the free reserves before disbursing a loan, subject however, to the restrictions mentioned below.

BONUS SHARES

Capitalisation of free reserves may be made by issuing of bonus shares. A banker always prefers this. But issue of bonus shares is not that easy. As per SEBI guidelines, a company has to fulfil the following conditions, before declaring a bonus issue:

1. A company cannot issue any bonus shares if any of its shares remain partly paid.
2. Bonus issue is permitted only out of free reserves created from genuine profits alone, or from the share premium amount collected in cash. A capital reserve created by revaluation of fixed assets, where there is no accrual of cash, cannot be capitalised.
3. A company cannot make a bonus issue in lieu of dividend.
4. No bonus issue can be made within 12 months of any public/rights issue.
5. No bonus issue shall be made, which will dilute the value or rights of the holders of debentures, convertible fully or partly.

6. Consequent to the issue of bonus shares, if the subscribed and paid-up capital exceeds the authorised share capital, the company must increase its authorised capital with the approval of the general body.

7. A company cannot make a bonus issue if it has defaulted in payment of interest or principal with respect to fixed deposits and debentures, which are due for redemption, and statutory dues of the employees, such as contributions to the provident fund, gratuity and bonus.

8. The issue of bonus shares must be approved by the general body meeting of the company. The board of directors must indicate in that meeting the management's intention regarding the rate of dividend in the year immediately following the bonus issue.

CAPITAL RESERVE

Revaluation reserve coming under this category is not a free reserve, hence, not available for distribution to shareholders as dividend. It is also not taken into consideration for calculating borrowing rights of a company or for computation of residual reserves in case of a bonus issue.

Revaluation of Assets

Capital reserve may be created by revaluation of fixed assets. Current assets may also be revalued, but that is not generally resorted to for creating a capital reserve.

The historical accounting system has been under fire for quite some time, because in times of fast-changing price levels as they are today, the affairs of a firm are not truly represented if assets and liabilities are shown at their historical costs, that is, at the price at which these were acquired in the past. However, this concept has yet to gain ground in our country. The cardinal principles of inflation accounting suggest that once started, it has to be followed consistently, to avoid confusion in the minds of shareholders and analysts. Alternatively, revalued items of assets and liabilities should be shown simultaneously with their historical costs.

A company may also desire to revalue its fixed assets for the ostensible reason that they have gone up in value substantially over the years and hence, the business is now worth more than what is shown in the balance sheet. The argument is that by charging depreciation, some of the assets might have been reduced almost to a value of nil, while their market value is now more than the price paid even at the time of purchase. This may be a good argument, but underneath it there is hidden, the gone-concern approach. Unless the company is on sale, or there is conversion of a proprietorship or partnership firm to a limited company, no tangible gain is achieved, except a 'face-lifting' of the company.

A banker receiving a revalued balance sheet must, therefore, be very careful. It is necessary for him to go into the methods of revaluation adopted by the company. If the company revalues its plant and machinery upward, a banker should be doubly cautious because fast technological developments affects the saleability, and hence the real value much more than the changing price level. A piece of machinery purchased five years before may not have any market at all, because a more efficient machine at a cheaper cost might have already come to the market making the old machine obsolete and unsaleable.

Land, and to some extent buildings, have really gone up in value very sharply in recent times. Technological innovations do not generally affect the value of land negatively. There is nothing wrong, therefore, in revaluing this item of fixed assets to reflect its true value in the balance sheet. In fact, a banker while appraising a credit proposal of a somewhat large company, may like to adopt a gone-concern approach to know the real net worth of the business for the purpose of assessing the risk involved in the event of its winding up.[10]

Revaluation of assets, however, does not enhance either the operating or the financial viability of a business. It only enhances its apparent credibility. There is no net inflow of resources due to revaluation. This is the reason why any profit arising out of a revaluation of assets is transferred to the capital reserve, and is not allowed to be distributed to shareholders either in the form of dividend or bonus shares. All these make a banker uneasy when he sees revaluation reserves in the balance sheet of a borrowing company. He is necessarily put on enquiry as to what prompted the company in the first place to revalue its assets.

Redemption Reserves

Capital reserve is also created for redemption of preference shares by transference from profit or from free revenue reserves. This reserve is not available to shareholders till the redemption of preference capital. But once the redemption is made, the reserve takes the place of redeemed capital and can be capitalised by issuing bonus shares.

Capital reserve is also created from out of any profit realised from the sale of assets at a price more than their book value.

Capital subsidies received from the government for export promotions, environmental projects, backward area development, bio-tech parks, and other industrial area development are treated as capital reserve. These are in fact part

---

[10] For this reason, it is desirable to calculate two sets of net worth, one with the revaluation reserve, and the other without it. Similarly, two sets of debt–equity ratio should also be calculated to put a clear financial picture before the decision maker.

of the paid-up capital 'contributed' as if by the government.

Tests to be Applied

There may be other types of capital reserves, which we are not taking up for discussion, but a banker is advised to apply the following tests to distinguish between revenue and capital reserves and their evaluation for purposes of credit appraisal:

- A reserve arising out of profit, which is not for any specific purpose is called a free reserve; and a reserve arising out of capital transactions or from profit, but for the purpose of a future designated capital transaction is denoted as a capital reserve.
- Unless there is an inflow of genuine funds into the business, a capital reserve does not enhance the financial strength of a firm.
- A tied capital reserve, such as capital redemption reserve, should not be taken into consideration for computing the capital structure of a company, if the redemption is due in the year for which a credit proposal is being considered, because it may amount to double counting.

Banker's Viewpoint

Before concluding on reserves, we want to emphasise that any reserve created out of profits or from *cash* (*assets*) received in the business (share premium account), by whatever name it is called (revenue reserve, free reserve, or capital reserve), strengthens the financial position of the business, or in other words, increases its net worth. This applies to the preference share redemption reserve also, because even if it is a capital reserve, the fund remains in the business in some form of assets until the capital is redeemed. When it is so redeemed the capital redemption reserve replaces the preference capital redeemed, and reduces the net worth to the extent of redemption. Some accountants do not want to include anything in the net worth which is not a free reserve, but a banker should not restrict himself to this narrow concept, and apply the broad test mentioned earlier.

Sinking Fund

The position is somewhat different in the case of a sinking fund. This fund is created from out of profit either for redemption of debentures or for replacement of assets (similar to that of a depreciation fund). In the former case, it is appropriated from profit, and in the latter, it is a charge on profit as depreciation.

The amount of a sinking fund is generally invested outside the business in gilt-edged securities. Even the interest received on such investments is similarly invested. On redemption of debentures, the sinking fund is transferred to the general reserve. But in case it is created for replacement of assets, the fund is transferred to the asset account (which was being shown at original cost in all the years) on its disposal, and the investment is realised for buying a new asset.

Should It form Part of Net Worth?

The question that now arises is whether a sinking fund for redemption of debentures should form a part of the net worth of the business. If we consider net worth as all tangible assets less all outside liabilities of the business, then a sinking fund investment, being an asset, will be automatically included in net worth. This, on the other hand, means that after deducting all outside liabilities, including debentures (for which the sinking fund is created), what is left as net worth is composed of share capital, other reserves, and the sinking fund. The net worth of a business does not change after the redemption of debentures. This is the reason why after the redemption of debentures from the proceeds of

the sinking fund investment, the sinking fund account is transferred to the general reserve. It is doubtful, however, whether this general reserve is a free reserve, and hence available for distribution as dividend. Still a banker should insist on its early capitalisation by issue of bonus shares.

In the case of a sinking fund for replacement of assets, the position is different. The fund may appear under liabilities in the balance sheet, while the asset for which it is created should be shown at full cost on the other side of the balance sheet. A sinking fund investment will also similarly appear as an asset. At the time of replacement of the designated asset, the sinking fund is transferred (credited) to the asset account, and the sinking fund investment is realised to buy a new machine. The net effect of all these transactions is the reduction of net worth to the extent of the amount of the sinking fund transferred to the asset account. This is in contrast to the treatment of a sinking fund created for the redemption of debentures. The latter is part of net worth, while the former is not. This is so because a sinking fund for replacement of assets is nothing but accumulated depreciation (which is a charge to the profit and loss account), reducing the value of assets, hence the net worth. If the asset is shown at full cost less the sinking fund, there would have been no confusion. However, if in addition to charging depreciation in the normal course, a separate sinking fund is created by appropriation of profit, then it would be part of the net worth.

DEBENTURES

Debenture is an acknowledgement of debt. A bond is also a debenture.

Companies may raise long-term loans from the capital market by issuing debentures, generally for financing long-term assets, but sometimes also for financing a portion of current assets. As per the stock exchange guidelines, the face value of a debenture shall be Rs 100. With effect from

1 August 1991 interest rate on debentures has been deregulated.

While making a debenture issue, public limited companies adopt almost the same procedure as they do for making a capital issue. A company issuing debentures, whether non-convertible or convertible (discussed later), must obtain a credit rating at least from one approved credit rating agency and disclose the rating in the prospectus. If the rating is obtained from more than one agency, all such ratings are to be disclosed.

Debentures can also be issued through private placement. A private limited company cannot make an invitation to the public by a prospectus for taking debentures, although it is entitled to issue debentures to any number of persons through private deals. Debentures are tradable in the market like the shares of the company. A debenture holder is, therefore, not dependent upon the company to realise his money. This adds attractiveness to debentures.

However, the marketability of debentures is dependent upon the ability of the company to pay interest regularly on the due dates. The auditor of a company is under legal obligation to report whether the company has defaulted in payment of dues to debenture holders along with the amount and period of such default. If the company skips interest payments in any year, its debentures lose marketability immediately, and the company also loses its credibility to make further issues of debenture in the future. This creates a problem for the company, which may try to pass it over to its banker. This is a ticklish situation. A bank is not supposed to finance interest payments, but this is a special situation. Stoppage of interest payments may prejudice the company's position against its present debenture holders as well as future subscribers. Debenture holders whose interest payment has been refused may also bring a suit against the company or enforce securities charged to them. All these actions and the dangerous possibilities inherent in them may ultimately prejudice a bank's finance already blocked in the company. A banker should, therefore, consider all these aspects and take a pragmatic view of the situation.

Interest on debentures has a bearing on the market rate, but it is usually less than the rate charged by commercial banks and financial institutions. Lending institutions should, therefore, insist on companies financing a part of their projects through debenture issues. It is also a safe method of financing, because so long as the annual payments due to the debenture holders are not in arrears, they cannot interfere with the business of the company, because, at present, debenture holders do not have any voting rights.

Secured and Unsecured Debentures

There is nothing in law against a company issuing unsecured debentures. However, unsecured debentures issued to the public other than companies are treated as public deposits and governed by rules made thereunder. When these are issued to companies and banks/financial institutions these are treated as inter-corporate deposits and loans respectively and are excluded from the definition of public deposits.

Secured debentures are secured by a charge on a company's assets whether present or future. Besides tangible assets, charge can be created on the following:

1. Uncalled share capital.
2. Calls made but not paid.
3. A share in a ship.
4. Goodwill, patent or license under a patent, trademark, copyright, and license under a copyright.

A charge may be in the form of a fixed charge on fixed assets, or a fixed and floating charge on future fixed or floating assets. The latter is an omnibus charge leaving almost nothing to a company to offer for obtaining further loans. A banker advancing to such a company can only have a secondary charge on the assets of the company, which, of course, is not a good security. A *pari passu* charge is a via media between the two extreme situations, but one that requires the previous consent of debenture holders, which is not easy to come by. In case of a fixed charge a company can deal with the assets in the ordinary course of business, but always subject to the charge. In case of a floating charge, however, the company can deal with the assets freely until the charge is crystallised. A fixed charge relates to a specific asset, while a floating charge does not fasten on any specific property but covers the whole of the company's property, whether it is subject to a fixed charge or not. A floating charge is, therefore, an equitable charge and remains dormant until the company ceases to be a 'going concern', or until the person in whose favour the charge is created intervenes on the violation of the terms of agreement of the loan. This is similar to banks taking hypothecation of the assets of a company as security against advances granted by them. In none of the cases (both fixed and floating), however, creditors (whether debenture holders, banks, or suppliers of goods and services) do not normally have any right of possession, except in case of a pledge where goods are directly taken under custody.

Redemption

Debentures are generally redeemable after a period of time specified in the debenture certificate. Redemption may be at par, at a discount, or at a premium. Redemption of debentures *should* be out of profit only. But debentures have to be redeemed even if there are no profits. Hence, unless a company has built up sufficient reserves out of profit and has also arranged for liquid resources, it would be difficult to meet the redemption in due time. For this purpose, a debenture redemption reserve (DRR) has to be created from out of the profit for all redeemable debentures with maturity periods of over 18 months. For manufacturing and infrastructure companies, the minimum DRR should be 50 per cent of the value of debentures issued through a public issue and 25 per cent for privately placed debentures. If sufficient reserve is built up but liquid resources are not available at the time of redemption, then banks or financial institutions may come to help by taking over the debenture liability of a company. This question should be dealt with in the same manner as in the case of redemption of the preference share capital discussed earlier. If a bank or financial institution decides to help a company redeem debentures, it can very well step into the shoes of the debenture holders, with all their rights and securities, by getting the same debentures issued to them. It may be pointed out here that debentures on redemption are not cancelled automatically; the company can reissue them if permitted by the Articles of Association.

Security against Loans

Banks and financial institutions may also accept debentures as collateral security against overdrafts granted to companies. This is good security because debentures are marketables that can be sold in case of necessity without resorting to any legal formalities. Besides, since debentures are covered by a strong security in the form of fixed or floating charges on the assets of the company, banks also enjoy this strength of security. Debentures lodged by a company with a bank as securities for advances granted in a current/cash credit account are not deemed to have been redeemed even when the account shows a credit balance. They continue to be alive until the company takes a decision to cancel them.

Irredeemable Debentures

Companies can issue perpetual debentures, irredeemable or redeemable only on the happening of a distant contingency. It is difficult to raise money on perpetual debentures, except from friends and relatives of major shareholders. In that case, they are simply part of the capital structure of the company.

Convertible Debentures

When the terms of issue so permit, debentures can be converted into shares, either partly or wholly. Such debentures are called convertible debentures. This was originally popularised by the International Financial Corporation for reconstruction of war-torn economies of Europe. Since then convertible debentures have gained popularity throughout the world, including in India. Debenture holders are given an option to convert a part or whole of the amount of debentures into equity shares after a period. This option is very attractive when a company is progressing and working profitably. Conversion may be at a premium, but it cannot be at a discount of the face value of shares unless previous permission of the government is obtained. In case of both convertible debentures conversion on or after 18 months shall be at the option of investors; if the period is less than 18 months conversion is compulsory.

Conversion is permitted only if the terms of issue so provide. But in case of any loan given to a company by the government or by any institution designated by the government, either by subscribing to debentures or by a term loan, then the government has the power to convert the debentures or loans into the shares of the company, even if the terms of the issue do not provide for such a conversion. Debentures can also be issued to public financial institutions (PFIs) and scheduled commercial banks (except cooperative banks, regional rural banks, and foreign banks) to be convertible to shares at the option of such PFIs and banks.

Companies can issue debentures of maturity of 18 months or less. This type of debenture is exempt from the requirements of the appointment of trustees and the creation of a debenture redemption reserve. This has opened up an important avenue for companies to access the short- and medium-term capital markets for their short-term fund requirements. It has lesser hassles as compared to other forms of debentures. The cost of raising and servicing the debentures is also low. This instrument stands somewhere between bank overdrafts and commercial paper.

Naked Debentures

The above relaxation has paved the way for issuing naked or unsecured debentures. As the name suggests, these debentures are issued without any charge on the assets of the company. In reality, these debentures are equivalent to fixed deposits. The rights of debenture holders do not go beyond those of ordinary unsecured creditors.

Roll over of Partly-non-convertible Debentures

Companies are permitted to roll over non-convertible debentures or the non-convertible portion of partly convertible debentures, with or without change in the interest rate, with the consent of individual debenture holders. Within a period of six months before the roll over, the company must obtain a fresh credit rating from an approved agency and execute a fresh trust deed. There is, however, no need to create fresh security if the existing trust deed or the securities document provide for continuation of the security until the redemption of debentures.

TERM LOAN

This is distinguished from debentures (which are a long-term liability of a special class) and also from a short-term loan, which is classified under current liabilities. Here we discuss term loans obtained from banks, financial institutions, friends, relatives, directors, and partners.

Repayment Problems

Generally, the repayment of a term loan is spread over a longer period of time. A loose distinction is sometimes made between medium- and long-term loans. In case of the former, the repayment period is more than three years but less than five years, and in case of the latter, it is five years and more. A question often pesters the mind of a credit appraiser at the time of calculating the long-term resources of a business as to what maturity period of term loans should come under this head. One way of going about it is to exclude all loans repayable within one year from the total loan fund, and treat the former as well as all instalments falling due for repayment of term loans of longer maturity (including debentures) within the year as current liabilities. This is a sound principle of credit appraisal, because it enables a banker to estimate the net cash outflow of the business in a particular year. It may, however, create some confusion, which should be cleared at this stage. Normally, current liability is also treated as a source of funds because of its average stability at any point of time through continuous liquidation and almost simultaneous acquisition. This stability enables it to partly take care of the funding of current assets, which are also acquired and disposed of continuously in the same manner, and therefore, imparts the same dynamic stability. But debentures or instalments of term loans which fall due in a particular year are nothing but long-term funds, transferred to the current liability by a mere book adjustment. They do not have the character and dynamic stability of a current liability arising out of the normal working of the business. The repayment will, of course, entail a definite outflow of cash, which will reduce current assets simultaneously with the reduction of this 'current liability'. However, if this part of current liabilities is also deducted from current assets along with other current liabilities to determine the working capital gap, and hence bank finance, as was originally held by the RBI, a borrower would always get a lesser amount of working capital finance from a bank, which would make it difficult for him to pay the proposed instalments. The RBI, after prolonged parleys with the industry and commerce, finally agreed to delete this item from the current liabilities while calculating permissible bank finance.[11] A banker is, however, required to see that sufficient arrangement is made by a borrower to discharge annual debt service obligations and that working capital finance is not utilised to meet these long-term obligations.

Purpose

Next comes the purpose. A term loan or deferred credit is generally contracted to acquire long-term assets. This is quite logical. Lending institutions would also not lend on a long-term basis for any purpose other than for acquisition of fixed assets. Without going into the details of the principles of term lending[12] at this stage we should mention that while matching a fixed asset against a term loan, an appraiser must see that the margin between the two has been financed from the shareholders fund only and not from any other long-term loan fund, including debentures, to ensure promoters' stake in every asset creation.

A long-term loan may also be contracted for financing a part of the working capital. In fact,

[11] See Chapter 12 for a full consideration of this item in credit appraisal of a proposal for working capital finance.

[12] Discussed in Chapters 17 and 18.

sound principles of lending require that a portion of the working capital requirement should be financed from long-term resources. Banks also insist on this requirement. We have already discussed the raising of working capital loans by issuing some special types of debentures. Directors, proprietors, or partners also give loans to the business, which are unsecured in nature. Normally, no repayment period is envisaged in the latter type of loans, and hence they can be bracketed under long-term loans. These loans are generally given for working capital purposes. The directors or proprietors may not like to put in more stake in the firm by way of equity capital, and therefore, they put funds in the form of a loan, with the hope that they will withdraw the loan amount when the financial condition of the business improves. When a banker finds such types of loans in the books or account of a business, he normally asks the directors or proprietors to give an undertaking that they will not call back their loans until a bank's advance is liquidated. This is not a very good solution, because bankers may not have any direct control over the observance of the undertaking. A better solution is to get them capitalised. There is no reason why the directors or proprietors would object to this proposal, because if they really want to do business and make an earning out of it, they should not feel shy of increasing their real stake in the business, particularly when a bank is intending to have no smaller a stake in their business.

LOANS FROM FRIENDS AND RELATIVES

Sometimes, however, loans appear in the names of friends and relatives. This is a very tricky item. Often this may not be anything but concealed profit shown in this manner to avoid taxes. A banker often gets perplexed when he finds that an apparently thriving business with high goodwill in the market is showing an exceedingly low rate of profit. He may be tempted to ask that if the return on investment is so low—at times, much below the rate available on bank deposits—it is advisable to wind up the business and invest the capital in fixed deposits with a bank to earn better and safer returns with much less trouble. But if he looks at the liability side of the balance sheet, he may discover that loans from friends and relatives are consistently on the increase. This may be nothing but concealed profit brought into the books in a clandestine manner. Whether a bank should insist on a full disclosure in the 'national interest' is a doubtful question, because there is a separate agency to take care of this, and if an entrepreneur produces an income tax clearance certificate, it may not be possible or desirable to go further in the matter. A bank's concern in this case is to ensure that these loans remain in the business, even with interest. A meaningful discussion with the proprietor(s) will enable a bank to explore the possibility of converting at least a portion of these 'loans' to capital. If this is not possible, then the only way left is to obtain written undertakings addressed to a bank from these friends and relatives to the effect that they would not withdraw their funds from the business so long as a bank's advance remains unpaid. The binding force of such an undertaking is, however, doubtful as mentioned earlier, but such undertakings are found to be generally honoured.

LOANS FROM SUBSIDIARIES

Loans may also be in the names of subsidiary, associate, or principal firms. These loans may be genuine advances made to firms to tide away financial stringency of the business, or the undisclosed profit of either of the firms arising out of apparently genuine business transactions between the two firms. A banker should view these items in the same manner as discussed in the earlier paragraphs.[13]

MODERN FINANCIAL INSTRUMENTS

One of the main objectives of financial liberalisation is enlarging the spread as well as the depth of the financial markets. While the number of varied types of financial instruments increases the spread of the financial market, the volume of transactions at finer two-way quotes deepens the market.

In response to liberalisation, a number of new debt instruments are coming to the market, and more are expected to come in the near future. In what follows, we describe a number of such instruments, some of which have already made their appearance, while some are likely to come later.

Zero Coupon Debentures/Bonds

These are sold at a discount on the nominal or face value of the bonds. On maturity, which generally varies between five and 12 years, the debentures or bonds are redeemed at par value. A variation of this, namely zero coupon convertible bonds, were first issued by Mahindra and Mahindra Limited. As in such types of instruments investors are not entitled to interest payments, the conversion price is suitably adjusted to take care of the interest loss.

This type of bond is very suitable for new project financing. The advantage to an entrepreneur is that there is no debt-servicing burden during the gestation period of the project. The beginning of the redemption, or the conversion period, can be planned in such a manner so that the project can pay for itself.

These debt instruments are very attractive to investors at a time of falling interest rates in the economy. As in the case of convertible bonds the

[13] See also Chapter 12 for its treatment under 'Classification of Current Assets and Liabilities'.

interest is only notional, it is not subject to tax. These instruments are especially beneficial for investors in high tax brackets.

Partly Convertible/Non-convertible Debentures with Buy-back Arrangements

The non-convertible portion of debentures (popularly known as 'khokha') can be bought back by financial institutions, including banks and other financial services companies at a discount on the face value. As per SEBI guidelines, buy-back of 'khokha' has to be made on a spot delivery basis, and the procedure for buy-back and its tradability should be disclosed in the offer document.

A partly convertible debenture without a buy-back arrangement is often disadvantageous to the issuing company because it may have to offer a fairly high coupon rate, while pricing equity at a steep discount. As against this, a debenture with a buy-back option provides greater liquidity at a lower cost. Presently, a good company with a high credit rating can access funds at 8 per cent per annum, which is less than the average coupon rate of the market. There is, however, the problem of maturity mismatch due to the prescribed lock-in periods. The problem can be largely resolved by broad basing the issue through the retail route.

Convertible Reset Debentures

This is a hybrid of convertible debentures with a provision for upward interest rate adjustment, typically effective several years after issuance. A company is required to reset the coupon rate high enough to give the debentures a market value at least equal to their face or par value. The objective of the reset is to compensate the bond holder for any credit deterioration. The reset may also be used by the company to refinance, or perhaps, to force conversion. The latter can be ensured by incorporating a mandatory provision in the debenture contract requiring the bond holder to buy sufficient shares of the company to retire the debt in full at its scheduled maturity date.

Deep-discount Bonds

These bonds are sold at a large discount on their par value. The maturity period may vary between 5 years to 25 years. The Industrial Development Bank of India came out with such an issue in 1992 on an unsecured basis. The success of this issue encouraged other national-level financial institutions to join the league.

This is similar to the zero coupon bond as there is no interest payment during the gestation period of the project. In some cases, investors are given an option to withdraw a pre-determined amount on the expiry of certain prescribed periods after a minimum lock-in period ranging between 3 and 5 years from the date of allotment. The issuer can also have a similar option of retiring the bond before maturity after the lapse of a certain period at a pre-determined value.

Investors prefer this instrument when the market expects declining rates of interest. The instrument is subject to the long-term capital gains tax.

Secured Premium Notes (SPN)

These instruments are sold at their face value, but do not carry any interest. These are redeemed in several instalments at a premium over their face value. The premium amount is distributed equally over the period of maturity of individual instalments.

A variation of this instrument carries a detachable warrant, which entitles an investor to claim allotment of a certain number of shares for cash at a certain price. This right is exercisable by the holder after a prescribed period.

These instruments are secured by a mortgage of immovable properties of the company. TISCO Limited first issued these instruments to its shareholders in 1992.

This mode of raising finance is advantageous to a company because during the initial years of the project there is no outflow of funds due to interest payments. A company issuing this instrument can plan the outflows commensurate with the inflows of the project. From an investor's point of view, besides the attraction of buying shares of the company through detachable warrants, this instrument being tradable provides easy liquidity.

Floating Rate Notes (FRN)

These instruments are issued with a fixed principal sum having a long or even indefinite life. The interest rate is set at a fixed margin over a reference rate. This is also an excellent interest-rate-swap instrument used widely in developed financial markets.

The floating rate envisaged in this type of instrument has the advantage of insulating both the issuer and the investor against interest rate movements. A variation of FRN is called the drop-lock floating rate note, which allows an investor additional protection by converting the FRN into a fixed-rate note when the reference rate drops below a pre-set trigger rate.

Although FRNs are very popular in American and European markets, in India these are yet to take off because of the absence of a true reference rate like LIBOR, and the investors' general preference for high fixed interest rates for long-term instruments.

Reverse Floating Rate Note

It is a very popular floating rate note in western financial markets. Here, the rate of interest *increases* as the market floating rate declines, and *falls* when the market floating rate rises. Typically, the rate paid on the note is set by doubling the appropriate fixed rate at the time the note is issued, and subtracting the floating reference index rate for each payment period from the doubled fixed rate. This note is also called a bull floater, bull floating rate note, or inverse floater.

Investors who desire higher current yields than are currently available in the short-term rate market, or who expect floating rates to remain low are the principal buyers of these notes. They, however, sacrifice some of the potential increase in future floating rates.

A variation of this note, called a leveraged reverse floating rate note, multiplies the fixed rate by three or four, and subtracts the floating rate multiplied by two or three from the fixed rate multiple. This provides investors with even greater inverse exposure to fluctuations in interest rates.

Contingent Takedown Option Bonds

These are debt instruments with debt warrants popularly known as 'kicker', which entitle the holder to invest in additional debt instruments on the same terms. This acts as an incentive to investors at a time of falling interest rates, to hold debt at higher than the market rate.

Deferred Coupon Bond

This instrument is becoming popular in India. It envisages no interest payment for an initial fixed period, and thereafter it pays interest at a relatively high rate for the remainder of the life of the instrument. This is also known as a stepped coupon bond. This instrument allows the issuing company to link the stepped up interest payment with the increased level of cash flows of the project after the initial take off. This also provides investors a much higher rate of return as compensation for the waiting time.

Extendable Notes

There are two types of these bonds:

(a) An open-ended debt instrument where rates of interest are re-set every few years

based on negotiations between the issuer and the investor. At each renegotiation date the investor has the option to put the bond back to the issuer if the new rate proposed by the issuer is unacceptable to him.

(b) The second is a combination of a traditional bond and an embedded option, which gives the issuer (or less frequently the investor) the right to call or to extend the maturity of the note at a pre-specified interest rate.

These bonds are generally issued for 10 years with the flexibility of reviewing the interest rate every two years. This instrument encourages long-term investor participation because of the periodical review of interest rates.

Revenue Bonds

These bonds are secured against a project's cash flows. They are suitable for specialised projects with more or less assured cash flows like telecom or power projects. Investors must have a high level of confidence in both the project and its sponsors.

Tax Free Bonds

In India, public sector units engaged in infrastructural activities like power, telecom, railways, and housing used to issue these bonds. Typical interest rates ranged between 9 and 10.5 per cent. These bonds are on their way out, except perhaps for government sponsored infrastructure projects, as they disturb the interest rate structure of the market.

CONCLUDING REMARKS

Long-term liabilities provide stability to the capital structure of a business, the most important among them being equity, which is considered as the ultimate risk capital to absorb shocks. What the optimal combination of debt and equity should be is a question that has been addressed by finance managers for long without a proper solution.

As will be explained in Chapters 11 and 16, low equity with high debt makes the capital structure highly geared. Shareholders may like this because it provides higher returns per share, but a company remains vulnerable to takeover bids, which may not always be liked by a lender as it destabilises the management. Bankers would also not like a highly leveraged company because of its low shock absorption capacity. During a recession, debt holders of such companies suffer the most, but in a boom their position does not change much because of the contracted terms of most long-term debts. External liability holders are not expected to take more than the normal risk, hence they must look for a capital structure which insulates them against more than the normal ups and downs of the fortunes of the borrowing company.

In India, debt–equity ratios remained very high as in any controlled economy. But as the country moves towards a market-driven economy, the risk-proneness of the business rises. The corporate sector all over the world has learnt through many a disaster that it is ultimately the equity base that can steer a company out of a crisis. The present move is towards enlarging the capital base of the corporate sector. Indian companies and their bankers should take a cue from what is happening around the world as the country moves more towards a market controlled economy.

9 Current Liabilities

INTRODUCTION

Current liabilities originate from current or short-term promises made to non-owners of a business, namely suppliers of goods and services, including suppliers of short-term cash. As current assets originate similarly, but on the other side of the balance sheet, it is normally expected that current liabilities are to be paid from out of current assets.

ORIGINATION

Besides actual dated transactions, certain liabilities grow continuously and naturally with the passage of time from out of standard promises made in the course of business, or implicit promises made by the operation of law. For example, interest payable, tax payable, and rates payable all accumulate with the passage of time. It is difficult to pinpoint at which moment an exchange has taken place giving rise to a promise and a corresponding liability. These promises, implicit or otherwise, are contracted continuously, giving rise to accrued liability.

Continuous exchanges are implicitly made with the passage of time or operation of law. Discrete exchanges occur instantaneously. Liabilities are entered as they occur, like creditors for purchase of goods. They do not naturally occur, but

are provided for as liabilities, like costs of services accrued. Generally, only service exchanges are continuous and give rise to accrued liabilities. Exchange of goods and cash settlements are discrete that give rise to trade creditors.

DANGER OF OVERTRADING

We have already talked about the dynamic stability of current liabilities and current assets. Under the fund concept, current liabilities finance a portion of current assets, that is, they provide funds to carry the working assets. One may thus be tempted to raise current liabilities to such an extent as to carry the entire volume of current assets. Let us look at it from another angle. Current liabilities do provide funds but they have to be paid (continuously) whenever they fall due for payment, to enable the business to have further credit in the market. Failure to honour commitments will not only destroy the goodwill of the business, but also bring the creditors tumbling at the door of the enterprise. It is necessary, therefore, to generate adequate liquid resources to pay up the creditors in due time, which is possible only when current assets are contracted in such a manner as to provide a continuous stream of realisation to meet the demand of creditors. *However, this sound principle of financial management is forgotten precisely at a time when the business is booming and its goodwill is soaring high.* The overenthusiastic entrepreneur tries to achieve too much by contracting too many liabilities to build up too high a level of current assets with too little of his own funds. He may already be on the wrong side of the borderline of genuine trade practices. In fact, he is overtrading. Any unexpected hitch in the smooth progress of production or sales, or delayed realisation of some of the current assets, will precipitate a crisis, because there is no margin of safety left between current assets and liabilities to meet the demand of creditors who may now be swarming in.

Safety Margin

This margin of safety is very important to avert a disaster. At any point of time, the level of current assets should be such as to completely meet all current liabilities on demand if there is some bottleneck in production, sales, or realisation. The latter condition requires a cushion of current assets over current liabilities, which can absorb shocks coming from both within and outside the business. Traditionally, financial analysts demanded that the level of current liabilities should not exceed half of the current assets. At one time, bankers also regarded this as an ideal condition. There was always a war between the bankers and the entrepreneurs in this respect, the former asking to set the ratio at the ideal level, with the latter wanting to bring it down as far as possible to take advantage of higher credit available in the market and making a quick profit while the going was good. Entrepreneurs were reluctant because this margin of safety, which is called the net working capital, is required to be financed from long-term sources. We shall elaborate on present-day norms for the current ratio later, but for the time being it should be remembered that any source of funds,

particularly current liabilities, should not be over utilised except at the risk of total disaster of the business.[1]

We now propose to discuss some important items of current liabilities.

Trade Creditors

Accounts Payable

Although all persons giving loans to a business or to whom the business owes money are creditors, the term accounts payable (or sundry creditors, as some people call them) applies specifically to suppliers of goods and services on credit. The length and quantum of credit available to a business is dependent on various factors. The most important factor is the goodwill of the business built over a long period by consistent honouring of commitments. As goodwill takes some time to build, a new business does not generally get credit in the market during the initial years of building up goodwill. This aspect should be borne in mind while appraising a proposal for a new business.

Monopoly versus Monopsony

When a business is a monopsonic buyer, it can command good credit by simply bullying the suppliers. But when a monopsonic buyer faces a monopoly supplier, the situation reaches an equilibrium, and no one can have an edge over the other. However, if the business is one of many in the market, but the supplier is enjoying a monopoly, or there are only a few suppliers, then

---

[1] While the danger of overtrading and the importance of a margin of safety must be emphasised, it should be pointed out that it is possible for a company enjoying both monopolistic and monopsonistic positions in the market to carry on business smoothly without any margin of safety, that is, zero net working capital. This is explained in Chapter 16.

it may not be possible to get any credit beyond the reasonable minimum.

A banker appraising a credit proposal should, therefore, examine the nature of raw materials required by the firm and the status of the business in the market to assess the length and quantum of credit available to the business for purchases. While discussing this aspect with an entrepreneur, a banker, almost always, is told that the unit has to give longer credit on sales than what it gets in the market for purchases. This experience is common to all bankers. One wonders who receives all this 'long credit'. Debtors of one unit are mostly creditors of other units, and hence there should be a balance between credit received and given by a borrower. This is the characteristic of a competitive economy. But when a borrower faces a monopsonic buyer or a monopoly seller, the balance is lost, as discussed earlier. However, at times, the fault may also lie with an entrepreneur. When easy credit is available from a bank, a borrower may not like to exert himself fully to obtain better credit terms from his suppliers.

Overtrading Again

On the other side of the coin lies the risk of overtrading. As indicated earlier, when the goodwill of the firm is soaring, or it is enjoying monopsonic buying power, or there is a glut of raw materials in the market forcing the suppliers to give long credit, an entrepreneur may be overenthusiastic about piling up stocks not warranted by the existing production level. He may simultaneously be tempted to give longer credit to the buyers of his products to increase market share, or become callous towards the realisation of debts (because raw materials are always available in the market on long credit). When, suddenly the market turns adverse or any bottleneck in production develops, the castle collapses in thirst of liquidity.

Need for Proper Synchronisation

The ideal condition is to ensure synchronisation of the maturity period of debtors and creditors. This is possible by the judicious contracting of creditors and debtors in such a manner that when the former fall due for payment, the latter get realised at or around that time. This being the standard, a banker should examine how close the business is towards this standard. If for genuine reasons average maturity periods of debtors are much longer than those of creditors; it is dangerous to allow a business to enlarge the volume of creditors. A high level of creditors with low maturity against a high volume of debtors with long maturity may threaten the very existence of the business. It is a case of assets–liabilities mismatch. *In such a situation a prudent banker should discourage an entrepreneur to increase the volume of creditors. He should finance the stocks directly. This important aspect is often forgotten by a banker in his desire to force an entrepreneur to obtain as much credit as available in the market, and seek as little as possible from a bank.*

A credit appraiser should call for the list of major creditors to find out the average maturity time, and compare it with that of debtors to make a judgement on the desirable level of creditors.

More or less the same judgement can be reached, though not with the same precision, by comparing creditors velocity with that of debtors. The former is computed by dividing it by the total level of debtors. If the creditors' velocity is very high (that is, shorter credit term or maturity period) and the debtors' velocity is very low (that is, longer credit term or maturity) a banker should delve into the reasons behind such a state of affairs. There may be one or more of the reasons mentioned earlier. But if it appears that the reasons are genuine and only the prevailing market conditions are reflected in these two ratios, a banker may finance the gap without forcing the business to increase the volume of creditors with shorter maturities. One thing is clear, therefore, that creditors' velocity cannot be considered in isolation; it has to be compared with the debtors' velocity to come to a decision. We elaborate further on this in Chapter 16 on Ratio Analysis.

Creditors include bills payable. The only difference is that a supplier draws bills containing the terms of credit on a buyer, which when accepted by the buyer become bills payable.

Accrued Liabilities

Under this head come expenses which have been contracted but not paid till the date of finalisation of the annual accounts. Accrued working expenses like salaries and wages are a charge to the profit and loss account, and hence debited as such and then carried over to the balance sheet as liabilities. These are very short-term liabilities, which are not expected to provide any funds for any *major assets* to be built. But they can take care of some of the assets of a similar short-term nature.

Accrued liabilities also include the dividend payable, proposed dividend, and taxation liabilities. These are almost immediately payable after the finalisation of the annual accounts. All these liabilities are also very short-term in nature though they have an almost perpetual periodical recurrence, and hence should be treated as such while assessing the working capital gap of a business. Similar is the case with prepaid expenses on the other side of the balance sheet.

Special Case

Liabilities may also accrue with respect to the capital expenditure made but not paid for. This happens mostly in the case of progress payment where jobs are certified as completed, but payment is yet to be made. Although this expenditure is due for acquiring fixed assets, which is shown as capital work-in-progress on the asset

side of the balance sheet, it is an immediate liability, which has to be paid from out of current assets, namely cash, hence this liability is shown under the head 'current liability'. However, this should not be confused with the funding of the expenditure. Since capital expenditure is meant for acquiring fixed assets, sound principles of lending suggest that funds should come from long-term sources and not from current liability. Whenever this type of accrued liability appears in the balance sheet of a firm, a banker should enquire about the arrangement made to liquidate it. Unless a long-term fund is contracted by the unit to meet this liability, it is desirable to hold back the sanction of working capital finance, because in the absence of the former, the unit may use up the latter to meet the pressing demand of the suppliers of fixed assets.

Provisions

The Indian Companies Act has defined provision as an amount written-off or retained by way of providing for depreciation, renewals, or diminution in the value of assets, or retained by way of providing for any known liability of which the amount cannot be determined precisely.

There are two aspects of this definition. The first calls for making a provision for future replacement of an asset, particularly fixed assets. This is nothing but savings made out of profit, for future requirements. So far as provisions constitute real savings, like depreciation which though is a charge for the usage of assets, they are similar to reserves from a financial viewpoint, and should necessarily be considered as part of the fund generated from operations.

The second calls for making a provision for meeting a liability for expenses, or to take care of a probable loss relating to a particular accounting year, which may, however, occur in the following year. It is nothing but a present charge which may be paid later. The fund created to provide for these expenses or losses, in fact, does not remain in the business for long.

Bad and Doubtful Debts

Provision for bad and doubtful debts is one such example. During the accounting year whenever certain debts become absolutely unrealisable, these may be charged to the profit and loss account directly. But if these debts relate to a past year, and the firm knew that these were going to be bad, then it should have provided for this eventuality in the profit and loss account of *that* year, without burdening the current year's profit. In the absence of such a provision, the firm must have taken a higher profit in the preceding year and, of course, paid taxes on it and distributed a higher dividend to shareholders, to which they were not entitled. It is essential, therefore, for a banker to see that adequate provisions for bad debts are made by an enterprise to prevent any unplanned outflow of funds. To this end, he should scrutinise the auditors report carefully.

DEPOSITS FROM CUSTOMERS AND PUBLIC

Security Deposits

A business may often require its dealers to keep a certain amount with it as a security deposit, calculated as a percentage of contracted or projected sales. Although the purpose behind taking such deposits is to take care of dealers' failures to pay for any instalment of delivery, the funds available from such deposits are akin to long-term funds, and can be used as such. It is preferable, however, to use them not for financing fixed assets, but for meeting a portion of the net working capital.

Fixed Deposits from Public

With the passage of the Companies (Amendment) Act, 1974 and subsequent Companies (Acceptance of Deposits) Rules 1975 as amended up to 2004 a non-banking company can also invite and accept deposits from the general public. This was primarily designed to help companies to meet a portion of their working capital requirements in the face of stringency of bank finance. This is also a cheap source of finance, because the rate of interest paid on such deposits, though higher than the rate paid by banks on their own deposits, is lower than the rate charged by banks on their working capital advances.

A company paying a consistently good rate of dividend and whose shares are quoted high in the market can make use of this avenue of profitably. As the principal aim of this scheme is to create a semi-permanent fund, the rules forbid acceptance of deposits repayable on demand, or earlier than six months.[2] In reality, however, deposits are generally accepted for at least 12 months, which go up to a permissible maximum of 36 months. If a company continues to show good results and pays dividend and interest regularly, depositors normally renew their deposits, unless the company itself decides otherwise. As these deposits are unsecured in nature, the goodwill of the company is very important to attract and retain such deposits.

However, no company can accept any amount of deposits and make its position vis-à-vis the depositors vulnerable. As per the rules, the maximum permissible limit of deposits is 10 per cent

---

[2] According to Indian Companies (Amendment) Act, 1988, if a company has failed to repay any deposit or part thereof in accordance with the terms and conditions of such deposit, the Company Law Board (since replaced by the Tribunal) may direct the company to make repayment of such deposit or part thereof forthwith, or within such time as may be specified in the order. The Companies Act was further amended in 1997, which provides that companies defaulting in payment of interest or repayment of principal amount of deposits will be debarred from raising further deposits until these defaults are remedied.

of a company's net worth that excludes accumulated losses, deferred revenue expenditure, and intangible assets.[3] The maximum rate of interest payable is 15 per cent per annum.

In order to ensure due repayment of deposits maturing in a given year, the rules at present demand that an amount equal to at least 15 per cent of the deposits falling due for repayment shall have to be deposited in a scheduled bank in a charge-free non-lien account, or invested in any unencumbered government or trust securities, or with HDFC limited.

A credit analyst may regard public deposits as a medium source of funds if it is taken for a period longer than one year, and is renewable. *However, it is not desirable to acquire fixed assets from this source.* It may create a problem of liquidity. Public deposits should be raised for financing a portion of current assets.

INTER-CORPORATE LOANS AND INVESTMENTS

This is an extension of the fixed deposit market on the short-term side, generally restricted among corporate players. Loans and investments include debentures and inter-corporate deposits (ICDs). The market provides both an inlet and outlet to short-term corporate funds. The Companies Act does not make any distinction between fixed deposits and inter-corporate deposits. The rules, which debar companies from raising further deposits if they default in payment of interest or repayment of the principal amount, are also applicable to inter-corporate deposits. Although ICDs are predominantly unsecured in nature, some companies are found to ask for collaterals if the amount is very large, or the borrowing company has a low credit standing in the market. The rate of interest in the ICD market is governed by the demand and supply of funds.

---

[3] For government companies the maximum limit is 35 per cent.

Inter-corporate loans and deposits are often bracketed with unsecured loans in the balance sheet of a company. A banker appraising a credit proposal of a company would ordinarily include it as a part of current liabilities, which would consequently have the effect of reducing the permissible bank finance. But he must enquire, at the same time, about the arrangement made by the company for repayment of the ICDs. Many a times, companies raise ICDs as a bridge loan against impending market issues, or against term loan commitments by financial institutions and banks. Failure of market issues, or the company's inability to finally launch the issue will ultimately devolve on the market, while the funds raised through ICDs might have already been invested in long-term assets, making it difficult for the company to pay up the ICDs on the due dates. A roll-over may just not be available, or if at all it would be at a high cost. Besides, it may send panic signals in the market.

It has been found that inter-corporate loans and investments are often used for diversion of funds. A banker should be very careful in this matter lest his working capital finance is diverted to other companies. The government has also risen to the occasion and made the following rules to check the diversion of funds:

1. Inter-corporate loans and investments shall include:
   i. Loans given to any corporate body
   ii. Giving any guarantee or providing security in connection with a loan made *by* any other person or *to* any body corporate (that is, loan given *to* a body corporate)
   iii. Giving any guarantee or providing security in connection with a loan made *to* any other person *by* a body corporate (that is, loan given *by* body corporate).

iv.   Acquiring by way of subscription, purchase, or otherwise the securities of any other body corporate.

2.   The overall limit for all these taken together cannot exceed 60 per cent of paid up capital and free reserves or 100 per cent of free reserves which ever is higher.

3.   The minimum interest shall not be less than the prevailing bank rate.

4.   The resolution of the board of directors authorising such loans and investments shall be *unanimous*. That is, a simple majority cannot pass it as in other cases.

BRIDGE LOANS

This is an interim finance obtained principally to bridge the gap between a capital or debt issue in the market, and the receipt of spendable money by the company issuing it, or to bridge the gap between the sanction of a term loan proposal by a financial institution or bank and the actual disbursement of the loan amount. This is also used, to a limited extent, to bridge the gap between entitlement of subsidies from the government and their actual receipt by the enterprise. The loan is purely temporary in nature. Its sole objective is to ensure that the project for which the money is being raised, is launched in time and according to plans, to avoid time and cost over-runs. In the case of capital and debt issues, spendable funds are available to the company after the lapse of considerable time spanning from one to four months, because of various legal formalities to be observed between the issue and the allotment. In the case of a term loan, it may just be that though the lending institution/bank has sanctioned the loan, it does not have enough funds at the moment to disburse the loan amount.

In situations like these, promoters have only three options to avoid time and cost over-runs:

first, to raise interim finance from the inter-corporate deposit market; second, to approach one or more non-banking finance companies (NBFCs); and the third, to ask a commercial bank to bridge the gap. In the first two cases there are problems of availability of sufficient funds, and even if they are available, the rate of interest is very high. However, till 1989 these two sources were meeting the demand of bridge loans to a large extent. But with the pace of industrial expansion gaining momentum due to the liberalisation of the economy, a large number of companies started entering the capital market or approaching term lending institutions. As a consequence the demand for bridge loans also rose. The Inter-Corporate Deposit Market or the NBFCs were just not capable of meeting the rising demand. Commercial banks had to come in in a big way from 1990–91 to bridge the temporary funds gap. The industry welcomed this because of the huge fund base of commercial banks and their lower rates of interest as compared to the other two sources. For banks also this source of investment appeared to be less risky and highly profitable. But industries did not behave by the rule book, and banks also failed to take required care and safeguards while sanctioning bridge loans, which resulted in a partial ban and stricter control imposed by the RBI, as we will see now.

Bridge Loan against Proceeds of Capital Issues/Market Borrowings

The RBI originally stipulated the following conditions for sanctioning bridge loans by commercial banks against public equity/debenture issues of private sector companies, and also against market borrowings of public sector undertakings:

1.   The public issue/market borrowings must have the approval of relevant public

authorities like the Company Law Board[4] and SEBI.

2. The extent of bridge loan sanctioned by an individual bank should not exceed 50 per cent of the issue/flotation and 75 per cent thereof if sanctioned jointly with other financial institutions.

3. The sanction is within the approval of the members of the consortium/financing bank, as the case may be.

4. The exposure is within the prudential norms laid down for exposure to individual groups of borrowers.

5. A bridge loan against a public issue must not devolve upon a bank through underwriting.

In addition to these terms and conditions governing bridge loans against market issues, the RBI also stipulated that: (a) banks should not extend bridge loans/interim finance for activities which are required to be legitimately met out of government resources or budgetary allocations, and (b) against amounts receivable from central/state governments by way of subsidies, refunds, reimbursements, and capital contributions except the subsidies receivable by the fertiliser industry under the normal retention price scheme (RPS) for periods up to 60 days. However, banks are allowed to grant interim finance to exporters against receivables from governments for exports (for example, duty drawback).

Originally, banks were not allowed to grant bridge loans/guarantees against commitments of other lending institutions. However, on the recommendations of the Standing Committee

[4] The Company Law Board (CLB) was dissolved by the Companies (Amendment) Act, 2002. The National Company Law Tribunal was formed in 2002 to take over the major functions of CLB; it started functioning from 2003.

for Coordination between banks and term lending institutions, the RBI revised its position in October 1995 and allowed banks to consider granting of bridge loans/interim finance against a commitment made by a financial institution and/or another bank only in cases where the lending institution faces a *temporary liquidity constraint*. This was subject to the compliance of the following conditions:

1. A bank extending bridge loan/interim finance must obtain prior approval of the other bank and/or financial institution which has sanctioned the term loan.

2. The bridge loan sanctioning bank must also obtain a commitment from the other bank and/or financial institution that the latter would directly remit the amount of the term loan to it at the time of disbursement.

3. The period of such bridge loan/interim finance should not exceed four months. Under no circumstances, extension of time should be allowed for repayment of bridge loans/interim finance.

4. A bank should ensure that the bridge loan/interim finance sanctioned and disbursed is utilised for the purpose for which the term loan has been sanctioned by the financial institution or the other bank.

A bridge loan against market issues of capital or debentures is beset with more problems than a bridge loan against a term loan sanctioned by another bank or financial institution. In the case of the latter, not only has another lending institution already made a full appraisal of the company and the project, the availability of funds to adjust the bridge loan is also more or less assured. But in case of a bridge loan against market issues, such a pre-appraisal may not be there if the company has not gone to a financial institution for raising a term loan in addition to capital issues. In cases like this, full appraisal of the project as well as the company promoting it should be made by a bank before granting the bridge loan. The lending decision should take on a worst-case-scenario approach, that is, if the market issue fails, whether a bank is prepared to fund the project on a full-term loan basis considering the creditworthiness of the project and a bank's own fund position. A banker must remember that if the market issue fails, the 50 per cent margin may not help. His vision should not be so clouded as to ignore the necessity of making a full appraisal of the proposal by looking at the list of well-known lead managers that the promoters have lined up. He should take a lesson from history that many 'best' issues have failed in spite of the 'best' lead managers. The arithmetic of a merchant banker is often different from that of a commercial banker.

When a full-scale appraisal is made as discussed earlier, and a bank is satisfied about the creditworthiness of the proposal and its bankability, there is nothing wrong in underwriting the issue besides granting a bridge loan (in fact, before underwriting an issue, a bank should always make a similar appraisal of the proposal, which is not being done by most banks, resulting in severe problems when unsubscribed issues devolve on them).

Unfortunately, during the post-liberalisation period, the spurt in capital and debt issues made all the parties forget the rules of the game, and the worst sufferers were commercial banks, who jumped on to the bandwagon with their bags full of bridge loans. The financial system was in chaos. The RBI, finding no other alternative, imposed a total ban on all bridge loans/interim finance by banks and financial institutions to all companies including finance companies from 17 April 1995. Later on, the ban on bridge loans against term loan

commitments by financial institution(s) or other bank(s) was withdrawn, as discussed earlier, but the ban continued against market issues. It was expected that when the financial market stabilised through the regulatory efforts of the SEBI, and commercial banks geared up their appraisal machinery, the RBI would withdraw the ban on granting bridge loans/interim finance against market issues also. However, the matter is now left to the boards of directors of commercial banks to formulate guidelines as part of their loan policies. Presently, bridge loans are sanctioned by banks generally to top rated borrowers against expected proceeds of equity issues, proceeds of non-convertible bonds, external commercial borrowings, global depository receipts, and foreign direct investments. Bridge loans serve a very important economic purpose in pacing the industrial growth of a country.

COMMERCIAL PAPER (CP)

Commercial paper as a short-term financial instrument, which originated in the US in the early nineteenth century. It gained popularity over the years and spread first to Canada and then to other financial markets of the world. The primary reason behind the popularity of CP was the credit restrictions imposed by commercial banks.

Although the CP markets of other countries were developed taking the US market as the model, some differences exist to take care of varying local conditions. For example, in Canada, Australia, the Netherlands, and Norway, no distinction is made between banking and non-banking companies for issuance of CPs. Similar is the case with the US. But in most other countries, including India, CPs cannot be issued by banking companies. In the United Kingdom, only the companies listed on the London Stock Exchange are entitled to issue CPs. Although in most countries the average maturity of CPs is about 30 days, in Canada CPs are issued for periods as short as seven days, and in France CPs can be issued for a period up to seven years. In India, CPs can now be issued for a maturity period between seven days and up to one year. In spite of the fact that there virtually exists no secondary market transaction for CPs in the US, the tremendous growth of the CP market in that country is due to banks coming in as guarantors by issuing letters of credit. In India, though secondary market transactions in CPs were on the rise, the market was not expanding as fast as it should because of prohibition on banks to offer any such guarantee. Earlier the RBI not only delinked the issue of CPs from working capital finance limits, it also withdrew the standby facilities hitherto being offered by commercial banks. However, the directive was moderated to a large extent in October 2000, as we will see later. It is true that CP must ultimately stand on its own feet in the marketplace and from that point of view the US position is questionable, but in India where the money market is yet to develop fully some support is necessary from the banking community for such an important money market instrument to explore its full potential.

Although the RBI considers CP a 'stand alone' product, the 2000 directive allows banks and financial institutions the flexibility to provide for a CP issue, and to offer credit enhancement by way of stand-by assistance/credit back stop facility. Banks are also allowed the flexibility to fix working capital limits duly taking into consideration the resources pattern of the company.

The CP market in India is restricted to blue-chip companies only. Although listing requirements have been withdrawn, this may ultimately not help the expansion of the market, because the credit enhancement facility available through the stand-by arrangement will no longer be available to not-so-good unlisted companies. Investors would not like to invest in the CPs issued by such companies.

In India, the CP market is of recent origin. The Working Group on the Money Market that was appointed in September 1986 under the Chairmanship of N. Vaghul to examine in detail the reform proposals contained in the Chakraborty Committee's report suggested, inter alia, the introduction of CPs in its report submitted in January 1987.

The CP was defined by the Vaghul Group as an *unsecured* promissory note negotiable by endorsement and delivery and sold directly by the issuers to investors or placed by the borrowers through merchant banks and security houses. The RBI has defined it simply as a privately placed unsecured money market instrument issued in the form of a promissory note.[5] As against a trade bill, the important feature of CP is that there is no self-liquidating trading transaction behind its issue. But it is not a 'kite' or accommodation bill, which generally records a fictitious commercial transaction, and hence is not above board.

It was expected that CP would ensure financial stability to the issuing commercial houses and discourage unhealthy practices of the inter-corporate credit market.

On the basis of the Vaghul Group's recommendations the RBI formulated and announced its scheme on CP in March 1989. The detailed guidelines were first issued in January 1990 by the RBI, which were subsequently modified to a large extent by various amendments to the extant guidelines.

Who can Issue Commercial Paper?

All non-banking companies, both financial and non-financial, including companies under the Foreign Exchange Management Act, primary

---

[5] RBI circular No. IECD.3/08.15.01/2000–2001 dated 10 October 2000. Available at http://rbidocs.rbi.org.in

and satellite dealers[6], and all-India financial institutions[7] are eligible to issue CPs. The objective of developing the CP market is to enable these companies to diversify their sources of short-term borrowings.

Eligibility Criteria

At present, a company can issue CPs only if it satisfies the following requirements:

1. Tangible net worth of not less than Rs 4 crore as per the latest audited balance sheet.
2. The issuing company must obtain a credit rating from approved credit rating agencies like the Credit Rating Information Services of India Limited (CRISIL), the Investment Information and Credit Rating Agency of India Limited (ICRA), Credit Analysis and Research Limited (CARE), and Fitch Ratings India Limited. The rating should be current and equivalent to the minimum P-2 of CRISIL, and it should not have fallen due for review at the time of issuing the CPs. While a rating agency can decide the validity period of the rating, it would have to closely monitor the rating assigned to the issuers vis-à-vis their track record at

---

[6] Primary dealers (PDs) regarded as merchant bankers to the government constitute the first tier of the government securities market. Satellite dealers (SDs) work in tandem with the PDs to form the second tier catering to the retail requirement of the market. PDs and SDs came up during 1994–96 to strengthen the market infrastructure and put in place an improvised and efficient secondary market for government securities.

[7] For financial institutions, issue of CPs together with term money borrowings, term deposits, certificates of deposit, and inter-corporate deposits should not exceed 100 per cent of their net owned funds.

regular intervals and make public the revisions in rating through their publications, and the website.

3. The issuing company must have been sanctioned a working capital limit by bank(s), financial institution(s), and the borrowal account of the company is classified as a standard asset by the financing bank(s)/institution(s).

Minimum and Maximum Period

The CPs shall be issued for maturities between seven days and less than a year from the date of issue. There will be no grace period for payment. Every issue of CP shall be treated as a fresh issue.

Denomination and Minimum Size of CP

The CPs may be issued in multiples of Rs 5 lakh (face value) and the minimum amount to be invested by a single investor in the primary market shall also be Rs 5 lakh. CPs may be issued on a single date or in parts on different dates within a period of two weeks from the date on which the issuer opens the issue for subscription. If the CPs are issued in parts on different dates, the maturity date will, however, be the same.

Mode of Issue and Discount Rate

CPs are issued in the form of usance promissory notes negotiable by endorsement and delivery or in dematerialised form through SEBI approved depositories. They are issued at such discount to the face value as may be determined by the company issuing the CPs. CPs will also be subject to payment of stamp duty as applicable.

Issue Expenses

All expenses (such as dealers' fees, rating agency fee, and other charges) for issue of CPs should be borne by the issuing company.

Investors in CP

CPs may be issued to any person or corporate body registered or incorporated in India (including banks and financial institutions), unincorporated bodies, non-resident Indians (NRIs), and foreign institutional investors (FIIs). In the case of FIIs, investment in CPs shall be within the limits set for their investments by the SEBI.

Procedure for Issue of CP

1. CPs can be issued only through an issuing and paying agent (IPA). A company intending to issue CPs shall appoint a scheduled bank as IPA to whom all documents pertaining to the placement of CPs should be submitted.

2. The IPA would scrutinise the documents, and on being satisfied that the eligibility criteria (credit rating etc.) and the terms and conditions for issue of CP are complied with by the company as per the rules, shall issue a certificate to that effect. All the original documents are to be held in the custody of the IPA.

3. The issuing company shall disclose to potential investors its financial position as per standard market practices.

4. The company thereafter makes arrangements for privately placing the issue within a maximum period of two weeks from the opening of the issue. Within three days from the date of completion of the issue, the IPA shall advise the RBI of the details of the CPs issued.

5. The initial investor in CPs shall pay the discounted value of the CPs by means of a crossed 'account payee' cheque to the account of the issuing company.

6. The issuer company then issues physical certificates to the investors or arranges for crediting the CPs to the depository accounts of individual investors.

Repayment of CP

On maturity of the CPs, the holder should present the instrument for payment to the issuing company. If there is a default in repayment of CP on due date, the IPA must immediately report it to the Reserve Bank of India.

Exemption from the Purview of Section 58 of the Companies Act, 1956

The central government has granted exemption to the issue of CPs from the provisions of Section 58A of the Companies Act, 1956 relating to public deposits.

Pricing of CP

While recommending the introduction of CP, the Vaghul Group observed that on the one hand, the CP market can provide highly-rated corporate borrowers with cheaper funds than they could obtain from banks, and on the other, it will allow institutional investors to earn higher rates of interest than they could get from banks. Besides bank deposits, CPs will also have to compete with other financial instruments available in the market. The pricing of CP should, therefore, be such that its issue price computes out to be lower than the cost of obtaining a working capital loan from banks, and high enough to remain competitive in the financial market.

It has already been said that CPs will be issued at a discount, the rate of which will be determined by the company issuing them. This rate must take into account various expenses connected with the launching and issuing of the CPs. The Vaghul Group estimated that these issue expenses could go up to 1 per cent of the amount, which included the management fees of merchant bankers (not exceeding 0.50 per cent), commitment charges for stand-by arrangements (say 0.25 per cent), fees for the credit rating agency (about 0.10 per cent), and stamp duty (about

0.15 per cent). However, presently the estimated expenses will be as follows:

Stamp duty	0.20 per cent
Rating fees	0.10 per cent subject to a minimum of Rs 1 lakh
IPA's fee	0.10 per cent
Stand-by fee	0.15 per cent
Management fee	0.20–0.25 per cent

The aggregate issue expenses being 0.75–0.80 per cent we can now examine the rates offered by major competing instruments.[8]

1. *Bank deposits:* 3.5 per cent per annum up to 14 days, 3.75 per cent per annum up to 3 months, 5.5 per cent up to 6 months and 6.5 per cent for one year.
2. *Banks' certificates of deposits:* These are offered at different rates depending upon the demand and supply of funds in the market, more particularly the need for funds by a bank issuing them. The ruling rate now varies between 4.15 per cent and 7 per cent per annum.
3. *Inter-bank call money:* The weighted average rate presently is 5.30 per cent per annum.
4. *Treasury bills:* The rate varies between 3.97–5.24 per cent for 91 days treasury bills, between 4.70–5.25 for 182 days, and between 5.06–5.22 for 364 days bills.
5. *Repo rate,* which is considered as the bank rate, is 5.5 per cent and the reverse repo rate is 4 per cent.
6. *Banks' base rate:* It varies between 8–8.5 per cent per annum.

The CP has to find a place within these competiting instruments.

[8] All the rates are average of rates prevalent in the market during the first half of 2010.

In India, short-term rates are not yet properly aligned as in developed countries, because barring the call money rate, many of the rates still suffer from some administered elements; the existence of CRR and SLR also contributes to this. However, looking at the rate structure of various instruments given here and keeping in mind the profile of issuers and investors as mentioned earlier, we may say that the rate offered on CPs should be higher than the rate offered on treasury bills and bank deposits of appropriate maturity and somewhat lower than or closer to a bank's base rate.

Effective Interest Rate

The effective rate on CPs is influenced by methods of placement—placed directly or through a dealer, commitment charges for back-up/guarantee/letter of credit (LC), if any, and finally the discount rate. The formula for calculating the effective interest rate (EIR) is:

$$\text{EIR} = \frac{Total\ Financing\ Costs}{Net\ Cash\ from\ CP} \times \frac{365}{Maturity\ Period\ of\ CP}$$

Example

A company intends to issue commercial paper for Rs 100 lakh. The discount rate is 7 per cent per annum. Total issue expenses, as shown earlier, can be taken at 0.75 per cent on the face value of the CP. EIRs for 30 days and 180 days maturity are calculated as:

(Rs in lakh)

30-days maturity

Total Financing Costs	
Discount cost $(0.07 \times 100 \times 30)/365$	0.5753
Issue expenses $(0.75 \times 100)/100$	0.7500
Total	1.3253

Cash receivable: $100 - 1.3253 = 98.6747$
Hence, EIR $= (1.3253/98.6747) \times (365/30) = 0.1634$ or 16.34 per cent.

180-days maturity

Total Financing Costs

Discount cost $(0.07 \times 100 \times 180)/365$	3.452
Issue expenses $(0.75 \times 100)/100$	0.750
Total	4.202

Cash receivable: $100 - 4.202 = 95.798$

Hence, EIR $= (4.202/95.798) \times (365/180) = 0.0889$ or 8.89 per cent.

It may be seen that under the given cost structure, 30 days maturity is cost prohibitive while it is feasible for 180 days maturity. The reason behind the lower EIR for 180 days maturity is that the issue expenses are spread over a period much longer than in the 30 days maturity.

A major component of issue expenses is the stamp duty, which is very high in India. There is a case for reducing it substantially or abolishing it altogether for CP to encourage its growth. There is no stamp duty on CP in countries like the US, UK, and France.

Present State of Affairs

The primary investors in CPs are generally banks and mutual funds. Other financial institutions, public sector undertakings and Discount and Finance House of India (DFHI) also buy CPs to park their surplus funds. In order to develop a secondary market in CPs the DFHI provides a forum for buying and selling CPs. They offer a two-way quote on a daily basis. But as yet, not much turnover is visible in the secondary CP market which is retarding its growth. The reason behind this is that major buyers of CPs hold them until maturity.

In India, default in repayment of CP is few and far between.

Securitised Commercial Paper

Although CPs were originally conceived to be unsecured in nature, in several countries of Europe and America collateralised commercial papers have already emerged. The first movers were large finance companies, which created specific pools of automobile loans to be tied to particular issues of securitised CP.

During recent times, small and less creditworthy firms have also been able to raise funds through securitised CPs. For example, a small firm could be the supplier to highly rated companies, and thus may have a pool of high quality receivables. But given the status of the firm it may not be able to get the required credit rating from a rating agency. In such a situation, the firm may form a financial subsidiary and transfer these receivables to the new company. Because of the high quality of the collateralised receivables this new company will be able to obtain a good rating of the CP. Due to this credit enhancement the not-so-creditworthy firms may often get a better rate in the CP market.

REGISTRATION OF CHARGES

It is advisable to discuss here in some detail the provisions of the Indian Companies Act regarding registration of charges with the Registrar of Companies in order to make charges enforceable, because it covers the entire gamut of loans, advances, and credit given to the company by debenture holders, banks, financial institutions, and other creditors.

1. Registration of charges is required only in the case of limited companies.
2. The following charges are to be compulsorily registered:
   i. A charge for purpose of securing any issue of debentures.
   ii. A charge on the uncalled share capital of the company. As capital uncalled is in no sense a 'property' of the company—it is more in the nature of a power or right—the company must have express authority to charge it either by a specific provision to this

effect, or by a general provision to mortgage all properties and rights in the Articles of Association. A banking company cannot create a charge on its own uncalled capital.

iii. A charge on any immovable property of the company or any interest therein, for example, land and buildings, whether freehold or leasehold.

iv. A charge on any book debt of the company.

v. A charge on any movable property of the company, not being a pledge, for example, stocks, plant and machinery not fastened to the earth, taken under hypothecation or lien, and also a floating charge on the undertaking or any property of the company.

vi. A charge on calls made but not paid.

vii. A charge on a ship or any share in the ship.

viii. A charge on goodwill, patent, or licence under a patent, trade mark, copyright or a licence under a copyright.

Notes

1. A charge includes a lien or equitable mortgage by deposit of the title deeds or even an agreement to deposit title deeds. All these need registration.

2. Plant and machinery when fixed to the earth become immovable property under the Transfer of Property Act. And as charges on all immovable properties are required to be registered under the Indian Registration Act, any charge on such plant and machinery is also to be registered with the Registrar of Assurances, in addition to their being registered with the Registrar of Companies. As a banker is not supposed to be an engineer who can distinguish between the movability and immovability of the plant and machinery installed in a factory, it is advisable that where the amount of advance is large and the installation is also big and complicated, the charge taken on it should be registered additionally as a regular mortgage with the Registrar of Assurances, because the borderline between immovability and movability in this case may be very thin.

3. A charge to be valid should be registered with the Registrar of Companies within 30 days of its creation. The date can be extended by another 30 days by the registrar if she/he is satisfied about the reason for delay, on payment of additional fees. *A recent amendment requires the charges to be filed in electronic form.*

4. A charge on properties situated outside India can be created either in India or abroad.

5. A hire-purchase agreement also needs registration because it makes the financier a secured creditor.

6. It should be remembered that if a charge required to be registered is not registered, it is void against the liquidator and other creditors of the company, but not against the company itself. So long as the company is a going concern, the mortgage or the charge is good and can be enforced. The company is also not entitled to avoid the debt which remains enforceable against it whether security is available to the creditor or not for want of registration. No company can itself have a cause of action arising out of non-registration.

7. Although the Companies Act apparently casts a duty on companies to register any charges created by them, it is not mandatory in nature. Till today, companies are

under no legal obligation to register the charges with the Registrar of Companies on their own. In fact, some companies do not want to register charges for reasons of prestige, but since creditors are always in a disadvantageous position if charges are not registered, it is necessary that they themselves get the charges registered immediately after creation.

8. Charges created by operation of law, for example, a vendor's lien on unpaid goods arising out of the Sale of Goods Act requires no registration.

9. When a bank advances money to a company against deposit of duly discharged fixed deposit receipts, the charge is deemed to be in the nature of a pledge, hence it need not be registered.

10. A charge, though expressed in words as a fixed charge or mortgage, will be treated as a floating charge if the intention was that the company should be allowed to continue to use the charged assets in the carrying on of its business.

11. The following tests should be applied to identify a floating charge:
    (a) If it is a charge upon all or one or more classes of assets, present and future;
    (b) If the assets charged would in the ordinary course of business be changing from time to time; and
    (c) If, expressly or by necessary implication the company has the power, until some step is taken by the charge holder, of carrying on its business in the ordinary way so far as the charged assets are concerned.

12. Registration of charge is a notice to all concerned, and any person acquiring such a property takes it with the previous charge.

13. A register for charges on a company's property is available for inspection by paying a small fee. It is necessary, therefore, to inspect this register before accepting a charge on a company's assets as a security for money advanced.

14. A charge takes effect from the date of registration only, and not from the date of creation.

15. The registrar will issue a certificate of registration on the registration of charges, which shall be conclusive evidence even if some defects are noticed later.

16. Every company is required to keep a register of charges, and also true copies of every instrument creating a charge on the company's assets at the registered office of the company. A lender is, therefore, advised to inspect this register and documents at the company's office in addition to carrying out an inspection at the office of the Registrar of Companies.

CONCLUDING REMARKS

Current liabilities are not the other face of current assets. Instruments of financing current assets are not necessarily restricted to current liabilities only. These can also be long-term capital or debt instruments. It all depends upon the capital structure policy of an enterprise and its market command. The principles of management of current assets and current liabilities are also different.

When granting working capital finance a banker's primary focus is on current liabilities, while sanctioning a term loan the focus is on long-term liabilities, but in the matter of appraisal of a credit proposal whether for working capital or term loans, a lender has to take a total view of the business and its capital structure.

When a company enjoys command in the supply market, it is often prone to 'overtrading' by obtaining larger and longer credit from suppliers. A banker should not keep his eyes closed to such a phenomenon thinking that he has to lay down a lesser amount of working capital finance, because when the supply market turns adverse, the snowball will finally stop at his door alone.

Besides CP and bridge loans, a number of modern financial instruments have emerged or are emerging with the spread of liberalisation. Some of these instruments are designed as short-term instruments also. These instruments are complex, and as the financial market deepens, their complexity will increase. A banker has to be very careful in evaluating the impact of these financial instruments on the capital structure of a firm, and ultimately on the working capital finance sanctioned by him.

Positive anything is better than negative nothing.

—Elbert Hubbard

10 Profit and Loss Account

INTRODUCTION

When a business has acquired assets (by contracting liabilities), the stage is set to start the operational process, the purpose being to produce outputs by adding value to the inputs. The process is a continuous flow of various operations which engage economic resources for production of outputs, the sale of which generates further economic resources. This continuous revolution of inputs and outputs, at times creates a problem for an entrepreneur when he wants to know the results of his operation as a feedback to what he is doing. The balance sheet, as we will see in the next chapter, can give him a snapshot status report of his business at a point of time only. From the balance sheet he may know the composition of his assets and liabilities and also their relative increment over a period. It is more a stock report than an operational report. An entrepreneur may not be satisfied with a stock report only. He may like to know how he has performed operationally; where he has gone wrong; where he has improved; which is the weakest chain of the productive process that needs immediate attention. In short, he wants to capture the entire flow of operations during a period. The profit and loss account is such a flow report which summarises the results of operations for a given period of time.

ACCOUNTING CONCEPTS

Input-Output

A profit and loss account can be viewed from an input-output angle. Inputs are economic resources which are put to production for manufacturing outputs. These inputs include not only physical and tangible items like raw materials, but also all the services used in the production and marketing process, for example, labour and publicity. Any service received is an input, and its cost is an expense. When a piece of plant and machinery is put to use, the process receives the services of the plant, which is an expense that we call depreciation. But when the same piece of plant and machinery has been bought, it is an expenditure and a cost, but not an expense till the time its services are used.

Outputs are meant to generate profit; that is the reason why an entrepreneur is in business. But sale of outputs does not necessarily generate profit in the strict sense of the term. It generates only revenue. Revenue is the value of goods sold. When the expenses of generating revenue are matched against it, we come to know whether the business has made a profit or a loss. The profit and loss account is a means of finding out how the revenue and expense are matched to each other, giving rise to a net result.

An entrepreneur can choose any period of time for calculating his profit or loss, that is, for matching expenses against revenues. The more frequently this is done, the better it is for him as well as for a banker. But the convention of closing the books of accounts at least once in a year has been an established practice for more than 500 years now, since Lucas Pacioli codified the book keeping methods. Taxation authorities have also fallen in line with this convention, and they assess the income of a business annually.

However, revenues and expenses are merely nominal in nature. Their net effect is felt only in decreasing or increasing the value of assets. Since the net assets of a business are the net worth or the owner's equity, revenues or expenses ultimately increase or decrease the owner's equity or net worth. Any analysis of a profit and loss account should begin keeping this concept in mind.

Income and Cash

Before we move over to the other aspects of a profit and loss account, we should make a distinction between income and cash, because it is often found that the cash concept of a business is confused by a banker with the income concept, giving rise to a wrong assessment of a credit proposal. An increase in cash need not necessarily be an income, because it may come from the sale of an asset, for example, a fixed asset or from realisation of debtors while an income need not always be available in cash, but may be blocked in debtors via sales, or simply blocked in unsold stocks. We should note here that all cash goes to the balance sheet, but all income goes to the profit and loss account.

There is a controversy, however, whether cash is more important than income. It manifests particularly at the time of assessing the viability of a sick unit. An otherwise profitable concern may be choked to death for want of sufficient cash, and a highly liquid concern may ultimately fall into an abyss if it cannot generate enough income to sustain its expenses. You cannot pay bills with profit, only by cash.[1] The cash flow concept of accounting emerged from this controversy. For a banker, liquidity is as important as profitability. A tilting of the balance between the two may ultimately be responsible for withering away both liquidity and profitability. A balance sheet throws light on liquidity, as we will see later, and a profit and loss account on the profitability of operations, and the two together indicate the health of a business.[2]

NATURE OF COSTS

Costs may be categorised into short-term and long-term costs.

Costs that are expected to be matched with revenues within the given accounting period may be called short-term costs (expenses), and costs that enable the firm to generate outputs for more than the given accounting period are called long-term costs. These two broad headings are then sub-divided into tangibles and intangibles.

Short-term Tangible Cost

Certain costs are incurred for acquisition of tangible assets, which when utilised during a given accounting period become expenses. For example, raw material, stores, tools, and dies are essential for the current operation of a business, and in fact, they themselves get converted into outputs after various services are brought into operation. The test of tangibility is physical existence.

Short-term Intangible Cost

The costs of various *services* that are used for conversion of physical short-term assets into

[1] Stancill, J.M., *When is the Cash in Cashflow? Harvard Business Review*, March–April 1987, pp. 38–52.
[2] See Chapters 9 and 12.

outputs are by their nature intangible, because it is not possible to visualise these services in a real form. The services of labour received, against which a cost is incurred, is an expense in the given year. This, we call wage.

Borrowing of funds is a service received. The cost of this service is the interest which has to be paid, though it appears only in the books of accounts of the lender and the business. It is very difficult to find out the physical existence of this fund service, except, perhaps, in the availability of real currency notes in the coffers of the business. Hence, the cost of borrowing or cost of funds is treated as an intangible cost, and it becomes an expense for the year of operation of the business. Income tax is slightly different from other intangible costs, because here the cost is not matched with the revenue directly, but via the net income before-tax. It is presumed that services from the government are received continuously throughout the life of a business, and a portion of them is recovered from the business in every financial year.

Long-term Tangible Cost

The costs of acquisition of any *pool of services* which will be realised in instalments over a long period of time are all long-term tangible costs. When a machine is bought, a capacity of production is installed. This capacity will be realised by a business over a long period of time, say 20 years. During this period, the machine will release its capacity, and hence lose its working value or life. When this machine releases its capacity, it charges the business for the capacity given (depreciation). To the business it is, therefore, a short-term cost (an expense), while the cost of acquisition of the machine is a long-term tangible cost. Other examples include land and buildings, motor vehicles, and furniture and fixtures.

Long-term Intangible Cost

A business incurs certain costs for a *block of services* spanning many years. For example, when a product or process is patented, the state takes care of its protection against copying. The patent right is available for a long period on payment of a fee to the government. The benefit received is the protection from infringement of patent rights. Hence, it is intangible in nature. It is like any other long-term asset, and the proportionate cost for the given year is charged to the revenue. Other examples include copyrights and trade marks.

In the terminology of cost accounting, however, expenses are termed as costs. As in the following paragraphs we will be using the concept of cost accounting, we are retaining the term 'cost', meaning thereby 'expense'.

Prime Cost

The costs that are incurred at the primary stage of production are called prime costs. The primary input, that is, raw materials, is directly brought into contact with the services of labour for initial conversion. Prime costs, therefore, include only direct raw material, direct labour, and other costs which can be directly *identified* with the output. Costs which cannot be so directly identified with a given output are excluded from this category. Since the major components of any product are raw materials and labour, the prime costs help an analyst to know the added value produced by the business by comparing it with the sales. If the value added is not significant, then at this stage itself an analyst will be able to say that the product would not be able to meet its indirect costs.

Factory Indirect Cost

Costs which cannot be identified directly with any single output come under this head. Indirect cost of labour for maintenance, the salaries of forklift operators, product inspectors, timekeepers, supervisors, works managers, cost of stores, spares and tools, depreciation, and insurance are some of examples of factory indirect costs. Other costs of services like electricity, heat, power, and maintenance of a testing laboratory also come under this head. These costs are essential for the production of output, but none of them can be identified with any single product. The aggregate of these costs help in the manufacture of all the products of a business. Hence, these are called factory indirect costs, which are added to prime costs to obtain full factory costs.

Full Factory Cost

The total cost of conversion, from raw material to the final product, is called the full factory cost. This is the cost at which goods are carried to the inventory. This excludes any cost incurred outside the factory gate.

It is time now to analyse in some greater detail certain important items of costs from a banker's point of view. Each element of cost is analysed from the angle of both a large-scale and a small-scale unit, so that a lender can bear in mind their differential treatment while analysing a credit proposal.

WAGES

The cost of labour is one of the most important items in any business process, whether manufacturing or trading. When incurred inside a factory, we call it wage and when incurred outside, we call it salary. For the business as a whole, it is the cost of labour. This dichotomy enables us to pinpoint the expenditure point and the intensity of its use. The level and type of technology used by any unit determines the extent of usage of labour as a factor of production. In case of labour-intensive technology, wages will be a bigger component in the output produced, while in

the case of capital-intensive technology, it will be lower.

When we look at small-scale industrial units, we find that in most of the cases labour-intensive technology is used. This is because these units do not have enough capital to install sophisticated capital-intensive technology that saves on cost of labour, and perhaps this is the reason why the government fosters small-scale units. In a country where capital is scarce but labour is abundant, the government has to decide on a policy of maximum employment with a lesser amount of capital. Small-scale units provide a reasonable solution to such a difficult problem, though for the time being the country may be deprived of the best quality output available from capital-intensive technology. The latter point, which had weighed in the mind of the government for quite some time, finally resulted in gradual the de-reservation of a number of products from the list reserved for small-scale industries.

Inter-firm Comparison

In case of small-scale industrial units, although the labour component in the product is high, the unit labour cost is cheaper as compared to a large business where labour overheads like provident fund, welfare expenses, and gratuity augment the unit cost of labour. It is difficult to make inter-firm comparisons of labour utilisation in case of small-scale units because of scanty data, but in the case of large units, it is possible to make inter-firm comparisons. A comparison of the cost of labour to the total production cost can be made among various large units manufacturing the same product. All the data, namely wages and the total cost of production, are available from published annual accounts. A standard can be fixed by taking the best ratio. Any deviation from the standard will explain whether labour is being used efficiently or not. It will also indicate whether a unit is functioning at a desired technological level. For an individual unit, it is possible to calculate the productivity of labour over time to see whether it is increasing or decreasing.

Materials

The progress of technology primarily means not only efficient utilisation of labour, but also efficient utilisation of materials: there should be less wastage on both counts. In case of small industrial units, because of less sophisticated technology, material efficiency is lower. In the initial periods, wastage will be high because a unit has to settle down and the entrepreneur has to learn the checks and balances required for running a production line. A lender has to bear this point in mind while assessing a proposal of a small unit. It will be wrong to assume optimal efficiency during the initial settling period. A new entrepreneur may not always be aware of this. He may project all his operations with standard efficiency. A lender will commit a mistake if he sanctions a proposal without taking into consideration the contingencies involved. *It will also be wrong for him to argue that since the borrower has not demanded additional elbow room, he has not included the contingencies in his assessment.* A borrower may not always know his need because he is yet to learn, but a banker cannot afford to be ignorant about it because he has to lay down the finance. By not considering contingencies, he might underfinance the unit, and by the time the borrower has learnt the lessons, both the unit and the bank might have lost the game.

Material Efficiency

A fall in material efficiency is a sure sign of falling efficiency of the management. When any unit becomes large, there is a possibility of greater wastage of materials through poor planning and pilferage, unless a well-coordinated management is at the helm of affairs. A banker should compare the raw material consumption with the total production cost, and thus calculate a ratio for the past few years to see whether the raw material efficiency is falling or increasing. This should be a starting point of appraising any credit proposal for large units. If the ratio is increasing (that is, the efficiency is falling) over the years, a lender should probe deeply into the matter to find out the real causes. If he does the exercise now, he may save an unpalatable similar exercise in the future when the unit falls sick. *It is generally found that when material efficiency starts falling, it is difficult to reverse the downward movement if not checked at the right time.*

Effect of Inflation

It may be possible that the rupee cost of the consumption of materials might be high, giving rise to a higher ratio because of inflationary increase in prices. If this is so, then a banker has to look at the sales also, and see whether inflation has increased their value as well. There is no problem if it is more or less matched, but if the increase in the price of raw materials is going to stay, and the sales price of the product is not expected to increase proportionately in the coming future, an entrepreneur is better advised to either change the technology (which may not always be possible because of high capital costs), or to diversify the product line. Unless either of the two is done, a lender may soon find himself financing a dying unit.

PRODUCTION OVERHEADS

This is perhaps the biggest area of strength for small-scale industrial units, and the weakness of large units. In the case of the former, costs like rent of a factory building, supervisory costs, loose tools, and spares are low because the unit is small and the process simple, hence easily manageable by an entrepreneur himself. However, one important point that has come to the notice of this writer should be mentioned here. A small-scale entrepreneur always thinks that he will be able to manage everything by himself; he may not appoint even a supervisor. As a result, he soon loses his grip on production. It has been found that one of the reasons behind failures of small-scales units is the absence of a supervisory hand and an accountant. We, therefore, suggest that *in case of a small unit where the capital investment is more than Rs 10 lakh, a banker should insist upon the appointment of a supervisor and an accountant, and include their salaries in the financial package sanctioned.*[3]

A large unit using sophisticated technology requires an elaborate management network at the factory. Production overheads are, therefore, high in such a unit. There is nothing wrong in this. But in order to absorb the high overheads, it must have a lower prime cost, leaving a larger margin for absorption of overheads. If the margin is lower, it can be presumed that the factory organisation is top-heavy.

Maintenance and Repairs

We have already mentioned that management of loose tools and spares—which are components of production overheads—is a big problem for a large unit. There is income leakage through mismanagement of this item of costs. This is, perhaps, the most neglected area, where neither the management nor a banker pays much attention. Besides small-scale units, even many large industries do not have any organised approach to the problem of maintenance of plant and machinery, and the management of its cost. It has been found that spare parts and tools often constitute 50 to 80 per cent of the total maintenance cost of a factory, and a substantial portion of these

articles are lost or poorly used, because of lack of proper control. If the consumption of tools and spares is increasing rapidly, it is not necessary that the plant and machinery are being maintained properly; there may simply be wastages. Although the cost of maintenance and repairs must increase with the age of a machine, a sharp increase in maintenance costs, particularly due to increased consumption of tools and spares, may well be an indication that maintenance is not being done in an organised manner, but costs are being incurred mostly for 'fire-fighting'. Poor maintenance results in increased costs and loss of production due to haphazard organisation of the maintenance department, frequent breakdowns, costly repairs, and increased downtime. In most Indian organisations, what we have really seen is 'repair maintenance'. Maintenance people gather around machines only when the 'smoke comes out'. This proves expensive with respect to both the cost of maintenance and the resultant loss in production.

In case of medium and large units, a lender should insist on the establishment of a regular maintenance department manned by qualified people. *Normally, the total maintenance cost should not exceed 1 per cent of the sales.* Based on this a lender can calculate, with reasonable accuracy, the total maintenance cost to be budgeted by a firm. If, however, it is found that actual costs have increased more than the standard, a lender could well surmise that the maintenance department is disorganised, and hence there is a leakage that needs to be plugged.

Contract Maintenance

In some western countries, contract maintenance is replacing in-factory maintenance, particularly in process industries. This has been found to be cheaper because of less overhead costs to a company. But in India, except in household equipments, contract maintenance is yet to catch

---

[3] See Bhattacharya, Hrishikes, *Entrepreneur, Banker and Small-Scale Industry*, Deep and Deep Publishers, New Delhi, 1984.

up. In units where the maintenance department is found to be disorganised and the cost high, a banker can suitably advise them to switch over to contract maintenance. Necessary information and consultancy services are available from the Indian Institute of Plant Engineers.

ADMINISTRATIVE COSTS

Production and marketing processes consist of several activities which are at once complementary to, and conflicting with, each other. It, therefore, calls for the services of a band of 'overseers' who can coordinate various activities towards the desired goal of a business. This involves cost, which is better termed as general management cost, though in the language of accountants, it is termed as the general administration cost.

In fact, expenditure incurred in formulating policy, directing the organisation, and controlling the operations come under this head. This is also called policy cost. This is a burden on the organisation, yet no organisation can run without it. It is very difficult to establish a standard for measurement and comparison with respect to this cost. Some relationship can, however, be established only with the net profit earned by a firm, and this net profit should be profit after interest and tax, because fund management and tax planning are the two most important areas dealt with by the general management. Administrative overheads increase both with the passage of time and the expansion of a unit. The cost would not be very high for a small unit where proprietors are themselves managers. Even for a large unit, the cost during the initial period would not be very high. There is, however, always a minimum, below which the organisation would not be able to function satisfactorily. This minimum includes salaries of accountant and watch-and-ward staff, besides fixed costs like rent, rates, insurance, lighting, depreciation of office buildings and furniture, costs of telephones and internet, postage, and printing and stationery.

MARKETING AND DISTRIBUTION COSTS

When goods are produced, these have to be sold for earning revenue. Bringing the goods outside the factory gate involves certain costs, which we call marketing and distribution costs. Goods may be distributed among a number of selling or distribution points, wherefrom these are delivered to the customers. The cost of renting these godowns, the maintenance of selling offices or a marketing network, and publicity campaign come under this head. While commission on sales is a fixed percentage on the quantum of goods sold, other marketing and distribution expenses cannot be so identified with individual outputs sold. The aggregate of these expenses ensures a given amount of sales. The cost of marketing management, advertising, sales promotion, commissions, and discount are also called order-getting costs, and the costs of carriage outward, management of depots, cost of warehousing, and billing are called logistic costs.

The ability of an organisation to survive and grow depends upon its ability to sell. To start with, a business has to 'push' its products, but if it stays in that condition for a long time, it is likely that it has ceased to grow, because the pushing mechanism cannot ensure the continuous growth of an organisation. The business has to move over to a 'pull' situation, where customers should demand its products continuously. The 'push' creates the market, while the 'pull' sustains it. The former is called selling, while the latter is called marketing. This marketing concept has gained over the selling concept in recent times. A marketing set-up requires substantial investments, which may at times be more than the cost of production, particularly in case of luxury and highly competitive consumer products. *A banker need not, therefore, be concerned if he finds heavy marketing and distribution overheads in the profit and loss account of a firm dealing in such kinds of goods.* The question, however, is whether he should finance the cost. Unfortunately, until recently bankers did not take a very liberal view of this. This is ironic, because in all the literature and the reports of various committees, marketing has been given the most important place. It is said that unless a company can sell and sustain its market share, it is bound to fall sick soon. But as marketing overheads are not included in the cost of sales, bankers are unwilling to finance them. However, by not financing them they are doing nothing but crippling an otherwise sound business. It is, therefore, suggested that if the marketing overheads are substantial, and an entrepreneur is not in a position to finance these from his own resources, a banker should come forward to help him, first by including it in the *total* cost of sales and then allowing him to value the finished goods inventory at the *total* cost of sales. This is particularly important for small units.

CONTROLLABLE VERSUS UNCONTROLLABLE COST

Accountants generally regard all indirect expenses as overheads. They use the two terms interchangeably. But a banker should make a distinction between the two to help him understand their nature correctly and counsel an entrepreneur appropriately. Rent is an indirect cost, so also is the cost of maintenance. Both are overheads, but the former is not controllable because it has to be paid for, whether the firm produces or not. The latter is controllable to a great extent, and therefore, this point should weigh in the mind of a lender while analysing a profit and loss account. If the maintenance cost is too high, he should call for a proper explanation from the entrepreneur, and if necessary, advise him on the curtailment of this cost. Rent, as an overhead, has to be absorbed by increasing

production, while maintenance cost is an overhead which though absorbable, can be curtailed as well. Accountants normally regard direct labour as a controllable cost. But there may be cases, and these are many in number, where even the direct labour cost is fixed. Workers may be paid fixed weekly or monthly wages irrespective of the hours of work they put in, or the units they produce. *In such a situation, it is a case of absorption like any other fixed overhead. The cost structure of the firm might have become sticky.*

TRADING, MANUFACTURING, AND PROFIT AND LOSS ACCOUNT

Even two decades back, accountants all over the world were very conservative in releasing information regarding operations of a business, but this conservatism is waning fast due primarily to the increasing role of market regulators and an evolving philosophy of corporate governance. Full disclosure is the norm today. A lot of information is now available from the published profit and loss account of a business. The Indian Companies Act and the SEBI have directed more disclosures in the profit and loss account of limited/listed companies. However, banks can still ask for any other relevant information, which has a bearing on the assessment of the credit proposal. There should not be any secrecy between a borrower firm and a bank in this respect. *The old adage that asking for too much information amounts to a bank interfering in the business no longer holds good.* A banker should view withholding of any information by the business seriously.

The purpose of analysing the profit and loss account is to know the earning capacity of a business. Conventionally, there are two indicators which we discuss now.

GROSS PROFIT

The method of determining gross profit varies slightly with different types of businesses. Profit made after charging to sales only those costs which are directly incurred in production in case of manufacturing unit or trade sales of goods and services, in case of trading units, is called gross profit.

A credit appraiser should examine whether the gross profit is rising or falling proportionately with sales. The ratio should be stable over a reasonably long period. If a variation is observed, a banker should probe deeply into the matter. It may be that wages have increased without any corresponding increase in sales, or the cost of materials has increased but the sale price could not be increased. It may also be that the sale price has been cut to increase the turnover, and hence the market share of the firm. There may also be a change in the valuation method of stocks, which has either inflated or deflated the gross profit. At this point, it is desirable to sound a warning note to a banker. *When a unit is going downhill, the management often tries to paint a glowing picture by showing an increased gross profit, while in fact there may be a gross loss.* This is done by debiting certain items of costs to the profit and loss account, which should have been charged to the trading or manufacturing account. A banker should carefully scrutinise these items of costs, and try to arrive at a correct gross profit for the purpose of comparison and evaluation.

OPERATING PROFIT

The profit figure arrived at after charging all the expenses of an enterprise against all its incomes is called net profit. When we deduct the tax payable from the net profit, we arrive at the after-tax profit earned by an enterprise. Some accountants treat this item in the profit and loss appropriation account.

However, a banker is more interested in knowing the *business profit* of an enterprise rather than its net profit. A profit figure can be swollen by bringing into account a substantial profit

made on the sale of fixed assets, investments, or rental income. Even a loss can thus be wiped out. A banker should, therefore, exclude all such incomes (including the income from investments made outside the business) and expenses incidental thereto, to arrive at the true profit of the *business*. When this profit is taken before interest and tax and other extraordinary items as above we arrive at the *operating profit*, which indicates the operating strength of the business. Interest is not taken into consideration because it is a finance cost, which depends not upon the operating structure of an enterprise but on its financial structure. If a firm has good operating strength, an enterprise can be made viable by suitable financial planning, but the converse is not always possible.

PBIT VERSUS PBT

After arriving at the operating profit before interest (also known as profit before interest and tax, or PBIT), a lender should compare it with the operating profit after interest, or simply profit before-tax (PBT), both for the past years and the projected year, to examine the impact of the interest burden on the results of the operations of a business, and advise a borrower to rationalise the financial structure, if necessary.

For the purpose of inter-company comparison, it is preferable to exclude depreciation also, because different companies may charge depreciation at different rates, beyond the minimum prescribed by the Companies Act or the Income Tax Act.

In the next section we first analyse the profit and loss of a trading and service company, followed by that of a manufacturing company.

TRADING COMPANIES

A typical trading and profit and loss account of a trade or an export house will look like the following:

Trading and Profit and Loss Account for the Year Ended 31 March 20X7

(Rs in thousand)

Dr					Cr
Opening stock of goods		3049	Sales	55100	
Purchase of goods	36611		Less:		
Less:			Return	2000	53100
Return	1000	35611	Closing Stock		3805
Carriage inwards		34			
Wages		1271			
Gross profit carried down		16940			
Total		56905	Total		56905
Salaries		768	Gross profit		
Welfare expenses		118	Brought down		16940
Rent		284	Cash assistance		
Rates and taxes		636	for exports		266
Insurance		56	Interest and		
Advertisement		473	dividend received		26
Carriage outward		1695	Misc. Income		52
Commission and brokerage		263			
Travelling expenses		356			
Postage, telegrams etc.		123			
Printing and stationery		55			
Interest paid		512			
Bank charges		76			
Depreciation		313			
Misc. expenses		556			
Net profit (before income tax)		11000			
Total		17284	Total		17284

No manufacturing expenses have been incurred by the trader/exporter because he is not manufacturing any goods, but dealing in finished goods of some other manufacturers. There is no conversion cost. Costs of services, namely, carriage and wages paid for handling, and repacking are added to the cost of goods sold. Depreciation is charged not to the trading account but to the profit and loss account because this depreciation is not on plant and machinery, but on office equipments and furniture and fixtures.

A problem arises in the case of service companies like consultancy firms, motels, and beauty salons where there is, in fact, no buying of goods, except perhaps some stores and provisions. There may not be much of a stock also. In such a case, it is very difficult to calculate any gross profit. The entire cost of labour, administration, rent, and depreciation of assets should be aggregated as cost of services sold and charged against the fees received. The profit or loss that comes out is the *business* or operating profit or loss.

Cost of Goods Sold

The cost of goods sold for a typical trading unit, as in the example given earlier, may be calculated as below:

	(Rs in thousand)
Opening stock of goods	3049
Add: Purchase of goods	36611
	39660
Less: Goods returned	1000
	38660
Add: Carriage inward	34
Add: Wages for handling and packaging	1271
Goods available for sale	39965
Less: Closing stock	3805
Cost of goods sold	36160

Selling and Administrative Expenses

In the case of a trading company, which lives virtually on commission on sales (which is almost always a fixed percentage), it is necessary that the turnover should be high, and the administrative and selling expenses low, so that it can earn a reasonable profit on the total investment. Although trading companies vary from one to another because of various types of goods dealt with by them, a relationship can be established between the gross profit and selling and administrative expenses. It has been found from a study of a number of trading concerns that for a successful trading unit, the selling and administrative expenses should not be more than one-third of the gross profit. The example given earlier is a typical one drawn up by keeping in mind the various standards available from the best-performing units. *If the ratio is high, it is likely that the concern is spending more on main-*

taining an office style rather than on doing business. A banker is also likely to be fooled by the 'show' of a luxuriously decorated office. Although firms dealing in luxury goods, domestic appliances, and gadgets may have to maintain a certain level of style in their offices and showrooms, in such cases also the selling and administrative overheads should not exceed one-third of the gross profit, because in luxury items the margins are also high.

MANUFACTURING COMPANIES

We can now move to the final accounts of a manufacturing concern. A manufacturing company buys raw materials and converts them into finished products. We have already seen in Chapter 6 that conversion costs include raw materials, wages, and other manufacturing expenses. The inventory or stock constitutes raw materials, work-in-progress, and finished goods. These items of costs and stocks mark the basic difference between a trading and a manufacturing concern. Raw materials include the acquisition cost, while work-in-progress includes raw materials, plus labour, plus other manufacturing expenses incurred in the process, which is yet to be completed. Finished goods are goods fully manufactured.

ABSORPTION COSTING VERSUS DIRECT COSTING

The cost incurred in a manufacturing concern takes on various names at different stages of production. There is, however, a controversy about the costing of products sold. The debate is primarily between the proponents of the absorption costing method and of the direct costing method.

The absorption costing method makes a functional classification of costs, that is, it separates costs on the basis of various functions of an enterprise like manufacturing, selling, and administrative, while direct costing, which is also called the marginal or variable costing method, separates costs on the basis of behaviour, namely, variable, semi-variable, and fixed. The latter gives importance to the contribution made by the units sold towards fixed cost and profit. This enables a firm to calculate the break-even point, as is elaborated upon in Chapter 15.

Under the direct costing method, manufacturing costs are taken as expenses for the *period*. This applies specially to fixed manufacturing expenses or manufacturing overheads. It treats this cost as a period cost only. No part of it should be carried forward to the ensuing year through absorption in work-in-progress and unsold finished goods. The presumption here is that manufacturing overheads being periodical burdens have to be paid for even if there is no production, and hence

should be treated separately and absorbed fully in the given period. If any portion of these is carried forward to the next year, it will vitiate the product costing for both the years, because the same amount of manufacturing overheads have to be incurred in the next year also, irrespective of the level of production.

Advocates of the absorption costing method enter into controversy at this stage. According to them, manufacturing overheads are to be absorbed in the periods of sale only and not in the periods of their occurrence. In other words, it means that total manufacturing overheads should be distributed among all the productive resultants, namely, work-in-progress and finished goods, so that the unsold or semi-manufactured goods carry with them a portion of these costs in the following period. The following example will make the distinction clear.

	Rs	Rs
Sales		16000
Opening Stock:		
Raw materials	4200	
Work-in-process	1200	
Finished goods	3600	9000
Purchase of raw materials		6000
Direct wages		3600
Manufacturing overheads		7200
Commission on sales @ 5%		800
Other marketing and administrative expenses		1200
Closing Stock:		
Raw materials	3000	
Work-in-process	4800	
Finished goods	6000	13800

The firm has sold 120 units during the year.
The raw material cost per unit is Rs 50.
Direct labour cost per unit is Rs 15.

Manufacturing Account

Absorption Costing Method	Rs	Rs	Direct Costing Method	Rs	Rs
Sales		16000	Sales		16000
Opening stock of raw materials	4200		Raw materials consumed 120 × Rs 50	6000	
Add: Purchase of raw materials	6000		Direct wages 120 × Rs 15	1800	
Total raw materials available	10200		Selling cost @ 5% on sales	800	
Less: Closing stock of raw materials	3000		Cost of goods sold (variable)		8600
Consumption of raw materials	7200		Contribution to overheads and profit		7400
Add: Direct wages	3600		Less: Manufacturing overheads	7200	
Add: Manufacturing expenses	7200		Less: Marketing and administrative overheads	1200	8400
Manufacturing costs	18000		Net loss		1000
Add: Opening stock of work-in-process	1200				
Available for completion	19200				
Less: Closing stock of work-in-process	4800				
Cost of goods manufactured	14400				
Add: Opening stock of finished goods	3600				
Goods available for sale	18000				
Less: Closing stock of finished goods	6000				
Cost of goods sold		12000			
Gross profit		4000			
Less: Selling and administrative expenses (including commission on sales @ 5%)		2000			
Net profit		2000			

DIFFERENCE IN PROFIT MEASUREMENT

It will be observed that under the direct costing method, only the cost of completed products sold is matched with the sales revenue that gives a contribution against which the aggregate of the manufacturing, selling, and administrative fixed overheads incurred during the whole period are matched. In the case of absorption costing, manufacturing overheads are spread out proportionately on goods sold, work-in-progress, and goods remaining unsold. In the former case, the cost of goods sold is principally variable in nature, where even the fixed commission on sales—a variable expense on the units sold—is included. In both the cases, except manufacturing overheads, other marketing and administrative overheads are charged in full against the sales of the year. One, therefore, wonders why manufacturing overheads should also not be treated similarly.

Under the absorption costing method, the difference between the sales revenue and the cost of goods sold is generally called gross profit or margin whereas under the direct costing method, it is called contribution. The value or cost of goods sold will obviously differ under these two methods. It is Rs 12,000 under the absorption costing method, while it is only Rs 8,600 under the direct costing method. Under the former method, there is a net profit of Rs 2,000, while in the latter method there is a loss of Rs 1,000.

Uses of Direct Costing Method

The full or absorption costing method is widely used and accepted by taxation authorities. The Tandon Committee had also advocated this method, which has now become an integral part of the appraisal format of banks. However, a banker is well-advised to use the direct or marginal costing method for an in-depth analysis of a credit proposal because of certain advantages of this method:

1. Under the direct costing method, profit responds to sales only, while in the case of absorption costing, profit is a function of both sales and production. In case of the latter, a large unsold stock may offset a fall in sales. A firm may have taken a profit on unsold stock (and pay taxes and dividend) which may not be sold at all. This may often fool a banker and make all his calculations go wrong. The direct costing method removes this income effect on inventory changes. Even when a borrower presents a manufacturing account under the absorption costing method, a banker should calculate the actual contribution and net profit on the basis of the direct costing method also, by making suitable adjustments as we have shown earlier. This will enable him

to know not only the operating strength or weakness of the business, but also the efficiency of the management in maintaining the competitive edge of the product line.

2. An incremental cost analysis is possible only under the direct costing method. This facilitates short-run price fixation to the advantage of a firm. When a large order is received and a bank is approached to finance it, the direct costing method enables a banker to know the incremental cost of producing the additional units, and thus argue effectively with the borrower, who may be claiming funds for the full factory cost.

3. It is claimed by the opponents of the direct costing method that under this the inventory value is understated because it does not include manufacturing overheads. But bankers would always like to have this method of valuation as it gives the true, though conservative, value of stocks by excluding manufacturing overheads. These overheads have to be paid for whether there is production or not.

Short-term and Long-term Effect

A critical look at the two methods will reveal that when *production exceeds sales*, net income under the absorption costing method is greater than it is under the direct costing method, because some fixed manufacturing overheads are absorbed in the inventory rather than being written-off as product costs. When, however, *sales exceed production*, net income under the absorption costing method is less than it is under the direct costing method, because some previously deferred fixed manufacturing overheads are included (along with current fixed manufacturing costs) in the cost of goods sold (through work-in-progress and finished goods). When sales and production are equal, there would obviously be no change in the net income under both the methods. In the long run, however, all costs are variable costs, and hence aggregate net income under the two methods will be equal provided all the goods produced are sold out.

In Chapter 12, absorption costing is reintroduced in the credit appraisal formats of banks and in Chapter 15 we explore marginal costing more fully through a break-even analysis.

Final Accounts

We now show extracts from the trial balance of a real company—National Industries Limited. Certain additional information, relevant to the drawing up of the final accounts, is also appended. With the help of this information, we first draw up various final accounts, and then interpret them from a banker's point of view. The trial balance will not tally, because items of assets and liabilities are excluded. A full trial balance is presented in the next chapter.

Extract from Trial Balance of National Industries Ltd. as on 31 March 20×7

(Rs in lakh)

	Dr	Cr
Sales		53100
Cash assistance and duty drawback		266
Interest and dividend received		26
Miscellaneous income		52
Excise duty	5287	
Purchase of raw materials	35611	
Wages including bonus	1271	
Salaries including bonus	768	
Contribution to PF and gratuity fund	283	
Carriage inward	34	
Welfare expenses	118	
Spares and stores	367	
Power, fuel, water	1908	
Repairs: Building	94	
Plant	305	
Others	<u>38</u>	437
Rent: Factory	180	
Office	<u>104</u>	284
Rates and taxes:		
Factory	392	
Office	<u>244</u>	636

(contd.)

(contd.)

Insurance: Factory	20	
Office and others	<u>36</u>	56
Advertisement		473
Carriage and freight outward		1695
Commission and brokerage		263
Travelling expenses		356
Postage, telegrams, and telephones		123
Printing and stationery		55
Audit expenses		7
Interest paid to bank		394
Interest paid for other loans		118
Bank charges		76
Miscellaneous expenses		556
Opening stocks:		
Raw materials	6614	
Work-in-progress	1372	
Finished goods	<u>3049</u>	11035

Other information

Closing stocks:			Provision for bad debt:	
Raw materials	7235		On debtors @ 2%	45
Work-in-progress	1432		On trade loans and advances @ 5%	<u>42</u>
Finished goods	<u>3805</u>			
	<u>12472</u>			<u>87</u>

Pre-paid expenses:				
Wages	90		Interest on bank loan accrued but not paid	43
Salaries	20			
Rates and taxes	50			
Insurance (office)	<u>20</u>			
	<u>180</u>			

Depreciation:		
Leasehold land	@ 2%	8
Buildings	@ 3%	44
Plant and machinery	@ 10%	462
Railway siding	@ 12.5%	1
Furniture and fixtures	@ 15%	11
Motor vehicles	@ 10%	<u>4</u>
		<u>530</u>

10% of share issue expenses to be written-off: Rs 3.

We move step-by-step from the conventional approach of drawing up a trading and profit and loss account to the most modern approach of drawing up a manufacturing, trading, and profit and loss account from these figures. A banker will come across both the approaches in his day-to-day dealing of credit proposals. The classical practice of drawing a straightforward trading and profit and loss account, where both the gross profit and net profit are calculated under one head, is still followed by many firms. This will look like the following:

Trading and Profit and Loss Account for the Year Ended 31 March 20X7

(Rs in lakh)

Dr					Cr
Opening stock:			Sales	53100	
Raw materials	6614		Less:		
Work-in-progress	1372		Excise duty	5287	47813
Finished goods	3049	11035	Closing stock:		
Purchase of raw materials		35611	Raw materials	7235	
Wages, including bonus	1271		Work-in-progress	1432	
Less: Pre-paid	90	1181	Finished goods	3805	12472
Carriage inward		34			
Power, fuel, water		1908			
Spares and stores		367			
Repairs—plant		305			
Rent—factory		180			
Rates and taxes (factory)		392			
Insurance—factory		20			
Depreciation:					
Leasehold land	8				
Plant and machinery	462				
Railway siding	1	471			
Gross profit carried down		8781			
Sub-total		60285	Sub-total		60285
Salaries	768		Gross profit brought down		8781
Less: Pre-paid	20	748			
Contribution to PF and gratuity fund		283	Cash assistance and duty drawback		266
Welfare expenses		118	Interest and dividend received		26
Repairs:					
Building	94		Miscellaneous Income		52
Others	38	132			

(contd.)

(contd.)

Rent—office		104
Rates and taxes—office	244	
Less: Pre-paid	50	194
Insurance—office	36	
Less: Pre-paid	20	16
Advertisement		473
Carriage and freight outward		1695
Commission and brokerage		263
Travelling expenses		356
Postage, telegrams, and telephones		123
Printing and stationery		55
Interest	512	
Add: Accrued	43	555
Bank charges		76
Miscellaneous expenses		556
Audit expenses		7
Depreciation:		
Buildings	44	
Furniture and fixtures	11	
Motor vehicles	4	59
Provision for bad debt:		
On debtors	45	
On trade loans and advances	42	87
Share issue expenses written-off		3
Net profit carried to Profit and loss appropriation account		3222
Total		9125	Total	9125

COST OF GOODS SOLD

The first part of the profit and loss account is similar to that of a trading account. Here all the opening stocks of raw materials, work-in-progress, and finished goods are charged to the debit of the profit and loss account, whereas the closing stocks are shown in its credit side. The gross profit is typically a manufacturing profit, as we will see later. However, it does not enable us to know the cost of goods sold, which is very important for a banker. It can be calculated under the *absorption costing method* once we segregate and group the costs as follows:

(Rs in lakh)

Manufacturing expenses:

Carriage inward	34
Power, fuel, and water	1908
Spares and stores	367
Repairs—plant	305
Rent—factory	180
Rent and taxes—factory	392
Insurance—factory	20
Depreciation—works	471
	3677

General administrative expenses:

Salaries	748
Contribution to PF and gratuity fund	283
Welfare expenses	118
Repairs—building	132
Rent	104
Rates and taxes	194
Insurance	16
Postage etc.	123
Printing and stationery	55
Bank charges	76
Miscellaneous expenses	556
Audit fees	7
Depreciation	59
Share issue expenses	3
	2474

Selling and marketing expenses:

Advertisement	473
Carriage	1695
Commission and brokerage	263
Travelling expenses	356
Provision for bad debt	87
	2874

With the help of these groupings of expenses, we now make an improvement on the previous method of presentation, which is practised by many enterprises.

Manufacturing, Trading, and Profit and Loss Account for the Year Ended 31 March 20X7

(Rs in lakh)

Debit				Credit
			Cost of production carried down	39788
Opening stock of materials	6614			
Add: Purchases	35611			
	42225			
Less: Closing stock	7235			
Material consumed		34990		
Wages, including bonus		1181		
Prime cost		36171		
Manufacturing expenses		3677		
		39848		
Add/Deduct:				
Difference in work-in-progress balance:				
Closing	1432			
Opening	1372	(–) 60		
Factory cost or Cost of production		39788		39788
			Sales	53100
Opening stock of			Less:	
finished goods		3049	Excise duty	5287
Add: Cost of production b/d		39788	Net sales	47813
		42837		
Less: Closing stock of finished goods		3805		
Cost of goods sold		39032		
Gross profit C/D		8781		
Total		47813	Total	47813
Selling and marketing expenses		2874	Gross profit b/d	8781
General administrative expenses		2474	Cash assistance and duty drawback	266
Interest		555	Interest and dividends received	26
Net profit carried over to Profit			Misc. Income	52
and Loss appropriation account		3222		
Total		9125	Total	9125

Excise Duty

It may be seen that excise duty is not included in the debit side of the account, but shown as a deduction from total sales. The reason behind this is that excise duty is a direct charge against sales revenue. Whenever finished goods leave the factory or designated godowns, excise authorities wait to have their share of the revenue. This indirect tax is passed on to the consumers by adding it to the price. It is not a production cost, but an incidence on sales. Hence, it is not included as cost, but deducted from sales to arrive at the net sales figure which is the real revenue of the business.

OPERATING PROFIT APPROACH

The manufacturing, trading, and profit and loss account shown earlier does not reveal the *operating profit*, but a net profit, which takes into account all non-trading expenses and incomes. Operating profit is calculated as:

		Rs in lakh
Net profit		3222
Less: Non-operating income:		
Interest and dividend received	26	
Miscellaneous income	52	78
Operating profit (after interest)		3144

A further development of the earlier system, which adopts the absorption costing method, calculates the operating profit far more analytically.

Manufacturing and Profit and Loss Account for the Year Ended 31 March 20×7
(Under Absorption Costing Method)

(Rs in lakh)

Sales		53100
Less: Excise duty		5287	47813
Opening stock of raw materials	6614	
Add: Purchases of raw materials	35611	
Raw materials available	42225	
Less: Closing stock of raw materials	7235	
Consumption of raw materials	34990	
Add: Direct wages including bonus	1181	
Add: Manufacturing expenses	3677	
Manufacturing cost	39848	
Add: Opening stock of work-in-progress	1372	
Available for completion	41220	
Less. Closing stock of work-in-progress	1432	
Cost of goods manufactured	39788	
Add: Opening stock of finished goods	3049	
Goods available for sale	42837	
Less: Closing stock of finished goods	3805	
Cost of goods sold	39032	
Gross profit (47813 – 39032)	8781	

(contd.)

(contd.)

Add: Cash assistance and duty drawback	<u>266</u>
	9047
Less: Selling, distribution, and administrative expenses	<u>5348</u>
Operating profit before interest	3699
Less: Interest	<u>555</u>
Operating profit after interest	<u>3144</u>

We may observe that cash assistance and duty drawbacks are excluded from the calculation of gross profit but they are not excluded for arriving at the final operating profit because these are incentives given by the government for export sales, though for a temporary period. *This is not exactly sales revenue but since it is arising out of (export) sales only, it should be taken into consideration while arriving at operating profit or loss.*

When we compare the last two systems of accounting, we will find that *factory cost* in the earlier system is called *cost of goods manufactured* in the latter system, while *cost of goods sold* and *gross profit* are similar under both the systems. Non-trading incomes are completely excluded from consideration in the latter system, and the operating profit before interest is calculated by deducting selling and distribution expenses and administrative expenses. As we will see in Chapter 12, the latter system has been recommended by the Tandon Committee for credit appraisal. Therefore, published final accounts of companies will have to be reconstructed by bankers to understand the flow of costs at each stage of production.

The attention of bankers should focus on the two most important figures—*goods available for completion and goods available for sale. A comparison of these two figures will reveal whether a firm is holding up funds in the process for a long time.* If the difference is high, then it can be presumed that some bottlenecks have developed

in the production process that need immediate attention. It may be that a crucial item needed for final conversion to finished goods is not available, or that labour trouble has slowed down the production.

Some General Observations

It may also be seen that the prime cost is 91 per cent of the cost of production, of which raw materials constitute 88 per cent and labour 3 per cent. This indicates that the company is a technology intensive enterprise. It is also volume driven as the low operating margin on sales suggests (6.97 per cent). The company is in a competitive market requiring a lot of effort in marketing the products; selling and distribution expenses constitute about 5.5 per cent of sales. Such a set-up also requires considerable management costs, both at the factory and head office levels for planning and coordination. Manufacturing overheads are found to be about 10 per cent of the cost of production, and the general management costs are about 4.5 per cent of sales. All these costs, particularly those of a fixed nature, do not tell much now. Figures for the past few years are required to make a comparative study and draw meaningful conclusions. This is taken up in Chapter 15 on ratio analysis.

UNUSUAL INCOMES

It is necessary to locate any unusual items of income, which may have a bearing on the operating health of a company. For this company, the non-operating income is not much as compared to the net profit (Rs 78 lakh against a net profit of Rs 3222 lakh). It is composed of interest and dividends received, besides some miscellaneous income. However, while on this subject, we must draw the attention of a banker to a situation where non-operating incomes comprise a substantial part of the profit. In some cases it may also be found that the size of non-operating incomes is such that but for it a company would have made a loss. Such situations indicate that the firm either has lost its operating viability or is on the verge of losing it. It may be making frantic efforts to keep the shareholders happy with a dividend by making earnings from investments made in the shares of other companies or simply by letting out either the whole or a part of the factory and office premises. The firm having already lost the business no longer requires the space! What will follow next is the selling out of plants and land buildings part by part, and crediting the surplus to the profit and loss account. If, however, the firm is doing it as part of a plan for diversifying to new business, it is a conscious business decision. There is nothing wrong in this, because the assumption here is that the profit so made will be invested in the diversified business line.

But if the funds are diverted from the business by paying dividend to cater to the interests of the controlling shareholders, the objective of the company is suspect.

At times, the credit side of the profit and loss account may feature depreciation credited back owing to a change in the method of calculating depreciation. This must be read with the notes of the auditors on this subject. It may have been done to give a 'face-lift' to the eroding net worth of a company, or to pay dividend where the company has, perhaps, made no profit at all. Both moves are suspect, but the latter is dangerous—*the company may be eating out of its own capital.*

Concluding Remarks

In conclusion, it can be said that a banker's immediate concern is the profit earning capacity of a business because as we have said in Chapter 3, a profitably-run unit is the best security of a banker. A banker doing credit appraisal must focus on this aspect of the business. With the help of the systems of accounting presented in this chapter, we will calculate and interpret certain important earning and expense ratios in Chapter 16 with a view to understanding the profitability of a business.

If for sins committed, I am to be punished, what about justice for desiring those uncommitted?
—Ghalib

11 Understanding the Balance Sheet

INTRODUCTION

We mentioned in the last chapter that a profit and loss account enables an entrepreneur to know the result of his operations for a given period. In addition to that, he also desires to know the status of his business as on a particular date. That is, he should know how his operations are affecting, or have affected, the financial structure of his business; whether the structure is still capable of supporting his operations further; if not, what are the corrective steps to be taken. Hence, when he draws up a profit and loss account for a period, he also takes stock of all assets and liabilities standing at the close of the business of that period. This 'stock-taking' is done in a format which is called a balance sheet.

As mentioned before, the choice of the time period and date for drawing up of the profit and loss account and the balance sheet respectively, follows some established conventions, but that does not preclude an entrepreneur from knowing the position of his business at any other interval or date. An accountant can do it simply by surrogating a closure and drawing up memorandum statements. It has now become a norm for many companies to publish results of their operations quarterly and biannually to keep the stakeholders informed. It is *invariably* done before declaring an interim dividend by a company, or taking on a new partner, or retiring one, in case of partnership firms. The memorandum statements are also drawn up at the desire of a financial institution or bank which may like to know the condition of the business on a date as close as possible to the date of consideration of a credit proposal.

TRIAL BALANCE

As accountants will record a transaction only when an exchange has taken place, the normal presumption is that at any point of time the aggregate of debit balances must tally with the aggregate of credit balances appearing in the books of accounts of a business. In the next three pages ledger balances are drawn from the books of accounts of the same multi-crore unit—National Industries Limited that we studied in Chapter 10. This is the basic statement for drawing up of both the profit and loss account and the balance sheet.

TREATMENT OF CLOSING STOCK

Readers would observe one peculiarity in the trial balance. While in all the cases, closing balances feature in the statement, in the case of stock it is the opening stock which appears there; the closing stock features below it.

National Industries Ltd.
Trial Balance as on 31 March 20XX

(Rs in lakh)

Serial No.	Account Head	Dr	Cr
1.	Paid-up capital		2916
2.	Share premium		5
3.	Revaluation reserve		1652
4.	Debenture redemption reserve		40
5.	Investment allowance reserve		520
6.	General reserve		3301
7.	Debentures		250
8.	Secured loan from ICICI Bank		160
9.	Unsecured loan from parent Co.		408
10.	Secured loan from WBIDC		251
11.	Fixed deposits		989
12.	Cash credit from bank (secured)		2121
13.	Trade creditors		7326
14.	Bills payable		281
15.	Creditors for capital expenditure		123
16.	Security deposits		508
17.	Unclaimed dividends		43
18.	Land (freehold)	171	
19.	Land (leasehold)	411	
20.	Buildings	1453	
21.	Plant and machinery	4620	
22.	Railway siding	8	
23.	Furniture and fixtures	76	
24.	Motor vehicles	39	
25.	Capital work-in-progress	1012	
26.	Investment in subsidiary Co.	2	
27.	Investment in unquoted shares and debentures	3	
28.	Investment in quoted shares and debentures	17	
29.	Amount due from subsidiary	4	
30.	Housing and other loans to employees	507	
31.	Trade loans and advances	847	
32.	Trade deposit with suppliers	168	
33.	Deposit with IDBI	50	
34.	Advance to suppliers of capital goods	179	

(contd.)

(contd.)

35.	*Opening stock:*			
	Raw materials	6614		
	Work-in-progress	1372		
	Finished goods	3049	11035	
36.	Sundry debtors		2225	
37.	Cash and bank		307	
38.	Share issue expenses not written-off		28	
39.	Sales			53100
40.	Cash assistance and duty drawback			266
41.	Interest and dividend received			26
42.	Miscellaneous income			52
43.	Excise duty		5287	
44.	Purchase of raw materials		35611	
45.	Wages including bonus		1271	
46.	Salaries including bonus		768	
47.	Contribution to PF and gratuity fund		283	
48.	Carriage inward		34	
49.	Welfare expenses		118	
50.	Spares and stores		367	
51.	Power, fuel, water		1908	
52.	*Repairs:*			
	Building	94		
	Plant	305		
	Others	38	437	
53.	Rent		284	
54.	Rates and taxes		636	
55.	Insurance		56	
56.	Advertisement		473	
57.	Carriage and freight outward		1695	
58.	Commission and brokerage		263	
59.	Travelling expenses		356	
60.	Postage, telegrams, and telephones		123	
61.	Printing and stationery		55	
62.	Audit expenses		7	
63.	Interest paid to bank		394	
64.	Interest paid on other loans		118	
65.	Bank charges		76	
66.	Miscellaneous expenses		556	
	Total		74338	74338

(contd.)

(contd.)

Adjustments:

Closing stock:

Raw materials	7235
Work-in-progress	1432
Finished goods	<u>3805</u>
	<u>12472</u>

Provisions for bad and doubtful debt:

On debtors @ 2%	45
On trade loans and advances @ 5%	<u>42</u>
	<u>87</u>

Pre-paid expenses:

Wages	90
Salaries	20
Rates and taxes	50
Insurance (office)	<u>20</u>
	<u>180</u>

Interest on bank loan accrued but not paid:		43

Depreciation to be provided:

Leasehold land	2% p.a.	8
Buildings	3% p.a.	44
Plant and machinery	10% p.a.	462
Railways siding	12.5% p.a.	1
Furniture and fixtures	15% p.a.	11
Motor vehicles	10% p.a.	<u>4</u>
		<u>530</u>

10% of shares issue expenses to be written-off every year:	3

When opening stock appears in the trial balance and closing stock below it, the obvious presumption is that in the stock account there is only one entry at the beginning of the year, that is, when the closing balance of the previous year is carried forward. This balance continues till the end of the year, and hence features in the trial balance as such. The question now is how the closing stock is calculated and entered in the accounts book. It is definitely not by entering all purchases to the debit of the stock account and all sales or cost of goods sold, or simply the issues to the credit side of the account. A look at the trial balance will reveal that the purchases account is shown separately from the stock account, which is to be closed by passing a credit entry to the debit of the profit and loss account. This leaves no scope for transferring the balance once again to the stock account. If we do this, we would charge the profit and loss account twice for the same amount of purchases, which is wrong. The riddle is solved if we look at the subsidiary books of a business.

Stock Registers

There is one book, the stock purchases register, that is not part of the accounts book. This is maintained separately for each item of stock, both by quantity as well as in rupees. Whenever purchases are made these are entered in this register and the aggregate figure in rupees is debited to the purchase account. When stocks are issued to production, these are entered in the stock register at a value pre-determined by the management based on either FIFO, LIFO, or average value etc. method as discussed earlier. Whatever method of valuation is adopted, the stock in hand at the end of the year, as found from this register, is an estimate of the value of stocks as on the date of closing. It should be noted here that when issues are made to production, these are entered only in the stock register; they are never credited to the stock account, which remains static. This opening stock is charged to the profit and loss account, closing it for the time being. Then the closing stock as estimated is credited there—as if a part of income to be reckoned with sales—and then brought to the stock account as a corresponding debit item to be carried forward to the next year as the opening stock.

CLASSIFICATION OF ACCOUNTS

The account heads featured in the trial balance can be divided into three categories:

Nature of Account	Item Nos.
1. Promises account	1 to 17
2. Real account	18 to 37
3. Nominal account	39 to 66

The only item left out is item no. 38—the share issue expenses account (not written-off). This is purely an expense item, but treated as a fictitious

asset. We have dealt with this item in detail in Chapter 7.

Nominal accounts exist for name's sake only, which are reflected either in diminution of or increase in assets at the end of a year or on a given date. Therefore, we can simply jot down the assets as on that date and match them against the liabilities standing on that date to know whether the business has made a profit or not. This way we can completely ignore all the nominal accounts, that is, income and expenses and also the profit and loss account. Let us see how this can be done.

BALANCE SHEET

Just below the trial balance, besides closing stock, certain additional items feature, which are to be taken into account to arrive at a true and fair view of the state of affairs of a business. We have first prepared a statement of assets and liabilities, after adjusting these items in the next page.

We shall find that against aggregate assets of Rs 24,159 lakh, the business has contracted liabilities aggregating Rs 20,937 lakh. Hence, the excess of assets over liabilities must be the profit of the business calculated as below:

	(Rs in lakh)
Aggregate of assets as on 31 March 20XX	24159
Less: Aggregate of liabilities as on 31 March 20XX	20937
Profit for the year	3222

Readers may recall that we have already arrived at exactly the same figure from the profit and loss account of the company drawn up in the last chapter. Principles of book keeping and accountancy maintain that every transaction is an exchange operation having two faces. If assets (debit) show a certain value as on a certain date, the other face, which is liabilities (credit), must be same as the first face. The gap may be filled up by contracting a capital liability or any outside

Statement of Assets and Liabilities as on 31 March 20XX

Liabilities	(Rs in lakh)	Assets		(Rs in lakh)
Paid-up capital	2916	Land (freehold)		171
Share premium	5	Land (leasehold)	411	
Revaluation reserve	1652	Less depreciation	8	403
Debenture redemption reserve	40	Buildings	1453	
Investment allowance reserve	520	Less: Depreciation	44	1409
General reserve	3301	Plant and machinery	4620	
Debentures	250	Less: Depreciation	462	4158
Secured loan ICICI Bank	160	Railway siding	8	
Secured loan WBIDC	251	Less: Depreciation	1	7
Unsecured loan from parent Co.	408	Furniture & fixtures	76	
Fixed deposits	989	Less: Depreciation	11	65
Cash credit from bank	2121	Motor vehicles	39	
Trade creditors	7326	Less: Depreciation	4	35
Bills payable	281	Capital work-in-progress		1012
Creditors for capital expenditure	123	Investment in subsidiary Co.		2
Security deposits	508	Investment in unquoted shares and debentures		3
Unclaimed dividend	43	Investment in quoted shares and debentures		17
Interest accrued and payable	43	Amount due from subsidiary		4
		Housing and other loans to employees		507
		Trade loans and advances	847	
		Less: Provision for bad debts	42	805
		Trade deposit with suppliers		168
		Deposits with IDBI		50
		Advances to suppliers of capital goods		179
		Sundry debtors	2225	
		Less: Provision for bad debt	45	2180
		Closing stock		12472
		Cash and bank		307
		Share issue expenses	28	
		Less: Written-off	3	25
		Pre-paid expenses		180
	20937			24159

loan liability. Since the trial balance does not show any other liability, the balancing fund must have been generated from the operations of a business, which we call profit. This fund concept is elaborated further in Chapter 14 on funds flow and cash flow analysis.

We should remember that whenever profit is made, the biggest partner, the government, wakes up to have the lion's share by way of income tax. Then come the shareholders or proprietor(s), who may decide to retain a portion of profit-after-tax in the form of a reserve, and take the balance by way of dividend or drawings. These are all appropriations or allocations from profit.

Prospects and Problems

It is clear by now that a balance sheet is the picture of a business, taken by a snapshot, as on a particular date. The business continues thereafter. The picture will be different even one day before or after that. It does not indicate much about its future shape, except perhaps a trend, if considered with the past years' balance sheets. For this reason, the balance sheet as a tool for credit appraisal has come under attack at the hands of the modern school of financial analysts. The old school, however, still maintains that a balance sheet analysis helps a banker in assessing the continued creditworthiness of a borrower. Under the 'going concern approach' a banker first interprets the balance sheet to see whether the required bank finance plus new debt or equity issues, if any, indicate the desired financial strength of the business to justify the advance. If the indication is negative, there is no need to proceed further in the matter. When the prima facie assessment is positive, a banker moves to the 'gone concern approach' and assesses the probable risk in the event of the failure of the business. This is done by evaluating every item of assets from the point of view of relisability.

'These arguments were alright,' claims the new school, 'so long as lending was really short-term and self-liquidating.' These days the principles of bank lending have undergone considerable change. Now, a banker has a long-term stake in a borrower's business. The cash credit system of working capital finance (whatever part remains) is in effect, more permanent than a term loan, as any banker will agree. The purpose is now more important than the collaterals as security cover. Under this changed situation, the classical 'going-gone' approach no longer holds good.

There is some validity in the arguments of both the schools. Without going into this controversy any further, *it will be sufficient to remember that no new methodology of financial appraisal can be handled properly, unless we develop a thorough understanding of the balance sheet.* Even the methodology of appraisal proposed by the new school, which came to be partially codified by various committees in India, cannot be made good use of unless we grasp the fundamentals of the balance sheet.

Funds Approach

We have indicated earlier that the liability side of the balance sheet is composed of various promises made by a business to a proprietor(s), lenders, and suppliers of goods and services. These promises constitute sources of funds, which are employed to acquire various assets needed for the operation of the business. Later, in a separate chapter, we make an in-depth study of the funds flow concept. Here we only classify various sources and usage of funds for making an alternative presentation of the balance sheet. Some broad outlines of this classification were given while we discussed liabilities in Chapters 8 and 9. We now try to draw a complete picture within that outline. The tabular presentation in the next page is an attempt in that direction.

This list is not exhaustive, though we have tried to include here possible sources and usage of funds in greater detail. The usage of funds proposed here is as per ideal standards evolved

Classification of Sources and uses of Funds

Concept	Constituents	Usage
Long-term funds		
(a) Shareholders' fund	i. Equity share capital ii. Preference share capital iii. Capital reserve iv. Debenture redemption reserve v. Investment allowance reserve vi. General reserve vii. Surplus credit balance in profit and loss account	i. Intangible and fictitious assets like goodwill, preliminary expenses, patents etc. debit balance of profit and loss account ii. Fixed assets iii. Investments iv. Long-term loan to staff etc. v. Deposits with port, customs etc. vi. Net current assets
(b) Long-term loan fund	i. Debentures ii. Term loan iii. Loan from parent company or those falling due in the year iv. Deposits of long maturities	
(c) Short-term funds Current liabilities and provisions	i. Trade creditors ii. Bills payable iii. Fixed deposits of shorter maturity or those falling due in the year iv. Bank overdraft/cash credit v. Loan instalments of term loan falling due for payment within the year vi. Accrued liabilities vii. Provision for bad debt viii. Taxation liability	Large portion of i. Current assets, e.g., stocks, debtors cash etc. ii. Loans and advances, trade advances, advances (short-term) to employees iii. Trade deposits

by financial analysts over a long period. Any deviation from the standard must be probed into, but as we will see in a later chapter, there should not be any rigidity about it: there are circumstances which may justify deviations from the standard. *However, the standard principle that as far as possible shareholders' funds together with long-term funds should cover not only the fixed assets but also a portion of current assets should apply,* except where the unit is sick and under a nursing programme. We will elaborate on this and other related aspects after we recast the balance sheet under the funds concept in the next page.

Funds Analysis of Balance Sheet
National Industries Ltd.
Balance Sheet as on 31 March 20XX (Before appropriation of profit)
Capital and long-term funds employed

(Rs in lakh)

I.	*Shareholders' fund*		
	Paid-up capital	2916	
	Share premium	5	
	Revaluation reserve	1652	
	Debenture redemption reserve	40	
	Investment allowance reserve	520	
	General reserve	3301	
	Profit and loss a/c (1)	<u>3222</u>	11656
II.	*Long-term loan fund*		
	Debentures	250	
	Loan from ICICI Bank	160	
	Loan from WBIDC	251	
	Loan from parent Co.	408	
	Security deposits (2)	<u>508</u>	<u>1577</u>
	A. *Long-term resources*		<u>13233</u>
III.	*Employment of long-term resources*		
	Net fixed assets	6248	
	Capital work-in-progress (3)	1012	
	Investments (unquoted)	5	
	Housing and other loans to employees (4)	507	
	Advances to suppliers of capital goods (5)	179	
	Deposit with IDBI (6)	50	
	Share issue expenses	<u>25</u>	8026
	B. Total		<u>8026</u>
	C. *Net working capital* (A–B)		5207
IV.	*Short-term assets*		
	Closing stock	12472	
	Sundry debtors (net)	2180	
	Cash and bank	307	
	Trade loans and advances (net)	805	
	Trade deposits with suppliers	168	
	Amount due from subsidiary	4	
	Investments (quoted)	17	
	Pre-paid expenses	<u>180</u>	
	D. Total		16133

(Rs in lakh)

V. *Short-term resources*		
Trade creditors	7326	
Bills payable	281	
Fixed deposits (7)	989	
Cash credit from bank	2121	
Creditors for capital expenditure (8)	123	
Interest accrued and payable	43	
Unclaimed dividend (9)	<u>43</u>	
E. Total		<u>10926</u>
F. *Net current assets* (D–E)		<u>5207</u>
VI. *Net worth*:		
Shareholders' fund		<u>11656</u>
Less: Share issue expenses	25	
Revaluation reserve	<u>1652</u>	<u>1677</u>
Tangible net worth (before appropriations)		<u>9979</u>

Explanatory Notes:

1. Net profit arrived at in the profit and loss account is the profit before taxation and allocation to various reserves. It changes its character the moment allocations are made. The company has now made the following allocations:

	(Rs in lakh)
Taxation (@ 50% assumed)	1600
Transfer to debenture redemption reserve	120
Proposed dividend @ 25% on paid-up capital	730
Transfer to general reserve	<u>772</u>
Net profit	<u>3222</u>

In this situation, the taxation liability and proposed dividend aggregating Rs 2,330 lakh would now move to the short-term fund, and Rs 892 lakh being the aggregate of debenture redemption reserve and general reserve would go under the shareholders fund.

The allocation immediately changes the financial structure and stake of the business. Not only is the net worth reduced, but the company will have to make immediate arrangement for cash to meet the taxation liability, and proposed dividend (within 42 days) aggregating Rs 2,330 lakh against the available cash and bank balance of Rs 307 lakh only. The net worth after appropriation has also come down to Rs 7,649 lakh. All these changes are incorporated in the percentage balance sheet drawn up later in this chapter.

2. Security deposits are received from dealers as caution money. These continue so long as the dealership arrangement continues, which is generally for a long term, particularly for this company, which holds

a monopoly position in the consumer goods market. Hence, these deposits are treated under long-term resources.[1]

3. 5 and 8

Capital work-in-progress 3, and advances to suppliers of capital goods 5 are necessarily part of fixed assets, and therefore, shown as such because these are supposed to have been funded from long-term sources. But *creditors for capital expenditure 8 cannot be part of long-term resources because these creditors are to be paid-off immediately*, and hence, included as short-term liability. No doubt that their payments might or should be funded from long-term sources, but the effect of the payments would be an immediate reduction in current assets.[2]

4. Housing and other loans to employees may sometimes be included under the head loans and advances. But as these loans are generally repayable in monthly instalments from the salary, and spread over a long period—perhaps till retirement—it is advisable to treat these loans as part of long-term assets, and get them financed from long-term resources.

6. This deposit with IDBI was made to obtain certain tax advantages. It is repayable after a long period. Hence, it is included under long-term assets. If, however, it is found that it is maturing within the given year, it should be treated as a short-term asset. We should remember, however, that it is an investment outside the business.

7. It is presumed that deposits are falling due for repayment within a short period. If, however, this is not so, or the company intends to renew the deposits as and when they fall due for repayment, they can be bracketed under long-term resources, and utilised to finance a portion of the net working capital requirements.[3]

9. Unclaimed dividends, though included under short-term resources, are in effect, a fund on which the business has no control, because under the Indian Companies Act the unpaid dividend account has to be maintained separately with a scheduled bank, and the company cannot utilise the fund except for the purposes of payment of dividend. Companies are under a legal obligation to transfer the unclaimed portion of dividend declared to the unclaimed dividend account within seven days of expiry of 42 days from the date of declaration of dividend. After the expiry of three days, the amount of dividend still lying unclaimed/unpaid has to be transferred to the general revenue account of the central government. It is clear, therefore, that this fund shown on the liability side of the balance sheet, and an equal amount from the cash and bank balance on the other side, should be deleted altogether from the purview of the consideration of a credit proposal by a banker.[4]

---

[1] See also Chapter 12 and Annexure 12.1 for its treatment under the Reserve Bank of India guidelines.

[2] Ibid.

[3] Although term loan instalments or fixed deposits falling due within the next 12 months do not any longer form part of current liabilities for calculation of bank finance, the current nature of this liability cannot be denied.

[4] See also Annexure 12.1 to Chapter 12.

NET WORTH

We have already indicated that net worth is the financial stake of proprietor(s) in a business. It is often claimed that a banker is interested in net worth mainly for the security of his advance. This is more so now under the changing principles of lending. A modern banker is more interested in the trend rather than the size of the net worth. If the net worth of a firm is increasing, a banker feels comfortable because his finance is in good hands. A banker's strongest security is the continuing good health of a business, a sure indication of which is increasing net worth. On the contrary, if the worst happens, then also it is the net worth that measures the magnitude of the risk undertaken by a bank.

Estimating the Net Worth

On the right hand side of the balance sheet, net worth is supposed to be represented by solid assets, the assumption being that on the sale or realisation of all assets, what is left after payment of all outside liabilities is the net worth. It follows, therefore, that in calculating the net worth of a business, we should also look at the assets side of the balance sheet and exclude all intangible or fictitious assets like goodwill and unabsorbed expenses (preliminary expenses, share issue expenses), and of course, any debit balance in the profit and loss account representing loss. The last item is the most important, because any loss eats into the capital of the firm, and hence into its net worth.

In our example of National Industries Limited, the shareholders fund is Rs 11,656 lakh from which the unabsorbed share issue expenses of Rs 25 lakh and revaluation reserve of Rs 1,652 lakh have been deducted to arrive at the *provisional* net worth, that is, 11656 – 1677 = Rs 9,979 lakh. This is before making provisions for payment of taxes and dividend, which aggregate to Rs 2,330 lakh. The resultant net worth of the firm therefore comes to 9979 – 2330 = Rs 7,649 lakh.[5]

Incidentally, for this company, net worth covers net fixed assets of Rs 5,787 lakh (that is, 6248 + 1012 + 179 – 1652) more than fully, which is a sure sign of the financial strength of the business. Its long-term outside liability (Rs 1,577 lakh) is only a fraction of the net worth (20 per cent).

It appears that the company has preferred to depend more on internal resources than going in for market borrowing for its growth. The company might have decided on this capital structure (long-term) for either one or more of the following reasons:

1. To keep the average cost of fund at a low level.
2. To avoid interference from financial institutions.
3. To conform to the conservative risk profile of the company.

[5] Net worth of the company is taken at net of the revaluation reserve, because as has been pointed out before, the revaluation reserve does not constitute any actual fund flow to the business. A similar amount should also be deducted from revalued fixed assets to arrive at net fixed assets. However, if a banker is satisfied with the revaluation and is convinced that the market value of the assets is more than their book value, it is advisable for him to make a note of it in the appraisal memorandum by showing two sets of net worth—one before revaluation and the other after—because maybe if the borrower fails, it is the latter net worth which may ultimately return the lent fund.

A banker may look at net worth from two angles: one, to determine the stake of a borrower in the business, and the other to assess the net realisable value of the business in the event of its failure. The former stems from the 'going concern approach', where all revaluations are excluded, and the latter from the 'gone concern approach', where the market value of assets becomes relevant.

Whichever may be the reason, prima facie, a banker likes a company with such a sound financial base. But such companies are not too many. The first reason is the difficulty to generate adequate internal resources, and the second is the desire of the company to gear its capital structure, as we will now see.

GEARING OF CAPITAL

A substantial general reserve creates an expectation in the minds of the shareholders for a bonus issue. A company cannot morally refuse this, though it may find it difficult to maintain the same rate of dividend on the expanded capital base.[6] Let us now imagine that the present company has decided to capitalise 50 per cent of its general reserve accumulated as on 31 March 20XX, that is, 3301 + 772 = Rs 4,073 lakh; 50 per cent of it, say Rs 2,034 lakh). The paid-up capital would, therefore, be 2916 + 2034 = Rs 4,950 lakh.

If the company intends to maintain its existing dividend rate of 25 per cent on the paid-up capital, it will require Rs 1,237 lakh as against Rs 730 lakh required before capitalisation of the reserve fund. This would not be so easy a proposition even for a profit-making company like the present one.

Let us imagine a completely different situation when paid-up capital was kept at Rs 1,000 lakh as against Rs 4,950 lakh, and the remaining amount of Rs 3,950 lakh was arranged by way of borrowing by issue of debentures at a rate of 15 per cent interest per annum. The tax remains at 50 per cent of the net profit. The two cases are analysed in the next page in Table 11.1.

---

[6] Under SEBI guidelines, the board of directors of a company while declaring a bonus issue have to indicate the rate of dividend payable in future on the expanded capital base.

SHAREHOLDERS VERSUS BANKER

Case II is a highly geared situation which may be liked by shareholders. As against 14.74 per cent dividend for Case I shareholders, Case II shareholders get a dividend of 42.30 per cent, even after payment of interest on additional debentures and making the same amount of transfer to the general reserve. If the company decides to transfer a lesser amount to the reserve, which it most likely would, then the rate of dividend will be much higher.

There are legal provisions forbidding a board of directors from raising external loans more than the aggregate of paid-up capital and free reserves, but with the permission of shareholders at a general meeting, it can well exceed the limit, and a situation as described in Case II is, therefore, not improbable. In fact, quite a few companies have this kind of capital structure. Their shares are quoted at extraordinarily high prices in the share market. The scrips are in great demand, not because they have solid asset backing, but because the company pays high dividends. Fast trading in these scrips enables an operator to make a 'quick buck' from loading and unloading operations.

To a banker, a highly geared company is vulnerable to shocks. Houses owning such companies invariably engage themselves in speculative activities. Examples are rife in the history of Indian banking to show that companies whose scrips were highly sought after at one time finally became sick and landed in the laps of banks and the government, (particularly after the nationalisation of banks). These companies borrowed up to their necks without expanding their capital bases, and being unable to redeem the loans due to the absence of reserves, they borrowed more and more, and finally succumbed to the demand of snowballing creditors.

TABLE 11.1   Effect of Capitalisation

(Rs in lakh)

	Paid-up Capital	Additional Debentures	Profit before Tax	Interest on Additional Debentures	Tax
	1	2	3	4	5
Case I	4950	—	3222	—	1600
Case II	1000	3950	3222	593	1314

	Profit after Interest and Tax	Transfer to Reserve	Available for Dividend	Rate of Dividend
	6	7	8	9
Case I	1622	892	730	14.74%
Case II	1315	892	423	42.30%

FORMAT OF A BALANCE SHEET

The profit and loss account and balance sheet discussed in the last chapter and in this chapter have been presented in a general 'T' form for ease of understanding. Once the operating and financial variables of a business are understood properly in their right context and connotation, culling and grouping the variables from any format of presentation to another becomes a simple exercise.

Different forms of presentations have been evolved and standardised keeping in mind the necessity of various user groups. For corporate entities, the Indian Companies Act has laid down two alternative forms of a balance sheet. One is in the conventional 'T' form, where assets and liabilities are grouped and arranged in the descending order of liquidity, in contrast to the American form of presentation. This has been done primarily for the ease of shareholders' understanding, who are mostly concerned about the net worth of the business or the net asset value of their shares. The other is the vertical form of a balance sheet giving sources and applications of funds. This is analytical about how the business operations of a unit have been financed for a given period. We have already introduced this form in this chapter while making a funds analysis of the National Industries Limited. This form was introduced by the Indian Companies Act on 12 March 1979 keeping in mind the recommendations of the International Accounting Standards Committee. This form is useful for trained analysts, particularly those belonging to a group of lenders and creditors who are interested in knowing how the funds supplied by them have been used by the borrowing company.

NON-CORPORATE BORROWERS

While for corporate borrowers, forms of presentation of financial statements had long been standardised, there had been no standard form for non-corporate enterprises like proprietary or partnership firms. Unlike corporate entities, the audit reports of these firms were also not standardised. This was creating problems for structuring the operating and financial variables of non-corporate borrowers for purposes of credit analysis. In order to remove this difficulty, the Indian Banks Association, in collaboration with the Institute of Chartered Accountants of India, prepared the following formats for presentation of financial statements of non-corporate firms:

1. Proforma of profit and loss account and balance sheet for *trading firms*.
2. Proforma of profit and loss account and balance sheet for *manufacturing firms*.
3. Proforma of funds flow statement.
4. Proforma of audit report.
5. Proforma of special audit reports in case of borrowal firms perceived by banks as important for regular and close monitoring.

In the meantime, the Central Board of Direct Taxes amended the Income Tax Rules to prescribe the forms in which the reports of *audit of accounts* of persons carrying on business or profession having a business turnover of over Rs 40 lakh and income receipts of over Rs 10 lakh respectively were to be submitted. This form of *audit report* was finally adopted by the RBI in place of the one suggested by the Indian Banks' Association (IBA) and Institute of Chartered Accountants of India (ICAI) team. Other formats of financial statements, as suggested by the team, were approved by the RBI with some modifications. Banks were advised on 12 April 1985 to ask their non-corporate borrowers, enjoying aggregate working capital limits of Rs 10 lakh and above from the banking system, to present their final accounts and audit reports in these formats. This standardised system has gone a long way in developing a uniform appraisal system in the banking industry. All these formats are given in Annexures 11.1 to 11.7.

PERCENTAGE BALANCE SHEET

For analytical purposes, a balance sheet can also be presented in percentage form. This form of presentation reveals a lot of information at one look. It is an excellent starting point for a credit appraiser in forming a prima facie opinion of a business. In a percentage balance sheet, each item is represented as a percentage of the total of the respective side of the balance sheet to facilitate a quick analysis. We have done it for the balance sheet of National Industries Limited in the next page.

PRELIMINARY OBSERVATIONS

From the percentage balance sheet the key figures can be picked up to form a prima facie opinion of the business:

Shareholders' fund	38.60%	Long-term assets	33.28%
Total long-term resources	45.13%	Short-term assets	66.72%
Trade creditors (including bills payable)	31.48%	Stocks	51.63%
Total short-term resources	54.87%		

The shareholders' fund (net worth) is the dominant component of long-term resources; it is providing nearly 40 per cent of the total fund requirements of the business. The company must have built up this fund by consistently ploughing back its profits, which is evident from the large general reserve fund (16.86 per cent). It is likely that the company may soon issue bonus shares to capitalise a part of this reserve. Whatever may be the reason for depending heavily on internal resource generation (as discussed earlier) it can be said that this is a growth-oriented company. The share of net worth in the total long-term resources also suggests that its unavailed borrowing capacity is considerably high. The picture is, however, different on the short-term side. Here the company relies more on market finance (trade creditors: 30.32 per cent) than on bank finance (8.78 per cent). The net worth of the company being good, the conclusion may be that the firm is holding a near-monopsonic position

National Industries Ltd.
Percentage Balance Sheet as on 31 March 20XX (after appropriations)

(Rs in lakh)

Liability	Amount	%	Assets	Amount	%
Paid-up capital	2916	12.07	Net fixed assets	6248	25.86
Share premium	5	0.02	Capital work-in-progress	1012	4.19
Revaluation reserve	1652	6.84	Investments	22	0.09
Debenture redemption reserve	160	0.66	Housing loan to employees	507	2.10
Investment allowance reserve	520	2.15	Advances to suppliers of capital goods	179	0.74
General reserve	4073	16.86	Deposits with IDBI	50	0.20
Shareholders' fund	9326	38.60	Share issue expenses	25	0.10
Debentures	250	1.03	Long-term Assets	8043	33.28
Loan from ICICI Bank	160	0.67	Closing stock	12472	51.63
Loan from WBIDC	251	1.03	Sundry debtors	2180	9.02
Loan from parent Co.	408	1.70	Trade loans and advances	805	3.33
Security deposits	508	2.10	Trade deposit with suppliers	168	0.70
Long-term loan fund	1577	6.53	Amount due from subsidiary	4	0.02
Total Long-term Resources	10903	45.13	Pre-paid expenses	180	0.76
Trade creditors	7326	30.32	Cash and bank	307	1.26
Bills payable	281	1.16	Short-term Assets	16116	66.72
Fixed deposits	989	4.10			
Cash credit from bank	2121	8.78			
Creditors for capital expenditure	123	0.50			
Interest accrued and payable	43	0.18			
Taxation liability	1600	6.63			
Proposed dividend	730	3.02			
Unclaimed dividend	43	0.18			
Short-term Fund	13256	54.87			
Grand total	24159	100	Grand total	24159	100

in the input market, which has enabled it to command larger credit from its suppliers, who may be small and numerous.

On the assets side, short-term assets are double the fixed assets. This indicates that the company is in the consumer goods market. This is also evident from the composition of the current assets. The closing stock constitutes nearly 52 per cent of the total assets and 77 per cent of total current assets. A consumer goods industry should have adequate stocks of finished goods, and consequently, an adequate inventory of raw materials.

This preliminary evidence suggests that there is a prima facie case for proceeding with the proposal further. In order to arrive at a final decision, deep probing into the entire financial and operating structure of the business is necessary.

This probing is done through ratio analysis in Chapter 16.

So far we have discussed the balance sheet of a firm that has a formal accounting system. But these days a banker has to deal with a large number of small businesses that do not have any formal accounting system; only incomplete records of accounts are available. A banker has to take a view of such a business to determine its creditworthiness. However, he cannot do it unless he captures the major financial and operating variables of the firms in a format amenable to further analysis. We do this with the help of the following case study.

A Business with no Formal Accounting System

Let us consider the case of a small entrepreneur who has come to a bank for the first time for a loan to expand his business. He cannot produce any balance sheet or profit and loss account because he does not maintain a regular set of books of accounts. He has no bank account also till date. He has his own method of keeping records, which he picked up from his fellow businessmen. His primary concern is cash. He counts his daily collections at the end of the day, writes them in a big cash *khata* (cash record) and then takes the cash home. He gives a part of this cash to his wife for meeting household expenses, and then makes an estimate of the following day's requirements of cash in the business—purchase of stocks, payment of wages, payments to creditors, and other expenses. Setting aside these requirements of cash, he puts the balance in his cash safe. He enters all these cash items in the cash *khata*, which is his only book of accounts, besides the *udhar khata* (loan record).

Every bank manager, particularly in rural and semi-urban branches, will agree that this is the type of customer he faces every day. The bulk of the loan accounts of such branches also belong

to this type. In his role partly as a development banker, a bank manager has to assist such businessmen. *But a bank manager cannot do this unless he knows what the customer is doing. For this purpose, he has to organise the accounts of the customer in a somewhat standard form, from whatever records are available.*

Let us now see what the customer has brought before us, and how the bank manager deals with the problem.

1. The bank manager examines the customer's cash *khata*, which now shows a cash balance of Rs 3,070. From this *khata*, and also from the *udhar khata*, he calculates his sales to be Rs 7,24,660 in the previous year.

2. The manager now pays a visit to the place of business. On reaching there, the manager asks his customer whether he buys goods on credit also, and if so, how he knows at any time to whom he owes money. The entrepreneur says that he keeps a copy of the challan, or when he does not receive a challan, he writes the transaction on a chit of paper. As and when he pays his suppliers, he simply writes it on the face of the challan or on the chit. During the next 10 minutes he rummages through his *khata* and files and tells the banker that as on this date he owes Rs 76,070 to his suppliers.

3. The intelligent entrepreneur knows the next question. He has already taken up the *udhar khata*, wherein he keeps records of persons to whom he sells goods on credit. He finally concludes that persons to whom he supplied goods on credit owe an amount of Rs 22,250 to him, out of which he is skeptical about realising Rs 450. The manager now starts scrutinising the cash *khata*. He picks up the following data.

(a) The entrepreneur has made an investment in the shares of a cooperative society amounting to Rs 260.

(b) He has given loans aggregating Rs 5,070 to his employees to be repayable over a long period.

(c) An amount of Rs 10,650 in aggregate has been paid to various suppliers to ensure prompt delivery of goods. He says that one such supplier with whom Rs 420 had been deposited long back would neither supply goods, nor return the advance.

(d) He has made an advance of Rs 1,790 for supplying a wooden rack to keep his stores.

(e) An amount of Rs 11,350 has already been paid to the electrician for electrical installations. An amount of Rs 1,230 is due to him.

(f) He has taken loans from his friends and relatives from time to time aggregating Rs 10,690. He does not have to bother about their repayment right now.

(g) Because he is a very reliable person, some people keep their money with him, to be adjusted against future supply of goods or otherwise, in cash. This aggregates to Rs 15,400.

(h) He has pre-paid wages and other expenses to the extent of Rs 2,050.

(i) He had borrowed earlier from a chit fund. The balance outstanding as on date is Rs 21,210 and the interest payable is Rs 430, which he has not yet paid.

4. After jotting down all these data, the banker asks him to value his stocks, to which he readily agrees, because he can always tell roughly what stocks he has on any day. The banker also asks him to bring his first cash *khata* and also a list of various fixed assets purchased by him at different dates with their original purchase price.

5. After a few days the entrepreneur presents him a detailed list of stocks aggregating Rs 1,24,720. He has also produced a list of fixed assets engaged in the business, which includes land and building, small equipments, furniture and fixtures, and also a motor cycle.

6. From the first cash *khata* the banker finds that he had brought in Rs 29,160 to the business from his personal savings.

7. The banker now takes up paper and pencil. The first thing he does is calculate depreciation on fixed assets from the date of purchase of each piece of fixed assets. He applies depreciation rates as:

Land (leasehold)	2%
Buildings	3%
Equipment	10%
Furniture	15%
Motor cycle	10%

8. Finally, he calculates the net fixed assets, aggregating Rs 62,480, after charging accumulated depreciation of Rs 12,500. Having done this, he now prepares the statement of assets and liabilities of the business as on that date, that is 2 April 20XX (see next page).

It would appear from the statement that almost all the major information sought for by the banker are now available. The accumulated profit of Rs 76,130 includes this year's as well as all the past years' profits net of drawings. The banker may also calculate drawings from the cash register, but in the present case it is not necessary. Assuming now that the financial year of the business has ended on 31 March of the last year all the drawings for the past year have already been made. Hence, the accumulated

Statement of Assets and Liabilities of the Small Business as on 2 April 20XX

Item No.	Liabilities	Rs	Item No.	Assets	Rs	
6.	Capital	29160	8	Net fixed assets		62480
3(f)	Loan from friends etc.	10690	3(e)	Capital expenditure		11350
3(g)	Deposits	15400	3(d)	Advance for capital expenditure		1790
3(i)	Loan from chit fund, including interest accrued	21640	3(a)	Investment in shares of a cooperative society		260
3(e)	Amount due for capital expenditure	1230	3(b) 3(c)	Loan to employees		5070
2	Creditors	76070		Advance to suppliers	10650	
	Sub-total	154190		*Less:* Provision for bad debt	420	10230
	Depreciation reserve	12500		Pre-paid expenses		2050
	Accumulated Profit		3(n)	Stocks		124720
	(being the difference between two sides)	76130	5	Debtors	22250	
			3	*Less:* Provision for bad debt	450	21800
			1	Cash		3070
	Total	242820		Total		242820

profit of Rs 76,130 may be added to the original capital of Rs 29,160 to arrive at the net worth of the business.

We refrain here from making any in-depth analysis of the business. With all the essential figures now available, the banker can calculate a few important ratios to arrive at a final decision about the creditworthiness of the business. The ratios are discussed in Chapter 16. We also make a full appraisal of a small business loan in Chapter 19.

CONCLUDING REMARKS

A balance sheet is a stock concept, while the profit and loss account is a flow concept. The former indicates the state of a business as on a particular date, while the latter tells us how the present state has come into being. The two together finally tell us how the funds flowed through the business during a given period. The accounting system first evolved the balance sheet, followed by the profit and loss account later. In fact, the balance sheet of a business is never static, in spite of its being labelled as such. It is changing every moment, no matter when we decide to draw up one. The balance sheet is a total concept, while the profit and loss account is a partial concept. One can do without a profit and loss account, as we have already seen, but not without a balance sheet. Although the 'how's' are important, as we find from a profit and loss account, 'what' is the ultimate for a banker. This is the reason why the balance sheet has received so much attention of lenders—not only to see whether the loan stands secured, but also to examine whether the value of the business is increasing or not. A profit and loss account tells us more about the operating management of the business, while the balance sheet indicates the efficiency of financial management. The ratios calculated between a stock variable (balance sheet) and a flow variable (profit and loss account) enable us to estimate the overall efficiency of a business. This we do in Chapter 16.

Annexure 11.1

Audit Report for Non-Corporate Borrowers

1. I/We have examined the balance sheet of .... as at .... and the profit and loss account and the funds flow statement for the year ended on that date which are in agreement with the books of account maintained at the head office at ....

    ....

    ....

    and branches at ....

    ....

    ....

    i.   I/We have obtained all the information and explanations which to the best of my/our knowledge and belief were necessary for the purpose of my/our audit.

    ii. In my/our opinion, proper books of account have been kept by the head office and the branches of the entity so far as appears from my/our examination of such books, subject to the comments given below:

    iii. In my/our opinion and to the best of my/our information and according to the explanations given to me/us, the said accounts and the funds flow statement give a true and fair view:

    (a) in the case of the balance sheet, of the state of affairs of the entity as at..........................
    and

    (b) in the case of the profit and loss account, of the profit or loss of the entity for the account year ending on

    (c) in so far as it relates to the funds flow statement of the movement of funds during the year ending on that date.

2. The auditor's report on the accounts of the entities shall be accompanied by a statement in respect of the following matters:

A. In the case of a manufacturing, mining, and processing entity:

    i.   Whether the entity is maintaining proper records to show full particulars, including quantitative details and situation of fixed assets, whether these fixed assets have been physically verified by the management and if any serious discrepancies were noticed on such verification, whether the same have been properly dealt with in the books of account.

    ii. In a case where the fixed assets have been revalued during the year, the basis of revaluation should be indicated.

    iii. Has physical verification been conducted by the management at reasonable periods in respect of finished goods, stores, spare parts, and raw materials, and if any significant discrepancies have been noticed on such verification as compared to book records, whether or not the same have been properly dealt with in the books of account; whether the auditor is satisfied that the valuation of these stocks is fair and proper in accordance with the normally accepted accounting principles and is on the same basis as in the earlier years; if there is any deviation in the basis of valuation, the effect of such deviation, if material, is to be reported.

    iv. If the entity has taken any loan whether secured or unsecured from firms, companies, or other parties, whether the rate of interest and the terms and conditions of such loans are prima facie prejudicial to the interest of the entity.

    v.   Whether the parties to whom the loans or advances in the nature of loans have been given by the entity are repaying the principal amounts as stipulated and are also regular in payment of the interest, and if not, whether reasonable steps have been taken by the entity for the recovery of the principal and interest.

vi.   Is there an adequate internal control procedure commensurate with the size of the entity and the nature of its business for the purchase of stores, raw materials, including components, plant and machinery, equipment, and other assets?

vii. Whether stores, raw materials, or components exceeding Rs 10,000 in value for each type thereof are purchased during the year from the associate firms or other parties in which the partners/ proprietor are/is interested; whether the prices paid for such items are reasonable as compared to the prices of similar items supplied by other parties.

viii. Whether any unserviceable or damaged stores and raw materials are determined, and whether provision for the loss, if any, has been made in the accounts.

ix.   Is the entity maintaining reasonable records for the sale and disposal of realisable by-products and scraps where applicable and significant?

x.   In relation to entities the capital of which at the commencement of the financial year concerned exceeds Rs 25 lakh, whether the entity has an internal audit system commensurate with its size and the nature of its business.

xi.   Is the entity regular in depositing provident fund dues with the appropriate authorities, and if not, the extent of arrears of provident fund dues shall be indicated by the auditor.

B. In the case of a service entity:

i.   All the matters specified in Clause (A) to the extent to which they are applicable.

ii.   Whether the entity has a reasonable system of recording receipts, issues, and consumption of materials and stores commensurate with its size and nature of its business, and whether such a system provides for a reasonable allocation of the materials and man-hours consumed to the relative jobs.

iii. Whether there is a reasonable system of authorisation at proper levels with necessary control on the issue of stores and allocation of stores and labour to jobs, and whether there is any system of internal control commensurate with the size of the entity and the nature of its business.

C. In the case of a trading entity:

i.   All the matters specified in Clause (A) to the extent to which they are applicable.

ii.   Have damaged goods been determined, and if the value of such goods is significant, has provision been made for the loss?

D. In the case of finance, investment, chit fund, *nidhi,* or mutual benefit entity:

i.   All the matters specified in Clause (A) to the extent to which they are applicable.

ii.   Whether adequate documents and records are maintained in a case where the entity has granted loans and advances on the basis of security by way of pledge of shares, debentures, and other similar securities.

iii. Whether the provisions of any special statute applicable to a chit fund, *nidhi,* or mutual benefit society have been duly complied with.

iv.   If the entity is dealing or trading in shares, securities, debentures, and other investments, whether proper records have been maintained of the transactions and contracts, and whether timely entries have been made therein; also whether the shares, securities, debentures, and other investments have been held by the entity in its own name.

3. Reasons to be stated for an unfavourable or qualified answer.

Where, in the auditor's report the answer to any of the questions referred to as in (2) above is unfavourable or qualified, the auditor's report shall also state the reasons for such unfavourable or qualified answer, as the case may be. Where the auditor is unable to express any opinion in answer to a particular question, his report shall indicate such fact together with the reasons why it is not possible for him to give an answer to such a question.

Annexure 11.2

PROFORMA OF BALANCE SHEET FOR NON-CORPORATE TRADING ENTITIES

Name of entity ....

Balance sheet as at..

Figures for Previous Year	Capital and Liabilities	Figures for Current Year
	I. *Capital* (In case of partnership, these particulars to be given separately for each partner, and if possible the fixed capital accounts may be segregated from the current accounts) as at the beginning of the year. Add/deduct net profit/net loss during the year. Interest of capital. Drawings. Any other items (give details).	
	II. *Reserves* (give details under each head)	
	1. Capital reserves (if any).	
	2. Other reserves (including retained profits to the extent not already added to the capital, give details).	
	3. Sinking funds (if any).	
	III. *Loans and borrowings*	
	1. Interest accrued and due on each category to be shown separately.	
	2. In case of secured loans, the nature of security to be shown separately.	
	3. Amounts due for repayments within one year from the balance sheet date to be shown separately.	
	4. Loans from partners and relatives of the proprietors or partners to be shown separately:	
	(a) Loans from financial institutions.	
	(b) Loans and borrowings from banks (specify the name of the bank, the relevant amount and nature of borrowings, e.g., cash credit, term loans, overdraft, packing credit etc. separately).	
	(c) Fixed deposits (from public and others).	
	(d) Others (give details).	
	IV. *Current liabilities and provisions* (Amounts due for payment beyond one year from the date of the balance sheet be shown separately).	
	A. CURRENT LIABILITIES	
	1. Sundry creditors for goods suppliers.	
	2. Sundry creditors (others).	

Figures for Previous Year	*Capital and Liabilities*	*Figures for Current Year*

3. Advances/progress payments from customers/ deposits from dealers, selling-agents etc.
4. Interest and other charges accrued but not due for payment.
5. Bills payable.
6. Statutory liabilities (overdue amounts to be shown separately).
7. Other current liabilities and provisions (major items to be shown separately).

B. PROVISIONS

1. For taxation, less: advance tax paid.
2. For provident fund.
3. For contingencies.
4. Other provisions.

A footnote to the balance sheet may be added to show separately:

1. Claims against the entity not acknowledged as debts.
2. Uncalled liability on shares partly paid.
3. Estimated amount of contracts remaining to be executed to capital account and not provided for.
4. Contingent liability for bills discounted.
5. Other moneys for which the entity is contingently liable (give details).
6. Aggregate amount of arrears of depreciation, if any.

NOTES ON BALANCE SHEET

i. In case of partnership firms, state whether it is registered with the Registrar of Firms, registration number, date of registration, and the state in which it is registered.
ii. Unless otherwise indicated, the terms used herein have the same meaning as they have in Schedule VI to the Companies Act, 1956.

TOTAL RUPEES

Figures for Previous Year	*Properties and Assets*	*Figures for Current Year*

I. *Fixed Assets*
1. Under each head the original cost, the additions thereto, the deductions therefore during the year, and the total depreciation written off or provided up to the end of the year to be stated.
2. Where the assets have been revalued, the revalued figures to be shown. Each balance sheet for the first five years subsequent to the date of revaluation to state the amount of revaluation.
3. Distinguishing as far as possible between expenditure upon:
    (a) Goodwill.
    (b) Land.
    (c) Buildings.
    (d) Leaseholds.
    (e) Railway sidings.
    (f) Plant and machinery.
    (g) Furniture and fittings.
    (h) Development of property.
    (i) Patents, trademarks, and designs.
    (j) Livestock.
    (k) Vehicles, etc.
        (i)   Cost.
        (ii) Less depreciation.

II. *Advances and deposits on capital account*

III. *Investments* (attach details of investment showing in each case nature of investment and mode of valuation, e.g., cost or market value).
1. Investment in shares, debentures, or bonds.
    (*Note:* Investments in concerns wherein proprietor, partner, or their relatives are interested to be shown separately).
2. Immovable properties.
3. Investments in the capital of partnership firms.
4. Other investments.

IV. *Loans*
1. The nature, security (if any), and amount of each type of loan to be specified.
2. Amounts due within one year to be shown separately.
3. Loans to proprietors, partners, or associated concern to be shown separately.
    Less provision for bad and doubtful loans.
4. Loans considered bad or doubtful to be shown separately.

Figures for Previous Year	*Properties and Assets*	*Figures for Current Year*

V. *Current assets*

  A. INVENTORIES

     (The mode of valuation to be shown separately)

    1. Stock-in-trade.

    2. Supplies and sundries.

      (If the trading organisation is also involved in any processing activity/ies, other categories of inventories, e.g., raw material and work-in-progress, should be separately disclosed).

  B. RECEIVABLES

    1. Debts due and outstanding for a period exceeding six months to be shown separately.

    2. Instalments of deferred receivables due within one year to be shown separately.

    3. Debts considered bad or doubtful to be shown separately.

    4. Amount due from proprietors, partners, or associated concerns to be shown separately.

      i.   On account of sales on deferred payment basis.

      ii. On account of exports.

      iii. Others.

      iv. Total receivables.

      v.   Less provision for bad and doubtful debts.

  C. BILLS OF EXCHANGE

     (Same information to be given as for 'receivables').

  D. ADVANCES ON CURRENT ACCOUNT

     (Same information to be given as for loans).

    1. Advances to suppliers of raw material and stores/spares consumables.

    2. Advance payment of taxes (in excess of tax payable).

    3. Pre-paid expenses.

    4. Others.

  E. CASH AND BANK BALANCES

    1. Fixed deposit account.

    2. Current and savings account.

    3. Cash on hand.

VI. *Miscellaneous expenditure*

To the extent not written-off or adjusted (specify the nature and amount of each item).

VII. *Accumulated losses* (if any):

  i. Before depreciation.

  ii. After depreciation.

TOTAL RUPEES

Annexure 11.3

Proforma of Profit and Loss Account for a Trading Entity

Name of entity ....

Profit and loss account for the year ending ....

Particulars		This Year Rs	Last Year Rs
1. Sales (net of sales tax) (income from services may be shown separately)		......	......
2. Cost of goods sold:			
(a) Opening stock Add purchases (less returns)	....		
	......		
Less closing stock	......		
		......	
(b) Other direct expenses (if any)	......		
		......	......
3. Gross profit (1–2)		......	......
4. Sales and administrative expenses	......		......
5. Other income/expenses* net (±)	......		......
6. Interest		......	
		......	......
7. Profit before depreciation and tax (item 3 minus items 4 + 5 + 6)	......	......	
8. Depreciation	......		......
9. Taxation (for example for registered firms)**	......		
		......	......
10. Profit after depreciation and taxation (item 7 minus items 8 + 9)		......	......

Note: * Any item of expenditure which forms a significant proportion, say 5 per cent or more of the total sales or has special significance otherwise should be shown separately under appropriate heads, e.g., (i) Salary, (ii) Commission, and (iii) Perquisites and money value thereof.

** Registered firms are subject to tax, before the profit is apportioned amongst partners.

Annexure 11.4

PROFORMA OF BALANCE SHEET FOR NON-CORPORATE MANUFACTURING ENTITIES

Name of entity ....

Balance sheet as at...

Figures for Previous Year	Capital and Liabilities	Figures for Current Year

I. *Capital* (In case of a partnership, these particulars to be given separately for each partner, and if possible the fixed capital accounts may be segregated from the current accounts) as at the beginning of the year.
Add/*deduct* net profit/net loss during the year
Interest on capital.
Drawings.
Any other items (give details).

II. *Reserves* (give details under each head)
1. Capital reserves (if any).
2. Other reserves (including retained profits to the extent not already added to the capital, give details).
3. Sinking funds (if any).

III. *Loans and borrowings*
1. Interest accrued and due on each category to be shown separately.
2. In case of secured loans, the nature of security to be specified.
3. Amounts due for repayments within one year from the balance sheet date to be shown separately.
4. Loans from partners and relatives of the proprietors or partners to be shown separately:
   i.   Loans from financial institutions.
   ii. Loans and borrowings from banks (specify the name of the bank, the relevant amount, and nature of borrowings, e.g., cash credit, term loans, overdraft, packing credit etc. separately).
   iii. Fixed deposits (from public and others).
   iv. Others (give details).

IV. *Current liabilities and provisions*
(Amounts due for payment beyond one year from the date of the balance sheet be shown separately).
A. CURRENT LIABILITIES
   (a) Sundry creditors for goods supplied.
   (b) Sundry creditors (others).

Figures for Previous Year	Capital and Liabilities	Figures for Current Year
	(c) Advances/progress payments from customers/deposits from dealers, selling-agents etc.	
	(d) Interest and other charges accrued but not due for payment.	
	(e) Bills payable.	
	(f) Statutory liabilities (overdue amounts to be shown separately).	
	(g) Other current liabilities and provisions (major items to be shown separately).	

B.   PROVISIONS
1.   For taxation.
     Less advance tax paid.
2.   For provident fund.
3.   For contingencies.
4.   Other provisions.

A footnote to the balance sheet may be added to show separately:
1.   Claims against the entity not acknowledged as debts.
2.   Uncalled liability on shares partly paid.
3.   Estimated amount of contracts remaining to be executed to capital account and not provided for.
4.   Contingent liability for bills discounted.
5.   Other moneys for which the entity is contingently liable (give details).
6.   Aggregate amount of arrears of depreciation, if any.

NOTES ON BALANCE SHEET
i.   In case of partnership firms, state whether it is registered with the Registrar of Firms, registration number, date of registration, and the state in which it is registered.
ii. Unless otherwise indicated, the terms used herein have the same meaning as they have in Schedule VI to the Companies Act, 1956.

GRAND TOTAL

Figures for *Previous Year*	*Properties and Assets*	*Figures for* *Current Year*

I. *Fixed assets*

1. Under each head, the original cost, the additions thereto, the deductions therefore during the year, and the total depreciation written-off or provided up to the end of the year to be stated.

2. Where the assets have been revalued, the revalued figures to be shown. Each balance sheet for the first five years subsequent to the date of revaluation to state the amount of revaluation.

3. Distinguishing as far as possible between expenditure upon:
    (a) Goodwill.
    (b) Land.
    (c) Buildings.
    (d) Leaseholds.
    (e) Railway sidings.
    (f) Plant and machinery.
    (g) Furniture and fittings.
    (h) Development of property.
    (i) Patents, trademarks, and designs.
    (j) Livestock.
    (k) Vehicles, etc.
        i.   Cost.
        ii. Less depreciation.

II. *Advances and deposits on capital account*

III. *Investments* (attach details of investments showing in each case the nature of investment and the mode of valuation, e.g., cost or market value).

1. Investment in shares, debentures, or bonds. (investments in concerns wherein proprietor/partner or their relatives are interested to be shown separately).

2. Immovable properties.

3. Investments in the capital of partnership firms.

4. Other investments.

IV. *Loans*

1. Nature, security (if any) and amount of each type of loan to be specified.

2. Amounts due within one year to be shown separately.

3. Loans to proprietors, partners, or associated concern to be shown separately.

4. Loans considered bad or doubtful to be shown separately.
    Less: provision for bad and doubtful loans.

Figures for Previous Year	Properties and Assets	Figures for Current Year

V.   *Current assets*
   A.   INVENTORIES
        (The mode of valuation to be shown separately)
        1.   Raw materials (including stores and other items used in the process of manufacture).
        2.   Work-in-progress.
        3.   Finished goods.
        4.   Consumable stores and spare parts.
        5.   Loose tools.
        6.   Others.
   B.   RECEIVABLES
        1.   Debts due and outstanding for a period exceeding six months to be shown separately.
        2.   Instalments of deferred receivables due within one year to be shown separately.
        3.   Debts considered bad or doubtful to be shown separately.
        4.   Amount due from proprietors, partners, or associated concerns to be shown separately.
             i.   On account of sales on deferred payment basis.
             ii.   On account of exports.
             iii.   Others.
             iv.   Total receivables.
             v.   *Less*: provision for bad and doubtful debts.
   C.   BILLS OF EXCHANGE
        (Same information to be given as for 'receivables').
   D.   ADVANCES ON CURRENT ACCOUNT
        (Same information to be given as for loans).
        1.   Advances to suppliers of merchandise, supplies and sundries etc., and stores/spares/consumables.
        2.   Advance payment of taxes (in excess of tax payable).
        3.   Pre-paid expenses.
        4.   Others.
   E.   CASH AND BANK BALANCES
        1.   Fixed deposit account.
        2.   Current and savings account.
        3.   Cash on hand.
VI. *Miscellaneous expenditure*
     To the extent not written-off or adjusted (specify the nature and amount of each item).
VII. *Accumulated losses* (if any):
     i.   Before depreciation.
     ii.   After depreciation.
GRAND TOTAL

Annexure 11.5

PROFORMA OF PROFIT AND LOSS ACCOUNT OF A NON-CORPORATE MANUFACTURING ENTITY

Name of entity..

Profit and loss account for the year ending...

(000's omitted)

Particulars		Current Year	Previous Year
1. Sales (income from services may be shown separately)		......	......
2. *Less*: excise duty	......	......	......
3. Net sales (item 1 minus item 2)	‾‾‾‾‾		
Add/deduct/increase/decrease in finished goods:			
i. Closing stock	......		
Less: opening stock	......	......	......
4. Cost of production:	‾‾‾‾‾		
(a) Raw materials consumption:			
i. Opening stock	......		
Add: purchases	......		
Less: closing stock	......		
(b) Stores and spare consumption	......		......
(c) Salaries and wages	......		......
(d) Other manufacturing expenses excluding depreciation	......		......
Add: opening stocks-in-process	......		
	......		
	......		
	......		......
Deduct: closing stocks-in-process	......		......
Cost of production	......		......
5. Gross profit/loss (item 3 minus item 4)	‾‾‾‾‾	......	
6. Sales and administration expenses		......	......
7. Interest and other overheads		......	......
8. Other income/expenses net ($\pm$)		......	......
9. Profit/loss before depreciation and tax		......	......
10. Depreciation on other assets		......	......
11. Profit after depreciation		......	......
12. Taxation		......	......
13. Profit after-tax		......	......
GRAND TOTAL		......	......

Notes: 1. Any item of expenditure which forms a significant proportion, say 5 per cent or more, of the total cost of production or has special significance otherwise should be shown separately under appropriate heads, e.g., (i) Salary, (ii) Commission, and (iii) Perquisites and money value thereof.

2. If audited accounts for the previous year are not available, the fact should be stated.

Annexure 11.6

PROFORMA OF FUNDS FLOW STATEMENT FOR NON-CORPORATE BORROWERS

Name of the entity ....

Funds flow statement for the year ending ....

(000's omitted)

Particulars	Current Year	Previous Year
SOURCES		
Profit before tax	....	....
Add: depreciation	....	....
Add: interest on capitals of partners/proprietors	....	....
Add: salaries, commission etc. paid/ payable to partners/proprietors	....	....
Gross funds generated	....	....
	....	
Less: taxes paid/payable on the profit of the firm (relating to the year) (applicable only to partnership firms)	....	....
Less: withdrawals (including personal taxes paid/payable on income of the partners/proprietors out of the income the entity) by the partners/proprietors		
Less: salaries, commissions etc. paid to partners/proprietors		
A. SUB-TOTAL	....	....
Increase in capital (only the fresh capital introduced by the partners/proprietors during the year)	....	....
Increase in term loans/deferred payment liabilities	....	....
Increase in fixed deposits	....	....
Increase in loans from partners	....	....
Increase in loans from relatives, friends etc.	....	....
Decrease in fixed assets	....	....
Decrease in investments in other partnerships/business	....	....
Decrease in advances and deposits on capital account	....	....
B. SUB-TOTAL	....	....

Particulars	Current Year	Previous Year
Increase in short-term bank borrowings	....	....
Increase in other current liabilities	....	....
Decrease in inventory	....	....
Decrease in receivables	....	....
Decrease in loans to partners/proprietors/associated concerns etc.	....	....
Decrease in other loans	....	....
Decrease in bills of exchange	....	....
Decrease in advance on current account	....	....
Decrease in cash and bank balances	....	....
C. SUB-TOTAL	....	....
TOTAL FUNDS AVAILABLE (A + B + C)	....	....
USES		
Decrease in term loans/deferred payment liabilities	....	....
Decrease in fixed deposits	....	....
Increase in fixed assets	....	....
Increase in investments of other partnerships/business etc.	....	....
Increase in advances and deposits on capital account	....	....
D. SUB-TOTAL	....	....
Decrease in short-term bank borrowings	....	....
Decrease in other current liabilities	....	....
Increase in inventory	....	....
Increase in receivables	....	....
Increase in loans to partners/proprietors/ associated concerns etc.	....	....
Increase in other loans	....	....
Increase in bills of exchange	....	....
Increase in advances on current account	....	....
Increase in cash and bank balances	....	....
E. SUB-TOTAL	....	....
Loss (See note 3)	....	....
Less: depreciation		
Less: interest on capitals of partners/proprietors	....	....
Less: salaries, commissions etc. paid/payable to partners/proprietors	....	....
Balance, that is, gross funds lost (−) or gross funds generated (+)	....	....

Particulars	Current Year	Previous Year
Add: taxes paid/payable on the profits of a registered firm relating to the year (applicable only to partnership firms)	......	......
Add: withdraws (including personal taxes paid/payable on income of the partners/proprietors)	......	......
Add: salaries, commissions etc. paid to partners/proprietors	......	......
F. SUB-TOTAL	......	......
TOTAL FUNDS USED (D + E + F)	......	......

SUMMARY

	Current Year	Previous Year
Long-term sources	......	......
Less: long-term uses	......	......
Changes in net working capital (±)	......	......
Short-term sources	......	......
Less: short-term uses	......	......
	......	......

Notes: 1. The valuation of current assets or current liabilities and recording of income and expenses in these forms should be on the same basis as adopted for the balance sheet submitted to the bank, and should be applied on a consistent basis.

2. Under the item increase/decrease in term loan/deferred payment liabilities, each of the term loans and deferred payment liabilities together with the names of the concerned lending/guaranteeing institutions should be indicated separately.

3. Figures should be filled in here only when the total effect is net funds lost. In case of loss, if the loss, taxes, withdrawals etc. are more than compensated for by depreciation, interest on capital etc., the amount of loss should be shown under 'sources' against the item 'profit before-tax', as a negative figure.

Annexure 11.7

SPECIAL AUDIT REPORT

In the case of accounts perceived by the bankers as important for regular and active monitoring, the following audit report may be given:

I/We have examined the information given below relating to quarter ending on .... In my/our opinion and to the best of my/our information and according to the explanations given to me/us:

1. The important operating data for the quarter is as below:

Actual production	......
Actual production as a percentage of rated capacity	......
Sales	......
Cost of goods sold	......
Gross margin	......
Interest on bank borrowings	......
Interest on others	......

    (actual fixed costs need not be worked out)

2. The age-wise classification of raw materials inventory and finished goods as on .... is as below:

	Raw Materials	Finished Good
(a) Above one year		
(b) Between six months and one year		
(c) Between three months and six months		
(d) Below three months		

3. The work-in-process of Rs .... as on .... represents .... days production.

4. The raw materials are valued at .... The stock-in-process is valued at .... (give detailed basis for valuation, including the manner of determination of cost, e.g., first-in-first-out). Accordingly the value of raw materials and the finished goods is as below:

    The said valuation of stock is fair and proper in accordance with the normal accepted accounting principles, and is on the same basis as in the earlier quarter.

    The discrepancies (if any) between the value given here and that shown in the stock statements to the bank and the reasons thereof are given below.

5. The age-wise classification of total bill receivables and receivables outstanding as at .... is as below:

	Domestic	Exports
(a) Above one year	—	—
(b) Between six months and one year	—	—
(c) Between three months and six months	—	—
(d) Below three months	—	—

6. The month and balances of the stocks, bills receivables, and receivables are as below (give the balances as at the end of each month in the quarter for major categories of stocks, receivables, and bills receivables).

7. Tax assessments and payments made during the quarter were as below:

8. Actual disbursements for capital expenditure during the quarter were as below:

9. Outstanding contracts on capital account as on .... are as below:

Name of the Party	Amount Rs
1.	....
2.	....
3.	....

10. Contingent liabilities which may or may not materialise, as on .... during the financial year, immediately succeeding the quarter in relation to which this information pertains.

11. i.   Investments made during the quarter were as below:
    ii. Income from investments, including profit on sale thereof was as below:

12. Loans given by the entity during the quarter were as below:

13. (a) From banks (give details).
    (b) From others.

14. The purchase and sale transactions of the entity exceeding Rs 10,000 per annum from/to the companies, partnership firms, or other entities in the same group appear to be in the normal course of business, and the transacted prices of such items are reasonable as compared to the prices of similar items in the market (if not, give details).

15. The funds from the bank have been utilised for the purpose for which they were lent. Details of the funds diverted for purposes other than for those for which they were lent are given below:

16. The overdue statutory liabilities as at the end of the quarter are as below (give details):

17. As per the annual accounts the cash losses during the last two years are as below:
    (state whether the accounts were audited or not.)

18. At the end of the quarter, the following were amounts due but not paid:
    (a) Loans from banks.
    (b) Other loans.
    (c) Public deposits.

19. We give below some important ratios of the entity as per the last audited accounts:

(a) Current ratio
$$= \frac{\text{Assets realisable within a year}}{\text{Liabilities due to be paid within a year}}$$

(b) Acid test ratio
$$= \frac{\text{Cash + bank balance + marketable securities + debtors due within two months}}{\text{Liabilities due to be paid within the next six months}}$$

(c) Raw materials turnover ratio
$$= \frac{\text{Raw materials consumed during the year}}{\text{Average raw materials stock}}$$

(d) Finished goods turnover ratio
$$= \frac{\text{Sales during the year}}{\text{Average finished goods in stock}}$$

(e) Receivables turnover ratio
$$= \frac{\text{Credit sales during the year}}{\text{Average receivables}}$$

(f) Return on investments $\quad = \quad \dfrac{Earnings\ before\ interest\ and\ tax}{Net\ capital\ employed}$

(g) Interest cover ratio $\quad = \quad \dfrac{Earnings\ before\ interest\ and\ tax}{Interest\ charge\ payable}$

(h) Net margin ratio $\quad = \quad \dfrac{Earnings\ before\ interest\ and\ tax}{Sales}$

(i) Capital turnover ratio $\quad = \quad \dfrac{Sales}{Net\ capital\ employed}$

(j) Debt–equity ratio $\quad = \quad \dfrac{Liabilities\ to\ outsiders}{Capital\ +\ Reserves\ -\ Miscellaneous\ expenditure}$

(k) Operating cash flow (PBIT plus depreciation)/sales (net of excise).

Let him that would move the world, first move himself.

—Socrates

12 New Era of Lending

Tandon Committee and Its Aftermath

INTRODUCTION

In Chapter 6 we discussed how current assets are generated both along the productive-distributive line of a business and also discretely, away from the pipeline, and how finally they find their place in aggregate forms in the balance sheet after being financed by working capital. We also indicated that certain norms for holding of principal current assets were first laid down by the Tandon Committee for the purpose of financing working capital requirements of firms by banks.[1] Although banks are no longer bound by the industry-wise norms for holding current assets as originally prescribed by the Tandon Committee, and as subsequently revised and enlarged by the RBI from time to time, it must be said that the Tandon Committee recommendations will go down in the history of Indian banking as the first attempt to reorient the technology of bank lending in India. This 'new' methodology continued to govern and shape lending operations not only of commercial

banks but also of other financial organisations engaged in these activities. The methodology of appraisal and the forms derived from the recommendations of the committee dominated the lending system for over two decades. Even the norms for current assets holdings, which are now only indicative in nature, have paved the way for individual banks to evolve their own norms.

Before the nationalisation of banks, credit decisions were mostly security oriented. Bankers were not so much concerned about how a borrower was conducting his business. But the nationalisation of 14 major banks in 1969 envisaged a qualitative change both in the pattern and content of bank advances. With the emergence of the priority sector claiming a substantial portion of bank credit, there was a strain on banks' resources for serving the traditional sectors. It was felt that the time had come to examine in depth the pattern and mode of financing by commercial banks and suggest changes in the existing methods of credit appraisal and administration to ensure judicious allocation of scarce resources of banks.

[1] Reserve Bank of India, 'Report of the Study Group to Frame Guidelines for Follow-up of Bank Credit', Mumbai, 1975.

I. Tandon Committee

A study group under the chairmanship of Mr P.L. Tandon, the then chairman and managing director of Punjab National Bank, was formed in July 1974 for this purpose. The group submitted its interim report in October 1974 and its final report in August 1975, which is popularly known as the Tandon Committee report. With the acceptance of the major recommendations of the committee by the RBI, the methodology of credit appraisal and management of bank lending underwent substantial changes. Here we concentrate only on the system and methodology of appraisal proposed by the committee and its relevance today.

The New Approach

Breaking away from traditional methods of credit appraisal, the system proposed by the committee enjoined upon the banker:

1. To assess the need-based credit of a borrower on a rational basis;
2. To ensure proper end-use of bank credit by keeping a closer watch on a borrower's business and thus to ensure safety of a bank's funds;
3. To improve the financial discipline of a borrower; and
4. To develop healthy banker-borrower relationships.

The committee examined the existing system of lending and recommended the following broad changes in the lending system:

1. The credit needs of borrowers should be assessed on the basis of their business plans.
2. Bank credit should only be supplementary to the borrowers' resources and not in replacement of them, that is, banks are not to finance 100 per cent of borrowers' requirements.
3. Borrowers should be required to hold inventories and receivables according to norms prescribed by the RBI from time to time (no longer applicable).
4. Credit be made available in different components only, depending upon the nature of holding of various current assets.
5. In order to facilitate a close watch on the operations of borrowers, they be required to submit at regular intervals data regarding their businesses and financial operations, both for the past and future periods.

The committee held that at any time a business is required to hold the following current assets for operations of the business:

1. Raw materials, including stores and other items used in the manufacturing process.
2. Stocks-in-process.
3. Finished goods.
4. Receivables.
5. Spares.

Classification of Inventories

A borrower needs working capital for carrying current assets. Of all these current assets, inventory and receivables comprise the bulk. The committee examined in depth the qualitative aspects of these two items of current assets, and made the following distinctions:

1. *Normal inventory:* Where inventories are based on a production plan, lead time of supplies, and economic ordering levels. Normal inventories will fluctuate primarily with changes in production plans. A normal inventory also includes a reasonable factor of safety.

2. *Flabby inventory:* Where finished goods, raw materials, and stores are held because of poor working capital management and inefficient distribution.
3. *Profit-making inventory:* Where stocks of raw materials or finished goods are held not for the purpose of genuine business operations, but only for realising stock profit.
4. *Safety inventory:* Where stocks are held to meet unexpected failures in supplies, spurt in demand etc. as a kind of insurance cover.
5. *Excessive inventory:* Where even an efficient management may be required to hold inventory more that the requirements for reasons beyond its control, as in the case of a strategic import, or as a measure of government price support of a commodity.

The committee recommended that a 'flabby inventory' should not be permitted, and a 'profit-making inventory' should be positively discouraged, because both are selfish and an inequitable and inefficient use of resources. With regard to the 'safety inventory', it was proposed that good management should bring it down to a reasonable level based on experience gained in the past, and by application of statistical techniques, if necessary. Carrying inventory in excess of the normal inventory should be discouraged by banks.

THE NORMS

The committee initially suggested norms for holding various current assets for 15 industries. The list was not an end in itself. It was meant to be extended in the future. The norms were also not fixed for ever. These could be revised both upwards and downwards, as and when necessary, depending upon changes in the economic situation and the needs of industries. Many of

these norms were revised, and the list extended to cover almost all major industries.

Expression of Norms

1. Raw materials are expressed as so many months consumption. These include stores and other items used in the process of manufacture.
2. Stocks-in-process are expressed as so many months cost of production.
3. Finished goods and receivables are expressed as so many months cost of sales and sales respectively. Generally, receivables should include only inland sales on a short-term basis, that is, excluding receivables arising out of deferred payment sales and exports (see note 3 of Annexure 12.1).
4. Stocks of spares are not included in the norms, since in financial terms they are not significant in many industries. Banks will ascertain the requirements of spares for individual units. They should, however, keep a watchful eye if spares exceed 5 per cent of total inventories.

The RBI set up a number of committees to review, and if necessary, to revise the norms prescribed by the Tandon Committee, and also to develop similar norms for other industries. One of the first sub-committees, headed by Mr J.N. Pathak, was asked to review the norms for the textile industry, after examining the changes that had taken place in the structure of the industry like the emerging power loom sector, the increasing role of synthetic and blended fabrics in the textile market, the adoption of the multi-fibre policy for the cotton textile industry, and the pattern of financing of working capital requirements of different segments of the industry. The sub-committee, after reviewing various aspects of the textile industry in the light of the above, and after considering representations made by the Indian Cotton Mills' Federation, submitted its report, which was accepted by the RBI (with some modifications) in the first week of July 1984.

The Pathak Committee, while recommending new norms, suggested, inter alia, that the textile group should be classified under five main heads: (1) cotton/blended textile mills; (2) silk and art silk textile mills; (3) woollen mills; (4) man-made/synthetic fibre industry; and (5) jute textiles. The sub-committee suggested separate norms with respect to (a) composite mills; (b) spinning mills; and (c) processing mills. Different norms were also suggested for different types of raw materials and different types of mills. The norms for stock-in-process also varied according to the types of mills. In case of composite cotton/blended textile mills, which purchase grey cloth as raw materials, norms as prescribed for processing mills were extended for such grey cloth.

Subsequently, the Committee of Direction, the RBI, revised the existing norms from time to time, and also took up other industries for suggesting new norms. These norms, which are now indicative in nature, are given in Annexure 12.1.

Operational Aspects of Norms

The industry-wise norms were to be treated as outer limits for holding various current assets. Borrowers were not expected to hold more than these levels. But the norms were not to be treated as entitlements to hold current assets up to this level. If a borrower had managed with less in the past, he should continue to do so.

The norms were for the average level of holding of a particular current asset. This was not applicable to any individual items of that current asset. A few examples will make this clear.

Suppose in a unit, the projected consumption of raw materials for the year is Rs 600 lakh, and suppose that the norm prescribed for the holding of raw materials for this industry is two months, then the maximum holding of raw materials can be:

$$600 \times \frac{2}{12} = \text{Rs } 100 \text{ lakh}$$

The figure of Rs 100 lakh represents only the average level of raw materials holding. Individual items of inventory could have been held for more than two months. The same situation may arise in the case of receivables also. Suppose the norm for holding of receivables for a particular industrial unit is three months, but if a particular debt was outstanding for five months, there was no violation of the norm as long as the average figure in rupees did not exceed three months of sales.

It may be observed from Annexure 12.1 that for most of the industries a combined norm was prescribed for finished goods and receivables. In such cases, the levels of finished goods and receivables were to be added together while applying the norms.

Exceptions

The Tandon Committee, however, was against any rigidity of the norms. It held that norms could not be absolute or rigid. Allowance would have to be made for some flexibility under circumstances justifying a need for re-examination. The committee visualised that there might be deviations from norms in the following circumstances:

1. When there is bunched receipt of raw materials including imports.
2. When there is interruption of production due to power cuts, strikes, or other unavoidable situations.
3. Transport delays or bottlenecks.

4. When there is accumulation of finished goods due to non-availability of shipping space for exports or other disruptions in sales.
5. There may be a build-up of stocks of finished goods, such as machinery, due to failure on the part of purchasers for whom these were specifically designed and manufactured.
6. There may also be a need to cover full or substantial requirements of raw materials for specific export contracts of short durations.

The committee, however, wanted banks to be very careful in allowing any deviation from the norms to prevent any enterprise/industry from taking this for granted and expecting concessions as a matter of course and thus destroying the very spirit of the new system of lending. The committee reiterated that the criteria for deviations must be fully justified. The deviations should be for known specific circumstances and situations (which should be recorded), and allowed for an agreed period (which should be relatively short), and there should be a return to the norms when the conditions returned to normal.

Methods of Lending

The Tandon Committee had come up with the term, 'core current assets', which though not defined properly in the body of the report, was presumed to be a kind of permanent current asset which any business was required to hold. In case of stocks of raw materials, the core line goes horizontally below the ordering level so that when stocks are ordered, materials are consumed down the ordering level during the lead time and touch the core level but are normally not allowed to go down further, except at the cost of stoppage of production. This core level provides a safety cushion against a sudden shortage of raw

materials, or a sudden increase in production demanding more than the usual supply of raw materials. This core level was considered to be equivalent to fixed assets, and hence was to be financed only from the long-term resources of a business.

As indicated earlier, the essence of the Tandon Committee's recommendations was to finance only a portion of a borrower's working capital requirement and not the whole of it. Gradually, a borrower should depend less and less on banks to fund his working capital requirements. Keeping this in focus, the committee proposed three alternatives for working out permissible levels of bank borrowings. Of these three methods of lending, the third method was never put into practice. The borrowers were first placed under the first method, and later moved to the second method of lending as suggested by the Chore Group (discussed in a later section). The second method of lending continues to dominate lending decisions of commercial banks for working capital finance even though it is no longer mandatory. All the three methods of lending suggested by the Tandon Committee are now discussed to understand, in particular, the philosophy behind the committee's recommendations.

Methods of Computation

All the three methods begin with the computation of working capital gap as given below:

Total current assets	Rs ....
Less: Current liabilities other than bank borrowings	Rs ....
Working capital gap	Rs ....

Under the first method, 75 per cent of this working capital gap would be financed by a bank, which was called Permissible Bank Finance (PBF), and the remaining 25 per cent would come from the long-term resources of a borrower.

In the second method, a borrower would be required to finance 25 per cent of the total current assets (not of working capital gap, as in the first method) from long-term resources. A certain level of credit for purchases and other current liabilities would be available, and a bank would provide the balance. However, total current liabilities inclusive of bank borrowings would not exceed 75 per cent of current assets.

In the third method, permissible bank finance should be calculated in the same manner as in the second method, but after deducting core current assets from the total current assets. Core current assets should be financed from out of the long-term funds of a borrower.

The committee illustrated the three methods of lending by taking the following example of a borrower's financial position, projected at the end of the next year.

Impact on Current Ratio

It will be observed that under the first method, a bank would finance 75 per cent of the working capital gap of Rs 220, that is, Rs 165, and a borrower will provide at least Rs 55 out of his long-term funds. This method has resulted in a current ratio of 1.17. The ratio could be higher, but it could never go below 1, because 25 per cent of the working capital gap has to come from the long-term funds of the borrower.

Current Liabilities		Current Assets	
Creditors for purchases	100	Raw materials	200
Other current liabilities	50	Stocks-in-process	20
	150	Finished goods	90
Bank borrowing, including bills discounted with banker	200	Receivables, including bills discounted with bankers	50
		Others current assets	10
	350		370

1st Method		2nd Method		3rd Method	
Total current assets	370	Total current assets	370	Total current assets	370
Less: Current liabilities other than bank borrowing	150	25% of above from long-term sources	92	Less: Core current assets (illustrative) from long-term sources	95
			278		
Working capital gap	220			Real current assets	275
25% of above from long-term sources	55	Less: Current liabilities other than bank borrowings	150	25% of above from long-term sources	69
					206
Maximum bank borrowings permissible	165	Maximum bank borrowings permissible	128	Less: Current liabilities other than bank borrowings	150
Actual bank borrowings	200	Actual bank borrowing	200	Maximum bank borrowing permissible	56
				Actual bank borrowing	200
Excess borrowing	35	Excess borrowing	72	Excess borrowing	144
Current ratio	1.17:1		1.33:1		1.79:1

Under the second method, the current ratio improves to 1.33 because a borrower is required to finance 25 per cent of the current assets, that is, Rs 92 (approximately). The ratio could improve only when the borrower contributes more than 25 per cent of the current assets. But if he conforms to this minimum requirement of net working capital (NWC), this ratio would never change. This is one of the differences between the first and the second methods of lending proposed by the committee.[2]

Under the third method, the current ratio would improve further, and permissible bank finance would be the least, because the 'core' portion of the current assets would have to be additionally financed by a borrower from his long-term resources.

From banks' point of view, the third method would have been ideal because of constraints in lendable resources. It was, however, felt that the time had not yet come to force borrowers to the third method. Banks were, therefore, asked to move gradually from the first method to the second method, and then to the third method. The last method was, however, not found to be feasible by the Chore Group, as we will see later.

While analysing the operations of many cash credit accounts of non-seasonal industries, the Tandon Committee observed that the outstanding in a cash credit account did not fall below a certain level, which represented the stable fund requirement during the year. The committee, therefore, suggested that permissible bank finance be made available to a borrower in the form of a demand loan for that minimum level, which constituted the stable fund requirement, and the fluctuating portion of the working capital be made available by way of cash credit. However, this bifurcation did not find acceptance with bankers because of difficulties in calculating the two components. It was finally abandoned by the Chore Group. Permissible bank finance was, therefore, made available in the form of cash credit and bills discounting.

SYSTEM MECHANICS

The mechanics of the lending system proposed by the Tandon Committee, as relevant today, are:

1. Under this system, a banker is to be concerned about the total operation of the business, and not merely its inventories or receivables. Hence, it is imperative that a banker examine the operational plan of the business. It is in the interest of a customer that he plans his operations so as to be assured of adequate bank credit. Adhocism and fire fighting should be replaced by proper planning.

2. A borrower should submit an operating statement and a funds flow statement for the projected year, as also the projected balance sheet along with past performance data, to enable a banker to analyse the operating and financial strength of the business and the viability of the proposal for the projected year (in addition to this, a borrower is now required to submit a cash flow statement). While making projections for the coming year, a borrower must have made certain assumptions. These assumptions should be conveyed

[2] The Jilani Committee, which submitted its report in October 1993, had suggested that borrowers enjoying working capital limits of Rs 10 crore and above from the banking system should be subjected to a minimum current ratio of 1.5. For those borrowers who enjoy working capital limits between Rs 50 lakh and Rs 10 crores, the minimum prescribed current ratio of 1.5 should be raised in a phased manner within a period of three years. See Reserve Bank of India, 'Report of the Working Group on Cash Credit System', Mumbai, 1993.

to a banker to enable him to examine the validity of the assumptions.

3. The current asset position should be examined to ensure conformity with the inventory and receivables norms in relation to the projected level of production (banks are now entitled to decide the level of holding of various current assets according to their own assessment. The norms are now only indicative).

4. A banker would then calculate the working capital gap and permissible bank finance depending upon the method of lending applicable in the manner stated earlier. Fixation of an overall limit is necessary for purposes of documentation, registration of charges with the Registrar of Companies, and also for submission of proposals to the RBI under the Credit Authorisation Scheme (since abandoned).

5. If after analysing the proposal it is found that the limit already enjoyed by a borrower is in excess of permissible bank finance, the excess will be segregated and placed on a repayment basis to be adjusted over a period of time, taking into account a customer's cash accruals, obligations, and his capacity to raise additional equity.

6. A customer shall submit quarterly budget and performance data, which will constitute a segment of the annual plan of a borrower. This will enable a banker to see whether the quarterly plan is more or less in line with the earlier expectations, and also to locate diversion of funds for non-productive purposes.

7. Fixation of a limit, however, is not be construed by a borrower as an authority to draw funds up to that limit. Permissible drawings within the limit would be restricted to the actual deficit in the funds as shown in the quarterly statement. That is, the permissible level of drawing in any quarter would be the level as at the end of the previous quarter, plus or minus the deficit or surplus shown in the funds flow statement. If the peak requirement in any quarter varies from the normal level, it should be specifically mentioned.

8. However, actual day-to-day drawal of funds should be determined based on the drawing power available, after providing for the necessary margin.

9. As no budget or plan can be perfect, variation within $\pm$ 10 per cent would be permitted, but if it is more than that, then the matter should be discussed in detail with a borrower, and corrective measures taken well in time.

END-USE

Unlike the earlier system of lending, where bank finance was directly related to the availability of security, the system proposed by the Tandon Committee took into account all current assets and liabilities and linked bank finance to the working capital gap thus arrived at. This was done to ensure that a bank advance went to support a reasonable level of current assets. The committee dealt with the question whether payment of cheques for wages, power, taxes, dividend and so on by a banker from a cash credit account would be a proper end-use of funds. It held that when all transactions of a borrower are put through the cash credit account, it becomes unrealistic for a banker to differentiate between the purpose of one drawing and another in the account. The only feasible manner in which he can satisfy himself with respect to proper end-use of funds would be to examine the level and relationship of current assets and current liabilities from time to time. So long as the agreed current ratio, the levels of various current assets, and the net working capital remained at the levels agreed, it would be presumed that the bank finance had gone for building up current assets, and hence discrimination between payments was unnecessary.

CLASSIFICATIONS OF CURRENT ASSETS AND CURRENT LIABILITIES

The committee made a departure from the norms for classification of current assets and current liabilities prescribed by the Companies Act, and recommended that this be made as per the usually accepted approach of bankers.

The recommended classifications, as amended by the RBI from time to time, are now discussed.

Current Assets

i. Cash and bank balances.
ii. Investments (see note 1 at the end of this list):
   (a) Government and other trustee securities (other than for long-term purposes, such as sinking fund and gratuity fund).
   (b) Fixed deposits with banks.
iii. Receivables arising out of sales other than deferred receivables (including bills purchased and discounted by bankers (see note 2 at the end of this list).
iv. Instalments of deferred receivables due within one year.
v. Raw materials and components used in the process of manufacture, including those in transit (see note 3 at the end of this list).
vi. Stock-in-process, including semi-finished goods (see note 4 at the end of this list).
vii. Finished goods, including goods in transit.
viii. Other consumable spares (see note 3 at the end of this list).
ix. Advance payment of tax.
x. Pre-paid expenses.
xi. Advances for purchase of raw materials, components, and consumable stores.
xii. Amount receivable from contracted sales of fixed assets during the next 12 months.
xiii. *Non-current Assets*: Deposits kept with public bodies and so on for normal business operations, that is, security deposits, earnest deposits kept by construction companies, tender deposits etc., whether maturing within the normal operating cycle of one year or not, should be classified as non-current assets.

Notes:

1. Investments in shares and advances to other firms/companies, not connected with the business of the borrowing enterprise should be excluded from current assets.

2. Export receivables could be included in the total current assets for arriving at the maximum permissible bank finance, but the minimum stipulated net working capital (that is, 25 per cent of total current assets under the second method of lending) should be reckoned after excluding the quantum of export receivables from the total current assets. Within the MPBF thus arrived at, banks might continue the existing practice of fixing suitable need-based post-shipment/pre-shipment credit facilities, taking into account a borrower's export performance, export orders, and other relevant factors where necessary.

3. 'Dead inventory', that is, slow moving or obsolete items, should not be classified as current assets. Projected level of spares based on past experience but not exceeding 12 months consumption for imported

items and nine months consumption for indigenous items should be treated as current assets for purposes of assessing working capital requirements.

4. While analysing current assets and current liabilities of construction companies and turnkey projects for determining a borrower's contribution under the second method, the net work-in-progress, that is, gross work-in-progress less advance/progress payments outstanding, should be taken into consideration.

Current Liabilities

i. Short-term borrowings, including bills purchased and discounted from:
    (a) Banks.
    (b) Others.
ii. Unsecured loans.
iii. Public deposits maturing within one year.
iv. Sundry creditors (trade) for raw materials and consumable stores and spares.
v. Interest and other charges accrued but not due for payment.
vi. Advance/progress payment from customers (see note 4 under current assets, and also note 3 at the end of this list).
vii. Deposits from dealers, selling agents and so on (see note 2 at the end of this list).
viii. Instalments of term loans, deferred payment credits, debentures, redeemable preference shares, and long-term deposits, payable within one year (instalments of term loans falling due within one year shall not form part of current liabilities).
ix. Statutory liabilities:
    (a) Provident fund dues.
    (b) Provision for taxation (see note 1 at the end of this list).
    (c) Sales tax, excise duty etc. (see note 4 at the end of this list).

    (d) Statutory obligations towards workers.
    (e) Others (to be specified).
x. Miscellaneous current liabilities:
    (a) Dividends (see note 1 at the end of this list).
    (b) Liabilities for expenses.
    (c) Gratuity payable within one year.
    (d) Other provisions.
    (e) Any other payments due within 12 months.

Notes:

1. In cases where specific provisions have not been made for these liabilities, and the liabilities will eventually be paid out of general reserves, estimated amounts should be shown as current liabilities.

2. These deposits might be treated as term liabilities irrespective of their tenure, if such deposits are accepted to be repayable only when the dealership/agency is terminated. Banks should satisfy themselves about the fulfilment of this condition before treating them as term liabilities. If necessary, they should verify the terms of agreement between the concerned borrower and the dealers/selling agents. Deposits, which do not satisfy this condition, should continue to be classified as current liabilities.

3. These advances should continue to be classified as current liabilities. However, in case of certain enterprises, for example, manufacturers of automobiles and two-wheelers who accept deposits while booking orders for new vehicles and are required in terms of regulations framed by the government, to earmark a part of such amount for investment in certain approved securities and so on, the benefit of netting is allowed to the extent of such

investment, and only the balance amount is to be classified as a current liability.

4. Previously disputed liabilities for payment of excise duty, income tax, sales tax, customs duty, and electricity charges were treated as current liabilities even where the liability for payment of these was shown as a contingent liability in the balance sheet, and accordingly no provision was made in the final accounts. As this method of treatment of disputed liabilities (not provided for and shown as contingent liabilities) as part of current liabilities resulted in reduced levels of permissible bank finance, the RBI reviewed the position in the light of representations made by the industry and advised that these disputed liabilities shown as contingent liabilities, or by way of notes to the balance sheet, would no longer be treated as part of current liabilities for calculating permissible bank finance, unless they had been collected or provided for in the accounts of a borrower, and certified as such by the statutory auditor of the company.

In terms of the above classifications of current assets and current liabilities, we have restructured the profit and loss account and balance sheet of a real-life company in the formats generally used by banks (Exhibit I–III).

II. CHORE GROUP

The Tandon Committee made a significant attempt towards modernising the methodology of credit appraisal and credit management in India. But the banking community was slow to implement the recommendations. The RBI became anxious and wanted to make a further in-depth study into the working of the lending system as a whole. A working group under the chairmanship of Mr K.B. Chore, the then additional chief officer of RBI's Department of Banking Operations and Development, the RBI, was appointed on 4 April 1979 for this purpose. The terms of reference of the group were:

1. To review the operation of the cash credit system, particularly with reference to the gap between a sanctioned limit and its utilisation.

2. In the light of the review, to suggest:
   (a) Modification in the system with a view to making it more amenable to rational management of the funds by commercial banks, and/or;
   (b) Alternative types of credit facilities, which would ensure greater credit discipline and also enable banks to relate credit limits to increases in output or other productive activities.

3. To make recommendations on any other related matter as the group may consider germane to the subject.

The group submitted its interim report in the middle of May 1979 and its final report on 31 August 1979.

The issues raised in the report are substantially valid even today. The Chore Group had gone deep into the prevalent system of working capital finance by commercial banks in India, and made a comparative study of different systems of financing prevalent in some of the advanced countries in the world. In what follows we critically analyse the main findings and recommendations of the Chore Group with the belief that a *banker should not only know how to appraise a credit proposal, he must also have a clear understanding of how the existing lending system works, its efficacy or otherwise vis-à-vis alternative systems of financing, and its impact on the monetary and banking policies of the country.*

REVIEW OF THE LENDING SYSTEM

It was observed by the Chore Group that though the share of term loans in the total advances of commercial banks was on the increase, the cash credit system was still the predominant form of bank lending. It was still more than 50 per cent of total advances. The committee, therefore, went deep into the operation of the cash credit system.

Under the cash credit system, limits were fixed according to the maximum requirements of individual borrowers, and drawals allowed according to the needs at any point of time. This resulted in the existence of unutilised portions of credit limits that often frustrated any endeavour of monetary authorities to contain the creation of credit by banks. The unutilised portion of credit limits acted as a source of readily available cash, which could be drawn upon in full the moment a credit restriction was imposed.

The gap between sanctioned limits and their utilisation was found to be roughly one-third of the sanctioned limits. The gap was more in the case of public sector units than in the private sector. This was an average estimate at the macro-level, and hence did not suggest that at no time were limits fully enjoyed.

The gap, however, was not unique to India. It was found in all the countries where the cash credit or overdraft system is prevalent. For example, in the UK the gap was around 60 per cent. Some of the reasons behind the existence of this gap, which are still valued today are:

1. As the peak level borrowing requirement of individual borrowers occurs at different times, borrowers as a whole would not utilise all their facilities at the same time.
2. Psychologically too, an Indian banker has been trained to view with approval large fluctuations in the credit limit. Full utilisation of the limit throughout the year is considered as a drawback, casting reflections on the financial soundness of a borrower. If the account comes in credit many times during the year, it is considered to be a good sign. The statistical format in the renewal proposal of any bank is indicative of it.
3. At the time of submitting their credit proposals, borrowers prefer to inflate their requirements because of the delay involved in getting the proposals sanctioned. They fear that by the time the proposal is sanctioned, the price level may increase requiring additional funds, which may take a longer time to be sanctioned. So why not get a larger limit sanctioned at the outset? It does not cost anything to have a larger limit!
4. Larger limits are also asked for to insure against imponderables like power cuts, flood, transport bottlenecks, changes in import policy, and budget uncertainties.
5. Under the cash credit system, bankers want all receipts of a borrower to be routed through the cash credit account. As these receipts include sales revenue with profit (which gradually reduces the availment), and also public deposits and unutilised portions of term loans, the balance in the cash credit account may often come to a credit.
6. The imperfections in the movement of economic variables make the projection of business parameters difficult. As a result, both borrowers and bankers play safe in setting up limits.

Problem of Potential Liquidity

As indicated earlier, this gap between limits and their availment creates potential liquidity in the economy, which frustrates any policy for containment of credit expansion. The duty to check this potential liquidity obviously falls largely on bankers. Bankers do try to check it by insisting on the submission of stock statements, and relating availment to drawing power calculated on the basis of such stock statements. But this has not been very effective. The Tandon Committee prescribed a quarterly information and control system to minimise this gap. The committee tried to relate productivity to the availment of credit limits. The Chore Group observed that the system proposed by the Tandon Committee could not find proper roots; but for increase in the term loan component of the bank credit, the gap between credit limits and their availment would have been much more.

The Chore Group laid down the following attributes of a good lending system:

1. It should be amenable to rational management of funds by banks.
2. It should be amenable to credit control measures by monetary authorities.
3. It should enable banks to relate credit limits to increase in output or other productive activities.
4. It should be operationally convenient to banks as well as customers, and the cost of administering the system should not be a burden either on a banker or on a borrower.

CASH CREDIT SYSTEM

The Chore Group examined the cash credit system in the light of the above attributes.

Merits-Demerits

Under the cash credit system, management of cash resources is shifted to the bank by the borrower. All receipts are deposited in the account, and as and when necessary the account is drawn up to the limit. There is no problem of managing investment of surplus cash, as is prevalent where the loan system is in vogue. While this relieves the borrower from installing a cash management system, it creates a problem for the banker, who does not know when the demand for funds will be made. Previously, banks were able to forecast the level of drawals during the busy and slack seasons, but with the fast industrialisation of the country, the seasonality of banking is waning, as a result of which it is now difficult to forecast the level of drawals even on a quarterly basis. This difficulty is partly due to the prevalence of the cash credit system.

The cash credit system is not conducive to efficiency. On the contrary, it encourages inefficiency. An efficient unit will get less finance because its inventory and receivable levels are less due to a high turnover of both. On the contrary, a producer may withhold output to take advantage of rising prices. His high inventory level will enable him to get more finance than the producer who sells his output faster and thus reduces the inventory.

The one year review generally practised for cash credit accounts is too long a period for short-term finance. More often than not, even the annual reviews are delayed. As such, it is difficult for bankers to know what the borrowers are doing with the bank's money. When reviews are made (generally at the time of renewal), it may be observed that a number of assumptions might have gone wrong, which if timely measures had been taken, could have saved the borrower's business as well as the bank's money.

Against the above disadvantages, the arguments in favour of the continuation of the cash credit system are:

The cash credit system has been in vogue for a long time, mainly because of its flexibility, which can take care of temporary requirements of funds by borrowers.

The cash credit system enables recycling of funds into a bank. The funds remain in the system because the borrowers are not forced to invest their surplus cash outside the system.

Because of recycling of funds into the cash credit account, a borrower's drawal is limited to the minimum requirement of funds at any point of time, and hence he can save on interest, which would otherwise have been payable in a loan system, where the full amount of the loan has to be drawn at one time.

Under the cash credit system, repetitive documentation is avoided.

In India, bankers and borrowers have long been accustomed to the cash credit system of financing. The system functions well during normal times, though at the times of economic strains and stresses, it is open to misuse.

Let us now examine the loan system in the Indian context.

LOAN SYSTEM

Merits-Demerits

In the US and Japan, term loans for short periods are the chief form of short-term finance. Overdrafts, or the cash credit system of financing, are virtually non-existent there.

Under this system, loans are sanctioned for definite purposes and periods. Usually borrowers are required to maintain a compensatory balance in the current account as a percentage of the loan sanctioned. This system forces a borrower to plan his cash budget, thus ensuring a degree of self-discipline.

Management of funds by banks would be easy in case of the loan system. Banks can plan their credit folio rationally. This, in turn, would enable monetary authorities to regulate credit expansion effectively. Banks can squeeze on credit expansion at any time by just stopping further loans. But during the currency of a loan, a borrower will not suffer because there will be no cut in the finance already made available to him.

Automatic review is built into the loan system. Unlike the cash credit system, where irrespective of a review, the advance continues, under the loan system every new loan has to be negotiated afresh. This gives an opportunity to a bank to deny a loan if the performance of the company is not found to be satisfactory.

From the banks' point of view, leakage of income can be plugged to a great extent under the loan system because of the ease of calculation of interest and maintenance of book keeping records.

It is also claimed that unlike the cash credit system with its cumbersome procedure of giving limits and sub-limits and maintenance of drawing power the loan system is simple to administer.

The main disadvantage of the loan system is its inflexibility. Normally, a borrower is expected to plan his needs in advance. He is not welcome to ask for any ad hoc sanction during the currency of a loan. This may take a heavy toll on the business of a borrower if economic and financial conditions change abruptly during the currency of the loan, which are beyond his control. It is desirable that in such contingencies, banks should come forward to tide away the difficulties, but under the loan system, it is generally not possible. Besides, a borrower is expected to repay the existing loan amount before seeking a fresh loan. If, for some reason, a borrower cannot repay the loan, he cannot negotiate for a fresh loan even if his needs are pressing. These inflexibilities in the loan system ultimately lead to its dilution. In many cases, fresh ad hoc loans are given and new loans are sanctioned just to repay the earlier loans. In this manner, the loan system has largely been diluted, taking it back to the cash credit system.

As every loan has to be negotiated, there may be a tendency on the part of a borrower to inflate the requirement to provide for contingencies. The situation is similar to the cash credit system. The excess funds thus obtained may be kept in deposit with the same bank, which will increase the deposit base, resulting ultimately in the expansion of credit. If it is kept outside, it also goes to increasing the money supply. In effect, whereas under the cash credit system the un-utilised limit acts as a potential source for expansion of credit, the unused portion of funds raised by way of loans creates a similar problem.

Under the loan system, although the purpose of a loan is determined at the time of granting the loan, once the funds are disbursed a bank has no further control over the end-use of the funds. It is difficult to ensure that the funds are utilised for the purpose for which they were granted.

Comparing the two systems, some critics hold that while the cash credit is a 'roll-over' credit (which, though for a short term, is never repaid), a loan, when usually combined with a revolving credit agreement and informal lines of credit, becomes virtually concomitant to giving loans arranged in advance and drawn as and when required by a borrower as in a cash credit account. A loan, similar to cash credit, is more often renewed than repaid. Besides, in the US and other countries where the loan system is prevalent, there are developed secondary markets to supplement bank finance. In India, these markets are still in the developmental stage.

These criticisms ascribed to the loan system are more due to implementation and monitoring mechanics, and not so much of principle and policy. The RBI also desires banks to move over to the loan system. It has advised that in case of borrowers enjoying working capital limits of Rs 10 crore and above from the banking system, the loan component should normally be 80 per cent. For limits below Rs 10 crore, banks should persuade borrowers to follow the same bifurcation by offering incentives in the form of lower interest rates for the loan component. Banks have, however, been given the freedom to change the composition by increasing the cash credit beyond 20 per cent or to increase the loan component beyond 80 per cent.[3]

BILL SYSTEM

Merits-Demerits

In India, the bill system is more or less an adjunct of the cash credit system. Several committees and study groups formed earlier than the Chore Group also recommended the progressive use of the bill system of financing.

This system enables banks and other financial agencies to invest their surplus funds by buying bills of various maturities. Simultaneously, it also helps those who are in need of funds to discount their bills in the market.

As the date of repayment is definite for bills, credit planning by banks is comparatively simplified. Moreover, the bill being a self-liquidating short-term instrument, it suits banks, as their resources are basically of a short-term nature.

From a supplier's point of view also, the bill system is preferable as he can expect payment of bills on a pre-determined date, and accordingly plan his production and prepare his cash budget.

However, there are certain disadvantages of the bill system, which make it applicable in limited spheres only. First, bills can be drawn only

---

[3] See, RBI circular DBOD. No. Dir. BC. 13/13.03.00/2010-11 dated 1 July 2010. Available at www.rbi.org.in.

for certain types of transactions, for example, for purchase and sale of raw materials and finished products and hence, it cannot totally replace other systems of lending.

Under the bill system, drawees become committed to a definite period of payment. As a result, they are often found to be reluctant to accept bills. Moreover, where part payment of a bill is an accepted business practice, like in government departments, the bill system cannot operate satisfactorily. It may probably take some more time for the system to be ingrained in the normal business practices in India, though an all-out endeavour is being made by monetary agencies to instill a bill culture in our economy.

Besides, cost of operations for borrowers under the bill system, and also the cost of administering the system by banks, are somewhat higher than other systems of lending because of stamp duties, detailed book keeping and so on.

However, the advantages of the bill system outweigh its disadvantages. The increased use of bills could have smoothened some of the undesirable features of a lending system based on cash credit and overdrafts.

PROPOSED SCHEME

After reviewing various systems of lending, the Chore Group came to the conclusion that even if increasing use of bills and loans was made in working capital finance, a borrower would still require cash credit limits mainly for holdings of stocks. Increasing use of a drawee's bill finance might, however, reduce this reliance to a great extent. The Chore Group, perhaps thought that the time then was not yet ripe to progressively replace the cash credit system by the loan system. Its approach was restricted to improving upon the use and administration of the cash credit system, and to supplement it with other forms of finance.

Abandoning the 'Core Current Asset' Concept

The Tandon Committee made a beginning in making the lending system amenable to credit planning by banks and to prevent speculative building up of inventories. The inventory norms and the mode of fixation of limits on the basis of peak level requirement as recommended by the Tandon Committee were implemented to a great extent, but the recommendations regarding bifurcation of the cash credit limit into a 'core' loan portion and a 'variable' cash credit portion were not put into practice to any significant extent. Similarly, the quarterly information system, which was an integral part of the Tandon Committee's recommendations, had not been implemented with the attention it deserved. The Chore Group observed that when a system was to be implemented in totality, implementation of it in part was not likely to achieve the desired result.

The Chore Group found that despite the lapse of a considerable period, the system of bifurcation of current assets into 'core' and 'variable' had not found acceptance either on the part of the banks or the borrowers. It was felt that the bifurcation might not serve the purpose of better credit planning by narrowing the gap between sanctioned limits and the extent of their utilisation. Unless the 'core' portion was fixed at a fairly high level, say about 80 to 85 per cent of the total cash credit, the disadvantages associated with underutilisation would remain even after bifurcation. Further, the 'core' idea would not be applicable in case of seasonal industries, where the cash credit accounts would usually remain in credit for a part of the year. Besides, in cases where fluctuations in the account were minimal, the hard 'core' portion would virtually be the same as the limit sanctioned. *In view of these, the Group abandoned the idea of bifurcation of limits into 'core' and 'variable' portions.*

Invoking the Second Method of Lending

At the same time, the Group felt that there was need for reducing the overdependence of medium and large borrowers on bank finance. Hitherto, it was believed that the surplus cash generation of a unit should be utilised for its expansion, without reducing the level of borrowing for working capital purposes. It was argued that unless this was done, industrial growth would be retarded. The Group, however, contended that with financial resources becoming scarce due to the increasing tempo of industrialisation, resources of banks should be more evenly distributed to a larger number of units. The existing medium and large borrowers should finance their expansion by raising capital from the market by way of share capital or debentures, or by raising loans from other institutional agencies. Additional cash generation should, therefore, reduce working capital advances gradually and thereby release funds to banks for broadbasing their advances portfolio. This way, the Group argued, it would check the potential danger of expansion of monopoly houses, which was in line with the declared policy of the government.

The Group examined the first and second methods of lending proposed by the Tandon Committee, and came to the conclusion that an owner's contribution for working capital purposes could be enhanced without structurally changing the system proposed by the Tandon Committee. The first method of lending gave a small current ratio, around 1.17, which was obviously on the low side, particularly from the point of view of a borrower's contribution to working capital. The Tandon Committee proposed that gradually borrowers would move to the second method of lending, which gave a minimum current ratio of 1.33, by reducing their reliance on bank finance gradually. But the Group found that borrowers were reluctant to move to the second method by enhancing their contributions to working capital requirements. *The group, therefore, recommended that banks should take steps to place these borrowers under the second method of lending immediately.*

Implementation Mechanism

As many borrowers might not be immediately in a position to work under the second method of lending, the excess borrowing should be segregated and treated as a *working capital term loan* repayable in instalments at a higher rate of interest. However, exception was allowed for units which had been identified as sick and were under a nursing programme, or where rehabilitation measures were under consideration.

The following two examples will make this clear.

Current Account Balance Sheet of a Hypothetical Firm

Current Liabilities		Current Assets	
Creditors for purchases	200	Raw materials	400
Other current liabilities	100	Stocks-in-process	40
Bank borrowings, including bills discounted with banks	400	Finished goods	180
		Receivables, including bills discounted with banks	100
	____	Other current assets	20
Total	700	Total	740

In the above illustration, the difference between current assets and current liabilities, which is 40, would represent the actual contribution from long-term sources. But the required contribution will be different under the second method of lending:

Current assets		740
25% of the above from long-term funds		185
Sub-total		555
Less: Current liabilities other than bank borrowing		300
Maximum permissible bank finance		255
Working capital gap comprises:		
Bank borrowing	255	
Contribution from long-term funds	185	
	440	

Under the second method, contributions required from long-term sources were 185, whereas the present contribution was only 40, which meant that the borrower was enjoying excess borrowing to the extent of 145. *The group proposed that in order to put the borrower under the second method, the excess borrowing of 145 should be segregated and converted into a working capital term loan on a repayment basis.* The repayment of such loan could also be ensured by appropriating a portion out of the proceeds of sales, bills collected, discounted, or purchased by the bank.

Peak-Level Requirement

It has been mentioned earlier that one of the reasons for the gap between the limits sanctioned and the availment is that the limits were hitherto sanctioned on the basis of the peak-level credit requirement. In order to bridge this gap to a large extent, the group recommended that there should be separate limits for 'normal non-peak level' requirements and 'peak-level' requirements, mentioning the periods for which these two types of limits would be operable. While fixing such limits, banks should examine a borrower's utilisation of credit limits in the past. Within such limits, drawings would be allowed based on quarterly projections submitted by the party. Any ad hoc or temporary accommodations suggested by a borrower should be critically examined, and if found satisfactory, these should be granted by way of a separate demand loan or a 'non-payable' cash credit limit. This limit should be availed of by a borrower only after utilising the regular cash credit limits in full, and it should be for a pre-determined short period. This ad hoc facility should carry an interest of 1 per cent more than the normal rate, except pre-shipment and post-shipment credits, financing of sick units, or units where the RBI had ordered exemption considering the financial position of the unit or industry.

Operative Limit

As indicated earlier, a borrower should indicate his quarterly requirements of funds in the appropriate format prescribed by the Group within a week preceding the commencement of the quarter for which it relates. The indicated requirement would be the operative limit for the current quarter. In addition to this, monthly stock statements should be obtained as usual, and the drawing power fixed. The actual availment would be the drawing power or operative limit, whichever was lower.

Banks should ensure that borrowers adhered to quarterly operative limits and for this purpose, borrowers should submit another quarterly statement within six weeks from the end of the relevant quarter, giving a comparative statement of projected availment and actual availment of the credit limit. Banks should see that at least the maximum outstanding in the account (and not the average utilisation) should closely adhere to the operative limit of the quarter. This statement should also act as the basis for determining the operative limit. While fixing an operative limit, banks should examine whether projected production and sales, current liabilities, and current assets of the ensuing quarter were realistic, by comparing past performance data as available from this form. Banks should also examine whether projected inventories and receivables were within the prescribed norms.

In addition, borrowers should also submit half-yearly operating statements and funds flow statements, along with half-yearly balance sheets within two months from the close of the half-year.

In case of a consortium advance, a borrower would submit the quarterly information statements to all the member banks. The leader of the consortium would advise the member banks of their respective shares of operative limits. The consortium leader would also take notice of non-submission of quarterly statements and other irregularities and convene a meeting of member banks to initiate such actions as charging of a penal rate of interest and freezing of accounts and so on. The group visualised the importance of information sharing among the members of the consortium to prevent any fraud on the banking system. But over the years, this importance has been diluted, particularly at the behest of the leader of the consortium. During the first half of 2008, a number of frauds came to light. The Central Vigilance Commission (CVC) was required to make an investigation into the matter. In its report, the CVC expressed concerns about the working of consortium lending and multiple banking arrangements. It attributed the incidence of frauds mainly to the lack of effective information sharing about the credit history and the conduct of the account of a borrower among various banks In order to prevent a recurrence of such frauds, the RBI in consultation with the Indian Banks Association, developed an additional information system to be followed by banks engaged in consortium lending or multiple banking arrangements.[4]

Emerging System

The system of lending proposed by the Tandon Committee and Chore Group, popularly known as the MPBF system, is no longer mandatory. Banks are now at liberty to retain the MPBF system or develop their own lending systems. As discussed earlier, the current assets holding norms, which are a part of the MPBF system, are presently indicative in nature. However, this norm structure now provides not only a general framework of reference, but also a benchmark for developing newer norms to take care of the changing needs of industry and trade. The minimum current ratio of 1.33 is also not mandatory any longer. The Jilani Committee had recommended a minimum current ratio of 1.5. For units having borrowal limits up to Rs 2 crore from the banking system, 25 per cent of output value would be reckoned as working capital requirement, of which one-fifth should be by way of promoters' contribution. During recent times, the RBI has advised that in case of small and medium enterprises (SMEs) working capital credit limits up to Rs 5 crore should be calculated on the basis of minimum 20 per cent of their estimated annual turnover.[5]

[4] See RBI circular DBOD No. BP. BC. 46/08.12. 001/2008-09 dated 19 September 2008.
[5] A small enterprise is defined as an enterprise where the investment in plant and machinery (excluding land) is more than Rs 25 lakh but does not exceed Rs 5 crore. In case of medium enterprise the investment in plant and machinery, is more than Rs 5 crore but does not exceed Rs 10 crore. If a small enterprise is engaged in providing services, investment in equipment should be more than Rs 10 lakh but not exceeding Rs 2 crore. For such medium enterprise,

In order to introduce further flexibility in the credit delivery system, the RBI has also advised that it would not be obligatory for banks to form a consortium even if the credit limit per borrower exceeded Rs 50 crore. Need-based finance required by borrowers may, therefore, be extended by banks either entirely on their own or in association with other banks. As an alternative to sole/multiple banking/consortium arrangements, banks are free to adopt the syndication route. A note on 'Syndication of Credit' is given in Annexure 12.2.

Penal Provision

Banks may continue the information system proposed by the Chore Group. In order to ensure compliance, there should be a penal provision for non-submission of these returns. If a borrower does not submit the returns within the prescribed period, he should be penalised by charging a penal rate of interest on the outstanding in all working capital limits.

Exporter-Borrower

Some relaxations are allowed to exporter-borrowers to boost exports. Firstly, banks have been advised by RBI that borrowing units engaged in exports need not have to bring in any margin for that portion of current assets as is represented by export receivables.

Secondly, additional credit needs of exporters arising out of firm orders/confirmed letters of credit should be fully met even if sanction of such an additional credit limit exceeds the overall limits sanctioned to a borrower.

---

the investment should be more than Rs 2 crore but not exceeding Rs 5 crore. See RBI master circular No. RPCD.SME & NFS. BC. No. 9/06.02.31/2010-11 dated 1 July 2010. The circular is available at www.rbi.org.in.

DRAWEE BILL SYSTEM

The Chore Group laid great emphasis on bill finance. The purchase and discount of bills by banks is quite well-known in the country for financing receivables, though its usage is still limited. For a long time, RBI had been advising banks to replace cash credit against book debts by the bill finance. As a part of this endeavour, the Chore Group proposed a drawees' bill system, in addition to the existing drawers' bill system of financing.

The System Mechanics

The group recommended that to begin with, banks must extend at least 50 per cent of the cash credit limit against *raw materials* by way of drawee bills in case of units (both in the public and private sectors) whose aggregate working capital limit from the banking system was Rs 50 lakh and above.

It is probable that for operational convenience, bills of large amounts could only be taken under the drawee bills system, and hence the system might tend to favour large suppliers only. Bills of small units, which are generally of small amounts, may not be taken under this system, and as a result these units would suffer. This was against the objective of the Group. It, therefore, suggested that large borrowers should maintain control accounts of sundry creditors with respect to small-scale industries and others separately, and report them in their quarterly information statement. A portion of the drawee bill limit should be utilised only for small-scale industries.

The group hoped that the drawee bill system would automatically ensure better inventory control of raw material purchases, and better discipline and planning consciousness among borrowers.

Under this system, a seller is assured of payment on a definite date. This would benefit small-scale industries, in particular, because they do not get payment of their bills from large and medium units promptly. Besides, when they obtain the acceptance of a bank, they can get the bill discounted promptly and at a better rate.

A buyer also gets advantages from the system. As his bills are accepted by a bank, he can obtain a higher rate of discount from suppliers. Procurement of additional stocks also becomes easy for him for the same reason. He would also have no difficulty in satisfying a bank of the amount of unpaid goods to the extent such goods are covered by bills.

A buyer's bank also runs no risk in accepting a drawee bill, as the goods covered by such a bill would form part of the stock charged to it in the cash credit account. The bank will also have ready information regarding paid or unpaid stocks of a borrower which form the security of the advance made to him at any time. A banker may not, therefore, depend solely on a borrower for this information.

For a seller's bank, its investment is safe because the bills are accepted by other banks. The bank can also discount such bills with other institutions as and when necessary.

Let us now see how a drawee bill system operates.

The system may operate in two ways: acceptance system and bill discounting system.

Acceptance System

In this system, a supplier (S) draws a bill on a buyer (B), which is accepted by the buyer's banker (BB). S may now discount this bill with his banker and get funds promptly. On the due date, BB debits the amount of the bill to B's account, and remits the proceeds to S's banker. If an alternative arrangement is not made, the goods covered under the bill may be taken as security from the date the bill is accepted by BB.

Under this system, B would give authority to his banker BB to accept bills drawn under this scheme. It is also possible for B to have an arrangement by which S may draw bills on BB directly, as 'BB–a/c B', up to a certain amount. BB, who is also maintaining the cash credit account of the buyer, will maintain an indirect liability ledger for bills accepted. In the stock statements submitted by the borrower, the amount of goods purchased on credit under the acceptance limit will be shown separately. While calculating the drawing power in the cash credit account of the borrower, the outstanding liability with respect to acceptance of bills (as available from the indirect liability ledger) will be excluded, and earmarked for making payments of bills accepted by the bank on their due dates. This earmarking can be done under two different methods illustrated below.

	(Rs in lakh)
Limit sanctioned against raw materials	200
Fifty per cent of the limit earmarked for drawee bill	100
Amount available for drawings against raw materials	100

Assuming that there are no other limits, and also no other current assets, the above limit might have been fixed on the basis of the following calculations:

	(Rs in lakh)
Gross working capital represented by stock	400
Less: Trade creditors	100
Working capital gap	300
Less: 25% of current assets as NWC (margin)	100
Permissible bank finance or limit sanctioned	200

Hence, classification of the stock will be as under:

Stock paid for	300
Stock unpaid for	100
	(represented by creditors)
Total stock	400

Normally, when a borrower submits stock statements, effective stock for calculation of drawing power will be only Rs 300 lakh. Assuming the margin on stock being 33.33 per cent, the drawing power available will be Rs 200 lakh, which is equal to the limit. If the drawee bill limit is carved out of the total limit, this margin on stock for calculation of drawing power will have to be increased, as we will see now.

Method I

Suppose 50 per cent of the limit, that is, Rs 100 lakh (which cannot exceed the amount of sundry creditors for raw materials) is granted by way of a drawee bill limit, and all bills aggregating Rs 100 lakh are accepted by a bank, drawing power will be calculated and earmarked in the following manner:

	(Rs in lakh)
Stocks paid for	300
Stocks represented by accepted bills	100
Total stocks available	400
Less: 50% margin	200
Drawing power available	200
Less: Drawing power earmarked for accepted bill	100
Drawing power available for cash credit	100

Now if the cash credit limit is drawn in full, the bank's books of records will show Rs 100 lakh in the indirect liability ledger as bills accepted, and Rs 100 lakh in the cash credit account of the party. When all bills are paid on the dates due, and assuming no other creditors are contracted, the indirect liability ledger will show a nil balance, and the debit balance in the cash credit account will go up to Rs 200 lakh; the paid-up stocks now being Rs 400 lakh, drawing power will be Rs 200 lakh. There will, therefore, be no irregularity in the account. This is Method I proposed by the Chore Group.

Criticism

It may be seen that if the drawee bill limit had not been there, the borrower would have been able to draw up to Rs 200 lakh against paid-up stocks of Rs 300 lakh with 33.33 per cent margin as shown earlier. But because of the drawee bill limit being carved out of the total limit, he is able to draw only Rs 100 lakh against the same stock, which means that for the time being at least, he is asked to provide for a higher margin (in this case 66.67 per cent). It is likely that the borrower may resist this on the ground that even if the bank had not accepted the bills of his creditors, he would have commanded the same length of credit from his suppliers. Moreover, to some extent his bargaining power over the creditors is impaired. Against this, it can be argued that when the bills drawn on the borrower are accepted by his banker, or discounted (as we will see later), it is done on the full value without keeping any margin. This counterbalances his higher margin on paid-up stocks. Moreover, because a bank is accepting the bills, the borrower's goodwill with the creditors increases, which enables him to contract more creditors at a bargain price. After all, he has to pay his creditors from realisation of his current assets or from his cash credit account only. What the bank is doing is just entering as an agent with its full financial weight for the benefit of both, with a little more emphasis on creditors, who may be small.

Method II

Continuing the same example, under Method II, drawing power will be calculated as:

Paid-up stocks	Rs 300 lakh
Drawing power at the rate of 50%	Rs 150 lakh

The borrower for reasons mentioned earlier, may like this method. But ultimately, it creates a problem for both the borrower and the banker.

For example, assume that the bank has accepted bills for Rs 100 lakh represented by unpaid stocks/creditors. The account will become irregular when these bills are paid by the bank on their due dates by debiting the cash credit account of the borrower, because the debit balance in the cash credit account will now become Rs 250 lakh, against a drawing power of Rs 200 lakh (50 per cent of Rs 400 lakh). The irregularity is to the extent of drawing power of Rs 100 lakh worth of goods now taken into stock after payment of the bills. This is so because bills are debited to the account with their full value. In order to regularise the account, the borrower must now be asked to bring in the amount of margin money on bills, which the borrower may not be in a position to do. In order to avoid this difficulty, the banker would prefer the first method.

Bill Discounting System

Under this system, a buyer's banker (BB) will discount the bill and remit the proceeds to the creditors of the buyer. The banker straightaway takes the goods covered under the bill as security cover against bills discounted, which appear separately in the drawee bill discounting ledger. The rate of interest will be the same as that applicable in case of cash credit against hypothecation/pledge of stocks. Fixation of limits and calculation of drawing power will be the same as in the acceptance system. The bank should suitably earmark the drawing power available against stocks after providing the prescribed margin. On the due dates, discounted bills are debited to the borrower's cash credit account, and the drawing power recalculated in the same manner as in the acceptance system.

In this system, creditors of the borrower are most favoured, but the borrower may object to this system on the ground that he is called upon to pay interest and discounting charges for the unexpired period of the credit

otherwise available to him free of cost from his creditors.

The drawee bill system has the excellent potential of infusing a bill culture among both the upper and lower ends of the market. It can also solve, to a large extent, the perennial problem of delayed payments suffered by small and medium-scale enterprises, and hence, of banks, because these small borrowers would approach the banks only with intermittent requests for higher limits, which in effect are implicitly enjoyed by large enterprises. But unfortunately, the system is yet to be implemented with as much vigour as is expected of bankers. There has been initial resistance from large borrowers, but that could be overcome by willing bankers. The system is straightforward. It can be implemented with little effort. The RBI has been advocating increasing use of the drawee bill scheme for many years now. It recently advised banks to fix sub-limits within the overall working capital limits to large borrowers specially for meeting the payment obligations with respect to purchases from SMEs.[6] In the emerging discipline of supply chain management, financial integration of the channel system can be effectively done within the format of the drawee bill system.[7]

RESTRUCTURING OF FINANCIAL STATEMENTS, CREDIT APPRAISAL, AND LENDING DECISIONS

Need for New Appraisal Formats

Balance sheet and profit and loss accounts are drawn up by accountants in terms of provisions of the Companies Act and/or the Income

---

[6] See RBI circular RPCD.SME & NFS.BC. No. 9/06.02.31/2010-11 dated 1 July 2010. Available at www.rbi.org.in.

[7] See Bhattacharya, Hrishikes, *Working Capital Management: Strategies and Techniques* (2nd edition), PHI Learning (P) Ltd. New Delhi, 2009, Chapter 8.

Tax Act. In published financial and operating statements, for example, it is not necessary for accountants to distinguish between salaries and wages. These can be clubbed together. It is also not necessary for them to show the calculation of cost of sales or operating profit. They are also not required to distinguish between current assets and non-current assets and gross working capital and net working capital. But a credit appraiser must have all these distinct classifications before him to judge the financial and operating health of a borrower. The formats for drawing up of a balance sheet and a profit and loss account, as used by accountants to conform to the statutory requirements, does not suit the purpose of a credit appraiser. He has to reclassify various assets and liabilities, and then restructure these statements to suit his requirements.

For this purpose, the RBI has laid down guidelines for the classification of current assets and current liabilities and also prescribed formats for operating statements, balance sheet spreads and so on. These formats, as they stand today, are the result of many revisions done to conform to the changing requirements of banks. In the process, what has evolved is an excellent instrument for credit appraisal and lending decisions, which can be used by any class of lenders as a basic tool for any type and amount of loan, with some modifications to suit any special requirements of a bank or other lending agencies.

LENDING DECISION: AN EXAMPLE

In the following pages, we first present financial and operating statements of a real company (though the original name has been changed to United Equipments Limited), restructure them as per banks' formats and classifications and then explain the major items under the head 'explanatory notes'. Next, we prepare an analytical note on credit appraisal and suggest appropriate lending decisions.

Guidelines for Filling up the Appraisal Formats

Form I

i. Information should be given separately with respect to each of the working capital credit facilities—cash credit/overdrafts, export packing credit, working capital term loan, bills purchased and discounted, both inland and exports etc. Details of quasi-credit facilities—letters of credit, co-acceptances, guarantees etc. should also be indicated. Data relating to term loans/DPGs, including foreign currency loans as also foreign currency loans not backed by DPGs issued by banks in India should be shown separately under sub-head 'B'. The exchange rate applied to arrive at the outstanding under existing foreign currency loans should be indicated.

ii. In the case of a multi-divisional company, if separate credit limits are sanctioned for different divisions, the data should be shown division-wise. Division-wise sub-totals should also be indicated.

iii. Details of credit facilities, if any, availed of by a borrower from non-consortium banks should be indicated separately. Details of deposit accounts, if any, maintained with other non-consortium banks should also be indicated.

iv. Maximum and minimum utilisation of the limits during the past 12 months and outstanding balances as on a recent date only should be given—month-wise figures need not be indicated.

v. In case the existing sanctioned limits have remained/are largely unutilised, the reasons therefor should be given.

Forms II, III, and IV

i. In case the audited balance sheet and profit and loss account for the previous accounting year are not available, estimated/provisional data for that year may be indicated in Column (2) of Forms II, III, and IV.

ii. The assumptions on which the projections of sales turnover, profitability, build-up of inventory and receivables, other current assets, current liabilities and so on have been based should be indicated.

iii. In the case of a multi-division company, division-wise data should be indicated separately for each division in Forms II and IV. In such cases, Form III/(analysis of balance sheet) should encompass data for the company as a whole. Wherever possible, separate data for each division may also be indicated in Form III.

iv. The valuation of sales projections should be based on the current ruling prices. Similarly, the valuation of various inputs of cost of sales in the projections should also be based on current costs. It should be ensured that price escalations are not built into the projections. Where the projections relating to production show wide variations in comparison with the past trend, information with regard to the physical quantity of goods produced/to be produced, their unit price and so on should also be furnished. Where the number of items manufactured is large, the information may be classified under three or four broad categories.

v. The projected carry of inventory and receivables shown in Form IV should normally be in conformity with the norms and/or the past trends/levels usually maintained by a borrower, whichever are lower. In case the level of projected inventory/receivables is higher than the norms/past levels, the reasons therefore should be explained. In such cases, a definite programme for conforming to the stipulated norms as prescribed by the bank should also be indicated.

vi. Spares should be classified as non-current assets. However, the projected levels of spares on the basis of past experience but not exceeding 12 months, consumption for imported items and nine months, consumption for indigenous items may be treated as current assets for the purpose of assessment of working capital requirements.

vii. The projected level of current assets, other than inventory and receivables, and that of current liabilities should also compare with past trends and prevailing market conditions. In case there are significant/abnormal variations, the position should be explained with respect to each item of variation.

viii. The basis of valuation of current assets should be in accordance with that adopted for a statutory balance sheet. Estimates of current liabilities and recording of income and expenses should also be on the same basis as that adopted for statutory financial statements.

ix. The classification of current assets and current liabilities should be done as per the usually accepted approach of banks, and not as per definitions in the Companies Act. The guidelines indicated in this regard by RBI should also be kept in view.

x. In case specific provisions have not been made for known liabilities like dividend payable and tax payable, and so on, estimates thereof should be made for eventual payment during the year, and the amounts though not provided for, should be shown as current liabilities.

xi. Details of term liabilities raised during the year (debentures, term loans, deferred payment credits, long term deposits etc.) should be furnished separately.

xii. Bills purchased and discounted (though shown as contingent liability in the balance sheet) should be included under items 28(i) and (ii) of Form III and 5 and 6 of Form IV.

xiii. Outstanding liabilities with respect to credit purchases under usance letters of credit/co-acceptances facility from the bank should be shown under item 3/Form III (sundry creditors [trade]).

xiv. In case of borrowers having seasonal activity where the working capital limits are to be sanctioned based on peak-level requirements (not coinciding with the balance sheet date) the corresponding data for the previous/preceding year(s) should also be indicated separately in Form IV. In such cases, the corresponding build-up of the balance sheet position as on the date of peak requirement should also be indicated.

xv. If the canalised items form a significant part of the raw material inventory, this may be shown separately.

xvi. Income received from and the expenses paid to or with respect to subsidiary companies/affiliates with respect to sales/purchases, should be indicated separately by way of footnote(s) to Form II.

xvii. If the borrowing company is a subsidiary, the name of the holding company and the extent and nature of interest of the holding company, should be furnished as a footnote to Form III.

xviii. If the borrowing company is a holding company, the extent and nature of its interest in subsidiary companies and their names should be furnished as a footnote to Form III.

xix. Three copies of the last audited balance sheet should be submitted along with the appraisal data.

Form V

i. In all cases other than sick/weak units, the computation of permissible bank finance should be done as per the second method of lending.

ii. In other cases where an appraisal of working capital requirements is sought to be done under the first method of lending, specific reasons thereof should be furnished.

Remark: The methods of lending as originally proposed by the Tandon Committee are no longer mandatory.

Form VI

i. Increase in carry of various items of inventory, which is disproportionate to percentage rise in sales turnover, should be explained in detail separately.

ii. Similarly, a decrease in current liabilities, which is not commensurate with the percentage rise or fall in sales turnover, should be explained in detail separately.

iii. In case the increase in the working capital gap is not commensurate with the increase in net sales, the position should be explained in detail separately.

iv. Item 7 (net surplus/deficit) and item 8 (increase/decrease in bank borrowings) would be algebraically opposite figures, and these should agree with each other.

An Example

EXHIBIT I
United Equipments Limited
Income Statement

(Rs in lakh)

	20X0	20X1	20X2	20X3 (projected)
INCOME				
Domestic sales	47696	57616	67274	70108
Export sales	3341	4042	4817	7896
Gross sales	51037	61658	72091	78004
Less: Excise duty	5289	6551	8297	8032
Net sales	45748	55107	63794	69972
Scrap sales	484	703	786	706
A. Income from operations	46232	55810	64580	70678
EXPENDITURE MANUFACTURING EXPENSES				
Direct materials:				
Imported	4063	5224	5853	5860
Indigenous	14996	16407	21847	25513
	19059	21631	27700	31373
Stores and consumables	430	416	653	600
	19489	22047	28353	31973
Spares consumed:				
Imported	9	63	47	127
Indigenous	32	37	87	121
Direct labour (Manufacturing wages and salaries)	4127	5132	5932	6523
Power and fuel	329	559	479	640
Repairs and maintenance (plant and machinery)	129	168	208	246
Depreciation (plant and machinery)	568	769	792	713
Insurance	134	162	222	252
Service charges	140	130	93	111
Total Manufacturing expenses	24957	29067	36213	40706
Add: Opening stock of work-in-process	2512	2681	2973	4610
	27469	31748	39186	45316
Less: Closing stock of work-in-process	2543	2972	4610	5484
B. Cost of production	24926	28776	34576	39832
Add: Opening stock of finished goods	2716	2334	2684	3463 (*contd.*)

Exhibit I (*contd.*)

Add: Finished goods purchased	<u>11237</u>	<u>15046</u>	<u>16097</u>	<u>15183</u>
C. Goods available for sale	38879	46156	53357	58478
Less: Closing stock of finished goods	<u>2328</u>	<u>2684</u>	<u>3463</u>	<u>3599</u>
D. Cost of goods sold	36551	43472	49894	54879
E. Gross profit (A–D)	9681	12338	14686	15799
SELLING, DISTRIBUTION, AND ADMINISTRATIVE EXPENSES				
Salaries (sales and marketing)	1061	1425	1597	1710
Salaries (others)	708	775	945	1086
Forwarding, godown, and packing	868	1204	1290	1311
Advertisement	336	492	502	529
Bad debts	158	23	88	496
Travelling (sales and marketing)	375	501	627	638
Travelling (others)	161	214	290	302
Vehicle expenses	36	51	62	73
Professional charges	68	45	63	91
Rent, rates, and taxes	558	660	781	774
Repairs of buildings, etc.	136	164	227	256
Depreciation (building, etc.)	150	174	205	300
Audit fees	9	9	12	13
Miscellaneous expenses	<u>1515</u>	<u>1960</u>	<u>2579</u>	<u>2900</u>
F. Total Selling, distribution, and administrative expenses	<u>6139</u>	<u>7697</u>	<u>9268</u>	<u>10479</u>
G. Operating profit (E–F)	3542	4641	5418	5320
Add: Other income (interest, dividend sale of fixed assets, etc.)	<u>695</u>	<u>780</u>	<u>817</u>	<u>1303</u>
H. Profit before interest and taxes	4237	5421	6235	6623
Less: Interest and commitment charges	<u>2257</u>	<u>3269</u>	<u>4508</u>	<u>5093</u>
I. Profit before taxes	1980	2152	1727	1530
Less: Taxation	<u>700</u>	<u>50</u>	<u>700</u>	<u>475</u>
J. Profit after tax	1280	2102	1027	1055
Less: Proposed dividend	<u>346</u>	<u>384</u>	<u>384</u>	<u>476</u>
K. Retained profit transferred to various Reserves and surpluses	934	1718	643	579

EXHIBIT II
Balance Sheet

(Rs in lakh)

ASSETS	20X0	20X1	20X2	20X3 (projected)
FIXED ASSETS				
Land and buildings	5573	6531	6830	7219
Less: Depreciation to date	873	1013	1160	1295
A. Sub-total	4700	5518	5670	5924
Plant and machinery	6774	9269	10330	10627
Less: Depreciation to date	3941	4680	5464	5573
B. Sub-total	2833	4589	4866	5054
Furniture, fixtures, vehicles, etc.	975	1325	1699	1892
Less: Depreciation to date	441	569	753	867
C. Sub-total	534	756	946	1025
D. Operating net block (A + B + C)	8067	10863	11482	12003
E. Capital work-in-progress	698	830	720	1725
F. Total fixed assets (D + E)	8765	11693	12202	13728
INVESTMENTS				
Govt. and trustee securities	35	43	43	84
Shares of subsidiary companies	156	50	50	1115
Other shares and debentures	227	538	638	665
G. Total investments	418	631	731	1864
CURRENT ASSETS				
Cash and bank balances	2	7	32	78
Fixed deposits with banks	16	43	209	34
Debtors (inland)	15240	18188	22948	25213
Debtors (foreign)	1025	1264	1650	2824
Loans and advances	4414	5012	5546	7352
Inventories				
Raw materials	2523	3103	3905	3969
Work-in-process	2543	2972	4610	5484
Finished goods	2328	2684	3463	3599
Stores and spares	66	174	139	160
H. Total current assets	28157	33447	42502	48713
I. Miscellaneous expenditure	241	670	792	818
J. Total assets (F + G + H + I)	37581	46441	56227	65123

(contd.)

Exhibit II (*contd.*)

(*Rs in lakh*)

LIABILITIES	20X0	20X1	20X2	20X3 (projected)
LONG-TERM LIABILITIES				
Share capital	1920	1920	1920	2920
Reserves and surpluses				
Revaluation reserve	2781	2720	2660	2605
Capital reserve	8	—	—	—
Share premium	—	—	—	4754
Other reserves	752	891	790	702
Capital subsidy	15	15	35	35
Debenture redemption reserve	36	144	252	432
General reserve	2891	2554	3156	3654
Profit and loss a/c	182	459	493	482
A. Shareholders' fund	8585	8703	9306	15584
Long-Term loans and deposits				
Debenture	2475	5667	5449	2257
Term loans	868	5538	5688	5579
Fixed deposits	1295	1567	1543	1650
Security deposits	1479	1305	1895	2561
Deferred payment credits	360	365	269	176
Incentive loans from govt.	311	322	375	448
B. Total long-term loans and deposits	6788	14764	15219	12671
C. Total long-term liabilities (A + B)	15373	23467	24525	28255
SHORT-TERM LIABILITIES CURRENT LIABILITIES				
Bridge loans	36	—	93	2503
Trade creditors	12818	14877	18230	18643
Advance payments	4036	5233	5432	5489
Expense creditors	277	365	485	235
Bank overdraft	4608	2059	6904	9481
Unclaimed dividends	2	3	2	3
D. Total current liabilities	21777	22537	31146	36354
PROVISIONS				
Taxation (net)	—	—	152	—
Premium on redemption of debentures	85	53	20	38
Proposed dividend	346	384	384	476
E. Total provisions	431	437	556	514
F. Total liabilities (C + D + E)	37581	46441	56227	65123

EXHIBIT III
United Equipments Limited
Annexure to Financial Statements

Notes and assumptions:

1. Capital reserve was the result of an amalgamation, which was ultimately adjusted against the general reserve.

2. Land and buildings were revalued on a date five years earlier than 20X0 by Rs 3114 lakh. Depreciation on the same is recouped from the revaluation reserve.

3. *Particulars of Debentures* (Rs in lakh)

Type	Amount	Interest	Terms of redemption	Premium
Non-convertible	508	12%	In 5 equal annual instalments starting from 30 June 20X4	5%
—do—	218	10%	Payable in full on 30 June 20X1	5%
—do—	249	13.5%	In full on 15 July 20X7	5%
—do—	1000	12.5%	In 3 equal annual instalments starting from 11 May 20X8	5%
—do—	500	14%	In full on 22 March 20X7	5%
Convertible	3192	12.5%	Convertible in 6.72 lakh equity shares of Rs 100 each during 20X3 at a premium of Rs 375 per share. Debentures were issued during 20X1	

4. Term loan repayment schedule.

(Rs in lakh)

	20X0	20X1	20X2	20X3	20X4
	125	780	800	800	800

5. Materials and wages are net of capitalisation.

6. Contingent liabilities not provided for

(Rs in lakh)

	20X0	20X1	20X2	20X3
(a) Disputed income tax, customs, excise duty, and sales tax	67	246	218	527
(b) Bank guarantees	9624	9664	11739	14170
(c) Sellers' bills discounted (drawers' bills)	922	412	1381	1896
(d) Suppliers' bills discounted (drawees' bills)	4958	5690	4608	6125

7. Miscellaneous expenses include:
   (a) Debenture issue expenses written-off.
   (b) Share issue expenses written-off.
   (c) Deferred revenue expenditure written-off.

Distribution of miscellaneous expenses (Rs in lakh)

	20X0	20X1	20X2	20X3
As above	22	100	190	170
Others	1493	1860	2389	2730
Total	1515	1960	2579	2900

8. *Interest and commitment charges*

	20X0	20X1	20X2	20X3
Term loans, etc.	529	1084	1463	2053
Debentures	302	367	733	513
Other short-term	1426	1818	2312	2527
Total	2257	3269	4508	5093

(*contd.*)

Exhibit III (*contd.*)

9. Consumption of raw materials and spare parts (including capitalised items)

(Rs in lakh)

	20X0		20X1		20X2		20X3	
Raw materials								
Imported	4076	(21.32)	5252	(24.15)	5868	(21.13)	5877	(18.68)
Indigenous	15037	(78.68)	16498	(75.85)	21895	(78.87)	25583	(81.32)
Total	19113	(100.00)	21750	(100.00)	27763	(100.00)	31460	(100.00)
Spare parts								
Imported	9	(21.95)	63	(63.00)	47	(35.07)	127	(51.21)
Indigenous	32	(78.05)	37	(37.00)	87	(64.93)	121	(48.79)
Total	41	(100.00)	100	(100.00)	134	(100.00)	248	(100.00)

Note: Figures in brackets represent percentage of the total.

10. *Repayment of deferred payment credits*

(Rs in lakh)

20X0	20X1	20X2	20X3	20X4
124	126	136	112	112

11. On an average, fixed deposits taken from the public are repaid at Rs 175 lakh per annum net of renewals.

12. Incentive loans from the government include interest-free sales tax loans and special incentives from the State Industrial Development Corporation, and sales tax deferral loans. None of them are due for repayment in the next seven years.

13. Bridge loans aggregating Rs 2503 lakh are taken during 20X3 against a rights issue of equity shares. Earlier bridge loans were against sanctioned term loans.

14. *Loans and advances are composed of the following items:*

(Rs in lakh)

		20X0	20X1	20X2	20X3
(a)	Advances to suppliers of materials	2291	3627	3754	5001
(b)	Advances to subsidiaries for materials and services	1210	107	62	390
(c)	Technical know how (net of adjustment)	251	252	607	588
(d)	Security deposits with landlord, excise and customs authorities	70	190	250	300
(e)	Deposits with the excise and customs authorities in current account	38	81	134	186
(f)	Advance income tax (net)	150	100	—	75
(g)	Staff advances (Vehicles and housing)	404	655	739	812
	Total	4414	5012	5546	7352

15. *Opening balance of inventories in 20X0*

(Rs in lakh)

Raw materials	2129
Spares	51
Work-in-progress	2512
Finished goods	2716
Total	7408

16. The amount of bad debt in 20X3 includes Rs 403 lakh being advances paid to a subsidiary company written-off under the scheme approved by the Board of Industrial and Financial Reconstruction.

17. Share premium account is net of Rs 61 lakh written-off as share issue expenses.

18. During the last quarter of 20X3, the company made a rights issue of 13.12 lakh equity shares of Rs 100 lakh at a premium of Rs 700 per share. The issue was fully subscribed. An amount of Rs 200 per equity share was received during the year as application money, representing Rs 25 towards share capital and Rs 175 towards premium. The remaining amount will be payable on allotment by the first quarter of the following year. Besides this, the company has 25.92 lakh fully paid-up equity shares of Rs 100 each as on 31 December 20X3. The authorised share capital of the company is Rs 6000 lakh divided into 60 lakh equity shares of Rs 100 each.

19. Pursuant to a scheme of amalgamation sanctioned by the Board for Industrial and Financial Reconstruction, Indian Electrical Lamp Works Limited was amalgamated with United Equipments Limited in 20X1. In terms of the scheme, United Equipments Limited took over all properties, assets and liabilities of Indian Electrical Lamps Works Limited. Excess of liabilities over assets taken over by United Equipments Limited on amalgamation of Indian Electrical Lamps Works Limited amounting to Rs 1539 lakh was adjusted against the capital reserve and general reserve.

20. For the sake of simplicity, assume that the company closes its annual accounts on 31 December.

FORM I
Assessment of Working Capital Requirements
Particulars of the existing/proposed limits from the banking system
(limits from all banks and financial institutions as on date of application)

(Amount Rs in lakh)

Sl. No.	Name of Bank/ Financial Institution	Nature of facility	Existing limits	Extent to which limits were utilised during the last 12 months		Balance o/s as on	Limits now requested
				Max.	Min.	(date......)	
(1)	(2)	(3)	(4)	(5)	(6)	(7)	(8)
A. Working capital limits							
1.							
2.							
3.							
4.							
5.							
6.							
7.							
8.							

Sl. No.	Name of Bank/ Financial Institution	Sanctioned limit	Outstanding as on	Overdues, if any	Remarks
B. Term loans/DPGs	(excluding working capital term loans)				

Note: This form has not been filled up to maintain the anonymity of the company under study.

FORM II
Assessment of Working Capital Requirements Operating Statement

(Rs in lakh)

Name: United Equipments Limited	31.12.20X0	31.12.20X1	Estimates for the year ended/ending 31.12.20X2	31.12.20X3
	Last 2 Years Actuals (as per audited accounts)		Current Year Estimates	Following Year Projections
	1	2	3	4
1. Gross sales				
i. Domestic sales	47696	57616	67274	70108
ii. Export sales	3341	4042	4817	7896
iii. Scrap sales	484	703	786	706
Total	51521	62361	72877	78710
2. Less excise duty	5289	6551	8297	8032
3. Net sales (1–2)	46232	55810	64580	70678
4. % age rise (+) or fall (–) in net sales as compared to previous year	—	20.72	15.71	9.44
5. Cost of Sales				
i. Raw materials (including stores and other items used in the process of manufacture)				
(a) Imported	4063	5224	5853	5860
(b) Indigenous	14996	16407	21847	25513
(c) Stores	430	416	653	600
ii. Other spares				
(a) Imported	9	63	47	127
(b) Indigenous	32	37	87	121
iii. Power and fuel	329	559	479	640
iv. Direct labour (factory wages and salaries)	4127	5132	5932	6523
v. Other mfg. expenses	403	460	523	609
vi. Depreciation (plant and machinery)	568	769	792	713
vii. Sub-total (i to vi)	24957	29067	36213	40706
viii. Add: Opening stocks-in-process	2512	2681	2973	4610
Sub-total	27469	31748	39186	45316
ix. Deduct: Closing stocks-in-process	2543	2972	4610	5484
x. Cost of production	24926	28776	34576	39832
xi. Add: Opening stock of finished goods	2716	2334	2684	3463
Add: Finished goods purchased	11237	15046	16097	15183
Sub-total	38879	46156	53357	58478
xii. Deduct closing stock of finished goods	2328	2684	3463	3599
xiii. Sub-total (Total cost of sales)	36551	43472	49894	54879
6. Selling, general, and administrative expenses	6139	7697	9268	10479
7. Sub-total (5 + 6)	42690	51169	59162	65358
8. Operating profit before interest (3 – 7)	3542	4641	5418	5320

9. Interest	2257	3269	4508	5093
10. Operating profit after interest (8–9)	1285	1372	910	227
11. i. *Add* other non-operating income (a) (b)				
Sub-total (income)	695	780	817	1303
ii. Deduct other-non operating expenses (a) (b)	—	—	—	—
Sub-total (expenses)	—	—	—	—
iii. Net of other non-operating income/ expenses [net of 11 (i) and 11 (ii)]	695	780	817	1303
12. Profit before-tax/loss 10+11 (iii)	1980	2152	1727	1530
13. Provision for taxes	700	50	700	475
14. Net profit/loss (12–13)	1280	2102	1027	1055
15. (a) Equity dividend	346	384	384	476
(b) Dividend rate	(18%)	(20%)	(20%)	(16.30%)
16. Retained profit (14–15)	934	1718	643	579
17. Retained profit/net profit (% age)	72.97%	81.73%	62.61%	54.88%

FORM III
Analysis of Balance Sheet

(Amount Rs in lakh)

Liabilities	As per balance sheet as at			
	31.12.20X0	31.12.20X1	31.12.20X2	31.12.20X3
	Last 2 Years *Actuals (as per* *audited accounts)*		*Current* *Year* *Estimates*	*Following* *Year* *Projections*
Current Liabilities	*1*	*2*	*3*	*4*
1. Short-term borrowings from banks (including bills purchased and discounted and excess borrowings placed on repayment basis)				
i. From applicant bank	5530	2471	8285	11377
ii. From other banks	—	—	—	—
iii. (of which BP and BD)	(922)	(412)	(1381)	(1896)
Sub-total (A)	5530	2471	8285	11377
2. Short-term borrowing from other (bridge loans)	36	—	93	2503
3. Sundry creditors (trade)	12818	14877	18230	18643
4. Advance payments from customers/deposits from dealers	4036	5233	5432	5489
5. Provision for taxation	—	—	152	—
6. Dividend payable	346	384	384	476

(*contd.*)

Form III (*contd.*)

7. Other statutory liabilities (due within one year)	—	—	—	—
8. Deposits/instalments of term loans/DPGs/ debentures etc. (due within one year)	424	1299	1111	1087
9. Other current liabilities and provisions (due within one year)				
– Expense creditors (specify major items)	277	365	485	235
– Premium on redemption of debentures	85	53	20	38
Sub-total (B)	18022	22211	25907	28471
10. Total current liabilities (total of 1 to 9)	23552	24682	34192	39848

Term Liabilities

11. Debentures (not maturing within one year)	2475	5449	5449	2257
12. Preference shares (redeemable after one year)	—	—	—	—
13. Term loans (excluding instalments payable within one year)	743	4758	4888	4779
14. Deferred payment credits (excluding instalments due within one year)	236	239	133	64
15. Term deposits (repayable after one year)	1120	1392	1368	1475
16. Other term liabilities	1792	1630	2272	3012
17. Total term liabilities (Total of 11 to 16)	6366	13468	14110	11587
18. Total outside liabilities (10 + 17)	29918	38150	48302	51435

Net worth

19. Ordinary share capital	1920	1920	1920	2920
20. General reserve	2891	2554	3156	3654
21. Revaluation reserve	2781	2720	2660	2605
22. Other reserves (excluding provisions)	811	1050	1077	5923
23. Surplus (+) or deficit (–) in profit and loss account	182	459	493	482
24. Net worth	8585	8703	9306	15584
25. Total liabilities (18+24)	38503	46853	57608	67019

Assets
Current Assets

26. Cash and bank balances	2	7	32	78
27. Investments (other than long-term investments)				
i. Government and other trustee securities	35	43	43	84
ii. Fixed deposits with banks	16	43	209	34
28. i. Receivables other than deferred and exports (including bills purchased and discounted by banks)	16162	18600	24329	27109
ii. Export receivables (including bills purchased/discounted by banks)	1025	1264	1650	2824

29. Instalments of deferred receivables (due within one year)	—	—	—	—
30. Inventory:				
i. Raw materials (including stores and other items used in the process of manufacture)				
(a) Imported	538	749	825	741
(b) Indigenous	1985	2354	3080	3228
ii. Stocks-in-process	2543	2972	4610	5484
iii. Finished goods	2328	2684	3463	3599
iv. Other consumable spares				
(a) Imported	14	110	49	82
(b) Indigenous	52	64	90	78
31. Advances to suppliers of raw materials and stores/spares	2291	3627	3754	5001
— Do — Subsidiaries	1210	107	62	390
32. Advance payment of taxes	150	100	—	75
33. Other current assets (specify major items)	38	81	134	186
34. Total current assets (Total of 26 to 33)	28389	32805	42330	48993

Fixed assets

35. Gross block (land and building, machinery, work-in-progress)	14020	17955	19559	21463
36. Depreciation to date	5255	6262	7357	7735
37. Net block (35–36)	8765	11693	12202	13728

Other non-current assets

38. Investments/book debts/advances/ deposits which are not current assets				
i. (a) Investments in subsidiary companies/affiliates	156	50	50	1115
(b) Others (shares and debentures)	227	538	638	665
ii. Advances to suppliers of capital goods and contractors	—	—	—	—
iii. Deferred receivables (maturity exceeding one year)	—	—	—	—
iv. Others (security deposits)	70	190	250	300
39. Non-consumable stores and spares	—	—	—	—
40. Other non-current assets, including dues from directors	655	907	1346	1400
41. Total: Other non-current assets (Total of 38 to 40)	1108	1685	2284	3480
42. Intangible assets (patents, goodwill, prelim. expenses, bad/doubtful debts not provided for etc.) (misc. expenditure not written-off)	241	670	792	818

(contd.)

Form III (*contd.*)

43. Total assets (Total of 34, 37, 41 and 42)	38503	46853	57608	67019
44. Tangible net worth (24–42)	8344	8033	8514	14766
45. Net working capital [(17 + 24) – (37 + 41 + 42)] To tally with (34 – 10)	4837	8123	8138	9145
46. Current ratio (items (34÷10)	1.20	1.33	1.24	1.23
47. Total outside liabilities/ Tangible net worth (18÷44)	3.58	4.75	5.67	3.48

Additional information
(A) Arrears of depreciation

(A) Arrears of depreciation	—	—	—	—
(B) Contingent liabilities:				
i. Arrears of cumulative dividends	—	—	—	—
ii. Gratuity liability not provided for	—	—	—	—
iii. Disputed excise/customs/tax liabilities	67	246	218	527
iv. Other liabilities not provided for	15504	15766	17728	22191

FORM IV
Comparative Statement of current assets and current liabilities

(Amount Rs in lakh)

		As per balance sheet as on			
		31.12.20X0	31.12.20X1	31.12.20X2	31.12.20X3
	*Norms**	*Last 2 Years Actuals*		*Current Years Estimates*	*Following Year Projections*
	1	2	3	4	5
A. Current Assets					

1. Raw materials (including stores and
    other items used in the process of
    manufacture)					

(a) Imported:		538	749	825	741
Months consumption:		(1.60)	(1.70)	(1.70)	(1.50)
(b) Indigenous:		1985	2354	3080	3228
Months consumption		(1.55)	(1.70)	(1.65)	(1.50)
2. Other consumable spares excluding those included in 1					
(a) Imported:		14	110	49	82
Months consumption		(18.67)	(20.95)	(12.51)	(7.75)
(b) Indigenous:		52	64	90	78
Months consumption:		(19.50)	(20.75)	(12.41)	(7.73)
3. Stocks-in-process:		2543	2972	4610	5484
Months cost of production:		(1.20)	(1.25)	(1.60)	(1.65)
4. Finished goods		2328	2684	3463	3599
Months cost of sales:		(0.75)	(0.75)	(0.85)	(0.80)

5. Receivable other than export and deferred receivables (including bills purchased and discounted by bankers	16162	18600	24329	27109
Months domestic sales excluding deferred payment sales	(4.00)	(3.85)	(4.35)	(4.65)
6. Export receivables (incl. bills purch. and disc.)	1025	1264	1650	2824
Months export sales:	(3.70)	(3.75)	(4.10)	(4.30)
7. Advances to suppliers of raw materials and stores/spares, consumable	3501	3734	3816	5391
8. Other current assets incl. cash and bank balances and deferred receivables due within one year (specify major items)	241	274	418	457
9. Total current assets (to agree with item 34 in Form III)	28389	32805	42330	48993
B. Current Liabilities (other than bank borrowings for working capital)				
10. Creditors for purchase of raw materials, stores and consumable spares	12818	14877	18230	18643
(months purchases)**	(7.75)	(7.90)	(7.50)	(7.00)
11. Advances from customers	4036	5233	5432	5489
12. Statutory liabilities (income tax)	—	—	152	—
13. Other current liabilities				
— Dividend payable	346	384	384	476
— Bridge loan	36	—	93	2503
— Expense creditors	277	365	485	235
— Premium on redemption of debentures	85	53	20	38
— Repayment of term loans etc.	424	1299	1111	1087
14. *Total* (To agree with sub-total of B-Form III)	18022	22211	25907	28471

Notes: * As RBI norms are no longer mandatory, we have not filled up this column. Banks are now free to follow those norms or develop their own norms.

** Months purchases are calculated ignoring direct finished goods purchased.

FORM V

Computation of Maximum Permissible Bank Finance for Working Capital (MPBF)*

(Including annual repayment of term loans etc. as part of current liabilities)

(Amount Rs in lakh)

		As per balance sheet as at			
		31.12.20X0	31.12.20X1	31.12.20X2	31.12.20X3
		Last 2 Years Actuals		Current Year Estimates	Following Year Projections
		1	2	3	4
1.	Total current assets (9 in Form IV)	28389	32805	42330	48993
2.	Other current liabilities (other than bank borrowing) (14 of Form IV)	18022	22211	25907	28471
3.	Working capital gap (WCG) (1–2)	10367	10594	16423	20522
4.	Min. stipulated net working capital, that is, 25% of total current assets as per second method of lending (export receivables excluded, that is, 6 of Form IV)	6841	7885	10170	11542
5.	Actual/projected net working capital (45 in Form III)	4837	8123	8138	9145
6.	Item 3 minus item 4	3526	2709	6253	8980
7.	Item 3 minus item 5	5530	2471	8285	11377
8.	Maximum permissible bank finance (item 6 or 7 whichever is lower)	3526	2471	6253	8980
9.	Excess borrowing representing short fall in NWC (4–5)	2004	(238)	2032	2397

Note: * MPBF system is no longer mandatory for banks. However, the above format is in use in most banks with or without any modification.

FORM V (A)

Computation of Maximum Permissible Bank finance for working CAPITAL (MPBF)

(Ignoring annual repayment of term loans etc. as part of current liabilities)

(Amount Rs in lakh)

		As per balance sheet as at		
	31.12.20X0	31.12.20X1	31.12.20X2	31.12.20X3
	Last 2 Years Actuals		*Current Years Estimates*	*Following Year Projections*
	1	2	3	4
1. Total current assets (9 in Form IV)	28389	32805	42330	48993
2. Other current liabilities (other than bank borrowing and repayment obligations) (14 of Form IV, 8 of Form III)	17598	20912	24796	27384
3. Working capital gap (WCG) (1–2)	10791	11893	17534	21609
4. Min. stipulated net working capital, that is, 25% of total current assets as per second method of lending. (export receivables excluded, that is, 6 of Form IV)	6841	7885	10170	11542
5. Actual/projected net working capital (45 in Form III) plus 8 of Form III	5261	9422	9249	10232
6. Item 3 minus item 4	3950	4008	7364	10067
7. Item 3 minus item 5	5530	2471	8285	11377
8. Maximum permissible bank finance (item 6 or 7 whichever is lower)	3950	2471	7364	10067
9. Excess borrowing representing short fall in NWC (4–5)	1580	(1537)	921	1310

FORM VI
Funds Flow statement

(Amount Rs in lakh)

	As per balance sheet as at		
	31.12.20X1	31.12.20X2	1.12.20X3
	Last 2 Years Actuals (as per audited balance sheet)	Current Year Estimates	Following Year Projections
	1	2	3
1. Sources			
(a) Net profit (after-tax)	2123	1084	1148
(b) Depreciation	1007	1095	378
(c) Increase in capital (share premium and capital subsidy)	—	20	5754
(d) Increase in term liabilities (including public deposits)	7102	642	—
(e) Decrease in			
i. Fixed assets	—	—	—
ii. Other non-current assets	—	—	—
(f) Others	—	—	—
(g) Total	10232	2841	7280
2. Uses			
(a) Net loss	—	—	—
(b) Decrease in term liabilities (including public deposits)	—	—	2523
(c) Increase in:			
i. Fixed assets	3935	1604	1904
ii. Other non-current assets	577	599	1196
iii. Misc. expenditure	429	122	26
(d) Dividend payments	384	384	476
(e) Others	1621	117	148
(f) Total	6946	2826	6273
3. Long-term surplus (+)/deficit (−) (1–2)	3286	15	1007
4. Increase/decrease in current assets *(as per details given below)	4416	9525	6663
5. Increase/decrease in current liabilities other than bank borrowings	4189	3696	2564
6. Increase/decrease in working capital gap (4–5)	227	5829	4099
7. Net surplus (+)/deficit (−) (difference of 3 and 6)	(3059)	5814	3092
8. Increase/decrease in bank borrowings	(3059)	5814	3092
Increase/decrease in net sales	9578	8770	6098

*Break-up of item (4)			
i. Increase/decrease in raw materials	580	802	64
ii. Increase/decrease in stock-in-process	429	1638	874
iii. Increase/decrease in finished goods	356	779	136
iv. Increase/decrease in receivables			
(a) Domestic	2438	5729	2780
(b) Export	239	386	1174
v. Increase/decrease in stores and spares	108	(35)	21
vi. Increase/decrease in other current assets	266	226	1614
Total	4416	9525	6663

Explanatory Notes

Form II: Operating Statement

Item No. 5 (i) and 5 (ii) : Percentage consumption of imported and indigenous raw materials follow the same pattern as in item no. 9 of Exhibit III. In case of consumption of spares, the same pattern is followed (ignoring the small capitalised items). Indigenous stores consumption [5 i(c)] is calculated after deducting the spares consumption from stores and spares as in Exhibit I.

Item No. 5 (v) : 'Other manufacturing expenses' are composed of service charges, repairs of plant and machinery, and insurance.

Item No. 6 : 'Selling, general and administrative expenses' include depreciation on building, etc.

Form III: Analysis of Balance Sheet

Item No. 1 (iii): The figure for 'bills purchased and discounted' is taken from item no. 6 (c) of Exhibit III, which amount is also added to the receivables figure of the balance sheet in item 28

(i), to reflect the true level of receivables.

Item No. 8 : *Repayment obligations are calculated as:*

Particulars	20X0	20X1	20X2	20X3
Term loans	125	780	800	800
Fixed deposits	175	175	175	175
Debentures	—	218	—	—
Deferred payments	124	126	136	112
Total	424	1299	1111	1087

Maximum permissible bank finance has been calculated first by considering these annual repayment obligations as part of current liabilities (Form V), and then by ignoring them (Form VA).

Item Nos. 13 and 14 : These are net of annual repayment obligations as in item no. 8.

Item No. 16 : 'Other term liabilities' are composed of security deposits, incentive loans, and unclaimed dividends. The latter item has lost its currentness, because the company has ceased to have any control over it. The corresponding bank account may have to be closed soon by transfer to the central government as per the rules. Some analysts prefer to include it under the head 'other current liabilities'. As long as the nature of this liability is understood properly and treated accordingly, it is not going to make much difference where one puts it.

Item No. 22 : 'Other reserves' include share premium, debenture redemption reserve, capital reserve, capital subsidy, and investment allowance reserve.

Item No. 30 : Bifurcation of the raw materials inventory and spares between imported and indigenous follows the same pattern as their consumption.

Item No. 31 : 'Advances to subsidiaries' are taken as part of trade advances, owing to their nature as revealed in their movement over the years.

Item No. 33 : 'Other current assets' include deposits with Excise and Customs Departments in current accounts.

Item No. 40 : 'Other non-current assets' include technical knowhow and staff advances.

Form VI: Funds Flow Statement

Item No. 2 (e) : For 20X1 'others' include doubtful debt reserve, decrease in revaluation reserve, and goodwill amounting to Rs 1539 lakh being excess of liabilities over assets of Indian Electrical Lamp Works Limited taken over by UEL (see item no. 19 of Exhibit III).

Form IV: Comparative Statement of Current Assets and Current Liabilities

(Rs in lakh)

Item No. 10	Calculation of Purchases			
	20X0	20X1	20X2	20X3
Raw materials consumption	19489	22047	28353	31973
Add: Closing stock	2523	3103	3905	3969
	22012	25150	32258	35942
Less: Opening stock	2129	2523	3103	3905
Purchases	19883	22627	29155	32037
Consumable spares consumption	41	100	134	248
Add: Closing stock	66	174	139	160
	107	274	273	408
Less: Opening stock	51	66	174	139
Purchases	56	208	99	269

CREDIT APPRAISAL

Sales of the company are falling both in percentage terms and in absolute value. At one time, the company was the leader in the market. In domestic appliances and equipments the company was a household name. Although with liberalisation the market is expanding both in depth and spread, the company's market position is being eroded gradually with increasing competition. In order to hold on to its market share it is giving a longer line of credit to its buyers, which is creating a severe liquidity problem as we will see later.

It appears that the company is in the process of consolidation and restructuring. It has made substantial investments for renewal/replacement of plant and machinery during the last three years as growth of fixed assets during this period will reveal. These investments are principally supported by long-term borrowings and capital issues. It might take a few more years to fully reap the benefits of these investments. During the consolidation period, the company has projected a moderate sales growth of approximately 9.5 per cent, which is conservative but reasonable.

The operating structure of the company is strong. It has a stable gross profit ratio as the following calculations will reveal (see Chapter 16 for a detailed ratio analysis).

	20X0	20X1	20X2	(Rs in lakh) 20X3 (Projected)
Net sales (item 3 of Form II)	46232	55810	64580	70678
Cost of sales (item 5 of Form II)	36551	43472	49894	54879
Gross profit	9681	12338	14686	15799
Gross profit ratio (% on sales)	20.94	22.10	22.74	22.35

Comparison of the following two operating ratios, however, reveals the weakness of the company.

	20X0	20X1	20X2	(% on Sales) 20X3 (Projected)
1. Operating ratio before interest (item 8 ÷ item 3 of Form II)	7.66	8.32	8.39	7.52
2. Operating ratio after interest (item 10 ÷ item 3 of Form II)	2.78	2.46	1.41	0.32

The fall in operating ratio before interest in the projected year is largely due to non-absorption of selling and general and administrative expenses (Item 6 in Form II) by sales, though the company appears to have taken steps to control its growth. These overheads grew at 25.38 per cent in 20X1, fell to 20.41 per cent in 20X2, and in 20X3 the company has projected a moderate 13.06 per cent rise which is quite tolerable. The company expects to bring this down further.

However, the sharp fall in the operating ratio after interest reveals the weakness of the financial structure of the company. All the benefits of the strong operating structure of the company are being negated by its weak financial structure. The ratio was just 1.41 per cent in 20X2 and in the projected year it is going to be only 0.32 per cent. In fact, the company is living on its non-operating income (Item 11 of Form II). The condition is serious. It calls for substantial restructuring of the finances of the company. The lending banker should call for the company's plans in this direction.

Presently, the company is paying an average interest rate of about 21 per cent on its total outside liabilities, including bank finance for working capital. The rate is too high to sustain. It is desirable that the company explores cheaper sources of finance, such as debentures and fixed deposits from the public, and pay back high cost loans from financial institutions and banks. As the company could successfully market its capital issues at a premium, it still enjoys goodwill in the market. The company has also not defaulted on servicing its fixed deposits and debentures. Therefore, it may not be difficult for the company to raise funds from these two sources.

In addition to this, the banker must require the company not to pay any dividend both in the projected and following years till it makes a financial turnaround. The company might not have been able to do so earlier because capital issues were in the offing but it can no longer be permitted to pay dividends for some time to come.

The total debt–equity ratio of the company (item 47 in Form III) is high. It went up to 5.67 in 20X2, though the company has decided to bring it down to 3.48 in the projected year. This high ratio is primarily due to a large volume of current liabilities. The small current ratio (item 46 in Form III) is indicative of this fact.

While some of the turnover ratios (given in brackets against items 1 to 3 in Form IV) support our earlier observations of the good operating strength of the business reflected by variability of expenses with sales. The finished goods stock turnover ratio (item 4 in Form IV) is of particular importance. It indicates fast movement of stock. The company is holding only about three weeks' stock, which apparently suggests efficiency of the marketing department in generating sales. But the low receivables turnover ratios (items 5 and 6 in Form IV) tell us at what cost the finished goods turnover ratio is kept low or, in other words, at what cost sales are being made. As indicated earlier, the marketing department of the company, in order to hold on to its market share, must be doling out longer credit lines to its buyers, or the collection machinery of the company might have slowed down. This is creating a severe liquidity problem, forcing the company to delay payments to its suppliers as is revealed by the creditors' turnover ratio (item 10 in Form IV). Presently, trade creditors are not being paid for seven months. The company is on the brink of a severe liquidity crisis.

It is time the lending banker intervenes. He must change his role from a passive lender to an active banker and ask the company to review its receivables policies. The first step in this direction would be to evolve a moderately stringent credit policy. Second, the company should undertake cost-benefit analyses of alternative cash discount policies. If it is found that the discount cost is lower than the carrying cost of receivables, it should be offered to both existing and future debtors for quicker generation of cash. Third, the company must gear up its collection machinery. One way of doing this is to place responsibility for collection of sales within the given credit period on the marketing personnel. It can no longer be the responsibility of the accounts department alone.

Lending Decisions: Problems with the MPBF System

A comparison of Forms V and VA reveals that the MPBF is lower by Rs 1087 lakh if we include annual repayments of term loans, etc. in current liabilities. As mentioned earlier, this is the reason why industry and trade opposed their inclusion in current liabilities for a long time, to which the RBI ultimately relented. One would also notice the inherent rigidity in fixing maximum permissible bank finance. The matter is now left to the boards of directors of banks. In what follows we try to remove this rigidity and take a pragmatic approach to resolve the problems faced by the company.

We have deliberately ignored the current assets-holding norms for calculation of available bank finance in order to take a realistic view of the company's position. By definition, the company is far from being sick, but if the financial structure of the company is not restructured properly then 'far' may not be too far. The banker must play an active role in such a restructuring process. He should be pragmatic, taking a total view of the business, and should provide a judicious level of finance which should not be so high as to make the company lax on its finances or so low as to suffocate it for want of liquidity.

For the projected year, the banker should require the company to bring down its average cost of finance on long-term borrowings (items 13–16 in Form III) from 22.6 per cent (2053/9087) to 17 per cent per annum, which will reduce the interest burden by about Rs 500 lakh in the projected year assuming that the present level of borrowings continues. Over the next four years, the company should aim to lower its interest further, at least to 15 per cent per annum. The bank must examine the company's plan towards achieving these goals. Interest rate on short-term finance should also be rationalised at 17 per cent per annum. As already mentioned, the company should refrain from declaring any dividend during the restructuring period.

The company's domestic receivables holding is presently 4.35 months of sales and its exports receivables holding is 4.10 months of export sales. This is the main culprit behind the liquidity crisis of the company. Urgent steps are called for to arrest the damaging impact of a high level of receivables on the company's finances and profitability. The banker should indicate that in the projected year both the domestic and export receivables should be brought down to three months of their respective sales. During the next four years, the objective should be to bring down all receivables to an average of two months of sales. As mentioned earlier, the company should review its existing credit and collection policies and devise alternative policies and action plans to attain these objectives.

Supply creditors must have been suffering for long. If the situation persists, they may be forced to stop supplies which will be dangerous for the company. At present, they do not receive payments for seven months. It is likely that the suppliers have a long-term relationship with the company (though it may not continue for long if the present situation persists). A meaningful negotiation with the suppliers should begin forthwith. It may be possible to get them to agree to a four months payment period for the projected year with a definite plan of reducing it to three months during the next four years.

It is imperative that the bank obtains and examines all these operative plans carefully before taking the lending decision. Assuming now that the proposed plans are implemented, working capital finance for the projected year should be recalculated as below:

(Rs in lakh)

Items	Revised level
Domestic receivables to be reduced to 3 months of domestic sales (ignoring scrap sales)	17527
Export receivables to be reduced to 3 months of export sales	1974
Total receivables	19501
Trade creditors to be reduced to 4 months of purchases $4[32037 + 269)/12]$	10768

Hence, Gross current assets
= Rs 48993 − 29933 + 19501 = Rs 38561
Less: Current liabilities
= Rs 28471 − 18643 + 10768 = Rs 20596
(excluding bank finance)
Working capital gap = Rs 17965

Considering the fact that the company is in the process of restructuring its finances, the bank should take a pragmatic view of the situation. The working capital finance sanctioned to the company should be enough to enable it to do business as per the projections without any further strain on its liquidity. As pointed out earlier, this must imply at the same time that the bank should not sanction a credit limit which would make the business lax in its financial restructuring process.

The company has projected a net working capital of Rs 9,145 lakh at the end of 20X3 (item 5 in Form V), assuming that it is able to discharge repayment obligations of term liabilities by that time. We should add to this Rs 500 lakh and Rs 476 lakh, being savings on interest due to restructuring of term finances and withholding of dividend payment respectively, as indicated earlier. On this assumption, net working capital at the end of the projected year should not be less than Rs 9145 + 500 + 476 = Rs 10,121 lakh. In ordinary circumstances and under the MPBF system the bank would sanction a working capital finance of Rs 17965 – 10121 = Rs 7,844 lakh on the assumption of uniform generation of profit. But in reality, the company will not be able to generate the projected sales, and hence profit, unless full finance is made available to it at the beginning of the projected period. The savings on interest on long-term finances may also not be possible right at the beginning of the projected year. A realistic view would be to take half of the projected profit and interest savings for the purpose of NWC calculation. Deducting this from projected net working capital calculated above we can determine the average level of NWC for the projected year. That is Rs 10,121 – 0.5 (1055 + 500) = Rs 9,343 lakh. Available bank finance should, therefore, be Rs 17,965 – 9,343 = Rs 8,622 lakh.

The company has projected working capital finance of Rs 11,377 lakh and on this basis it calculated interest, which featured in the operating statement (item 9 in Form II). Assuming a rate of interest at 17 per cent per annum, savings of interest due to lower level of working capital finance will be Rs 0.17 (11377 – 8622) = Rs 468 lakh, which will be added to the net working capital of the company in the projected year, which will strengthen the financial structure of the company.

Working capital finance of Rs 8,622, or say Rs 8,620 lakh, will be made available to the company in the following forms:

	(Rs in lakh)	
Cash credit	1085	(13%)
Bill purchased and discounted:		
Export bills	1975	(23%)
Domestic bills	4060	(47%)
Working capital term loan	1500	(17%)
Total:	8620	(100%)

It may be seen that 70 per cent of the finance is made available to the company in the form of bill finance since even after restructuring of bills receivables, they still constitute more than 50 per cent of current assets.

Working capital term loan will be repaid in three years' time in half-yearly instalments of Rs 250 lakh (exclusive of interest). Rate of interest will be 17 per cent per annum. The bank will closely monitor the performance of the company in terms of its operative plans to see that during the projected year:

A. Long-term borrowings are rationalised in such a manner as to bring down the average interest paid to 17 per cent.
B. Receivables holding (both domestic and export) is brought down to an average of three months sales.
C. The company stops declaring dividend until it makes a full turnaround.

Concluding Remarks

The lending system proposed by the Tandon Committee in 1975 was perfected by the Chore Group in 1980. The greatest strength of the system lies in its simplicity, and flexibility to adapt to changes in the economic environment without tilting its basic framework. By highlighting the necessity of developing industry-wise norms for holding inventories and receivables, the committee laid down the foundation of a lending discipline hitherto unheard of in the history of Indian banking. It is expected that commercial banks will follow up the basic tenets of this approach, and develop their own in-house norms.

The Chore Group took pains in raising various issues around the prevalent cash credit system of financing working capital. The Group did look beyond, but stopped short of recommending gradual replacement of the cash credit system by the loan system. It took about a decade and a half for the RBI to germinate the seed sown by the Chore Group. In April 1995 the RBI made a beginning by announcing that 25 per cent of the maximum permissible bank finance would be made available by way of short-term loans to borrowers enjoying working capital limits of Rs 20 crores and above from the banking system. Gradually, the cash credit component was drastically reduced to 20 per cent. For borrowers with sanctioned limits falling between Rs 10 and 20 crores, the cash credit component would be 25 per cent, and the loan component 75 per cent. The RBI made a beginning and showed the way. It is desirable for banks to move towards scraping the cash credit system for all categories of borrowers. The credit limits should be a judicious mixture of both loans and bills, the latter being not less than 25 per cent of aggregate limits to ensure continued development of the bill market, as spearheaded by the Discount and Finance House of India Limited. With the rising spread and depth of the financial market in terms of availability of financial instruments, it should not be difficult for large borrowers to install and/or develop their own cash management systems, instead of relying on the cash credit system.

The Tandon Committee visualised the need for reducing the dependence of borrowers on bank finance. It proposed to achieve this objective by gradually increasing the current ratio. The Jilani Committee followed up this approach (like the Chore Group) and proposed that large borrowers enjoying working capital limits of Rs 10 crores and above from the banking system should be placed on a current ratio of 1.5. The move was in the right direction, but presently bankers are still taking time to implement it because of industry resistance, and also their own anxiety to withstand the growing pressure of competition and disintermediation.

The mandatory provisions of the MPBF system have finally been withdrawn by the RBI. In his monetary policy announcements on 16 April 1997, the RBI governor said that 'since major corporates have adopted cash budgeting as a tool of funds management, banks may follow cash budget system for assessing the working capital requirement in respect of large borrowers. Individual banks may also, if they so decide, retain the present Maximum Permissible Bank Finance System with necessary modifications or develop any other system'. Banks are now given full operational freedom in assessing the working capital requirements of borrowers.

The cash budgeting system of assessing working capital needs of a borrower is discussed in Chapter 14. In this chapter we have restructured the profit and loss accounts and balance sheets of a real-life company in the assessment formats evolved originally by the RBI and later modified by banks to suit their individual requirements. The credit needs of the borrowing company were appraised under the liberalised system of lending.

Annexure 12.1

Current assets holding norms as given below are as prescribed by different committees/groups/task force appointed by the RBI from time to time. The norms are no longer binding on banks. Banks are free to use these norms or develop their own norms.

NORMS FOR INVENTORIES AND RECEIVABLES

(In months of holding)

Industry	Raw Materials (including stores and other items used in the process of manufacture)	Stocks-in-Process/Semi-Finished Goods	Finished Goods	Receivables
1	2	3	4	5
1. Textiles				
(a) Cotton/Blended Textile Mills	(a) Raw Cotton 2.00 (Bombay and Ahmedabad areas) 3.00 (Eastern areas) 2.50 (Other than the above areas)	1.5 (Composite Mills) 0.50 (Spinning Mills) 0.75 (Processing Mills for non-job work)	3.00 (Combined for Composite Mills) 2.50 (Combined for processing mills for non-job work)	
	(b) Synthetic Fibre/ Yarn 1.50	0.50 (Processing Mills for job work)	2.25 (Combined for Processing mills for job work)	
	(c) Cloth 0.50 (for processing mills and composite mills using grey cloth as raw material)			
	(d) Other raw materials 2.00			
(b) Silk and Art Silk Mills	i. Synthetic yarn 1.00	0.50 (Weaving Mills)	2.50 (Combined for Weaving Mills)	
	ii. Cloth 0.50 (for processing mills)	0.75 (Processing/ composite mills for non-job-work)	2.50 (Combined for Processing/ Composite mills)	
	iii. Other raw materials 2.00	0.50 (Processing/composite mills for job work)		

1		2	3	4	5
(c) Woollen Mills	i.	Raw wool 3.00	1.25 (Weaving Mills)	4.00 (Combined Off-season: April–September)	
	ii.	Rags and Waste 3.00		3.00 (Combined Busy season: October–March)	
	iii.	Synthetic fibre/yarn 1.00			
	iv.	Other raw materials 2.00			
(d) Man-made/ Synthetic Fibre		1.50	0.50	2.00 (Combined)	
(e) Jute Textiles		2.50	0.33	1.00 (for domestic sales) 1.50 (for exports)	
2. Rubber (a) Tyres		2.00 (Combined for imported and indigenous) 1.25 (additional for peak season only)	0.50	2.00 (Combined)	
(b) Other Rubber Products		2.00	0.25	1.75 (Combined)	
3. Fertilisers* (a) Nitrogenous		0.75 (Units near refinery)	Negligible	1.75 (Busy season: Oct–February)	1.50
		1.50 (Units away from refinery)		2.25 (Off-season– March–Sept.)	1.75
(b) Single Super-Phosphate		2.00 (Units in port areas)	Negligible	1.50 (Busy season: Oct.–February)	1.25
		3.00 (Units away from port areas)		2.25 (Off season: March–Sept.)	1.50
(c) Complex Fertilisers		2.00 (Units in port areas)	Negligible	1.75 (Busy season: Oct.–February)	1.25
		3.00 (Units away from port areas)		2.50 (Off-season: March–Sept.)	1.75

* In addition to the above norms spares holding for 12 months consumption for all the three types of fertiliser industry were permitted.

1	2	3	4	5
4. Chemicals (other than fertilisers)				
(a) Drugs & Pharmaceuticals)	2.75	0.75	1.50	1.50
(b) Pesticides, Weedicides, etc.	2.75	0.75	2.00	1.50
(c) Paints and Varnishes	2.25	0.50	1.50	2.00
(d) Petro chemicals	1.50	0.50	1.00	1.50
(e) Speciality chemicals#	1.50	0.75	1.50	2.00
(f) Inorganic chemicals (other than fertilisers)	2.00	0.50	1.00	2.00
(g) Dyes and Dye Intermediates (a) Imported/ canalized 2.50	1.00		3.50 (Combined)	
(b) Indigenous/ non-canalized 2.25				
(h) Basic Industrial Chemicals	2.75	0.25	1.00	1.75
(i) Essential Oil-based	1.50	0.25	1.75	1.50
5. Paper Imported				
i. Pulp, Waste Paper, Paper Cutting etc.	4.00	7 days	1.00 __ 2.00 __ (Combined level: 2 months)	
ii. Felts and Wires	6.00			
Indigenous				
i. (a) Bamboo, Wood bagasse, Straw etc.	6.00			
(b) Waste Paper, Rags Leads etc.	3.00			
ii. Chemicals	2.00			
iii. Coal + 2 months for mills using bagasse as raw material)	2.00			
iv. Felts and Wires	3.00			

Speciality chemicals include (i) Adhesives, (ii) Rubber Chemicals, (iii) Textile Auxiliaries and Miscellaneous Speciality Processing Chemicals, (iv) Leather Chemicals, (v) Foundry and Smelting Chemicals, (vi) Surface Finishing & Electroplating Chemicals, and (vii) Industrial Explosives.

1	2	3	4	5
6. Cement				
(a) Gypsum	2.25	0.50	2.50 (Combined)	
(b) Limestone	1.25			
(c) Coal	2.00			
(d) Packing materials	1.50			
7. Engineering				
(a) Four-wheelers and commercial vehicles	2.25	0.75	2.50 (Combined)	
(b) Two-wheelers and auto-rickshaws	2.25	0.75	2.50 (Combined)	
(c) Agricultural Machinery	2.25	0.75	2.50 (Combined)	
(d) Ancillary Industry	2.25	0.75	2.50 (Combined)	
(e) Machinery other than Electrical Machinery	2.75	1.50	3.50 (Combined)	
(f) Electrical Machinery	2.75	1.25	3.50 (Combined)	
(g) Machine Tools	2.75	1.25	3.50 (Combined)	
(h) Electrical Cables, Wires, etc.	2.00	0.75	2.75 (Combined)	
(i) Steel, Tubes, Pipes, Nuts, Bolts, Bars, etc.	2.00	0.75	2.50 (Combined)	
(j) Bearings	3.00	1.00	3.00 (Combined)	
(k) Consumer Durables	2.00	0.75	2.50 (Combined)	
(l) Bulbs, flourescent tubes and dry cell batteries	4.00 (imported)			
	2.50 (Indigenous)	0.50	3.00 (Combined)	
(m) Storage Batteries	4.00 (Imported)		3.00 (Combined)	
	2.50 (Indigenous)	1.00		
(n) Fans	3.00 (Imported)	0.50	4.00 (Combined: Off-Season)	
	1.00 (Indigenous)		2.50 (Combined: Seasons)	

1	2	3	4	5
(o) Other (excluding Heavy Engg. Industries)^π	2.25	0.75	2.50 (combined)	
8. Glass	2.50	Nil	3.25 (Combined)	
9. Ceramics:				
i. Insulators	3.00	1.00	3.50 (Combined)	
ii. Others	3.00	0.50	1.00	1.00
10. Breweries:				
(a) Hops	3.00			
(b) Malt and others	2.00	0.50	0.75	1.00
11. Distilleries^§	3.00	0.25	1.00	1.00
12. Leather manufacturers (processing of raw hides and skins into finished leather and leather products	3.50 (Combined)		2.00 (Combined)	
13. Food and Food Products:				
(a) Flour mills	2.00	—	0.25	2.00
(b) Biscuits and Bakery products	1.00	0.10 (3 days)	0.50	0.50
(c) Vegetable and Hydrogenated Oils	1.00	Negligible	0.75 (Combined)	
14. Diamond Exporters*	2.5 (Combined)		1.00	3.00
15. Power Generation/ Distribution Industry	Coal 1.50 Fuel oil 2.00 Consumable Spares (i) Indigenous (ii) Imported	— 9.00 12.00	—	2.50

^π Heavy engineering would include supply of whole or substantial plants involving a long manufacturing period, for example, Sugar, Cement, Steel, and Textile plants. Inventories and Receivables for the Heavy Engineering industry would be assessed on the basis of past actuals.

^§ If the allotment of molasses is on a monthly basis, the norms should be suitably reduced, say to one month.

* The combined norm for raw materials includes work-in-process (to be computed based on so many months consumption of raw materials). Further, the combined norm of 3.5 months with respect to raw materials, work-in-process, and finished goods is inclusive of the transit period of 15 days for receipt of rough diamonds in the case of sight holder; in the case of non-sight holders, the norm applicable should be reduced to three months (combined), within which the normal processing cycle should be completed.

1	2	3	4	5
16. Bicycle Tyres	1.75	0.50	_____ 3.00 _____ (Combined)	
17. Consumer Electronics (e.g. Radio Receivers, Tape Recorders, Television Sets, etc.)	Imported 4.00 Indigenous 2.00	0.75	_____ 2.50 _____ (Combined)	
18. Communication Equipment (e.g. Telephones, Tele-printers, Railway signalling equipment etc.)	Imported 4.00 Indigenous 3.00	1.50	_____ 3.50 _____ (Combined)	
19. Computers (including calculators)	Imported 4.00 Indigenous 3.00	1.25	_____ 4.00 _____ (Combined)	
20. Control instruments and industrial electronics (e.g. Electronic meters, Oscilloscopes, Testers, Measuring instruments, etc.)	Imported 4.00 Indigenous 3.00	1.25	_____ 3.50 _____ (Combined)	
21. Electronic components, (e.g. Resistors, Capacitors, Connectors, Relays, etc.	Imported 4 Indigenous 2	1.00	_____ 2.50 _____ (Combined)	
22. Aerospace and Defence	Imported 4 Indigenous 3	1.25	_____ 3.50 _____ (Combined)	

Notes: 1. Raw materials are expressed as so many months 'consumption'. They include stores and other items used in the process of manufacture.

2. (a) Stocks-in-process are expressed as so many months 'cost of production'.

(b) In individual cases, banks may deviate from the norm for stocks-in-process if they are satisfied that the actual process time involved in any particular unit, say in view of the nature of production, past experience, and technology employed, is more than the norm suggested.

3. (a) Finished goods and receivables are expressed as so many months 'cost of sales', and 'sales' respectively. These figures represent only the average levels. Individual items of finished goods and receivables could exceed the indicated norms so long as the overall average level of finished goods and receivables does not exceed the amounts as determined in terms of the norm.

(b) The norm prescribed for receivables relates only to inland sales on a short-term basis (that is, excluding receivables arising out of deferred payment sales and exports).

4. Stocks of spares should be classified as non-current assets. However, the projected levels of spares on the basis of past experience but not exceeding 12 months consumption for imported items and nine months consumption for indigenous items, may be treated as current assets for the assessment of working capital requirements.

Annexure 12.2

A Note on Syndication of Credit

A syndicated credit is an agreement between two or more lending institutions to provide a borrower a credit facility using common loan documentation. A prospective borrower intending to raise resources through this method awards a mandate to a bank commonly referred to as the 'lead manager' to arrange credit on his behalf. The mandate spells out the commercial terms of the credit and the prerogatives of the mandated bank in resolving contentious issues in the course of the transaction. The mandated bank is required to prepare an information memorandum about the borrower in consultation with the latter, and the bank distributes this amongst prospective lenders, soliciting their participation in the credit to be extended to the borrower. The mandated bank does not sell the credit risk, but presents an opportunity to lend by extending an offer containing terms agreed upon between the mandated bank and the borrower. The information memorandum provides the basis for each lending bank making its own independent economic and financial evaluation of the borrower, if necessary, by seeking additional supporting information from other sources as well. Thereafter, the mandated bank convenes a meeting to discuss the syndication strategy relating to coordination, communication, and control within the syndication process, and finalises the deal timing, charges towards management expenses and cost of credit, share of each participating bank in the credit and so on. The loan agreement is signed by all the participating banks. The borrower is required to give prior notice to the lead manager or his agent for drawing the loans amount to enable the latter to tie up disbursements with the other lending banks. While syndication is very similar to the system of consortium lending in terms of dispersal of risk, the freedom the borrower has in terms of competitive pricing and the discipline that is sought to be achieved through a fixed repayment period under syndicated credit are absent in the present system of lending through the consortium arrangement. Thus, syndication of credit is a convenient mode of raising long-term funds by borrowers.

Source: Reserve Bank of India Circular No. IECD/20/08.13.08/93–4 dated 28 October 1993.

Take calculated risks. That is quite different from being rash.

—General George Patton

13 Business Forecasting and Credit Decisions

INTRODUCTION

One of the terms of references of the Tandon Committee[1] was to make recommendation for obtaining from borrowers the following periodical forecasts:

1. Business/production plans, and
2. Credit needs.

In accordance with this term of reference, the committee also included a question in the questionnaire sent to various industrial units: Is there a system of forecasting production/business plans for your unit? If so, on what basis and at what intervals is it drawn up? ... (Question 13).

The report of the committee, however, did not contain any analysis of responses to this question. It merely ended by suggesting quarterly information system formats in which to obtain forecast data from borrowers. The question of the quality of forecasts of different operating variables of a business, particularly sales, which form the basis for taking credit decisions by a banker, was not

[1] Report of the Study Group to Frame Guidelines for Follow-Up of Bank Credit, headed by P.L. Tandon, Reserve Bank of India, Bombay, 1975.

awarded the seriousness it deserved. Most bankers even today do not know on what basis and by which technique various operating variables like sales and current assets are projected in the annual plan of a business. As a result, a banker has no option but to apply the age-old thumb-rule to determine the projected levels of operations, which is often at variance with the desired levels. Not that business firms do not apply any modern technique of forecasting: a number of professionally managed business houses have been making forecasts of their operating variables by applying rigorous statistical techniques. But they are unable to make the other party appreciate this, because many bankers are either not aware of, or they feel uneasy with statistics and mathematics, and as such would not like to hear of them from borrowers. The communication gap widens. As a result, borrowers are often found to generate two sets of data: one for their internal use which they have developed by using modern statistical techniques, and the other to feed in a banker's format.

It is, however, heartening to note that of late, particularly at the head office level of banks, there is a growing desire to appreciate and install statistical forecasting methods in the methodology of credit appraisal. The system is gaining ground because of bankers' disheartening experience of seeing many of the projections given in the appraisal formats by borrowers going awry by the end of the year.

In this chapter we discuss one of the most reliable and commonly used techniques of business forecasting, and work out an appraisal methodology by applying this technique. The presentations are kept as simple as possible, assuming that most of our readers have only a limited knowledge of statistics.

THE BASIC THEORY

As the business grows and/or economic conditions become complex, simple rules of thumb become unruly in predicting the future. Environmental variables, both internal and external, exert influence on the operating variables of a business. These are so many variables and they are so inter-connected that it is very difficult to grasp the exact effect of each. Let us take the example of sales. Sales are dependent upon the proactive decision of an entrepreneur tempered by environmental variables. If now, we take the sales figures over a period of time, the aggregates reflect the aggregate influence of external economic conditions, say demand and supply of finished products and raw materials, and internal conditions like productivity of labour and managerial efficiency. Over a period of time, the sales figures may show a certain degree of association with time: either increasing or decreasing at a certain rate. It is not that time itself is the variable on which sales depend, meaning thereby that sales will automatically increase with the passage of time even if nothing is done; it only means that time captures the influence of various internal and external factors of an organisation on the growth or decline of sales in the aggregate. Sales,

therefore, show a certain degree of association with time.

However, we know that operating expenses, level of current assets and so on depend on sales, and naturally they show a certain degree of association. On this basis, we can project various operating variables of a business that are needed for appraisal of a credit proposal.

Of all the statistical methods of forecasting, regression analysis has been found to be the most dependable. We use this technique to analyse a proposal for the working capital finance of a real company (whose name, however, is changed). However, before we do this, it is necessary to make a short run-down of some statistical concepts relating to regression analysis.

VARIABLES

Elements of statistical data, which are changeable, for example, sales, purchases, and working capital are called variables. These are of the following kinds.

Dependent and Independent Variables

An independent variable is the influencing variable that is used as the basis of estimating the value of another variable with respect to *a particular statistical analysis*. For example, if we are measuring the quantum of working capital in terms of sales, then sales is an independent variable, and working capital is a dependent variable. However, dependency or independency is not a static concept. An independent variable in one analysis may be a dependent variable in another analysis. In this example sales is an independent variable, but it will be a dependent variable when we are estimating sales in terms of demand of the product. However, it must be clearly understood that in statistical analysis dependency or independency between variables does not necessarily imply *causation*. It indicates *direction of relationship*, for example, savings and personal spending tend to increase with an increase in income, but savings do not *cause* personal spending! It is a contradictory concept, but these two variables can be related in a statistical analysis.

Discrete and Continuous Variables

Whenever elements of a population are counted, we get distinct full numbers—integers, 1, 2, 3, 4 and so on. This is called a discrete variable. It does not include any fraction.

When elements are measured, continuous data are generated, which may be expressed in fractions. These are called continuous variables.

REGRESSION ANALYSIS

When two continuous variables are so related that a change in one variable (independent) is associated with a change in the other (dependent), we use regression analysis to develop an equation by virtue of which the value of one variable (dependent) can be estimated when the value of the other variable (independent) is known. This can be done with the help of regression analyses, which are of the following types.

Simple Linear Regression

Here, one dependent and one independent variable are related to each other linearly. That is, the resultant regression equation will be of the first degree. It will contain no variable with a power more than one.

Multiple Linear Regression

Here, one dependent and more than one independent variables are related linearly to each other. The resultant equation, however, will be of the first degree, as above.

Non-linear Regression

The dependent and independent variable(s) are related to each other non-linearly or exponentially.

For the purpose of our study, we concentrate only on simple linear regression.

Steps:

1. Choose correct variables and decide which is independent and which is dependent. For example, between sales and working capital requirement, we treat the former as an independent and the latter as a dependent variable.
2. Plot the data on a graph, the horizontal axis (base) is for the independent variable (x), and the vertical axis for the dependent variable (y). Each dot in the graph will represent the value of the two variables $(x$ and $y)$.
3. Observe whether the plotting of points indicates a linear relationship. If so, decide on the following equation:

$$y = a + bx \qquad \ldots \qquad (13.1)$$

where

y is a dependent variable;

x is an independent variable;

a is the intercept which determines the level of the regression line; and

b is the slope which indicates and measures the direction of change in y that is associated with a given change in x.

4. In fitting a regression line through a given data set, several methods have been developed, of which the least square method is the best, because it has been found that the sum of the square of differences (residuals) between the estimated and actual values of a dependent variable is the least. It is also regarded as a kind of 'mean line', in the sense that it represents the average relationship between the two variables for all possible values.

This regression equation (13.1) indicates the value of y when $x = 0$, that is, only the value of a remains, which is the minimum level of the dependent variable. Slope b is also regarded as the slant of the line—the position or direction of an angle less than 90 degrees.

When, we fit the regression line with equation 13.1, the resultant equation with the value of the coefficients (a, b) is written in the following manner:

$$y_c = a + bx \qquad \dots \qquad 13.1(a)$$

The subscript c below y indicates that it is the estimated value of y.

b in the above equation is calculated by the following formula:

$$b = \frac{\Sigma xy - n\bar{x}\,\bar{y}}{\Sigma x^2 - n\bar{x}^2} \qquad (13.2)$$

and

$$a = \bar{y} - b\bar{x} \qquad \dots \qquad (13.3)$$

The notation Σ indicates summation or addition of all values represented under its cover; '—' above the variable indicates the arithmetic mean of the variable; and n is the number of observations.

5. Let us now take the following example and develop a regression equation:

Year	Additional Capital Employed (x)	Additional Sales (y)	xy	x^2	y^2
1	3	9	27	9	81
2	2	8	16	4	64
3	1	5	5	1	25
4	3	10	30	9	100
5	1	8	8	1	64
	$\Sigma x = 10$	$\Sigma y = 40$	$\Sigma xy = 86$	$\Sigma x^2 = 24$	$\Sigma y^2 = 334$

$n = 5$.

Arithmetic mean of x or $\bar{x} = \dfrac{\Sigma x}{n} = \dfrac{10}{5} = 2$

Arithmetic mean of y or $\bar{y} = \dfrac{\Sigma y}{n} = \dfrac{40}{5} = 8$

$$b = \frac{86 - 5\,(2 \times 8)}{24 - 5\,(2)^2} = \frac{86 - 80}{24 - 20} = \frac{6}{4} = 1.5$$

Hence, $a = 8 - 1.5(2) = 5$

The resultant regression equation can now be written as follows:

$$y_c = a + bx$$
$$\text{or } y_c = 5 + 1.5x$$

On the basis of this equation, the estimated value of y, that is, y_c is calculated for all values of x and tabulated by the side of the actual values of y as below:

Year	y	y_c	Residuals $y - y_c$	Square of residual $(y - y_c)^2$
1	9	9.5	– 0.5	0.25
2	8	8.0	0.0	0
3	5	6.5	– 1.5	2.25
4	10	9.5	+ 0.5	0.25
5	8	6.5	+ 1.5	2.25
Total	40	40.0	0	5.00

It may be observed from the values of estimated y_c that they differ from the actual values, which should obviously be the case, because in social sciences, business, and economics, there is invariably a degree of error in estimation, and hence prediction. The least square method only minimises the difference.

The regression equation developed from the observed data enables us to predict the future value of the dependent variable (y_c) when the value of the independent variable (x) is given. That is, we may like to know what would be the increase in sales (y_c), if additional capital (x) of Rs 15 lakh is brought into the business. We may calculate it with the help of the derived equation:

$y_c = 5 + 1.5x$
or, $y_c = 5 + 1.5 \times 15$
or, $y_c = 5 + 22.5$
or, $y_c = 27.5$

That is, there will be additional sales of Rs 27.5 lakh when the capital employed is increased by Rs 15 lakh.

Standard Error of Estimate

But due to the error element mentioned earlier, our prediction may be wrong. As bankers, we would like to know the total estimate of error, and then predict the value with a certain level of accuracy, say 90 per cent.

The standard error of estimate (SE) is developed to measure the degree of scatter of the actual values of a dependent variable with regard to the regression line used for estimating that variable. It is indicative of the amount of discrepancy between the estimated and the actual values of the dependent variable. The formula for calculating SE is:

$$SE = \sqrt{\frac{(y - y_c)^2}{n - 2}} \tag{13.4}$$

In the table above, we have already calculated the values of $(y - y_c)^2$. Hence, SE can now be calculated as:

$$SE = \sqrt{\frac{5}{5 - 2}} \tag{13.5}$$

$$= \sqrt{1.67}$$

$$= 1.29$$

There is also a straightforward formula for calculating SE.

$$SE = \sqrt{\frac{\Sigma y^2 - a\Sigma y - b\Sigma xy}{n - 2}}$$

$$SE = \sqrt{\frac{334 - 5(40) - 1.5(86)}{5 - 2}}$$

$$SE = \sqrt{\frac{334 - 200 - 129}{3}}$$

$$= 1.29$$

In both the cases, the standard error of estimate is Rs 1.29, or say, Rs 1.30 lakh.

The concept of SE is that the estimated value of the dependent variable (y_c) will differ from the actual value on either side with 68 per cent probability. That is, $y_c \pm SE$

or, $y_c \pm 1.30$ (in lakh)

t-Distribution

If we like to increase the probability, to say 90 per cent, we may use a pre-calculated table called the t-distribution table, which is also called the 'student's t-distribution' table, named after W.S. Gosset, who published it under his pseudonym 'Student'. This table is given at the end of this chapter as Annexure 13.1.

There is a unique t-distribution associated with each of the possible degrees of freedom. When there are two elements in a sample, and a sample statistic depending upon these values has been computed, the number of sample elements which can vary freely is one. In case of a regression equation where there are two constants, two degrees of freedom are lost. We have, therefore, deducted 2 from n while calculating the SE. The same concept is applicable while locating the value of t with a given probability. Suppose we want to raise the prediction level to 90 per cent probability, there is a chance that in 10 per cent cases our predicted value will not be correct. We can now locate the t value in the table with a degree of freedom: $n - 2 = 3$ (located in the first column). The corresponding value of 10 per cent probability (that the estimated value will fall outside it) is then located against it in the fourth column under 0.10 probability, which is 2.353.

The SE is now multiplied with the standard t value, and the predicting equation is finally written as follows:

$$y_c = (5 + 1.5x) \pm (SE \times t)$$
$$\text{or,}\quad y_c = (5 + 1.5x) \pm (1.30 \times 2.353)$$
$$\text{or,}\quad y_c = (5 + 1.5x) \pm 3.06$$

hence, if x = 15 then:

$$y_c = 5 + 1.5 \times 15 \pm 3.06$$
$$\text{or,}\quad y_c = 27.5 \pm 3.06$$

The value of the dependent variable will, therefore, fall within the following range:

Rs 24.44 lakh
to
Rs 30.56 lakh

It signifies that the actual value of the dependent variable will differ by more than the value derived, in either direction, from the estimated or predicted value of the dependent variable with a probability of $(0.10 \div 2) = 0.05$.

COEFFICIENT OF CORRELATION

When two variables are fully correlated, the ratio will be equal to 1. For example, when a 10 per cent increase in one variable is associated with a similar increase in the other variable, the ratio will obviously be 1. This ratio may also be negative. That is, when an increase in one variable is associated with a proportionate decrease in the other variable, the ratio will be -1.

Correlation analysis enables us to know the degree of association between two variables. The degree or coefficient of correlation will fall within the range -1 to $+1$. The formula for calculating the coefficient of correlation (which is denoted as r) is given below:

$$r = \frac{n\Sigma xy - \Sigma x\, \Sigma y}{[\sqrt{n\Sigma x^2 - (\Sigma x)^2}\,][\sqrt{n\Sigma y^2 - (\Sigma y)^2}\,]}$$

The values derived from the example given earlier can be used to determine the value of r:

$$n = 5,\ \Sigma xy = 86$$
$$\Sigma x = 10,\ \Sigma x^2 = 24$$
$$\Sigma y = 40,\ \Sigma y^2 = 334$$

Hence,

$$r = \frac{5 \times 86 - 10 \times 40}{[\sqrt{(5 \times 24) - (10)^2}\,]\ [\sqrt{(5 \times 334) - (40)^2}\,]}$$

$$= \frac{430 - 400}{(\sqrt{120 - 100})\ (\sqrt{1670 - 1600})}$$

$$= \frac{30}{(\sqrt{20})\ (\sqrt{70})}$$

$$= +0.80$$

The coefficient of correlation between the two variables is $+0.80$. It signifies that the degree of association is high, and the variables are positively related. In statistical analysis of business situations, we should reject data which show a coefficient of correlation of less than 0.50 in either direction, because the degree of scatter will be very high in that case, which may make a statistical inference unreliable.

We now apply the statistical techniques discussed so far in the following example.

ILLUSTRATION

International Cranes and Tractors Limited was established in India as a subsidiary of John Steel Limited of the United Kingdom. For about six years since its inception, the company was engaged solely in marketing the products of its parent company, but the establishment of a factory was already underway. The first batch of indigenous production of cranes came out in the seventh year. The company, however, continued to market the products of its parent company simultaneously for 10 more years, when import of the principal's products was stopped. However, with rapid industrialisation of the country, the demand for the company's products increased. The company moved into the production of earthmovers, construction equipment, drilling machines, and agricultural heavy equipment, and soon established itself as the market leader.

Later, another subsidiary of the parent company manufacturing the same products was merged with this company, and it diluted its foreign shareholding to the extent of 49 per cent. With the merger, the company's capacity increased.

The company was able to maintain cordial industrial relations all through, except that five years back, one of its factories was closed for some time due to a lockout.

Eight years back the company went in for major structural changes, including replacing British members on the board by Indian entrepreneurs. The present working capital facilities of the company are shown in Table 13.1.

Other relevant operating figures are given in Table 13.2.

The net working capital of the company at the end of the seventh year was Rs 425 lakh. Public fixed deposits will be Rs 250 lakh in the projected year. It has submitted a proposal for working capital finance of Rs 750 lakh in the projected year.

The composition of current assets and current liabilities at the end of seventh year are given in Table 13.3 and their projections are shown in Table 13.4.

CHECKING THE ASSUMPTIONS

The company has made certain projections. It would be advisable to know the basis of these projections and the techniques used. A banker's job will be simplified if there is an agreement in the choice of bases and techniques of forecasting.

The great advantage of regression analysis is that the forecasting parameters remain stable for quite some time. Subsequent changes can also be programmed with ease in the forecasting model. Before we start the exercise of checking the projections of the borrower, we would like to

(Rs in lakh)

TABLE 13.1   Existing Working Capital of International Cranes and Tractors Ltd.

Name of Facility	Existing Limits	Availment during the last 12 Months		Balance Outstanding
		Maximum	Minimum	
Cash credit	450	455	174	410
Bills discounting	350	204	138	204
Letter of credit	405	240	24	70

TABLE 13.2   Operating Figures

(Rs in lakh)

Year	Sales	Operating Expenses	Gross Profit	Net Profit before Tax	Gross Working Capital or Current Assets	Trade and Expenses Liabilities (excluding bank finance)
1.	1144	931	405 (35%)	240 (21%)	630	206
2.	1232	966	481 (39%)	268 (22%)	724	161
3.	1332	1090	434 (33%)	246 (18%)	921	219
4.	1602	1427	384 (24%)	216 (13%)	900	175
5.	1854	1595	493 (27%)	236 (13%)	1158	273
6.	2251	1964	597 (27%)	262 (12%)	1311	277
7.	2605	2252	737 (28%)	311 (12%)	1443	361
8. (Projected)	3200	2596	972 (30%)	350 (11%)	1800	475

TABLE 13.3   Existing Current Assets and Liabilities

(Rs in lakh)

Current Assets			Current Liabilities (excluding bank finance)		
1.	Stock of raw materials	603	(5.6 months)	1.	Trade creditors (1.5 months)	200
2.	Work-in-process	155	(1 month)	2.	Expense creditors	10
3.	Stock of finished goods	243	(1.7 months)	3.	Others	151
4.	Receivables	312	(1.25 months)			
5.	Others	130				
	Total	1443			Total	361

TABLE 13.4   Projections of Current Assets and Liabilities

(Rs in lakh)

Current Assets			Current Liabilities		
1.	Stock of raw materials	640	(5 months)	1.	Trade creditors (1 month)	120
2.	Work-in-process	196	(1.5 months)	2.	Expense creditors	11
3.	Stock of finished goods	300	(1.6 months)	3.	Others	344
4.	Receivables	534	(2 months)			
5.	Others	130				
	Total	1800			Total	475

emphasise that any projection of the future cannot be accurate throughout. We have mentioned earlier that there will definitely be variations from the actual. What we intend to do is to minimise the variations by making use of various concepts of regression analysis, and point out the extent of the reliability of the projections. A banker is not fastidious about precision. It is not possible. If he can come to a decision with 90 per cent probability, he is satisfied. He can always take care of the 10 per cent aberrations.

PROJECTION OF SALES

We start with sales, as it is the basis of all other projections. We have taken data for the last seven years only, because the history of the company reveals that there had been major structural changes eight years ago. Hence, the performance of the company earlier to that year would definitely be different from the later period. *In making use of time series data for business forecasting, it is desirable that we choose as the base year a more or less stable year, otherwise the instability in time series data may influence the result adversely.* Let us now subject the existing and past data to regression analysis for projection of sales (Table 13.5).

Here we have coded the year as x_s which is the independent variable. We want a projection for the year $x_s = 8$. 'Sales' is the dependent variable, which we designate as y_s (the subscript s indicates that the variables used are for projection of sales). The number of observations is denoted by n, which is 7 in this case.

Hence $\bar{x}_s = \dfrac{28}{7} = 4; \bar{y}_s = \dfrac{12020}{7} = 1717.14$

We can now compute the coefficient of correlation (r_s), or the degree of association between the two variables by the following formula:

$$r_s = \frac{n\Sigma x_s y_s - \Sigma x_s\, \Sigma y_s}{\left[\sqrt{n\Sigma x_s^{\,2} - (\Sigma x_s)^2}\,\right]\left[\sqrt{n\Sigma y_s^{\,2} - (\Sigma y_s)^2}\,\right]} \quad \text{or,}$$

$$r_s = \frac{7 \times 55023 - 28 \times 12020}{\left[\sqrt{7 \times 140 - (28)^2}\,\right]\left[\sqrt{7 \times 22457530 - (12020)^2}\,\right]}$$

$$\text{or, } r_s = \frac{48601}{\left[\sqrt{196}\,\right]\left[\sqrt{12722310}\,\right]} = \frac{48601}{49936}$$

or, $r_s = 0.97$

It appears that the coefficient of correlation between the two variables is very high. Hence,

TABLE 13.5   Regression Equations for Sales Projection

Year Code (x_s)	Sales (y_s)	$x^2{}_s$	$y^2{}_s$	$x_s y_s$
1.	1144	1	1308736	1144
2.	1232	4	1517824	2464
3.	1332	9	1774224	3996
4.	1602	16	2566404	6408
5.	1854	25	3437316	9270
6.	2251	36	5067001	13506
7.	2605	49	6786025	18235
$\Sigma x_s = 28$	$\Sigma y_s = 12020$	$\Sigma x_s^2 = 140$	$\Sigma y_s^2 = 22457530$	$\Sigma x_s y_s = 55023$

n = 7.

we can now proceed to compute the coefficients of regression equation from the following formulae:

$$y = a_s + b_s x_s$$

where,

$$b_s = \frac{\Sigma x_s y_s - n\bar{x}_s \, \bar{y}_s}{\Sigma x_s^{\,2} - n\bar{x}_s^{\,2}}$$

$$a_s = y_s - b_s \bar{x}_s$$

by the method of the least square.

Putting the derived values in the above formulae, we get the value of coefficients b and a in the following manner:

$$b_s = \frac{55023 - (7 \times 4 \times 1717.14)}{140 - (7 \times 16)}$$

$$\text{or, } b_s = \frac{6943.08}{28}$$

$$\text{or, } b_s = 247.97$$

and

$$a_S = 1717.14 - 247.97 \times 4$$
$$\text{or, } a_S = 725.26$$

The regression equation, therefore, becomes:

$$y_{cs} = 725.26 + 247.97\, x_S$$

We may now proceed to calculate the Standard Error (SE) by the treatment of the residuals (Table 13.6).

$$SE = \sqrt{\frac{(y_s - y_{cs})}{n-2}}$$

$$SE = \sqrt{\frac{95516}{7-2}} = 138 \text{ (approx.)}$$

TABLE 13.6   Calculation of Standard Error of Estimate

Observed Value (y_S)	Estimated Value (y_{CS})	Residuals ($y_S - y_{CS}$)	Square of Residuals ($y_C - y_{CS})^2$
1144	974	+ 170	28900
1232	1221	+ 11	121
1332	1469	− 137	18769
1602	1717	− 115	13225
1854	1965	− 111	12321
2251	2213	+ 38	1444
2605	2461	+ 144	20736
Σ = 12020	12020	0	95516

$n = 7$.

We can also estimate SE by the following straight-forward formula:

$$SE = \sqrt{\frac{\Sigma y_s^{\,2} - a_s \Sigma y_s - b_s \Sigma x_s y_s}{n-2}}$$

By putting derived values in the above equation:

$$SE = \sqrt{\frac{22457530 - 725.26 \times 12020 - 247.97 \times 55023}{7-2}}$$

$$SE = \sqrt{\frac{95851}{5}} = 138.45$$

$$\text{or, } SE = 138 \text{ (approx.)}$$

The SE when adjusted with the predicting regression equation, as derived earlier, indicates that the estimated value of the dependent variable which is sales, will differ from the actual value by Rs 138 lakh on either side with 68 per cent probability. If we want to increase the probability of accuracy, to say, 90 per cent as is normally desired by a banker, we have to multiply the SE with the appropriate figure from the Student's t-distribution table (Annexure 13.1).

As there are two constants in the regression equation, we have lost two degrees of freedom from our n number of data series. In the present case, therefore, we have $n - 2$ or $7 - 2 = 5$ degrees of freedom. As we want to predict with 90 per cent accuracy, we are prepared to tolerate a 10 per cent probability that the predicted value may fall outside the actual observation. That is, we have to find out from the t-distribution table, the corresponding figure under the 0.10 column against 5 degree of freedom, which is 2.015. This figure has now to be multiplied with the derived SE. The predicting regression equation finally takes the following form:

$$y_{cs} = (a_s + b_s x_s) \pm SE\,(t)$$

or, $y_{cs} = (725.26 + 247.97 x_s) \pm 138 \times 2.015$

Projected sales (y_{cs}) for the eighth year, or when $x_s = 8$ will, therefore, fall within the following range:

$$y_{cs} = (725.26 + 247.97 \times 8) \pm 138 \times 2.015$$

or, $y_{cs} = 2709 \pm 278$

Or, projected sales will vary between Rs 2,987 lakh and Rs 2,431 lakh. For say the next two years, sales can be similarly projected with the help of the above equation by simply changing the value of x_s. We do not want to go beyond three years of projections with this derived equation, because the predicting strength of the parameters may not exist beyond three years in a business situation. For years beyond three, a fresh equation has to be derived by incorporating the actual data for the intervening years in the time series.

If sales show an increasing trend, it is preferable to take the predicted value in the maximum of the range, and be prepared for a fall in sales to the minimum of the range. We, therefore, take the projected sales for the company as Rs 2,987 lakh and not Rs 3,200 lakh, as projected by the company.

PROJECTED OPERATING EXPENSES

We now project operating expenses in terms of sales. The underlying presumption is that the level of operating expenses each year varies with the volume of sales. Although, theoretically the general overheads are not expected to vary with the volume of sales, but in actual business situations, overheads constitute only a small portion of the total operating expenses, which do not influence the aggregate significantly. In reality also, overheads are not strictly fixed; they do vary with the volume of sales, may be not proportionately. Such situations can be captured by the intercept (a) of the regression equation.

We can derive a regression equation for operating expenses in the same manner. But here, sales is the independent variable, which we denote by x_o. The dependent variable is the operating expense (excluding interest, because it is a financial expense), which we denote by y_o. The calculations are given in Table 13.7.

$$n = 7,\ \bar{x}_o = 1717.14;\ \bar{y}_o = 1460.71$$

(The subscript 'O' indicates that the variables are used to project operating expenses). The coefficient of correlation is now calculated by the formula given earlier:

$$r_o = \frac{7 \times 19237664 - 12020 \times 10225}{\left[\sqrt{7 \times 22457530 - (12020)^2}\right]\left[\sqrt{7 \times 16497171 - (10225)^2}\right]}$$

TABLE **13.7**   Regression Equations for Projection of Operating Expenses

(Rs in lakh)

Year	Sales	Operating Expenses (y_0)	$x^2{}_0$	$y^2{}_0$	$x_0 y_0$
1.	1144	931	1308736	866761	1065064
2.	1232	966	1517824	933156	1190112
3.	1332	1090	1774224	1188100	1451880
4.	1602	1427	2566404	2036329	2286054
5.	1854	1595	3437316	2544025	2957130
6.	2251	1964	5067001	3857296	4420964
7.	2605	2252	6786025	5071504	5866460
Σ=	12020	10225	22457530	16497171	19237664

or, $r_0 = 0.99$

The variables are, therefore, highly correlated.

The coefficients of regression equations are now calculated below:

$$b_0 = \frac{19237664 - 7 \times 1717.14 \times 1460.71}{22457530 - 7\,(1717.14)^2}$$

or, $b_0 = 0.92$

and

$a_0 = 1460.71 - 0.92 \times 1717.14$
or, $a_0 = -119.05$

The SE is:

$$SE = \sqrt{\frac{16497171 - (-119.05)(10255) - 0.92\,(19237664)}{7 - 2}}$$

or, $SE = 56.22$

As before, the t-value from the t-distribution table with 5 degrees of freedom and a probability of 0.10, is 2.015.

Hence, the predicting regression equation for operating expenses will be as follows:

$$y_{co} = (-119.05 + 0.92\,x_0) \pm (56.22 \times 2.015)$$

(where y_{co} is the estimated operating expense, and x_0 is sales).

Therefore, for projected sales of Rs 2987 lakh, the operating expenses will be as below:

Operating expenses or $y_{co} =$
$(-119.05 + 0.92 \times 2987) \pm 113.28$
or, between   Rs 2,743 lakh
and   Rs 2,515 lakh

The negative intercept ($a_0 = -119.05$) is a very important decision criterion for choosing between the two points of the range of projected operating expenses as derived above. If we look at the regression equation as a production function of the Cobb-Douglas type, then the intercept (a_0) can be regarded as an efficiency parameter. The only difference is that the dependent variable here is operating expenses, not the output as in the Cobb-Douglas function.

Hence, while it is true that the marginal rate of change (b_0) in operating expenses will not be affected by a change in (a_0), any decrease in the latter will represent an increase of efficiency reflected in the savings of operating expenses. Another interpretation of this is that the company has a built-in cost reduction mechanism, which is more efficient in reducing fixed overheads. In such a situation, that is, when the intercept (a_0) is negative, we should preferably take the lowest of the range of derived operating expenses. In the present case, it is Rs 2515 lakh. Therefore:

	Rs in lakh
Projected sales	2987
Projected operating expense	2515
Projected net profit	472

Having thus decided on the major operating variables of the company, we can proceed to compute the working capital requirement by the methods of the operating cycle theory, the operating expense cycle theory, or by statistical methods. Here we use statistical methods of computation of the working capital requirement.

PROJECTION OF GROSS WORKING CAPITAL

Let us first compute the projected gross working capital (GWC) or current assets. We proceed with the assumption that the level of GWC is dependent on the level of sales. When we calculate the coefficient of correlation, we shall know the degree of association between the two variables.

Calculations necessary for projection of gross current assets are shown in Table 13.8.

$n = 7, \overline{x}_g = 1717.14; \overline{y}_g = 1012.43$

The coefficient of correlation, or

$$r_g = \frac{7 \times 13138268 - 12020 \times 7087}{[\sqrt{7 \times 22457530 - (12020)^2}] [\sqrt{7 \times 7721251 - (7087)^2}]}$$

or, $r_o = \dfrac{6782136}{6974223} = 0.97$, which is very high.

We can now calculate the regression coefficients.

$$b_g = \frac{13138268 - 7 \times 1717.14 \times 1012.43}{22457530 - 7 (1717.14)^2}$$

or, $b_g = \dfrac{968879.65}{1817541.60}$

$b_g = 0.53$

and

$a_g = 1012.43 - 0.53 \times 1717.14$
or, $a_g = 102.35$

SE will be:

$$\sqrt{\frac{7721251 - 102.35 \times 7087 - 0.53 \times 13138268}{7 - 2}}$$

or, $\sqrt{\dfrac{32614.51}{5}}$

or, 80.76

TABLE 13.8   Deriving Regression Equations for Projection of GWC

Year	Sales x_g	GWC (y_g)	x^2_g	y^2_g	$x_g y_g$
1.	1144	630	1308736	396900	720720
2.	1232	724	1517824	524176	891968
3.	1332	921	1774224	848241	1226772
4.	1602	900	2566404	810000	1441800
5.	1854	1158	3437316	1340964	2146932
6.	2251	1311	5067001	1718721	2951061
7.	2605	1443	6786025	2082249	3759015
$\Sigma =$	12020	7087	22457530	7721251	13138268

As before, t being 2.015 for 90 per cent accuracy, we can now write the predicting regression equation for projection of the gross working capital requirement as:

$$y_{cg} = (102.35 + 0.53\, x_g) \pm (80.76 \times 2.015)$$
where, x_g is the projected sales (Rs 2987 lakh).

Hence, the projected GWC will be:

GWC = $(102.35 + 0.53 \times 2987) \pm 163$
or, GWC = will be 1685 ± 163
that is between Rs 1848 lakh and Rs 1522 lakh.

Of these two figures, we are taking the maximum of the range. That is, GWC for the projected year will be Rs 1,848 lakh.

PROJECTION OF TRADE AND EXPENSE LIABILITIES

We can now project the level of trade and expenses liabilities (y_L) relating it with operating expenses (x_L). The former is exclusive of bank finance, because the latter is exclusive of interest. Calculations are shown in Table 13.9

$$n = 7: \overline{x}_L = \frac{10225}{7} = 1460.71; \overline{y}_L = \frac{1672}{7} = 238.86$$

The coefficient of correlation is

$$r_L = \frac{7 \times 2628182 - 10225 \times 1672}{[\sqrt{7 \times 16497171 - (10225)^2}]\,[\sqrt{7 \times 428522 - (1672)^2}]}$$

$$= \frac{1301074}{1493004}$$

$$= 0.87$$

Here, the degree of association, though high for statistical purposes, is low as compared to the earlier cases. Now let us calculate the regression coefficients.

$$b_L = \frac{2628182 - 7 \times 1460.71 \times 238.86}{16497171 - 7\,(1460.71)^2}$$

or, $b_L = 0.12$

and $a_L = 238.86 - 0.12 \times 1460.71$

or, $a_L = 63.57$

The SE will be:

$$SE = \sqrt{\frac{428522 - 63.57 - 1672 - 0.12 \times 2628182}{7 - 2}}$$

or, $SE = 37$ (approx.)

TABLE 13.9   Deriving Regression Equations for Projection of GWC

Year	Operating Expenses (x_L)	Trade and Expense Liabilities (y_L)	x_L^2	y_L^2	$x_L y_L$
1.	931	206	866761	42436	191786
2.	966	161	933156	25921	155526
3.	1090	219	1188100	47961	238710
4.	1427	175	2036329	30625	249725
5.	1595	273	2544025	74529	435435
6.	1964	277	3857296	76729	544028
7.	2252	361	5071504	130321	812972
Σ =	10225	1672	16497171	428522	2628182

Now the *t*-value being 2.015 as before, we can write the predicting equation as below:

$$y_{c_L} = (63.57 + 0.12\, x_L) \pm (37 \times 2.015)$$

Where y_{c_L} is the projected trade and expenses liabilities, and x_L is the projected operating expense for the year under projection (operating expenses for the projected year have already been derived as Rs 2515 lakh). Hence, the estimated level of trade and expense liabilities for the projected year will be:

Projected trade and expense liabilities =
$(63.57 + 0.12 \times 2515) \pm 75$
or, $= 365 \pm 75$
or, between Rs 440 lakh and Rs 290 lakh

Taking the maximum of the range, the trade and expense liabilities for the projected year will be Rs 440 lakh.

BANK FINANCE FOR WORKING CAPITAL

We have now before us, the following projected figures:[2]

	Rs in lakh
1. Sales	2987
2. Operating expenses	2515
3. Gross working capital	1848
4. Trade and expense liability	440
5. Profit before interest and tax	472

We have calculated available bank finance for working under Method I and Method II as

[2] These figures are arrived at through statistical techniques. There is no need to apply industry-specific norms for current assets holding which have come under fire during recent times as these do not always reflect the genuine credit need of the borrower at the unit level.

		Rs in lakh
Calculation of working capital gap:		
Projected gross working capital		1848
Less: Projected trade and expense liability	440	
Projected fixed deposit	250	690
Working capital gap		1158

Calculation of bank finance		
First Method		Rs in lakh
1. Working capital gap		1158
2. Minimum stipulated net working capital (25% of item No. 1)		290
3. Actual net working capital at the beginning of the year		425
4. Item No. 1 minus item No. 2		868
5. Item No. 1 minus item No. 3		733
6. Maximum permissible bank finance (item No. 4 or item No. 5, whichever is lower)		733

Second Method		Rs in Lakh
1. Working capital gap		1158
2. Minimum stipulated net working capital (25% of total current assets)		462
3. Actual net working capital at the beginning of the year		425
4. Item No. 1 minus item No. 2		696
5. Item No. 1 minus item No. 3		733
6. Maximum permissible bank finance (item No. 4 or item No. 5, whichever is lower)		696

originally proposed by the Tandon Committee. It may be seen that while calculating the maximum bank finance available for the projected working capital requirement, we have taken the net working capital at the beginning of the year. This means that the company would require bank finance of Rs 733 lakh under Method I, and Rs 696 lakh under Method II, at the beginning of the projected year. This requirement will go on decreasing or increasing with the increase or decrease of the net working capital. Now, the net working capital is affected by any change in the long-term capital structure (and also its utilisation in fixed assets) of the company. Infusion of fresh share capital, long-term loans, and finally profit, expand this structure, while contraction occurs when the contrary happens. In the projected year, there would not be any other inflow of long-term capital from outside sources. Profit is the single source of expanding the net working capital of the company in the projected year. The projected profit before interest and tax of the company is Rs 472 lakh.

From the PBIT, the amount of interest and tax will be deducted to arrive at the net profit. Assuming a working capital advance of Rs 733 lakh the amount of interest @ 16.5 per cent per annum comes to Rs 120 lakh, and on fixed deposits it is Rs 35 lakh @ 14 per cent per annum. The total outgoing by way of interest is, therefore, Rs 155 lakh.

	Rs in lakh
Hence, PBIT	472
Less: Interest	155
Profit before-tax	317
Less: Taxation (50%)	158
Profit after-tax	159

As the company has to pay advance income tax, there is an outflow of funds from the profit generated, and hence it has to be deducted from the calculation of the net working capital generated out of profit. We have, therefore, taken profit after-tax as the source of the net working capital of the company. Assuming that the profit is generated uniformly throughout the year, the monthly generation of net profit will be Rs 13.25 lakh. It follows, therefore, that the requirement of bank finance will be reduced at the rate of Rs 13.25 lakh every month till the proposed dividend is paid out, when it will rise once again to that extent. As banks want to sanction an overall limit for a definite period, a ticklish question arises about whether the limit should be fixed after taking into account the net working capital at the beginning of the year, or at the end of the projected year. If we take the NWC of the projected year, the company will get a lower amount of bank finance, as calculated below:

		Rs is lakh
I. NWC at the beginning of the year		425
Add: Profit after-tax in the projected year	159	
Less: Dividend, say	59	
Amount transferred to reserves		100
NWC at the close of the projected year		525
II. Working capital gap in the projected year		1158
Less: NWC at the close of the projected year		525
Available bank finance		633

It appears, therefore, that if we take NWC at the beginning of the year, the company can get Rs 696 lakh under Method II, while under the second assumption it gets Rs 63 lakh less. By now, it must be clear that the company would not be able to achieve the budgeted sales with the bank finance of Rs 633 lakh, because budgeted sales can be achieved only with the budgeted finance, which is Rs 696 lakh. A bank may take two positions under the circumstances. It may sanction a limit of Rs 696 lakh straightaway and ask the company to limit its drawings to actual requirements, that is, the projected requirements less the monthly accrual of profit. Alternatively, it may bifurcate the aggregate finance among the following limits:

	(Rs in lakh)
Bills purchased and discounted	Rs 173 (25%)
Working capital term loan	Rs 313 (45%)
Cash credit	Rs 210 (30%)
Total	Rs 696

Working capital term loan will be repayable in three years @ Rs 52.17 lakh (exclusive of interest) payable half-yearly.

CONCLUDING REMARKS

Statistical techniques for predicting business variables are in wide use in the corporate sector. Their applications in lending decisions are, however, of recent origin. It is expected that in the present era of liberalisation and globalisation of both the real and financial sectors, banks and financial institutions will update their methodology of credit appraisal to match the forecasting techniques employed by the corporate sector. Of the various statistical techniques used for forecasting, the least square regression analysis is robust and it has stood the test of time. The standard error of estimate (SE), aided by the 't' distribution table enables a decision maker to take a position within a range depending upon the risk profile of the customer, and that of the lending organisation.

In business forecasting at the unit level, time-series data beyond 10 years and less than five years may not give meaningful coefficients of business variables because in the former case, the impact of changes in environment, both external and internal, may get smoothened out over a long time-series data and in the latter case, the data period is too small to capture any trend. However, it is desirable to begin the data series with a more or less stable year.

If the distribution of a predicting variable is found to be highly scattered it is not advisable to employ simple linear regression analysis. In such a situation, one may be tempted to apply the non-linear model. But unlike economic forecasting, non-linear models may not be suitable for the kinds of variables we have attempted to forecast in this chapter.

Annexure 13.1

Distribution of 't'

Degrees of Freedom	Probability						
	0.50	0.30	0.20	0.10	0.05	0.02	0.01
1.	1.000	1.963	3.078	6.314	12.706	31.821	63.657
2.	0.816	1.386	1.886	2.920	4.303	6.965	9.925
3.	0.765	1.250	1.638	2.353	3.182	4.541	5.841
4.	0.741	1.190	1.533	2.132	2.776	3.747	4.604
5.	0.727	1.156	1.476	2.015	2.571	3.365	4.032
6.	0.718	1.134	1.440	1.943	2.447	3.143	3.707
7.	0.711	1.119	1.415	1.895	2.365	2.998	3.499
8.	0.706	1.108	1.397	1.860	2.306	2.896	3.355
9.	0.703	1.100	1.383	1.833	2.262	2.821	3.250
10.	0.700	1.093	1.372	1.812	2.228	2.764	3.169
11.	0.697	1.088	1.363	1.796	2.201	2.718	3.106
12.	0.695	1.083	1.356	1.782	2.179	2.681	3.055
13.	0.694	1.079	1.350	1.771	2.160	2.650	3.012
14.	0.692	1.076	1.345	1.761	2.145	2.624	2.977
15.	0.691	1.074	1.341	1.753	2.131	2.602	2.947
16.	0.690	1.071	1.337	1.746	2.120	2.583	2.921
17.	0.689	1.069	1.333	1.740	2.110	2.567	2.898
18.	0.688	1.067	1.330	1.734	2.101	2.552	2.878
19.	0.688	1.066	1.328	1.729	2.093	2.539	2.861
20.	0.687	1.064	1.325	1.725	2.086	2.528	2.845
21.	0.686	1.063	1.323	1.721	2.080	2.518	2.831
22.	0.686	1.061	1.321	1.717	2.074	2.508	2.819
23.	0.685	1.060	1.319	1.714	2.069	2.500	2.807
24.	0.685	1.059	1.318	1.711	2.064	2.492	2.797
25.	0.684	1.058	1.316	1.708	2.060	2.485	2.787
26.	0.684	1.058	1.315	1.706	2.056	2.479	2.779
27.	0.684	1.057	1.314	1.703	2.052	2.473	2.771
28.	0.683	1.056	1.313	1.701	2.048	2.467	2.763
29.	0.683	1.055	1.311	1.699	2.045	2.462	2.756
30.	0.683	1.055	1.310	1.697	2.042	2.457	2.750
40.	0.681	1.050	1.303	1.684	2.021	2.423	2.704
60.	0.679	1.046	1.296	1.671	2.000	2.390	2.660
120.	0.677	1.041	1.289	1.658	1.980	2.358	2.617
∞	0.674	1.036	1.282	1.645	1.960	2.326	2.576

A journey of a thousand miles, begins with one step

—A Chinese Proverb

14 Funds Flow and Cash Flow Analysis

I. Funds Flow Analysis

Introduction

We have shown in Chapter 8 that promises are sources of funds for a business. Promises stay in the books of accounts as liabilities and funds flow to the business for buying assets. It, therefore, follows logically that when any of the promises are met, and hence a liability is reduced, there will be a flow of funds outside the business. The matching concept tells us that whenever a piece of asset is acquired, whether fixed or current, somewhere in the business there has already been an inflow of funds. In any business, funds come first, then the assets. Funds may come by a cash contribution either from the proprietor, or from creditors who agree to receive payments later for goods supplied. A fund is, therefore, a broader term than cash. Some writers look for funds on the assets side of the balance sheet. They argue that though the liability side of the balance sheet constitutes the sources of funds, this is actually found in its utilisation on the assets side. Their opinion differs, however, on the constitution of funds. Some writers would include only cash and marketable securities in the definition of funds; some want to add debtors to it, but desire that it should be net of current liabilities, while others go a bit further and declare that only net current assets should be regarded as funds. The evolution of the three concepts is explained in Figure 14.1.

It may be observed that all the three concepts emanate from the liquidity need of an enterprise. Net current assets, as is found in the third concept, are nothing but net working capital, which some writers simply call working capital. However, a banker should continue to regard it as net working capital, because he regards total current assets as gross working capital. Net working capital is also the amount that is available from

First Concept	*Second Concept*	*Third Concept*
Cash + marketable securities	(Cash + marketable securities + debtors) – (current liabilities)	(Cash + marketable securities + stock + all other current assets – (current liabilities)
Cash	*Quick Assets*	*Net Current Assets*

Figure 14.1 Evolution of Fund Concepts

long-term sources of the business after paying for fixed assets.[1] It is, therefore, claimed that any inflow or outflow of funds will ultimately affect the net working capital position of a business, which is not always true, as we will see later.

FINANCING THE TOTAL OPERATION: FOURTH CONCEPT

It is not that a finance manager's only concern is liquidity. He is concerned with the financing of the total operation of a business, and naturally, a banker will also be so interested while evaluating the financial and operating strength of a business. A change in net working capital is not his only concern. There may be situations where in spite of a definite inflow or outflow of funds, the net working capital of a firm is not affected at all. For example, if a machine is bought by issue of shares, debentures, or against a term loan, then there is a definite inflow of funds to the business, but the net working capital will not be affected by such fund flows. The converse will also be true when a liability is extinguished against disposal of an asset. Similarly, when creditors supply stocks, or they are paid-off by sale of stocks of an equivalent amount, then also in spite of a definite inflow and outflow of funds, there would not be any change in the net working capital. Again, if a piece of fixed or current assets is sold and the amount is invested in buying another fixed or current asset, there will be no change in the net working capital. Similar will be the case when a long-term or short-term liability is replaced by another liability of a similar nature. But if there is a flow of funds between long-term sources and short-term assets, or between short-term sources and long-term assets, or between long-term sources and short-term sources, or between long-term assets and short-term assets, the net working capital will be immediately affected.

[1] For details, see Chapters 6 and 11.

The Rules

We can now formulate certain rules which govern the movement of funds in a business.

1. Any *horizontal movement* of funds of the same value between two sides of the balance sheet is a definite flow of funds, *but it will not affect the net working capital.*
2. Any *inter-se movement* of funds amongst groups of liabilities or assets (namely short-term and long-term) will be a definite flow of funds, *but it will not affect the net working capital.*
3. Any *vertical movement of funds* between two groups of sources on the left hand side of the balance sheet, or between two groups of assets on the right hand side of the balance sheet, is a definite flow of funds, and *it affects the net working capital immediately.*
4. Any *diagonal movement* of funds between long-term sources and short-term assets, or between short-term sources and long-term assets, is a definite flow of funds, and *it affects the net working capital immediately.*

This body of rules governs the funding of the total operation of a business, which may be termed as the *fourth concept*. It is pictorially presented in Figure 14.2.

The fourth concept is elaborated further while analysing each item of the sources and uses of funds in the following section.

SOURCES AND USES OF FUNDS

1. Capital
We have already discussed capital as the primary source of funds. As funds, capital includes the share premium account also, whether received in cash or in kind. In the latter case, there is no increase in working capital, hence according to

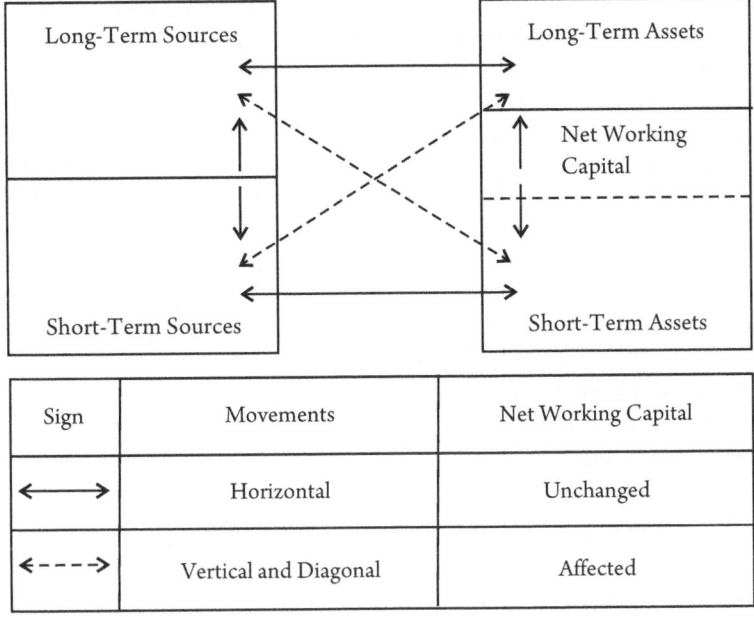

Sign	Movements	Net Working Capital
←——→	Horizontal	Unchanged
←---→	Vertical and Diagonal	Affected

FIGURE 14.2   Balance Sheet

the third concept, share premium account is not a source of funds unless it is received in cash. But the total fund concept or the fourth concept, as discussed earlier, will definitely include the share premium account, whether received in cash or in kind, as source of funds, because assets have been acquired through it, whether it is a piece of machinery, a plot of land, or simply cash. *Between two periods, any increase in the amount of capital and the share premium account is a source of funds, and any decrease, like redemption of preference shares, is a diminution of funds.*

2. Term Loans and Debentures

Any increase in term loans and debentures is a source of funds, even if no cash is received. Machinery acquired under a deferred payment arrangement and issue of debentures as payment to shareholders of a business acquired by the company are examples of non-cash funds movements. *Any reduction under this head will mean*

repayment, hence outflow of funds. However, if cash is neither received nor paid out, there is no change in the net working capital of a business.

3. Current Liabilities

Any increase in current liabilities is a source of funds. Conversely, any decrease in current liabilities, that is, repayment, is an outflow of funds. The net working capital will not change if the transaction is restricted between current assets and current liabilities only, as we have seen earlier. The net working capital is adversely affected if funds flow from short-term sources to long-terms assets. This situation is a concern for a banker. A funds flow analysis sharply brings this point into focus.

4. Long-term Assets

As acquisition of assets is utilisation of funds, their disposal is an inflow of funds. Any receipt from disposal is definitely a cash inflow. But how is the fund position of a business affected due to this transaction? If the book value of a piece of assets is Rs 100, then it has been funded exactly at Rs 100. When it is sold for Rs 80, the business is immediately short of funds to the extent of Rs 20. This amount of Rs 20 is an outflow of funds. The reverse will happen in case of sale of assets at a profit.

5. Current Assets

Like any other assets, current assets block funds. *Any increase, therefore, would mean utilisation of funds, and a decrease the release of funds.* From this it follows that even a reduction in cash is an inflow of funds. This may apparently confuse the reader but a deeper understanding of the fund concept will enable the reader to distinguish between cash and fund. In order to have an amount of cash as a piece of current assets, there must have been a certain fund flow from the liability side of the balance sheet. That fund is carrying the burden of cash like any other current asset. If this cash is now utilised to pay-off a certain liability, then that burden is released. We know that when a liability is extinguished, there is an outflow of funds. But to match this outflow, there must have been some inflow of funds somewhere. This inflow of funds is provided by reduction of cash.

This discussion can be represented graphically in Figure 14.3.

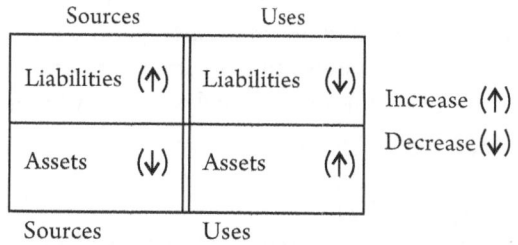

Sources	Uses	
Liabilities (↑)	Liabilities (↓)	Increase (↑)
Assets (↓)	Assets (↑)	Decrease (↓)
Sources	Uses	

FIGURE **14.3**   Sources and Uses of Funds

GENERATION OF FUNDS FROM OPERATIONS

Our discussions will not be complete unless we discuss the internal generation of funds from operations. A business in a running condition is expected to generate funds continuously. When sales revenue is in excess of the total funded cost of sales, an additional fund flows into the business in the form of profit. We have used here the term 'funded cost of sales', which means that only those costs which require laying down of actual funds are to be deducted from sales revenues. Non-cash costs like depreciation should be excluded for the purpose of calculating net funds outflow. Though depreciation is a cost, it remains in the business. Some people regard depreciation as a source of funds, which is wrong because no additional funds flow from this 'source'. It should be added back to the net profit for calculating the total funds generated from operations.

Provision for Expenses

A question may arise whether provisions for expenses, particularly for bad and doubtful debts, are to be added back to profit or not, because in this case also there is no immediate laying down of funds. Technically speaking, this supposition is true because these are also shown as current liabilities, which at any point of time are funding some assets on the other side of the balance sheet. An accountant may have to take this position because he has to tally the two sides of a balance sheet, the inflows and outflows. But a financial analyst will take a realistic view. Provisions are so short-term in nature that they do not serve any useful purpose. Besides, when provisions are made, the business has already decided to accept lesser funds from revenues. Hence, no financial analyst would regard provisions as part of funds generated from operations.

Provision for Tax and Dividend

The second question arises as to the treatment of provision for taxation and proposed dividend. When advance tax is paid, there is definite outflow of funds. It is included under the head 'loans and advances', as part of current assets. But when taxes are paid at the end of the financial year, no funds are laid down from income, which is generated continuously throughout the year. Hence, for the full year, the business enjoys the usage of funds, which in fact belong to the Income Tax Department. Similar is the case with dividend, which is generally payable once a year after the conclusion of the annual general meeting (though some companies pay interim dividend also), while profit is generated throughout the year. If monthly or quarterly funds flow statements are prepared, profit before depreciation will appear as an inflow throughout the year; tax and dividend will appear as outflows only in the months of their payment. However, when a funds flow statement is prepared, the previous year's provisions for taxation and dividend usually features in it as an outflow of funds, but the current year's provisions are not taken into account. An in-company funds flow statement is prepared on this basis for internal financial management. But a banker who likes to know the likely net fund position of a borrower at the end of the year would treat both the proposed dividend and taxation as an outflow. Funds position under these two systems would only differ marginally, because taxation and dividend are more or less stable. While calculating funds generated from operations as on the balance sheet date, transfer of profits to reserves should be ignored. Similar treatment should be given to writing-off of crystallised expense items like preliminary expenses, patents, and copyrights.

Estimation of funds flow may be vitiated due to valuation of stocks. A portion of profit may be due to overvaluation of closing stock. But if a uniform valuation method is followed, there shall be no problem. A banker should, therefore, enquire whether there has been any change in the method of valuation of stocks.

RECOMMENDATIONS OF IASC

Various accounting standards committees formalised treatment of funds items and presentation of funds flow statements.[2] Recommendations, which are useful for a banker's understanding of the problem are given below.

1. The funds flow statement summarises the resources made available to finance the activities of an enterprise, and the uses to which such resources have been put for a given period. This is useful for improving the understanding of the operations and activities of an enterprise for the reporting period.
2. The term 'funds' generally refers to cash and cash equivalents, or to working capital. In a statement of changes in financial position, the particular use of the term is to be made clear.
3. Funds provided from or used in the operations of an enterprise should be presented in the statement of changes in the financial position separately from other sources or uses of funds. Unusual items or

<hr>

[2] In some countries 'Statement of Source and Application of Funds', or a similar title, is used. The importance of a Cash flow statement and its relationship with the Funds flow statement is discussed in the next section. In Chapter 16, the problems associated with singular use of the Funds flow approach is further elaborated, and the importance of the Cash flow approach is highlighted. The new standards of Cash flow statements along with illustrative examples are given as Annexure 14.1 after this chapter.

items which are not part of the ordinary activities of an enterprise should be separately disclosed in the statement. Unusual items are also adjusted to the extent that they do not involve a movement of funds in the current period.

This practice improves the usefulness of financial statements.

4. A method commonly used for presentation is to show the net income (or loss) and to make adjustments for those revenues or expenses that do not involve a movement of funds in the current period, for example, depreciation. An alternative method is to begin with revenues that provided funds during the period, and deduct the costs and expenses that involve a movement of funds. The resulting amount is described as funds from operations.

Other sources and uses of funds

1. Other sources and uses of funds are stated separately from the funds provided from or used in operations. These include, for example:
   (a) Proceeds from the sale of long-term assets.
   (b) Outlays for the purchase of long-term assets.
   (c) Dividends in cash or in other assets.
   (d) Issue of long-term debts.
   (e) Redemption and repayment of long-term debts.
   (f) Issue of shares for cash or other assets.
   (g) Redemption or repurchase of shares for cash or other assets.

2. Some financing transactions of an enterprise involve the exchange of one form of security for another. When such

exchanges are equivalent to the issue of one security and the redemption of the other, these transactions are part of the financing and investing activities of an enterprise, and are disclosed in the statement of changes in the financial position. An example of such a transaction is the conversion of long-term debt to common or ordinary shares.

3. It may be necessary to disclose separately the investment and financing aspects of each type of transaction. For example, the proceeds on disposal of long-term assets are presented separately from the outlay for acquisition of long-term assets, and when an asset is acquired through the issue of long-term debt or equity, the issue of debt or equity and the acquisition of the asset are disclosed separately.

4. In the statement of changes in financial position, there are two methods of dealing with income from an investee company:
   (a) The funds provided from or used in the operations as a result of such an investment may be restricted to the dividends received or currently receivable. This method is based on the view that the unremitted earnings of such an investee company do not represent current resources available to the investor.
   (b) Alternatively, the investor's entire share of investee earnings can be included in the funds provided from or used in operations, and no adjustment is required in determining funds provided from or used in the operations. Under this method, the unremitted portion of the income from the investee company is shown separately as a use of funds.

ACQUISITION OR DISPOSAL

The acquisition or disposal of subsidiaries may be presented in the statement as a single amount. Alternatively, the amounts of individual assets and liabilities acquired or disposed of may be included with separate sources and uses of funds of each asset and liability dealt with in the statement. The following supplementary information should be provided:

(a) The total purchase or disposal price of the subsidiary.
(b) The portion of the purchase or disposal price discharged by cash and cash equivalents.
(c) The amount of cash and other working capital items in the subsidiary acquired or disposed of.
(d) The amounts of other assets and liabilities in the subsidiary acquired or disposed of.

AN ILLUSTRATION

We are now set to do an exercise on cash flow and funds flow analysis.

This exercise is based on a real-life case. The name of the company has been changed for purposes of anonymity. The figures are also approximated to facilitate calculation.

Rajendra Plastics Limited manufactures industrial consumable coatings. This is a niche market. The company has a market share of 35 per cent and is considered a leader in the field. Its annual turnover reached its peak at Rs 160 crore when a prolonged labour strike followed by a lockout brought everything to a halt. The uncertainty continued for about a year, during which time the company had to sell all its accumulated stocks pledged with the bank as security against working capital advance. This step, besides wiping out the entire borrowing

from the bank, left a reasonable sum to maintain overheads for some time. When the factory opened at last after a settlement with the workers at the intervention of the chief minister of the state, the company had to start afresh, because besides exhausting its accumulated stocks, it spent the debtor's realisation also to pay for overheads and satisfy pressing creditors. It ended up with a loss of Rs 398 lakh and a cash balance of Rs 10 lakh. Trade creditors, (the amount of credit stood at Rs 114 lakh as on the date of the opening), agreed to supply the materials under the old terms and conditions, and to accept payments of the overdue amount in equated monthly instalments spread over a year.

Projections

1. Presently, the company is not in a position to achieve its previous years' sales. It wants to move gradually. For this year, it has projected a sale of Rs 8670 lakh.
2. As a matter of policy, the company wants to keep three months of sales as finished stock, valued at sales price net of excise duty. The company's product and process is such that is has negligible work-in-process.
3. It is not a seasonal industry. Both sales and procurement of raw materials are done uniformly throughout the year.
4. Twenty per cent of the sales are made in cash, the rest on one month's credit. Debtors' turnover was found to be 15 in the past years, which is likely to be maintained this year also.
5. Consumption of raw materials is estimated at 50 per cent of the net sale price.
6. The company wants to build a stock of raw materials for two months consumption in two months time.

7. Twenty per cent of purchase of raw materials is paid in cash, the rest on two months credit. The creditors' turnover is around 8, which the company wants to maintain for current transactions.

8. With the increase in cost of wages, the company estimates that it will be 20 per cent of raw material consumption. Wages are paid weekly.

9. Salaries will be about Rs 370 lakh a year, paid monthly.

10. With the new settlement, bonus is estimated at Rs 35 lakh to be paid in October.

11. Contribution to provident fund is Rs 170 lakh per annum payable along with salaries and wages.

12. Welfare expenses are estimated at Rs 125 lakh per annum, payable along with salaries and wages.

13. Excise duty is calculated at Rs 590 lakh on total sales, payable as and when sales are made.

14. Sales tax is calculated at Rs 72 lakh on total sales, payable quarterly.

15. Four per cent commission on sales is payable in the month following the sales.

16. Other variable production expenses are estimated to be 15 per cent of the raw materials consumed.

17. Fixed production overheads are Rs 25 lakh per month.

18. The cost of insurance is Rs 14 lakh, payable in March.

19. Depreciation is Rs 224 lakh.

20. Interest on debentures amounting to Rs 16 lakh to be paid in January this year.

21. Auditors' fees are Rs 2 lakh, payable in December.

22. Other administrative overheads are Rs 33 lakh per month.

23. The company is expected to receive a dividend of Rs 4 lakh from its investments in April.

24. It proposes to dispose of its entire investments, which stood at Rs 26 lakh in the books of accounts, and expects to realise Rs 31 lakh net of expenses in June.

25. The interest on security deposits and loans and advances is estimated to be Rs 14 lakh to be realised in April.

26. The company has already contracted to sell some of its old machinery (book value nil) at Rs 26 lakh. Payment is expected in February.

27. The State Financial Corporation has agreed to grant a term loan of Rs 30 lakh, which will be available in March. Another term loan of Rs 32 lakh is expected from IDBI in the same month. In both cases, repayment will start after two years.

28. The company has a loan of Rs 100 lakh outstanding with ICICI. It is repayable @ Rs 9 lakh every June and December. Other term-lenders (amounting to Rs 600 lakh) have agreed on a moratorium of repayment for two years.

29. Aggregate interest on all term loans is Rs 21 lakh, payable quarterly.

30. The company has fixed deposits amounting to Rs 340 lakh. Interest @ 10 per cent on an average will fall due for payment in April. Out of these fixed deposits, Rs 30 lakh will be due for repayment in the same month. However, the company has already made arrangements to raise further deposits. It expects to receive Rs 140 lakh in April.

31. A deposit with the Port Trust, which stood at Rs 76 lakh, is to be increased to Rs 80 lakh in January.

32. Advance Income tax to be paid @ Rs 23 lakh quarterly.
33. Loans and advances, which stood at Rs 195 lakh, will be recovered @ Rs 1.25 lakh per month.
34. The company has plans to purchase/renew fixed assets in the following manner:
    February—Rs 25 lakh; March—Rs 65 lakh; and April—Rs 40 lakh.
35. Further capital expenditure is planned in November (Rs 5 lakh) and December (Rs 5 lakh).

The company opened with the balance sheet given below.

a business is planning or projecting operations for future period(s), the statement holds, though in the reverse. That is, a matching inflow of funds into the business must be planned in advance, if the projected operations for the future period(s) generate current assets or require acquisition of fixed assets. In planning such inflow of funds, the policy of a company should be such that as far as possible, short-term funds are not engaged in the acquisition of long-term assets.

What is also implicit in this statement, or the subsequent variation of it, is that an inflow of funds is necessitated only when there is generation/acquisition of assets. No inflow of funds is required if there is no acquisition/generation of assets. For example, if the projected sales of

Balance Sheet as on 31-12-20X7

(Rs in lakh)

Liabilities			Assets	
Authorised capital		2000	Fixed assets	2803
Issued, subscribed, and paid-up capital		1178	Investments	26
Debenture redemption reserve		90	Deposits with Port Trust	76
General reserve		886	Other loans and advances	195
8% Debentures		200	Cash and bank balances	10
Term loans			Profit and loss a/c	398
From ICICI	100			
IFC	260			
IDBI	340	700		
Fixed deposits		340		
Sundry creditors		114		
Total		3508	Total	3508

SUGGESTED APPROACH

We indicated in our introduction of funds flow analysis that in a going concern whenever there is an acquisition of assets, there must have been a flow of funds somewhere in the business. When

Rs 8,670 lakh of Rajendra Plastics Limited were all realisable in instant cash, and there was no need to hold an inventory of raw materials and finished goods, the company would not require any additional inflow of funds for current operations (except perhaps for some small items like advance tax) over and above the first dose of working capital comprising raw materials and expenses spent on the conversion cycle, which in this case is in the nature of a transient current asset, as the processing time is negligible.

We should, therefore, first see what are the assets that are likely to be acquired and/or generated during the projected operations of the business:

(Rs in lakh)

Acquisition of Long-term (Fixed and Non-Current) Assets

Item No.	Head	Amount	Remarks
34	Fixed assets	130.00	
35	Capital expenditure	10.00	
	Sub-total	140.00	
31	Deposit with Port Trust	4.00	See notes to this table.
	Total	144.00	

Generation of Short-term (Current) Assets

Item No.	Head	Amount	Remarks
2	Inventory of finished goods	2020.00	For calculation, see notes to this table.
6	Inventory of raw materials	840.00	–do–
4	Debtors	578.00	–do–
32	Advance income tax	92.00	
	Total	3530.00	

Notes: (Rupees in lakh)

1. *Inventory of finished goods*[3]

Projected sales	8670.00
Less: Excise duty	590.00
Net sales	8080.00

Three months net sales as inventory $= (8080/12) \times 3 =$ Rs 2020 lakh

2. *Debtors*

Projected sales per month $(8670 \div 12)$	722.50
Less: 20% realised in cash	144.50
Debtors for one month of credit sales	578.00

Check

Turnover of debtors is to remain at 15

$$\frac{Sales}{Debtors} = \frac{8670}{578} = 15 \ Q.E.D$$

3. *Inventory of Raw Materials*

As the company is starting its production anew with no opening stock, a projected inventory of finished goods worth Rs 2,020 lakh at net sale price as calculated above will have to be built in addition to the projected net sales of Rs 8,080 lakh. The projected level of production at net sale price is, therefore, Rs 8080 + Rs 2020 = Rs 10,100 lakh.

Consumption of raw materials is 50 per cent of projected production at net sale price, that is, Rs 5,050 lakh. Inventory of raw materials at two months consumption, therefore, comes to $(5050/12) \times 2 =$ Rs 840 lakh (approx.).

4. *Deposit with Port Trust*

As per RBI guidelines, this is to be treated as a non-current asset, to be funded from long-term sources only.

We shall now see how the company proposes to fund these assets in the projected year. First, we calculate *funds from operations,* which are the most important sources of funds.

[3] Although here we are following the company's mode of valuing finished goods inventory, it would have been preferable to value it at cost of goods sold.

Generation of Funds from Operations

(Rs in lakh)

Item No.	Head	Amount	Remarks
1	Sales	8670.00	
13	*Less:* Excise duty	590.00	
	A. Net sales	8080.00	
5	Consumption of raw materials	5050.00	See notes to this table.
8, 10	Wages and bonuses	1045.00	–do–
16	Variable production expenses	757.56	–do–
17	Fixed production overheads	300.00	
19	Depreciation	224.00	
	B. Cost of production	7376.56	
	Less: Closing inventory of finished goods	2020.00	
	C. Cost of goods sold	5356.56	
	D. Gross profit $(A - C)$	2723.44	
9	Salaries	370.00	
11	Contribution to PF, etc.	170.00	
12	Welfare expenses	125.00	
18	Insurance	14.00	
14	Sales tax	72.00	
23	Other administrative overheads	396.00	
22	Auditor's fee	2.00	
15	Commission on sales (including outstanding, Rs 29 lakhs)	348.00	
	E. Selling and adm. expenses	1497.00	
	F. Operating profit $(D - E)$	1226.44	
Interest			Interest on fixed deposits
21	Term loans	84.00	includes accrued
20	Debentures	16.00	interest @ 10% for
30	Fixed deposits	44.50	9 months on Rs 140 lakh
	G. Finance cost	144.50	of new deposits.
	H. Operating profit after interest $(F - G)$	1081.94	
	Add: Other incomes		
26	Interest on loans and advances, etc.	14.00	
24	Dividend on investment	4.00	
25	Profit on sale of investment	5.00	
	I. Net profit	1104.94	
	Add: Back depreciation	224.00	
	J. Gross funds from operations (excluding interest on bank finance)	1328.94	

Notes:

1. Gross funds from operations as calculated above exclude:

   (a) *Interest on cash credit finance by the bank:* We are yet to determine the working capital gap, and hence the bank finance on which interest is payable. Once that is done, the interest on it will reduce the profit, and if not paid out, will form part of current liabilities and appear in the balance sheet as expense creditors.

   (b) *Provision for income tax:* Once the tax is estimated, the provision will reduce the profit and form part of current liabilities until it is paid off in cash after adjusting against the advance tax paid.

(c) *Insurance premium*: Although insurance premium payable in March will have an unexpired portion left at the close of the projected year, we have ignored it for ease of calculation.

(d) *Transfer of net surplus to various reserve funds*: These transfers are book transfers. They do not change the fund position of the company.

(e) *Profit from sale of fixed assets (Rs 26 lakh book value being nil)*: Although it will ultimately enter the credit side of the profit and loss account under the head 'other income', it is treated separately (as we will see later) because it is an unusual income.

2. Though outstanding commission on sales (Rs 29 lakh) has been deducted from profit to arrive at the gross funds from operations, it will remain as funds from other sources (expense liability) till it is paid off.

3. Consumption of raw materials

Net sales + 3 months finished goods inventory = Aggregate production, or Rs 8080 lakh + Rs 2020 lakh = Rs 10,100 lakhs.

Consumption of raw materials is 50 per cent of Rs 10,100 lakh, or Rs 5,050 lakh.

4. Wages

It is 20 per cent of raw materials consumption.

That is, Rs $5050 \times 20/100$ lakh = Rs 1,010 lakh.

5. Variable production expenses

It is 15 per cent of raw materials consumed.

That is, Rs $5050 \times 15/100$ lakh = Rs 757.5 lakh.

6. Interest accrued on new fixed deposits of Rs 140 lakh @ 10 per cent for nine months = $140 \times 10/100 \times 9/12$ = Rs 10.50 lakh.

Gross funds inflow from other sources are tabulated below:

(Rs in lakh)

Item No.	Head	Amount		Remarks
Inflow of Long-term Funds				
	Term loans:			
28	From SFC	30		
28	From IDBI	32		
	Sub-total	62		
29	*Less:* Repayment of ICICI loan	18		
	Net inflow from term loans:		44	
30	Fixed deposits	140		
30	*Less:* Repayment	30		
	Net inflow from fixed deposits:		110	
27	Sale of fixed assets (book value nil)		26	As the book value is nil, the
	Total		180	entire amount is to be treated as profit, hence as funds inflow.
Inflow of Short-term Funds				
Item No.	Head	Amount		Remarks
7	Net sundry creditors (trade)	558.00		See notes to this table
15	Net sundry creditors (expense)	29.00		See notes to this table
25	Reduction (sale) of investments	26.00		Profit of Rs 5 lakh was included
30	Interest accrued on FDs	10.50		in gross funds from operations.
33.	Reduction (repayment) of loans and advances	15.00		
	Reduction of cash	10.00		See the opening balance sheet and notes after this table.
	Total	648.50		

Notes:

1. Calculation of incremental sundry creditors (trade)

A. Aggregate production at net sale price   Rs 10100 lakh

Consumption of raw materials at 50% of 'A' above (see item No. 5)   5050 lakh

Add: 2 months consumption as stock (see item no. 6)   840 lakh

Total purchases: Rs 5890 lakh

B. Buying Pattern

The company does not have any raw materials in store. Hence, it is proposed that it will build up an inventory of Rs 840 lakh in two months. It may also be seen that although we have taken a month's consumption at Rs 420 lakh, the exact figure is Rs 420.83 lakh, which means that over a period of one year, there will be a shortage of Rs 10 lakh against projected consumption of raw materials. In order to take care of this problem, the following buying pattern is proposed:

Ist month, Rs 425 lakh + Rs 420 lakh = Rs 845 lakh.

2nd month, Rs 425 lakh + Rs 420 lakh = Rs 845 lakh.

Thus, in two months a stock of Rs 840 lakh will be built. From the third month onwards, the company will buy @ Rs 420 lakh per month (the company may also decide to hold inventory at Rs 850 lakh, and buy as usual @ Rs 420 lakh per month. Whatever may be the decision, it will not have any effect on total purchases and the level of creditors).

(Rs in lakh)

Paying Pattern and Level of Creditors

Month	Purchases	Cash Payment (20%)	Creditors
1st month	845	169	676
2nd month	845	169	676 + 676 = 1352
3rd month	420	84	1352 + 336 – 676 = 1012
4th month	420	84	1012 + 336 – 676 = 672
5th month onwards	420	84	672 + 336 – 336 = 672

C. Paying Pattern

It may be seen that the level of creditors varies during the first three months, and then settles at Rs 672 lakh from the fourth month. Although for funds flow analysis we take creditors at Rs 672 lakh only, ignoring different levels in the initial months, the payment pattern will feature exactly as above in cash flow analysis, as we will see later.

It is proposed that existing creditors amounting to Rs 114 lakh will be repaid in equated monthly instalments during the year. The net inflow of funds from trade creditors is, therefore, Rs 672 – Rs 114 = Rs 558 lakh.

2. Sundry creditors (expenses)

Four per cent commission on sales is payable in the month following the sales (item No. 15 of the illustration). Hence, one month's commission will remain outstanding.

That is Rs $\dfrac{8670 \times 4}{100 \times 12}$ = Rs 28.9

or Rs 29 lakh (approx.)

3. Reduction of cash

The opening balance sheet of the company shows a cash balance of Rs 10 lakh. It is presumed that the company will not keep this cash balance idle, but reduce it to lower the requirement of a loan, or utilise it by investing it in short-term securities.

The funds gap in the projected operations of the business can now be calculated.

(Rs in lakh)

Determination of Funds Flow Gap

A. Long-term assets to be acquired		– 144.00
Inflow of long-term funds		+ 180.00
(+/–) Contribution towards gross current assets (incremental NWC)		+ 36.00
B. Gross current assets to be generated		3530.00
To be financed by:		
Inflow of short-term funds	648.50	
Gross funds from operations	1328.94	
Contribution from long-term sources as above	36.00	2013.44
Net funds flow gap		1516.56

The net funds flow gap of Rs 1,516.56 lakh calculated above obviously represents a shortfall in current operations, because the funds requirement for incremental fixed assets has been more than what has been met by inflow of long-term funds. If it were otherwise, that is, if contribution towards proposed generation of current assets was negative, then the banker might normally raise a question because this meant that a portion of the current funds was being utilised to finance long-term assets. Although raising this question at this stage by the banker is justified because it leads him to further enquiry, it may be found after detailed analyses that the existing level of contribution from long-term sources (NWC) is sufficient to take care of the shortfall in incremental NWC. Besides, gross funds from operations (which also includes depreciation) cannot be preciously bracketed under current funds, because a portion of it is ordinarily transferred to reserves to augment the long-term resources of the firm. However, a fund analysis of the projected operations of a business along this line enables a banker to understand how and from what sources the proposed activities of the

business are to be financed. All said and done, a banker would definitely be happy if incremental fixed assets are financed from incremental long-term funds only, because if the existing NWC is not very large, and if due to a bottleneck in production and/or marketing, funds from operations fail to leave a sufficient balance to augment the reserve funds, then acquisition of fixed assets must have already blocked the current funds of the business almost permanently.

Let us now see whether the current operations can be financed by the bank under the second method of lending.

CALCULATION OF BANK FINANCE FOR WORKING CAPITAL

(Rs in lakh)

Existing level of current assets (see the opening balance sheet)			307.00
Add: Projected generation of current assets (including non-current assets)			3534.00
Sub-total			3841.00
Less: Sale of investments		26.00	
Reduction of cash		10.00	
Repayment of loans and advances		15.00	51.00
Projected gross current assets			3790.00
Less: Deposit with Port Trust (76 + 4) being non-current assets			80.00
Projected chargeable current assets			3710.00
Less: Current liabilities			
Existing level of trade and expenses creditors		114.00	
Add: Incremental trade and expenses creditors		587.00	
Accrued interest on fixed deposits		10.50	
			711.50
Projected working capital gap			2998.50
Less: 25% margin on chargeable current assets			927.50
Bank finance (BF) I			2071.00

	Or	
Working capital gap (as above)		2998.50
Less: Existing level of NWC (see note 2)	117.00	
Incremental NWC from long-term sources	36.00	
Net Funds from operations (see note 1)	984.70	1137.70
Bank finance (BF) II		1860.80

Bank may choose to sanction the lower of BF I or BF II.

Notes:

1. Calculation of gross funds flow gap and net funds from operations

		(Rs in lakh)
Working capital gap as above		2998.50
Less:		
1. Existing level of NWC	117.00	
2. Incremental NWC from long-term sources	36.00	
3. Gross funds from operations	1328.94	1481.94
Net funds flow gap (tallied with our earlier calculation)		1516.56

The net funds flow gap of Rs 1,516.56 lakh should be made available to the business to run its projected operations. This means that this amount must be net of payment of interest on bank finance. The bank interest being 18.5 per cent, the net gap of Rs 1,516.56 lakh should represent 81.5 per cent of bank finance made available to the business. Hence, gross funds flow gap comes to $(1516.56/81.5) \times 100$ or Rs 1,860.80 lakh, and interest payable on it is Rs 344.24 lakh.

The amount of interest payable must be funded from gross funds from operations. Hence, net funds from operations will be $1328.94 - 344.24 =$ Rs 984.70 lakh.

2. Calculation of existing level of net working capital

Opening Balance Sheet

(Rs in lakh)

(1)	Gross Current Assets, Including Non-Current Assets (2)	Gross Current Assets, Excluding Non-Current Assets (3)
Investments	26	26
Loans and advances	195	195
Cash and bank	10	10
Deposit with Port Trust	76	0
	307	231
Less: Current liabilities		
Sundry creditors	114	114
Net working capital	193	117

Note: Deposit with the Port Trust is a non-current asset to be funded from long-term sources. See 'Classification of Current Assets and Current Liabilities' in Chapter 11.

Bank Finance (BF II) amounting to Rs 1,860.80 lakh (being the lower of the two), matches with the gross funds flow gap calculated earlier. When the bank funds this gap, the entire operation of the business in the projected year will also stand funded. We have assumed that the entire amount of working capital finance is to be sanctioned by way of loans repayable in three years (see our argument for this in Chapter 4) after a moratorium of repayment for one year. The amount of interest shall be paid quarterly @ Rs 86.06 lakh per quarter.

Projected Balance Sheet

The funds flow analysis will not be complete until we prepare the projected balance sheet of the company. Before doing so, we should make the following adjustments/appropriation from the gross funds from operations, assuming 40 per cent income tax is payable on net profit after providing for depreciation and interest; and making an adjustment of accumulated losses of Rs 398 lakh.

		(Rs in lakh)
Gross funds from operations		1328.94
Add: Profit from sale of fixed assets		26.00
		1354.94
Less: Depreciation	224.00	
Interest on bank finance	344.24	
Provision for income tax	155.48	723.72
Net surplus		631.22

Assuming no dividend is declared, the following appropriation of the surplus is made.

	(Rs in lakh)
Writing off accumulated loss	398.00
Transfer to Debenture redemption fund	22.00
Transfer to general reserve (assumed)	200.00
Surplus retained in profit and loss a/c	11.22
	631.22

Projected Balance Sheet as on 31-12-20X8

(Rs in lakh)

Liabilities			Assets		
Authorised share capital		2000.00	*Fixed assets*:		
Issued, subscribed, and paid-up share capital		1178.00	Opening balance	2803	
			Addition	130	
				2933	
General reserve	886				
Addition	200	1086.00			
			Less: Depreciation	224	2709.00
			Capital expenditure		10.00
					2719.00
Debenture redemption reserve	90				
Addition	22	112.00	Deposit with Port Trust	76	
Profit and loss a/c		11.22	Addition	4	80.00
8% Debentures		200.00			
Term loans	700		Loans and advances	195	
Less: Repaid	18		*Less*: Repaid	15	180.00
	682				
Add: New loan	62	744.00			
Fixed deposits	340				
Less:	30		*Closing stock*		
	310				
Add: New deposits	140	450.00	Finished goods	2020	

Bank borrowing		1860.80	Raw materials	840	2860.00
Sundry creditors					
(Trade and expense)			Sundry debtors		578.00
Trade creditors	672.00		Advance income tax		92.00
Provision for income tax	155.48				
Outstanding comm.	29.00	856.48			
Accrued interest		10.50			
Total		6509.00	Total		6509.00

We now draw up a comparative balance sheet for the two years under the funds flow concept to enable us to draw some meaningful conclusions.

Balance Sheet
(*Funds Flow Concept*)

(Rs in lakh)

	Actual as on 31.12.20X7 1		*Projected as on* 31.12.20X8 2	
Capital and long-term funds				
Paid-up capital	1178		1178	
Debenture redemption reserve	90		112	
General reserve	886		1086	
Profit and loss account	—		11	
A. Shareholders' fund		2154		2387
8% Debentures	200		200	
Term loans	700		744	
Fixed deposits	340		450	
B. Long-term loan fund		1240		1394
C. Total Long-term funds (A + B)		3394		3781
Employment of long-term funds				
Net fixed assets	2803		2709	
Capital expenditure	—		10	
Profit and loss account (loss)	398		—	
Non-current assets (deposit with Port Trust)	76		80	
D. Long-term assets		3277		2799
E. Net working capital (C – D)		117		982
Short-term assets				
Cash and bank balances	10		—	
Closing stock	—		2860	

(*contd.*)

(*contd.*)

(Rs in lakh)

	Actual as on 31.12.20X7 1	Projected as on 31.12.20X8 2
Debtors	—	578
Loans and advances	195	180
Advance income tax	—	92
Investments	<u>26</u>	—
F. Current assets	231	3710
Short-term resources		
Sundry creditors (trade)	114	672
Sundry creditors (expense, including provision for income tax)	—	184
Bank borrowing	—	1861
Accrued interest	—	<u>11</u>
G. Current liability	<u>114</u>	<u>2728</u>
H. Net current assets (F – G)	<u>117</u>	<u>982</u>

Some Observations

Before trouble, the company had a commendable market share. Its sales touched Rs 16,000 lakh. As against this, the company has projected a conservative figure of Rs 8,670 lakh for the next year, which is approximately 50 per cent of the previously achieved sales. Due to closure, the company might have lost some of its market, which it may take some time to regain, but it can be assumed with all reasonableness that company will be able to achieve at least 50 per cent of its last year's sales.

Even with this moderate level of sales and increased cost of operations due to the recent wage settlements, the company is still be able to make an operating profit of Rs 1,226.44 lakh, which is approximately 14 per cent of sales, and 19 per cent of the total assets employed.

It is wise for the company to propose disposal of some old machinery and use the funds to partly finance the purchase of new fixed assets.

The decision to dispose of the entire investment is in the right direction. The investments might have been built up by the company in its good years to take care of such an eventuality. Non-declaration of dividend will not only enable the company to wipe out its past year's loss, but strengthen its reserves also, which is essential if it desires to regain its market share in the years to come. No reasonable shareholder will object to this proposal. Shareholders may wait till the company's business is revived. All these decisions will enable the company to increase its net working capital via net worth from Rs 117 lakh to Rs 982 lakh. The banker will also be happy to observe that the company has planned to fund its incremental fixed assets from long-term sources; a portion is also available to augment its NWC.

However, the current ratio, which was 2 in the last year, will worsen to 1.36 in the projected year. There is no reason for the banker to be alarmed. We have shown in Chapter 16 on ratio analysis that a mere worsening of the current ratio is not always an indication of bad financial health. On the contrary, it may be a reflection of improved financial management. A high current ratio may often indicate a risk-averse management, which tries to fund current assets mostly from its owned resources, without exploiting the rather cheap market credit. We have also mentioned that the classical standard current ratio of 2 has lost most of its importance to a modern finance manager. During the past two decades, the standard has been diluted to a great extent. Even the banks in our country, till recently, were prepared to accept a current ratio of 1.33 under the second method of lending. The projected current ratio of 1.36 for Rajendra Plastics Limited is above this. However, the banker is still advised to compare this ratio with that of past years, when the business was normal. If it compares well, it is good. But even if it does not compare so well, then also the banker should not feel alarmed, because when the company is trying to revive its operation after a year of closure, it is likely that it would go for more market borrowing (and thereby worsen its current ratio), because it may not be easy for it to raise resources at this stage by issue of share capital. Although banks do not normally allow dilution of the existing current ratio, considering the difficult situation through which the company is passing, an exception to the rule will be in order.

The company has planned to raise additional fixed deposits amounting to Rs 140 lakh, partly to repay some of the existing deposits, which will fall due for repayment, and partly to augment its net working capital. A question may be raised as to whether the company will be able to raise additional deposits from the public under the given circumstances. The public deposit market will obviously be somewhat cold towards the company now. Under the circumstances, the best strategy would be to first repay the deposits that have fallen due for payment, and then invite fresh

deposits. It is likely that in the past the company had not defaulted on repayments. If in the coming year also the company does not default, much of the fear in the minds of the depositors will be allayed. Above all, if the depositing public has faith in the management, then whether in some years the company made losses or skipped dividends for explainable reasons, will not generally shake their confidence. The management may also appeal to the shareholders of the company, who may be too willing to subscribe to the deposits not so much for the additional incentive interest of 0.5 per cent, but for their faith in the management.

Although we do not have more data (particularly of past years) to enable us to do a further in-depth analysis of the company's performance and projections, on the basis of available data it appears that the case merits favourable consideration by the bank.

II. Cash Flow Analysis

CLEARING THE GROUND

Before we set ourselves to the task of preparing projected cash flow statements or cash budgets, we must clearly understand the nature of cash flow, and how it is distinguished from funds flow.

We have already seen that obligations are the sources of funds, but these obligations also demand to be relinquished at the appointed time as per the promises made by a firm, by exchange of some assets, which have been created earlier by the fund itself. In the barter economy of the olden days, obligations were met only by exchange of goods (assets). At the firm level, for instance, the obligation to a supplier of raw materials could be met by supply of finished goods produced by the firm; workers might also be paid similarly. Thus, in any given period the discharge of any obligation (reduction of funds) must be equal to the exchange of a pre-determined quantity of goods. When the entire business is liquidated, the total fund is wiped out by the exchange of all the assets created by such a fund.

With the advent of money, all goods (assets) came to be expressed in terms of monetary units. An obligation, which previously began with the supply of a quantity of goods, and ended also with the return of a quantity of goods, now began in the same way as before, but ended with the return of cash instead of goods. This gave tremendous freedom of choice to the obligation holder to hold and spend his wealth the way he liked. He was also freed from the worry of delivering back a particular asset or goods to discharge his obligation. As all goods and assets were now convertible in cash, he had a choice of selecting any one, or a combination of them, to discharge his obligation. In modern times, any outflow of funds (to discharge obligations) should ordinarily be by way of reduction of cash on the other side of the balance sheet, though an inflow of funds need not necessarily be so restricted, for example, acquisition of fixed assets against deferred liability.

VALUE AND OBLIGATION

We know that a business lives on creating and discharging obligations. When an obligation is contracted on the liability side of the balance sheet, a value is stored in some assets on the other side. Some of these assets may be highly transient in nature. For example, when raw materials are being converted into finished products by the services of workers, at every moment of its progress, value is created and obligations contracted with the workers. The storage of value becomes visible only in work-in-process, which may soon be transformed into finished goods. As with the discharge of any other obligation, this obligation to the workers is paid in cash. Now, if this cash (as any other asset) is funded by capital liability, the obligation to workers having been relinquished,

the fund now returns to the shareholders against the additional value stored in the finished goods. If, however, this cash is funded by any loan liability, the obligation to the workers will now be transferred to the lenders. When finished goods are sold, say at a profit (but on credit), the former are transformed into debtors. The debtors will, of course, be higher in value under the circumstances than the finished goods stock, because of the profit element. This additional value in the form of profit now becomes the obligation of the business to the shareholders. When the debtors discharge their obligations (which should be in cash only, as with the discharge of any obligation in a non-barter cash economy), this asset is transformed back to cash.

CASH AND FUNDS FLOW

It should, however, be remembered that when the debtors pay, though there will be a definite cash inflow into the business, no further inflow of funds would occur, because no additional value is created. The debtors who already stood funded are now merely converted into another asset, cash; the value of the business remains the same. This cash can now be used to discharge any obligation of the business contracted previously (and value created), including obligation to shareholders (dividends). The net effect will be reduction of funds, and hence, the value of the business.

In the ultimate analysis, any reduction of cash due to discharge of obligations, will reduce the funds and the value of the business, but not when it is used to acquire any other asset. Now, if the firm wants to maintain its previous value (or to the extent it wants to do that), it has to find matching funds by a positive inflow from outside. For example, when a firm sells Rs 10,000 on credit, and the operation is funded as trade creditors, Rs 8,000 and profit margin Rs 2,000, there will be no change in the funds position or in the value of the business (which has already been increased by the profit) when the debtors are realised in cash. If now the firm wants to discharge the entire credit or some of it, there will be a matching reduction in cash, and consequent reduction in the value and level of the funds of the firm. If, however, the firm wants to discharge the obligation to the present creditors without reducing the value of the firm, it has to contract fresh obligations either with the creditors or with the bank, or directly with the shareholders. There will, of course, be no change in the funds position or value of the firm when a portion of the cash is used to acquire another asset, though in such a case, there will be a definite cash outflow.

There are, therefore, two components in cash outflows: one to discharge obligations, and the other to acquire assets. The former will affect the fund position, the latter will not. From the aggregate cash outflow if we now deduct those outflows which have been used to acquire other assets (because these already stand funded, and for which matching cash inflows are available),

what remains can be attributed only towards discharge of obligations and consequent reduction in the value of the firm, against which no additional funding arrangement has been made.

When a firm plans its future operations, it in effect, plans to achieve a particular value of the firm at the end of the projected period. When operations of the business result in a negative net cash flow, then the firm is unable to achieve its planned value: a gap remains, which is nothing but a funds flow gap, because in the arithmetic of finance, value is equivalent to funds. We can, therefore, say that a funds flow gap in the projected operations of a business will always be equal to the net cash flow gap.

Let us explain this further with the help of the example of Rajendra Plastics Limited. We first draw up a cash book summary of the projected operations by picking up only its cash components.

Cash Book Summary

We have seen in the earlier section that funds flow gap of the projected operations was Rs 1,860.80

(Rs in lakh)

To Opening balance	10.00	By Purchases (raw materials)	1178.00
" Sales (cash sales)	1734.00	" Sundry creditors (new)	4040.00
" Sundry debtors	6358.00	" Sundry creditors (old)	114.00
" Dividends received	4.00	" Wages	1010.00
" Investments (sale)	31.00	" Variables production expenses	757.56
" Interest received	14.00	" Salaries	370.00
" Fixed asset disposal	26.00	" Bonus	35.00
" Term loan-SFC	30.00	" PF., etc.	170.00
" Term loan-IDBI	32.00	" Welfare expenses	125.00
" Fixed deposits	140.00	" Excise duty	590.00
" Loans and advances	15.00	" Sales tax	72.00
(repayment)		" Commission on sales	319.00
		" Fixed production overheads	300.00
		" Insurance	14.00

(contd.)

(contd.)

		" Other administrative expenses	396.00
		" Auditor's fees	2.00
		" Advance income tax	92.00
		" Interest paid—Debentures	16.00
		" Interest paid—Term loan	84.00
		" Interest paid—Fixed deposit	34.00
		" Interest paid—Bank finance	344.24
		" Term loan—Repayment ICICI	18.00
		" Fixed deposits—Repayment	30.00
		" Port Trust Deposit	4.00
		" Fixed assets (purchase)	130.00
		" Capital expenditure	10.00
Sub-total (receipts)	8394.00	Sub-total (payments)	10254.80
Bank cash credit (being the net cash flow gap)	1860.80		–
Total	10254.80	Total	10254.80

lakh, which now exactly matches with the net cash flow gap calculated above. This gap when funded by the bank creates a liability to the bank against which an equal amount of cash is made available.

DETAILED CASH FLOW STATEMENT

What we have done so far is to make an estimate of the cash or funds flow gap of the projected operations of the business at the aggregate level. In the day-to-day operation of a business the actual cash requirements will vary. Whenever there is a cash gap, the finance manager has to find a source to fund it, so that the business proceeds according to plan. A detail break-up of cash flows is, therefore, as essential as to estimate the aggregate fund requirement of the business. While the latter answers the question 'How much?', the former answers, 'When?'. As cash is the 'only' item of the assets with which to meet the obligations, and it is only by meeting obligations that a business thrives, proper synchronisation between cash receipts and payments becomes

an essential part of day-to-day financial management. When cash receipts and payments are synchronised for the projected operations of a business by a proper funding of the gap, if any, then we have what is called a cash budget. The operational part of the cash budget is the cash flow statement, which we have drawn up on a monthly basis for Rajendra Plastics Limited (Table 14.1). We shall then discuss in some detail the principles and methods of drawing up of cash budget and analyse the nature of the various components of cash flows from a banker's point of view.

The projected cash flow statement indicates that the company's cumulative cash deficit increases gradually from Rs 352.59 lakh to Rs 1,860.80 lakh at the end of the year, which is also the funds flow gap, as we have seen earlier. The statement shows that although the aggregate cash requirement for the projected operations is Rs 1,860.80 lakh, the company does not require all the cash at one time. The cash credit system of financing prevalent in India so far allowed the

TABLE **14.1** Projected Cash Flow Statement

(Rs in lakh)

Cash Inflows	Jan.	Feb.	March	Apr.	May	June	July	Aug.	Sept.	Oct.	Nov.	Dec.	Total
1. Opening cash	10.00	–	–	–	–	–	–	–	–	–	–	–	10.00
2. Cash sales	144.50	144.50	144.50	144.50	144.50	144.50	144.50	144.50	144.50	144.50	144.50	144.50	1734.00
3. Realisation from debtors	–	578.00	578.00	578.00	578.00	578.00	578.00	578.00	578.00	578.00	578.00	578.00	6358.00
4. Dividend on investment	–	–	–	4.00	–	–	–	–	–	–	–	–	4.00
5. Sale of investment	–	–	–	–	–	31.00	–	–	–	–	–	–	31.00
6. Interest on security deposit, loans and advances	–	–	–	14.00	–	–	–	–	–	–	–	–	14.00
7. Sale of fixed assets	–	26.00	–	–	–	–	–	–	–	–	–	–	26.00
8. Term loan from SFC	–	–	30.00	–	–	–	–	–	–	–	–	–	30.00
9. Term loan from IDBI	–	–	32.00	–	–	–	–	–	–	–	–	–	32.00
10. Fixed deposits	–	–	–	140.00	–	–	–	–	–	–	–	–	140.00
11. Repayment of loans and advances	1.25	1.25	1.25	1.25	1.25	1.25	1.25	1.25	1.25	1.25	1.25	1.25	15.00
Sub-total (A)	155.75	749.75	785.75	881.75	723.75	754.75	723.75	723.75	723.75	723.75	723.75	723.75	8394.00

(Rs in lakh)

Cash Outflows	Jan.	Feb.	March	Apr.	May	June	July	Aug.	Sept.	Oct.	Nov.	Dec.	Total
1. Cash purchases of raw materials	169.00	169.00	84.00	84.00	84.00	84.00	84.00	84.00	84.00	84.00	84.00	84.00	1178.00
2. Payment to trade creditors (current)	—	—	676.00	676.00	336.00	336.00	336.00	336.00	336.00	336.00	336.00	336.00	4040.00
3. Wages	84.16	84.16	84.16	84.16	84.17	84.17	84.17	84.17	84.17	84.17	84.17	84.17	1010.00
4. Variable production expenses	63.13	63.13	63.13	63.13	63.13	63.13	63.13	63.13	63.13	63.13	63.13	63.13	757.56
5. Salaries	30.84	30.84	30.84	30.84	30.83	30.83	30.83	30.83	30.83	30.83	30.83	30.83	370.00
6. Bonus	—	—	—	—	—	—	—	—	—	35.00	—	—	35.00
7. Contribution to PF, etc.	14.16	14.16	14.16	14.16	14.17	14.17	14.17	14.17	14.17	14.17	14.17	14.17	170.00
8. Welfare expenses	10.40	10.40	10.42	10.42	10.42	10.42	10.42	10.42	10.42	10.42	10.42	10.42	125.00
9. Excise duty	49.15	49.15	49.17	49.17	49.17	49.17	49.17	49.17	49.17	49.17	49.17	49.17	590.00
10. Sales tax	—	—	18.00	—	—	18.00	—	—	18.00	—	—	18.00	72.00
11. Commission on sales	—	29.00	29.00	29.00	29.00	29.00	29.00	29.00	29.00	29.00	29.00	29.00	319.00
12. Fixed production overheads	25.00	25.00	25.00	25.00	25.00	25.00	25.00	25.00	25.00	25.00	25.00	25.00	300.00
13. Insurance	—	—	14.00	—	—	—	—	—	—	—	—	—	14.00
14. Other administrative overheads	33.00	33.00	33.00	33.00	33.00	33.00	33.00	33.00	33.00	33.00	33.00	33.00	396.00
15. Auditors' fees	—	—	—	—	—	—	—	—	—	—	—	2.00	2.00
16. Advance Income tax	—	—	23.00	—	—	23.00	—	—	23.00	—	—	23.00	92.00
17. Interest on debentures	16.00	—	—	—	—	—	—	—	—	—	—	—	16.00

(Rs in lakh)

Cash Outflows	Jan.	Feb.	March	Apr.	May	June	July	Aug.	Sept.	Oct.	Nov.	Dec.	Total
18. Interest on term loans	—	—	21.00	—	—	21.00	—	—	21.00	—	—	21.00	84.00
19. Interest on bank loan for working capital	—	—	86.06	—	—	86.06	—	—	86.06	—	—	86.06	344.24
20. Repayment of loan to ICICI	—	—	—	—	—	9.00	—	—	—	—	—	9.00	18.00
21. Interest on fixed deposits	—	—	—	34.00	—	—	—	—	—	—	—	—	34.00
22. Repayment of fixed deposits	—	—	—	30.00	—	—	—	—	—	—	—	—	30.00
23. Deposit with Post Trust	4.00	—	—	—	—	—	—	—	—	—	—	—	4.00
24. Purchase of fixed assets	—	25.00	65.00	40.00	—	—	—	—	—	—	—	—	130.00
25. Capital expenditure	—	—	—	—	—	—	—	—	—	—	5.00	5.00	10.00
26. Payment to creditors (old)	9.50	9.50	9.50	9.50	9.50	9.50	9.50	9.50	9.50	9.50	9.50	9.50	114.00
Sub-total (B)	508.34	542.34	1335.44	1212.38	768.39	925.45	768.39	768.39	916.45	803.39	773.39	932.45	10,254.80
(A – B) = (Deficit/surplus)	(352.59)	207.41	(549.69)	(330.63)	(44.64)	(170.70)	(44.64)	(44.64)	(192.70)	(79.64)	(49.64)	(208.70)	(1860.80)
Cumulative deficit (before bank loan)	(352.59)	(145.13)	(694.87)	(1025.50)	(1070.14)	(1240.84)	(1285.48)	(1330.12)	(1522.82)	(1602.46)	(1652.10)	(1860.80)	
Cumulative surplus (after bank loan)	1508.21	1715.62	1165.93	835.30	790.66	619.96	575.32	530.68	337.98	258.34	208.70	0	

borrower to be sanctioned a limit of Rs 1860.80 lakh in the present case, but to draw the sum only as per his requirements, and pay interest only on the amount drawn. When the entire working capital finance is made available to the company through a cash credit account, and the business progresses according to plan, the cumulative monthly deficit as shown in the cash flow statement would be reflected as a debit balance in the cash credit account of the company. Interest is charged on daily balances, though payable, say quarterly. But under the evolving loan system of working capital finance, the entire amount of bank finance should be made available to the borrower at a time in the form of a term loan repayable within, say three years, as we have proposed in this chapter (with a moratorium, of one year as a special case). Unlike as in the cash credit system, this may often result in excess monthly cash balances (equivalent to unutilised portions of the limit in the cash credit account) in the current account of the borrower. The cumulative surplus appearing at the bottom of the cash flow statement of Rajendra Plastics Limited reveals this phenomenon. No well-meaning borrower would like to keep these balances idle. Besides a bank's own range of short-term deposits, expanding money and capital markets provide ample opportunities to park idle cash balances in short-term securities. With the firming up of the loan system in working capital finance, the corporate sector is expected to establish or gear up its treasury department for profitable investments of excess cash balances. Some companies have already converted their treasury departments as a profit centre: the objective is to compensate a part of the interest payable on working capital loan accounts.

Budgetary Drill

We have indicated earlier that when the cash components of various budgets are taken out and inflows and outflows are matched for a given period, we get a cash budget. Cash budget is an operational gist of the business for the projected year. It enables a banker to control and monitor the course of the business. But, for that he has to evaluate the operational plan of the business, which flows from various operational budgets of the enterprise. It is necessary, therefore, to understand the mechanics of formulation of various budgets.

For medium and large units, budgeting should be a normal exercise every year. In western countries it has been found that almost 99 per cent of the companies (except the smallest ones) prepare budgets. With an increase in uncertainties in the business world, a planned approach to business problems has gained importance during the past four decades. Multinational companies operating in India started this exercise simultaneously with their parent companies. In fact, they set examples before Indian companies to switch over to a planned approach to business. The Tandon Committee championed this approach, and implored upon bankers to insist upon their medium and large borrowers to internalise the budgetary drill in their management processes. Therefore, a banker should ask a borrower to submit the following budgets for consideration, and of course, the master budget, preferably in the form of a projected profit and loss account and a balance sheet:

1. Sales budget.
2. Operating and expense budgets.
3. Capital expenditure budget.
4. Cash budget.

A number of assumptions go into the preparation of budgets. A firm may make a statistical forecast of sales on the basis of an analysis of past achievements, general business conditions, trends in the market and so on or may simply make an internal estimate by analysing the opinions of executives and salespersons. But it must be remembered that a forecast by itself is merely passive. To make it achievable, a constructive plan is required. A budget reflects the positive actions that the management desires to take in achieving goals.

Sales Budget

Any budgetary exercise should begin with a sales budget. The budget should not only indicate projected sales in quantitative and monetary terms, but also lay down plans to achieve it. Besides the strategy for achieving the targeted sales, the latter also includes the expense budget to finance the strategy. It may be an increase in sales personnel, a plan for an advertisement campaign and other promotional activity, redesigning of products, or additions to product lines. A banker has to examine whether the projected sales are achievable. The past trend is a good guideline. It rests on the assumption that the future is likely to resemble the past. If sales have been increasing at the rate of 10 per cent a year, it is likely that in the year under consideration too sales will increase at the same rate. This is the simplest assumption. But it may fool a banker if he does not take environmental factors into consideration. It may be that a recession has already set in that particular product whose total market is falling, or there may be a general recession in the economy pulling down all the products. The percentage increase in projected sales may also be misleading. A 100 per cent increase in the case of a starter cannot be comparable with a 5 per cent increase of a giant organisation, which has been in the business for a long time, with a high figure of sales in the base year. This confusion can be avoided if a banker examines the market share of the unit instead of examining the percentage increase in absolute sales. Stability and efficiency of a business is ensured if the unit can increase its market share gradually or at least hold on to it for

different lines of products at their different stages of growth.

A banker should also examine whether the projected sales are producible and whether the existing capacity is sufficient, with reasonable margin, to take care of increased production. If not, what the plans of the company are to increase its capacity. At this point, a banker should examine the capital expenditure budget to ensure correspondence with the planned increase in sales.

Expense Budgets

Next comes an examination of various expense budgets. Primary attention should be given to operating and sales expenses: whether variable expenses are proportionate to the increase in volume, and overheads are being fully absorbed or they are out of line; whether the existing margin on sales is being affected adversely or not; and is there any case for increasing the price of the product without affecting its sales? These are the various points which should be examined by a banker. It may be possible for a new entrant to cut back prices, or to spend heavily on promotional activities to increase its market share. A banker need not be alarmed in such a case so long as the entrepreneur operates near the break-even point. A lower margin may be desirable in such a situation to ensure future growth.

Cash Budget

Cash components from all the budgets when dated in a standard format form part of the cash budget. Cash inflows and outflows are now calculated weekly, monthly, or quarterly. For in-company management, cash flows may be calculated even daily, but it is sufficient for a banker to have these monthly, and in some cases quarterly. We have already said that a calculation of cash flows does not itself constitute a cash budget. When outflows are balanced with inflows, we get the cash budget. This balancing is a joint exercise of both a borrower and a banker.

CASH INFLOWS

Sales Revenue

In any business, the major source of cash inflow is sales revenue. In case of non-seasonal products, sales can be presumed to be uniform throughout the year. In such a case, the total annual projected sales can be divided by 12 to get the average monthly sales. It would be better, however, if a borrower makes a monthly projection of sales, because in real life sales are not often uniform. In case of seasonal products, sales are concentrated during a few months. A cash budget will be very important in such a case to determine peak-level cash requirements. Seasonality may be with respect to the procurement of raw materials like tea, coffee, jute, cotton, sugarcane, and oilseeds, while the demand of the products may be non-seasonal, that is, uniform throughout the year. On the other hand, demand for products like woollen garments, rainwear, fertilisers, and agricultural inputs may be seasonal, while raw materials for these products are available throughout the year. When raw materials suffer from seasonality, cash requirements during the procurement period will reach a peak level and then start falling throughout the year, often showing a positive cash balance as the sales realisation outweighs disbursements. On the other hand, when sales are seasonal, cash requirements during the season will fall, showing a positive balance, but it will increase during the off-season for maintenance of production and payment of overheads.

Realisation of Sales

Sales may be made wholly in cash or on credit or a mixture of both. The normal pattern is that a certain percentage of total sales is made in cash and the rest on credit. Credit sales may also be realised in instalments, say a portion after one month, and the remaining part in the following month. A borrower will be able to indicate the realisation pattern of sales from his past experience, which can be verified from the credit turnover in his current or cash credit account. The debtors' turnover ratio will indicate fairly well the monthly realisation of sales. With the help of this ratio a banker will be able to check the cash inflow from sales every month, if no other information as to the realisation pattern of sales is available. After all, a banker is interested only in the average monthly realisation of sales, and not in its minute division.

Other sources of cash inflow are discrete in nature—capital and debenture issues, long-term borrowings from financial institutions, sale of fixed assets, fixed deposits, and loans from directors, partners, friends, and relatives. Working capital advance from a bank can be discrete or continuous in nature, depending upon whether it is given under a loan or a cash credit system.

MOTIVES FOR HOLDING CASH

While assessing working capital requirements, a banker has to take into consideration the raw cash requirements of a business. Technically speaking, this cash-in-the-till is unproductive in nature as it remains idle unless invested in short-nature securities as mentioned earlier. The inventory of cash finds a place amongst other working assets to satisfy the following three motives of an entrepreneur:

Transaction Motive

It holds that the firm should maintain a minimum level of cash to meet day-to-day expenses in the ordinary course of the business. Expenses are generally for payment of operating costs, taxes, dividend and so on. If there were proper synchronisation between cash receipts and payments, this need would not arise. From a banker's point of view, no business needs to hold any additional cash for this purpose. It is taken care of in financing the gap between total cash inflows and outflows. In fact, the entire cash budgeting exercise is based on analysing and closing the gap in cash transactions. No business can claim any additional cash over and above the transactional gap revealed in the cash budget.

Precautionary Motive

In a world of uncertainties, a businessperson has to be cautious. Many of his assumptions may go wrong, and when they do, he needs some breathing time to rectify the situation. He needs a cushion or buffer to withstand contingencies. If cash flows could be predicted very accurately, there would be minimum need for precautionary cash holding. A firm's ability to borrow cash at short notice will also reduce the level of precautionary cash holdings. A banker must take care of this precautionary cash need of a business. But since this cash is not ordinarily expected to earn anything from within the business, it should be kept at its minimum. Some studies by the RBI show that, on an average, a business requires to hold cash to the extent of 6 to 7 per cent of its current assets. Some other studies suggest that on an average, a week's cash outflow would be sufficient.

The precautionary cash balance should be invested in liquid securities. Earlier a banker did not like this idea, because a cash credit limit would take care of this precautionary cash requirement. Any portion of the limit unutilised was equivalent to ready cash. But in the loan system of working capital finance, there should be no such resistance.

Speculative Motive

It requires holding of cash outside the productive activity of a business. This is cash-in-waiting to seize speculative opportunities in securities, materials, and commodities to earn pure trading profit. Banks, as a matter of policy, discourage speculative activities and hence, they should not finance speculative cash holdings.

CASH OUTFLOWS

In estimating cash outflows, major attention is given to payments made for purchase of raw materials. Like sales, the payment pattern for purchases can be known from the borrower. This can be checked similarly by reference to the debit turnover in the cash credit or current account of the borrower and aggregate creditors' turnover ratio. Besides dated capital expenditure, the other expenses include payment of wages, salaries, other fixed expenses, taxes, and dividend. Workers are paid weekly, fortnightly, or monthly, but salaries are generally paid monthly. Similarly, fixed overheads like rent and electricity are paid monthly. The payment pattern of these expenses is almost uniform and there is no difficulty in dating their disbursements. All non-cash expenses, like depreciation, are excluded from the cash budget, as there is no cash outflow in such cases.

CONCLUDING REMARKS

In conclusion, we should point out that a cash budget or a projected cash flow statement is more of a tool for the control and monitoring of finances of a business than for appraising the viability of the credit proposal. Its purpose is important, but somewhat limited. When a banker is satisfied about the reliability of the projections and creditworthiness of a borrower by using other tools of analysis, he generally embarks on a cash flow analysis. It should invariably be preceded by a funds flow analysis as we have done in this chapter.

Annexure 14.1

Accounting Standard—Cash Flow Statements

Objectives

Information about the cash flows of an enterprise is useful in providing users of financial statements with a basis to assess the ability of the enterprise to generate cash and cash equivalents, and the needs of the enterprise to utilise those cash flows. The economic decisions that are taken by users require an evaluation of the ability of an enterprise to generate cash and cash equivalents and the timing and certainty of their generation.

This statement deals with the provision of information about historical changes in cash and cash equivalents of an enterprise by means of a cash flow statement, which classifies cash flows during the period from operating, investing, and financing activities.

Scope

An enterprise should prepare a cash flow statement and should present it for each period for which financial statements are presented.

Users of an enterprise's financial statements are interested in how the enterprise generates and uses cash and cash equivalents. This is the case regardless of the nature of the enterprise's activities, and irrespective of whether cash can be viewed as the product of the enterprise, as may be the case with a financial enterprise. Enterprises need cash for essentially the same reasons, however different their principal revenue-producing activities might be. They need cash to conduct their operations, to pay their obligations, and to provide returns to their investors.

Benefits of Cash Flow Information

A cash flow statement, when used in conjunction with the other financial statements, provides information that enables users to evaluate the changes in net assets of an enterprise, its financial structure (including its liquidity and solvency), and its ability to affect the amounts and timing of cash flows in order to adapt to changing circumstances and opportunities. Cash flow information is useful in assessing the ability of an enterprise to generate cash and cash equivalents, and enables users to develop models to assess and compare the present value of the future cash flows of different enterprises. It also enhances the comparability of the reporting of operating performances by different enterprises, because it eliminates the effects of using different treatments for the same transactions and events.

Historical cash flow information is often used as an indicator of the amount, timing, and certainty of future cash flows. It is also useful in checking the accuracy of past assessments of future cash flows, and in examining the relationship between profitability and net cash flow and the impact of changing prices.

Definitions

The following terms are used in this statement with the meanings specified:

Cash comprises cash on hand and demand deposits with banks.

Cash equivalents are short-term, highly liquid investments that are readily convertible into known amounts of cash and which are subject to an insignificant risk of changes in value.

Cash flows are inflows and outflows of cash and cash equivalents.

Operating activities are the principal revenue-producing activities of an enterprise, and other activities that are not investing or financing activities.

Investing activities are the acquisition and disposal of long-term assets and other investments not included in cash equivalents.

Financing activities are activities that result in changes in the size and composition of the owners' capital (including preference share capital in the case of a company) and borrowings of an enterprise.

Cash and Cash Equivalents

Cash equivalents are held for the purpose of meeting short-term cash commitments rather than for investments or other purposes. For an investment to qualify as a cash equivalent, it must be readily convertible to a known amount of cash, and be subject to an insignificant risk of changes in value. Therefore, an investment normally qualifies as a cash equivalent only when it has a short maturity, of say, three months or less from the date of acquisition. Investments in shares are excluded from cash equivalents, unless they are, in substance, cash equivalents; for example, preference shares of a company acquired shortly before their specified redemption date (provided there is only an insignificant risk of failure of the company to repay the amount at maturity).

Cash flows exclude movements between items that constitute cash or cash equivalents, because these components are part of the cash management of an enterprise rather than a part of its operating, investing, and financing activities. Cash management includes the investment of excess cash in cash equivalents.

Presentation of a Cash Flow Statement

The cash flow statement should report cash flows during the period classified by operating, investing, and financing activities.

An enterprise presents its cash flows from operating, investing, and financing activities in a manner which is most appropriate to its business. Classification by activity provides information that allows users to assess the impact of those activities on the financial position of the enterprise, and the amount of its cash and cash equivalents. This information may also be used to evaluate the relationships among those activities.

A single transaction may include cash flows that are classified differently. For example, when the instalment paid with respect to fixed assets acquired, on deferred payment basis includes both interest and loan, the interest element is classified under financing activities and the loan element is classified under investing activities.

Operating Activities

The amount of cash flows arising from operating activities is a key indicator of the extent to which the operations of an enterprise have generated sufficient cash flows to maintain the operating capability of an enterprise, pay dividends, repay loans, and make new investments without recourse to external sources of financing. Information about the specific components of historical operating cash flows is useful, in conjunction with other information, in forecasting future operating cash flows.

Cash flows from operating activities are primarily derived from the principal revenue-producing activities of an enterprise. Therefore, they generally result from transactions and other events that enter into the determination of net profit or loss. Examples of cash flows from operating activities are:

(a) Cash receipts from the sale of goods and the rendering of services.
(b) Cash receipts from royalties, fees, commissions, and other revenue.
(c) Cash payments to suppliers for goods and services.
(d) Cash payments to and on behalf of employees.
(e) Cash receipts and cash payments of an insurance enterprise for premiums and claims, annuities, and other policy benefits.
(f) Cash payments or refunds of income taxes, unless they can be specifically identified with financing and investing activities.
(g) Cash receipts and payments relating to futures contracts, forward contracts, option contracts, and swap contracts when the contracts are held for dealing or trading purposes.

Some transactions, such as the sale of an item of a plant, may give rise to gain or loss, which is included in the determination of net profit or loss. However, the cash flows relating to such transactions are cash flows from investing activities.

An enterprise may hold securities and loans for dealing or trading purposes, in which case they are similar to inventory acquired specifically for resale. Therefore, cash flows arising from the purchase and sale of dealing or trading securities are classified as operating activities. Similarly, cash advances and loans made by financial enterprises are usually classified as operating activities since they relate to the main revenue producing activity of that enterprise.

Investing Activities

The separate disclosure of cash flows arising from investing activities is important because the cash flows represent the extent to which expenditures have been made for resources intended to generate future income and cash flows. Examples of cash flows arising from investing activities are:

(a) Cash payments to acquire fixed assets (including intangibles). These payments include those relating to capitalised research and development costs and self-constructed fixed assets.

(b) Cash receipts from disposal of fixed assets (including intangibles).

(c) Cash payments to acquire shares, warrants, or debt instruments of other enterprises and interests in joint ventures (other than payments for those instruments considered to be cash equivalents, or those held for dealing or trading purposes).

(d) Cash receipts from disposal of shares, warrants, or debt instruments of other enterprises and interests in joint ventures (other than receipts for those instruments considered to be cash equivalents, and those held for dealing or trading purposes).

(e) Cash advances and loans made to other parties (other than advances and loans made by a financial enterprise).

(f) Cash receipts from the repayment of advances and loans made to third parties (other than advances and loans of a financial enterprise).

(g) Cash payments for future contracts, forward contracts, option contracts, and swap contracts except when the contracts are held for dealing or trading purposes, or the payments are classified as financing activities.

(h) Cash receipts from futures contracts, forward contracts, option contracts, and swap contracts except when the contracts are held for dealing or trading purposes, or the receipts are classified as financing activities.

When a contract is accounted for as a hedge of an identifiable position, the cash flows of the contract are classified in the same manner as the cash flows of the position being hedged.

Financing Activities

The separate disclosure of cash flows arising from financing activities is important, because it is useful in predicting claims on future cash flows by providers of funds (both capital and borrowings) to an enterprise. Examples of cash flows arising from financing activities are:

(a) Cash proceeds from issuing shares or other similar instruments.

(b) Cash proceeds from issuing debentures, loans, notes, bonds, and other short or long-term borrowings.

(c) Cash repayments of amounts borrowed.

Reporting Cash Flows from Operating Activities

An enterprise should report cash flows from operating activities using either:

(a) The direct method, whereby major classes of gross cash receipts and gross cash payments are disclosed; or
(b) The indirect method, whereby net profit or loss is adjusted for the effects or transactions of a non-cash nature, any deferrals or accruals of past or future operating cash receipts or payments, and items of income or expense associated with investing or financing cash flows.

The direct method provides information, which may be useful in estimating future cash flows, and which is not available under the indirect method and is, therefore, considered more appropriate than the indirect method. Under the direct method, information about major classes of gross cash receipts and gross cash payments may be obtained either:

(a) From the accounting records of the enterprise; or
(b) By adjusting sales, cost of sales (interest and similar income and interest expenses and similar charges for a financial enterprise), and other items in the statement of profit and loss for:
   i.   Changes during the period in inventories and operating receivables and payables.
   ii.   Other non-cash items.
   iii.   Other items for which the cash effects are investing or financing cash flows.

Under the indirect method, the net cash flow from operating activities is determined by adjusting net profit or loss for the effects of:

(a) Changes during the period in inventories and operating receivables and payables.
(b) Non-cash items, such as depreciation, provisions, deferred taxes, and unrealised foreign currency gains and losses.
(c) All other items for which the cash effects are investing or financing cash flows.

Alternatively, the net cash flow from operating activities may be presented under the indirect method by the operating revenues and expenses, excluding non-cash items disclosed in the statement of profit and loss and the changes during the period in inventories and operating receivables and payables.

Reporting Cash Flows from Investing and Financing Activities

An enterprise should report separately major classes of gross cash receipts and gross cash payments arising from investing and financing activities, except to the extent that cash flows are reported on a net basis as described below.

Reporting Cash Flows on a Net Basis

Cash flows arising from the following operating, investing or financing activities may be reported on a net basis:

(a) Cash receipts and payments on behalf of customers, when the cash flows reflect the activities of the customer rather than those of the enterprise.
(b) Cash receipts and payments for items in which the turnover is quick, the amounts are large, and the maturities are short.

Examples of cash receipts and payments referred to above are:

(a) The acceptance and repayment of demand deposits by a bank.
(b) Funds held for customers by an investment enterprise.
(c) Rents collected on behalf of, and paid over to, the owners of properties.

Examples of cash receipts and payments referred to above are advances made for, and the repayments of:

(a) Principal amounts relating to credit card customers.
(b) The purchase and sale of investments.
(c) Other short-term borrowings, for example, those which have a maturity period of three months or less.

Cash flows arising from each of the following activities of a financial enterprise may be reported on a net basis:

(a) Cash receipts and payments for the acceptance and repayment of deposits with a fixed maturity date.
(b) The placement of deposits with and withdrawal of deposits from other financial enterprises.
(c) Cash advances and loans made to customers, and the repayment of those advances and loans.

Foreign Currency Cash Flows

Cash flows arising from transactions in a foreign currency should be recorded in an enterprise's reporting currency by applying to the foreign currency amount the exchange rate between the reporting currency and the foreign currency at the date of the cash flow. A rate that approximates the actual rate may be used if the result is substantially the same as would arise if the rates at the dates of the cash flows were used. The effect of changes in exchange rates on cash and cash equivalents held in a foreign currency should be reported as a separate part of the reconciliation of the changes in cash and cash equivalents during the period.

Cash flows denominated in foreign currency are reported in a manner consistent with Accounting Standard 11 titled, Accounting For The Effects Of Changes In Foreign Exchange Rates. This permits the use of an exchange rate that approximates the actual rate. For example, a weighted average exchange rate for a period may be used for recording foreign currency transactions.

Unrealised gains and losses arising from changes in foreign exchange rates are not cash flows. However, the effect of exchange rate changes on cash and cash equivalents held or due in a foreign currency is reported in the cash flow statement in order to reconcile cash and cash equivalents at the beginning and the end of the period. This amount in presented separately from cash flows from operating, investing, and financing activities, and includes the differences, if any, had those cash flows been reported at the end-of-period exchange rates.

Extraordinary Items

Cash flows associated with extraordinary items should be classified as arising from operating, investing, or financing activities as appropriate and disclosed separately.

Cash flows associated with extraordinary items are disclosed separately as arising from operating, investing, or financing activities in the cash flow statement to enable users to understand their nature and effect on the present and future cash flows of an enterprise. These disclosures are in addition to the separate disclosures of the nature and amount of extraordinary items required by Accounting Standard 5 titled, Net Profit Or Loss For The Period, Prior Period Items, and Changes In Accounting Policies.

Interest and Dividends

Cash flows from interest and dividends received and paid should each be disclosed separately. Cash flows arising from interest paid and interest and dividends received in the case of a financial enterprise should be classified as cash flows arising from operating activities. In the case of other enterprises, cash flows arising from interest paid should be classified as cash flows from financing activities while interest and dividends received should be classified as cash flows from investing activities. Dividends paid should be classified as cash flows from financing activities.

The total amount of interest paid during the period is disclosed in the cash flow statement, whether it has been recognised as an expense in the statement of profit and loss or capitalised in accordance with Accounting Standard 10 titled, Accounting For Fixed Assets.

Interest paid and interest and dividends received are usually classified as operating cash flows for a financial enterprise. However, there is no consensus on the classification of these cash flows for other enterprises. Some argue that interest paid and interest and dividends received may be classified as operating cash flows, because they enter into the determination of net profit or loss. However, it is more appropriate that interest paid and interest and dividends received are classified as financing cash flows and investing cash flows respectively, because they are costs of obtaining financial resources or returns on investment.

Some argue that dividends paid may be classified as a component of cash flows from operating activities in order to assist users to determine the ability of an enterprise to pay dividends out of operating cash flows. However, it is considered more appropriate that dividends paid should be classified as cash flows from financing activities, because they are cost of obtaining financial resources.

Taxes on Income

Cash flows arising from taxes on income should be separately disclosed, and should be classified as cash flows from operating activities unless they can be specifically identified with financing and investing activities.

Taxes on income arise on transactions that give rise to cash flows that are classified as operating, investing, or financing activities in a cash flow statement. While a tax expense may be readily identifiable with investing or financing activities, the related tax cash flows are often impracticable to identify and may arise in a different period from the cash flows of the underlying transactions. Therefore, taxes paid are usually classified as cash flows from operating activities. However, when it is practicable to identify the tax cash flow with an individual transaction that gives rise to cash flows that are classified as investing or financing activities, the tax cash flow is classified as an investing, or financing, activity as appropriate. When tax cash flows are allocated over more than one class of activity, the total amount of taxes paid is disclosed.

Investments in Subsidiaries, Associates, and Joint Ventures

When accounting for an investment in an associate or a subsidiary or a joint venture, an investor restricts its reporting in the cash flow statement to the cash flows between itself and the investee/joint venture, for example, cash flows relating to dividends and advances.

Acquisitions and Disposals of Subsidiaries and Other Business Units

The aggregate cash flows arising from acquisitions and from disposals of subsidiaries or other business units should be presented separately, and classified as investing activities.

An enterprise should disclose, in aggregate, with respect to both acquisition and disposal of subsidiaries or other business units during the period each of the following:

(a) The total purchase or disposal consideration.
(b) The portion of the purchase or disposal consideration discharged by means of cash and cash equivalents.

The separate presentation of the cash flow effects of acquisitions and disposals of subsidiaries and other business units as single line items helps to distinguish those cash flows from other cash flows. The cash flow effects of disposals are not deducted from those of acquisitions.

Non-cash Transactions

Investing and financing transactions that do not require the use of cash or cash equivalents should be excluded from a cash flow statement. Such transactions should be disclosed elsewhere in the financial statements, in a way that provides all the relevant information about these investing and financing activities.

Many investing and financing activities do not have a direct impact on current cash flows, although they do affect the capital and asset structure of an enterprise. The exclusion of non-cash transactions from the cash flow statement is consistent with the objective of a cash flow statement, as these items do not involve cash flows in the current period. Examples of non-cash transactions are:

(a) The acquisition of assets by assuming directly related liabilities.
(b) The acquisition of an enterprise by means of issue of shares.
(c) The conversion of debt to equity.

Components of Cash and Cash Equivalents

An enterprise should disclose the components of cash and cash equivalents, and should present a reconciliation of the amounts in its cash flow statement with the equivalent items reported in the balance sheet.

In view of the variety of cash management practices, an enterprise discloses the policy which it adopts in determining the composition of cash and cash equivalents.

The effect of any change in the policy for determining components of cash and cash equivalents is reported in accordance with Accounting Standard 5 titled, Net Profit Or Loss For The Period, Prior Period Items, and Changes In Accounting Policies.

Other Disclosures

An enterprise should disclose, together with a commentary by the management, the amount of significant cash and cash equivalent balances held by the enterprise that are not available for use by it.

There are various circumstances in which cash and cash equivalent balances held by an enterprise are not available for use by it. Examples include cash and cash equivalent balances held by a branch of the enterprise that operates in a country where exchange controls or other legal restrictions apply, as result of which the balance is not available for use by the enterprise.

Additional information may be relevant to users in understanding the financial position and liquidity of an enterprise. Disclosure of this information, together with a commentary by the management is encouraged, and may include:

(a) The amount of undrawn borrowing facilities that may be available for future operating activities and to settle capital commitments, indicating any restrictions on the use of these facilities.
(b) The aggregate amount of cash flows that represent increases in operating capacity separately from those cash flows that are required to maintain operating capacity.

The separate disclosure of cash flows that represent increases in operating capacity and cash flows that are required to maintain operating capacity is useful in enabling the user to determine whether the enterprise is investing adequately in the maintenance of its operating capacity. An enterprise that does not invest adequately in the maintenance of its operating capacity may be prejudicing future profitability for the sake of current liquidity and distribution to owners.

Appendix 1 to Annexure 14.1

CASH FLOW STATEMENT FOR AN ENTERPRISE OTHER THAN A FINANCIAL ENTERPRISE

The appendix is illustrative only, and does not form part of the accounting standard. The purpose of this appendix is to illustrate the application of the accounting standard.

The example shows only current period amounts.

Information from the profit and loss statement and balance sheet is provided to show how the statements of cash flows under the direct method and indirect method have been derived. Neither the statement of profit and loss nor the balance sheet are presented on conformity with disclosure and presentation requirements of applicable laws and accounting standards. The working notes given towards the end of this appendix are intended to assist in understanding the manner in which the various figures appearing in the cash flow statements have been derived. These working notes do not form part of the cash flow statement and, accordingly, need not be published.

The following additional information is also relevant for the preparation of the statements of cash flows (figures are in Rs'000):

(a) An amount of 250 was raised from the issue of share capital, and a further 250 was raised from long-term borrowings.

(b) Interest expenses was 400, of which 170 was paid during the period. Interest expense of the prior period which was 100 was also paid during the period.

(c) Dividends paid were 1200.

(d) Tax deducted at source on dividends received (included in the tax expense of 300 for the year) amounted to 40.

Statement of Profit and Loss for the period ended 31.12.1996

	(Rs'000)
Sales	30650
Cost of sales	(26000)
Gross profit	4650
Depreciation	(450)
Administrative and selling expenses	(910)
Interest expense	(400)
Investment income	500
Foreign exchange loss	(40)
Net profit before taxation and extraordinary item	3350
Extraordinary item—Insurance proceeds from earthquake disaster settlement	180
Net profit after extraordinary item	3530
Taxes on income	(300)
*Net profit	3230

(e) During the period, the enterprise acquired fixed assets for 350. The payment was made in cash.

(f) Plant with original cost of 80 and accumulated depreciation of 60, was sold for 20.

(g) Foreign exchange loss of 40 represents the reduction in the carrying amount of a short-term investment in foreign currency designated bonds arising out of a change in the exchange rate between the date of acquisition of the investment and the balance sheet date.

(h) Sundry debtors and sundry creditors include amounts relating to credit sales and credit purchases only.

Balance Sheet as at 31.12.1996

		1996		1995
				(Rs'000)
Assets				
Cash on hand and balances with banks		200		25
Short-term investments		670		135
Sundry debtors		1700		1200
Interest receivable		100		—
Inventories		900		1950
Long-term investments		2500		2500
Fixed assets at cost	2180		1910	
Accumulated depreciation	(1450)		(1060)	
Fixed assets (net)		730		850
Total assets		6800		6660
Liabilities				
Sundry creditors		150		1890
Interest payable		230		100
Income taxes payable		400		1000
Long-term debt		1110		1040
Total liabilities		1890		4030
Shareholders' Funds				
Share capital		1500		1250
Reserves		3410		1380
Total shareholders' funds		4910		2630
Total liabilities and shareholders' funds		6800		6660

NOTES TO THE CASH FLOW STATEMENT
(Direct and Indirect Method)

1. *Cash and Cash Equivalents*

Cash and cash equivalents consist of cash on hand and balances with banks, and investments in money market instruments. Cash and cash equivalents included in the cash flow statement comprise the following balance sheet amounts:

	1996	1995
Cash on hand and balances with banks	200	25
Short-term investments	670	135
Cash and cash equivalents	870	160
Effect of exchange rate changes	40	—
Cash and cash equivalents as restated	910	160

Cash and cash equivalents at the end of the period include deposits with banks of 100 held by a branch, which are not freely remissible to the company because of currency exchange restrictions.

The company has undrawn borrowing facilities of 2000 of which 700 may be used only for future expansion.

2. Total tax paid during the year (including tax deducted at source on dividends received) amounted to 900.

Direct Method Cash Flow Statement

(Rs'000)

1996

Cash flows from operating activities		
Cash receipts from customers	30150	
Cash paid to suppliers and employees	(27600)	
Cash generated from operations	2550	
Income taxes paid	(860)	
Cash flow before extraordinary item	1690	
Proceeds from earthquake disaster settlement	180	
Net cash from operating activities		1870
Cash flows from investing activities		
Purchase of fixed assets	(350)	
Proceeds from sale of equipment	20	
Interest received	200	
Dividends received	160	
Net cash from investing activities		30
Cash flows from financing activities		
Proceeds from issuance of share capital	250	
Proceeds from long-term borrowings	250	
Repayments of long-term borrowings	(180)	
Interest paid	(270)	
Dividends paid	(1200)	
Net cash used in financing activities		(1150)
Net increase in cash and cash equivalents		750
Cash and cash equivalents at beginning of period (see note 1)		160
Cash and cash equivalents at end of period (see note 2)		
		910

Indirect Method Cash Flow Statement (paragraphs 17b)

	(Rs'000) 1996	
Cash flows from operating activities		
Net profit before taxation, and extraordinary item	3350	
Adjustments for:		
Depreciation	450	
Foreign exchange loss	40	
Investment income	(500)	
Interest expense	400	
Operating profit before working capital changes	3740	
Increase in sundry debtors	(500)	
Decrease in inventories	1050	
Decrease in sundry creditors	(1740)	
Cash generated from operations	2550	
Interest paid	(270)	
Income taxes paid	(900)	
Cash flow before extraordinary item	1380	
Proceeds from earthquake disaster settlement	180	
Net cash from operating activities		1560
Cash flows from investing activities		
Purchase of fixed assets	(350)	
Proceeds from sale of equipment	20	
Interest received	200	
Dividends received	200	
Net cash used in investing activities		70
Cash flows from financing activities		
Proceeds from issuance of share capital	250	
Proceeds from long-term borrowings	250	
Repayment of long-term borrowing	(180)	
Dividends paid	(1200)	
Net cash used in financing activities		(880)
Net increase in cash and cash equivalents		750
Cash and cash equivalents at beginning of period (see note 1)		160
Cash and cash equivalents at end of period (see note 1)		910

ALTERNATIVE PRESENTATION
(Indirect Method)

As an alternative, in an indirect method cash flow statement, operating profit before working capital changes is sometimes presented as follows:

Revenues excluding investment income	30650	
Operating expense excluding depreciation	(26910)	
Operating profit before working capital changes		3740

WORKING NOTES

The working notes given below do not form part of the cash flow statement and, accordingly, need not be published. The purpose of these working notes is merely to assist in understanding the manner in which various figures in the cash flow statement have been derived.

		(Rs'000)
1.	*Cash receipts from customers*	
	Sales	30650
	Add: Sundry debtors at the beginning of the year	1200
		31850
	Less: Sundry debtors at the end of the year	1700
		30150

2.	*Cash paid to suppliers and employees*		
	Cost of sales		26000
	Administrative and selling expenses		910
			26910
	Add: Sundry creditors at the beginning of the year	1890	
	Inventories at the end of the year	900	2790
			29700
	Less: Sundry creditors at the end of the year	150	
	Inventories at the beginning of the year	1950	2100
			27600

3.	*Income taxes paid (including tax deducted at source from dividends received)*	
	Income tax expense for the year (including tax deducted at source from dividends received)	300
	Add: Income tax liability at the beginning of the year	1000
		1300
	Less: Income tax liability at the end of the year	400
		900

Out of 900, tax deducted at source on dividends received (amounting to 40) is included in cash flows from investing activities and the balance of 860 is included in cash flows from operating activities.

4.	*Repayment of long-term borrowings*	
	Long-term debt at the beginning of the year	1040
	Add: Long-term borrowings made during the year	250
		1290
	Less: Long-term borrowings at the end of the year	1110
		180

5.	*Interest paid*	
	Interest expense for the year	400
	Add: Interest payable at the beginning of the year	100
		500
	Less: Interest payable at the end of the year	230
		270

Appendix 2 to Annexure 14.1

Cash Flow Statement for a Financial Enterprise

The appendix is illustrative only and does not form part of the accounting standard. The purpose of this appendix is to illustrate the application of the accounting standards.

1. The example shows only current period amounts.
2. The example is presented using the direct method.

	(Rs'000)
	1996
Cash flows from operating activities	
Interest and commission receipts	28447
Interest payments	(23463)
Recoveries on loans previously written off	237
Cash payments to employees and suppliers	(997)
Operating profit before changes in operating assets	4224
(Increase) decrease in operating assets:	
Short-term funds	(650)
Deposits held for regulatory or monetary control purposes	234
Funds advanced to customers	(288)
Net increase in credit card receivables	(360)
Other short-term securities	(120)
Increase (decrease) in operating liabilities:	
Deposit from customers	600
Certificates of deposit	(200)
Net cash from operating activities before income tax	3440
Income taxes paid	(100)
Net cash from operating activities	3340
Cash flows from investing activities	
Dividends received	250
Interest received	300
Proceeds from sales of permanent investments	1200
Purchase of permanent investments	(600)
Purchase of fixed assets	(500)
Net cash from investing activities	650
Cash flows from financing activities	
Issue of shares	1800
Repayment of long-term borrowings	(200)
Net decrease in other borrowing	(1000)
Dividends paid	(400)
Net cash from financing activities	200
Net increase in cash and cash equivalents	4190
Cash and cash equivalents at beginning of period	4650
Cash and cash equivalents at end of period	8840

Source: The Chartered Accountant, February 1996.

Praise the sea, but keep on the land.

—Herbert

15 Cost, Profitability, and Break-Even Analysis

INTRODUCTION

While introducing the concept of marginal costing in Chapter 10, we indicated that the appraisal format, first standardised by the RBI and later modified by different banks to suit their requirements, prescribes an absorption costing method of presenting a profit and loss account to assess the profitability of a business. But it is important for a banker to make a marginal analysis of the profitability for a deeper understanding of the cost and profit behaviour of a business or a product. In the long run, however, the two methods may lead to similar conclusions, but in the short run—in which a banker is more interested as he lays down mostly short-term finance—marginal analysis gives a much better understanding of the profitability of a firm.

In this chapter we introduce the concept while dealing with a real problem of an entrepreneur. The purpose is two-fold: one, to acquaint a lender with the usage of this important tool in the appraisal of a business; and the other to enable him to counsel entrepreneurs, particularly the first-generation type, about the operating and financial viability of product(s).

DILEMMA OF AN ENTREPRENEUR

An Example

Mr Pankaj Verma is an electrical engineer from the Indian Institute of Technology, Kanpur. While in service for about five years in a fan manufacturing industry, he found that in all machine shops, workers used imported electrical hand drilling machines to bore holes of various sizes in metal plates. These tools were heavy and quite noisy; their cost was also very high. He gathered that the company had once tried low-cost indigenous tools, but soon these were discarded due to intermittent breakdowns.

Mr Verma, having a researcher's bent of mind, went through all the engineering aspects of these tools, and finally developed a model tool, which more than met international standards. It was light and there was minimal noise. He surmised that as the product was better than the imported variety, he would get a ready market. He finally decided to quit his job and embark on manufacturing hand drilling tools on his own.

He started in a small way. In the first year, he could produce only 100 units. He thought that he would be able to fetch a better price in the market and compete successfully with the imported brand. The market price of the imported brand was Rs 6,000 per unit, but he could not sell his product at that price. As he was new, no one was willing to buy his product at that price. Though his product was of better quality, he could not sell it at more than Rs 5,400 per unit. However, at this price, not only were all his products sold, he was flooded with more orders.

While he was enjoying the pleasure of his creation, a feeling was creeping into his mind that somewhere things were going wrong. Despite the fact that his sales were mostly in cash due to the high demand for his product even in the first year, quite often he had to pour in more funds to meet various expenses of his business. As he did not know much about book keeping, he had appointed an accountant from the beginning. At the end of the year, he now asked the accountant to bring before him the results of his operation. The accountant presented him the following profit and loss account of the business:

Now Mr Verma knew why he was feeling the pinch of occasional financial stringency. He was making a loss!

From the profit and loss account, he calculated the total cost of producing 100 units of hand drilling tools. It was Rs 6,60,000, which meant that his cost per unit was Rs 6,600 and he was selling it at Rs 5,400 and basking in the impression that he had really made it a roaring business! He had to price the product at Rs 7,200 to make a profit of at least Rs 600 per unit, or else he would have to close down the business and go back to service.

He moved around the market, but found that though many were willing to buy his product because it really worked better than the imported variety, they would not buy it at Rs 7,200. They could at best offer him Rs 6,000, the price of the imported variety.

Should he close down the business?

A sulking Mr Verma returned to his office. Selling the tools at Rs 6,000 would still mean a loss of

Profit and Loss Account for the Year Ended 31 March

Dr	Rs	Cr	Rs
Raw materials consumed	180000	Sales	
Wages	90000	(100 units @ Rs 5400)	540000
Fuel and power	30000		
Gross profit c/d	240000		
	540000		540000
Rent (@ Rs 6000 p.m.)	72000	Gross profit b/d	240000
Salaries of work supervisors (@ Rs 9000 p.m.)	108000	Net loss	120000
Salaries of accountant and office staff (@ Rs 10500 p.m.)	126000		
Salary of Darwan (@ Rs 3000 p.m.)	36000		
Depreciation @ 10%	18000		
	360000		360000

Rs 600 per unit, which meant another year of loss and stringencies. He would not be able to bear this loss, because he was already at his lowest financial ebb. After all, what fun was there in business if it made a loss? He started thinking of winding up his business.

When Mr Verma was so sulking on the cruelty of the business world, a representative of an engineering company came to his place. His company had purchased 20 hand drilling tools from Mr Verma that year. The works manager was very satisfied with the product. The company now wanted to buy 200 more such units. Mr Verma was elated. He had the capacity to produce 400 units per year. So, 200 units would not be a problem. But the price? The representative said that though it was a bulk order, the company would not want to reduce the price at which it had bought the products that year. It would pay the same price of Rs 5,400 per unit. Mr Verma had already become wiser. He would not sell at Rs 5,400. He said 'sorry', and was about to turn down the deal when his accountant intervened.

Since it was a small open office, the accountant was hearing the discussion with great interest. For some time, he had been hearing that Mr Verma was thinking of closing down the business. He thought that here was an opportunity to save the business. He implored upon Mr Verma to accept the offer. Mr Verma glowered at him, 'What are you telling me! If I accept the offer at Rs 5,400 a unit, I will have a loss of Rs 2,40,000. Already I have made a loss of Rs 1,20,000. I have no capacity to bear with any further loss. So, forget it.'

The accountant was a polite and intelligent young man. He requested Mr Verma not to reject the order right then. He could tell the representative to meet him tomorrow for a final decision. Mr Verma looked at his accountant with bewilderment. However, he liked him very much, so he acceded and asked the representative to meet him the next day. He was sure that then too

he would reject the offer, but in the meantime, what was the harm in listening to the young man?

However, the next day when the representative of the company came to Mr Verma, he readily accepted the offer. His accountant had already shown him that with this order itself he would make such a profit as to wipe out last year's loss completely.

How the Accountant Saved the Business

Was the accountant right, or was he just trying to save his service tactfully for another year?

How did the accountant convince Mr Verma?

The conversation between Mr Verma and the accountant went as follows:

Accountant: Do you agree, Sir, that the cost of raw materials per unit of the drilling machine is Rs 1,800, and it is not likely to change in the near future?

Mr Verma: Yes.

Accountant: Do you agree, Sir, that the wages for the workers for producing one unit of the machine will not be more than Rs 900, and the fuel and power as we have calculated will also be only Rs 300 per machine produced?

Mr Verma: Yes.

Accountant: In that case, the total direct cost for producing one unit of machine comes to Rs 3,000. As our production increases, only this part of the cost will increase proportionately. I think you will agree with my logic.

Mr Verma: Yes, but what about the rent, salary, and other expenses?

Accountant: Sir, I am sure, the landlord would not ask for an increase in rent, nor are you going to increase our salaries in the near future, and the depreciation is always a fixed percentage of the plant and machinery. Hence, all these are more or less fixed in nature. Now, let us see what happens in case you accept the present order of 200 units.

The accountant's calculations are given below:

	Rs	Rs
Sale price quoted by the company per unit		5400
Less: Variable cost per unit		
Raw materials	1800	
Wages	900	
Fuel and power, etc.	300	3000
Contribution per unit		2400
Hence, total contribution for 200 units comes to be:		480000
Less: Fixed cost		
Rent (@ Rs 6000 p.m.)	72000	
Salaries of accountant and other office staff (@ Rs 10500 p.m.)	126000	
Supervisors' salary (@ Rs 9000 p.m.)	108000	
Darwan's salary (@ Rs 3000 p.m.)	36000	
Depreciation	18000	360000
Net profit		120000

FULL COST VERSUS MARGINAL COST

It appears, therefore, that even if the machines were sold at Rs 5,400 per unit, Mr Verma would make a profit of Rs 1,20,000 which would wipe out last year's loss. Mr Verma understood that the full cost of the product as calculated by him from last year's operation, namely, Rs 6,600, was misleading. But it still did not lead him anywhere with respect to his production and pricing policies. He now wondered that somewhere along the production path there must lie a point where sales revenues would match with the total cost, leading to a 'no profit/no loss' situation. If he could know this, he would be in a position to understand how far away he was from this point. This would not only indicate the strength or weakness of his productive operations, it would also help him in quoting the right price. The accountant calculated this in the following way:

$$Break\text{-}even\ Sales = \frac{Total\ fixed\ cost}{Contribution\ per\ unit}$$
$$= \frac{Rs\ 360000}{Rs\ 2400} = 150\ units$$

The accountant advised Mr Verma that at the point of sale of 150 units of this product, his operations would break even, which he might call the break-even point of sales or simply break-even sales, where he would have neither a profit nor a loss, that is, revenues would exactly match the expenses. Let us now check the conclusion of the accountant:

Sale price for 150 units at Rs 5400	810000
Less: Variable cost for producing 150 units (Rs 3000 × 150)	450000
Contribution	360000
Less: Fixed cost	360000
Profit/Loss	nil

It should be clear by now that contribution is nothing but marginal revenue, which contributes first to the fixed costs and then to the profit. Hence, when the fixed costs are fully provided for by the break-even level of the sales volume, marginal revenue (contribution) from any additional unit sold beyond the break-even (BE) point will be pure profit. In the present example, if Mr Verma sold 151 units, he would earn a profit of Rs 2,400, which is nothing but the contribution from one unit of the product.

Let us now discuss the nature of the two types of cost discussed above.

Variable Cost

Variable simply means changeable. But in accounting practices this changeability takes on a special meaning. It is changeable not in relation to time, season, or period, but only in relation to the volume of sales. If any item of cost increases/decreases proportionately with the increase/decrease in volume, then we call this a variable cost. In the above example, the variable cost increased proportionately when the volume of production increased. It was Rs 3,00,000 for 100 units and Rs 6,00,000 for 200 units. That is, Rs 3,000 is fixed per unit for all the units produced. This immediately leads us to another aspect of the variable cost, that is, while the total variable cost increases with the increase/decrease in volume the *variable cost per unit remains fixed.*

We have already seen that variable cost includes direct wages, raw material, power, and fuel which are directly engaged in the production of goods and services. At this point, we may tend to conclude that all direct costs are also variable. This is wrong; only the converse is true, because depreciation is a direct cost, but it is fixed in nature. We can, therefore, say that all items of variable cost are direct in nature, but all items of direct cost are not variable.[1]

Fixed Cost

Fixed costs do not vary with volume. These remain fixed for a given period. A better term for

[1] Certain selling and distribution costs, for example, selling commission are variable with the volume of sales. But to call them direct costs will invite the wrath of cost accountants. For the purpose of a break-even analysis, however, a banker should take into account the variable selling and distribution costs as part of total variable costs.

fixed costs would be non-variable costs. However, the present term is used widely and understood commonly by all engaged in and associated with manufacturing activities. Examples of fixed costs are salaries, administrative expenses, rent and taxes on properties, and occupancy costs like heating and lighting. Fixed costs can be regarded as period costs, because these are incurred during a period, and calculated for a given period only. Two months' salary of a manager is double of one month's salary, but any increase or decrease in the volume of production does not affect it. Let us now see what happens to fixed costs when volume of production increases or decreases.

No. of Units Produced	Total Variable Cost	Variable Cost per Unit	Total Fixed Cost	Fixed Cost per Unit
100	300000	3000	360000	3600
200	600000	3000	360000	1800

It is now clear that *fixed costs per unit decreases with an increase in the volume of production and vice versa, while total fixed costs remain the same.*

The Rules

We may now make the following rules:

1. *Per unit* variable cost is fixed. It does not vary with the volume of output.
   Per unit fixed cost changes with the volume of output.
2. *Total* variable cost increases proportionately with the increase in the volume of output, and decreases with the decrease in the volume of output.
   Total fixed cost does not increase or decrease with the volume of output.

If, in any year, there is no production, the business continues to incur fixed costs but not variable costs. Only production can absorb fixed costs. The more the production, the more will be the absorption. This is the reason why fixed costs are also called overhead cost. They hang on the business perpetually. *A banker while analysing a profit and loss account should see whether production could be increased to such an extent as to cover fixed costs.* It may be observed that variable costs of a product may be low, leaving a substantial contribution per unit, but fixed costs are so high that the production and its consequent sale may have to be increased to a large extent so that the absolute contribution can take care of the entire fixed costs, and also leave a net profit. But this may not always be possible.

We should point out, however, that fixed costs remain fixed only for a given period of time, though sufficiently long. In the long run when the capacity of the plant and machinery is increased requiring more rent and more salaries, the fixed costs also increase. But, thereafter, for another period they will once again remain fixed. Fixed costs may also vary by deliberate management decisions. For example, the management may decide to work on three shifts instead of one. This will necessitate the engagement of one more guard, two shift supervisors, and so on. This immediately increases fixed costs. A banker should take into consideration this aspect when a borrower wants an additional credit facility, because he wants to increase his production by running extra shifts. *He should enquire what the additional fixed costs for this purpose would be.*

Types of Fixed Costs

Fixed costs may also be divided into two groups—direct fixed costs and indirect fixed costs. The former include production overheads, such as depreciation, indirect wages, and salaries of supervisors and works managers. Indirect fixed costs, which are popularly called general overheads, include selling and administrative expenses. They also include interest on borrowings

but that needs a little more clarification. Interest is a finance cost which depends on the financial structure of a business. It may not have anything to do with the operating structure. For example, gross working capital (GWC) is composed of various current assets. How these current assets are to be financed is a financial decision of the business. It may choose to finance them entirely from capital, from trade credit, by borrowings, or by a combination of all three. Similar options are available for financing fixed assets. Each such method of financing will give rise to a particular interest cost. Under the full cash credit system of financing, the interest on working capital is variable to a large extent. But that may not be the case under the loan system of financing working capital. One has to study the nature of a loan to decide the fixity or otherwise of the interest cost. It may be necessary to calculate two break-even points, one before interest and the other after interest. This we do later in this chapter.

Semi-Variable Cost

The name itself suggests that in this type of cost there is an element of both fixity and variability. The cost varies, but not proportionately like the full variable cost. For example, a 10 per cent increase in volumes may increase only 3 per cent of the cost. This is also called a semi-fixed or partially variable cost. Indirect wages, maintenance, and some of the administrative costs fall under this head. Let us take the following example to analyse the nature of semi-variable cost and try to break it into two parts—fixed and variable—so that the fixed portion can be added to the other general fixed costs and the variable portion can be added to the other variable costs.

No. of Units	20	25	30
Nature of cost	Rs	Rs	Rs
Variable cost	800	1,000	1,200
Fixed cost	600	600	600
Semi-variable cost	300	350	400

We can see from this example that variable costs increase directly and proportionately with the volume of output. The semi-variable cost increases, but not proportionately. There is an element of fixedness, which we should try to separate. We can do it with the help of simultaneous equations. Let 'a' be the fixed portion in the total semi-variable cost and let 'x' be the coefficient of the variable portion of the cost. Hence:

$$a + 25x = 350 \qquad \ldots \qquad (15.1)$$
$$a + 20x = 300 \qquad \ldots \qquad (15.2)$$

Solving the two equations, we get:

$$5x = 50$$
$$\text{or, } x = 10$$

Solving it now for equation (15.1) we get:

$$a + 25 \times 10 = 350$$
$$\text{or,} \quad a + 250 = 350$$
$$\text{or,} \quad a = 100$$

Hence, the fixed portion of the semi-variable costs is Rs 100. The variable portion varies at Rs 10 per unit of output.

Those who have an aversion towards algebra may approach the problem arithmetically in the following manner:

Increase in production: 25 − 20 = 5 units
Incremental cost: Rs 350 − Rs 300 = Rs 50

Hence, when the production increases by 5 units, the cost increases by Rs 50. That is, the per unit increase in cost is Rs 10. Hence, the variable portion is 25 × 10 = Rs 250, and the fixed portion is 350 − 250 = Rs 100.

Let us now allocate the fixed and variable portions of the semi-variable cost to the original variable and fixed costs in the following manner:

	20 Units	Cost per Unit	25 Units	Cost per Unit	30 Units	Cost per Unit
Variable cost	800	40	1000	40	1200	40
Add: Variable portion of semi-variable cost	200	10	250	10	300	10
Total variable cost	1000	50	1250	50	1500	50
Fixed cost	600		600		600	
Add: Fixed portion of semi-variable cost	100		100		100	10
Total fixed cost	700	35	700	28	700	23.33
Total cost	1700	85	1950	78	2200	73.33

Calculation of Break-Even Sales

The nature of these three types of costs can be depicted in the three diagrams shown in Figure 15.1.

Sales Price (assumed)
  Rs 70 per unit
Variable cost
  Rs 50 per unit
Contribution
  Rs 20 per unit

BE sales = Fixed cost/
    Contribution
    per unit or
    700/20 = 35 units

Check: Sales price
for 35 units   = 35 × 70 = Rs 2450
  Variable cost for 35 units = 35 × 50 = Rs 1750
  Contribution   Rs 700
  Fixed costs   Rs 700

The break-even point of sales is that point when fixed costs divided by the contribution is unity. That is, 700/700 = 1

The break-even analysis enables us to pinpoint certain other important aspects of operations of a business. We discuss only two of them here, which are useful for a banker to evaluate the strength of a credit proposal.

MARGIN OF SAFETY

The margin of safety indicates the amount by which the present volume of sales exceeds the

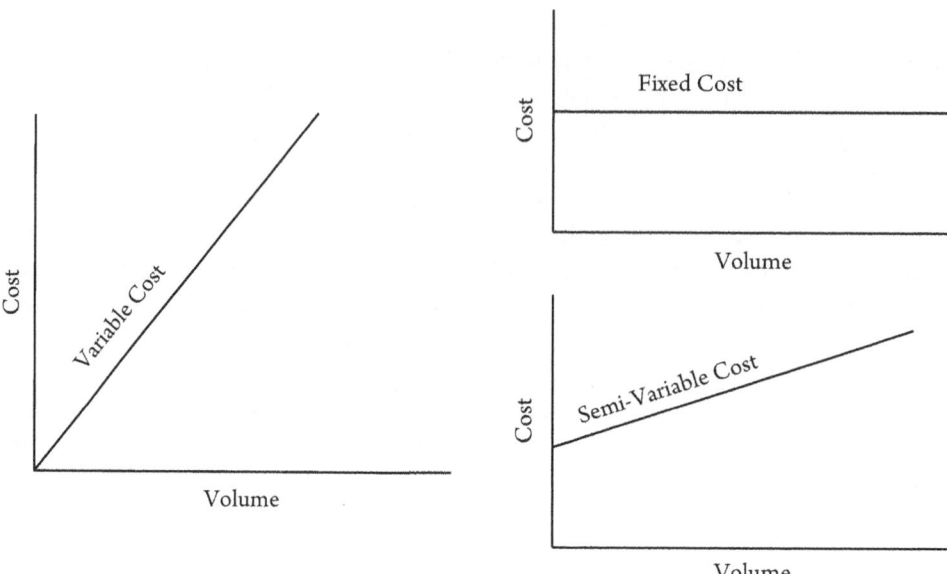

FIGURE 15.1   Types of Costs

break-even point. A business operates in an uncertain situation. Various economic, social, and political factors may affect sales, and hence the profit of a firm adversely. A banker who is taking a calculated risk may want to know if sales fall below a certain point, what the condition of a business would be, that is, whether the business will be able to withstand a fall in sales, and if so, to what extent. The margin of safety is a very robust tool by which he can estimate the sensitivity of a business to variation in sales.

This is calculated in the following two ways:

(a) $\dfrac{Profit}{Contribution} \times 100$ or

(b) $\dfrac{Sales - Break\text{-}even\ Sales}{Sales} \times 100$

For a banker the simple method as in (a) is more helpful because it requires less calculations than the latter.

Let us take the following example of a business:

	Rs
Net profit	3000
Sales	54000
Variable cost	44000
Fixed cost	7000

The contribution is Rs 54,000 – Rs 44,000 = 10,000.

Hence, the margin of safety will be (using formula 'a'):

$$\frac{3000}{10000} \times 100 = 30\%$$

It indicates that if, at any time, the sales volume falls by 30 per cent, the firm can still pay for the full cost without making a loss. This is the margin of safety presently available to the firm. On the other hand, it also means that 70 per cent of the existing sales is the break-even sales. It can be checked as:

70% of the existing sales
   $54000 \times 70/100$ =   Rs 37800
Less: 70% of variable cost
   $44000 \times 70/100$ =   Rs 30800
Contribution   Rs 7000
Less: Fixed cost   Rs 7000
                      No profit, no loss

Minimum Requirement

The margin of safety calculated above essentially indicates the operating strength of a business. Normally, a banker should expect a margin of safety beyond 25 per cent, because the market of the products going adverse by 20 per cent plus minus is highly probable. Hence, a 20 per cent margin of safety is not a desirable situation. It also points to the existence of high overheads that require a higher volume of sales to absorb them. A banker should probe into the matter deeply to see why the overheads of a company are so high, against a low volume of sales. If it is found that it is difficult to increase sales, a banker should be on guard in sanctioning such a credit proposal, because working capital finance may probably go towards financing the overheads only. A realistic plan for reduction of overheads should be made a pre-requisite for considering the credit proposal further.

Usefulness during Depression

At times of depression, either in general or in a particular product, the margin of safety becomes very important, because sales are always decreasing. A banker would like to know to what extent a business can withstand the fall in sales. This, however, does not suggest that during depression bankers should put their hands off a business for fear that the company may fail. On the other hand, it is imperative in such a situation to come forward and help the business to carry increasing levels of stocks, though unsold due to depression, so that production is not hampered. In a depression, the worsening economic situation is aggravated if production falls below a certain threshold limit. The margin of safety in such a situation indicates the extent of risk that a banker can bear so that he can plan the utilisation of resources in a meaningful way, because in a recessionary situation, demand for a bank's funds is also reduced.

Some possible steps to improve the margin of safety are:

1. Increase in sale price.
2. Increasing the volume of sales of existing products.
3. Substituting the existing product lines with more marketable and profitable products.
4. Reduction of fixed costs.
5. Reduction in variable costs by efficient use of plant, raw materials, and stores.

Any one or a combination of some or all of these steps may be of help depending upon market conditions. A banker should discuss all these possible steps with a borrower and settle on a constructive plan of action. *The margin of safety indicates the shock-absorbing capacity of a business. It is a valuable guide to judge the operating strength of a unit.*

PROFIT–VOLUME RATIO

This ratio indicates the intrinsic strength of a product. It is calculated as:

$$\frac{Contribution}{Sales} \ or \ \frac{Sales - Variable\ Cost}{Sales} \ or \ \frac{Fixed\ Cost + Profit}{Sales}$$

This is expressed in percentage form.

From this example, we can calculate the profit–volume (P/V) ratio.

Sales	Rs 54000
Variable cost	Rs 44000

Therefore, the P/V ratio will (using the second formula)[2] be:

$$\frac{54000 - 44000}{54000} \times 100 = \frac{10000}{54000} \times 100 = 18.52\%$$

If this ratio is declining, the conclusion could be that the product is losing in the market, which may be due to general obsolescence that occurs during the life cycle of a product; a banker may be financing a dying product at his peril. The ratio may also decline when the variable group of costs has lost proportionality with sales, indicating stickiness of the operating structure of the business.

When a company is producing more than one product, the profit–volume ratio becomes a very useful tool to analyse the relative strength of a particular product. If the ratios for two products are 20 per cent and 30 per cent, then a company should choose to increase the sales of the latter product. However, this should be taken with a pinch of salt, because other factors, like the operating cycle, investment required in both fixed assets and working capital, and realisation of sales may weigh heavily in favour of the former product. We elaborate on this point through an example later in the chapter.

The P/V ratio is also helpful in comparing the performance of two units selling the same products. A credit appraiser may often deal with proposals of firms producing the same product or product range. He may very well make a comparison among these firms and pick up the best unit giving the highest P/V ratios as a standard, and compare the performance of other firms in terms of their P/V ratios. It is also possible to have a standard ratio calculated for the industry as a whole. This may help a banker to come to a judgement on the performance of various companies producing the same product.

FURTHER PROBLEMS OF PANKAJ VERMA

Let us now see what our entrepreneur, Mr Pankaj Verma is doing presently.

He has now become an ambitious businessman. He has seen the success of his electric hand drill. It is selling well in the market. He feels now that he should introduce a smaller variety of the same drilling machine that can be used by small fabricators, who cannot use the bigger type because of high costs. The product has already been developed, the trial run made, and the first batch of commercial production is awaiting a 'go ahead'.

On making enquiries in the market Mr Verma has found that similar products, though of inferior quality, are being sold at Rs 1,800 per unit. He decided to sell his product at Rs 1,500 to start with. He has now asked his accountant to give him product-wise elements of cost. The accountant has given him the following figures, marking the bigger drilling machine as 'A' and the smaller as 'B'.

		(Rs per unit except depreciation)
	Product A	Product B
Raw materials	1800	600
Wages	900	300
Fuel and power, etc.	300	150
Depreciation	18000	15000
Price per unit	5400	1500

---

[2] The reader may also calculate it by the other two formulae. The result will be the same.

He has also submitted the following yearly establishment expenses of the firm.

Rent	Rs 72000
Salaries	Rs 670000
Total	Rs 742000

Mr Verma is confused. He has learnt a bit of the break-even analysis by now. He can see that product 'A' is more profitable, but he knows that because of high costs he will not be able to increase its sales faster. He is also facing difficulties in getting immediate payments from big customers. Product 'A' also requires more investments and larger space in the factory. But product 'B' can sell very quickly because of its low price. Large numbers of small fabricators are looking for a cheap drilling tool. Additional investment in this equipment also is small. The new product can be manufactured within the given factory set-up, though in a separate plant. Although rent has not increased, salaries have gone up owing to a larger administrative set-up.

Should He Take the Second Product?

Of late, Mr Verma has been thinking of having a second product to fall back upon, in case the demand for the bigger variety falls. He has already found that he will not be able to sell more than 360 units of the bigger variety in a year unless he breaks into other markets (which he does not want to do now because of more overhead costs). He, therefore, wants to know whether his new product will be profitable or not, and at which point of sale it will reach its break-even point. He can very well produce 100 units of product 'B' per month and sell 1200 units a year all in cash, whereas in case of product 'A' he can produce 30 units a month. It now takes about two months to realise the sale proceeds of product 'A'.

He calls his accountant once again, and asks him to consider all these points and advise him whether he should go for product 'B'.

Allocation of Overheads

The accountant now distinguishes the fixed overheads into fixed production overheads and fixed general overheads, because Mr Verma now has two separate plants to produce the two products. The depreciation cost of product 'A' is Rs 18,000 and that of 'B' Rs 15,000 (which are to be allocated to the two products separately), and the general overheads of Rs 7,42,000 have to be allocated between the two products in some manner so that a break-even analysis for the two products can be made.

		(Amount in Rs)
	Product A	*Product B*
Sales p.a.	360	1200
	units	units
Sale price per unit	5400	1500
Total sales revenue	1944000	1800000
Less: Variable cost	1080000	1260000
Contribution (total)	864000	540000
Contribution (per unit)	2400	450
Production overhead:		
Depreciation	18000	15000

Now the question of allocating general overheads of Rs 7,42,000 between the two products arises. There are various ways by which these allocations can be made. But a realistic way to allocate them is in proportion to the variable costs incurred by each product, because it is ultimately the raw materials and workers that occupy the space and demand administrative attention. Therefore, the proportion should be:

A:B = 108 : 126 or, 6 : 7

General overheads are allocated by this ratio:

Product 'A'	Rs 342461
Product 'B'	Rs 399539
Total	Rs 742000

Total overheads, including production overheads for products 'A' and 'B' will be:

Product 'A'	Rs 342461 + 18000 = 360461
Product 'B'	Rs 399539 + 15000 = 414539
	775000

Relative Strength of a Product

Stage I

We can now calculate the break-even sales for both the products.

Product	Contribution per unit	Fixed costs	Break-even sales (in units)
'A'	2400	360461	360461/2400 = 150
'B'	450	414539	414539/ 450 = 921

The total cost of sales of 360 units of product 'A' = Rs 1080000 + 18000 + 342461 = Rs 14,40,461 (per unit Rs 4,000), and the same for producing 1200 units of product 'B' = Rs 1260000 + 15000 + 399539 = Rs 16,74,539 (per unit Rs 1,395).

This analysis shows that product 'A' reaches a break-even sales point with a much lower volume of sales, but this still cannot be taken to indicate the strength of this product. A comparison of the relative strengths of the two products should first be done through a P/V analysis.

Product	P/V Ratio		Remarks
A	$\dfrac{2400}{5400} \times 100$	= 44.44%	Calculated on the basis of per unit sales and contribution
B	$\dfrac{450}{1500} \times 100$	= 30%	

It appears that once again product 'A' has relatively more strength than product 'B'.

The accountant now takes into consideration other information given to him by Mr Verma: that only 30 units of product 'A' could be produced in a month, and it now takes about two months to realise its sales proceeds, while 100 units of product 'B' could be produced in a month, which are all saleable in cash. The accountant also finds that on an average the firm has to hold in stock product 'A' equivalent to two months' sales. For product 'B', he estimates it to be not less than 15 days' sales. The firm's normal practice of holding the raw materials inventory for one month's consumption would be extended to product 'B' also. The raw materials market is such that all materials are bought in cash.

Stage II

Investment in current assets for both product 'A' and 'B' are calculated below:

	Product 'A' Rs
1. Raw materials inventory (Rs 1800 × 30)	54000
2. Finished goods inventory at cost of sales (Rs 4000 × 30 × 2)	240000
3. Debtors at cost of sales (Rs 4000 × 30 × 2)	240000
Total current assets	534000

	Product 'B' Rs
1. Raw materials inventory (Rs 600 × 100)	60000
2. Finished goods inventory (Rs 1395 × 100 × 1/2)	69750
Total current assets	129750

We now calculate below the return (contribution) on current assets for products 'A' and 'B':

	Investment in Current Assets	Contribution	Return (contribution) on Current Assets
Product 'A'	534000	864000	161.80%
Product 'B'	129750	540000	416.18%

This analysis indicates that in spite of product 'A' having a better P/V ratio and a lower break-even sales point, in the ultimate financial analysis, product 'B' appears to be much stronger, because it not only demands much lower investments in working capital, but its return (contribution) on investment is also considerably higher than product 'A's'. Generally, the P/V analysis is restricted to Stage I only, as has been shown above. That is, the analysis stops at knowing only the relative operating strength of a product. It is not extended to a financial analysis as has been done in Stage II. *No doubt, a banker is interested in knowing the operating strength of a product, but he cannot consider financing a new venture unless he knows its financial strength also.* A P/V analysis indicates the profitability of sales, which remains partial unless it is extended to the financial analysis as we have done here. When a proposal for diversification to a new product line is received by a banker, he should not stop at knowing its operating strength only, but also its financial strength vis-á-vis the existing product line.

In this analysis, while calculating the investments required for working capital, we have ignored work-in-progress, assuming it to be small. But a lender is advised to include it whenever he finds it significant.

PROBLEM OF MULTIPLE PRODUCTS

When a unit is manufacturing more than one product, a banker may often be wrongly advising the customer to drop a product if it shows a nil or negative profit. The importance of a P/V analysis is once again felt here. The robustness of this tool can be explained by taking the following example. Overheads are allocated in the ratio of machine-hour consumed by each product, which is 50 hours each for products 'X' and 'Y', and 40 hours for product 'Z'.

	Product X	Product Y	Product Z	Total
Sales	13600	15000	8400	37000
Variable cost	7600	9000	4400	21000
Contribution	6000	6000	4000	16000
Allocation of overheads in the ratio of 5:5:4	5000	5000	4000	14000
Operating profit	1000	1000	nil	2000

From this contribution analysis, a banker may be prone to advise the entrepreneur to discontinue product 'Z', because it is not making any profit. This situation often arises when a banker is nursing a sick unit. If the entrepreneur agrees with him or is forced to agree, then both the banker and the entrepreneur may be inviting trouble, because the unit as a whole may soon be more sick for want of adequate profit generation. This can be explained if we do a P/V ratio analysis for all the three products.

Product	P/V Ratio
X	$\dfrac{6000}{13600} \times 100 = 44.12\%$
Y	$\dfrac{6000}{15000} \times 100 = 40.00\%$
Z	$\dfrac{4000}{8400} \times 100 = 47.62\%$

The entire picture has changed now. Product 'Z', which is making no profit, appears to be the best product among the three, because its rate of contribution is the highest as manifested in the P/V ratio of 47.62 per cent. There is no reason, therefore, why the entrepreneur should stop producing product 'Z'. On the contrary, there is a case for increasing its sales.[3]

[3] It may also be a case for misallocation of overheads. In such a situation a P/V analysis should be done only after proper allocation of overheads.

The reader must have noticed that in the P/V ratio analysis, we have used the contribution and not the profit. The term itself, therefore, is a misnomer. The better term will be contribution–volume ratio, but the nomenclature P/V ratio has been in use since the invention of the break-even analysis. We have retained the old name as it is commonly understood. As long as we understand that it is the contribution and not the profit which matters in a P/V ratio analysis, there is nothing wrong in continuing to use the old nomenclature.

A Simple Method for a Break-Even Analysis

The methodology of a break-even analysis discussed so far may not be of any use to a lender unless he knows the most important element—the number of units produced or proposed to be produced by a firm. Although these days, large companies publish some data on the number of units produced, these are not amenable to a break-even analysis. Moreover, when the products manufactured are many, it is very difficult to make an item-wise break-even analysis. Often it is observed that an entrepreneur is not willing to part with detailed product-wise cost information claiming confidentiality. In such a situation, a lender is unable to make any headway towards a break-even analysis, and hence for quite some time this tool of analysis could not be made much use of by lending organisations. An example will make the position clear.

Illustration

In searching for an illustration we can once again turn to Mr Pankaj Verma and see what he is doing at present, because a number of years have passed since he first ventured into business.

Mr Verma is now a big industrialist. He has diversified his interests to consumer electronics. He is now the chairman of National Industries Limited, which holds a commendable position in the market. The young accountant he started with is now the chief accountant of the company. Presently, he has asked him to negotiate with the bank for an increase in overdraft. The chief accountant has submitted the profit and loss account and balance sheet to the bank manager, Mr Ramesh Shah, for the past three years, including the last year ending 31.12.20X7.

Mr Shah now looks at the relevant profit and loss account figures of National Industries Limited for the year ended 31.12.20X7 (after adjustments) (see Chapter 10 for a full profit and loss account).

(Rs in lakh)

1.	Opening stock:		
	(a) Raw materials	6614	
	(b) Work-in-progress	<u>1372</u>	7986
2.	Purchase of raw materials		35661
3.	Wages, including bonus		1181
4.	Carriage inward		14
5.	Stores and spares		367
6.	Power, fuel, and water		1908
7.	Excise duty		5287
8.	Repairs		437
9.	*Rent:*		
	Factory	180	
	Office	<u>104</u>	284
10.	*Rates and taxes:*		
	Factory	392	
	Office	<u>194</u>	586
11.	Salaries		748
12.	Welfare expenses		118
13.	Contribution to PF and gratuity		283
14.	Insurance		36
15.	Advertisement		473
16.	Carriage and distribution expenses		1695
17.	Commission and brokerage		263
18.	Postage, telegrams, and telephones		123
19.	Travelling expenses		356
20.	Printing and stationery		55
21.	Depreciation		530
22.	Interest		555

23.	Bank charges	76
24.	Misc. expenses	556
25.	Audit expenses	7
26.	Sales	53100
27.	Closing stock:	
	(a) Raw materials 7235	
	(b) Work-in-progress 1432	8667
28.	Opening stock of finished goods	3049
29.	Closing stock of finished goods	3805

Banker's Dilemma

Mr Shah wants to know the operating strength of the business. He must, therefore, find out the break-even point followed by margin of safety and the P/V ratio. But he is bewildered, because to start the exercise, he must know the number of units produced by the company. He asks the chief accountant of the company to submit the figures to him. The list submitted by the chief accountant makes him more confused, because it contains 25 items of consumer electronic goods produced by the company. How is he going to calculate break-even points with 25 items of goods produced? It may require a complicated analysis by a full-fledged costing department, which neither the company nor the bank has.

Let us see if we can help the bank manager.

Variable Costs

Item No.	Account Head	(Rs in lakh)	
(1a+2) –27(a)	Raw materials consumed	35040	
3	Wages and bonus	1181	
4	Carriage inward	34	
5	Stores and spares	367	
6	Power, fuel, and water	1908	
7	Excise duty	5287	
		43817	say, 43820
Fixed Costs Item No. 8 to 25		7181	say, 7180
	Total cost	50998	say, 51000
	Sales	53100	say, 53000

As a banker, Mr Shah should be more interested in knowing the following:

1. What percentage of existing sales makes the break-even point?
2. What is the margin of safety available to the business?
3. What is the P/V ratio of the *whole* business, so that he can make a meaningful comparison with other units in the same industry?

Let us make two arbitrary assumptions with respect to the units produced, and see whether it is possible to fulfil the requirement under (1) above.

(Rs in lakh)

	Revenue/ Cost	Assumption-I	Assumed per Unit Revenue/ Cost	Assumption-II	Assumed per Unit Revenue/ Cost
Sales	53000	1000 units	53.00	700 units	75.72
Variable cost	43820	1000 units	43.82	700 units	62.60
Contribution	9180	1000 units	9.18	700 units	13.12
Fixed cost	7180	1000 units	—	700 units	—

Break-even sales under Assumption-I

$$\frac{Fixed\ cost}{Contribution\ (per\ unit)} = \frac{7180}{9.18}$$

Break-even sales as a percentage of

$$existing\ sales = \frac{7180 \times 100}{9.18 \times 1000}$$

$$= 78.20\%$$

Break-even sales under Assumption-II

$$\frac{Fixed\ cost}{Contribution\ (per\ unit)} = \frac{7180}{13.12}$$

Break-even sales as a percentage of

$$existing\ sales = \frac{7180 \times 100}{13.12 \times 700}$$

$$= 78.20\%$$

We can see that under both the assumptions, break-even sales as a percentage of existing sales comes to be about 78.20 per cent, which is Rs 41,446 lakh.

If the calculation is made by assuming any other figure of units produced, the result will be the same.

If the reader has understood the underlying principles, she/he would understand that what remains in the ultimate analysis is the comparison between contribution and fixed costs in absolute value. Let us do the calculations accordingly.

$$\frac{Total\ Fixed\ Cost}{Contribution\ in\ absolute\ value} \times 100$$

$$= \frac{7180}{9180} \times 100 = 78.20\%$$

Margin of Safety

We now proceed to calculate the margin of safety.

$$Margin\ of\ Safety = \frac{\begin{array}{c}Total\ Sales -\\ Break\text{-}even\ Sales\end{array}}{Sales} \times 100$$

$$= \frac{53000 - 41446}{53000} \times 100$$

$$= 21.80\%$$

This means that if the volume of sales falls by 21.80 per cent, the company will be just at the break-even point.

A P/V analysis may similarly be done as:

$$\frac{Contribution}{Sales} \times 100 = \frac{9180}{53000} \times 100 = 17.32\%$$

FINANCIAL BREAK-EVEN POINT

We find from this analysis that the break-even point of sales of National Industries Limited is high, and consequently its margin of safety is low, at around 20 per cent. This suggests that the shock absorption capacity of the company is low. It goes down further as we consider the finance cost of the company.

We find from Chapter 16 (where the company is dealt with in further detail) that the finance cost of the company inclusive of bank charges is Rs 588 lakh. Considering this as a fixed cost, we calculate below the financial break-even point of sales and the financial margin of safety of the company.

Financial Break-Even Sales

(Rs in lakh)

$$\frac{\begin{array}{c}Fixed\ Cost +\\ Finance\ Cost\end{array}}{Contribution} = \frac{Rs\ 7180 + 588}{9180} \times 100 = 84.62\%$$

The financial break-even point of sales, therefore, increases to Rs $53,000 \times 0.8462 = $ Rs 44,848 lakh.

FINANCIAL MARGIN OF SAFETY

$$\frac{\begin{array}{c}Tales\ Sales - Financial\\ Break\text{-}even\ Sales\end{array}}{Total\ Sales} \times 100 = \frac{53000 - 44848}{53000} \times 100$$

$$= 15.38\%$$

This is the true margin of safety of the business as a whole, which for National Industries Limited is considerably low. A fall in sales by 15 per cent is just an ordinary possibility even if the company is not facing a cyclical downturn. With such a low margin of safety, the company enters the high-risk category. A high break-even point of sales and consequently a low margin of safety indicate the presence of a high fixed overhead burden, which can be carried only by increasing sales. If the present line of products is reaching a saturation point, the company has to look for opportunities to diversify into other profitable products.

Projected Break-Even Point of Sales

When an enterprise is operating below the point of break-even sales, a lender may like to know at what percentage increase in the existing sales the business will reach break-even point to enable him to decide on a particular loan amount. We use the same simple technique developed earlier to calculate the desired level of break-even sales with the help of the following example.

Revenue/Cost

Total sales	Rs 6000
Total variable cost	Rs 5000
Contribution	Rs 1000
Total fixed cost	Rs 2000

With the help of the formula developed in the earlier example, we can now calculate what percentage of the present level of sales represents the break-even point.

$$\frac{Fixed\ Cost}{Total\ Contribution} \times 100 = \frac{2000}{1000} \times 100 = 200\%$$

That is, if the existing level of sales of Rs 6000 is increased by 200 per cent, the firm will reach break-even point. Break-even sales in absolute value will, therefore, be:

$$\frac{6000 \times 200}{100} = Rs\ 12000$$

Check: Total sales increased by 200%	12000
Less: Variable cost also increased by 200%	10000
Total contribution	2000
Less: Fixed cost	2000
	0

A break-even analysis has many other uses, namely selection of product-mix, price determination, fixation of production targets, and ensuring increasing return on sales. But these are the domain of the management accounting discipline; and are not of much use to a banker, who mainly deals in aggregates.

LIMITATION AND LAWS OF MARGINAL ANALYSIS

It is often claimed that the break-even method of marginal analysis suffers from certain limitations that render it a useless tool for practical use. Let us examine these limitations carefully and suggest ways to overcome them.

1. *In a break-even analysis, a linear or directly proportional relationship is assumed amongst the variables, which may not always hold good.* Necessary adjustments should, therefore, be made similar to a semi-variable analysis to circumvent this difficulty as and when a non-linear relationship is observed.

2. *A change in one factor may influence a change in other factors also. This is kept out of the purview of the present break-even analysis.* For example, an increase in the price of sales may reduce the volume of sales also. Therefore, a company dealing in goods and services having a highly elastic demand structure should take this point into account. But a banker in such a situation may easily know, by using this tool, at which level of sales the firm can reach the break-even point under the existing demand structure, and at which point it is difficult for the company to increase its sale price.

3. *One of the biggest limitations of a break-even analysis is that it does not take into account the capital employed in a business. It only looks at the operating strength and not the financial strength of a product or business.* The two, however, can be combined and an informed decision taken by a banker as we have shown in this chapter.

4. *Fixed costs are fixed in the short-term only, and hence it is argued that a break-even*

analysis cannot contribute anything towards the long-term planning of operations. The charge is true, but one should recall that even if fixed costs change, for example, when capacity is increased, the new level of fixed costs will be fixed for the new period.

5. *A break-even analysis, like a balance sheet, gives a static picture of a firm's operations, while a business is a continuous process. The conditions, both internal and external, may change even immediately after an analysis is made, making the conclusions totally inapplicable.* It is true that a business always operates in uncertainty, but in an uncertain situation, planning is the most important tool to take care of uncertainties. The margin of safety is one such tool of operational planning, which can help a banker to know the inherent operating strength of a business in absorbing sudden shocks.

6. *Of late, a charge is leveled against the manner in which variable costs are determined. It is claimed that the classic concept of the variability of wages no longer holds good. Wage has become more a fixed cost than other overheads because of the growing strength of trade unions.* We have shown earlier that a cost which is semi-variable or semi-fixed in nature can be broken down into two parts—variable and fixed—and then added to the respective cost-heads for purpose of a break-even analysis. This method is applicable for cost of labour also. If the wage is found to be totally fixed in nature—which is still not a likely situation—then the entire cost can be treated as a fixed cost.

At one time, limitations ascribed to a break-even analysis, as mentioned earlier, gave vent to the idea that a break-even analysis is not a dynamic concept but a static one. It cannot take care of the changing realities of business. The charge is not true, as we have already seen. Certain laws are evolved from an analytical study of the break-even concept that can take care of almost all probable changing situations. The most important of these laws, as relevant to a banker, are enumerated below with the reasons for their occurrence, and a banker's points of caution, so that he can take pre-emptive steps to prevent the laws operating against the business.

Law I

A change in fixed costs will change the break-even point but not the marginal revenue (contribution).

Reasons:
Increase in fixed costs falls into two typical categories—*positive* decisions and *default* decisions.

Positive decisions:
(a) Addition to plant to expand capacity.
(b) Addition to sales offices to expand market.
(c) Increase in research and development activities.
(d) Changing compensation method of sales staff from commission on sales to fixed salaries.
(e) Redesigning the organisational structure by splitting general functions and creating new job titles.
(f) Establishing in-house manufacturing facilities for items hitherto purchased from the market.

Default decisions:
(a) Permitting slackness in control.
(b) Deferring maintenance because 'we can't lose the production'.
(c) Stretching work to fit the workforce—when decline occurs, using all forms of specious reasoning.

(d) Elaborating record keeping.

(e) Allowing what is 'nice to have' because 'we must do things in a big way' popularly nicknamed as 'YMCA engineering'.

A banker must be very watchful of 'default decisions', because any such decisions may sow the seeds of future sickness of the unit. With regard to 'positive decisions', a banker must point out to a borrower that unless, within a reasonable time, variable costs are reduced enough to more than off-set the increase in the break-even point, a decision to increase fixed costs may be disastrous for the unit.

Law II

A change in variable costs will change both the break-even point and marginal revenue (contribution).

Reasons:
(a) Change in technology may change the variable cost per unit.
(b) Changing the nature of a cost item—from variable to fixed and will versa.

Positive decisions:
(a) Change in the specification and grade of raw materials.
(b) Change in product design.
(c) Revision of engineering design frequently causing obsolescence of stock and increased storage costs.
(d) Change in the rate and method of wage payments.
(e) Change in trade discount and commission policies.

Default decisions:
(a) Elaboration of factory administration, requiring multiplication of various orders.

(b) Allowing multifarious forms of lag, which lowers the rate of productivity of either labour, or materials, or both.
(c) Allowing publicity and advertisement fees based on volume.
(d) Application of grades of labour other than the standard for the work to be done.

We should remember that variable cost per volume generally increases, but only slowly. The management does not care till it has increased considerably. Unless, therefore, the process is arrested when there is a signal, a higher level of sales will be increasingly required to reach the break-even point, which may not always be possible. A banker should keep a careful watch on the variable expense ratios. If these are rising rather fast, he must probe deeply into the operating conditions of a borrower.

Law III

A change in the selling price will change the break-even point and the contribution rate.

Reasons:
(a) Change in selling price due to a competitive situation.
(b) Change in the internal relationship in the total sales value between high margin and low margin items.

When this law starts operating, a banker's attention should focus on the margin of safety and the P/V ratio. If they show a downward trend, it may possibly be time for the diversification of the product line or for the closing down of a particular product.

Law IV

When both fixed costs and variable costs change, the effect on the break-even point is extremely marked and definite if they move in tandem, but minor if they move in opposite directions.

Reasons:
  (a) Increase in fixed, or variable costs, or both, due to poor cost control.
  (b) Balance or lack of balance between the added depreciation resulting from new plant and machinery and the amount contributed towards the reduction of the variable cost rate.
  (c) Faulty plant or technology selection.

If the effect of the change is to push up the break-even point markedly, the situation is dangerous. If it is due to reason (c), it may be advisable to disband the new product line well in time before it starts affecting the performance of the unit as a whole.[4]

Concluding Remarks

Before we conclude our discussion on the break-even analysis, we should mention that a banker may often take two different positions while looking at the following break-even chart (Figure 15.2) of a unit depending upon his attitude towards financing a growing unit.

Let us assume that a banker is standing at the cross-section of the two lines facing the break-even point. If he looks towards his left, he will find that the firm is making losses, and hence, he may put his hands off the credit proposal submitted by a borrower. But if he looks to his right, he will find that it is a growing business, which, in course of time, will cross over to the profit zone. Which way should a banker look? Should he look to the left side only and refuse the proposal, acting as a traditional banker, or turn his head to the right and help the entrepreneur cross the loss zone smoothly? A modern banker looks to the right—the bright side of the picture. A break-even analysis enables him to change his attitude.

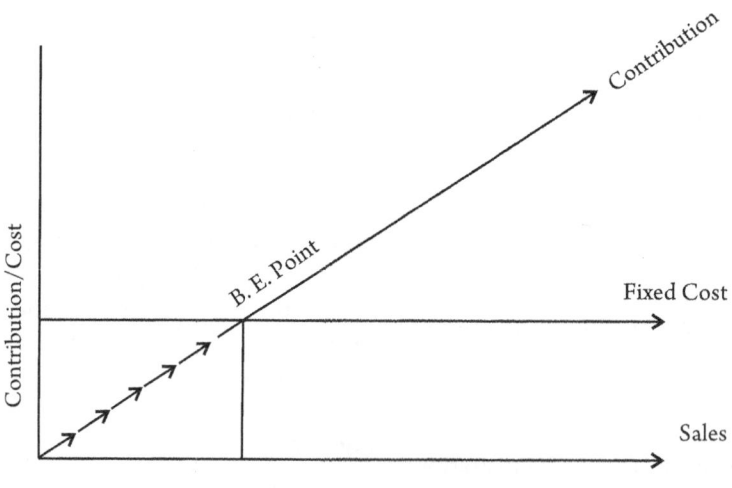

Figure 15.2 Break-Even Chart

[4] For details, see Gardner, V.F., *Profit Measurement and Control*, Macdonald and Co. Ltd., UK, 1971.

Dyspepsia is the remorse of a guilty stomach.

—A. Kerr

16 Appraisal and Monitoring through Ratios

INTRODUCTION

In describing the importance of a ratio analysis, we can use the analogy of the dashboard of a car. The state of the car on the road at any point of time is given by the signals on the dashboard. The driver by looking at the meters on the dashboard would know the speed of the vehicle, the engine speed, the oil pressure, and the rate of charge/discharge of the battery. All this information is available in ratio form—kilometres per hour, revolutions of the engine per second, kilograms per square centimetre and amperes per hour. The driver adjusts the controls and propels the car to the destination based on the information available to him. Everybody concerned with the car will use these ratios to judge its present state and future ability to reach a destination. The same holds true for a business. The management uses the information contained in a ratio for purposes of controlling and monitoring, a banker for securing his funds, and a shareholder for ensuring his yield.

Ratios relate absolute figures and bring forth meaningful information. Absolute figures are only data. They do not reveal anything without processing. Ratios are processed data. Yet, interpretations of these ratios vary from person to person depending upon the relative purposes and goals and a lot of individual judgement. By the same analogy of a car, we may say that the dashboard may reveal certain ratios about the speed of the engine or the state of the battery, but ultimately it is the judgement of the driver who has to reach a place by a certain time, in a certain condition of the road, weather, and lighting on the street.

Ratio analysis as a concept or technique is as old as accounting concepts. R.A. Foulke mentions that ratio analysis was being used in the last few years of the nineteenth century.[1] It was the duPont company which first used an integrated set of ratios in 1919, but kept it a closely guarded secret until 1949 when it was made public. Since then important developments in ratio analysis have taken place. In 1950, extensive studies were done on the choice and use of productivity ratios and finance and operating ratios. Bankers started using ratios as early as 1870. The first such ratio was the current ratio. In India, the Tandon Committee[2] proposed a comprehensive usage of ratio

---

[1] Foulke, Roy A., *Financial Statement Analysis*, Prentice-Hall Inc., Englewood Cliffs, New Jersey, 1978.

[2] *Report of the Study Group to Frame Guidelines for Follow-Up of Bank Credit*, Reserve Bank of India, Bombay, 1975.

analysis. Ratio analysis is now an important tool for taking credit decisions by bankers.

PRESENTATION AND USES OF RATIOS

Absolute figures, howsoever big or small they might be, do not speak anything by themselves unless they are related to some other variable. The following example explains this.

	Profit
Firm 'A'	Rs 1000
Firm 'B'	Rs 1000

As both the firms are earning a profit of Rs 1,000, one may tend to conclude that they are operating with the same efficiency. But if we say that firm 'A' has sales of Rs 10,000 and firm 'B' has a sales of Rs 1 lakh, our conclusion will immediately change, because in the case of firm 'A' the return on sales is 10 per cent, while in the case of firm 'B' it is only 1 per cent. We may now tend to conclude that firm 'A' is better than firm 'B'. This conclusion will however, be reversed if we consider the total investment of the two firms. In firm 'A' the investment is Rs 20,000 and in firm 'B' it is Rs 10,000. Hence, the return on investment for firms 'A' and 'B' will be 5 per cent and 10 per cent respectively, which indicates that firm 'B' is earning the same amount of profit by a lower amount of investment. Ratio analysis helps us to judge the efficiency or otherwise of one firm vis-à-vis another.

A ratio is thus the result of comparing or dividing one number (numerator) by another (denominator). Suppose the numerator is Rs 10,000 and the denominator is Rs 5,000, the ratio between the two can be expressed in one of the following forms:

1. A proportion (2:1).
2. A pure number (2).
3. A percentage (200%).

Conventionally, some ratios are presented in one or the other form for ease of presentation and understanding. For example, profitability ratios like return on sales, investments, or capital employed are invariably expressed in percentage form, while solvency ratios like current ratio and debt–equity ratios are expressed either as proportions or in pure numbers. Certain ratios like turnover of debtors and creditors are also expressed either in pure numbers or by converting them into days, weeks, or months, as we will see later.

MANIPULABILITY OF RATIOS

An analyst while calculating a ratio should also examine the nature of the two variables that will indicate the manipulability of each variable for purposes of making any improvements in the ratio. The manipulability depends, to a large extent, on the relationship between two variables. When two variables are mutually interdependent, it is very difficult to manipulate one variable by keeping the other constant. One such example is the operating profit ratio, which is calculated as a percentage of operating profit on sales. Operating profit will generally increase or decrease with the increase or decrease in sales, hence the ratio will remain constant. If sales could be reduced by keeping the operating profit constant, or the operating profit is increased by keeping the sales constant, then the ratio will also improve, but in reality such a situation, though not impossible, is difficult to achieve. The ratio can be improved only when we go back to some other variable(s) that has produced this particular variable. For instance, in order to improve upon operating profit independent of sales, we have to take on its influencing variable, namely, cost of sales, and find out ways of reducing it.

But in the case of current ratio, which is the ratio between current assets and current liabilities, both the variables can be manipulated independent of each other. Generation of current assets and their funding are two distinct operations. For example, it is not necessary to finance entire current assets from current liabilities only. A part of such financing can be or should be done from long-term resources. Hence, the current ratio can be improved by increasing long-term liabilities rather than current liabilities.

OBJECTIVITY IN RATIO ANALYSIS

A number of ratios have been developed since its advent in the nineteenth century. Managers and analysts at different times wanted to have a set of their own ratios to analyse, plan, and control their respective functions. One set of ratios used by one manager or analyst may not be useful for another. This brings us to the question of objectivity in ratio analysis. An analyst must have a set of clear objectives before him, and then decide which are the ratios needed by him under each such objective. There may be sub-goals for an objective, which, however, may conflict with each other, or at times the objectives themselves may come into conflict. Ratio analysis should be made in such a way as to enable conflicting objectives or sub-goals to yield to the overall goal of the business.

For a banker the objectives will broadly be:

1. To judge the operating efficiency of a borrower.
2. To judge the financial health.
3. To ensure safety and security of the advance.

In fact, the third objective will be satisfied largely if the first two objectives are achieved. The new approach to lending draws the attention of a banker to the fact that if the business is performing well with sound financial health, his advance is safe and secured. If it is not, then any amount of security will ultimately be useless.

But the objectives of a lender may, at times, come into conflict with one another, or the objectives of a banker may also change depending upon the condition of the borrower. For example, when a unit has fallen sick, the objective of safety and security may have to yield place to the objective of reviving the operating health of the business, thus giving second place to financial health. A worse current ratio or debt–equity ratio may have to be tolerated, at least for some time, to ensure improvements in operating ratios. For a sick firm under a nursing programme, financial ratios take the second place yielding the first place to operating ratios.

DIFFICULTIES WITH RATIOS

Like all other management tools, ratios can be misused and be misleading if used mechanically. For example, if a firm registers a sales growth of only 10 per cent and its return on sales is only 1 per cent, it will be wrong to conclude that the firm is doing bad business unless we look into the other ratios, including the market share of the firm. The firm's volume of sales may be Rs 500 crore but its total operating assets is Rs 10 crore, hence its return on investments is as high as 50 per cent. This is the picture of successful cigarette manufacturing companies. On the other hand, a unit may register a growth of sales of 100 per cent on its base figure of Rs 1 lakh only, but its market share may be insignificant as compared to a giant whose market share was 50 per cent at the base year but increased to 60 per cent in the year under review. Ratios should, therefore, be interpreted in their context.

As ratios are derived from a comparison of two variables, what constitutes these variables is more important. That is, a *proper valuation of each variable has to be done before calculating a ratio.* Figures may be cooked up in published financial statements to hide a falling trend in certain important ratios where a banker is more interested, or a group of assets or liabilities may or may not include certain figures for genuine accounting reasons. Unless these are taken into consideration and adjusted properly before calculating a ratio, wrong interpretations may vitiate the analysis. Ratio analysis is not a mechanical arithmetic exercise. Careful assessment of variables is a pre-requisite for an intelligent interpretation of a ratio.

Problems also arise in interpretation of ratios derived from variables that are valued conventionally at historical cost, for example, fixed assets. How much reliance is to be placed on such ratios is once again a matter of judgement of an analyst (these problems are discussed in greater detail while discussing individual ratios. The conflict between balance sheet ratios and profit and loss account ratios is highlighted at the end of this chapter).

CLASSIFICATION OF RATIOS

Banker's Ratios. A banker is interested in knowing the following aspects of a borrower's business:

A. Efficiency of operational management.
B. Efficiency of financial management.

C. Efficiency of debt-service management.

The chart (Figure 16.1) pictorially analyses these three aspects of management.

In Tables 16.1 through 16.3, we have identified certain important ratios under the three groups mentioned earlier.

We now discuss and calculate each of these ratios with the help of the financial statements of National Industries Limited, as presented in Chapters 10 and 11.

EFFICIENCY OF OPERATIONAL MANAGEMENT

Fixed Assets–Turnover Ratio

This is the ratio of fixed assets to sales turnover. By fixed assets, we mean operating fixed assets that contribute to the production of goods and services. Fictitious assets are excluded. Any revaluation of fixed assets is to be ignored, because it does not in any way augment the produceability of fixed assets. Capital expenditure made for a partly completed plant which is yet to be commissioned (capital work-in-progress) should also be excluded. Operating fixed assets

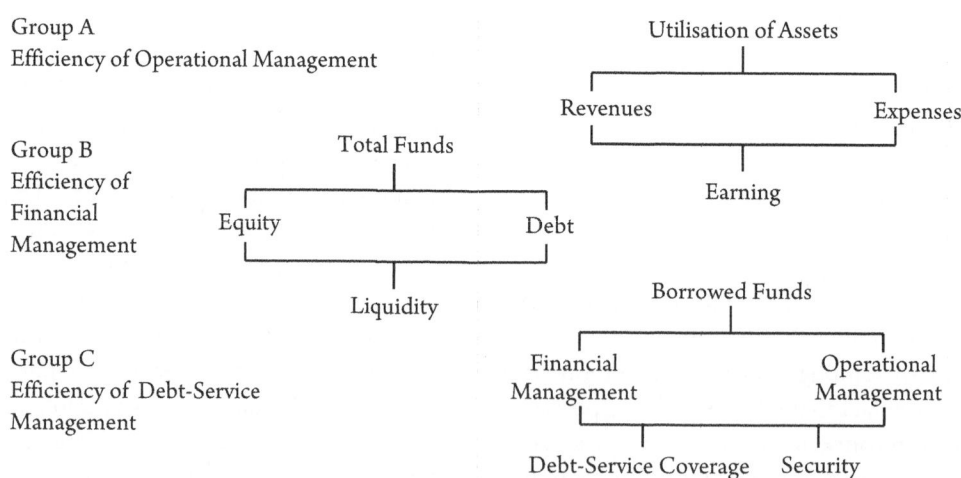

FIGURE 16.1   Different Aspects of Management

TABLE **16.1**   Group A: Ratios to Judge Efficiency of Operational Management

Item No.	Name of Ratio	Computation	Unit of Measurement	Particular Purpose
1.	Fixed Assets Turnover Ratio	$\dfrac{\text{Net Sales}}{\text{Operating Fixed Assets}}$	Number	To determine fixed asset utilisation
2.	Capital Turnover Ratio	$\dfrac{\text{Net Sales}}{\text{Capital employed}}$	—do—	To determine how judiciously long-term funds are employed
3.	Total Assets Turnover Ratio	$\dfrac{\text{Net Sales}}{\text{Total Operating Assets}}$	—do—	To determine the level of asset utilisation
4.	Return on Investment (ROI)	$\dfrac{\text{PBIT}}{\text{Total Operating Assets}}$	Percentage	To determine profitability of total assets employed
5.	Current Assets– Turnover Ratio	$\dfrac{\text{Total Sales}}{\text{Operating Current Assets}}$	Number	To determine the revenue generating capacity of current assets
6.	Materials Inventory Turnover Ratio	$\dfrac{\text{Consumption of Raw Materials}}{\text{Raw Materials Inventory}}$	—do—	To determine the efficiency of materials planning
7.	Work-in-Process Inventory Turnover Ratio	$\dfrac{\text{Cost of Production}}{\text{Work-in-Process Inventory}}$	—do—	To determine the stability of the operating structure
8.	Technology Updation Ratio	$\dfrac{\text{Capital expenditure}}{\text{Depreciation}}$	—do—	To determine the level of replacement, and hence technology
9.	*Export-Import Ratios* (a) Export Ratio	$\dfrac{\text{Export Sales}}{\text{Sales}}$	Percentage	To determine the sensitivity of the business to changes in international markets
	(b) Import Ratio	$\dfrac{\text{Imported raw materials}}{\text{Total raw material consumed}}$	—do—	—do—
10.	Protection Ratio	$\dfrac{\text{Domestic cost of the product}}{\text{Landed cost of the same imported product}}$	Percentage or Number	To determine product sensitivity to any withdrawal of government protection
11.	*Earning Ratios* (a) Gross Profit Ratio	$\dfrac{\text{Gross Profit}}{\text{Net Sales}}$	Percentage	To determine the operating efficiency of the business in keeping the rate of gross profit stable or increasing
	(b) —do—	$\dfrac{\text{Gross Profit}}{\text{Cost of goods sold}}$	—do—	—do—
12.	Operating Profit Ratio	$\dfrac{\text{Operating Profit}}{\text{Net Sales}}$	Percentage	To determine the operating efficiency of the business in keeping the rate of operating profit stable or increasing

13.	Net Profit Ratio	$\dfrac{\text{Net Profit}}{\text{Net Sales}}$	—do—	To determine the net earning capacity of sales
14.	*Expense Ratios*			
	a) Direct Operating Ratio	$\dfrac{\text{Cost of goods sold}}{\text{Net Sales}}$	—do—	To determine the operating efficiency of the management in controlling expenses
	b) Expense Group Ratios	$\dfrac{\text{Each group of expense}}{\text{Net Sales}}$	—do—	—do—
15.	Tax Incidence Ratio	$\dfrac{\text{Indirect taxes}}{\text{Sales}}$	—do—	To determine the vulnerability of the business to the vagaries of revenue authorities

TABLE 16.2   Group B: Ratios to Judge Efficiency of Financial Management

Item No.	Name of Ratio	Computation	Unit of Measurement	Particular Purpose
1.	Debt–Equity Ratio	$\dfrac{\text{Long-term outside liability}}{\text{Shareholders' Fund}}$	Percentage or Number	To determine the level of permanent stake of the borrower
2.	Total Debt–Equity Ratio	$\dfrac{\text{Total debt}}{\text{Shareholders' Fund}}$	—do—	To determine the level of a borrower's overall stake in the business
3.	Ratio of Net Working Capital to Current Assets	$\dfrac{\text{Net working capital}}{\text{Current assets}}$	—do—	To determine the level of buffer funds available to withstand financial shocks
4.	Current Ratio	$\dfrac{\text{Current assets}}{\text{Current liabilities}}$	A number or a ratio	To determine the general liquidity of the business
5.	Diversion Ratio	$\dfrac{\text{Net working capital}}{\text{Working capital gap}}$	Percentage	To determine diversion or loss of current funds
6.	Finished goods stock turnover Ratio	$\dfrac{\text{Cost of goods sold}}{\text{Finished goods stock}}$	Number of days or months	To determine the reasonableness of stock holding
7.	Debtors–Turnover Ratio	$\dfrac{\text{Gross Sales}}{\text{Trade debtors}}$	—do—	To determine the saleability of the product and efficiency of the collection department
8.	Creditors–Turnover Ratio	$\dfrac{\text{Purchases}}{\text{Trade Creditors}}$	—do—	To determine the ability of a firm to obtain market credit
9.	Market Command Ratio	$\dfrac{\text{Creditors turnover (by days)}}{\text{Debtors turnover (by days)}}$	Ratio	To determine the market position of a borrower

TABLE **16.3**   Group C: Efficiency of Debt-Service Management

Item No.	Name of Ratio	Computation	Unit of Measurement	Particular Purpose
1.	Interest Cover Ratio	$\dfrac{\text{Profit before interest and tax}}{\text{Annual interest obligation}}$	Number	To determine the interest-paying capacity of a firm
2.	Debt–Service/ Coverage Ratio	$\dfrac{\text{Profit after-tax + Interest + Depreciation}}{\text{Interest + Annual Repayment of term loans}}$	—do—	To determine the ability of a firm to service its total debt-service obligations
3.	Priority obligation Ratio	$\dfrac{\text{Net operating cash flows}}{\text{Priority outflows}}$	Percentage	To determine the cash position of a business to meet priority obligations
4.	Asset–Margin Ratio	$\dfrac{\text{Fixed Assets–Term Loans}}{\text{Fixed assets}}$	—do—	To determine the margin of safety of a lender, or the borrowing capacity of a borrower

for National Industries Limited may now be calculated.

Total fixed assets		Rs 7260 lakh
Less: Capital exp.	Rs 1012 lakh	
Revaluation reserve as per contra	Rs 1652 lakh	Rs 2664 lakh
Operating fixed assets		Rs 4596 lakh

Turnover here means turnover of goods, that is sales. For the purpose of calculating this ratio it is preferable to take net sales by deducting returns and excise duty from gross sales. For the company under consideration, net sales are Rs 47,813 lakh. We can now calculate the ratio.

$$\frac{\textit{Net Sales}}{\textit{Operating fixed assets}} = \frac{47813}{4596} = 10.40 \textit{ times}$$

It is expected that in a capital-intensive industry like National Industries Limited where capital spins faster, this ratio would be higher. The higher the ratio, the better the efficiency of fixed assets or, in other words, the higher the capacity utilisation. If the ratio is less than 3, a banker should probe deeply into the matter, because it would soon force the company to demand more working capital. A low fixed assets–turnover ratio

may be reflected in low profits and a low level of net working capital. A low and falling ratio also indicates outdated technology.

We have taken operating fixed assets net of depreciation for calculating this ratio. Some writers suggest that if fixed assets gross of depreciation are taken, it gives a better understanding of this ratio, particularly for inter-firm comparison, because depreciation policies differ from firm to firm. Although there is some validity in this argument, we should point out that the depreciation fund, if not invested outside the business, remains within the firm and contributes towards increasing sales. If, as a matter of policy, a firm depreciates its assets faster (which will give a higher ratio), it makes a savings of its income without giving it away as dividend. Hence, such a firm should be given due credit for its growth-oriented policy reflected in a higher fixed asset–turnover ratio, as against a firm which provides only minimum permissible depreciation.

Before we conclude our discussion on this ratio, we should raise a point of caution. The ratio in its present form is unable to cancel the impact of an inflationary price rise in sales. If an actual fall in the volume of sales is off-set by an inflationary rise in the price of the product, then the actual fall in operating efficiency of the business may be suppressed by the ratio. One way to tackle this problem is to make proper adjustments to off-set the inflationary rise in the rupee value of sales, and the other way is to take the operating cost of sales as the numerator, instead of sales.

Capital–Turnover Ratio

This is a variation of the earlier ratio. It is calculated by comparing net sales with the capital employed by a business. Sales should be taken as net of excise duty. By capital employed we mean long-term funds employed in the business, which are calculated for the company in two different ways.

		(Rs in lakh)
I. (a) Shareholders' fund (before appropriation)		11656
Less: Provision for taxation	1600	
Less: Proposed dividend	730	2330
		9326
Less: Revaluation reserve		1652
Net shareholders' fund		7674
(b) Add: Long-term borrowed fund		1577
Capital employed		9251
II. (a) Long-term assets and investments		8043
Less: Revaluation reserve as per contra		1652
Net long-term assets		6391
(b) Add: Net current assets		2860
Capital employed		9251

The ratio will, therefore, be:

$$\frac{Net\ Sales}{Capital\ employed} = \frac{47813}{9251} = 5.17$$

This ratio is very important in case of trading firms where a low level of capital is expected to turn over faster, giving rise to a large volume of sales and faster turnover of stocks. However, in case of a capital-intensive industry, like the pres-

ent one, the ratio will generally not be as high as in a trading firm. A ratio of around 5 is quite reasonable.

Total Assets–Turnover Ratio

This third variation takes a total view of a business as a producing unit. A banker may like to know the *produceability of the assets of a business*. This also indicates the managerial capability of an entrepreneur in putting the assets to best use.

Here also by total assets we mean operating assets, as discussed earlier and calculated as:

		(Rs in lakh)
Total assets		24159
Less: Revaluation reserve	1652	
Less: Capital work-in-progress	1102	
Less: Advances to suppliers of capital goods	179	
Less: Investment in shares	22	
Less: Share issue expenses	25	2980
Total operating assets		21179

The ratio is:

$$\frac{Net\ Sales}{Total\ operating\ assets} = \frac{47813}{21179} = 2.26$$

A manufacturing unit should generate sales, which should at least match with the total funds (assets) employed, that is the minimum ratio should be at least 1. But in case of trade, where the value added is very small as compared to manufacturing industries, this ratio should not be less than 2. For example, if the total investment in a business is Rs 1 lakh and the expected rate of return is 10 per cent on the capital invested, an entrepreneur in a manufacturing business will be able to ensure this return by making a sale of Rs 1 lakh only, the return being 10 per cent of Rs 1 lakh, or Rs 10,000. But in case of trade, where net commission say is only 5 per cent, he will need total sales of Rs 2 lakh to ensure a 10 per cent return on investment. Table 16.4 will clarify the situation.

This brings us to the next important ratio, return on investment or ROI, as it is popularly known.

Return on Investment (ROI)

The earlier ratios do not consider the profit made on the use of funds. The ROI ratio takes care of this aspect. In fact, this is a combination of operating profit ratio and assets turnover ratio as we will see now.

Profit here means profit before interest and taxes (PBIT). Non-operating income is excluded. This is calculated as:

	(Rs is lakh)
Profit before taxes	3222
Add: Interest	555
	3777
Less: Non-operating income	78
PBIT	3699

Let us first calculate the operating profit ratio:

$$\frac{PBIT}{Net\ Sales} \text{ or } \frac{3699}{47813} = 7.74\%$$

Later, we shall elaborate on this particular ratio.

Next, we find out the total asset–turnover ratio as calculated earlier and now repeated as:

$$\frac{Net\ Sales}{Total\ operating\ assets} = \frac{47813}{21179} = 2.26$$

We now combine these two ratios to find out ROI. The size of a firm's return on investments is a function of the margin of profit on sales and the amount of sales generated on the asset base. Hence:

$$ROI = \frac{PBIT}{Sales} \times \frac{Sales}{Total\ operating\ assets}$$

$$= \frac{PBIT}{Total\ operating\ assets}$$

or, $$ROI = \frac{3699}{47813} \times \frac{47813}{21179} = \frac{3699}{21179}$$

$$= 0.1746 \text{ or } 17.46\%$$

or, simply, ROI = 7.74 × 2.26 = 17.46% (approx.)

Figure 16.2 portrays the derivation of ROI through a flow chart, popularly known as the duPont Chart.

The purpose of deriving this ratio through such an elaborate method is to draw the attention of an analyst to the two ratios which give rise to ROI—improvement in any one of them should ordinarily improve ROI. But, as we have discussed before, certain ratios are not easily amenable to manoeuvrability due to the existence of a high correlation between the numerator and denominator variables. For example, it is difficult to improve upon the operating profit ratio because sales and operating profit are found to be highly correlated, giving rise to a more or less constant ratio with the increase or fall in sales. Attention should, therefore, be focused on the other ratio the total assets–turnover ratio— where the variables are not so closely related. Sales can be increased by increasing the capacity

TABLE 16.4   Comparative Total-Assets Turnover Ratios for Industry and Trade

Type of Venture	Total Investment	Sales	Return on Sales	Total Return	Turnover of Assets/Investment
Manufacturing	Rs 1 lakh	1 lakh	10%	10,000	1
Trade	Rs 1 lakh	2 lakh	5%	10,000	2

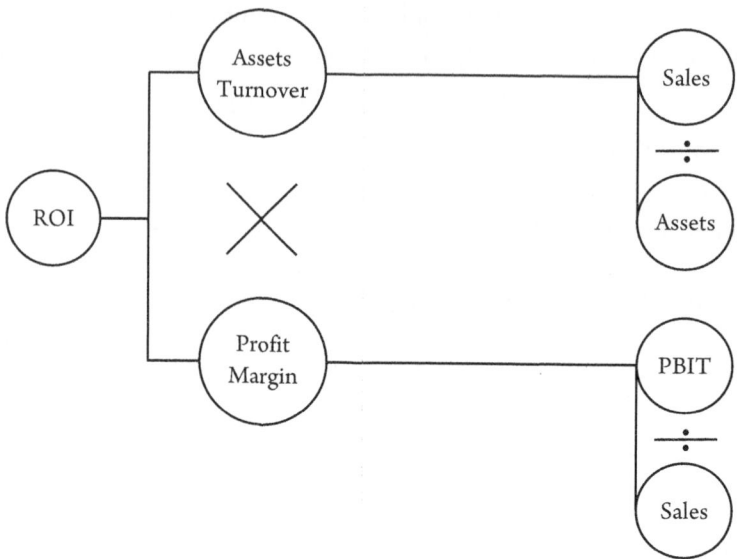

FIGURE 16.2   Return on Investment

utilisation of assets without increasing the latter's value. Non-moving assets could be removed without affecting sales. Both will have the effect of increasing the turnover of assets and hence, ROI.

The ROI matches the operating profit with the assets which earn this profit. Efficient utilisation of assets will ensure a relatively high return, while less efficient use will show a low return. A 12 per cent ROI is reasonable. A lower ratio will call for thorough investigation. A low ROI with a highly geared capital structure may keep an entrepreneur happy (because earning per share will be high), but a banker would question its veracity because at times of shortage of credit the highly geared capital structure may turn against the unit itself. A banker should also wonder why with a ROI of less that 12 per cent an entrepreneur is in business at all, because the same money, if invested in gilt-edged security, will earn a similar income. It is also a pointer to the inefficient use of scarce economic resources of the nation.

Current Assets–Turnover Ratio

Current assets here mean operating current assets (for a detailed evaluation of this variable see ratios under the head 'Efficiency of Financial Management' in this chapter). The balance sheet of National Industries Limited reveals aggregate operating current assets of Rs 16,133 lakh, from which Rs 43 lakh representing balance in the unclaimed dividend account and Rs 17 lakh representing investments are deducted (see Chapter 10) to arrive at an operating current assets figure of Rs 16,073 lakh. For turnover we should take total sales, gross of excise duty, because it enters into debtors through credit sales. The ratio will be:

$$\frac{Sales}{Operating\ current\ assets} = \frac{53100}{16073} = 3.30$$

This ratio indicates the sales generation capacity or mobility of current assets. If this ratio is falling, it may mean, on the one hand, that in order to hold or expand the market share larger credit is being given to buyers, which may also necessitate holding of a larger inventory. On the other hand, it may also mean that current assets include slow moving, or dead stocks, or bad debtors. The latter situation is of more concern for a banker, but even in the former case a banker must see that the firm is not overtrading in its zeal to expand the market.

Materials Inventory Turnover Ratio

This ratio measures the ability of an enterprise to integrate production and materials planning in such a manner as to hold a minimum inventory of materials in store, because every piece of material held in stock contributes negatively to the fund position and profitability of an enterprise. For National Industries Limited the ratio is calculated as:

$$\frac{Consumption\ of\ raw\ materials}{Inventory\ of\ raw\ materials} = \frac{34990}{7235} = 4.84$$

It terms of the number of days, the company is holding $365/4.84 = 75$ days of consumption in stock, which on the face of it is high. When a substantial part of the materials is imported or when a company has a highly diversified product range, it is likely that it has to carry somewhat larger inventories for fear of stock-outs. If this is not so, then a low turnover ratio can only suggest either poor material planning or simply overtrading in the materials market.

Work-in-progress Inventory Turnover Ratio

We have seen in Chapter 6 that work-in-progress inventory represents the core working capital of a business. As the core working capital cycle is technology given, this particular ratio should remain constant over a technology period. For National Industries Limited, the ratio is calculated as:

$$\frac{Cost\ of\ production}{Work\text{-}in\text{-}progress\ inventory} = \frac{39778}{1432}$$

$$= 27.78\ or\ 13\ days\ (approx.)$$

This ratio is akin to the gross profit ratio, as we discuss later. This ratio should be considered over a period of time. It may increase only gradually during the initial period of steaming off, but after that the ratio should stabilise. A decreasing trend indicates hardening of the operating structure of a business.

Technology Updation Ratio

Although there is a controversy about whether depreciation is a cost for usage of fixed assets or a provision for replacement, there can be no doubt that a firm has to make provisions for replacement of fixed assets. A bulk of the future expenditure should come from accumulation of depreciation over the life of a given asset. This is perhaps one of the reasons why depreciation is allowed as a deduction from profit by income tax authorities. A good management will replace its fixed assets well before they become unserviceable or at a time when a better machine has come into the market making the existing one obsolete. The following ratio indicates whether the management is replacing fixed assets regularly:

$$\frac{Capital\ expenditure}{Depreciation}$$

As fixed assets are generally replaced only after a period, the ratio should also be calculated over a number of years, say for three years. This ratio is essential for a capital-intensive industry, because if proper replacements are not made, a unit might fall sick soon. If at any time this ratio is found to be much less than unity, it is likely that the fixed assets are being run down without replacement: the business is investing the depreciation fund for some other purpose. *A banker should be very cautious about this aspect of a business, because when the unit falls sick because of non-replacement of fixed assets, and hence old technology, it is the banker who has to suffer the most.* The present state of affairs of the jute and cotton textile industries may be due to this reason. For these two industries, the ratio has been much below unity for a long period of time, which escaped the attention of bankers.

However, when a firm depreciates its fixed assets faster by adopting the reducing or double declining method of charging depreciation for reasons of prudence or accounting conservatism, the ratio may fall below unity without implying that the assets are being run down. But if the straight-line method is followed and the ratio falls below unity, it is invariably true that the business is not replacing its fixed assets as and when due, and hence these are being worn out. This is particularly true in times of inflation when the cost of replacement is high and provision of depreciation under the straight-line method is low.

In short, this ratio indicates the level of replacement of assets and hence, the state of technology of a business. We are unable to calculate this ratio for National Industries Limited for want of appropriate data.

Export-Import Ratios

These ratios are given by:

(a) *Export Ratio:* $\dfrac{Export\ sales}{Total\ sales}$

(b) *Import Ratio:* $\dfrac{Imported\ raw\ materials}{Total\ raw\ material\ consumption}$

These two ratios have become very important these days due to growing uncertainty in international trade and exchange rates.

As export and import figures for National Industries Limited are not available, we are unable to calculate these two ratios here, but some explanations are necessary because of their present day importance.

(a) *Export ratio:* Although a high export ratio may be welcomed in view of the present policy of the government, one should remember that it also makes a business vulnerable to the vagaries of the international market and volatile exchange rates. A drop in the international price of a product, a change in fashion, or an adverse movement in the exchange rate may at times, be responsible for even wiping out a business. This ratio is very crucial for export of food items like fish, meat, and milk products. The importing country may suddenly impose a complete ban or lay down stringent health safety conditions for export of these goods; the ban or regulations may be universal or country specific. During the mid-1990s, the entire seafood export industry of India became sick due particularly to such ban/restrictions imposed by the European Union and the US.

When the ratio exceeds 80 per cent, it is time for a firm to modify its business strategy; it may be necessary now to look inward and increase its domestic sales base to at least 30 per cent of it total sales.

Highly leveraged firms in the export business are wiped out faster when the market turns adverse. A bank financing an export-oriented unit should, therefore, consider the net worth position to gauge the ability of a firm to withstand shocks emanating from international markets. The debt–equity ratio should not be more than 2.

(b) *Import ratio:* The import of raw materials suffers from all the vagaries of the international market as mentioned earlier. The import ratio indicates the extent of a firm's dependence on foreign suppliers. Materials could be commodities, semi-finished products, or components of a product manufactured locally. Many units shut down when there is a shortage of critical components of raw materials or consumable spares in the international market. The riskiness of a firm reaches the critical level when the import ratio exceeds 60 per cent. There is a global trend now to develop materials indigenously and/or locate manufacturing facilities in the materials supplying countries not only to save on transport costs but also to ensure uninterrupted supply of materials.

Protection Ratio

This is calculated as:

$$\frac{Domestic \ cost \ of \ the \ product}{\substack{Landed \ cost \ of \ the \ same \ imported \ product \\ (net \ of \ customs \ duty)}}$$

This ratio is very critical for industries, which have hitherto been under a protective umbrella.

Government policies of liberalisation of imports and gradual withdrawal of protection in response to policy guidelines of World Trade Organisation (WTO), the World Bank, and the International Monetary Fund (IMF) have posed a threat to industries under protection. If the ratio is more than 2, a company becomes highly vulnerable to international competition. There are still companies, which are surviving or even doing well at present, thanks to a ban on imports or a high tariff wall, but they could just be washed away once the protection is lifted. This ratio quantifies this threat.

Earning Ratios

We discuss here only three ratios which are of utmost importance to a banker.

Gross Profit Ratio

This is the ratio of gross profit to turnover. By turnover we mean net sales, that is, sales minus excise duty. This ratio is expressed as a percentage. For National Industries Limited the ratio is calculated as:

$$(a) \ \frac{Gross \ Profit}{Net \ Sales} \times 100 = \frac{8781}{47813} \times 100 = 18.36\%$$

This is the standard method of calculation, but a banker can make a further variation for his own use. He may take cost of goods sold instead of sales for arriving at the ratio. This is better, because by taking the cost of goods sold figure, price fluctuations in sales are neutralised to a great extent. This is calculated in the following manner:

$$(b) \ \frac{Gross \ Profit}{Cost \ of \ goods \ sold} \times 100 = \frac{8781}{39032} \times 100 = 22.50\%$$

As the cost of goods sold consists mainly of variable expenses, the gross profit ratio should be more or less stable from year to year. A marginal increase is good, but a variation on the lower side is dangerous. A downward movement in the gross profit ratio suggests that the prices of raw materials and/or the labour cost has/have increased, which cannot be passed over to customers because of competitive market conditions or consumer resistance. Or, that the cost structure of a firm has turned sticky, that is,, more and more variable costs are becoming fixed. *It may be found in some extreme cases that a firm is selling raw materials instead of finished goods and concealing this fact from the banker. This is a sure sign of an impending catastrophe.*

We have already indicated earlier that at times a tricky businessperson might window-dress the gross profit figure by excluding certain items of costs normally chargeable to the manufacturing account. In some cases it has been found that this window-dressing is also done by taking into credit the previous year's sales into the current year's sales, or taking into credit sales contracted in the current year but deliverable only in the following year. Whether this is window-dressing or under-dressing, a banker should be concerned. He should probe deeply into the matter to find out the real cost and true gross profit. The GP ratio is the single most important ratio to judge the operating condition of a business.

Operating Profit Ratio

This is the ratio of operating profit to sales. Here also we take net sales instead of total sales. Like the GP ratio, this is also shown as a percentage. We have already calculated this ratio as a part of ROI, which is repeated as:

$$\frac{Operating\ Profit}{Net\ Sales} \times 100 = \frac{3699}{47813} \times 100 = 7.74\%$$

The ratio for this company is not very encouraging. In case of a trading company, it may be all right, because the margin on trade sales is generally low. A trading company can do with a lower ratio because investment per rupee of sales is also low, indicating a fast turnover of current assets manifested in large volume of sales. But for a manufacturing industry to survive on such a low operating profit ratio, it must have some element of trading in it, or it must have a large volume of sales, which is generally possible in the consumer goods industry. In Chapter 10, while analysing the prime cost we indicated that National Industries Limited is a capital-intensive industrial unit. Therefore, unless the turnover is high giving a high level of absolute total profit, it will not be able to earn a reasonable return on investments. This is the reason for this ratio to be a part of ROI as we have seen earlier.

The other side of the picture is that in some industries, for example, public utilities like electricity, gas, and public transport, return on sales, that is, the operating profit may be very high, but ROI is low because of heavy capital investment. *A banker should understand the nature of the business first to arrive at a definite conclusion.*

Net Profit Ratio

For National Industries Limited the ratio is as:

$$\frac{Net\ Profit}{Net\ Sales} \times 100 = \frac{3222}{47813} \times 100 = 6.74\%\ (approx.)$$

This is a tricky ratio. The operating profit of a company may be low, but it may well cover its operational inefficiency by earning a substantial non-operating income. Shareholders may not always bother, but a banker has to, because he is financing only the productive activity. It is the operating profit ratio which signifies the efficiency of the management, not the net profit ratio. A banker should know the range of the non-operating income and its influence on the total profitability of a business. A banker should compare the net profit ratio with the operating profit ratio to know the extent of the non-operating income.

For National Industries Limited the difference between this ratio and the operating profit ratio is not much. But if for any unit the net profit ratio is significantly higher, it is a concern for a banker. It may be that all his finances are going for investments outside the business, or that a part of the fixed assets has been put on rent. A widening gap between the operating profit ratio and the net profit ratio may suggest that a firm is losing on its main line of business.

Expense Ratio

The other side of earning ratios are expense ratios. All expenses are matched with net sales to bring out the ratios in a percentage form.

(a) Direct Operating Ratio:

$$\frac{Cost\ of\ goods\ sold}{Net\ Sales} \times 100 = \frac{39032}{47813} \times 100 = 81.64\%$$

(b) *Expense Group Ratios:*

　(i) *Administrative Expenses Ratio:*

$$\frac{General\ Admn.\ Exp.\ (excluding\ interest)}{Net\ Sales} \times 100$$

$$= \frac{2474}{47813} \times 100 = 5.18\%$$

　(ii) *Selling Expenses Ratio:*

$$\frac{Selling\ /\ Distribution\ Expenses}{Net\ Sales} \times 100$$

$$= \frac{2874}{47813} \times 100 = 6.01\%$$

　(iii) *Financial Expenses Ratio:*

$$\frac{Interest}{Net\ Sales} \times 100 = \frac{555}{47813} \times 100 = 1.17\%$$

Aggregate of Operating Expense Ratios = 94%

Normally, if the aggregate of operating expenses ratios is deducted from 100, we should get the operating profit ratio, but in this case, it will not match exactly, because an amount of Rs 266 lakh as cash assistance and duty drawback has been added to gross profit, which has increased the operating profit to that extent.

However, the gross profit ratio can be calculated by deducting the direct operating ratio from 100, that is, 100 – 81.64 = 18.36%

Note: *All these groups of expenses for National Industries Limited have been calculated in Chapter 10.*

When expenses are variable or semi-variable in nature, for example, direct operating expenses, the expense ratio remains more or less the same from year to year. Where the expenses group is fixed in nature, the ratio will decline with an increase in sales, and increase with a fall in sales. *The efficiency of the management can be judged by looking at the expense ratios over a period of time. An efficient management keeps the expense ratios declining.*

A banker's eye will obviously be drawn towards the financial expense ratio, because his basic interest is to see whether a firm is in a position to pay interest on borrowed funds. He would like to see whether the level of sales is enough to take care of the cost of finance. In the case of National Industries Limited, it is the composite interest cost on working capital finance and the term loan raised from financial institutions and others. It has generally been observed that a total interest cost exceeding 3 per cent of sales revenue is uneconomical. Although no firm rule can be laid down, generally speaking, interest on bank finance only should not exceed 1.5 per cent of sales. A banker, while considering a proposal for additional working capital finance, should ensure that the additional finance generates sufficient additional sales so that the additional cost of interest remains well within the standard.

In the case of National Industries Limited, the composite financial expense ratio is 1.17 per cent. The following additional ratio can be carved out to know the interest burden on bank finance.

$$\frac{Interest\ on\ bank\ borrowing}{Total\ Sales} \times 100$$

$$= \frac{394}{53100} \times 100 = 0.74\%$$

Here we have used total sales instead of net sales, because payments of excise duty, at times, have to be provided for from current bank finance and secondly, the debtors, which are part of chargeable current assets, include excise duty via full sales value at which invoices are raised.

Tax Incidence Ratio

This ratio is given by: $\dfrac{Indirect\ taxes}{Total\ Sales}$

Indirect taxes include excise duty, sales tax, export duties, octroi etc. These days one of the major components of sales is these taxes. These are also the most volatile since they are subject to frequent changes in government policy. Introduction of excise duty on computer software and sales tax on lease rentals are two such examples. In the case of cigarette companies, indirect taxes alone constitute 60 to 80 per cent of sales. In recent years, some companies engaged in manufacturing cigarette and cosmetics with medical properties faced tremendous financial difficulties due to change in excise rules. Hence, companies having a high tax incidence ratio are vulnerable to the vagaries of fiscal policies. One way to withstand this vulnerability is to diversify into low tax-incidence products, which many such companies are now doing.

EFFICIENCY OF FINANCIAL MANAGEMENT

Debt–Equity Ratio

A finance manager of a company may try to prove to a banker that the total long-term resources of the company not only cover the entire fixed assets, but also contribute reasonably towards current assets, that is, they are well within the norms. But a banker should immediately question the magnitude of the outside loan liability in the long-term funds. The question is even broader; a banker would like to know the extent of the financial stake of the entrepreneurs in the business.

This brings us to the debt–equity ratio. Let us approach the issue with the same example of National Industries Limited. After making appropriations from the profit of 20X7, the fund position is as:

1. Equity: Shareholders' fund   7674
   (net of revaluation reserve)
       Less: Share issue expenses not written-off   25
   (see Chapter 10 for detailed calculation)   7649
2. Debt: Long-term outside liability   1577
                   Total long-term resources   9226

First, we will find out the share of long-term outside liability in the total long-term resources of the company in percentage form:

$$\frac{1577}{9226} \times 100 = 17.10\%$$

The ratio indicates that the outside long-term creditors (debt) have only a 17.10 per cent stake in the long-term resources of the company. On the face of it, this is an extremely favourable situation, most liked by bankers. But it could also be that the company cannot afford to enlarge its loan base because of a low margin of safety as we have seen in Chapter 14.

Let us now evaluate the shareholders' stake (equity) in the long-term resources of the company by the following ratio:

$$\frac{7649}{9226} \times 100 = 82.90\%$$

The implication is quite obvious. The shareholders have the largest stake in the long-term resources of the company.

If we now combine these two ratios, we get what we call the debt–equity ratio. For National Industries Limited this ratio is 17.10 : 82.90, or 1 : 4.84, or 0.20 : 1.

The last form of presentation is more in vogue now.

The higher the debt–equity ratio the lower is the stake of shareholders.

The debt–equity ratio can also be calculated in a rather simple way by comparing the aggregate debt with the equity as:

1577 : 7649 or 0.20 : 1

However, calculating the same in the stages mentioned earlier enables us to understand the relationship of both internal and external resources to the aggregate long-term resources of a business.

Devolution of Debt–Equity Ratio

Since the classical days of credit analysis, the debt–equity ratio has undergone much devolution both with respect to the definition of debt and also its standard. Earlier, various committees recommended gradual relaxation of this ratio, because it was thought that when the country needed more and more entrepreneurial ventures to come up, banks and financial institutions were expected to dilute the debt–equity ratio so that a genuine entrepreneurial venture would not suffer due to lower equity. In fact, financial institutions till some years ago allowed a debt–equity ratio of 3:1 for small-scale industrial units, 2:1 for large- and medium-scale industrial units, and in case of very large-scale industrial units—which though was decided on a case-to-case basis—the ratio was even allowed to go up to 5:1. However, with the liberalisation of the financial sector, that provided a level playing field between the financial and the real sectors of the economy, banks and financial institutions have gradually moved towards lowering the debt–equity ratio to 1.5:1 to fall in line with the global standard.

List of Debts and Equities

Although the financial statements of National Industries Limited do not include many items of debt and equity, and hence we could not have a full list, it will be pertinent here to lay down a list of long-term debts and equities, which are taken into consideration by financial institutions and banks while calculating the debt–equity ratio.

1. Debts
   (a) *Long-term loans*: Include interest-bearing unsecured loans from the government/government agencies/promoters.
   (b) *Debentures*: Convertible debentures are treated as debt until converted into equity, but such debentures should invariably be treated as equity if convertible within one year.
   (c) *Deferred payments*: Include all loans and leases payable over a period of time.
   (d) *Preference shares*: Those due for redemption between 1 and 3 years are treated as part of debt by financial institutions. In case of banks, redeemable preference shares not maturing within 1 year but not exceeding 10 years are treated as part of long-term debt.

2. Equity
   (a) *Ordinary share capital*: Issued and paid up capital.
   (b) *Preference share capital*: Due for redemption after 3 years in case of financial institutions and after 10 years in case of banks. See also (d) above.
   (c) *Premium on issue of shares*: All premiums whether in cash or in kind.
   (d) *Free reserves and surplus*: This should be net of accumulated losses, arrears of depreciation not provided for and miscellaneous expenses not written-off but *including* the debenture redemption reserve and dividend equalisation fund.
   (e) *Amount of central/state subsidy*.
   (f) *Long-term interest-free unsecured loans*: These constitute loans from the government, government agencies (for example, sales tax loans), and promoters. When these loans are subordinated to institutional loans these are treated as quasi equity.

Total Debt–Equity Ratio

We have so far included only long-term outside liabilities in debt. Current liabilities have been kept outside the purview. For an appraisal of term-loan proposals this method of calculating the debt–equity ratio may be useful, but for banks appraising a credit proposal for working capital finance, the concept of debt has to be enlarged to include current liabilities also, because the average level of current liabilities has a dynamic stability as a source of funds. A banker is, therefore, interested to know the overall leverage of a company by calculating the total debt–equity ratio as:

		(Rs in lakh)	
Debt (1)	Long-term outside liability	1577	
(2)	Current liabilities	13256	(Rs 10926 lakh + Rs 730 lakh for proposed dividend + Rs 1600 lakh for taxation)
A.	Total debt	14833	
B.	Equity	7649	

The total debt–equity ratio of National Industries Limited is, therefore, 14833:7649 or 1.94:1. This means that total debt is 94 per cent higher than equity. In other words, equity and total debt have contributed 34 per cent and 66 per cent respectively, towards the total resources of the company. The former is the real margin that the company has provided to the total fund raised by it from various sources.

Let us now compare the two ratios as calculated above:

1. Debt–equity ratio—0.20:1 (long-term debt vs equity)
2. Total debt–equity ratio—1.94:1 (total debt vs. equity)

The second ratio is about 9.7 times greater than the first ratio, which proves at once that the volume of current liabilities is much higher than long-term outside liabilities. The heavy reliance on current liabilities may be due to the company's inability to raise and service long-term loans or the company may just be over-trading (as explained below). Whatever be the reason, pressure on the net working capital is very high.

NET WORKING CAPITAL

The above position will be clearer when we move up and down the balance sheet and deal with all assets and liabilities together. For this purpose, let us recalculate the balance sheet figures *after taking into account various adjustments* of proposed dividends and transfer to reserves made from the profit of the year as shown before.

We have already observed from the fund analysis of the balance sheet made in Chapter 14 that net working capital and net current assets are

		(Rs in lakh)	
A.	Equity (net)		7649
	Add: Long-term liabilities		1577
	Total long-term resources		9226
	Less: Utilisation by long-term assets		6366
	(Net of fictitious assets and revaluation increase)		
	Contribution towards short-term assets or		2860
	Net working capital		
B.	Gross current assets		16116
	Less: Current liabilities before adjustments	10926	
	Provision for taxation made in the year	1600	
	Proposed dividend	730	13256
	Net current assets		2860

Note: We can arrive at the same NWC or NCA figure by calculating from gross figures also.

the same. From an analyst's point of view, this is the contribution of long-term resources towards gross working capital as manifested in aggregate current assets. From a finance manager's point of view, this is the short-term fund available to the company from realisation of current assets after meeting current liabilities. The importance of net working capital is ascribed to the following situations:

When the volume of current assets is equal to the volume of current liabilities and they are maturing for realisation and payment respectively at the same time, a company would be left with no margin of safety in case the realisation of current assets (say debtors) is delayed. In that event, unpaid creditors may snowball upon the firm, forcing it towards liquidation. This is akin to walking on thin ice which may break at any time. In financial terminology, it is overtrading.

However, modern day financial management does not subscribe to the above view fully.

A Situation with Zero Net Working Capital

While normally bankers would not like a zero net working capital situation considering it to be the worst condition of a business as they are traditionally led to believe, it may be just the other way round. A firm maintaining itself with a zero net working capital may as well be an extremely good firm having very good command in the market. We may explain this by way of an example.

For simplicity's sake, let us assume that a firm is engaged in trading activity. Its (cost of) sales per month is Rs 1,000. It makes uniform purchases throughout the year to conform to sales demands but maintains a stock of one month's consumption (that is, cost of sales). All purchases and sales are on credit. Debtors make payments in the month following the sales, while creditors are paid in three months.

Barring the first three months of the first year, the balance sheet of the firm will show the following current assets and current liabilities:

Current Liabilities	Rs	Current Assets	Rs
Trade creditors	3000	Stock	1000
		Debtors (at cost of sales)	1000
		Cash	1000
Total	3000	Total	3000

The firm obviously does not have any net working capital. But can we say that it is in imminent danger? After three months, creditors aggregating Rs 1000 will mature for payment every month against which a matching amount of debtors will be realised. The firm should, therefore, have no difficulty in meeting the claims. But what happens when some of the debtors fail to pay in time? Although we have assumed that the firm has good command in the market, that is, it is operating in a seller's market, occasional failure of debtors is not an unlikely situation. To guard against such eventualities, the firm has already built a cash reserve of Rs 1,000. This sum will enable it to tide over temporary difficulties.

The firm has also been careful in another aspect of the management of current assets. Although as assumed, the firm commands a good influence on its suppliers also who are ready to supply goods according to the sales programme of the firm, and always on three months' credit, it may so happen that some of them may fail to supply goods in time, or there could be a temporary shortage in the market. In such an eventuality also the firm can fall back on the one month's buffer stock that it has already built.

It is clear, therefore, that if this firm can pull its strings carefully, it can manage its business without any net working capital.

Points for Consideration

A lender should not, therefore, be unnecessarily touchy about a zero or low net working capital of a business. Before coming to a definite conclusion, he has to examine the following aspects of a business:

(a) Market standing of the unit.
(b) Composition of current assets.
(c) Maturity classifications of debtors and creditors.
(d) Whether the debtors and creditors are fairly widespread.

We have already discussed the first point. In point (b), we emphasise the importance of cash as a component of current assets. In the earlier example, uncertainty of debtors' realisation is insured against not by another fund source, namely liability, but by another item of current asset, cash. A proper contingency plan will always enable a firm to allocate its current fund into various current assets to optimise risk at a minimum cost—trade credit being the least-cost source of funds.

In points (c) and (d), we intend to stress that both the creditors and debtors should be widely spread and their maturities matched to the advantage of the firm. The old adage that not all the eggs should be put in one basket must be kept in mind. If debtors and creditors are fairly well-dispersed, it is not probable that all debtors will fail to pay at one time, or all creditors will demand payment at the same time or will fail to supply goods in time.

Implicit Credit

The reader must have noticed that in this example we have raised debtors at the cost of goods sold, which does not include either any other cost or the profit. This is a trading firm, which may not have to spend anything on the goods it receives from suppliers. But it has to pay wages. Normally, a month's credit is always available from labourers (though it does not feature in the balance sheet) and even if some repackaging materials are needed to make the product marketable, these could be obtained under the same credit terms from the market. Hence, there would still be no necessity to arrange for net working capital. If the debtors are raised to sale value, say Rs 1,200, the margin of Rs 200 may represent Rs 50 as labour and Rs 150 as profit. The current asset would immediately be raised to Rs 3,200, while the current liability will remain at Rs 3,000. Should there now be a necessity of raising net working capital? Technically speaking, it has already been raised. The margin of Rs 200 comprises implicit credit given by the labourers amounting to Rs 50, and undistributed profit of Rs 150 due to shareholders. As implicit credit given by the labourers is not brought into the books of accounts of the firm, the whole amount of Rs 200 will represent net working capital via a technical increase in net worth. This is a theoretical increase in net working capital. The firm is still doing its business on trade creditors only.

This example is not an extreme situation. Quite a number of monopolistic companies are found to be enjoying such market command. Without, therefore, closing our eyes on any 'worst' net working capital position, we should probe into the matter and examine all relevant aspects mentioned earlier.

Ratio of Net Working Capital to Current Assets and Current Ratio

However, we should not forget that for firms who are not enjoying such market command, the general rule is that net working capital should be positive to finance a portion of the current assets. To judge this aspect, we should now calculate two important ratios for National Industries Limited with the help of the following figures:

Current assets   Rs 16073 lakh   Net of unclaimed
Current liabilities   Rs 13213 lakh   dividend
Net working capital   Rs   2860 lakh

(a) *Net Working Capital to Current Assets*

This ratio for National Industries Limited is as:

$$\frac{Net\ Working\ Capital}{Current\ assets} \times 100 = \frac{2860}{16073} \times 100 = 18\%$$

The ratio indicates that only 18 per cent of current assets are financed from long-term resources of the company, the remaining 82 per cent being provided by creditors. Normally this is not a very enviable situation for a banker. On the face of it, for every Rs 100 realised by the company it has to pay out as much as Rs 82 to meet the creditors—only Rs 18 is left as a margin. Unless, therefore, the company's creditors are well spaced, as mentioned earlier, the company would find it difficult to run the operations smoothly. It would obviously demand more and more bank finance. In order to know the exact position it would be necessary to find out the maturity periods of the short-term assets and liabilities as mentioned earlier and draw up a detailed cash flow statement.

Firms that thrive on this kind of financial management will have a high level of trade creditors against a comparatively low level of debtors at any point of time. The example of National Industries Limited proves this point. Its trade creditors are Rs 7,326 lakh while debtors are only Rs 2,180 lakh against a closing stock of Rs 12,472 lakh. It is obvious that the company is living largely on the intrinsic funds provided by creditors.

(b) *Current Ratio*

This ratio is the generalised form of the last ratio. It is the ratio of current assets to current liabilities. In the case of National Industries Limited it can be calculated as:

16073:13213 or 1.22:1

This means that for every Rs 1.22 collected by the company, Re 1 is paid out to meet the creditors, leaving only 22 paise for the day-to-day operations of the company. This leftover of 22 paise is the net working capital. If we calculate its percentage on Rs 1.22, we once again obtain the figure of 18 per cent, which is the ratio of net working capital to current assets as shown earlier.

On the face of it, this small current ratio may toll a danger signal for the company. It may be a borderline case of an impending liquidity crisis. However, for National Industries Limited, this is still not a problem probably because of the longer maturity of creditors and quick realisation of debtors.

The Ideal Current Ratio?

Analysts for long regarded a current ratio of 2:1 as ideal, which means a net working capital of 50 per cent on current assets. The presumption was that for every two rupees collected by a business, one rupee went for discharging the current liabilities, leaving another rupee as the margin of safety. But undesirable composition and slow realisability of current assets may make a very high current ratio meaningless. If turnover of stocks and debtors is low, then a high level of current ratio endangers liquidity, rather than easing it. If all sales are converted into debtors of long maturity, the current ratio would obviously be high. The author, in his capacity as a consultant of a large travel agency, found that its current ratio was as high as 40. The firm was surviving only by continuous influx of funds from its holding company. On the other hand, a low current ratio, as in the case of National Industries Limited, with a high turnover of debtors and low turnover of creditors, may well be a viable one though it is much below the standard. It is, therefore, necessary to consider any current ratio not in isolation, but along with the debtors' and creditors' velocity, as we discuss later in this chapter.

Some analysts calculate another liquidity ratio, which is called the quick ratio. This is done by comparing relatively more liquid current assets, like debtors and cash, with impending current liabilities, like trade and expense creditors and dividend payable to know whether the company is in a position to meet immediate liabilities as and when they fall due. This ratio is primarily useful for the finance manager of a company, who calculates it a number of times during a year when he has to discharge liabilities falling due for payment within a short period, say in the ensuing month. However, this ratio becomes important to a banker at the time of declaring a dividend by the company, because a low quick ratio at such a point of time would definitely force the company to fall back upon the bank for ready cash.

TREATMENT OF CONTINGENT LIABILITIES

While evaluating a current ratio, a banker should evaluate contingent liabilities also, which may include commitments for capital expenditure and bills discounted with banks. These figures are available from the published balance sheet of a company in the form of footnotes.

A commitment for capital expenditure has to be funded. A banker should enquire how a company plans to fund this expenditure. If long-term funds have not been arranged, there will be an erosion of current assets and consequently a diversion of funds. When, however, long-term funds have already been arranged, this will be reflected in cash. In such a situation a current ratio calculated without taking into consideration the contingent liability relating to capital expenditure will lead to a wrong conclusion.

When a company raises bills on its debtors, the outstanding balance in the latter is reduced to the debit of the bills receivable account. When these bills are discounted with a bank, this account also gets adjusted to the debit of the cash/bank account. In the books of accounts of the *bank*, a bills purchased account appears besides the cash credit account of the company. But no such account as a bills discounted account appears in the books of the *company*. In such situations, the debtors' account appearing in the body of the balance sheet of the company would not reflect the true level of debtors. Unlike 'without recourse' full factoring, discounting of bills is not encashment of debtors. If a bill is returned unpaid, the bank account is reduced by the debit entry made by the bank.

The liability of a company with respect to bills discounted with a bank continues till these bills are paid. This appears as a contingent liability below the balance sheet of a company. A banker can evaluate this liability by examining the bills purchased account of a company. He will first make an estimate of the percentage of bills returned unpaid in a particular year, and then calculate how much of the contingent liability on the bills discounted would mature into a real liability. Only after that should he calculate the current or quick ratio.

Diversion Ratio

This is a ratio of net working capital to the working capital gap. The working capital gap should be calculated before accounting for bank advance on working capital. For National Industries Limited it is computed as:

	(Rs in lakh)
Current assets	16073
Less: Current liabilities	11092
Working capital gap	4981
Financed by:	
Bank (cash credit account)	2121
Net working capital from long-term sources	2860
	4981

The ratio will, therefore, be:

$$\frac{Net\ Working\ Capital}{Working\ Capital\ Gap} \times 100 = \frac{2860}{4981} \times 100 = 57.42\%$$

On the face of it, this ratio appears to be very sound. The borrower's dependence on bank finance is at a low level. This ratio, however, is to be read with the ratio of net working capital to current assets. We have found that the borrower is financing a large portion of its current assets from trade creditors. As the borrower has a good command over the suppliers in demanding larger credit from them, he can keep his working capital gap at a low level resulting in a higher diversion ratio. This can be a case of overtrading as we have already discussed. The case would have been far more dangerous if the value of this ratio was low, or if it was showing a declining trend simultaneously with a low or declining net working capital to current assets ratio. It would have been a case of diversion of current funds and a lowering down of the stake of the borrower. The diversion can take any of the following forms:

(a) Investment of current funds in long-term assets.
(b) Current funds used to finance losses.
(c) Pure diversion of funds from out of the business by over-invoicing of raw materials or by booking salaries and wages for non-existent employees.

Although this year, National Industries Limited has transferred 55 per cent of its profit-after-tax

to reserves raising the total figure to Rs 4753 lakh, we do not know what the rates of transfer in earlier years were. It might be that they were low in earlier years. *The existence of a revaluation reserve in the balance sheet makes us uneasy.* If the company was regularly transferring a reasonable amount of profit to general reserves, what was the necessity of raising the revaluation reserve in its books of accounts? A banker must raise these questions.

The company may claim that as it is in the consumer electronics goods industry, its current assets would ordinarily be high. But we find that they are a little too high—almost double the fixed assets—and the bulk of the current assets are in stock, which itself constitutes one and a half times the fixed assets. While agreeing that companies having such a high market command can hold on with a low net working capital and can afford to pay high dividends without building up adequate reserves, it must be pointed out that these companies are also prone to overtrading as we have already indicated. The low stock turnover ratio may be a pointer to this. *It is a market tautology that no company can remain monopolistic for all times to come.* Some day it would face competition, as many giant consumer goods industries are facing now. Nirma's competition to Hindustan Lever (now Hindustan Unilever) is an eye-opener. Although market credit could still be available as demanded, a prudent management should build up its permanent resources systematically. Shareholders can be satisfied by paying high dividends as by well as issue of bonus shares.

As discussed earlier, this particular ratio is very important to a banker to know whether there has been diversion or loss of current funds of a firm. If this ratio is falling over a period, it is a signal that a firm is diverting current funds. *It may happen even in the face of increasing sales or even a stable gross profit ratio. A banker is warned not to be carried away by these two glowing aspects of the business. Behind them may be hidden a bad or dishonest financial management.*

Finished Goods Stock Turnover Ratio

This ratio measures the rate of movement or velocity of the finished goods inventory.

The ratio for National Industries Limited is calculated as:

$$\frac{Cost\ of\ goods\ sold}{Finished\ goods\ inventory}\ Or = \frac{39032}{3805} = 10.25$$

The ratio can be expressed in number of days also. That is, 365/10.25 = 35 days. It is moderately good for an enterprise which is engaged in consumer electronics.

For the trade and consumer goods industry, the ratio should generally be much higher than other industries. If the ratio falls over time, then the first presumption is that there is a glut in the market. It may suggest a prolonged recession. However, if the industry or the economy is not suffering from recession, and the ratio for the unit is still falling, it indicates that the unit is losing in competition, probably due to high marginal costs and/or low quality of goods. If this ratio, though low but is not very much above the past years' average, then it may be the general nature of the business.

Debtors–Turnover Ratio

Similar to the finished goods stock turnover ratio, this ratio also measures the rate at which debtors are converted into cash. This is calculated as:

$$\frac{Total\ Sales}{Trade\ debtors^3} = \frac{Rs\ 53100\ lakh}{Rs\ 2180\ lakh}$$
$$= 24.36\ or\ 365/24.36 = 15\ days\ (approx.)$$

[3] We have taken net debtors here after provision of bad debt, so that the true velocity in reflected. Net debtors is the true level of debtors.

The value of this ratio suggests that in National Industries Limited debtors turn over approximately 24 times in a year. Assuming that sales are made uniformly throughout the year, per month sales will be approximately Rs 4,425 lakh. As the turnover ratio is 24, we can say that 50 per cent (or Rs 2,212 lakh) of monthly sales is realised approximately in the same month, and the balance is carried over to the next month. This process continues from month to month, which is reflected in the balance sheet as on any date.

The debtors velocity of 24 converted to number of days holding is 15, which means that the company has to carry 15 days of unpaid sales throughout the year. This low holding of debtors suggests that the company's products are in high demand. The company may be operating in a seller's market, enjoying a very good command over its buyers.

Creditors–Turnover Ratio

This is given by:

$$\frac{Purchases}{Trade\ Creditors} = \frac{Rs\ 35611\ lakh}{Rs\ 7326\ lakh}$$
$$= 4.86\ or\ 365/4.86 = 75\ days$$

If purchases are made uniformly throughout the year, then for every month purchases will be Rs 2,968 lakh, which the company need not have to pay until the 76th day. In the meantime, the company can buy further goods on the same credit terms, so that it will have an average level of creditors for 75 days of purchases.

During this period of 75 days, the company would have realised total sales of:

$$\frac{(2212 \times 75)}{15} = Rs\ 11060\ lakh$$

On the 76th day it has to pay only Rs 7,326 lakh to trade creditors, leaving a surplus cash of

Rs 3,734 lakh, which can take care of other working capital requirements. If the company's requirements of stock were equal to the level of credit purchases available, namely Rs 7,326 lakh, then it would not need any working capital finance from a bank. However, in the case of National Industries Limited the level of stock is Rs 12,472 lakh; 60 per cent of this is financed by trade creditors.

Comparisons of these two ratios can very well evolve into a new ratio as is now shown.

Market Command Ratio

This is calculated as the ratio of debtors' velocity to creditors' velocity. For National Industries Limited the two velocities as calculated above are repeated as:

Creditors' velocity	=	75 days
Debtors' velocity	=	15 days

Hence, the ratio between the two will be 75:15 or 5:1

The higher the ratio, the better it is for a company. It at once indicates the position of a company at both ends of the market. A high ratio, such as this one, suggests that a company is not only a near-monopoly seller, but a monopsonic buyer as well. This is the level of command enjoyed by the company as both a buyer and a seller. This is the reason why it is termed as the market command ratio.

EFFICIENCY OF DEBT-SERVICE MANAGEMENT

All lending institutions, including banks are anxious to know whether:

(a) The profit of a borrowing firm is enough to cover not only the interest payment, it is also sufficient to provide a reasonable cushion against future uncertainty.

(b) The profit is also sufficient to provide enough coverage for repayment obligations.

(c) The assets of the firm provides adequate security for the loans sanctioned.

The following ratios enable a lender to judge these three aspects of lending.

Interest Cover Ratio

For National Industries Limited the ratio is as follows:

$$\frac{Profit\ before\ depreciation,\ interest\ and\ tax\ (PBDIT)}{Annual\ interest\ obligation}$$
$$=\frac{3222+530+555+3}{555}=7.76$$

We have taken PBDIT because in the first place we want to know how many times the interest payment could be covered by cash profit, and secondly tax is not considered because interest is a deductible expense under the Income Tax Act. The last figure in the numerator (Rs 3 lakh) represents share issue expenses that have been written off. It is a non-cash item like depreciation.

In case of a manufacturing firm, a coverage of 3 is a reasonable standard. The high ratio of National Industries Limited is indicative of the fact that its reliance on interest-bearing borrowed funds is very low. We have already seen that the company depends more on its net worth and free trade credit. If this is not the case for a firm, then a high interest cover ratio will generally indicate a risk-averse management. On the contrary, a very low ratio, say below 2, may indicate a risk-prone management with a highly-geared capital structure.

Debt–Service Coverage Ratio

For National Industries Limited we calculate the ratio as:

$$\frac{\text{Profit after tax + interest + depreciation + other non-cash expenses}}{\text{Interest + annual repayments of term loans}} = \frac{(3222 - 1600) + 555 + 471 + 3}{555 + 150 \text{ (assumed)}} = 3.76$$

We have assumed Rs 150 lakh to be the annual repayment of term loans, because nothing is mentioned in the trial balance of the company as given in Chapter 10. It is preferable to include annual repayment of fixed deposits also in debt obligations to know the overall debt-service capacity of a borrower.

The standard ratio is 1.5. In case of the present company the ratio is quite high for reasons mentioned above. *If the ratio is above 1 but below 1.5, and the firm is operationally viable, then a lender need not reject the proposal outright. Suitable spacing of the repayment period, thereby lowering the annual repayment obligations, may raise the ratio and make the proposal financially viable.* If, however, the ratio is one or less than that, then the company may just be 'thriving on balance'. It is not in a position to either pay dividend or accumulate reserves; financial erosion may already be there. The declining trend in the ratio may indicate an overly ambitious expansion. A banker should cry a halt at some stage and ask the firm to consolidate its position. A persistently low ratio indicates heavy repayment obligations, which the business is at pains to meet. It may soon eat into short-term funds causing persistent irregularity in the working capital finance account. Alternatively, the firm might be borrowing continuously to repay the current obligations and thus entering into a debt trap. The bank should, therefore, ask the borrower to renegotiate with the lending institutions for lengthening the repayment period to reduce the instalment burden.

We have calculated the debt–service coverage ratio by taking after-tax profit. Some analysts want to take before-tax profit, because they hold that service coverage should be seen as the ability of the firm to meet debt obligations before such tax shields as depreciation, other non-cash charges, and various incentive-deductions are applied to reduce the taxable profit. There is definitely some strength in this argument, and in case of some public corporations, the government (as the owner) does accept pre-tax profit as the basis for calculating this ratio, but for a banker, taxation is routine and unavoidable for a business, and hence he must base this ratio on after-tax profit.

Priority Obligation Ratio

Although the debt-service coverage ratio has been in use for a long time to measure the debt-service capacity of an enterprise, it often fails to serve its purpose because the numerator variable, PBDIT, does not always contain sufficient cash to discharge the obligations. It is cash alone, not profit, by which to discharge obligations. The reason behind this is that profit may contain working capital items like debtors and inventories. The profit of a firm will not be affected whether sales are made in cash or on credit, but the cash position of the firm will definitely be affected by the mode of sales. It is necessary, therefore, to prepare an operating cash flow statement of an enterprise to measure its ability to discharge priority obligations, which include payment of interest, lease rentals, repayment of term loans and fixed deposits, and redemption of debentures.

In addition to profit and loss and balance sheet figures given in Chapters 10 and 11, balances of certain working capital items are given below to calculate the incremental blockage of cash in the year under consideration.

(Rs in lakh)

Debtors		Creditors (including bills payable)	
Closing balance	2180	Closing balance	7326
Less: Opening balance	1244	Less: Opening balance	6305
Increase in debtors	936	Increase in creditors	1021

Raw materials inventory		Opening cash and bank balance	139
Closing balance	7235		
Less: Opening balance	6614		
Increase in raw materials inventories	621		

All other figures are taken from the chapters mentioned earlier to draw up the operating cash flow statement of National Industries Limited in Table 16.5.

Priority obligations remaining the same as in the case of the debt-service coverage ratio, we can now calculate the priority obligation ratio of National Industries Limited:

$$\frac{Net\ operating\ cash\ flow}{Priority\ obligations} = \frac{2420}{705} = 3.43$$

This ratio should at least be 1.5 to provide a reasonable cushion against sudden lengthening of the working capital cycle. The priority obligation ratio is a vastly superior ratio than the debt-service coverage ratio because profit is often a matter of opinion, it can be 'manufactured' also, but cash is the real thing.[4]

[4] For details, see Bhattacharya, Hrishikes, *Total Management by Ratios—An Analytic Approach to Management Control and stock Market Valuations*, 2nd edition Sage Publications India (P) Ltd., New Delhi, 2007.

Assets–Margin Ratio

This ratio indicates the debt capacity of the fixed assets of an enterprise. For National Industries Limited we calculate the ratio as follows:

$$\frac{Fixed\ assets - Term\ loans}{Fixed\ assets} = \frac{5608-661}{5608} \times 100 = 88.20\%$$

Fixed assets include capital work-in-progress but exclude profit on revaluation taken to reserve. Term loans exclude loans from the parent company and security deposits, because these may not have any charge on fixed assets.

TABLE 16.5   Operating Cash Flow Statement of National Industries Ltd. for 20X7

(Rs in lakh)

Gross sales		53100
Cash assistance and duty drawback		266
		53366
Less: Increase in sundry debtors		936
A: Operating cash inflows		52430
Consumption of raw materials		34990
Other manufacturing expenses (excluding depreciation)		3206
Excise duty		5287
General administrative expenses (excluding depreciation and share issue expenses written-off)		2412
Selling and marketing expenses		2874
Income tax		1600
		50369
Add: Increase in raw materials inventory	621	
Add: Increase in loans and advances (pre-paid expenses)	180	801
		51170
Less: Increase in creditors (including bills payable)		1021
		50149
Less: Opening cash and bank balance		139
B. Operating cash outflows		50010
C. Net operating cash flows (A–B)		2420

Normally, a 50 per cent margin is considered sufficient for a lender to feel secure. This ratio also indicates the reserve borrowing capacity of a company, to which it can turn in case of a financial crisis. For the present company, the reserve capacity is $(88.20 - 50) = 38.2$ per cent. That is, the company has the reserve strength to borrow against $[(5608 \times 50)/100] - 661 = 2143$ lakh of free assets in case of necessity. A company doing overtrading should have a high assets margin to protect itself against sudden adverse movements in the market. This ratio should be compared with the debt–equity ratio of an enterprise. It is often found that an enterprise has a low debt–equity ratio, but no asset margin left to withstand shocks.

STANDARDS OF COMPARISON

Just as no absolute figure is meaningful in isolation, so also no ratio is. A 2:1 current ratio may not itself speak anything of a business unless we have in mind some standards to compare. Since a banker is not doing the business of a borrower, he should have before him certain standards of ratios with which to compare the ratios revealed by a borrower's business. Standards can be developed in either of the following three ways or by a combination of all.

Firm's Past Standards

These are most readily available and most frequently used. A firm generates its own data, which are consistent in method of accounting and approach, and hence comparison is also consistent. It is comparing the 'like with the like'. In the absence of any inter-firm standards, a banker has to rely most often on the internal standards of a firm whose credit proposal is being assessed. However, while doing so he should guard against certain pitfalls in using the internal standards.

1. The past standards of a firm may not be very meaningful when these are established from a few years' data only. Comparison with past standards in such a case may give rise to complacency. For example, a 100 per cent increase in sales over the past year, may give misleading information where the past year may just be the first year of the business with a small sales base.

2. A perfectly satisfactory standard in the past may not be valid now due to a change in technology. An improvement over the past internal standards may conceal the fact that a unit is losing out to its competitors who might already have improved their performance by adopting a new technology in production methods.

3. There may be an environmental change in the economy resulting in either a general fall or rise in the economic activity, which may render the past standards of a firm useless.

4. An inflationary price increase may suppress a real fall in certain ratios. In case of depression, the converse may also happen.

Budgetary Standards

This is better than an internal ratio standard, as it takes into account changes in the economy, the state of technology, and also the value of money. But unfortunately a budget cannot be prepared as objectively as it should. Subjective influences of individuals creep into the fixation of budgetary standards. It is also found to be grossly influenced by what had happened in the past. Moreover, people in the management may try to lower targets so that they can show better performance. Although forecasts and projections are fallible, a banker can infuse objectivity by inviting a dialogue with the borrower and help the latter in setting realistic standards of ratios which would be mutually useful to both.

External Standards

Comparing ratios with those of other firms has the following advantages over the above two standards:

1. When it is found that past standards of a firm are poor, and therefore not good for comparison, standards derived from a reasonably wide and representative sample of other firms can be used. After all, the objective is to examine how a particular unit is performing in comparison to the others in the market.
2. Comparison of firm-level ratios with those of the industry over similar economic and technological periods can take care of aberrations caused by using only internal standards.
3. The subjective elements of budget preparation and the fallibility of future forecasts can be avoided to a large extent by comparing the performance of a firm with external standards.

These three advantages, however, give rise to the following two problems:

(a) *Standards of similarities* may encompass various aspects of a business, namely the product, the size, and also the location. One may hold that standards should be established for firms manufacturing the same product because in that case only is comparison possible in accordance with principle of 'like with like'. But universal ratios—the most important of them being return on investment—should not only be compared with firms producing the same goods, but also firms engaged in other activities, because this may indicate the desirability or otherwise of diversification. As against this, a ratio peculiar to a particular product line, for example, winding rate of compressor units per hour per employee can be compared with the standard derived from other compressor manufacturing units.

Some analysts claim that size is not a major consideration for deciding on inter-firm standards. Sizes of firms do not have any significant or measurable effect on many ratios. This may appear to be surprising at first sight, but if we go a little deeper into the matter, we will find that size affects both the numerator and the denominator of a ratio, and hence it ultimately cancels out its own effect.

(b) *Sources of information* are the biggest problem for using inter-firm standards. In advanced countries there are many specialised agencies, which do this job and their services are also available cheaply, but in India there are only a few agencies which do this job and that too only intermittently. The Tandon Committee undertook this study for certain selected industries, but it ended with the submission of its report. The RBI occasionally undertakes this job, but not regularly. The Centre for Monitoring of Indian Economy and Tata Services Limited are more or less regular in publishing selected industry-wise ratios. Various stock exchanges also publish selected industry-wise ratios. These standards can be internalised for use of credit departments of banks.

Published sources of information are cheap and readily available when published, but they suffer from a number of disadvantages:

(a) The information available in published accounts is often arrived at in different ways by different firms, hence making it incomparable to a great extent.

(b) Published information is available after the lapse of a considerable period of time, which reduces its relevance to the current situations.

(c) Published accounts give only period-end figures, which may suffer from window-dressing.

Although external standards suffer from all the disadvantages mentioned earlier, a banker handling a credit portfolio gains much additional information about the actual operating condition of a particular business vis-à-vis the industry.

Concluding Remarks

In concluding our discussion on ratio analysis, we would like to mention that some researchers have found that in diagnosing the health of a business, ratios derived from the profit and loss account of a firm are more reliable than those derived from the balance sheet. The reason ascribed to this finding is that the health and status of a business can be better judged by ratios drawn from variables valued at current prices, and since the profit and loss account figures are always nearer to current prices, ratios drawn from them are more reliable than ratios drawn from balance sheets, which are mostly recorded in historical rupees. While there exists strong theoretical support behind this finding, by the same argument it can be said that certain balance sheet variables like current assets and current liabilities are also valued closer to current prices, hence ratios drawn from them should be as good as those drawn from income and expenditure variables. The controversy may continue for some time to come. What is important for an analyst is to remember that if the composition of concerned variables are carefully analysed and properly valued, whether at current cost or historical cost, and the ratios are considered over a period of time to discern the trend, he will definitely get a good insight into the state of affairs of a business.

Decision of character will often give to an inferior mind command over a superior.

—W. Writ

17 Project Appraisal
Methods and Techniques

INTRODUCTION

The major approach of every treatise on project appraisal is to present alternative choices of investment proposals to the decision maker. When the choice is finally made, a particular proposal out of the alternatives proposed is presented to a financial institution or bank for consideration.

In selecting a project, an entrepreneur has to strike a balance between profitability and risk and select a proposal where there is a quick return of shareholders' funds at minimum risk. This is not an easy task. In order to help the management in resolving this perennial contradiction of business, a number of techniques have been developed. With the help of these techniques, analysts draw up alternative project proposals and aid the management in selecting the best among them.

A credit appraiser's approach is different because his problem is also somewhat different. It is not his job to suggest alternative projects. He has to assess the creditability of the project presented to him, and also its bankability. Credit risk is not the same as financial risk. A project may be financially viable, but not creditworthy. This is the reason why a credit appraiser gives much importance to net working capital, while to a

borrower this is a bother which reduces the rate of return per share.

A credit appraiser may use the same concepts as used by a borrower to arrive at an investment decision, but with a different objective in mind. He modifies some of the techniques to suit his requirements.

BANKS' INVOLVEMENT IN PROJECT FINANCING

Before nationalisation of banks, term financing was a domain almost exclusively reserved for term lending institutions. Banks restricted themselves to short-term financing. But after nationalisation, banks gradually entered into the field of term financing. The share of term loans in the advances portfolios of commercial banks has increased substantially during the last 30 years.

Although term loan portfolios of banks are on an increase, it is unfortunate that sufficient expertise is yet to develop in banks to handle project financing. Hitherto, banks were used to relying upon assessments made by financial institutions about the viability of a project, and restricted themselves to assessing the working capital requirement only. Project appraisal takes a total view; working capital assessment is only a part of it. Even under the modified system of cash credit lending, need-based financing can be ensured only if bankers take a total view of a business.

Besides laying down cash, banks and financial institutions help borrowers acquire fixed assets by undertaking deferred payment guarantees or acceptance limits on deferred terms. These are treated at par with term loans, and hence require a full-scale appraisal of a project.

POLICY CHANGES

During the past few decades the RBI has gradually liberalised its policy to encourage banks to extend term loans for acquisition of fixed assets, as can be seen from many of its directives during this period. The circular of 8 July 1985 was a landmark in this direction. It enabled banks to take up project financing on a bigger scale. The RBI empowered banks to grant term loans to industrial borrowers for acquisition of fixed assets without prior authorisation up to the cut-off point of Rs 1 crore. This was independent of working capital limits available to borrowers, irrespective of whether a borrower was covered under the credit authorisation scheme for its working capital or not. For arriving at this cut-off point, the aggregate of the balances outstanding in the existing term loans and the balances outstanding under deferred payment guarantees or the acceptance limit on deferred terms were taken into account.

The above liberalisation came on top of a number of measures already taken by both the central and state governments, and also public financial institutions, particularly for setting up industrial projects in backward areas. Under the central subsidy scheme, industrial units set up in notified backward areas were eligible for non-refundable subsidy up to 15 per cent of the fixed capital investment, or Rs 15 lakh, whichever was lower. Industrial projects located in certain hilly regions were also eligible for a transport subsidy under the central government transport subsidy scheme. The subsidy was restricted to 50 per cent of the transport cost of raw materials and finished goods within specified points. Financial institutions extended concessions for projects established in backward areas with respect to margin requirements and interest rates. Banks and financial institutions also relaxed debt–equity ratio norms for giant projects, especially in the joint sector and projects set up by qualified entrepreneurs. The Controller of Capital Issues (now defunct) permitted a debt–equity ratio up to 4:1 with respect to capital-intensive industries like cement and fertilisers.

Many of these subsidies are now either withdrawn or substantially modified and/or not likely to continue for long during the current phase of liberalisation. The present move is towards providing a level playing field across projects and their locations for productive allocation of lendable resources as in a market-driven economy, and also across banks and financial institutions to take part as equals in such competitive processes. To this end, the RBI announced major policy changes during 1993–95. The first such change was brought out by linking the banks' participation in term loans to quantum instead of cost of the project. Simultaneously, banks were allowed to lend up to Rs 50 crore individually and up to Rs 200 crore collectively from the banking system. Later on, the individual ceiling of Rs 50 crore was withdrawn, and the limit of loans from the banking system as a whole was raised to Rs 500 crore for each project inclusive of non-fund-based facilities carrying a weight of 50 per cent. For power generation projects, the limit was raised to Rs 1,000 crore inclusive of fund and non-fund-based facilities—both carrying 100 per cent weightage, but the former was limited to Rs 400 core only. This short history tells us that the RBI was gradually moving away from a directed regime to full deregulation of project financing by banks.

Non-Financial Appraisal

Expansion Project (existing product)

A proposal for a term loan may come either for installation of a new project, or for expansion of existing capacity. In the latter case, the task of a credit appraiser becomes easier because he has before him the performance of the company, which enables him to discern valuable indications about its future performance. The need for expansion may arise due to pressure of demand for the products of a company. If there is delay in forecasting additional demand, or banks and financial institutions take longer than the usual time for sanctioning the proposal, it may be found that others have already expanded their capacity to the disadvantage of the borrower.

When a credit appraiser receives an expansion proposal, he should first find out the existing demand situation of the product of the borrower, and the relative position of the competitors. If the forecasting data are dated, he may ask for a fresh market study.

New Project New Product

In case of a new project for a new product, the problems are substantially different. A 'new product' can be of different types:

(a) *The product is new to the company, but it already exists in the market.* Either a company desires to enter into the product market to find a place for itself by cutting into the market share of other players, or it intends to participate in the rising demand of the product, or both. A majority of the new projects come under this type. In appraising a project of this nature, the first problem that an appraiser faces is in the analysis of market research and forecasting data submitted by the prospective borrower.

Although the lender may not be an expert in market research, he is expected to at least evaluate the information put forward in such reports. He should be moderately well-informed about the general demand situation of a product. Industry-wise or even product-wise data are available from published sources.[1] A systematic study of these data and other related information available from published sources will enable him to keep himself abreast of the latest developments in product markets. It will also enable him to locate the gaps in the market research data submitted by the applicant company.

The principal focus of any market research report is on estimating the demand-supply gap of the product, which ultimately forms the basis of any project report. As this is the most crucial part of the project, the lender would have to critically evaluate the claim made by the borrower in his project report. Let us take an example.

The market research report for product X reveals the following information (figures may be in units or amounts):

Case I Present demand for the product: 50,000
Present market size of the product: 25,000
(that is, present supply)

Case II Present demand for the product: 50,000 but expected to grow @ 10% per annum during the next three years.
Present market size of the product: 25,000
(that is, present supply)

---

[1] For example, the *Annual Survey of Industries,* published by the Government of India; publications of the Centre for Monitoring Indian Economy; the Reserve Bank of India Bulletin, and the Survey of Industries published annually by *The Hindu* etc.

Case I

In this case the demand for the product exceeds supply by 50 per cent, which we may denote as $d = 0.50$. When such a supply gap exists in the market, the industry manufacturing the product must be growing at a rate which will cover up the gap within a period of, say three years (which should normally be the period in a competitive economy where market information is available to the participants uniformly). The supply gap will, therefore, be reflected in the growth rate of the industry. The expected growth rate of the industry manufacturing the product can be calculated by the following formula:

$$d(1 + r)^n = 1$$

where,
1. 'd' is the supply gap as explained above, which in the present case is 0.5.
2. 'r' is the expected rate of growth (to be derived) of the industry.
3. 'n' is the period within which the supply gap is expected to be met, which in the present case is three years.

Putting respective values in this equation, we get the following:

$$0.5 (1 + r)^3 = 1$$

or,	$\log 0.5 + 3 \log (1 + r) = \log 1$	
or,	$-0.30103 + 3 \log (1 + r) = 0$	
or,	$3 \log (1 + r)$	$= 0.30103$
or,	$\log (1 + r)$	$= 0.100343$
or,	$1 + r$	$= \text{Antilog } 0.100343$
or,	$1 + r$	$= 1.26$
or,	r	$= 0.26 \text{ or } 26\%$

Hence, if the market research report estimates a supply gap of 50 per cent, the product-industry should grow @ 26 per cent per annum. If the actual rate of growth of the industry deviates substantially from the expected rate of growth, the lender should point out the discrepancy to the prospective borrower and ask him to explain the position and recast the project report, if necessary.

Case II

Here the demand for the product is growing @ 10 per cent per annum, which we denote as $g = 0.10$. The above formula can now be modified as below to determine the required rate of growth (r):

$$d(1 + r)^n = (1 + g)^n$$

Putting respective values in the above equation, we get the following:

$$0.5 (1 + r)^3 = (1 + 0.10)^3$$
$$\text{or Log } 0.5 + 3 \log (1 + r) = 3 \log 1.10$$

Solving the above equation, we obtain $r = 0.386$ or 38.6 per cent. That is, under the given supply gap and the expected rate of increase in demand, the industry should reflect a growth rate of 38.6 per cent per annum.

We have assumed $n = 3$ years, which is likely to be the case as indicated earlier. Normally, the expected time horizon is mentioned in the market research report. In its absence, it should be settled by a discussion with the borrower, and his consultant who prepared the report. Similar analysis can be done for an expansion project of an existing product, as mentioned at the beginning of this section.

(b) *The product is new to the domestic market, but established in markets abroad.* The number of such products has been increasing in India in recent times with the liberalisation of the economy. Such products can be totally new in the domestic market, for example, pagers, mobile telephones, internet services, high-end perfumes and cosmetics, and ready-to-cook cereals and packaged foods launched in India some years back. Or the product has substantially new features which differentiate the existing domestic product so much that it virtually becomes a new product, for example, micro-detergents. The product features could also be such that it appeals to a particular market segment for which the product was just not available in the domestic market, for example, premium range automobiles.

As the product was not available in the domestic market previously, demand estimation is rather difficult. Market research reports for these kinds of products generally include product experience in other countries. Attempts are then made to simulate this on a targeted market segment through local research, as has been done for the introduction of pagers or cellular telephones in India. While analysing such a market research report, a lender should be careful to see that the product experience of countries of dissimilar cultural orientation are avoided as far as possible, to estimate domestic market demand. Experience of a product in the American market may not always be suitable for launching it in India. An Asian country experience is more preferable. This important point has often been missed even by well-known multinationals while introducing a 'new' product in India from their international portfolio. The recent failures of quite a few such products are a pointer in this regard.

(c) *The product may be a totally new/innovative product in the world market.* The success of this type of product depends upon a correct assessment of the latent need of the customer group in the market of its first launch. This is the most difficult task for a market researcher. A product may just be too early in a market, or in the world as such. As the risk for such a product is very high, a lender is well-advised to suggest to the prospective borrower not to rely on only one consultant. There should be at least three independent consultants to conduct market research for a totally innovative product.

Under this category we may also include products which are not new to the domestic market, but whose process of manufacture is totally new (though after India having joined the World Trade Organisation on signing the General Agreement on Tariffs and Trade for patented products like drugs and pharmaceuticals, the advantages hitherto enjoyed by Indian manufacturers in process innovation are not available after amendments to the Indian Patents and Copyright Act). For non-patented products, process innovations would continue to provide competitive advantages to innovative firms. An innovative process suffers from the same type and magnitude of risk as a totally innovative product. The project report would generally contain the result of a successful laboratory run, which has first to be verified from a similar run at the National Test House. Besides, the prospective borrower should be advised to obtain reports from at least two private agencies on the feasibility of the new process. The lender should remember that success in a laboratory run does not always get repeated in a commercial run. The new process may be scientifically valid, but it may ultimately turn out to be commercially non-viable.

As the risk is very high in these cases, the project should have high equity backing. It would not be unwise for a lender to insist on a very low debt–equity ratio, say 1, or even less than that.

In addition to analysing the projected demand–supply gap of products coming under various categories mentioned earlier, a banker should evaluate critically the following points mentioned in the project report, as a part of market research findings, in order to take a total view of the viability of the product:

(a) Competitive advantage of the proposed product over similar products already in the market.

(b) Economic and social trends—favourable or unfavourable—that would have a bearing on the future consumption of the product.

(c) Pace of consumer acceptance of the product.

(d) Whether the product market is stable or there is likelihood of violent ups and downs in the market.

(e) Extent and possibility of competition from abroad.

(f) Range of substitutes already available in the market, and the possibility of future substitutes.

(g) Price structure of similar products in the market and the sensitivity of consumers to variation in prices.

(h) Who the major buyers of the product are—government or private consumers.

(i) Whether the present technology of manufacture is stable or a new technology is in the offing that can change both the marketability and cost of the product.

(j) Whether markets for raw materials and other inputs required for the product are stable, or there is a likelihood of sudden shortages in supply.

We have indicated earlier the importance of market research in assessing the demand and saleability of a product. However, it must be made clear here that market research does not always mean an elaborate time-consuming exercise demanding a lot of expertise, and consequently, services of specialised agencies. In case of big projects such an elaborate exercise may be necessary, but in case of small- and medium-sized projects, a moderate level of research will enable both an entrepreneur and a banker to form an opinion about the saleability of a product. We have already said that secondary published data are available for various products and industries

manufacturing them. Valuable information can also be obtained from chambers of commerce and product associations. An intelligent analysis of these data followed by a moderate range of surveys will enable an analyst to know the potential demand and the supply gap of the proposed product.

TECHNICAL AND MANAGERIAL VIABILITY

Technical Feasibility

After establishing the demand and saleability of the product, a appraiser should determine the *technical feasibility* of the project. The promoter would have done the technical analysis of the project. All the cost estimates flow from this technical analysis and form the basis of studying the financial and economic feasibility of the project.

When the product is chosen after market analysis, technical people take over to design the product and the production process. In case of a well-established product, standard production processes are available. Even a credit appraiser may often find one in his portfolio—there may already be some units which manufacture similar products. He may, therefore, be familiar with the production process of such a product. If not, he may visit one or two such factories to get first-hand knowledge of the production process.

However, a number of proposals that come to a credit appraiser may not fit in this category. There are ventures where the promoters have developed certain special features of the product and they might insist, which is often right, that because of these features their product stands out uniquely against their competitors' products. On the other hand, it may also be found in some new ventures that though the product is of a standard variety, the production process is either novel, or contains some new features which save on the marginal cost of the product, and because of this the promoters can stand in competition with the existing manufacturers of the same product. In case the process innovations are untried and unproven, there must be a detailed technical feasibility study starting from the laboratory run of the production process to the testing report of the sample product. We have already pointed out that the laboratory efficiency of the production process or that of the product may not always be realised in an actual commercial run. Hence, *if the project proposal is based on laboratory experiments only, a credit appraiser must discuss this with the borrower and bring him down to reality.*

Structural and Infrastructural

The next step in project appraisal is to analyse the structural and infrastructural aspects of the project. These are discussed below.

Legal Formalities

Because of various controls imposed upon industries by various acts of Parliament and state legislations, industrial units are required to obtain more than one license or permission from appropriate government departments and municipal authorities. Particular attention should be paid to units producing drugs and chemicals, where government regulations and controls are many. If a banker does not check the observance of these legal formalities, then it may so happen that when the project is half-way through, government officials may suddenly intervene and stop the project altogether resulting in the sinking of bank's advances.

If a firm intends to enter into any collaboration agreement or tie-up arrangement with any foreign collaborator, it may require sanction by the central government, and RBI clearance under the Foreign Exchange Management Act. When it is a case of using a foreign trade mark or patented brand names, royalty in foreign currency has to be paid to the foreign owners of the trade mark or patent. In certain cases, previous clearance from the RBI is necessary.

Location

A project may be located in an industrially backward area to take advantage of various concessions given by the government and other agencies, but a credit analyst has to weigh various locational factors needed for the optimum functioning of a unit. Some of the factors may not be present, particularly those relating to external economies, if the location of the unit is in a backward area. In such a case, an analyst must see that the loss of external economies is compensated by the concessions available from the government and other agencies.

Generally, for the development of backward areas the government creates industrial estates. It is preferable to have a unit situated in such an estate to take advantage of the package of infrastructural facilities provided by the government.

The following locational factors should weigh in the mind of an analyst when appraising a project:

(a) Transportation of both raw materials and finished products.
(b) Topography of the place.
(c) Energy requirements (like coal, electricity, and natural gas) versus local availability of energy; frequency of load-shedding and alternative power generation arrangements.
(d) Requirement of workers (skilled and unskilled) versus availability.
(e) Disposal of waste.
(f) Water requirement versus availability.
(g) Proximity to residential areas.
(h) State laws and regulations.
(i) Local taxes.
(j) Isolation requirements from environmental or security point of view.

(k) Site layout—one building or several, provision for storage, staff quarters and so on.

(l) Future expansion plans versus availability of adjoining land.

(m) Parking facilities.

Plant and Machinery

Depending upon the production process—conventional or new—plant and machinery are purchased or designed. In case it is an outright purchase of standard machines, details of technical specifications, including capacity, are available from reputed suppliers. These may be studied by a banker to arrive at conclusions regarding capacity utilisation and lead time on which to base the production plan and financial outlay.

The problem becomes a little more ticklish when because of some newness in the production process the plant and machinery has to be uniquely designed. Although normally a banker is used to asking for quotations from three fabricators, it may sometimes be dangerous to settle for the lowest quotation, because the firm submitting such a quotation may not have the necessary technical expertise to manufacture the plant and machinery in accordance with the design given by the borrower. *It is always advisable for a banker to inspect the factory of the fabricator and examine for himself not only the technical ability of the fabricator, but also his financial strength to undertake the job.*

If the plant and machinery are to be imported, it has to be seen whether it is a turnkey arrangement or specific supply of machines. The contract with the foreign supplier should be examined to see whether it provides for after-sales service, and if so, at what cost; whether any special skills are required to operationalise the plant, in which case there should be provision for imparting necessary training to the Indian staff.

When getting machines from abroad, the level of technology is a question which bothers both the government as well as bankers. Normally, a foreign manufacturer would not part with the latest technology. In some cases, the latest foreign technology may also not be suitable for Indian conditions. Entrepreneurs in their over enthusiasm may try to buy the latest foreign technology. These cases must be examined thoroughly from the point of view of availability of skilled workers, servicing of equipment, and availability of raw materials. However, if the unit is 100 per cent export-oriented, or a major portion of its product is meant for export, then it is almost inescapable that the latest technology be imported, so that the product can withstand foreign competition.

All projects have a normal gestation period. The borrower must have drawn up a PERT/CPM chart to control and follow up the implementation of the project. A banker would do well to obtain a copy of the PERT/CPM, which will help him not only to follow up the project, but also to release funds in accordance with the progress made in the implementation of the project. However, in spite of best estimates, there may be unforeseen circumstances that may delay the completion of the project. Delay causes cost over-runs and increase in overheads. Suitable contingency plans should, therefore, be developed to take care of these eventualities.

Managerial Set-up

Next comes the assessment of the *managerial ability* of the promoters handling the project. Managerial competence includes technical competence. It is not necessary that the promoters themselves must have technical competence with respect to the project at hand. It will be sufficient if they can line up suitable technical staff, who can take care of the technical aspects of the project. Promoters themselves are not always good managers. This is not an unusual situation, because it has often been found that entrepreneurs are not necessarily good managers. A credit appraiser need not feel alarmed on this count. As in the case of judging the technical competence of the promoters, here also a credit appraiser should feel satisfied if the promoters have appointed well-qualified and experienced managers (these points have been analysed in detail while discussing the credit risk of a borrower in Chapter 20). A credit appraiser should keep those points in mind while judging the managerial and technical competence of the promoters.

We have so far analysed different attributes of a product and its project, which should enable a lender to finally establish the viability, or otherwise, of the proposed project. In order to help him further, we have developed a Product-Project Viability Questionnaire in Appendix 17.1. The 39 attributes that form the questionnaire were found to be highly discriminatory from amongst a list of 110 attributes originally chosen for elaborate statistical tests. A lender can take a decision on the acceptability or otherwise of a project on the basis of the scores obtained from the questionnaire. Subsequent exercise on analysing the financial viability of the project rests on this decision.

A lender is advised to supplement the above instrument with the Credit Risk Analysis Questionnaire given in Chapter 20, which assesses the creditworthiness of a borrower.

FINANCIAL APPRAISAL

Financial appraisal, in effect, means assessing the cost and profitability of a project. After the initial viability of the project has been determined as above, the next question an analyst asks is whether the proposed project is financially viable. To answer this, an operating plan is drawn up covering the entire life of the project.

Project Life

The first problem an analyst faces is regarding determination of the life of the project, that is, of the plant and machinery. In fact, it is a difficult task because the working life of a machine cannot be known with certainty. A machine may wear out normally, say within 10 years, but in-between if there is a technological breakthrough, the existing machine may become obsolete well before its actual working life. In order to obtain a favourable instalment plan, borrowers may project a longer life of the plant and machinery than their estimated life. A good way of solving this problem is to derive the life by referring to the annual depreciation proposed to be charged by the borrower, the minimum being the rates prescribed in Schedule XIV to the Indian Companies Act.

Operating Plan

The operating plan of a project begins with the sales plan, which is then matched with the manufacturing plan. The sales plan is restricted by the overall installed capacity of the plant. Generally, it is not possible to reach the full capacity in the first year of production. It increases gradually; but after reaching a certain level of capacity utilisation, it may not be possible to increase the utilisation further to the level of the installed capacity; it may not also be desirable because that may result in faster wear and tear of the machines. Installed capacity is an engineering estimate based on the assumption of standard upkeep of the machines.

Based on the sales plan, a detailed manufacturing plan is drawn up which is then supported by an administrative plan. Once these three plans are available, we obtain separate and aggregated costs and the flow of revenue over the life of the project. A projected income statement is then drawn up, on the basis of which a projected cash flow statement is prepared.

COST STRUCTURE

Cost structure flows from the manufacturing and administrative plans. The following are the main heads of the cost structure:

A. Preliminary expenses
   i.   Expenses for forming the company.
   ii. Legal expenses.
   iii. Market research.
   iv. Expenses for a technical feasibility study.
   v.   Consultants' fees.
   vi. Cost of registration of patents and copyrights.
   vii. Expenses for raising capital and borrowed funds.
B. Fixed investment cost
   i.   Land.
   ii. Buildings and associated arrangements of electricity, water, and air supply to pneumatic tools (if any), safety and security, and disposal of waste.
   iii. Machines for production and support systems, like material handling equipments (including cost of freight and installation).
   iv. Furniture and fixtures.
   v.   Office machines, including computers and computer software.
   vi. Motor vehicles and carts.
   vii. Other construction, like staff quarters (if any), and workers' welfare support systems.
C. Start-up cost
   i.   Training of specialised staff.
   ii. Consultants' fees.
   iii. Cost over-runs due to inefficiency and delay.
   iv. Cost of initial trial production.

D. Current assets
   i.   Inventory of raw materials, stores, and spares.
   ii. Inventory of work-in-process and finished goods.
   iii. Receivables.
   iv. Other current assets.
E. Manufacturing costs
   i.   Direct materials, including stores, spares, loose tools, and scrap.
   ii. Direct wages.
   iii. Factory overheads for:
       (a) Supervision.
       (b) Staff salaries (factory).
       (c) Fuel, power, and water.
       (d) Repairs and maintenance.
       (e) Depreciation.
       (f) Rent, rates, and taxes.
       (g) Insurance.
       (h) Telephones.
       (i) Postage and stationery.
       (j) Security.
F. Distribution, selling, and general administrative expenses
   i.   Managerial remuneration.
   ii.   Staff salaries, allowances, and commissions.
   iii. Packing and forwarding.
   iv.   Postage and stationery.
   v.   Advertisement.
   vi.   Travelling and entertainment.
   vii. Conveyance expenses.
   viii. Rent, rates, and taxes.
   ix.   Insurance.
   x.   Telephones and internet services.
   xi.   Research and development.
   xii. Miscellaneous.

Except depreciation [under head 'E' (iii/e)], all costs involve an actual outflow of cash. We shall deal with depreciation separately.

Although the bulk of the expenditure like that mentioned under heads 'A', 'B', and 'C' is incurred during the installation of the project, and therefore is of a fixed nature, manufacturing, distribution, and selling expenses vary over the life of the project depending upon the actual utilisation of capacity. So also is the case with net current assets, popularly known as margin on working capital.

Cash Flows

A project will, therefore, have the following cash flows:

Cash outflows:
  i. Preliminary expenses.
  ii. Fixed asset acquisition costs.
  iii. Start-up costs.
  iv. Manufacturing expenses (excluding depreciation).
  v. Distribution, selling, and administrative expenses.
  vi. Incremental net current assets.

Cash inflows:
  i. Sales revenue.
  ii. Sale of salvage on the winding up of the project.

The objective of a financial analysis is to find out whether cash inflows over the estimated life of the project exceed the cash outflows. If the difference is positive, we may conclude that the project is financially viable. In case there is no positive difference and the two sides of the cash flow just match, the project may still be taken up because of its economic viability. This applies mostly in infrastructural projects, or projects having a social angle.

DEPRECIATION

Annual profit for purposes of investment appraisal should be before depreciation. There are three reasons behind this. One, though depreciation is a charge in the profit and loss account, there is no outflow of cash. Second, since we are considering the entire life of the project, the general presumption is that at the end of the working life of the project, the plant and machinery would be replaced. When there is a positive net inflow or the flows just balance, it is immaterial whether the adjustment with respect to depreciation is made or not, because the project has already recovered its investment, hence replacement will not be a problem. If we take profit after adjustment of depreciation, it might happen that the aggregate of after depreciation profits of the company may fall short of the investment made in the project, but the company can still replace the machines from out of the cash retained in the business by way of accumulated depreciation. Third, depreciation is nothing but the total cost of fixed assets annually spread over the life of the project. Since we have already taken the cost of fixed assets as an outflow of cash, we would be double charging the project by taking annual depreciation once again.

TAXATION

The next question is the treatment of taxation in arriving at profit for purpose of investment appraisal. In case of big infrastructural projects or those having a social orientation where a social cost-benefit analysis is made, pre-tax cash inflows are taken into account, because taxed revenue ultimately goes to the national coffers. But in case of commercial ventures, taxation is considered as a net outflow of cash, hence after-tax profit is taken into account to calculate the viability of an investment proposal. As banks and financial institutions mostly undertake commercial projects, our analysis is based on after-tax profit.

INTEREST

Generally, the cash flow projections made in the project report include interest as an outflow of cash. But when an analyst is considering the viability or otherwise of an investment proposal, he would first like to know whether the investment itself is viable or not. The question of financing the project comes only after this. A finance manager takes over at that stage and decides at what interest rate can the net inflow of cash be held at a positive level. The actual interest cost may vary from one project to the other, though they may be of the same value. In fact, one of the principal objectives of a finance manager is to find out that rate of interest at which the project breaks-even, and then to compare it with the average cost of capital. We will be elaborating upon this when we discuss the net present value of a project and the internal rate of return. For the present, we exclude interest cost from our calculation. A summary of relevant cash flows for project evaluation follows:

Inflows
1. Cash flow from operations, that is, profit after-tax but before interest and depreciation.
2. Salvage value.

Outflows
1. Capital expenditure.
2. Increase in net current assets.

DISCOUNTED CASH FLOW

A project involves outlay of funds at one point of time (though marginal investments are made in subsequent years also), but revenue from sales flows over the whole life of the project. Entrepreneurs or shareholders who invest their present funds expect that they will get a better yield in the future. This expectation is the basis of the investment motive that generates economic activities. Let us translate this motive into a practical example. A person who invests Rs 100 will expect to get back something more than Rs 100 in the future. If he gets back only Rs 100 against an investment of the same amount, he simply has no incentive to invest. Suppose now that he expects Rs 105 in the future, this means that, for him the future value of Rs 100 is Rs 105, or in other words, the present value of Rs 105 is Rs 100.

Time Value of Money

The concept of the time value of money simply means that Rs 100 today is more important to a person than Rs 100 a year hence, because he can enjoy the value of money right now. When he is investing this fund for a future return, he is depriving himself of present-day consumption. He expects, therefore, to get a price for his sacrifice. Secondly, any investment involves some amount of risk. Therefore, he may also expect an additional compensation for the risk he is taking. These two elements taken together comprise the rate of return he expects from his present investment.

As an illustration, let us assume this rate or interest to be 5 per cent per annum. An investor expects capital growth every year at this rate, that is, interest is added to the initial capital every year. This is popularly known as a compound rate of interest. When an investor invests Rs 100 at this rate, he gets Rs 105 at the end of the first year. He has an option to withdraw this money and consume its value. But if he chooses to invest it further, he will now expect 5 per cent on Rs 105, that is, Rs 110.25 in the second year, Rs 115.76 in the third year, Rs 121.55 in the fourth year, Rs 127.63 in the fifth year, and so on.

Future Value

This example makes it clear that the future value of Rs 100, in say, the fifth year, will be Rs 127.63. This arithmetical exercise can be modelled in a simple algebraic formula for ease of calculation:

$$FV = PV \left(1 + \frac{r}{100}\right)^n \tag{17.1}$$

where, FV = Future value.
   PV = Present value.
   r = Rate of interest (per cent).
   n = Number of years.

Let us check this formula with the help of the above example where $PV = 100$; $r = 5$; and $n = 5$.

$$hence, FV = 100\left(1 + \frac{5}{100}\right)^5$$

$$\begin{aligned} or, FV &= 100\,(1.05)^5 \\ &= 100\,(1.2763) \\ &= 127.63 \end{aligned}$$

We can overlap one stage in the above sum by expressing straightaway the interest as on Re 1 instead of on Rs 100, which can be denoted as i to distinguish it from r. The formula will then look like the following:

$$FV = PV\,(1+i)^n; \qquad (17.2)$$

where i denotes interest on Re 1 per annum, that is, $\frac{r}{100}$

The above calculations can be made manually with the help of a logarithm table or a scientific calculator. But the job was made easier by someone else long back who took the trouble of calculating future values of 1 monetary unit at various rates of interest, and over a number of years. This is given in the Future Value Table at the end of this chapter as Annexure 17.2. An example will make the use of this table clear. Suppose we want to know the future value (FV) of Rs 50,000 (PV) invested at the rate of 10 per cent (r) for 10 years (n), we would simply pick up the future value of Re 1 mentioned under the column for 10 per cent interest against the row for 10 years. This value is 2.5937. We now multiply the given present value with this value to obtain the future value.

That is, FV = Rs 50000 × 2.5937 = Rs 129685.

Present Value

If we now look at the above derivation inversely, we can very well say that the present value of Rs 1,29,685 at 10 per cent discount rate receivable after 10 years is Rs 50,000. When we are moving forward from the present value to the future value, we go on adding interest to the principal every year at a given rate (i) but when we are moving backward from the future value to the present value, we discount the future value at the same rate (i).

A project appraiser is more interested in discounting future values, that is, the future cash flows of a project, to decide on its viability.

As PV is just the inverse of FV, we can adopt an inverse approach and discount the future sum back to its present value. The inverse of formula (17.2) will then be as follows:

$$FV = PV\,(1+i)^n \text{ as in } (17.2)$$

$$or, PV = \frac{FV}{(1+i)^n} \qquad (17.3)$$

By breaking it up we get $PV = FV \times \dfrac{1}{(1+i)^n}$

$1/(1+i)$ is nothing but the inverse of the future value of Re 1 at a given rate of interest. This we call the discounted value of Re 1.

As in case of calculation of future value, the discounted value can also be calculated manually or by a reference to the table given in Annexure 17.1. Let us use the same example to familiarise the reader about the use of this table.

Earlier we found out that the FV of Rs 50,000 (PV) at 10 per cent interest per annum after 10 years is Rs 1,29,685.

We now find out the PV of Rs 1,29,685 (FV) obtainable after 10 years at 10 per cent discount rate.

From the Present Value Table given in Annexure 17.1, we simple pick up the discounted value of Re 1 given under the column for 10 per cent discount rate against the row for 10 years. This value is 0.3855. We now multiply the given FV with this value to obtain the PV.

$$
\begin{aligned}
\text{That is,} \quad PV &= \text{Rs } 129685 \times 0.3855 \\
\text{or,} \quad PV &= \text{Rs } 49993.57
\end{aligned}
$$

(The small difference in PV is due to approximation of decimal points in the Discounted Value Table.)

It will be interesting to note here that in the first part of the example we obtained the future value of Re 1 as 2.5937, and in the second part of the example we got the discounted value of Re 1 as 0.3855, the rate of interest and period being the same. That the discounted value is nothing but the inverse of the future value can be proved in the following manner:

$$
PV = \frac{1}{FV}
$$

$$
\text{That is, } 0.3855 = \frac{1}{2.5937} = 0.3855
$$

In other words, all discounted values given in Annexure 17.1 are nothing but the inverse of corresponding future values given in Annexure 17.2.

Effect of Inflation

We have so far taken the interest or discount rate in real terms without considering the effect of inflation. If an investor expects a 10 per cent return in the future, he expects it in real terms. But if the general or specific price level increases in-between, his 10 per cent return would not enable him to buy as many goods in the future as he expected to. No investor will like such a situation where the value of his money is eroded. He would, therefore, like to build, in the interest or discount rate, an inflation component which will cover up the expected increase in price level.

Although the rate of inflation in the ensuing years of the operation of the project cannot be predicted with certainty, an analysis of past trends and future expectations will enable an appraiser to arrive at an estimation of the annual rate of inflation. Inflation can, however, be specific or general. The former refers to an increase in the price level of specific goods and services, while the latter refers to an increase in the general price level calculated by taking the weighted average of prices of all major goods and services. These indices of price level are available from a number of publications. For bankers, the handy publication is the Reserve Bank of India Bulletin published quarterly. If a specific price index for the product is not available, it will be safe to take the general wholesale price index to estimate the expected annual rate of inflation in the future.

Let us assume that the expected rate of annual inflation is 6 per cent. In our earlier example, the expected interest rate is 10 per cent. That is, at the end of one year an investor expects to get Rs 10 for every Rs 100 invested. But in the meantime, the price level has increased by 6 per cent. This means that a unit of goods, which he was buying at Rs 10 earlier, will now cost him 6 per cent more, or Rs 10.60. To protect his real income he must fix his nominal rate of interest in such a way that in the next year he gets Rs 10.60. The following formula will help him fixing the nominal rate:

$$
m = r + r \left(\frac{f}{100} \right) \tag{17.4}
$$

where, m is the monetary rate of interest in per cent
r is the real rate of interest.
f is the rate of annual inflation.

The new interest rate thus arrived at in m will now be used as the rate for discounting cash flows.

Important: It must be remembered here that if cash flows are projected at an inflation adjusted price (that is, after taking into account the rate of annual inflation), then only inflation adjusted discount rate (m) should be applied. If, however, projections are based on the present price level, no adjustment is necessary for inflation, and (m) should not be used as the discount rate. The original (i) will then be the rate for discounting cash flows. An analyst should make necessary enquiries with the borrower before deciding on the actual rate. *In a majority of the proposals received by bankers, cash flow projections are based on the present price level.* However, an enquiry is necessary before deciding the appropriate discounting rate.

RISK ELEMENT

We have already indicated that risk is associated with every investment activity, and hence the rate of interest should not only include the compensation payable to an investor for sacrificing his present consumption, but also for the element of risk. There is, of course, a normal business risk, which is uniformly applicable to all business ventures. But over and above this normal risk, some businesses are more risky than others. An entrepreneur will not venture into any high-risk project unless the return is also high.

We have already seen that the risk element is high in a project whose product or the production process is new.

Risk also increases in uncertain socioeconomic conditions, where probability of failure is higher than the normal level.

In a risky project, or a project in a risky situation, the return must be high not only because greater compensation is required for the higher risk taken, but also because a risky project should pay for itself quickly.

The risk element is calculated by an analysis of the probability of failure of a firm engaged in a risky business or working in a risky situation. It is not difficult for a banker to know the probability of failure of a risky business from his own experience of handling varied nature of businesses. In Chapter 20 we undertake an elaborate study to estimate credit risk. Presently, we can make use of the Product-Project Viability Score Table (Appendix 17.1) to estimate the riskiness of a project and apply the risk score to obtain the risk-adjusted discount rate as below:

Risk-Adjusted Discount Rate

$$D_R = D \left[1 + \left(\frac{5R_i}{48 - 5R_i} \right) \right]$$

where, 'D' is the interest (discount rate) for *most viable*, or 'O' risk category project. This may be regarded as the risk-free interest rate of the economy, for example, the interest rate on treasury bills.

D_R is the required risk-adjusted discount rate.

R_i is the risk category of the project.

Figure 48 appearing in the denominator of the right-hand side of the equation is the midpoint of the score attributed to 'O' risk-category (most viable) of the project.

The model is based on the premise that the riskiness of a project increases more than proportionately with the rise in its risk-category. The discount rate follows the same rule. That is, the discount rate applicable for a project with risk-category 3 will be more than proportionate to projects with risk-category 1 or 2. This is explained below assuming a risk-free interest rate of 12 per cent per annum.

Risk Category	Risk-adjusted Discount Rate (%)	Percentage charge in Risk-adjusted Discount Rate
1. $D_R = 12 \left[1 + \dfrac{5 \times 1}{48 - 5 \times 1} \right]$ = 13.40		11.67
2. Calculated as above = 15.16		13.13
3. –Do– = 17.45		15.10
4. –Do– = 20.57		17.88

Net Present Value (NPV)

We have indicated earlier that if cash inflows of a project exceed outflows, a project can be considered viable. Earlier, we have explained the necessity of discounting these cash flows to arrive at a meaningful conclusion. When all the relevant cash flows (both inflows and outflows) are discounted, we obtain a net present value (NPV). If NPV is positive, a project is considered viable; if it is zero, the project just breaks even; and if it is negative, the project cannot be considered viable.

The NPV method is also used by finance managers as a tool for wealth maximisation. The greater the positive value of NPV, the higher the generation of wealth.

We can explain the NPV concept with the help of an example.

A project with an expected life of five years, takes one year for implementation and generates the relevant cash flows given in Table 17.1.

The discount rate is 15 per cent per annum, including the risk element. All projections are made at the price level of 'O' year, hence the discount rate need not be adjusted for inflation.

Note: 'O' year denotes the year of implementation of the project. All cash flows are expressed in the price level of this year. Hence, the discount factor for this year will be 1.

TABLE 17.1   Cash-flow Statement

(Rs in '000s)

Head of Cash flows	0	First	Second	Year Third	Fourth	Fifth
1. Capital expenditure	(10000)	—	—	—	—	—
2. Increase or decrease in net working capital		(2000)	(500)	(700)	400	200
3. Net profit after-tax		2000	3000	4000	6000	1000
4. *Add* back depreciation		2000	2000	2000	2000	2000
5. *Add* back interest		*3000	1350	1250	800	550
6. Proceeds from salvage		—	—	—	—	1000
Present cash flows	(10000)	5000	5850	6550	9200	4750

Note: * Represents interest for the first two years. Amounts in brackets indicate cash outflow. In case of net working capital, the bracketed figures indicate increase (outflow), and figures without brackets indicate decrease (inflow) in the net working capital.

Discount factors at 15 per cent per annum for five years as taken from the Present Value Table in Annexure 17.3 are given below.

Year	Discount Factor at 15 per cent p.a.
0	1.0000
First	0.8696
Second	0.7561
Third	0.6575
Fourth	0.5718
Fifth	0.4972

Discounted values of cash flow projections are calculated in Table 17.2 by multiplying cash flows with the corresponding discount factor.

From this, we can now calculate the NPV of the project as follows:

Present value of cash inflows	Rs 20700
Less: Present value of cash outflows	Rs 10000
NPV of the project	Rs 10700

If we have understood the principles of NPV correctly, we can quickly calculate it by drawing the net annual cash flow figures from the cash flow statement and treating them with the relative discount factors as in Table 17.3.

As the NPV of the project is positive and substantial, we can consider the project as financially viable.

OPPORTUNITY COST

Promoters arrive at the rate for discounting cash flows of a project by making a study of the rates of return on comparable investments in the market place, the aim being wealth maximisation. When there are more than one investment opportunities in the market, an investor evaluates the rates of return on alternative investment opportunities and chooses the best rate to evaluate the project chosen. In other words, discount rate is the cost of foregoing other opportunities available in the market as compared to the one chosen. This is known as the opportunity cost of capital, or the discount rate for evaluation of cash flows. One simple example will make this clear.

Suppose an investor wants to invest Rs 10,000. The first opportunity available to him is to invest this fund in a long-term fixed deposit of a commercial bank, which offers a return, of say 13 per cent per annum. If he wants to invest this fund, in say, mutual funds, he would like to find out whether the rate of return in the alternative

TABLE **17.2**   Discounted Cash-flow Statement

(Rs in '000s)

Head of Cash flows	0	First	Second	Year Third	Fourth	Fifth	Total
1. Capital expenditure	(10000)	—	—	—	—	—	(10.000)
2. Increase or decrease in net working capital		(1739)	(378)	(460)	229	100	(2248)
3. Net profit after-tax		1739	2268	2630	3431	497	10565
4. *Add* back depreciation		1739	1512	1315	1144	994	6704
5. *Add* back interest		2609	1021	822	457	273	5182
6. Proceeds from salvage		—	—	—	—	497	497
Present value of cash flows	(10000)	4348	4423	4307	5261	2361	10700

Note: Figures in brackets indicate outflow of cash.

TABLE 17.3   Net Present Value

Year	Discount Factor 15% p.a.	Net Annual Cash Flow	Present Value of Cash Flows
0	1	(10000)	(10000)
1	0.8696	5000	4348
2	0.7561	5850	4423
3	0.6575	6550	4307
4	0.5718	9200	5261
5	0.4972	4750	2361
		Net Present Value = 10700	

investment is more than 13 per cent. That is, he will evaluate the net cash flows of the proposed investment at 13 per cent per annum, which is nothing but the cost of foregoing the opportunity available to him.

In this example, the opportunity cost of investment is equal to the marginal value of investment. In a perfectly competitive capital market, opportunity cost becomes equal to the market cost of raising capital. While making an economic analysis of a project, this approach is adopted. But in financial analysis—the one in which we are presently engaged—the opportunity cost of capital is always the average cost of capital. (When the capital market is imperfect, or administered interest rates prevail, as in India till some time ago, weighted average cost of capital is a better estimate of opportunity cost).

A *conflict may arise between the discount rate chosen by a borrower and that chosen by a banker, because the latter may like to apply his own lending rate for evaluating cash flows of the project.* This conflict needs to be resolved before determining the optimum discount rate. It may be observed that the NPV derived by a promoter by applying a particular discount rate may get substantially reduced when a banker discounts the cash flow by applying his lending rate for that particular type of advance. However, the magnitude of

the difference between the two NPVs enables a banker to enter into a dialogue with a borrower to decide an optimum capital structure, so that the final NPV can be kept at a positive level.

INTERNAL RATE OF RETURN

A banker would, therefore, like to know at which point the rate of return from the project meets the opportunity cost of capital. It is obvious that at a point where the rate of return from the project meets the cost of capital, NVP will be zero. That is, the discounted value of cash inflows will just meet the discounted value of cash outflows. The final rate at which the two sides tally (or the NVP becomes zero), is called the internal rate of return (IRR). In the language of financial analysis, the internal rate of return is that rate at which the project breaks even, and in the language of economics it is that rate where the marginal revenue of a project is equal to the marginal cost of raising capital.

Under this concept, an appraiser will not accept any discount rate *prima facie*, but will start discounting the cash flows at various rates till the resultant NVP becomes zero. For ease of calculation, he may, however, estimate a range between which the IRR is likely to fall. He will start discounting at the lowest of the range, and then go on increasing the rate till the NVP becomes zero.

Let us understand this with the help of an illustration given in Table 17.4, where present values are calculated at different discount rates.

From Table 17.4 it is clear that NVP will become zero at a rate somewhere between 15 per cent and 20 per cent, because at the former rate, NVP has come down to a negligible sum (7), and at 20 per cent, it has become negative. It is possible by an elaborate exercise to arrive at the exact rate between 15 per cent and 20 per cent, where NVP becomes zero. But such a time-consuming process is not necessary because we

TABLE 17.4   Search of Internal Rate of Return

Year	Net Annual	Present Values of Cash Flows at Various Discount Rates				
	Cash Flows	5%	10%	15%	20%	25%
(1)	(2)	(3)	(4)	(5)	(6)	(7)
0	(8000)	(8000)	(8000)	(8000)	(8000)	(8000)
1	4000	3810	3636	3478	3333	3200
2	3600	3265	2975	2722	2500	2304
3	1500	1295	1127	986	868	768
4	1000	823	683	572	482	410
5	500	393	310	249	201	164
NVP of the project	—	1586	731	7	(616)	(1154)

can find out the approximate rate by doing a little arithmetical exercise.

It is clear that the desired rate is 15 per cent plus *something*. This *something* will not, however, be greater than the difference between 15 per cent and 20 per cent, that is, 5 per cent. This 5 per cent increase in the rate is responsible for a decline in the NVP to the extent of 7 + 616 = 623.

Hence, IRR will be approximately:

$$15 + \frac{7}{623} \times 5 = 15 + 0.056, \text{ or } 15.056 \text{ per cent}$$

At this rate, the net present value of the project comes closer to zero.

IRR as A Decision Tool

A project is not viable when the IRR is less than the opportunity cost of capital, because NVP becomes negative, as will be evident from columns 6 and 7 of Table 17.4. When the opportunity cost of capital equals the IRR of the project, a banker may be moderately satisfied because the project can pay for the instalments and interest, but a profit-oriented investor may not be so interested, because the project becomes similar to any other investment opportunity available in the market, and there may be no reason why he should settle for *this* particular project. He will be indifferent. If, however, the opportunity cost of capital is less than the IRR, an investor will have a positive NVP, as will be evident from the NVPs shown in columns 3 and 4 of Table 17.4. For a banker, the interest rate on a particular type of loan will be the opportunity cost of capital when the major part of the funds (75 per cent and above) is provided by a bank, otherwise it will be the weighted average cost of funds raised from different sources.

When the derived IRR of the project is less than the lending rate of a bank or the weighted average cost of capital, then a banker should impress upon the borrower to plan his capital structure in such a way that the weighted average rate of raising the total funds from all sources, including the bank is less than the IRR, so that the project registers a positive NVP.

Besides banks, there are other opportunities in the market for raising capital, for example, fixed deposits from the public, debentures, loans from other financial institutions, and share capital. A promoter should raise various types of

PAY BACK METHOD

The pay back method (PBM) is a simpler but relatively imperfect method as compared to the NVP or IRR methods, though it has long been in use for investment appraisal. According to this method, the original investment is divided by the annual stream of net cash inflows (profit after-tax plus depreciation) to find out the period by which the original investment is fully realised.

The assumption of PBM is that net cash inflows are constant over the years. But the constancy of net cash inflows is not a reality. What we mostly find are uneven cash flows. In such a case, we may go on adding together the annual cash flows from the first year onwards, until an aggregate sum is obtained which is equal to the original cash outlay. The period by which this is achieved is called the pay back period.

Table 17.5 makes this clear.

We may notice that besides Project 'A', all the other projects have uneven cash flows. Both projects 'A' and 'B' have a pay back period of four years, but 'A' has a total cash flow of Rs 15,000 while 'B' has a total cash flow of Rs 21,000. The question is which of the two will be selected. The pay back method cannot give a satisfactory answer to this question because in the absence of discounted cash flow figures, we are unable to know the intrinsic value of the two projects. The PBM ignores the time value of money, and this is its greatest defect. Under the NVP method, selectivity of a project can be determined easily.

Despite its defects PBM is still much in use. The main reason for its continuance is that some investors believe that the return of invested capital in a shorter period of time is better than a return, though more in aggregate, over a longer period. They are not always incorrect because of present-day uncertain socioeconomic conditions of business. A risky project or a project in a risky situation must pay back quickly. For this reason, multinational corporations often make use of PBM while appraising investment proposals in developing countries.

AVERAGE AND EFFECTIVE RATE OF RETURN

The PBM can give us a crude estimate of the *average rate of return* of a project. We can calculate it by simply taking the reciprocal of the pay back period and multiplying it with 100. For example, projects 'A' and 'B' have a pay back period of

TABLE 17.5   Calculation of Pay Back Period

(Amount in Rs)

Project (1)	Initial Investment (2)	Net Cash Flows (Year)						Pay Back Period (9)
		First (3)	Second (4)	Third (5)	Fourth (6)	Fifth (7)	Sixth (8)	
A	10000	2500	2500	2500	2500	2500	2500	4 years
B	10000	1000	2000	3000	4000	5000	6000	4 years
C	10000	500	1000	1400	2600	2400	2100	6 years
D	10000	200	2000	3200	3800	800	—	5 years

four years. The estimated average rate of return will be:

$$\frac{1}{4} \times 100 = 25\%$$

We can also calculate the *effective rate of return* of a project after taking into account the interest payable on the capital invested. The following example explains and distinguishes the three methods.

A project that requires an investment of Rs 10,000 gives a uniform net cash flow of Rs 2,500 per annum for 10 years. The cost of raising capital is 15 per cent per annum.

Hence,

(i) *pay back period* $= \dfrac{10000}{2500} = 4\ years$

(ii) *Pay back average rate of return* $= \dfrac{1}{4} \times 100 = 25\%$

Calculation of pay back effective rate of return is shown below.

Assuming that the investment of Rs 10,000 is recovered within four years in equated annual instalments of Rs 2,500 at 15 per cent interest per annum, the aggregate interest payable on the reducing balances will be Rs 3,750. The aggregate return from the project is Rs 2500 × 10 = Rs 25,000. After deducting the interest of Rs 3,750 from this, we obtain a net return of Rs 25000 – 3750 = Rs 21,250. Hence, the annual average return will be Rs 21250/10 = Rs 2,125 on an investment of Rs 10,000.

(iii) *Pay back effective rate of return*

$$= \frac{2125}{10000} \times 100 = 21.25\%$$

As the effective rate of return of 21.25 per cent is more than the cost of capital (15 per cent), the project may be considered viable.

PROFITABILITY INDEX

This is another method of evaluating a project.

The index is calculated by the following formula:

$$\frac{Present\ value\ of\ cash\ flows}{Presnt\ value\ of\ cost\ of\ investment}$$

If this ratio is more than 1, the project is considered viable.

However, this ratio is no more informative than the NVP or IRR. Rather, as with any other ratio, an appraiser may often be trapped in confusion while interpreting this ratio. The NVP and IRR methods are more simple and straightforward. These also enable an appraiser to recast the capital structure, if necessary, in order to make the project bankable.

REPAYMENT CAPACITY

Having made all the analysis about the viability of a project, a lender will still not be satisfied until he knows the safety margin available to him regarding recovery of loan instalments and interest. The debt–service coverage ratio can quell his anxiety to a great extent. In fact, this is the most commonly used ratio for judging the creditworthiness of a project.

We have already shown in Chapter 16 how to calculate and interpret this ratio. But some points need to be emphasised here.

This ratio should be calculated for all the years of the existence of long-term debt. A declining trend in this ratio over the projected period of the project may indicate that the project is overly ambitious, or a banker has insisted on a much shorter period for the repayment of the term loan, which the project is not capable of adhering to, except at the cost of a sudden liquidity crisis. In such a situation, a banker should make a careful analysis of the income-generating capacity of the project, and reschedule the repayment programme, if necessary.

If the ratio is 1, there is no safety cushion; the project can just meet its obligation to the term lender. The lender will definitely not like such a situation. He would want the ratio to be more than 1. For him the larger the ratio the better it is. However, an unreasonably high debt–service coverage ratio may indicate that the lender has been too lax in fixing the repayment schedule. He might have allowed a much longer period for repayment than what is warranted by the cash flows.

In calculating this ratio, we should take the current values of particular cash flows. These should not be discounted, because payment of instalments and interest is made in actual rupees, not in their discounted values.

A good debt–service coverage ratio should fall somewhere between 1.5 and 2.5.

Concluding Remarks

The purpose of this chapter is to provide a basic framework for appraising the overall feasibility and bankability of a term loan proposal. We have selectively presented certain tools of analysis that are relevant to a banker.

In the next chapter we apply some of the techniques presented here and in Chapter 6 for making a comprehensive assessment of a project where a bank is expected to finance both its term loan and working capital requirements.

We have avoided loading this chapter with various formalities, procedures, and legal requirements for launching a project. The reader may consult different government publications on these subjects, and also consult some standard books available in the market.

Appendix 17.1

PRODUCT-PROJECT VIABILITY QUESTIONNAIRE

Serial No.	Questionnaire
1.	The product has widespread use.
2.	Customers are restricted to a special class.
3.	The product satisfies a basic need.
4.	It is a luxury product.
5.	The product will sell itself. Repeat sales likely.
6.	Intensive sales effort required.
7.	Some amount of sales effort required.
8.	The product has a large domestic and international market.
9.	The product can be sold only in the export market.
10.	The product can be sold only in the domestic market.
11.	The market for the product is not crowded. Competitors are relatively few in the domestic market.
12.	There are many competitors in the domestic market.
13.	The product is needed both in good and bad times.
14.	The demand for the product will fall drastically in bad times.
15.	The demand for the product is steady in all seasons.
16.	The demand for the product is seasonal.
17.	The product is either protected against international competition, or there is no threat from international competition.
18.	The product is open to international competition. It can be imported by any one and at any time.
19.	No single competitor can affect the market share substantially by reducing the price of the product.
20.	Powerful competitors can capture a substantial share of the market by reducing the price of the product.
21.	The product is new—can be protected by patent.
22.	Product design is difficult to protect. It can be copied easily.
23.	Raw materials needed to manufacture the product are widely available domestically.
24.	Imported raw materials are mostly required to manufacture the product.
25.	Raw materials for the product though available domestically, are closely controlled.
26.	Raw materials for the product are generally in short supply.
27.	The project is located within a reasonable distance from the source of raw materials.
28.	The project is far away from source of raw materials.
29.	Skilled workers are locally available.
30.	Skilled workers are to be brought from other areas, involving high wages.
31.	Technology of production is reasonably stable.
32.	The product and its production process can be easily modified in response to a new product or process technology.
33.	Technological advances in the product and process are very rapid.
34.	The manufacturing process of the product does not create environmental hazards. No control is likely.

35.   The manufacturing process of the product does create environmental problems. Controls are already there or are likely to be imposed.

36.   The market concentration of the product is within the command area of the manufacturing installations.

37.   The market for the product is widely dispersed while manufacturing is located in one place only.

38.   The project is located in a backward area.

39.   The project is not located in a backward area.

Instructions

1.   39 attributes of a product-project are listed above.

2.   Tick ($\sqrt{}$) the most appropriate ones.

3.   Award the following marks for the attributes ticked:

Serial No. of Attributes	Marks to be awarded
(a) 1, 3, 5, 8, 11, 13, 15, 17, 19, 23, 27, 29, 31, 34, 36	3 for each attribute
(b) 2, 4, 7, 10, 16, 21, 24, 25, 32, 35, 38	2 for each attribute
(c) 6, 9, 12, 14, 18, 20, 22, 26, 28, 30, 33, 37, 39	1 for each attribute

4.   *Add* up the total score, put it under appropriate risk category along the following scale to decide the viability or otherwise of the project:

	RISK CATEGORY					
	0 *Most viable*	*1* *Viable*	*2* *Moderately viable*	*3* *Just viable*	*4* *Doubtful viability*	*5* *Poor viability*
Score	50–46	45–41	40–36	35–31	30–26	25 and less
Percentage Score	100–91	90–81	80–71	70–61	60–51	50 and below

Annexure 17.1

PRESENT VALUE TABLE

(The Present Value of Re 1)

Year	1%	2%	3%	4%	5%	6%	7%	8%	9%	10%
1	0.9901	0.9804	0.9709	0.9615	0.9524	0.9434	0.9346	0.9259	0.9174	0.9091
2	0.9803	0.9612	0.9426	0.9246	0.9070	0.8900	0.8734	0.8573	0.8417	0.8264
3	0.9706	0.9423	0.9151	0.8890	0.8638	0.8396	0.8163	0.7938	0.7722	0.7513
4	0.9610	0.9238	0.8885	0.8548	0.8227	0.7921	0.7629	0.7350	0.7084	0.6830
5	0.9515	0.9057	0.8626	0.8219	0.7835	0.7473	0.7130	0.6806	0.6499	0.6209
6	0.9420	0.8880	0.8375	0.7903	0.7462	0.7050	0.6663	0.6302	0.5963	0.5645
7	0.9327	0.8706	0.8131	0.7599	0.7107	0.6651	0.6227	0.5835	0.5470	0.5132
8	0.9235	0.8535	0.7894	0.7307	0.6768	0.6274	0.5820	0.5403	0.5019	0.4665
9	0.9143	0.8368	0.7664	0.7026	0.6446	0.5919	0.5439	0.5002	0.4604	0.4241
10	0.9053	0.8203	0.7441	0.6756	0.6139	0.5584	0.5083	0.4632	0.4224	0.3855
11	0.8963	0.8043	0.7224	0.6496	0.5847	0.5268	0.4751	0.4289	0.3875	0.3505
12	0.8874	0.7885	0.7014	0.6246	0.5568	0.4970	0.4440	0.3971	0.3555	0.3186
13	0.8787	0.7730	0.6810	0.6006	0.5303	0.4688	0.4149	0.3677	0.3262	0.2897
14	0.8700	0.7579	0.6611	0.5775	0.5051	0.4423	0.3878	0.3405	0.2992	0.2633
15	0.8613	0.7430	0.6419	0.5553	0.4810	0.4173	0.3624	0.3152	0.2745	0.2394
16	0.8528	0.7284	0.6232	0.5339	0.4581	0.3936	0.3387	0.2919	0.2519	0.2176
17	0.8444	0.7142	0.6050	0.5134	0.4363	0.3714	0.3166	0.2703	0.2311	0.1978
18	0.8360	0.7002	0.5874	0.4936	0.4155	0.3503	0.2959	0.2502	0.2120	0.1799
19	0.8277	0.6865	0.5703	0.4746	0.3957	0.3305	0.2765	0.2317	0.1945	0.1635
20	0.8195	0.6730	0.5537	0.4564	0.3769	0.3118	0.2584	0.2145	0.1784	0.1486
21	0.8114	0.6598	0.5375	0.4388	0.3589	0.2942	0.2415	0.1987	0.1637	0.1351
22	0.8034	0.6468	0.5219	0.4220	0.3418	0.2775	0.2257	0.1839	0.1502	0.1228
23	0.7954	0.6342	0.5067	0.4057	0.3256	0.2618	0.2109	0.1703	0.1378	0.1117
24	0.7876	0.6217	0.4919	0.3901	0.3101	0.2470	0.1971	0.1577	0.1264	0.1015
25	0.7798	0.6095	0.4776	0.3751	0.2953	0.2330	0.1842	0.1460	0.1160	0.0923

(contd.)

(*contd.*)

Year	11%	12%	13%	14%	15%	16%	17%	18%	19%	20%
1	0.9009	0.8929	0.8850	0.8772	0.8696	0.8621	0.8547	0.8475	0.8403	0.8333
2	0.8116	0.7972	0.7831	0.7695	0.7561	0.7432	0.7305	0.7182	0.7062	0.6944
3	0.7312	0.7118	0.6931	0.6750	0.6575	0.6407	0.6244	0.6086	0.5934	0.5787
4	0.6587	0.6355	0.6133	0.5921	0.5718	0.5523	0.5337	0.5158	0.4987	0.4823
5	0.5935	0.5674	0.5428	0.5194	0.4972	0.4761	0.4561	0.4371	0.4190	0.4019
6	0.5346	0.5066	0.4803	0.4556	0.4323	0.4104	0.3898	0.3704	0.3521	0.3349
7	0.4817	0.4523	0.4251	0.3996	0.3759	0.3538	0.3332	0.3139	0.2959	0.2791
8	0.4339	0.4039	0.3762	0.3506	0.3269	0.3050	0.2848	0.2660	0.2487	0.2326
9	0.3909	0.3606	0.3329	0.3075	0.2843	0.2630	0.2434	0.2255	0.2090	0.1938
10	0.3522	0.3220	0.2946	0.2697	0.2472	0.2267	0.2080	0.1911	0.1756	0.1615
11	0.3173	0.2875	0.2607	0.2366	0.2149	0.1954	0.1778	0.1619	0.1476	0.1346
12	0.2858	0.2567	0.2307	0.2076	0.1869	0.1685	0.1520	0.1372	0.1240	0.1122
13	0.2575	0.2292	0.2042	0.1821	0.1625	0.1452	0.1299	0.1163	0.1042	0.0935
14	0.2320	0.2046	0.1807	0.1597	0.1413	0.1252	0.1110	0.0985	0.0876	0.0779
15	0.2090	0.1827	0.1599	0.1401	0.1229	0.1079	0.0949	0.0835	0.0736	0.0649
16	0.1883	0.1631	0.1415	0.1229	0.1069	0.0930	0.0811	0.0708	0.0618	0.0541
17	0.1696	0.1456	0.1252	0.1078	0.0929	0.0802	0.0693	0.0600	0.0520	0.0451
18	0.1528	0.1300	0.1108	0.0946	0.0808	0.0691	0.0592	0.0508	0.0437	0.0376
19	0.1377	0.1161	0.0981	0.0829	0.0703	0.0596	0.0506	0.0431	0.0367	0.0313
20	0.1240	0.1037	0.0868	0.0728	0.0611	0.0514	0.0433	0.0365	0.0308	0.0261
21	0.1117	0.0926	0.0768	0.0638	0.0531	0.0443	0.0370	0.0309	0.0259	0.0217
22	0.1007	0.0826	0.0680	0.0560	0.0462	0.0382	0.0316	0.0262	0.0218	0.0181
23	0.0907	0.0738	0.0601	0.0491	0.0402	0.0329	0.0270	0.0222	0.0183	0.0151
24	0.0817	0.0659	0.0532	0.0431	0.0349	0.0284	0.0231	0.0188	0.0154	0.0126
25	0.0736	0.0588	0.0471	0.0378	0.0304	0.0245	0.0197	0.0160	0.0129	0.0105

Year	21%	22%	23%	24%	25%	26%	27%	28%	29%	30%
1	0.8264	0.8197	0.8130	0.8065	0.8000	0.7937	0.7874	0.7813	0.7752	0.7692
2	0.6830	0.6719	0.6610	0.6504	0.6400	0.6299	0.6200	0.6104	0.6009	0.5917
3	0.5645	0.5507	0.5374	0.5245	0.5120	0.4999	0.4882	0.4768	0.4658	0.4552
4	0.4665	0.4514	0.4369	0.4230	0.4096	0.3968	0.3844	0.3725	0.3611	0.3501
5	0.3855	0.3700	0.3552	0.3411	0.3277	0.3149	0.3027	0.2910	0.2799	0.2693
6	0.3186	0.3033	0.2888	0.2751	0.2621	0.2499	0.2383	0.2774	0.2170	0.2072
7	0.2633	0.2486	0.2348	0.2218	0.2097	0.1983	0.1877	0.1776	0.1682	0.1594
8	0.2176	0.2038	0.1909	0.1789	0.1678	0.1574	0.1478	0.1388	0.1304	0.1226
9	0.1799	0.1670	0.1552	0.1443	0.1342	0.1249	0.1164	0.1084	0.1011	0.0943
10	0.1486	0.1369	0.1262	0.1164	0.1074	0.0992	0.0916	0.0847	0.0784	0.0725
11	0.1228	0.1122	0.1026	0.0938	0.0859	0.0787	0.0721	0.0662	0.0607	0.0558
12	0.1015	0.0920	0.0834	0.0757	0.0687	0.0625	0.0568	0.0517	0.0471	0.0429
13	0.0839	0.0754	0.0678	0.0610	0.0550	0.0496	0.0447	0.0404	0.0365	0.0330
14	0.0693	0.0618	0.0551	0.0492	0.0440	0.0393	0.0352	0.0316	0.0283	0.0254
15	0.0573	0.0507	0.0448	0.0397	0.0352	0.0312	0.0277	0.0247	0.0219	0.0195
16	0.0474	0.0415	0.0364	0.0320	0.0281	0.0248	0.0218	0.0193	0.0170	0.0150
17	0.0391	0.0340	0.0296	0.0258	0.0225	0.0197	0.0172	0.0150	0.0132	0.0116
18	0.0323	0.0279	0.0241	0.0208	0.0180	0.0156	0.0135	0.0118	0.0102	0.0088
19	0.0267	0.0229	0.0196	0.0168	0.0144	0.0124	0.0107	0.0092	0.0079	0.0069
20	0.0221	0.0187	0.0159	0.0135	0.0115	0.0098	0.0084	0.0072	0.0061	0.0053
21	0.0183	0.0154	0.0129	0.0109	0.0092	0.0078	0.0066	0.0056	0.0048	0.0040
22	0.0151	0.0126	0.0105	0.0088	0.0074	0.0062	0.0052	0.0044	0.0037	0.0031
23	0.0125	0.0103	0.0086	0.0071	0.0059	0.0049	0.0041	0.0034	0.0029	0.0024
24	0.0103	0.0085	0.0070	0.0057	0.0047	0.0039	0.0032	0.0027	0.0022	0.0018
25	0.0085	0.0069	0.0057	0.0046	0.0038	0.0031	0.0025	0.0021	0.0017	0.0014

(contd.)

Annexure 17.2

Future Value Table

(The Future Value of Re 1)

Year	1%	2%	3%	4%	5%	6%	7%	8%	9%	10%
1	1.0100	1.0200	1.0300	1.0400	1.0500	1.0600	1.0700	1.0800	1.0900	1.1000
2	1.0201	1.0404	1.0609	1.0816	1.1025	1.1236	1.1449	1.1664	1.1881	1.2100
3	1.0303	1.0612	1.0927	1.1249	1.1576	1.1910	1.2250	1.2597	1.2950	1.3310
4	1.0406	1.0824	1.1255	1.1699	1.2155	1.2625	1.3108	1.3605	1.4116	1.4641
5	1.0510	1.1041	1.1593	1.2167	1.2763	1.3382	1.4026	1.4693	1.5386	1.6105
6	1.0615	1.1262	1.1941	1.2653	1.3401	1.4185	1.5007	1.5869	1.6771	1.7716
7	1.0721	1.1487	1.2299	1.3159	1.4071	1.5036	1.6058	1.7138	1.8280	1.9487
8	1.0829	1.1717	1.2668	1.3686	1.4775	1.5938	1.7182	1.8509	1.9926	2.1436
9	1.0937	1.1951	1.3048	1.4233	1.5513	1.6895	1.8385	1.9990	2.1719	2.3579
10	1.1046	1.2190	1.3439	1.4802	1.6289	1.7908	1.9672	2.1589	2.3674	2.5937
11	1.1157	1.2434	1.3842	1.5395	1.7103	1.8983	2.1049	2.3316	2.5804	2.8531
12	1.1268	1.2682	1.4258	1.6010	1.7959	2.0122	2.2523	2.5182	2.8127	3.1384
13	1.1381	1.2936	1.4685	1.6651	1.8856	2.1329	2.4098	2.7196	3.0658	3.4523
14	1.1495	1.3195	1.5126	1.7317	1.9799	2.2609	2.5785	2.9372	3.3417	3.7975
15	1.1610	1.3459	1.5580	1.8009	2.0789	2.3966	2.7590	3.1722	3.6425	4.1772
16	1.1726	1.3728	1.6047	1.8730	2.1829	2.5404	2.9522	3.4259	3.9703	4.5950
17	1.1843	1.4002	1.6528	1.9479	2.2920	2.6928	3.1588	3.7000	4.3276	5.0545
18	1.1961	1.4282	1.7024	2.0258	2.4066	2.8543	3.3799	3.9960	4.7171	5.5599
19	1.2081	1.4568	1.7535	2.1068	2.5270	3.0256	3.6165	4.3157	5.1417	6.1159
20	1.2202	1.4859	1.8016	2.1911	2.6533	3.2071	3.8697	4.6610	5.6044	6.7275
21	1.2324	1.5157	1.8603	2.2787	2.7860	3.3996	4.1405	5.0338	6.1088	7.4002
22	1.2447	1.5460	1.9161	2.3699	2.9253	3.6035	4.4304	5.4365	6.6586	8.1403
23	1.2572	1.5769	1.9736	2.4647	3.0715	3.8197	4.7405	5.8715	7.2579	8.9543
24	1.2697	1.6084	2.0328	2.5633	3.2251	4.0490	5.0724	6.3412	7.9111	9.8497
25	1.2824	1.6406	2.0938	2.6658	3.3864	4.2919	5.4274	6.8485	8.6231	10.8347

Year	11%	12%	13%	14%	15%	16%	17%	18%	19%	20%
1	1.1100	1.1200	1.1300	1.1400	1.1500	1.1600	1.1700	1.1800	1.1900	1.2000
2	1.2321	1.2544	1.2769	1.2996	1.3225	1.3456	1.3689	1.3924	1.4161	1.4400
3	1.3676	1.4049	1.4429	1.4815	1.5209	1.5609	1.6016	1.6430	1.6852	1.7280
4	1.5181	1.5735	1.6305	1.6890	1.7490	1.8106	1.8739	1.9388	2.0053	2.0736
5	1.6851	1.7623	1.8424	1.9254	2.0113	2.1003	2.1924	2.2878	2.3864	2.4883
6	1.8704	1.9738	2.0820	2.1950	2.3131	2.4364	2.5652	2.6996	2.8398	2.9860
7	2.0762	2.2107	2.3526	2.5023	2.6600	2.8262	3.0012	3.1855	3.3793	3.5832
8	2.3045	2.4760	2.6584	2.8526	3.0590	3.2784	3.5115	3.7589	4.0214	4.2998
9	2.5580	2.7731	3.0040	3.2519	3.5179	3.8030	4.1084	4.4355	4.7854	5.1598
10	2.8394	3.1058	3.3946	3.7072	4.0456	4.4114	4.8068	5.2338	5.6947	6.1917
11	3.1518	3.4786	3.8359	4.2262	4.6524	5.1173	5.6240	6.1760	6.7767	7.4301
12	3.4985	3.8960	4.3345	4.8180	5.3503	5.9360	6.5801	7.2876	8.0642	8.9161
13	3.8833	4.3635	4.8980	5.4924	6.1528	6.8858	7.6987	8.5994	9.5964	10.6993
14	4.3104	4.8871	5.5348	6.2613	7.0757	7.9875	9.0075	10.1472	11.4198	12.8392
15	4.7846	5.4736	6.2543	7.1379	8.1371	9.2655	10.5387	11.9737	13.5895	15.4070
16	5.3109	6.1304	7.0673	8.1372	9.3576	10.7480	12.3303	14.1290	16.1715	18.4884
17	5.8951	6.8660	7.9861	9.2765	10.7613	12.4677	14.4265	16.6722	19.2441	22.1861
18	6.5436	7.6900	9.0243	10.5752	12.3755	14.4625	16.8790	19.6733	22.9005	26.6233
19	7.2633	8.6128	10.1974	12.0557	14.2318	16.7765	19.7484	23.2144	27.2516	31.9480
20	8.0623	9.6463	11.5231	13.7435	16.3665	19.4608	23.1056	27.3930	32.4294	38.3376
21	8.0492	10.8083	13.0211	15.6676	18.8215	22.5745	27.0336	32.3238	38.5910	46.0051
22	9.9336	12.1003	14.7138	17.8610	21.6447	26.1864	31.6293	38.1421	45.9233	55.2061
23	11.0263	13.5523	16.6267	20.3616	24.8915	30.3762	37.0062	45.0076	54.6487	66.2474
24	12.2392	15.1786	18.7881	23.2122	28.6252	35.2364	43.2973	53.1090	65.0320	79.4968
25	13.5855	17.0001	21.2305	26.4619	32.9190	40.8742	50.6578	62.6686	77.3881	95.3962

(contd.)

(contd.)

Year	21%	22%	23%	24%	25%	26%	27%	28%	29%	30%
1	1.2100	1.2200	1.2300	1.2400	1.2500	1.2600	1.2700	1.2800	1.2900	1.3000
2	1.4641	1.4884	1.5129	1.5376	1.5625	1.5876	1.6129	1.6384	1.6641	1.6900
3	1.7716	1.8158	1.8609	1.9066	1.9531	2.0004	2.0484	2.0972	2.1467	2.1970
4	2.1436	2.2153	2.2889	2.3642	2.4414	2.5205	2.6014	2.6844	2.7692	2.8561
5	2.5937	2.7027	2.8153	2.9316	3.0518	3.1758	3.3038	3.4360	3.5723	3.7129
6	3.1384	3.2973	3.4628	3.6352	3.8147	4.0015	4.1959	4.3980	4.6083	4.8268
7	3.7975	4.0227	4.2593	4.5077	4.7684	5.0419	5.3288	5.6295	5.9447	6.2749
8	4.5950	4.9077	5.2389	5.5895	5.9605	6.3528	6.7675	7.2058	7.6686	8.1573
9	5.5600	5.9874	6.4439	6.9310	7.4506	8.0045	8.5948	9.2234	9.8925	10.6045
10	6.7275	7.3046	7.9259	8.5944	9.3132	10.0857	10.9153	11.8059	12.7614	13.7858
11	8.1403	8.9117	9.7489	10.6571	11.6415	12.7080	13.8625	15.1116	16.4622	17.9216
12	9.8497	10.8722	11.9912	13.2148	14.5519	16.0120	17.6053	19.3428	21.2362	23.2981
13	11.9182	13.2641	14.7491	16.3836	18.1899	20.1752	22.3588	24.7588	27.3947	30.2875
14	14.4210	16.1822	18.1414	20.3191	22.7374	25.4207	28.3957	31.6913	35.3391	39.3738
15	17.4494	19.7423	22.3140	25.1956	28.4217	32.0301	36.0625	40.5648	45.5875	51.1859
16	21.1138	24.0856	27.4462	31.2426	35.5271	40.3579	45.7994	51.9230	58.8079	66.5417
17	25.5477	29.3844	33.7588	38.7408	44.4089	50.8510	58.1652	66.4614	75.8621	86.5042
18	30.9127	35.8490	41.5233	48.0386	55.5112	64.0722	73.8698	85.0706	97.8622	112.4554
19	37.4043	43.7358	51.0737	59.5679	69.3889	80.7310	93.8147	108.8904	126.2422	146.1920
20	45.2593	53.3576	62.8206	73.8642	86.7362	101.7211	119.1446	139.3797	162.8524	190.0496
21	54.7637	65.0963	77.2694	91.5915	108.4202	128.1685	151.3137	178.4060	210.0796	247.0645
22	66.2641	79.4175	95.0413	113.5735	135.5253	161.4924	192.1684	228.3596	271.0027	321.1839
23	80.1795	96.8894	116.9008	140.8312	169.4066	203.4804	244.0538	292.3003	349.5935	417.5391
24	97.0172	118.2050	143.7880	174.6306	211.7582	256.3853	309.9483	374.1444	450.9756	542.8008
25	117.3909	144.2101	176.8593	216.5420	264.6978	323.0455	393.6344	478.9049	581.7582	705.6410

Lucidity (Perhaps it's worth writing across the purity of this page) is not lucid.

—Octavio Paz

18   Project Appraisal and Lending Decisions

INTRODUCTION

In this chapter we apply some of the knowledge gained so far in appraising a project proposal, which has been received by the manager of a branch of a nationalised bank located in a jute growing area. We have used a different name for the borrower for purposes of anonymity.

The promoters seek to obtain composite finance from the bank—both term loan and working capital advance.

SUMMARY OF THE PROJECT

The project report for Modern Furnishers (P) Limited has been prepared by the Jute Technological Research Laboratory (JTRL), an organisation under the Council of Scientific and Industrial Research, Government of India. A summary of the project report is given below.

Location

It is proposed to be located in the hinterland of a jute growing area for manufacturing jute stick boards. The hinterland produces about 30000 metric tonnes (MTs) jute fibre and 88000 MTs jute sticks annually.

Jute sticks are agricultural waste left after extraction of the jute fibre. This will form the principal raw material of the project. It is cheap, abundant, and annually renewable material.

It has been found in a study that jute growers of the district are going below the poverty line because of the unremunerative price now available in the market for jute fibre, owing to a sharp fall in demand from jute mills. Sale of jute sticks, which are presently being wasted as country fuel, will provide them additional money for their livelihood. From this point of view, the project has a social value.

Due to the high cost of hardwood and plywood boards manufactured by large industries, the entry of cheap jute stick boards manufactured by small-scale industries has been rather easy. The market is competitive in the sense that these boards have to compete with wood boards, but the scope is wide because of the cheap cost of jute stick boards. However, the quality of boards presently being manufactured is not very good. As such, jute boards have not yet been able to catch the fancy of the quality-conscious segment of the market. The present promoters intend to bring in a new technology, which will not only compete in price but in quality as well.

The typical uses of these boards are:

1.   Partition walls.
2.   False ceilings.

3. Decorative soundproof panels.
4. Printing blocks.

Process

There are two known processes for making these boards:

(a) An emulsion is first prepared by neutralising formaldehyde solution with diluted sodium hydroxide. Urea is then dissolved in this neutral formaldehyde solution. The resultant emulsion is kept at room temperature for three to four hours. Ammonium crystals are then added to bring the pH down to six. The solution is then thoroughly mixed with the jute sticks powder. The mixed material is laid on a 8' × 2' tray under a press in a frame covered with a stainless steel plate. Pressure is maintained, with the temperature being kept at 130–160°C for 15 minutes, and then released. The particle board is then taken out, cooled, and stored. Most of the existing manufacturers are using this technology.

(b) The second one, which is called the resin process, is an improved version of the existing process. Here, one obtains particle boards of a higher impact strength and lower water absorbency rate. These boards will also not disintegrate when soaked or boiled in water.

In this process, the formaldehyde solution is brought to pH 7.5 to 8 with sodium hydroxide solution. Urea is then added. The resultant mixture is then refluxed for two hours on a heating mantle.

The mixture is now distilled to remove water. The resin thus obtained is then mixed with acid catalyte, formic acid, or sulphuric acid to bring down the pH to six. The active resin is then mixed with jute stick powder and processed to make particle boards in the same manner as in the previous method. Both the processes are continuous.

The promoters are adopting the second process. Under this process 4 kg of jute sticks, 1 kg of urea, and 2 litres of formaldehyde solution are needed to manufacture one unit of board.

Plant and Machinery

A major part of the plant and machinery is to be fabricated. The import content is, however, low. The jute technological research laboratory (JTRL) has recommended two firms which are technically competent and capable of supplying the plant and machinery. Out of these, the promoters have selected the one which has quoted the lowest price.

Details of the plant and machinery are given below:

		(Rs in lakh)
i.	Resin plant (1000 kg capacity)	5.00
ii.	Roller for hot press	15.00
iii.	Disintegrator for grinding jute sticks	2.00
iv.	Mixed-blender	2.00
v.	Hot press sleeve heaters with hydraulic (8' × 4') planer	27.00
vi.	Drill	2.00
vii.	Electric saw	1.00
viii.	Miscellaneous spare parts and tools	3.00
ix.	Motors with transformer including installation and connection	35.00
	Total cost of machinery	92.00

Land

The proposed site is on National Highway No. 34 connecting North Bengal, Assam, Bihar, and West Bengal. A railway junction station is about 6 km from the site. The company has already purchased a plot of land measuring 2.5 acres for Rs 12.25 lakh, which can take care of the present planned capacity and future expansion by 50 per cent.

Water

Underground water is within a depth of 40'. There is also a reserve tank near the site of the proposed factory.

Shed and Building

The plant capacity is estimated at 384000 boards annually of 8' × 4' with 0.5' thickness or 2250 MTs. The JTRL has estimated that in order to run such a capacity the company requires the following shed and buildings.

		(Rs in lakh)
i.	Shed measuring 40000 square feet (sft)@ Rs 150 per sft	60.00
ii.	Office building and godown for storage of raw materials and stores measuring 15375 sft @ Rs 200 per sft	30.75
	Total	90.75

The promoters have also submitted the sanctioned plans of the building and the shed.

Office Equipment and Furniture

These are estimated at Rs 3 lakh.

Capital expenditure will thus be as follows:

	(Rs in lakh)
Plant and machinery	92.00
Land	12.25
Shed and building	90.75
Office equipment and furniture	3.00
Total	198.00

Consumption of Raw Materials

It is estimated that at 100 per cent capacity utilisation, the project will consume the following raw materials per month:

		(Rs in lakh)
i.	Jute sticks—375 MTs @ Rs 500 per MT	1.88
ii.	Urea—93.30 MTs @ Rs 5000 per MT	4.66
iii.	Formaldehyde—17,600 litres @ Rs 11 per litre (approx)	1.95
iv.	Components for resin	0.71
	Total	9.20

Cost estimates are made at 5 per cent more than the ruling market price to take care of price fluctuations in the future.

Manufacturing, Selling, and Distribution Expenses

The following monthly estimates are made at 100 per cent capacity utilisation.

		(Rs in lakh)
1.	Power and fuel	1.50
2.	Wages	0.84
3.	Wastage	0.20
4.	Salaries	2.10
5.	Repairs and maintenance	0.10
6.	Packing and forwarding (variable)	1.00
7.	Selling and other administrative expenses	2.70
8.	Depreciation	1.16
	Total	9.60

Notes:

1. Depreciation is charged on the written down value method @ 10 per cent on plant and machinery, and furniture and fixtures, and 5 per cent on shed and building.
2. Monthly production at 100 per cent capacity utilisation is estimated at 32000 boards of 8' × 2'—or 64000 boards of 4' × 2' size.
3. Selling and other administrative expenses include Rs 1 lakh as miscellaneous expenses. The selling price of each board of 8' × 2' size is Rs 90 in the market.
4. Manpower requirement:

The project at 100 per cent capacity utilisation will require the following personnel.

1. One electrician.
2. Two mechanics.
3. Ten skilled workers.
4. Eight unskilled workers.
5. Two clerk-cum-typists.
6. One mazdoor.
7. One security guard.

8. Manager—a mechanical/chemical engineer
9. Two supervisors.

Other Information

(a) The procurement period of jute sticks is from August to October.
(b) The storage of jute sticks requires a huge space. The company has the capacity to store only three months' consumption of jute sticks.
(c) It is possible to buy jute sticks during the off-season from wholesalers based in town. One month's credit is available for such purchases.
(d) It is also possible to book the jute sticks with the growers by paying 10 per cent advance. They also allow one month's credit. The advance deposit is, however, adjustable only at the end of the cropping season.
(e) Suppliers of chemicals normally give one month's credit.
(f) As already indicated, jute stick boards manufactured by small units have to compete with the wood board manufactured by large and established manufacturers. Hence, a longer line of credit has to be allowed to the buyers. It has also been found that the biggest buyers of these boards are interior decorators, who have to give one and a half to two months' credit to the main contractor.
(g) On an average, materials remain in the process for seven days.
(h) Boards of this variety are generally sold against orders. Retail sales will not be much. If the demanded credit is allowed, stock turnover will be very high.
(i) For the day-to-day functioning of the company, it is necessary to hold cash for seven days expenses.

Consultancy Arrangement

An agreement has been entered into with the Jute Technological Research Laboratory for supplying technical know-how and consultancy services.

Gestation Period of the Project

The time for implementation of the project is six months as mentioned in the project report. However, it appears from discussions with the promoters that one year will be a reasonable period, considering various uncertainties.

Promoters

The following are the promoters of Modern Furnishers:

1. Mr Aswini Pandey
2. Mr Diwakar Chaturbedi
3. Mr Anil Burman
4. Mr Mahabir Rai

They are also the first directors of the company.

At present, the promoters are engaged in plywood trading, construction, and cereal trading business. Their involvement in these firms and investments in land and building are given in Table 18.1.

Other investments of the promoters are given below the table.

Capital Structure of the Company: The company will have an authorised capital of Rs 150 lakh and paid-up capital of Rs 75 lakh contributed by the promoters and their friends and relatives.

The company has applied for a term loan of Rs 150 lakh and a working capital loan of Rs 30 lakh.

Relevant figures, as obtained from the projected profit and loss account for five years, are given in Table 18.2.

TABLE **18.1**   Statement of Wealth of the Promoters

(Rs in lakh)

Name of Firm	Capital and Reserves of Partners			
	Aswini Pandey	Diwakar Chaturbedi	Anil Burman	Mahabir Rai
M/s Adam Plywood (plywood dealers)	98.46	52.36	38.25	—
M/s Sree Ganesh Bhander (cereal dealer)	23.40	3.82	7.80	—
M/s Mahabir Builders (construction firm)	—	—	—	28.57
M/s Chatur (construction firm)	—	25.53	—	—
Sub-total	121.86	81.71	46.05	28.57
Land and building	17.00	14.00	12.00	8.00
Total	138.86	95.71	58.05	36.57

(Rs in lakh)

Particulars of Deposit	Aswini Pandey	Diwakar Chaturbedi	Anil Burman	Mahabir Rai
Fixed deposit and mutual funds	13.00	6.00	7.00	8.25
Shares	2.25	0.25	0.60	2.00
Savings accounts with this bank	0.25	0.05	0.15	0.20
Savings accounts with other banks	0.05	0.01	0.00	0.10
Total	15.55	6.31	7.75	10.55

TABLE **18.2**   Projected Profit and Loss Account

(Rs in lakh)

Particulars	1st year	2nd year	3rd year	4th year	5th year
1. Capacity utilisation	50%	60%	70%	80%	100%
2. Sales net of stock adjustment	172.80	207.36	241.92	276.48	345.60
3. Depreciation					
(a) Shed and building @ 5%	4.54	4.31	4.10	3.89	3.70
(b) Plant and machinery, furniture and fixtures @ 10%	9.50	8.55	7.70	6.93	6.23
Total	14.04	12.86	11.80	10.82	9.93
4. Profit after depreciation but before interest and tax (PBIT)	24.12	44.45	64.66	84.80	124.00

Sales are projected at the market price—@ Rs 90 per unit. Later, we made a conservative estimate of the sale price. The rates of depreciation used in the project report are at variance both with those prescribed under the Indian Companies Act and the Income Tax Act.

For purposes of the financial evaluation of the project, we use the rates prescribed under the Income Tax Act. However, the rates of depreciation used by the consultant in the project report have some bearing on the estimated life of the project, which we examine later.

FINANCIAL ANALYSIS OF THE PROJECT

The project will have the following installed capacity, assuming 25 working days in a month.

1.   Annual 100% capacity—3,84,000 boards of 8' × 2' or 2250 MTs, or
2.   Monthly 100% capacity—32,000 boards of the same size or 187.5 MTs, or
3.   Daily 100% capacity—1280 boards of the same size or 7.5 MTs

COST STRUCTURE

Although the projected profitability, as calculated in the project report, is based on the market price of Rs 90 for one 8' × 2' board, considering the fact that the market is competitive, and is going to be more intense in the future, and also that the borrower is a new entrant in the field, it is preferable to take a conservative but reasonable estimate of the price at which the borrower can sell his products. Five per cent below the present market price is a reasonable estimate. Being a little more conservative, we can take the sale price at Rs 85 per board. However, the conservative cost estimates made in the project report are reasonable.

Based on our estimate of the sales price, and the cost estimates made in the project report, calculations of monthly and annual working results are made at 100 per cent capacity utilisation in Table 18.3.

LIFE OF THE PROJECT

There is no indication in the project report about the approximate life of the project. Nevertheless, we can make an estimate of it through the rate of depreciation proposed to be charged by the company.

Although 25 per cent depreciation allowance under the written down value method is available now on plant and machinery under the amended Income Tax rules, the company has chosen to charge depreciation at the rate of 10 per cent on the written down value of the plant and machinery. The latter may be the true depreciation as envisaged by the consultant, and should be taken for calculating the life of the project and drawing up of the final accounts. But for calculating the after-tax cash flow from operations, depreciation allowance as prescribed in the Income Tax rules should be taken. Under the written down value method, the time required to completely depreciate a machine is infinity. Hence, under this method, theoretically a machine remains on the books of account perpetually. However, when the written down value of a machine reaches one-fifth of its original value, we may treat the machine as having run out its useful life. On this basis, the written down value of the plant and machinery proposed to be installed by the company will reach one-fifth of its original values in 15 years at a 10 per cent annual rate of depreciation. The life of the project is, therefore, estimated as 15 years.

SALVAGE VALUE

The shed and building, which is depreciated at 5 per cent per annum, will have some salvage value at the end of 15 years. The land which is presently valued at Rs 12.25 lakh will have a shed

TABLE **18.3**   Projected Funds Generation of the Project

(Rs in lakh)

Monthly 100% capacity production of 32000 Boards		
Consumption of raw materials		9.20
Direct wages		0.84
Power and fuel		1.50
Wastage		0.20
Repair and maintenance		0.10
*Depreciation (as per the Income Tax Act)		2.70
Cost of production		14.54
Sales		27.20 (32000 boards at the rate of Rs 85 each)
Gross profit		12.66
Less:		
Salaries	2.10	
Packing and distribution (variable)	1.00	
Selling and other administrative expenses	2.70	5.80
Profit before Interest and income tax		6.86
Add: Back depreciation*		2.70
Net fund inflow before interest and tax		9.56
Annual sales projected at 100% capacity utilisation		Rs 27.20 × 12 = Rs 326.40 lakh
Annual fund generated before interest and tax at 100% capacity utilisation		Rs 9.56 × 12 = Rs 114.72 lakh

Note: * This will be different in later years (see Table 18.7).

on it costing Rs 60 lakh and a building costing Rs 30.75 lakh. The depreciated value at the end of 15 years of both the shed and the building will be Rs 40 lakh approximately. A shed normally loses its value faster. Moreover, a shed specially designed for one project may not always be useful for another project. Hence, generally the resale value of a shed is not much. A reasonable estimate of the salvage value of both the land and building can be taken as Rs 18 lakh. The shed and machines may together fetch another Rs 5 lakh. The realisable value of current assets net of current liabilities (that is, the money provided by the company) may be taken at 50 per cent of Rs 14.36 lakh or Rs 7 lakh approximately (see Table 18.6). The total salvage value of the project

at the end of 15 years is, therefore, estimated as Rs 30 lakh.

ESTIMATING PROJECTED REVENUE

The consultant has projected that in the first year the project will be able to utilise 50 per cent of its installed capacity. It will increase gradually over the next four years and reach 100 per cent in the fifth year. An enquiry with JTRL revealed that it was possible for similar projects to reach near 100 per cent capacity utilisation in less than five years. The projections, therefore, appear to be reasonable, except that it would not be wise to assume that the project will continuously generate 100 per cent capacity sales from the fifth year onwards.

We know that due to the operation of natural laws, any plant will produce a lesser and lesser amount of output as it ages.[1] Although it is possible to determine with precision such gradual fall in capacity, and project year-wise realisable revenues accordingly, such a precision may not be necessary for the purpose at hand. We can approach the problem once again via the rate of depreciation of the machines (the main part of the plant) on the basis of which we have determined that when the machines have reduced to 20 per cent of its value the life of the project will end. We interpret this as follows.

The plant is expected to reach its full capacity sales of Rs 326.40 lakh (27.20×12) in the fifth year (at the revised price), and in the next 10 years it will gradually expend 80 per cent of its capacity, which is equivalent to Rs 261.12 lakh worth of sales. Assuming now that the plant's capacity starts deteriorating from the first day of the fifth year itself (that is, its average production throughout the year shall not be Rs 326.40 lakh, but less than that), we can say that in 11 years the plant will lose Rs 261.12 lakh worth of sales, or Rs 23.74 lakh in sales every year, which is 7.27, or say, 7 per cent of full capacity sales. Average sales from the fifth year onwards can, therefore, be taken as 93 per cent, or say, 90 per cent of full capacity sales, or Rs 293.76 lakh.

RELEVANT CASH FLOWS

We have learnt from the last chapter that in making a financial evaluation of a project, we should begin with estimating the relevant cash flows, which are recapitulated below.

---

[1] Bhattacharya, Hrishikes, 'Towards a Theory of the Value of Capital Goods—A Techno-Economic Approach', *Economic and Political Weekly*, 26 November, 1988.

Cash Inflows
1. Cash flow from operations.
2. Salvage value.

Cash Outflows
1. Capital expenditure.
2. Incremental current assets.

We have already calculated salvage value. The estimate for capital expenditure as given is verified to be true. The cash flow from operations is calculated after-tax, but before depreciation. Since interest and depreciation are allowable deductions from income under the Income Tax Act, we have to first calculate profit after interest and depreciation, and then apply the relevant rate of tax to arrive at the after-tax profit. Depreciation and interest are then added back to arrive at the cash flow from operations.

For purpose of calculating interest, it is necessary to make a comprehensive assessment of the term loan and working capital requirements of the project and the bank finance there against, assuming, for the present, that the project is being financed by the bank. This exercise will also enable us to estimate the incremental net current assets.

WORKING CAPITAL AND TERM LOAN

As mentioned in Chapter 6, the assessment of working capital requirements of a project should begin with the determination of the core working capital (CWC).

We learn from the project report that the conversion process for producing jute stick board takes seven days, and it is a continuous process. The banker should call for the process diagram and check the actual conversion time involved in the process. Assuming that it is at par with the project report, we now estimate the funds blocked in the conversion process.

At 100 per cent capacity, the cost of production per month is Rs 14.54 lakh, as calculated before. Cost of production includes depreciation of Rs 2.70 lakh, which does not claim any fund outlay, and hence should be ignored for computation of working capital requirements. The cash cost of production is, therefore, Rs 11.84 lakh.

We have noted that the conversion time is one week. Assuming now that the components of the cash cost of production are variable in nature (though, one such component, namely repair and maintenance, need not exactly be so), we can estimate the funds blocked in the conversion process, or the conversion fund cycle as follows.

	(Rs in lakh)
Cash cost of production blocked in conversion process or work-in-progress: Rs 11.84 lakh/4	2.96
Variable packing and distribution expenses: Rs 1 lakh/4	0.25
Funds blocked in conversion process	3.21
Annual cash cost of production at 100 per cent capacity = Rs 11.84 lakh × 12	142.08
Variable packing and distribution expenses = Rs 1 lakh × 12	12.00
Total	154.08

Hence, (1) The velocity of conversion fund cycle = 154.08/3.21 = 48 times a year.

(2) The unit velocity of the conversion fund cycle = 1/48 or 0.020833.

We now allocate fixed overheads to the conversion fund cycle and determine CWC as:[2]

[2] It can also be calculated in the following manner as laid down in Chapter 6. UV = work-in-process fund/annual cash cost of production: 2.96/142.08 = 0.020833

Hence, CWC = UV (cash cost of production + variable packing and distribution expenses + fixed costs) = 0.020833 (142.08 + 12.00 + 57.60) = Rs 4.41 lakhs (approximately).

	(Rs in lakh)
Conversion fund cycle	3.21
Allocation of fixed overheads*	1.20
4.80 × 12 × 0.020833	
Core working capital	4.41

Fixed overheads per month

	(Rs in lakh)
1. Salaries	2.10
2. Selling and other admn. exp.	2.70
Total	4.80

We now proceed to estimate other current assets that are likely to be generated from the operations of the project.

Let us recall that at 100 per cent capacity utilisation per month, raw material consumption is as follows.

	(Rs in lakh)
a. Jute sticks—375 MTs @ Rs 500 per MTs	1.88
b. Urea—93.30 MTs @ Rs 5000 per MTs	4.66
c. Formaldehyde—17,660 litres @ Rs 11 per litre	1.95
d. Components for resin	0.71
Total	9.20

Jute sticks have to be lifted in sizeable quantities immediately after harvesting. The procurement period is from August to October. During these three months, the company has to lift sticks for its current consumption, and also for consumption during the rest of the year, jute being a one-time annual crop. One way is to procure stocks for the entire nine months' consumption during the harvesting season, but that will require a lot of space in the godown, which will be unremunerative in the long run. Another way is to lift a certain quan-

It should now be clear that CWC can be calculated straightaway by multiplying the aggregate cost with the derived UV as shown in this footnote. It is not necessary to go through the second stage of allocation of fixed overheads to the conversion fund cycle, which has been shown to explain the concept.

tity of stocks, for say, three months consumption (thereby assuring six months production, that is, three months current consumption plus three months stocks for future consumption), and book the future requirement with the growers against some advance, say 10 per cent of the stock holding. It is preferable to give this advance at the time of retting the crop. The third alternative is to procure stocks for three months future consumption during the harvesting period and rely on wholesalers for the remaining six months. The cost of materials lifted from wholesalers will, however, be higher than that from growers.

The second alternative appears to be feasible. We, therefore, propose the following buffer stock at 100 per cent capacity utilisation.

			(Rs in lakh)
A.	(1)	Stocks of jute sticks for 3 months consumption: 1.88 × 3	5.64
	(2)	One months' stock of chemicals and resin components	7.32
		Total buffer stock of raw materials	12.96
		Say,	13.00
B.		10% advance to growers for 6 months consumption of jute sticks (Rs 11.28 lakh)	1.13

The market for the boards is competitive. Presently, it is dominated by large wood board manufacturers, though small producers are making steady inroads in the market. In that sense, the market for jute stick boards is growing. Being a new entrant, the company may have to give a longer credit period to the buyers. The credit period may be estimated as two months, because the buyers of these boards are mostly interior decorators, who give a similar length of credit to the main contractors. Two months total cash cost of sales can, therefore, be taken as funds blocked in debtors. That is, 2 (Rs 11.84 + Rs 5.80) = Rs 35.28 lakh.

As the boards are generally supplied against orders, retail sales will not be much. For this reason, 15 days stock of the finished product will be sufficient to take care of over-the-counter sales, which at cost of sale comes to Rs 8.82 lakh.

The company will be required to hold buffer cash for one week's cash expenses. At 100 per cent capacity utilisation, monthly cash expenses are as below:

	(Rs in lakh)
Repair and maintenance	0.10
Power and fuel	1.50
Packing and distribution	1.00
Miscellaneous expenses	1.00
Total for one month	3.60
One week's requirement	0.90

Gross current assets at 100 per cent capacity utilisation are tabulated in Table 18.4 with their CWC multipliers.

One month's credit is normally available for chemicals. Although 10 per cent advance has to be given to growers for holding stocks for the company, a month's credit will be available from them because of supply exceeding the demand. In effect, credit for one month's consumption of aggregate raw materials will be available, which is Rs 9.20 lakh at 100 per cent capacity utilisation. In terms of CWC multipliers, it is 9.20/4.41 = 2.09.

We can now calculate the working capital requirement of the project at 100 per cent capacity utilisation.

	(Rs in lakh)	
	Amount	CWC Multipliers
Gross current assets (or gross working capital requirement)	62.05	14.05
Less: Sundry creditors	9.20	2.09
Working capital gap or net current assets for purpose of project evaluation	52.85	11.96

TABLE **18.4**   Gross Current Assets at CWC Multipliers

Particulars of Current Assets (1)	Rs in lakh (2)	CWC Multipliers (col. 2/4.41) (3)
1. Stock of raw materials	12.96	2.93
2. Advance to growers of jute sticks, 10% of six months consumption	1.13	0.25
3. Work-in-process (cash)	2.96	0.67
4. Debtors—two months cost of sales	35.28	8.00
5. Stocks of finished goods—15 days cost of sales	8.82	2.00
6. Cash—one week's cash expenses	0.90	0.20
Gross current assets/CWC multipliers	62.05	14.05

The requirement of gross working capital, working capital gap, and their CWC multipliers are calculated at 100 per cent capacity utilisation. We have mentioned before that in the first year, the project starts with 50 per cent capacity utilisation. The capacity utilisation gradually increases, reaches its maximum at 90 per cent in the fifth year, and stays there for the rest of the life of the project. While due to these different levels of capacity utilisation the quantum of CWC will vary, the working capital structure in terms of CWC multipliers will remain the same. We now calculate gross working capital requirement and the working capital gap for different levels of capacity utilisation (Table 18.5).

As during the subsequent years of the project life, capacity utilisation will remain at the 90 per cent level, the gross working capital and working capital gap will remain at Rs 57.45 lakh and Rs 48.90 lakh respectively at the present price level.

Working Capital Finance

	(Rs in lakh)
Gross current assets in the *first year* (Table 18.5, Item No. 7)	39.34
Less: Sundry creditors	5.85
Working capital gap	33.49
Less: 25% of gross current assets	9.84
Permissible working capital finance	23.65
Say,	Rs 24 lakh

Interest on both term loan and working capital finance may be taken as 18.5 per cent per annum.

In the next four years the requirement of working capital will increase, so also the bank advance. The bank may sanction a working capital term loan (WCTL) of Rs 24 lakh repayable in 5 years, and a cash credit limit for incremental requirements, which will continue during the life of the project. The equated annual instalment for repayment of WCTL @ 18.5 per cent per annum will be Rs 7.76 lakh (see Appendix 18.1). Annual incidence of interest cost and other calculations are shown in Table 18.6.

Term Loan

	(Rs in lakh)
Cost of acquisition of fixed assets	198.00
Less: 33.33% being margin requirement	66.00
Term loan	132.00

Assuming that the amount of term loan will be disbursed in stages depending upon the progress of implementation, we may take an average interest of six months on the loan amount of Rs 132 lakhs, which comes to Rs 12.20 lakh (approximately). Capitalising the first year's interest, the loan burden on the company at the beginning of the first year will be 132 + 12.20 = Rs 144.20 lakh. The capitalised interest of Rs 12.20 lakh will also be added to the cost of acquisition of

TABLE 18.5   WC Requirement at Different Levels of Capacity Utilisation

(Rs in lakh)

Serial No.	Particulars	Capacity Utilisation				
		50% (1st year)	60% (2nd year)	70% (3rd year)	80% (4th year)	90% (5th year)
1.	Yearly cash cost of production	71.04	85.25	99.46	113.66	127.87
2.	Variable packing and distribution expenses	6.00	7.20	8.40	9.60	10.80
3.	Total variable costs	77.04	92.45	107.86	123.26	138.67
4.	Conversion fund cycle ([3] multiplied by u.v., 0.020833)	1.60	1.93	2.25	2.57	2.89
5.	Allocation of fixed overhead (Rs 5760 × 0.020833)	1.20	1.20	1.20	1.20	1.20
6.	Core working capital	2.80	3.13	3.45	3.77	4.09
7.	Gross current assets or gross working capital requirement ([6] multiplied by CWC multipliers for GWC = 14.05)	39.34	43.98	48.47	52.97	57.45
8.	*Less:* Sundry creditors (CWC multiplied by CWC multipliers for creditors = 2.09)	5.85	6.54	7.21	7.88	8.55
9.	Working capital gap	33.49	37.44	41.26	45.09	48.90
10.	Relevant cash outflow for project evaluation (incremental)	(33.49)	(3.95)	(3.82)	(3.83)	(3.81)

TABLE 18.6   Projected Working Capital Requirements for Five Years and Interest Payable

(Rs in lakh)

	1st year	2nd year	3rd year	4th year	5th year and onwards
Working capital gap	33.49	37.44	41.26	45.09	48.90
Less: 25% on GCA	9.84	11.00	12.12	13.24	14.36
Bank finance (BF)	23.65	26.44	29.14	31.85	34.54
Incremental BF or cash credit (see note 2 to this table)	—	2.44	5.14	7.85	10.54
Interest payable	4.44	4.00	3.61	3.23	2.83

Notes: 1. See Table 18.5 for calculation of working capital gap and GCA.

2. Incremental BF or cash credit is calculated assuming base level advance of Rs 24 lakh in the form of a loan (WCTL).

3. Interest payable is calculated both on WCTL of Rs 24 lakh on reducing balance and on cash credit @ 18.5% per annum.

4. From the sixth year onwards, interest of Rs 1.95 lakh per annum will be payable only on cash credit of Rs 10.54 lakh, WCTL having been already paid off.

fixed assets to feature as capital expenditure in the 'O' year (see Table 18.8). The equated yearly instalment inclusive of interest, as calculated in Appendix 18.1, will be Rs 32.66 lakhs. The yearly interest that will be charged to the loan account by the bank is given below for the entire 10-year repayment period.

(Rs in lakh)

Year	Interest chargeable	Remarks
1.	26.88	Interest calculation is based on
2.	24.00	annual repayment of Rs 14.42
3.	21.34	lakh towards the principal
4.	18.67	amount. In case of payment by
5.	16.00	equated instalments, the aggregate
6.	13.34	incidence of interest will be
7.	10.67	somewhat higher.
8.	8.00	
9.	5.33	
10.	2.67	

CASH FLOW FROM OPERATIONS

We have already mentioned that in estimating cash flows from operations, we have to first calculate the net profit after interest, depreciation, and tax. We have already calculated interest on term loan and working capital advance. We now calculate the depreciation allowance on fixed assets.

The project will have the benefit of the following depreciation allowance on fixed assets under the Income Tax Act.

Building etc.	10 per cent on written down value
Plant and machinery	25 " " " " " "
Furniture and fixtures	10 " " " " " "

Assume that the present rate of income tax on the business income of a domestic company is 40 per cent. We have ignored surcharge while calculating the cash flows.

In Table 18.7, we show cash flows from operations by taking the above into account. We recall that interest on the working capital term loan will cease after five years, and that on the term loan will cease after 10 years on their full repayment. But interest on cash credit will continue during the life of the project.

We can now proceed to calculate the net present value (NPV) of the project (Table 18.8).

The NPV of the project can also be derived as below:

(Rs in lakh)

Present value of net cash inflows	278.89
Less: Present value of net cash outflows	214.36
NPV	64.53 (as in Table 18.8)

As NPV is comfortably positive, the project can be regarded as financially viable.

PROFITABILITY INDEX (PI) AND INTERNAL RATE OF RETURN (IRR)

Profitability Index

Although the profitability index (PI) is primarily used to rank competing projects in terms of profitability, it can also be used by a banker (to whom only the selected project comes) to know the profitability status of a project. The index takes the following form.

$$PI = \frac{Present\ value\ of\ cash\ Inflows}{Present\ value\ of\ cash\ outflows}$$

For the project under consideration, the PI will be 278.89/214.36=1.30

It is obvious that the higher the PI, the higher is the return. When the PI of the project falls below unity, it fails to meet the desired rate of return. The present project has a good profitability index.

TABLE 18.7 Cash Flow from Operations

(Rs in lakh)

Year	1	2	3	4	5	6	7	8	9	10	11	12	13	14	15
Capacity Utilisation	50%	60%	70%	80%	90%	90%	90%	90%	90%	90%	90%	90%	90%	90%	90%
A. Sales	163.20	195.84	228.48	261.12	293.76	293.76	293.76	293.76	293.76	293.76	293.76	293.76	293.76	293.76	293.76
B. Cost of Ssales															
1. Operating variable cost (COP + packing cost)	77.04	92.45	107.86	123.26	138.67	138.67	138.67	138.67	138.67	138.67	138.67	138.67	138.67	138.67	138.67
2. Operating fixed cost	57.60	57.60	57.60	57.60	57.60	57.60	57.60	57.60	57.60	57.60	57.60	57.60	57.60	57.60	57.60
3. Depreciation															
(a) Building, etc. (10%)	9.07	8.17	7.35	6.62	5.95	5.36	4.82	4.34	3.91	3.52	3.16	2.85	2.56	2.31	2.08
(b) Plant and machinery (2.5%)	23.00	17.25	12.94	9.70	7.28	5.46	4.09	3.07	2.30	1.73	1.30	0.97	0.73	0.55	0.41
(c) Furniture and fixtures (10%)	0.30	0.27	0.24	0.22	0.20	0.18	0.16	0.14	0.13	0.12	0.10	0.09	0.08	0.07	0.07
Total	167.01	175.74	185.99	197.40	209.70	207.27	205.34	203.82	202.61	201.64	200.83	200.18	199.64	199.20	198.83
Operating profit (A – B)	(3.81)	20.10	42.49	63.72	84.06	86.49	88.42	89.94	91.15	92.12	92.93	93.58	94.12	94.56	94.93
Less: Interest	(31.57)	(28.50)	(25.45)	(22.40)	(18.83)	(15.29)	(12.62)	(9.95)	(7.28)	(4.62)	(1.95)	(1.95)	(1.95)	(1.95)	(1.95)
Net profit	(35.38)	(8.40)	17.04	41.32	65.23	71.20	75.80	79.99	83.87	87.50	90.98	91.63	92.17	92.61	92.98
Less: Income tax	—	—	—	—	—	21.36	22.74	24.00	25.16	26.25	36.39	36.65	36.87	37.04	37.19
Profit after tax	(35.38)	(8.40)	17.04	41.32	65.23	49.84	53.06	55.99	58.71	61.25	54.59	54.98	55.30	55.57	55.79
Cash flow from operations (Profit after tax + interest + depreciation)	28.56	45.79	63.02	80.26	97.49	76.13	74.75	73.49	72.33	71.24	61.10	60.84	60.62	60.45	60.30

Note: Income tax is charged as follows:

Tax holiday for 5 years followed by 30 per cent tax for the next 5 years under Section 80–9A of the Income Tax Act, and thereafter at 40 per cent. Surcharge is ignored.

Table 18.7 (*contd.*)

Notes: 1. We have not shown any gradual increase in the operating costs of the project. In reality, operating costs tend to rise with the age of the machinery. In the case of variable operating costs, it is possible to have some idea of this rate of increase by studying the movement of the operating expenses of similar firms. Since such information is not available to us, we have ignored it.

2. In the present case, we have taken fixed overheads constant at Rs 57.60 lakhs per annum for the entire working life of the plant at 100 per cent capacity utilisation for ease of calculations. Moreover, the higher-than-real cost taken here will off-set the future rise in overheads. In a real-life situation fixed overheads (excluding depreciation) are expected to rise with time. Since this group of expenses is not so much technology-dependent, the rate of increase across the industry is generally known. A rise of 2 to 2.5 per cent per annum is a fair estimate. Though the incidence of fixed overheads, to a large extent, is independent of capacity utilisation, it is unlikely that a firm will appoint all the personnel and buy all the stationery in the first year of production, when it is working only at 50 per cent of its capacity. The burden increases only gradually, and in effect, may settle down at full office costs in the fourth and fifth years of its operation.

TABLE 18.8   Discounting of Relevant Cash Flows

(Rs in lakh)

Year	Capital Expenditure (inclusive of Interest of Rs 12.20 lakh Capitalised)	Cash flow from Operations (Table 18.7)	Increase/ Decrease in Net Current Assets (Table 18.5)	Salvage Value	Net Annual Cash Flows	Discount Factor at @ 18.5%	Present Value of Net Cash Flows
0.	(210.20)	—	—	—	(210.20)	1.0000	(210.20)
1.	—	28.56	(33.49)	—	(4.93)	0.8439	(4.16)
2.		45.79	(3.95)	—	41.84	0.7121	29.80
3.		63.02	(3.82)	—	59.20	0.6009	35.58
4.		80.26	(3.83)	—	76.43	0.5071	38.76
5.		97.49	(3.81)	—	93.68	0.4280	40.09
6.		76.13	—	—	76.13	0.3612	27.49
7.		74.75	—	—	74.75	0.3048	22.78
8.		73.49	—	—	73.49	0.2572	18.90
9.		72.33	—	—	72.33	0.2170	15.70
10.		71.24	—	—	71.24	0.1832	13.05
11.		61.10	—	—	61.10	0.1546	9.44
12.		60.84	—	—	60.84	0.1304	7.94
13.		60.62	—	—	60.62	0.1101	6.67
14.		60.45	—	—	60.45	0.0929	5.61
15.		60.30	—	30.00	90.30	0.0784	7.08
Net present value							64.53

Internal Rate of Return

The IRRs of the project at different discount rates are calculated in Table 18.9.

It is clear from Table 18.9 that NPV will be zero somewhere between 18.5 per cent and 24 per cent discount rate. The internal rate of return at which NPV becomes zero is calculated below.

IRR = 18.5 + (64.53/66.19) × 5.50 = 23.86 per cent

As the IRR of 23.86 per cent is sufficiently higher than the average cost of capital, that is, 18.5 per cent (which for our purposes is the oppor-

tunity cost of capital), the project is financially viable.

One may observe from Table 18.9 that as we increase the discount rate, NPV does not fall at a constant rate, but at a declining rate. Due to this reason, the IRR calculated by the simple formula shown above may overestimate it. We can make a more precise estimate by evaluating the fall in NPV for discount rates, of say, between 23.85 and 23.86. Although it is not difficult to make such a minute evaluation with the help of a scientific calculator or by a computer package, for most purposes we do not need such precision, as we can very well observe from column 5

TABLE **18.9**   Internal Rates of Return at
Various Discount Rates

(Rs in lakh)

Year (1)	Net Annual Cash Flows (2)	Present Values of Cash Flows at Various Discount Rates		
		18.5% (3)	24% (4)	23.86% (5)
0.	(210.20)	(210.20)	(210.20)	(210.20)
1.	(4.93)	(4.16)	(3.98)	(3.98)
2.	41.84	29.80	27.21	27.28
3.	59.20	35.58	31.04	31.16
4.	76.43	38.76	32.33	32.48
5.	93.68	40.09	31.95	32.14
6.	76.13	27.49	20.94	21.09
7.	74.75	22.78	16.58	16.72
8.	73.49	18.90	13.15	13.27
9.	72.33	15.70	10.44	10.55
10.	71.24	13.05	8.29	8.39
11.	61.10	9.44	5.73	5.81
12.	60.84	7.94	4.60	4.67
13.	60.62	6.67	3.70	3.76
14.	60.45	5.61	2.98	3.03
15.	90.30	7.08	3.58	3.65
Net present value		64.53	–1.66	–0.18

of Table 18.9 that at 23.86 per cent, NPV is close to zero.

NPV VERSUS IRR

Although in the present case both the NPV and IRR methods have given the same 'viable' verdict, this may not always hold true. For a one-period investment, the same conclusion is reached under both the methods. Similarly, for a project that requires a single cash outflow in return for a stream of future inflows, the NPV and IRR methods will recommend the same accept or reject decision. But if a project's cash flows

do not follow this simple pattern, there may be more than one IRR, of which at least one may be imaginary. Besides, in the evaluation of mutually exclusive projects, the NPV and IRR methods may rank projects in a different order. Further, the IRR does not tell us how much the investment is and for how long. It is only a relative measure of wealth arising out of a project, whereas the NPV method enables us to assess the absolute value of the project, which is the primary concern of both an entrepreneur and a banker. In that sense, the NPV method can be considered superior to the IRR method. However, a banker is well-advised to calculate the IRR of the project also to know 'what rate of interest the project can bear' or what is the margin of safety available to him.

BREAK-EVEN POINT

Although some idea can be formed about the probable break-even point of sales from Table 18.7, it is preferable to determine it more precisely at this stage.

At 100 per cent capacity utilisation, the unit is expected to produce 384000 boards of 8' × 2' size per annum under the following cost structure.

		(Rs in lakh)
Variable cost		154.08
Fixed costs:		
Salaries and other selling and distribution costs	57.60	
Depreciation (average of 5 years)	35.13	
Interest (average of 5 years)	25.35	118.08
Total cost	Rs	272.16
Sale price per unit	85.00	
Less: Variable cost per unit (Rs 154.08 lakh/384000)	40.13	
Contribution	44.87	

Hence, the break-even point of sales will be:
Fixed costs/Contribution per unit = 11808000/44.87 = 263160 units of 8' × 2' boards.

The company will reach this break-even point of sales at $(263160/384000) \times 100 = 68.5\%$ (approx.) of capacity utilisation, which the company is reaching around its third year of operation.

DEBT–SERVICE COVERAGE RATIO

Although the project is found to be financially viable, the banker may not accept it as a lendable project unless he is satisfied about the repaying capacity of the project. This is judged by the debt–service coverage ratio, as we have explained in an earlier chapter. It should be remembered that the debt–service coverage ratio has to be calculated for all the years till the repayment of the loan amount. In the present case, the bank is sanctioning both the term loan and working capital advance. However, a part of the latter (cash credit), is not repayable except on the winding up of the project, hence that part of the principal amount of working capital advance (cash credit) need not be included in the debt-service burden, but interest payable on it should be considered.

We have calculated the debt–service coverage ratio of the project for 10 years in Table 18.10.

We have mentioned in the last chapter that the minimum debt–service coverage ratio should be 1.50. Table 18.10 shows that the project reaches this minimum ratio around the third year. It is unable to service its debt obligation in the first year, and just meets it in the second year. But the project cannot be rejected on this ground, because in subsequent years the ratio is well above the minimum required. Although the deviation in this case is not much and that too during the first two years only, still if the bank insists it may suggest one of the four alternatives mentioned below, or a suitable combination of them.

1. The borrower may be asked to put in more funds as share capital and hence, take a lower quantum of term loan. At present, the proposed share capital is on the lower side. The directors' statement of personal wealth suggests that they can bring in more share capital.

TABLE **18.10**   Debt–Service Coverage Ratio

(Rs in lakh)

Year (1)	Profit before Interest and Depreciation (2)	Equated Annual Instalment of Term Loan* (3)	Equated Annual Instalment of Working Capital Term Loan* (4)	Interest on Cash Credit (5)	Total Debt-Service Burden (cols. 3 + 4 + 5) (6)	Ratio (col. 2/col. 6) (7)
1.	28.56	32.66	7.76	0.45	40.87	0.70
2.	45.79	32.66	7.76	0.95	41.37	1.11
3.	63.02	32.66	7.76	1.45	41.87	1.51
4.	80.26	32.66	7.76	1.95	42.37	1.89
5.	97.49	32.66	7.76	1.95	42.37	2.30
6.	76.13	32.66	7.76	1.95	42.37	1.80
7.	74.75	32.66	7.76	1.95	42.37	1.76
8.	73.49	32.66	7.76	1.95	42.37	1.73
9.	72.33	32.66	7.76	1.95	42.37	1.71
10.	71.24	32.66	7.76	1.95	42.37	1.68

Note: * See Appendix 18.1 for calculation.

2. The borrower should seek an alternative (cheaper) source to finance a portion of fixed assets to bring down the average cost of capital.

3. The bank should allow a longer repayment period of term loan, so that the annual debt-service obligation is reduced.

4. The bank should allow the borrower to carry over the unpaid portion of the debt-service obligation to the following years.

Concluding Remarks

In this chapter we made a comprehensive credit appraisal—both for working capital and term loan—of a real-life project by applying the methods and techniques that we have learnt so far, particularly those in Chapters 6, 15, and 17.

Project evaluation and financing decisions should begin with establishing the viability of a product (Chapter 17). Once this is done, we proceed to determine the technical and financial viability of the project. But a lending decision does not always rest on financial viability. A project may be financially viable but not always lendable. In order to make an otherwise financially viable project lendable, it may be necessary to re-engineer the capital/financial structure of the project.

Appendix 18.1

CALCULATION OF EQUATED INSTALMENTS

We use a discount factor for discounting future sums to arrive at the present value. We now calculate a capital recovery factor which when multiplied with the principal amount of loan gives that equated instalment which will repay the loan by a certain period with a certain rate of interest charged on the unpaid balance.

The capital recovery factor is calculated on Re 1, as in the case of the discount factor, by using the following formula:

$$C_f = \frac{i}{1 - \dfrac{1}{(1+i)^n}}$$

where,

C_f = The capital recovery factor for Re 1
i = The interest on Re 1 for the given period (yearly, half-yearly, quarterly, monthly, etc.) at a given rate
n = Number of instalments

As an example, let us calculate the capital recovery factor of Re 1 (C_f) repayable in five years in equal annual instalments with interest at 13 per cent per annum.

Here,

$$i = 0.13$$
$$n = 5$$

Hence,

$$C_f = \frac{0.13}{1 - \dfrac{1}{(1 + 0.13)^5}}$$

$$\text{or, } C_f = \frac{0.13}{0.4572}$$

$$\text{or, } C_f = 0.2843$$

If the term loan for a project is Rs 10 lakh repayable in five years and the implementation period of the project is one year, we should adopt the following procedure to determine the equated annual instalment inclusive of interest.

In 'O' year (that is, the year of implementation of the project) interest will accrue but no repayment will be made. Repayment will start only from the next year, that is, the first year of operations of the project. As in 'O' year disbursement of loan will be made not on the first day of the year but in stages only, interest on the entire loan amount of Rs 10 lakh for the whole year will not be chargeable; interest will be calculated only on the disbursed amounts from the date of such disbursements. Let us assume that on this basis the interest cost comes to Rs 0.65 lakh. Hence, at the beginning of the first year of operation the term loan liability will be Rs 10.65 lakh, which shall be repaid in five equal annual instalments. Equated annual instalments can now be calculated by multiplying Rs 10.65 lakh with the capital recovery factor (C_f) derived earlier. That is, 10.65 × 0.2843 = Rs 3.03 lakh.

The capital recovery factors for Re 1 repayable by annual instalment at various rates of interest and number of years are given in Annexure 18.1. The analyst only has to pick up the appropriate factor from this table, and multiply with it the principal amount of the term loan to determine the equated annual instalment.

However, Annexure 18.1, which is meant for calculating yearly instalments under rates of interest expressed in whole numbers, will not always be of help to a banker, who generally recovers term loans at monthly, quarterly or half-yearly instalments, and at rates of interest which are often in fractions.

In the example of Modern Furnishers (P) Limited, the term loan to be sanctioned is Rs 132 lakh repayable in 10 years by annual instalments with an interest at the rate of 18.5 per cent per annum. The capital recovery factor table as given in Annexure 18.1 will not be of much help in finding the equated yearly instalment. We have to use the formula given earlier, and calculate capital recovery factors as follows for both types of loan.

Term loan

$$C_f = \frac{0.185}{1 - \dfrac{1}{(1.185)^{10}}} \quad \text{where } i = 0.185 \text{ and } n = 10$$

or, $C_f = 0.226481$

Working capital loan

$$C_f = \frac{0.185}{1 - \dfrac{1}{(1.185)^5}} \quad \text{where } i = 0.185 \text{ and } n = 5$$

or, $C_f = 0.323407$

Equated annual instalments can now be calculated as below:

Term loan	Rs 132.00 lakh
Add: Half of interest chargeable @ 18.5% p.a.	
in 'O' year	Rs 12.20 lakh
Total amount	Rs 144.20 lakh
Amount of equated annual instalment	= Rs 144.20 lakh × 0.226481
	= Rs 32.66 lakh

Working capital term loan	Rs 24 lakh
Amount of equated annual instalment	= Rs 24 lakh × 0.323407
	= Rs 7.76 lakh

Annexure 18.1

Capital Recovery Factor

(Annual payment that will repay a Re 1 loan in X years with compound interest on the unpaid balance)

Year	1%	2%	3%	4%	5%	6%	7%	8%	9%	10%
1.	1.010000	1.020000	1.030000	1.040000	1.050000	1.060000	1.070000	1.080000	1.090000	1.100000
2.	0.507512	0.515050	0.522611	0.530196	0.537805	0.545437	0.553092	0.560769	0.568469	0.576190
3.	0.340022	0.346755	0.353530	0.360349	0.367209	0.374110	0.381052	0.388034	0.395055	0.402115
4.	0.256281	0.262624	0.269027	0.275490	0.282012	0.288591	0.295228	0.301921	0.308669	0.315471
5.	0.206040	0.212158	0.218355	0.224627	0.230975	0.237396	0.243891	0.250456	0.257092	0.263797
6.	0.172548	0.178526	0.184598	0.190762	0.197017	0.203363	0.209796	0.216315	0.222920	0.229607
7.	0.148628	0.154512	0.160506	0.166610	0.172820	0.179135	0.185553	0.192072	0.198691	0.205405
8.	0.130690	0.136510	0.142456	0.148528	0.154722	0.161036	0.167468	0.174015	0.180674	0.187444
9.	0.116740	0.122515	0.128434	0.134493	0.140690	0.147022	0.153486	0.160080	0.166799	0.173641
10.	0.105582	0.111327	0.117231	0.123291	0.129505	0.135868	0.142378	0.149029	0.155820	0.162745
11.	0.096454	0.102178	0.108077	0.114149	0.120389	0.126793	0.133357	0.140076	0.146947	0.153963
12.	0.088849	0.094560	0.100462	0.106552	0.112825	0.119277	0.125902	0.132695	0.139651	0.146763
13.	0.082415	0.088118	0.094030	0.100144	0.106456	0.112960	0.119651	0.126522	0.133567	0.140779
14.	0.076901	0.082602	0.088526	0.094669	0.101024	0.107585	0.114345	0.121297	0.128433	0.135746
15.	0.072124	0.077825	0.083767	0.089941	0.096342	0.102963	0.109795	0.116830	0.124059	0.131474
16.	0.067945	0.073650	0.079611	0.085820	0.092270	0.098952	0.105858	0.112977	0.120300	0.127817
17.	0.064258	0.069970	0.075953	0.082199	0.088699	0.095445	0.102425	0.109629	0.117046	0.124664
18.	0.060982	0.066702	0.072709	0.078993	0.085546	0.092357	0.099413	0.106702	0.114212	0.121930
19.	0.058052	0.063782	0.069814	0.076139	0.082745	0.089621	0.096753	0.104128	0.111730	0.119547
20.	0.055415	0.061157	0.067216	0.073582	0.080243	0.087185	0.094393	0.101852	0.109546	0.117460
21.	0.053031	0.058785	0.064872	0.071280	0.077996	0.085005	0.092289	0.099832	0.107617	0.115624
22.	0.050864	0.056631	0.062747	0.069199	0.075971	0.083046	0.090406	0.098032	0.105905	0.114005
23.	0.048886	0.054668	0.060814	0.067309	0.074137	0.081278	0.088714	0.096422	0.104382	0.112572
24.	0.047073	0.052871	0.059047	0.065587	0.072471	0.079679	0.087189	0.094978	0.103023	0.111300
25.	0.045407	0.051220	0.057428	0.064012	0.070952	0.078227	0.085811	0.093679	0.101806	0.110168

(*contd.*)

Year	11%	12%	13%	14%	15%	16%	17%	18%	19%	20%
1.	1.110000	1.120000	1.130000	1.140000	1.150000	1.160000	1.170000	1.180000	1.190000	1.200000
2.	0.583934	0.591698	0.599484	0.607290	0.615116	0.622963	0.630829	0.638716	0.646621	0.654545
3.	0.409213	0.416349	0.423522	0.430731	0.437977	0.445258	0.452574	0.459924	0.467308	0.474725
4.	0.322326	0.329234	0.336194	0.343205	0.350265	0.357375	0.364533	0.371739	0.378991	0.386289
5.	0.270570	0.277410	0.284315	0.291284	0.298316	0.0305409	0.312564	0.319778	0.327050	0.334380
6.	0.236377	0.243226	0.250153	0.257157	0.264237	0.271390	0.278615	0.285910	0.293274	0.300706
7.	0.212215	0.219118	0.226111	0.233192	0.240360	0.247613	0.254947	0.262362	0.269855	0.277424
8.	0.194321	0.201303	0.208387	0.215570	0.222850	0.230224	0.237690	0.245244	0.252885	0.260609
9.	0.180602	0.187679	0.194869	0.202168	0.209574	0.217082	0.224691	0.232395	0.240192	0.248079
10.	0.169801	0.176984	0.184290	0.191714	0.199252	0.206901	0.214657	0.222515	0.230471	0.238523
11.	0.161121	0.168415	0.175841	0.183394	0.191069	0.198861	0.206765	0.214776	0.222891	0.231104
12.	0.154027	0.161437	0.168986	0.176669	0.184481	0.192415	0.200466	0.208628	0.216896	0.225265
13.	0.148151	0.155677	0.163350	0.171164	0.179110	0.187184	0.195378	0.203686	0.212102	0.220620
14.	0.143228	0.150871	0.158667	0.166609	0.174688	0.182898	0.191230	0.199678	0.208235	0.216893
15.	0.139065	0.146824	0.154742	0.162809	0.171017	0.179358	0.187822	0.196403	0.205092	0.213882
16.	0.135517	0.143390	0.151426	0.159615	0.167948	0.176414	0.185004	0.193710	0.202523	0.211436
17.	0.132471	0.140457	0.148608	0.156915	0.165367	0.173952	0.182662	0.191485	0.200414	0.209440
18.	0.129843	0.137937	0.146201	0.154621	0.163186	0.171885	0.180706	0.189639	0.198676	0.207805
19.	0.127563	0.135763	0.144134	0.152663	0.161336	0.170142	0.179067	0.188103	0.197238	0.206462
20.	0.125576	0.133879	0.142354	0.150986	0.159761	0.168667	0.177690	0.186820	0.196045	0.205357
21.	0.123838	0.132240	0.140814	0.149545	0.158417	0.167416	0.176530	0.185746	0.195054	0.204444
22.	0.122313	0.130811	0.139479	0.148303	0.157266	0.166353	0.175550	0.184846	0.194229	0.203690
23.	0.120971	0.129560	0.138319	0.147231	0.156278	0.165447	0.174721	0.184090	0.193542	0.203065
24.	0.119787	0.128463	0.137308	0.146303	0.155430	0.164673	0.174019	0.183454	0.192967	0.202548
25.	0.118740	0.127500	0.136426	0.145498	0.154699	0.164013	0.173423	0.182919	0.192487	0.202119

The smallest hair throws its shadow.

—Goethe

19 Small Business Loan

INTRODUCTION

One of the objectives of the nationalisation of major banks in India was to help self-employed and small businesspersons to better their economic conditions. Over the years, this objective has gained momentum and a number of schemes have been formulated to accommodate these hitherto neglected people. Liberalisation has not changed the course of this policy-objective in a major way. We mentioned in Chapter 3 that commitment to priority sectors would continue in spite of liberalisation of the banking industry. Branch managers, particularly of rural and semi-urban branches, continue to receive a number of loan applications from these people under various schemes.

There is a feeling that undue pressure is being brought upon the branch managers, who have no time to appraise individual loan applications carefully, and hence they are just giving away loans like doles. While the claim of time constraint may be partially true, the author, in his dealings with hundreds of branch managers of nationalised banks, got the feeling that in reality many of them really do not know how to appraise a proposal for a small business loan. As a result, they first take the shelter of time constraint to deny a proposal, and when the pressure from public authorities becomes unbearable, they just give away loans.

It is also claimed that techniques of credit appraisal, as have been taught, learnt, and suggested by various committees constituted by the RBI from time to time are applicable only to the assessment of credit proposals of large borrowers—these just cannot be used for appraising a small loan proposal. While it is true that if the credit proposal is only, for say, Rs 20000, a credit appraiser need not calculate all the ratios or draw up detailed funds flow and cash flow statements, or go into details of the proposal by using the techniques mentioned so far in this book, the fact remains that the principles of credit appraisal are independent of the amount of loan applied for. The difference lies in approach only: the basic principles remain the same. This is explained below with the help of a real-life case.

THE CASE

Mr S. Roy had recently taken over the charge of a rural branch of a nationalised bank. Before the present posting, he was a field officer for a group of three adjoining branches in another district of the same state. He was happy to get full charge of a branch at a young age, and hence was full of enthusiasm.

A few days after his taking over charge, he was approached by a person who identified himself as Mr M. Alam, proprietor of a small drug store. Some time back he had made an application to the branch for a loan of Rs 25,000. The previous manager was not willing to sanction the loan because many such small loans granted by the branch turned out to be bad debts. Mr Alam said that he was not like others: he was an honest person, which the manager could easily verify from the market.

Mr Roy found the person interesting. From the heap of pending papers, he fished out Mr Alam's one-page application in the bank's standard form. This is reproduced below:

1. Name and address : M/s ALAM MEDICO
   Village _____
   Distt. _____
2. Proprietor   : Mr M. Alam—
   qualified pharmacist
3. Business   : Medicine shop
4. Date of establishment: 20X5
5. Amount of   : 25000
   loan required
6. Marital status   : Married with two children
   of the proprietor
7. Financial data   : Fixed assets (land, house
   Amount invested in   etc.): Nil.
   business: Rs 61000

	20X5	20X6	20X7
Gross sales	182000	213500	246050
Expenses	127400	152250	171675
Net annual profit	54600	61250	74375
Annual stock purchases	163625	157500	171325
Other income	Rs 1500 per month as part-time attendant to the PHC		

8. Sources of supply : Wholesalers in the city, about 20 kms from the shop.
9. Practice of sales : Mostly cash
10. Guarantors   : 1. Mr Aslam Chowdhury—
    proposed   worth Rs 280000 (house and land measuring about 10 acres)
    2. Mr Abhoy Pandey—worth Rs 260000 (house and land measuring about 7 acres).
    Both are agriculturists.

The next day Mr Roy visited Mr Alam's shop. He found that it was situated opposite the public health centre (PHC). The proprietor had good relations with the doctor. In fact, while working as a part-time attendant at the PHC, he was encouraged by the doctor to set up this business. When he obtained his license as a pharmacist with the help of the doctor, he sold out his small piece of land and opened this shop with that money. He is continuing with the PHC, and intends to do so in the future also. The doctor was all praise for Mr Alam.

There was no medicine shop nearby. The demand for medicines was good. But Mr Alam explained that the turnover of his shop was low, because he could not keep adequate stocks in his shop owing to lack of finance. Many bulk orders from the PHC had to be declined often owing to lack of finance.

The books of accounts available with the proprietor revealed that the information given in the application was more or less correct. While verifying the stocks, the bank manager observed that Mr Alam was keeping cheaper varieties of medicines manufactured by not-so-well-known drug manufacturers, because the inhabitants of the village could not afford to pay for high value medicines. The margin of profit on these types of medicines was high. On enquiry, the proprietor said that his price of medicines included transportation costs. He also told him that since the previous year he had a young boy working in the shop to whom he paid Rs 600 per month. His other expenses (mainly on tea) were Rs 150 per month.

On asking why he had applied for a loan of Rs 25,000 only, Mr Alam said diffidently that it was his fear that if he had applied for a larger amount, he would not get the loan at all. This had been the experience of others who had obtained loans from the branch in the past.

Having gathered and verified the relevant information, Mr Roy came back to the branch and set himself to the task of making a real appraisal of the proposal. He did not agree with those fellow managers who normally held that since the amount of loan asked for was small and well within their discretionary powers, it could just be given without taking the trouble of assessing the proposal.

THE NEED OF THE BORROWER

The crucial question now was to determine the financial need of the prospective borrower. Mr Roy knew from his experience as a field officer that the most important aspect of appraising the credit proposal of a person with small means was to determine first the personal need of the borrower. The need of the business must then flow from it. The approach must be quite different from that of appraising the proposal of a big business.

Mr Alam's annual income from the business was Rs 74,375, or Rs 6,198, say Rs 6,200 per month. Adding to this, his income of Rs 1,500 per month as an attendant at the PHC, the aggregate monthly income came to around Rs 7,700. The total members of his family, including his widowed mother were five, of whom three were adults, and one a school-going boy. Even assuming that the cost of living in a village was lower than it was in a town or city, it was difficult to maintain a family of this size with the bare minimum necessities of life at a monthly income of Rs 7,700. But how had he maintained himself for so long? And if he could do so in the past, then why could he not be able to do it in the future? Yes, he did maintain himself in the past with such a meagre income, and he could also do it in the future, but he would continue to remain poor. A beggar also 'lives'; but it is no living, mere existence. If finance from a nationalised bank could not uplift him from his poverty level, there was

no need for the bank to remain in the village. Mr Roy firmly believed in this approach. Besides, he also believed that if a borrower was not given adequate finance to do a business which could earn for him an income sufficient to ensure a minimum livelihood, the loan itself would be wasted. The borrower would not be able to repay the loan, and the account would become bad. He had observed during his tenure as a field officer that before obtaining a bank loan, a poor man might have been honest. The bank, having given him a loan, which was inadequate for the purpose, would put a burden on him which he could not carry. He succumbed to the pressure, default in repayment, and hence would turn out to be 'dishonest'.

Mr Roy did not want to do this to Mr Alam. He estimated that Mr Alam must have at least a net income of Rs 15,000 per month from his *business*, which together with his salary of Rs 1,500 per month, would ensure him a minimum decent living. Therefore, his net aggregate income should not be below Rs 16,500 per month. But this is not all. He should also have another Rs 3,500 per month, partly as a saving to take care of contingencies, and partly for paying instalments towards the repayment of a loan, if sanctioned by the bank.

APPRAISAL

Mr Alam should, therefore, have Rs 15000 + 3500 = Rs 18,500 per month from the *business*, or Rs 2,22,000 per annum.

In 20X7, Mr Alam sold medicines for Rs 2,46,050 against which the total cost of sales was Rs 171675, leaving a profit of Rs 74,375. Return on sales, therefore, came to 30.23, say 30 per cent. Therefore, to ensure a return of Rs 2,22,000, he must have the following sales:

$$(100/30) \times 222000 = Rs\ 740000.$$

Now came the question of determining the investment required in stocks to ensure the required sales. Calculations shown in Table 19.1 would reveal the movement of stocks of the business since its inception in 20X5.

The level of closing stocks held in the business when compared with the original amount of Rs 61,000 invested by Mr Alam indicates that he had not eaten away his capital. Out of the capital of Rs 61,000, he must have spent about Rs 6,000–7,000 in furniture and fixtures for setting up his shop, and the remaining amount in stocks.

The stock turnover ratio is somewhat on the low side. Further, it has also fallen marginally in 20X7. However, considering that a medicine store situated in a remote village had to stock a variety of medicines to service the demand of the patients and the PHC, the stock turnover ratio could not be regarded as very low. Mr Roy, however, felt from a discussion with the proprietor that the stock turnover could be increased to 3.5 by proper planning in stockholding and increasing the frequency of purchases, which at present, was once in a fortnight. He, however, decided to be conservative and took the expected stock turnover at 3.20.

Mr Roy could now find out the amount of investment required in the stock to ensure a sale of Rs 7,40,000 as below.

Mean percentage of cost of goods sold on sales is 69 for the year 20X5 (Table 19.1). Hence, for a sale of Rs 7,40,000, the cost of goods sold will be Rs 740000 * 69/100 = Rs 5,10,600. The expected stock turnover being 3.20, Mr Alam must have a stockholding of 510600/3.20 = Rs 1,59,562, say Rs 1,60,000. He already had a stock of Rs 53725. So, he should get a loan of Rs 160000–53725 = Rs 1,06,275, say Rs 1,00,000 from the bank, which he could repay in three years in equated monthly instalments inclusive of interest @ 12 per cent per annum (for calculation of equated monthly instalments, see Appendix 18.1 in Chapter 18.)

ALTERNATIVE SCENARIOS

Mr Roy had also calculated various alternative quantum of loans to see their impact on the improvement of the financial condition of the applicant. Table 19.2 gives these alternatives.

Looking at Table 19.2, Mr Roy contemplated that alternatives (a) and (b) should be rejected, as these did not generate the targeted level of net monthly income of Rs 15000. The choice should be limited among alternatives (c), (d), and (e). Personally, he would have preferred alternative (e), but that required an aggregate sale of Rs 8,02,572 per annum. Although the proprietor said that he could increase his sales substantially

TABLE 19.1   Movement of Stocks and Related Ratios

	20X5	20X6	20X7	Remarks
Aggregate annual expenditure	127400	152250	171675	1. Other expenses are
Less: Other expenses	1800	1800	9000	tea, etc. @ Rs 150 p.m.
Cost of goods sold	125600	150450	162675	and wages @ Rs 600 p.m.
Opening stock	—	38025	45075	from 20X7.
Add: Purchases	163625	157500	171325	2. Stock turnover ratios
Cost of goods available for sales	163625	195525	216400	are calculated on the cost
Less: Cost of goods sold (as above)	125600	150450	162675	of goods sold against
Closing stock	38025*	45075	53725	year-end closing stock.
Stock turnover ratio	3.30	3.33	3.03	
Cost of goods sold as percentage of sale	69	71	67	

Note: * Purchases of Rs 163625 minus cost of goods sold Rs 125600.

TABLE **19.2**   Alternative Scenarios of Loan, Sales, and Monthly Income

Alternative Amount of Loan (1)	Probable Incremental Sales (2)	Probable Incremental Profit (3)	Repayment of Loan p.m. (approx.) (4)
Rs	Rs	Rs	Rs
(a) 80000	$\dfrac{100 \times 80000 \times 3.2}{69}$ 371015 $\dfrac{371015 \times 30}{100 \times 12}$	9275	2666
	(617065)		
(b) 90000	417391	10435	3000
	(663441)		
(c) 100000	463768	11594	3333
	(709818)		
(d) 110000	510145	12754	3666
	(756195)		
(e) 120000	556522	13913	4000
	(802572)		

Net Addition to Income per Month (5)	Expected Net Monthly Income from Business (6)
(col. 3 – col. 4)	(col. 5 + existing income from the business @ Rs 6200 p.m.)
Rs	Rs
(a) 6609	[6200+6609] = 12809
(b) 7435	13635
(c) 8261	14461
(d) 9088	15288
(e) 9913	16113

Note: Figures in brackets under col. (2) denote total sales calculated with the base sales of Rs 246050 in 20X7.

if proper finance was made available, could he really do so? Alternative (c) required annual sales of Rs 7,09,818. This appeared to be more feasible. Here, the projected net income of Rs 14461 per month was meeting the target closely.

To firm up his decision Mr Roy decided to meet the PHC doctor the next day to have an idea of the expected range of demand for medicines in the village. He would particularly examine the orders of the PHC, which could not be executed by Mr Alam in the previous year for want of finance.

CONCLUDING REMARKS

The purpose of this case study is not to arrive at a right or wrong answer. One may not agree with many assumptions made by Mr Roy. For example, his estimate of a minimum level of income to ensure a minimum standard of living for Mr Alam may be high or low, but that does not matter for the purpose at hand. The emphasis of this case analysis is on highlighting the approach to be taken by a branch manager, and the techniques to be used in appraising a small credit proposal.

You can't hold a man down without staying down with him.

—Booker T. Washington

20 Credit Risk Analysis

INTRODUCTION

Credit risk is simply defined as the risk of non-payment of services due to a loan, in time. The services include payment of interest and other charges, and repayment of the principal amount by instalments or otherwise. If these are not paid as and when due, credit risk is involved, because a bank not only has to incur the cost of funds to carry this loan for a further period, but also the profit that would have been earned on the simultaneous investment of this amount. A default, therefore, reduces the present value of the loan and consequently the value of a bank's business. According to prudential norms, a loan-asset becomes a sub-standard asset where there is 90 days default on interest and instalment payment. A sub-standard asset immediately entails provisioning for losses. A bank is also not entitled to book profit for unpaid interest.

The technical capacity of a business to service its loan is estimated by the debt–service coverage ratio or the priority obligation ratio, as discussed in Chapter 16. In this chapter, we intend to analyse why a business or a project fails to meet its debt-service commitments. There is not one, but a number of 'whys' that cause a default. These 'whys' constitute the credit risk of a lending decision.

Credit risk has two components: business risk and borrower risk. We first discuss business risk, followed by borrower risk.

BUSINESS RISK

Business risk is defined as the inability of a business or a project to service its debt in time. This inability stems from the income generation capacity of a business, which is again affected by the nature of the business or the products it sells, the external economic or market environment, and the internal manufacturing organisation and product mix of an enterprise. If all these variables are in a steady state, a business suffers no risk. But if any one of them is not in a steady state, a business will suffer from volatility. And this volatility is first reflected in sales, and as a consequence, on the profitability of a business. For example, a company engaged in oil prospecting will have a very large volatility in sales and profitability, because the nature of the business is such that in one year, oil may be struck, in another year it may not.

No one likes volatility—neither a business nor a bank—because volatility causes uncertainty. But unfortunately, volatility is the reality of the business world, and uncertainty is the only certain thing in business. Since volatility is certain, what is important is to measure it to estimate the risk involved and then take a lending or investment decision based on the risk bearing capacity of a lender or investor. It also helps a decision maker to chalk out alternative plans to minimise the impact of risk on lending or investment objectives if the risk becomes a reality.

The sum total of business risk is made up of systematic risk and unsystematic risk. The first type of risk is exogenous to an enterprise, and hence unavoidable. It is the overall market risk affecting all business enterprises or an industry, like the general political environment, changes in a country's economy, the fiscal policies of the government, infrastructural changes, and the energy situation. Unsystematic risk, on the other hand, is unique to a particular enterprise, independent of political, economic, and other factors that affect the fortunes of all enterprises in a systematic manner. Examples of unsystematic risks are a massive breakdown of plant and machinery, a strike or lock-out, a technological breakthrough making the existing product obsolete, or a new competitor entering the market with the same product. All these affect a particular business unit directly and create volatility in sales and profitability larger than the industry average. In terms of portfolio analysis, unsystematic risk accounts for around 70 per cent of the total risk, the remaining 30 per cent is due to systematic risks. Therefore, a bulk of the total risk is internal. This is contrary to the claims often made by borrowers that due to changes in the external environment, their businesses have been so adversely affected that they are unable to register growth, and hence service their loans.

Business risks essentially comprise sales risks (which is the principal component), followed by operating risk, financial risks, and industry risk. We analyse these risks in this order.

MEASUREMENT OF SALES RISKS

This is done by measuring the volatility of the sales of an enterprise. By volatility, we mean the extent of variation in the annual sales from the average or mean sales for a given period. For example, if the aggregate sales of an enterprise for five years are Rs 100 crore, the average yearly sales come to Rs 20 crore. How nice it would have been if the total sales were Rs 100 crore for a five-year planning period and every year the business had sales of Rs 20 crore uniformly. There would be no volatility, and hence no sales risk.[1] But suppose, in the past five years the sales have moved as below:

Year		Sales	
1		Rs 10	crore
2		10	
3		30	
4		15	
5		35	
	Total	100	crore

Obviously, this situation is not a likeable one. Although the enterprise has met the plan target, the strain created in the system and the cost associated with it could have been enormous. It is not the ups and downs in sales that are important, because if this has been the regular pattern of sales of the company, period after period, then in the ultimate analysis, riskiness cannot be supposed, because the variation from the mean value of sales will also show a regular pattern. One will know for certain what the sales are going to be in the next year. But unfortunately, this does not happen in business, except when

---

[1] This situation may not, however, be liked by an aggressive manager. For him, it may just be boring. There is no challenge, because there is no risk, and hence, there will only be moderate profit, which may not appeal to his ego.

it is seasonal in nature. Volatility is the general pattern, not the 'regularity' of it. What is important, therefore, is the irregularity in the pattern of sales, or the irregularity of the occurrence of an event that creates volatility in the measuring variable. The chance that sales may go up by 10 per cent, but may also fall by 10 per cent, is the kind of volatility that causes sales risk. Assuming that this is the case with our hypothetical enterprise, which is also most commonly observable in a business situation, we now measure the volatility of sales. This is done by a simple statistical tool called standard deviation (SD). The following steps are to be followed in calculating SD:

1. Calculate the mean value $(\bar{X})$ of the sales (X_i) for the given period, which in the present case, is Rs 20 crore.
2. Subtract the mean from sales of each year $(X_i - \bar{X})$.
3. Take the square of the differences in step 2, $(X_i - \bar{X})^2$.
4. Add up all the squared differences Σ $(X_i - \bar{X})^2$.
5. Divide the sum of all the squared differences by the number of years (N). That is,

$$\frac{\Sigma(X_i - \bar{X})^2}{N}$$

6. Take the square root of the value obtained in step 5 to arrive at SD,

$$\sqrt{\frac{\Sigma(X_i - \bar{X})^2}{N}}$$

Let us do it for the example cited in Table 20.1.

$$\text{Mean} = \bar{X} = \frac{\Sigma X_i}{N} = \frac{100}{5} = 20$$

We can now calculate SD by the following formula:

$$SD = \sqrt{\frac{\Sigma(X_i - \bar{X})^2}{N}} \quad \text{where } i = 1, 2, \ldots\ldots N$$

$$SD = \sqrt{\frac{550}{5}}$$

$$SD = \text{Rs } 10.48 \text{ crore.}$$

The calculated SD can be interpreted as follows:

While the annual average sales (Mean = $\bar{X}$) of the firm is Rs 20 crore, the actual sales varied by Rs 10.48 crore on an average on either side of the mean. That is, sales in one year might have been as high as 20 + 10.48 = Rs 30.48 crore, and in another year as low as 20–10.48 = Rs 9.52 crore.

TABLE 20.1   Calculating Standard Deviation

Year (i)	Sales (x_i)	(x_i − x̄)	(x_i − x̄)²
1	10	− 10	100
2	10	− 10	100
3	30	+ 10	100
4	15	− 05	25
5	35	+ 15	225
Total N = 5	$\Sigma x_i = 100$	$\Sigma (x_i - \bar{x}) = 0$	$\Sigma (x_i - \bar{x})^2 = 550$

The range of the variation in sales is extremely high, between Rs 30.48 crore and Rs 9.52 crore. One can, therefore, easily understand the extent of volatility or riskiness of the business. Figure 20.1 plots the annual sales figure to capture the nature of this volatility.

Figure 20.1 reveals that the sales are highly scattered in nature, and hence, their variation from mean sales, as represented by their SD, is also very high. What is the extent of this variation? To answer this question we now move to another simple statistical concept (henceforth, we shall know SD by the standard Greek letter, σ).

Coefficient of Variation (CV)

A SD of Rs 10.48 crore by itself does not convey any meaning except when it is compared with the mean value. The standard method of comparison is to reduce the SD as a percentage of the mean. The percentage so computed is called the coefficient of variation (CV). This is calculated for the above example in the following manner:

$$CV = \frac{\sigma}{\bar{X}} \times 100$$

or, $\quad CV = \dfrac{10.48}{20} \times 100$

or, $\quad CV = 52.4\%$

The CV so calculated is a very important piece of information for a decision maker about the extent of risk he is undertaking. For a lender, the decision parameters could be as follows:

(a) He may set an outer limit of CV beyond, which the proposal is not acceptable for further consideration. This limit could be, say, 50 per cent.

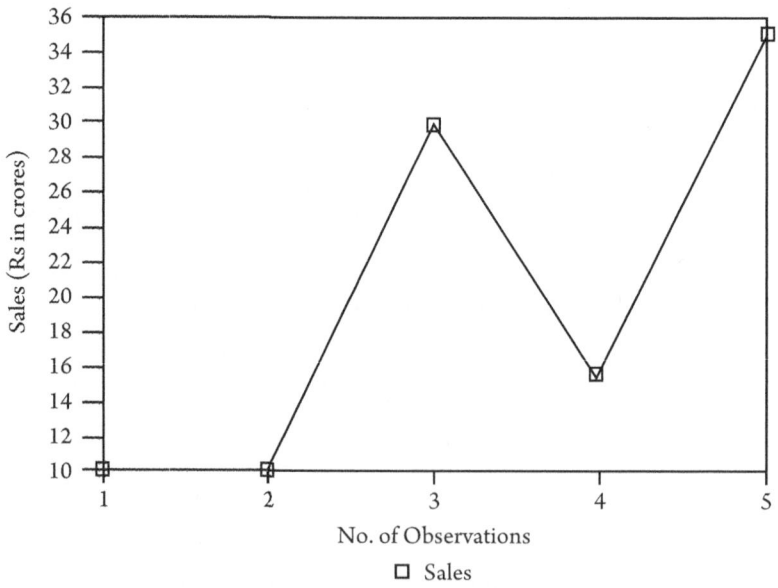

FIGURE 20.1 Sales Volatility of the Firms

(b) He may set out a range of CV bordering on this outer limit within which the credit proposal is eligible for consideration, but that calls for taking special protective measures. This range could be, say, 35–50 per cent.

(c) Proposals with a CV of, say, less than 35 per cent will ordinarily be eligible for consideration.

In a sense, the scales shown in (a), (b), and (c) reflect the risk-appetite of the lender. The risk-appetite of lending institutions varies depending upon their own risk profile, so also is the case with borrowing organisations. When the two profiles match, a meaningful dialogue starts for a fruitful relationship. Risk profiles can be improved by strengthening the capital base, acquiring skills, and developing the right kind of attitude among decision makers.

The CV in its percentage form acquires a universal character, hence it is amenable for comparison among distributions of the variable, which are different in size and form. For example, the sales of one enterprise may be measured quarterly while for another enterprise they may be measured yearly, or there might be a substantial difference in the volume of sales of these two enterprises. But these differences will not have any impact on CV. This particular property of CV enables an analyst to compare the CV, of say, the sales of an enterprise with that of the industry to which it belongs, and develop alternative standards for acceptable credit risks. It can be done both within the parameters established above, or independent of them. Since the CV of a specific industry reflects its overall volatility or its risk characteristics, any substantial negative deviation of the CV of a member enterprise from that of the industry represents an additional 'unsystematic risk' peculiar to that enterprise only. A bank may fix an outer limit, of say, 30 per cent adverse variation between the two for a credit proposal to be eligible for consideration.

Case of International Cranes and Tractors Limited

Let us recall the sales figures of this company from Chapter 13, and estimate the volatility (risk) in the manner discussed above (Table 20.2)

$$\bar{X} = \frac{12020}{7} = 1717.14$$

TABLE 20.2   Standard Deviation of Sales of International Cranes and Tractors Ltd.

(Rs in lakh)

Year	Sales (X_i)	$(X_i - \bar{X})$	$(X_i - \bar{X})^2$
1	1144	(–) 573.14	328489.46
2	1232	(–) 485.14	235360.82
3	1332	(–) 385.14	148332.82
4	1602	(–) 115.14	13257.22
5	1854	136.85	18727.92
6	2251	533.86	285006.54
7	2605	887.85	788277.62
$N = 7$	$S x_i = 12020$	0	$\Sigma (x_i - \bar{x})^2 = 1817452.40$

Hence, SD of sales is;

$$\sigma_A = \sqrt{\frac{1817452.40}{7}}$$

or, σ_A = Rs 509.54 lakh.

The above value of σ_A = Rs 509.54 lakh means that sales of the company had varied between Rs 1717.14 lakh + 509.54 lakh = Rs 2,226.68 lakh, and Rs 1717.14 lakh – Rs 509.54 lakh = Rs 1,207.6 lakh during the above period (this should not be confused with the results of the regression analysis done in Chapter 13 for projection of sales of the company for the eighth year, which was expected to vary between Rs 2,987 lakh and Rs 2,431 lakh). Here, we are not concerned with the projection of sales, but with the determination of the extent of volatility in sales.

For measuring the extent of volatility or riskiness of sales (CV_s) we calculate the coefficient of variation as follows:

$$CV_V \text{ of sales} = \frac{509.54}{1717.14} \times 100$$

or 29.67%

A question may be raised at this stage that although the sales of the company reflect inherent volatility, they also show a rising trend, which in a real-life situation reduces the riskiness of future sales. This claim is also justified when we find that the company's rate of growth in sales from the fourth year onwards is more than double the rate of earlier years. Hence, the coefficient of variation derived above must be qualified by the trend factor. That is, if the trend is upward, the riskiness of sales should be lower than the value given by the CV of sales; if the trend is downward, the riskness should be more than what is reflected in the CV_s; and if it is level, the riskiness remains at the given CV_s.

The derived CV_s is thus trend adjusted (CV_A) in the following manner:

$$CV_A = CS_S \frac{x_1 + x_2 + x_3 \ldots x_n}{x_1 + 2x_2 + 3x_3 \ldots nx_n} \times \frac{N + 1}{2}$$

where: 1. $x_1, x_2 \ldots \ldots x_n$ are the values of sales in years 1, 2, 3.....n years
        2. N = Total number of years

In the present case, it is calculated as below:

$$CV_A = 29.67 \left[\frac{1144 + 1232 + 1332 + 1602 + 1854 + 2251 + 2605}{1144 + 2 \times 1232 + 3 \times 1332 + 4 \times 1602 + 5 \times 1854 + 6 \times 2251 + 7 \times 2605} \times \frac{7 + 1}{2} \right]$$

or, $29.67 \left[\dfrac{12020}{55023} \times 4 \right]$

or, 29.67×0.8738

or, 25.93%

The derived CV_A can now be compared against the standards set earlier to decide the acceptability of the credit proposal of the company. Since it is less than 35 per cent, the proposal is ordinarily eligible for consideration.

In Table 20.3 we calculate the volatility of the sales of the industry group (CV_I), namely 'machinery manufacturing', to which International Cranes and Tractors belongs. For a better comparison, it would have been preferable if we could obtain the data for the cranes and tractors industry separately, because the industry group, 'machinery manufacturing' constitutes a variety of other products too. The findings are qualified to that extent. It is preferable to take this by way of illustration only, which in fact, is the purpose of this study.

$$\bar{X} = 28391/7 = 4055.86$$

$$\sigma_I = \sqrt{\frac{3964428.40}{7}} = \text{Rs } 752.57 \text{ crore}$$

$CV_I = (752.57/4055.86) \times 100 = 18.56\% \times 0.9586 = 17.79\%$, after adjusting it by the trend factor of 0.9586 calculated in the manner prescribed above.

It now appears that International Cranes and Tractors Limited has a larger volatility in sales than the industry to which it belongs. We must point out at this stage that though we have used time series data for the company as well as the industry, time has no impact on the value of the mean, SD, or CV. Volatility is measured in terms of observed values of the variable (for example, sales) during a given period, namely seven years, but it ignores their movement along a time scale. For the purpose at hand, sales of seven years are just seven observations. Volatility is measured among these observed values. Hence, for the purpose of a graphical presentation as in Figure 20.2, the sales figures of both the company and the industry are arranged in ascending order, and then indexed to neutralise the impact of the scale difference between company sales (in lakh) and industry sales (in crore).

The company's volatility is higher by $25.93 - 17.79 = 8.14$ or 45.76 per cent more than the industry. On the face of it, this might

TABLE 20.3   Standard Deviation of Sales of Industry Group: Machinery Manufacturing

(Rs in crore)

Year	Sales (X_i)	$(X_i - \bar{X})$	$(X_i - \bar{X})^2$	
1	2760	(–) 1295.85	1679227.22	
2	3525	(–) 530.85	281801.74	
3	4573	517.14	267433.78	$\bar{X} = \dfrac{28391}{7}$
4	4583	527.14	277876.58	or 4055/.86
5	5194	1138.14	1295362.70	
6	3655	(–) 400.86	160688.74	
7	4101	45.14	2037.64	
$N = 7$	$\Sigma X_i = 28391$	0	$\Sigma (X_i - \bar{X})^2 = 3964428.40$	

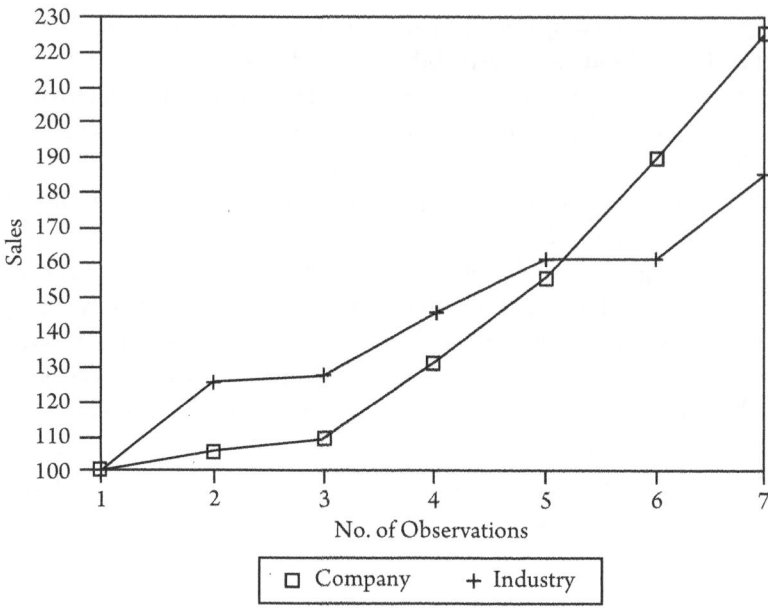

FIGURE **20.2**   Sales Volatility of a Company and Industry

indicate that the company is suffering from high 'unsystematic risk' peculiar to itself. It might just be losing out in competition. But the low value of industry CV_I must be interpreted by looking at the growth rate of the industry, which is much lower than that of the company. A lower growth rate may suggest low volatility, but it may also indicate stagnancy, which may ultimately affect the company, which in spite of industry-stagnancy, is growing at a faster rate. The industry stagnancy may soon bring the company down to a lower level equilibrium, and hence it may turn out to be a high-risk borrower. It is time that the company understands this and moves towards diversification to avoid the stagnancy in the industry.

EVALUATION OF SALES FORECAST

The 'scatter diagram' as in Figure 20.1 can be changed to a normal distribution as in Figure 20.3. This enables us to determine quite accurately where the values in a distribution are located relative to their mean. For example, we can measure the percentage of items in a population of sales, which fall within specific ranges under normal distribution. An examination of Figure 20.3 reveals the following:

1. About 68 per cent of the values in the population fall within plus or minus 1 SD from the mean.
2. About 95 per cent of the values in the population fall within plus or minus 2 SDs from the mean.
3. About 99 per cent of the values in the population fall within plus or minus 3 SDs.

All these indicate that the riskiness of the business increases with the number of SDs. The probability of reaching a sales target diminishes with the risk as measured by the number of SDs.

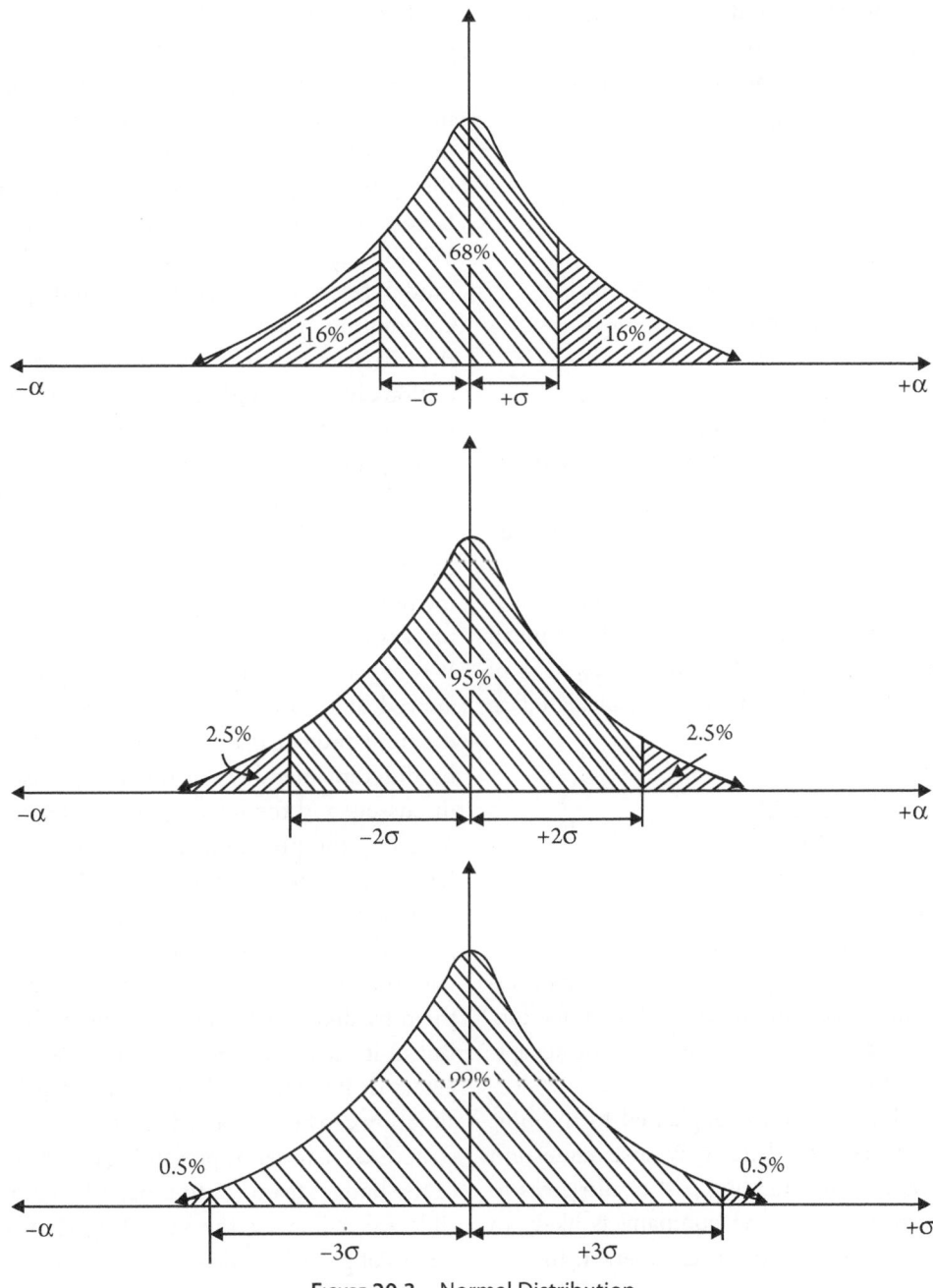

FIGURE **20.3**   Normal Distribution

However, this also poses a challenging situation before a business. An enterprise with a high risk-appetite may go up to 3 SDs in targeting its sales, while another with a low level of confidence may feel comfortable with one SD. Similar is the case with a lender.

In order to understand the riskiness of a sales projection, we need to know how many SDs away it is from the mean. This can be calculated by using the following formula:

$$Z = \frac{x - \bar{X}}{\sigma}$$

where,

x = the value of the random variable (for example, projected sales)

$\bar{X}$ = mean of the distribution of this variable

σ = SD of this distribution

Z = the number of SDs from x to the mean

We now evaluate the riskiness of the sales forecast of Rs 3,200 lakh made by International Cranes and Tractors Limited. We know from the calculations made earlier that the company has a mean ($\bar{X}$) sales of Rs 1717.14 lakh with a SD (σ_A) of Rs 509.54 lakh. Z_A can now be calculated as below:

$$Z_A = \frac{3200 - 1717.14}{509.54}$$

or, Z_A = 2.91 SDs.

The calculated Z_A appears to be very high, indicating high riskiness of the sales projection, which on the face of it, is unlikely to be acceptable to a bank.

When this position is explained to the borrowing company, the latter may raise a question on the validity of extending past occurrences to future projections as the company is likely to take a proactive position in the market. In fact, the sales volatility model presented earlier is often criticised for being backward looking. The approach is *ex-post*: it tells us something about the risks already encountered. But at the same time it assumes that the same level of risk remains while going forward. Although this criticism is genuine to an extent, the present model has stood the test of time because of its simplicity, which makes it amenable to managerial decision making. Findings of many empirical studies uphold that sensitivities of a business to different risk factors do have a bearing on its past behaviour. Without sacrificing the properties of the basic model described earlier, we can modify it by incorporating in our mode the present thinking of the management of the company about its future outlook of sales, holding at the same time that in weighing different possible future scenarios, the management will always have at the back of its mind how the company had fared in the past.[2]

Presently, the question raised by the company can be handled by re-enacting the decision making process of the company that has led to a sales projection of Rs 3200 lakh in the coming year. It is expected that the final projection has been arrived at through a budgetary process where different projected levels of the sales presented by different members of the budget team were discussed, and the final figure was decided after weighing the probabilities of achieving the different levels of sales projections. It would have been better if the figures of such alternative sales projections were made available to the bank, with the probabilities of occurrences attached to them by different members of the budget team. But in its absence—and even if no formal budgetary drill has taken place in the company—the situation can be re-enacted or freshly enacted in a structured manner by presenting to the members of the budget team (or to those who are responsible for achieving the sales target) of certain ranges of probable sales figures, and asking them to indicate their own estimation of the chances

---

[2] A very precise solution is possible, but we must warn that in its search there always lurks the danger of statistical overkill.

(within a 100 point scale) that the organisation will end up with a particular sales level in the projected year. Assuming now that we have done so with three members of the management team, the average of their observations is tabulated in Table 20.4, along with calculations of weighted sales and SD thereof.

The following formula for calculating SD of a probabilistic distribution of various outcomes is somewhat different from the one we have used earlier, though the mathematical properties of the two remain the same.

$$\sigma_B = \sqrt{\sum_{i=1}^{n}(R_i - \bar{R})^2\, P_i}$$

where

R_i = Possible levels of sales as in column 1.

P_i = Probability distribution of various possible levels of sales as given in column 3.

$\bar{R}$ = Weighted average given by

$\sum_{i=1}^{n} R_i\, P_i$. This is derived by multiplying corresponding figures appearing under column 1 with those under column 3,

and taking summations of them as in column 4. $\bar{R}$, therefore, replaces $\bar{x}$ of the earlier model. Since $(R_i - \bar{R})^2$ is multiplied by P_i, that is, the weights, there is no need now to divide it once again by N as in our earlier model.

Hence, $\sigma_B = \sqrt{189000}$ = Rs 434.74 lakh

$$CV_B = \frac{\sigma}{\bar{R}} \times 100 = \frac{434.74}{2900} = 15\%$$

$$Z_B = \frac{R - \bar{R}}{\sigma} = \frac{3200 - 2900}{434.74} = 0.69\ SD$$

where, 'R' is the targeted level of sales. Subscript 'B' indicates budgetary estimations.

The variation of the probability distribution of possible outcomes, as in Table 20.4, reflects the degree of the management's uncertainty. The low SD (Rs 434.74 lakh) relative to its expected value, and an equally small CV (15 per cent), indicates little dispersion and a high degree of confidence in the outcome. But at the same time, its Z_B value reflects a highly cautious approach of

TABLE 20.4 Probability Distribution of Various Levels of Possible Sales and Standard Deviation

(Rs in lakh)

Level of Sales (R_i) (1)	Chances of Occurring (%) (2)	Converting col. 2 in Decimal Points (P_i) (3)	Weighted Sales (x_i) (col. 1 × col. 3) (4)	($R_i - \bar{R}$) (5)	($R_i - \bar{R}$)^2 (6)	$P_i(R_i - \bar{R})^2$ (7)
3800	5	0.05	190	900.00	810000	40500
3500	10	0.10	350	600.00	360000	36000
3200	20	0.20	640	300.00	90000	18000
2900	30	0.30	870	0.00	0	0
2600	20	0.20	520	(–) 300.00	90000	18000
2300	10	0.10	230	(–) 600.00	360000	36000
2000	5	0.05	100	(–) 900.00	810000	40500
	100	1.00	$\bar{R}$ = 2900	0	2520000	189000

the management in projecting sales of Rs 3,200 lakh, which varies only by 0.69 SD. This low risk-appetite of the management, bordering on conservatism, may be due to their knowledge of the high volatility of sales experienced by the company in the past (CVs was almost 30 per cent as against the industry standard of 18.5 per cent), which is likely to be repeated in the near future.

The lender can repose his own confidence in the confidence of the borrower, and accept the projected sales target of Rs 3,200 lakh, which deviates only moderately from the mean sales of the probabilistic estimates, but at the same time he must bear in mind the following facts:

1. Past volatility of sales of the company, as reflected in modified CV_A is 25.93 per cent.
2. The deviation of the company's modified CV_A from the industry's modified CV_I is 8.14, which is about 46 per cent adverse.
3. The CV_B of the probabilistic estimation is 15 per cent.

SALES RISK INDEX

We can now develop a risk index for the company based on the three CVs, by applying appropriate weights to the above risk criteria with the lowest risk weight given to CV_B that resulted from the company's own probabilistic estimates, as it reflects the management's current thinking of the future, and its own risk profile. This is shown in Table 20.5.

It may be noted that if the company's own CV_A is lower than that of the industry (CV_I) to which it belongs, then the figure against risk parameter 3 will be negative, resulting in a lowering of the overall sales risk. The presumption here is that the company is performing better than the average players of the industry with respect to sales volatility.

Table 20.5 shows the weighted sales risk index (SRI) of the company as 30.

Generally, a SRI beyond 50 is an unacceptable risk for a lender. Taking this as the lowest benchmark, the remaining risk categories are determined at a 10 point interval as in Table 20.6. The index is finally converted to make it comparable with other risk indices that are developed later in this chapter. Conversion is done in the following manner:

$CRI_S = 100 - (SRI - 1)$. The higher the value of CRI_S, the lower is the risk.

MEASUREMENT OF OPERATING RISKS

We have so far analysed the business risks of an enterprise in terms of the volatility or uncertainty of sales. The impact of this volatility on the operating and financial structure of a business adds to the total risk of the enterprise. This can be measured by what are known as operating leverage (OL) and financial leverage (FL), which

TABLE 20.5   Sales Risk-Index of the Company

Risk Parameters	Value (%)	Weights	Weighted Index
1. CV_A	25.93	0.35	09.07
2. CV_B	15.00	0.25	03.75
3. $\dfrac{CV_A - CV_I}{CV_I} \times 100$	45.76	0.40	18.30
	—	1.00	31.12 (say, 30)

TABLE 20.6   Risk Categorisation in Terms of Sales Risk-Index

	Risk Category					
	0 *Excellent*	*1* *Very Good*	*2* *Good*	*3* *Fair*	*4* *Doubtful*	*5* *Poor*
Sales Risk-Index (SRI)	001–10	11–20	21–30	31–40	41–50	Below 50
Converted Risk						
Index (CRI$_S$)	100–91	90–81	80–71	70–61	60–51	50 & below

are nothing but an extension of the break-even concept that we have discussed in Chapter 15.

Operating Leverage (OL)

Although theoretically speaking all costs of a business are variable in the long run, in the short run (which is not necessarily always short), fixed costs loom as overheads in a business, which must be met regardless of the volume produced and sold. With fixed costs thus existing, the percentage change in profit due to a change in volume will be greater than the percentage change in volume. This phenomenon is called operating leverage, which is calculated by the following formula:

$$\text{Operating Leverage (OL)} = \frac{Contribution}{Contribution - Fixed\ Costs}$$

$$\text{or,} \quad \frac{Contribution}{Operating\ Profit}$$

Let us explain this by the following example.

Sales	Rs 100000
Variable cost (80%)	80000
Contribution	20000
Less: Fixed costs	10000
Operating profit	10000
Hence, operating leverage is	20000/10000 = 2

By virtue of the above definition of OL, if sales increase by 10 per cent, the operating profit will rise by two times the increase in sales, that is, 10% × 2 = 20%.

Check

Sales increases by 10%	Rs 110000
Less: Variable cost (80%)	88000
Contribution	22000
Less: Fixed costs	10000
Operating profit	12000

Therefore, the rise in operating profit is:

$$\frac{12000 - 10000}{10000} \times 100 = 20\%$$

OL shows symmetrical behaviour. That is, if there is fall in sales by a certain percentage, the operating profit will fall by OL times the percentage decrease in sales. For example, if sales decreases by 10 per cent, the operating profit will decrease, by 10 × 2 = 20%.

Check

Sales falls by 10%	Rs 90000
Less: Variable cost (80%)	72000
Contribution	18000
Less: Fixed costs	10000
Operating profit	8000

The decrease in operating profit is, therefore:

$$\frac{10000 - 8000}{10000} \times 100 = 20\%$$

The existence of fixed costs and the symmetrical property of OL make a business risk-prone.

For example, if the OL of a business is 4, a 20 per cent rise in sales increases the operating profit by 80 per cent, but if there is a 20 per cent fall in sales (which is not an unlikely event in a business), then it wipes out 80 per cent of the operating profit. It is more or less similar to sales behaviour with a high SD that operates both ways.

An operating leverage of 1.5 suggests a moderate amount of risk; 2 is challenging with a reasonable amount of risk. The risk-proneness of a business increases with the rise in OL, and beyond 3.5 it may be unacceptable to a lender.

MEASUREMENT OF FINANCIAL RISKS

The principal source of financial risk is the gearing of its capital structure. A highly leveraged company is one which has high debt-financing relative to its capital. Firms are motivated towards a highly leveraged capital structure in order to maximise the return on the shareholders fund. With tax deductible interest and a low level of equity, earning per share (EPS) increases. Shareholders can thus maximise the value of shares by higher level of debt financing. But it is often at the cost of the lender, because the riskiness of a business rises with the increase in leverage. All is well when the business is booming, but in a downswing it is the lender who loses the most. A very good company paying a very high dividend may not be able to service its debt even during the early phase of the downturn. A lender should, therefore, know the extent of the financial risk of a business. Financial risk is measured by a simple tool called FL.

Financial Leverage (FL)

The FL is given by the following formula:

$$FL = \frac{Operating\ Profit}{Operating\ Profit\ -\ Interest\ Cost}$$

$$or,\ \frac{Operating\ Profit}{Profit\ Before\ Tax\ (PBT)}$$

The interest cost is assumed to be fixed. This is so in the short-term under the existing system of financing. The FL attempts to capture the impact of a percentage rise or fall in the operating profit on the PBT of an enterprise. It also behaves in the same way as OL.

From our earlier example:

Operating profit	Rs 10000
Less: Interest cost	5000
Profit before tax (PBT)	5000

Hence, FL will be = 10000/5000 = 2

In our earlier example, operating profit has increased by 20 per cent with a 10 per cent increase in sales. Therefore, the PBT will, rise by $20 \times 2 = 40\%$.

Check

From the earlier example:

Operating profit	Rs 12000
(due to an increase in sales by 10%)	
Less: Interest cost	5000
Profit before tax (PBT)	7000

Percentage rise in PBT is, $\dfrac{7000 - 5000}{5000} \times 100 = 40\%$

Similar to OL, if there is a fall in operating profit, by say, 20 per cent then by virtue of the existence of the FL of 2, PBT will fall by $20 \times 2 = 40\%$. As with OL, the riskiness of a business increases with the increase in FL. Let us once again recall an example from Chapter 15, where we discussed the concept and application of a break-even analysis in lending decisions.

National Industries Limited has the following sales and cost components:

	(Rs in lakh)
Sales	Rs 53000
Fixed costs	7180
Variable costs	43820
Interest and bank charges	630

The operating leverage and financial leverage of the company are calculated below:

Operating Leverage:

Sales	Rs 53000
Less: Variable costs	43820
Contribution	9180
Less: Fixed costs	7180
Operating profit	2000
Less: Interest, etc.	630
Profit before tax (PBT)	1370

$$OL = \frac{\text{Contribution}}{\text{Operating Profit}}; \quad FL = \frac{\text{Operating Profit}}{\text{PBT}}$$

$$OL = \frac{9180}{2000}; \quad FL = \frac{2000}{1370}$$

$$= 4.59 \qquad\qquad = 1.46$$

The OL of the company is very high due to a high level of fixed costs relative to contribution. If there is a 21.8 per cent fall in sales, the fall in operating profit could be as high as 100 per cent! This also corresponds to the low level of the margin of safety (21.8 per cent) that we have already observed in Chapter 15. However, the operating leverage is not just another way of looking at the margin of safety of a business. By bringing out the symmetrical property of the margin of safety, it provides a simple but important tool in the hands of a manager to measure the impact of volatility of sales on the operating profit of an enterprise.

The FL of the company is moderate, though somewhat on the lower side, which is due to a low incidence of interest relative to the operating profit. This indicates that the financial structure of the firm is moderately leveraged. The debt burden relative to capital is not high, which suggests a low debt–equity ratio. It is 0.20:1 as we have already seen in Chapter 16. Presently, the value of FL suggests that the financial risk of the company is low.

By looking at the mathematical arrangement of these two leverages, some readers may be tempted to marry them to obtain a hybrid composite leverage. Our suggestion is to avoid such an exercise, because the two are of two different species altogether, though they may look somewhat alike, like a man and a monkey. The operating structure of a business is distinct from its financial structure. There are two different sets of rules for operating decisions and financial decisions. Two firms may have exactly the same operating assets, but their funding operations could be different: one may decide to fund them entirely from equity, while the other may do it by a combination of equity and debt resulting in different levels of interest burdens, and hence different FL. Multiplication of these two leverages is wrong, because it may suppress their individual differences through what we call 'compensating error'.

Although, as indicated earlier, a low FL of a company suggests a low level of financial risk, there is no reason for a lender to be happy, because the fundamental of a business is its operating strength. If the fundamental is not good, it may soon eat into the financial structure of the business. An enterprise having a bad financial structure (high FL) can be turned around by a rearrangement of its financial structure, but it can be done only when its operating structure is good (low OL). If it is the other way around, the task is difficult to perform except by making a complete technological overhauling of the productive organisation which, however, has the effect of making the company a substantially new one.

We are now ready to categorise a business in terms of operating and financial risks. The highest risk category is taken to be beyond 3.45 for both OL and FL. Other risk categories are then determined at a 50 decimal-point interval.

TABLE 20.7 Operating and Financial Risk Categorisation of a Business

	Risk Category					
	0 *Excellent*	*1* *Very Good*	*2* *Good*	*3* *Fair*	*4* *Doubtful*	*5* *Poor*
Operating risk (OL) (RI_O)	1.00–1.45	1.50–1.95	2.00–2.45	2.50–2.95	3.00–3.45	More than 3.45
Financial risk (FL) (RI_F)	1.00–1.45	1.50–1.95	2.00–2.45	2.50–2.95	3.00–3.45	More than 3.45
Converted Risk Index for both OL & FL $(CRI_{O/F})$	100–91	90–81	80–71	70–61	60–51	50 and below

Note: Both the Risk Indices $(RI_{O/L})$ are drawn on a scale with a class interval of 0.05. Hence, RIs falling between such a class interval should be approximated nearest to 0.05. For example, if an RI comes to 1.48, it should be taken as 1.50, and if it is 1.47, it should be approximated to 1.45.

Converted Risk Indexes (CRI) are calculated in the following manner:

$$CRI_{O/F} = 100 - 20 \, (RI_{O/F} - 1)$$

The risk indexes and risk categorisation are shown in Table 20.7.

Apparently, a FL of 1 and below could be considered safe, but this also indicates that the business might have lost most of its dynamism in as much as it has lost its capacity to take risks. A business grows only by taking risks; if it ceases to take risks, it might soon be dead by atrophy. It is much better then to put the money in gilt-edged securities than in business. Risk and return are two highly correlated variables. Risk rises with debt, but so also the returns. What is important, therefore, is to make a trade-off between the two, not to avoid debt altogether. A very low FL may satisfy a lender, but it may not satisfy the shareholders, because they may not get much of a return. They may soon desire the business to wind up.

This, however, is not true for OL. A low OL always means a low incidence of fixed costs relative to contribution, suggesting a high margin of safety to withstand shocks. The goal of modern day cost management is to maximise contribution and minimise fixed costs.

MEASUREMENT OF INDUSTRY RISK

Several studies, including a very elaborate one conducted by the Deutsche Bundesbank (German Federal Bank),[3] have revealed the significance of industry risk as an indicator of the default risk of a borrower. It has been observed that while under-capitalisation is the primary cause of default, the next most important cause is unfavourable sales (or order trends) of the industry to which the borrower belongs.

A lender should always keep in mind that it is the financially weak companies that become insolvent during a cyclically induced decline of the industry. The incidence of insolvency is high at the bottom of the boom phase and at the recovery phase from a recession. In the former case, labour costs and interest continue to remain unaltered or become high against a fall in sales, and in the latter case, firms are unable to support a rising demand for their products due to erosion of the capital base during reces-

---

[3] See the website of the bank at http://www. bundesbank.de under the head 'Publications'.

sion. It is important, therefore, to capture the cyclical trend in an industry to evaluate the lending risk.

Industry risk has two components: cyclical (short-term), and structural (long-term), but the two are not always aligned in the same direction. Both can diverge strongly at short notice and may change all the calculations of lending risks. It is important, therefore, to monitor at least the monthly movement of industry variables to locate any short-term cyclical trend. In developed nations, industry data are published monthly or even fortnightly. In India, such data are being made available in recent times though not in an organised manner, and often after a long delay, when these become dated for the immediate purpose at hand. What we intend to do, therefore, is to estimate the structural or long-term risks of various industry groups keeping in mind this limitation. We intend to keep the number of risk variables small and the techniques simple for easy installation of the system as an aid to credit managers in assessing the industry risk of a borrower. The following risk variables are selected from among the list of variables used by well-managed international banks, keeping in mind their suitability in Indian conditions and the availability of data.

Growth Rate of Value Added

It would have been better to take inflation-adjusted value-added data, but in the absence of a consistent long-term series, we are using value added at current prices. Value added is defined as profit before interest and taxes (PBIT), plus depreciation, plus salaries and wages. We have taken value added instead of sales to measure the growth of an industry, because the value added is the ultimate source of profit.

By this parameter we intend to find out whether the industry is growing or shrinking. Companies in growth industries are in a better position

than those operating in a shrinking market. In a growth cycle, competition is less intense and enterprises have better chances of increasing their sales, and can more easily achieve economies of scale. The contrary is true when an industry is in a downward cycle.

Volatility of the Value Added

Production volatility measures the degree to which production can be affected by demand fluctuations and related liquidity risks. Firms belonging to an industry characterised by a high degree of volatility usually suffer from lower capacity utilisation and higher adjustment costs. Volatility is measured (as before) by SD and CV.

Productivity of Labour

Generally, this is calculated as the change in value added per employee. But in India, the employment structure of all the industries is not available owing to the presence of large unorganised sectors in almost every industry. In the absence of consistent series of employee data, we may use data for salaries and wages as proxy. That is, we intend to find out how much value is added to the industry per Re 1 spent on salaries and wages. It has been observed that the sectors that have substantial scope for progress on productivity also have large potential for cutting costs.

Productivity of Capital Employed

This is a partial measure of the productivity of capital. The capital employed constitutes paid up capital, reserves and surpluses, debentures, and other long-term borrowings. The variable is derived as value added to capital employed. That is, how much value is added per Re 1 invested in capital.

By way of illustration we have used annual data for a ten-year period for ten industry groups to show how these four variables are calculated. As the number of companies in an industry continues to change year after year, an analyst should normalise the annual gross data by dividing it with the number of companies in the industry in that year. The relative data sets for a 10 year period are given in Tables 20.8 through 20.10.

METHODOLOGY AND RESULTS OF ANALYSES

Growth Rate of Value Added

For calculating cumulative growth of value added for different industries, we have used a geometric average growth model of the following type:

Growth (G) =

$$m\sqrt{\frac{P_1}{P_0} \times \frac{P_2}{P_1} \times \frac{P_3}{P_2} \times \frac{P_4}{P_3} \times \frac{P_5}{P_4} \cdots \frac{P_m}{P_{m-1}}} - 1$$

where, P_i = value added for ith year and
$i = 0, 1, 2, 3, \ldots m$
m = number of years for which growth rate is calculated

It may be seen that by cross-multiplication, all P_{m-1}, that is, the denominators get cancelled out excepting P_O, and all numerators get cancelled out except P_m. Hence, the formula can be simplified as below:

Growth (G) = $m\sqrt{\dfrac{P_m}{P_o}} - 1$

Let us explain this by calculating the growth rate of value added for the metal products (non-ferrous) industry. From the data in Table 20.8, we find the following:

Year	Value added
1 (P_o)	Rs 15.67 crores
10 (P_m)	Rs 45.75 crores
m = 9 years	

Hence, $G = 9\sqrt{\dfrac{45.75}{15.67}} - 1$

or, $G = 9\sqrt{2.919592} - 1$

or,

Log $G = \dfrac{Log\ 2.919592}{9} = \dfrac{0.4653221}{9} = 0.0517024$

or,   G = $antilog$ 0.0517024
or,   G = 1.1265 − 1 = 0.1265 or 12.65%

Note that the −1 will not form part of the calculation till the root function is calculated. It only helps in the calculation of the percentage.

In column 3 of Table 20.11 we present the cumulative growth of all the 10 industries calculated by this method.

Relative percentage marks in column 4 of Table 20.11 are calculated first by setting the percentage growth rate of the first rank holder at 100, thereby obtaining a factor which is then multiplied with the growth rate of other industries to determine their relative percentage marks. For example, the first rank holder in Table 20.11 has a growth rate of 15.61 per cent. Setting 15.61 = 100, we obtain the factor 100/15.61 = 6.406, which is then multiplied with the growth rate of other industries to obtain their relative percentage marks (ignoring decimals) as shown in column 4. The relative percentage will change with the change in rankings, which makes the system dynamic by periodical reviewing.

We may observe that the growth rate is the highest in the food and food products (excluding sugar) industry, closely followed by automobiles; it is the lowest in drugs and pharmaceuticals. But this does not tell the whole story. From a lender's point of view, we have to examine other parameters, the most important being the volatility of its output.

TABLE 20.8 Industry-group-wise Value Added Data (Average of Companies)

(Rs in crore)

Industry Group	Year									
	I	II	III	IV	V	VI	VII	VIII	IX	X
Automobile	58.45	66.09	72.45	87.00	107.20	111.67	125.33	148.17	163.50	214.60
Metal products (non-ferrous)	15.67	18.22	18.11	18.78	23.90	31.50	38.00	46.88	40.94	45.75
Metal products (ferrous)	18.42	21.69	19.09	20.09	26.63	23.39	23.41	29.77	44.21	47.96
Pulp, paper, and paper products	11.76	14.59	14.69	13.38	16.38	19.62	20.26	24.70	25.41	28.82
Rubber and rubber products	18.67	25.22	31.67	42.11	45.50	39.89	57.14	65.00	45.22	50.78
Machinery manufacturing	9.98	11.26	12.41	15.52	19.67	20.97	19.05	23.05	18.92	20.19
Electrical equipment	8.50	9.54	11.45	15.52	15.50	16.31	15.43	18.00	19.22	21.61
Drugs and pharmaceuticals	15.43	16.14	17.00	14.44	15.44	17.77	15.91	18.23	18.22	23.43
Food and food products (other than sugar)	16.82	16.36	16.25	19.08	20.58	29.17	21.00	22.68	46.88	62.04
Cement and cement products	25.40	27.80	26.36	28.18	30.11	30.83	46.20	62.53	55.73	57.27

TABLE 20.9 Industry-group-wise Capital Employed Data (Average of Companies)

(Rs in crore)

Industry Group	Year									
	I	II	III	IV	V	VI	VII	VIII	IX	X
Automobile	84.74	104.18	114.09	153.90	167.70	172.16	200.50	262.49	355.50	435.00
Metal products (non-ferrous)	25.33	27.55	37.56	42.66	46.50	56.42	109.58	127.40	109.31	145.82
Metal products (ferrous)	31.89	35.15	36.00	38.12	48.98	58.27	58.17	70.73	144.54	180.18
Pulp, paper, and paper products	27.06	30.11	34.69	37.63	45.31	39.91	42.60	54.21	70.23	86.05
Rubber and rubber products	33.56	41.67	42.11	54.45	63.26	58.44	86.00	116.86	119.78	134.11
Machinery manufacturing	16.88	19.89	22.96	27.56	31.43	36.30	30.64	39.37	34.96	45.77
Electrical equipment	11.23	12.21	16.41	27.56	21.09	22.10	27.54	31.87	30.24	49.13
Drugs and pharmaceuticals	18.00	19.72	23.29	22.67	26.11	28.53	23.82	27.96	32.87	48.22
Food and food products (other than sugar)	15.46	19.00	20.84	25.50	30.41	37.91	29.36	33.50	67.72	89.12
Cement and cement products	56.10	64.90	73.10	84.45	105.22	85.25	91.41	111.87	171.67	203.52

TABLE 20.10 Salaries and Wages (Average of Companies)

(Rs in crore)

Industry Group	I	II	III	IV	V	VI	VII	VIII	IX	X
Automobile	29.35	34.28	38.37	42.01	55.62	64.39	60.15	66.11	79.50	89.98
Metal products (non-ferrous)	7.16	9.68	10.76	9.64	9.89	12.15	10.25	13.90	9.70	12.50
Metal products (ferrous)	8.52	9.86	9.34	10.49	11.13	12.82	10.83	11.27	15.07	19.05
Pulp, paper, and paper products	5.30	5.42	5.96	7.02	7.15	8.91	7.68	6.85	9.12	9.60
Rubber and rubber products	10.09	11.16	12.00	14.05	15.38	18.26	19.46	25.24	15.56	15.49
Machinery manufacturing	4.90	5.66	6.24	7.09	8.90	11.38	11.19	8.96	7.56	8.07
Electrical equipment	4.82	5.39	6.29	7.05	8.14	9.11	8.85	7.70	13.78	15.79
Drugs and pharmaceuticals	9.82	8.20	9.40	9.93	8.92	8.28	8.72	7.98	7.95	10.20
Food and food products (other than sugar)	6.68	7.00	7.24	8.12	9.06	11.15	12.03	8.16	14.15	18.88
Cement and cement products	10.63	12.45	11.97	12.61	13.68	16.63	13.60	12.18	15.97	17.90

TABLE 20.11   Cumulative Growth Rate of Value Added of Industry Groups
Year I to X (Rank-wise)

Rank (1)	Name of Industry Group (2)	Growth Rate (%) (3)	Relative Percentage Marks (col. 3 × 6.406) (4)
1.	Food and food products (other than sugar)	15.61	100
2.	Automobiles	15.55	100
3.	Metal products (non-ferrous)	12.65	81
4.	Rubber and rubber products	11.76	75
5.	Metal products (ferrous)	11.22	72
6.	Electrical equipments	10.92	70
7.	Pulp, paper, and paper products	10.47	67
8.	Cement and cement products	9.45	61
9.	Machinery manufacturing	8.14	52
10.	Drugs and pharmaceuticals	4.75	30

Volatility of Value Added

This is estimated by calculating the arithmetic mean $(\bar{X})$, SD, and CV for each industry group in the manner discussed earlier. The calculations are given in Table 20.12.

Relative percentage marks for volatility measurement are awarded by a somewhat different method. As the first rank holder in Table 20.12 has the lowest CV (lowest risk), and the last rank holder has the highest CV (highest risk), we first take the reciprocal of the CV of the first rank holder. Then setting this reciprocal value at 100, we obtain a factor which is then multiplied with the reciprocals of the CV of other industries to determine their relative percentage marks. For example, the CV of the first rank holder in Table 20.12 is 13.99. Its reciprocal, $1/13.99 = 0.07148$. Now setting $0.07148 = 100$, we obtain the factor 1399, which is then multiplied with the reciprocals of CV of other industries to obtain their relative percentage marks as shown in column 6.

It may be seen that two industry groups—food and food products, and automobiles—which have registered the highest growth rate are also the highest in terms of volatility of value added. This led us to calculate the degree of association between these two variables, that is, between growth and volatility, by calculating coefficient of correlation (r) in the manner demonstrated in Chapter 13. 'r' is found to be 0.89, which is considerably high. It suggests that volatility (risk) is the condition of growth, though it creates problems for a banker. Historically, being conservative a banker prefers to invest in the least risky industries, but his profit motivation and desire to grow force him to stretch out to high-risk-high-return investment opportunities. Both these two phenomena are observable in the history of banking. In some periods, the risk profile of the banking industry came down so low that it necessitated government intervention to pull it up, while in some periods the risk appetite of bankers went so high that they put all their money in high growth/high risk sectors that ultimately resulted in massive bank failures. Prudence, therefore, demands a moderate approach towards generating a loan

TABLE 20.12   Industry Group-wise Mean, Standard Deviation, and Coefficient of Variation of Value Added (Ranked by lowest CV value)

Rank (1)	Name of Industry Group (2)	Arithmetic Mean (3)	Standard Deviation (4)	Coefficient of Variation (%) (5)	Relative Percentage Marks (1/col. 5 × 1399) (6)
1.	Drugs and pharmaceuticals	17.20	2.41	13.99	100
2.	Machinery manufacturing	17.10	4.28	25.00	56
3.	Electrical equipment	15.11	3.97	26.26	53
4.	Pulp, paper, and paper products	18.96	5.48	28.93	48
5.	Rubber and rubber products	42.12	13.40	31.81	44
6.	Cement and cement products	39.04	13.97	35.79	39
7.	Metal products (ferrous)	27.47	9.90	36.03	39
8.	Metal products (non-ferrous)	29.77	11.69	39.27	36
9.	Automobiles	115.45	46.62	40.38	35
10.	Food and food products (other than sugar)	27.09	14.56	53.74	26

portfolio, wherein return and risk are optimally spread.

Productivity of Labour

This is estimated first by calculating the ratio of value added to salaries and wages for each industry group. We then calculate the average growth rate of this ratio by the formula discussed earlier to arrive at the growth in the productivity of labour.

Industry group-wise ratios of value added to salaries and wages are calculated in Table 20.13. From this data set growth in the productivity of labour is calculated for industry groups. This is shown in Table 20.14.

Relative percentage marks are obtained in the same manner as in Table 20.11. Comparing Table 20.14 with Table 20.11, we find that the variation in ranking is very high in some cases. For example, while the food and food products industry group registered the highest growth rate in value added, immediately followed by automobiles, their ranks went down to 6 and 8

respectively in terms of productivity of labour. The worst performer in labour productivity is electrical equipment, which suffered a negative growth rate on this parameter, but it did not fare very badly with respect to value added. Since the variation is not so high in the case of other industry groups, we are not entitled to draw any general conclusion; still the belief that growth is *always* associated with the productivity of labour cannot also be upheld. The truth is brought out more sharply when we use value added as the numerator variable rather than sales, and salaries and wages as the denominator variable rather than the number of employees, as we have done here.

A manager is more interested in knowing how much value is added to the production, by spending say, Rs 1,000 on labour, rather than what the productivity of one employee engaged by the enterprise is. To him it is always the rupee investment that matters, whether in men or machines, and the return from that investment.

TABLE 20.13 Industry-group-wise Ratio of Value Added to Salaries and Wages (Average of Companies)

Industry Group	Year									
	I	II	III	IV	V	VI	VII	VIII	IX	X
Automobile	1.99	1.93	1.89	2.07	1.93	1.73	2.08	2.24	2.06	2.38
Metal products (non-ferrous)	2.19	1.88	1.68	1.95	2.42	2.59	3.71	3.37	4.22	3.66
Metal products (ferrous)	2.16	2.20	2.04	1.91	2.39	1.82	2.16	2.64	2.93	2.52
Pulp, paper, and paper products	2.22	2.69	2.46	1.91	2.29	2.20	2.64	3.61	2.79	3.00
Rubber and rubber products	1.85	2.26	2.64	3.00	2.96	2.18	2.94	2.58	2.91	3.28
Machinery manufacturing	2.04	1.99	1.99	2.19	2.21	1.84	1.70	2.57	2.50	2.50
Electrical equipment	1.76	1.77	1.82	2.20	1.90	1.79	1.74	2.34	1.39	1.37
Drugs and pharmaceuticals	1.57	1.97	1.81	1.45	1.73	2.15	1.82	2.28	2.29	2.30
Food and food products (other than sugar)	2.52	2.34	2.24	2.35	2.27	2.62	1.75	2.78	3.31	3.29
Cement and cement products	2.39	2.23	2.20	2.23	2.20	1.85	3.40	5.13	3.49	3.20

TABLE 20.14   Industry-Group-wise Growth in Productivity of Labour (Year I to X)
(Rank-wise)

Rank (1)	Industry Group (2)	Cumulative Growth Rate (%) (3)	Relative Percentage Marks (col. 3 × 15.244) (4)
1.	Rubber and rubber products	6.56	100
2.	Metal products (non-ferrous)	5.88	90
3.	Drugs and pharmaceuticals	4.31	66
4.	Pulp, paper, and paper products	3.41	52
5.	Cement and cement products	3.30	50
6.	Food and food products (other than sugar)	3.00	46
7.	Machinery manufacturing	2.31	35
8.	Automobiles	2.02	31
9.	Metal products (ferrous)	1.71	26
10.	Electrical equipments	(–) 2.78	(–) 42

Return on Capital Employed

As was said earlier, this is a partial estimate of the productivity of capital employed. While there is a convergence of opinions amongst economists in defining output as value added, there are considerable differences of opinion about what constitutes capital. These differences come into focus sharply while calculating the trend on capital/output ratio of an economy. Some researchers consider only fixed assets, while others include working capital as well in defining capital. For some, fixed assets are gross of depreciation, while for some others these are net of depreciation.[4] Without entering into this controversy, we can simply find out (as before) how much value has been added to the production by investing capital of Re 1 in the business. This is the major concern of a business, and this is the reason why this ratio is so popular amongst

entrepreneurs and enterprise managers. In Table 20.15 we have calculated value added to the capital employed ratio for all the ten industry groups. In Table 20.16, we present the average cumulative growth rate of productivity of the capital employed. Relative percentage marks are obtained in the same manner as in Table 20.12 for determining industry rank.

Table 20.16 indicates that none of the ten industry groups has shown a positive growth rate in the productivity of capital employed. The worst performer is metal products (ferrous), followed by metal products (non-ferrous). The 'best' among the 'worsts' are pulp, paper, and paper products and machinery manufacturing. The majority of the industries are capital-intensive. The two worst performers, ferrous and non-ferrous metal products are of the highest capital-intensity. It is often argued that industries with high capital intensity are not expected to show a high return on capital employed as compared to industries requiring low capital deployment. While there is some truth in this argument, this does not explain a negative growth

---

[4] See *Productivity in Indian Manufacturing*, Industrial Credit and Investment Corporation of India Ltd., Mumbai, 1994, for a number of studies made by various researches highlighting these differences.

TABLE 20.15   Industry-group-wise Ratio of Value Added to Capital Employed
(Average of Companies)

Industry Group	I	II	III	IV	V	VI	VII	VIII	IX	X
Automobile	0.6899	0.6344	0.6351	0.5653	0.6392	0.6486	0.6251	0.5644	0.4599	0.4933
Metal products (non-ferrous)	0.6184	0.6613	0.4822	0.4401	0.5140	0.5583	0.3468	0.3683	0.3745	0.3138
Metal products (ferrous)	0.5775	0.6174	0.5304	0.5268	0.5437	0.4013	0.4023	0.4209	0.3059	0.2662
Pulp, paper, and paper products	0.4348	0.4844	0.4234	0.3555	0.3614	0.4916	0.4755	0.4555	0.3618	0.3349
Rubber and rubber products	0.5563	0.6053	0.7520	0.7735	0.7194	0.6825	0.6645	0.5562	0.3776	0.3786
Machinery manufacturing	0.5909	0.5666	0.5404	0.5631	0.6260	0.5776	0.6219	0.5855	0.5416	0.4412
Electrical equipment	0.7570	0.7816	0.6981	0.5631	0.7348	0.7382	0.5602	0.5649	0.6355	0.4398
Drugs and pharmaceuticals	0.8571	0.8188	0.7301	0.6373	0.5915	0.6226	0.6679	0.6520	0.5542	0.4860
Food and food products (other than sugar)	1.0882	0.8612	0.7800	0.7484	0.6717	0.7692	0.7152	0.6771	0.6923	0.6961
Cement and cement products	0.4528	0.4284	0.3607	0.3337	0.2862	0.3617	0.5055	0.5590	0.3247	0.2814

TABLE 20.16   Industry Group-wise Cumulative Growth of Productivity of Capital Employed
(Rank-wise Ratio of Value Added to Capital Employed)

Rank (1)	Industry Group (2)	Cumulative Growth Rate (%) (3)	Relative Percentage Marks (1/col. 3 × 286) (ignoring signs) (4)
1.	Pulp, paper, and paper products	(–) 2.86	100
2.	Machinery manufacturing	(–) 3.19	90
3.	Automobiles	(–) 3.66	78
4.	Rubber and rubber products	(–) 4.19	68
5.	Food and food products (other than sugar)	(–) 4.84	59
6.	Cement and cement products	(–) 5.15	56
7.	Electrical equipments	(–) 5.85	49
8.	Drugs and pharmaceuticals	(–) 6.11	47
9.	Metal products (non-ferrous)	(–) 7.26	39
10.	Metal products (ferrous)	(–) 8.25	35

rate in the productivity of capital employed across all the ten industry groups that we have chosen to study.

The ten industry groups that we have chosen for analysis are by way of illustration only; they also do not represent the entire industrial structure of the country. Our findings are only incidental to the main purpose on hand. But they appear to be in conformity with the findings of more rigorous studies made on the productivity of labour and that of capital employed covering the entire industrial economy of the nation. For example, both the Ahluwalia[5] and ICICI[6] studies have observed that though labour productivity has been rising only moderately, the productivity of capital has been continuously declining.

[5] Ahluwalia, L.J., *Productivity and Growth in Indian Manufacturing*, Oxford University Press, New Delhi, 1991.

[6] Ibid.

INDUSTRY RISK CATEGORY

The reader must have observed that the parameters of four variables that we have chosen for an industry risk analysis do not together point to one direction of risk. For example, while a high growth rate in an industry minimises the risk of default, large volatility increases the risk (automobiles, food and food products etc.); both labour and capital productivity are found to be unmatched not only among themselves, but also with respect to the growth rate in value added, pointing to different directions of risk. There is nothing surprising about this; instead, here lies the beauty of this analysis. From a lender's point of view it is necessary now to assign relative weights to the parameters of the four variables for developing an optimum risk profile of industries.

A lender will obviously put major emphasis on volatility (because this makes the industry most unstable in debt-service commitments) followed by growth, capital productivity, and labour productivity in descending order. As against this, an individual enterprise may have a different order of emphasis: growth may be the first, followed by productivity of labour, and then of capital, while volatility may have the least relative emphasis. In Table 20.17, we have developed a risk index of industries by assigning different weights to the four variables.

Applying the weights assigned to the four risk variables, we have finally determined the risk profile of the 10 industries and developed a loan portfolio in Table 20.18. The method of determining the risk profile is explained in Table 20.19 through the illustration of the automobile industry.

Risk-adjusted values of different industry groups, as they appear in column 3 of Table 20.18, also enable us to determine a loan portfolio with optimum exposure to different industry groups. This is done by setting the total of column 3 at 100 and obtaining the factor $100/563 = 0.177$, which is then multiplied with the relative risk-adjusted values of different industry groups to determine the maximum exposure to any of the industry group in the loan portfolio of the lender (column 4).

BORROWER RISK

Borrower risk focuses on the promoters and management of an enterprise. In spite of the emergence of the fee-based banking school, lending still continues to be a relationship-based activity. Mutual confidence and clear understanding are the bases of good lending. Knowing a borrower means knowing him vis-à-vis his business. It has always been the combination of

TABLE 20.17   Relative Weights of Different Risk Variables

	Name of Variables	Weight (%)
1.	Growth rate of value added	25
2.	Volatility of value added	40
3.	Productivity of labour	15
4.	Productivity of capital employed	20
	Total	100

TABLE 20.18   Risk Profile of Different Industry Groups (Rank-wise) and Determination of Loan Portfolio

Rank (1)	Industry Group (2)	Risk-Profile (3)	Loan Portfolio Exposure (%) (col. 3 × 0.177) (4)
1.	Drugs and pharmaceuticals	67	12
2.	Rubber and rubber products	66	12
3.	Pulp, paper, and paper products	64	11
4.	Automobiles	60	11
5.	Machinery manufacturing	58	10
6.	Metal products (non-ferrous)	56	10
7.	Food and food products (other than sugar)	54	9
8.	Cement and cement products	50	9
9.	Metal products (ferrous)	45	8
10.	Electrical equipments	43	8
	Total	563	100

TABLE 20.19   Risk-Profile of Automobile Industry

Risk	Parameters (1)	Risk Weights (2)	Relative Percentage Marks (3)	Risk Adjusted Value (col. 3 × col. 2) (4)
1.	Growth rate of value added (Table 20.11)	0.25	100	25
2.	Volatility of value added (Table 20.12)	0.40	35	14
3.	Productivity of labour (Table 20.14)	0.15	31	05
4.	Productivity of capital employed (Table 20.16)	0.20	78	16
	Total	1.00	—	60

the five Cs—Character, Capacity, Capital, Condition, and Collateral—that make a prospective borrower creditworthy.

CHARACTER

Promoters/Directors

The business character of a borrower rests on such traits as honour, trustworthiness, and commitment. Good customers are basically the honest ones. The first of the Cs is always the character. It is ultimately the character that determines the creditworthiness of a borrower. How a borrower would respond to a real emergency when all the other Cs have turned bad is the real test of the character of a borrower. This is also the most difficult part of credit analyses, as it is predominantly judgemental. It is necessary, therefore, to probe into this most important of Cs in greater depth.

A good borrower is expected to maintain a code of conduct with regard to disclosing his business affairs to a banker. This may often go beyond the balance sheet and profit and loss account; losses can be hidden to face-lift a balance sheet, or profit can be suppressed to evade taxes. A banker would, however, question the integrity of the borrower if full disclosures are not made to *him*. Another code of conduct relates to the use of a fund by a borrower for the purpose for which it was lent. Not only that funds given for production purpose should not be used for consumption, but diversion of funds for some other purpose—may be, for another business venture—without the knowledge of a banker is equally questionable. Diversion of a working capital loan for fixed capital formation also falls within this ambit, though a negative net working capital is not viewed as seriously under modern day financial management as it was before. A borrower breaking these codes of conduct taints his business character, which may finally result in non-fulfilment of debt-service obligations.

An assessment of the integrity of a borrower is a vexed question for a credit appraiser, particularly when he is dealing with a first generation entrepreneur. For a corporate borrower subject to statutory audit and having past dealings with the bank, the question of integrity can be settled with a little more ease. But this is not so with a small borrower having no records of past dealings with any bank. A credit appraiser gropes in the dark to delve into the 'physical and mental state' of the prospective borrower. In Appendix 20.1, we have dealt with this typical problem in some depth. In what follows, we first make an attempt to lay down an 'approach to judge the integrity or character of a corporate borrower'.

Corporate Borrowers

In the earlier days of Indian banking, the identity of a borrowing company was of little importance to a bank; what mattered was the managing agency/house behind it. At one time, men of high business repute and acumen peopled these managing houses. Their creditworthiness as well as their business ability was also high. Banks would invariably take the guarantee of the agency managing the company. However, the managing agency system later came to disrepute and ultimately it was delinked from the management of companies. The vacuum was filled by a new generation of corporate entrepreneurs besides the existing big industrial and trading houses. Management of companies also got professionalised very fast in the face of stiff competition. All these require a systematic approach towards assessing the management of a company.

A corporate customer is represented by its board of directors, the chairperson being at the helm of affairs. The composition of the board has to be examined to see whether it is a diversified board. A truly professionalised board will have representatives from different broad areas of management—sales, production, and finance. The chairperson may have expertise in any of these areas, or he may be a professional in general management. Such professionalised boards, however, are not many in India, particularly in the private sector. Instead, we have boards of directors filled with entrepreneurs—who are more businesspersons than professional experts—connected with a number of units. There is nothing wrong in this, provided the lower hierarchy of management is filled with professional managers with the board laying down policies and giving general direction to the organisation. Entrepreneurs need not necessarily be good managers also: researches have shown that they are, in fact, not. However, successful entrepreneurs line up good managers to work for them. It is essential, therefore, that an entrepreneurial board has a diversified managerial structure below it.

If the directors are from established business families and connected with a number of industrial units, their business acumen can be judged by evaluating the success or failure stories of the units controlled by them. A good indication will be market quotations of shares of the units in which they are directors. A reference to their bankers may also help. Although these directors, being connected with a number of units, may be prone to diverting funds from one unit to the other (against which a banker must always be on guard), they also bring together a pool of experience in managing different units. This interconnectedness also helps in marketing products and buying inputs, because the finished products of one unit may often be the raw materials for another unit.

A banker should call for the following information from each director for analysis and record:

1. Name of the director.
2. Father's name (to know the family or house to which the director belongs).
3. Names of companies or firms wherein he is a director/partner or proprietor.
4. Business of these companies or firms.
5. Shareholding of the director in these companies or firms singly and with relatives.
6. Dividend declared or profit made by these companies or firms during the past three years.
7. EPS and present market quotations of the shares of these companies.

If necessary, this information can be verified easily by referring to published annual reports, referring to the share departments of these companies, and market quotations available from leading financial dailies.

In addition to these, a banker will, of course, obtain income tax and wealth tax returns of each director of an entrepreneurial board for the last three to five years to see whether his income and wealth are increasing or decreasing. At present, these returns are taken as a matter of routine to evaluate the creditworthiness of a director. A comparative analysis of these returns will indicate the ability of a director to prosper. Since his personal prosperity is directly related to the prosperity of the companies or firms where he has a controlling or managing interest, it may be taken as a safe indication of the prosperity or otherwise of these companies, and his business ability to direct them.

Management

For a corporate customer it is also necessary to look at the second tier of management that implements the policies laid down by the board. This tier of management must be broad-based, with professional managers heading broad functional areas like production, sales, and purchase, and a leader, or managing director, or general manager coordinating the departments. The bigger the unit, the larger will be the sub-divisions of various departments. The management team should be a balanced combination of the young and the old, experience and talent, to ensure continuation of the organisation's philosophy and to fill up the generation gap in management technology.

Particulars of managers—designation, remuneration, qualifications, age, and experience—are generally available from the published annual reports of a company or these may be called for. Analysis of these particulars will enable a credit appraiser to examine whether the criteria mentioned above are fulfilled or not.

Proprietary Corporates

Some corporate units, even though large, are still managed as proprietary concerns with sinecure nominee directors filling the board to conform to the requirements of law. In the face of fast professionalisation of business ventures, these concerns are found to lose ground in a competitive world. The 'old ways', howsoever effective in the 'good old days', can no longer rule the roost. These corporate customers are risky borrowers, because besides the professional handicap, the very continuation of the organisation is often at stake. The death of the proprietor-chairman may throw an organisation out of gear. The artisanal behaviour of the proprietor forbids grooming of the second line of management to take over the reins of the organisation. A banker assessing the credit proposal of such a corporate customer should insist on the appointment of professional managers in the organisation with proper delegation of authority. If this is not done, a banker will make an advance only at his peril.

A final word before we conclude our discourse on corporate customers. A banker can obtain valuable information from the auditors of a company, which is not revealed in their statutory report to the published annual account. This, however, requires prior authorisation by the company to the auditors for revealing information to a banker. It is not difficult to obtain this from a serious corporate borrower.

Capacity

The capacity to honour commitments depends upon the ability of a business to generate cash flows. Cash flows are often equated with profit after-tax, plus depreciation, and all other non-cash expenditure. But all the profit may not always be available in cash, because a part of it is blocked in current assets. It is not by profit that one can pay bills or repay loans, but only by cash. A company may have a level of profit, but at the same time, it may be technically insolvent, because it may not have enough cash to meet its obligations, the reason being the high level of current assets, where profits get blocked. Companies, particularly those on a high growth path, often miss this point. They are propelled by the rising level of profit. As a consequence, many well-known companies have been found to collapse because their capacity to pay did not increase, rather it fell with the rise in profits.[7] In times of steady sales growth, profit after-tax indicates more or less a realistic cash position of a business. But during the phase of faster growth the cash curve of an enterprise differs significantly from the profit curve, because of the increasing level of working capital items, which do not feature in the income statement of an enterprise but in the balance sheet. In fact, when the rate of growth is very rapid, both inventories and receivables may grow so fast as to absorb most of the cash accruing from profits. On the other hand, a business can frequently repay debts while operating without a profit (though it may not be able to do so for a long period as losses ultimately eat away the cash). A cash flow statement that measures the ability of a business to repay debt may often justify granting of a short-term credit to an unprofitable business.[8] High profit figures often give a disastrously euphoric feeling in the minds of corporate managers. But a lender is warned against sharing the same euphoria with the managers, because it is not the profitability but its cashability on which depends the repayment capacity of a borrower. If profit is the purpose of a business, cash is the condition of its survival.

In order to estimate the repayment capacity of a borrower, a lender should make a detailed cash flow analysis of the business as laid down in Chapter 14. Alternatively, if profit plus depreciation is used as a measure of the repayment capacity of a business, it must be qualified by an impact analysis of working capital items. A summary of cash flow position drawn in terms of accounting standard (AS 3) is available from published accounts of listed companies since 2001.

Capital

Capital is the net worth of a business. It provides a cushion to withstand shocks coming from adverse changes in external (economic, financial, legal, and so on) and internal (strikes, lock-outs, breakdown) environment of the business. Equity or net worth is, therefore, defined as the risk capital whose operational purpose is to absorb external and internal shocks, and its financial purpose is to insulate the outside liability holders from the impact of such shocks. Most of the outside liabilities contracted by a business have to be serviced by interest and pre-determined instalments. It is often dangerous to fail in servicing these obligations, hence the necessity to insulate them from shocks by providing a capital cushion.

The absolute amount of net worth remains meaningless to an analyst until it is compared with the volume of debt of an enterprise. The equity–debt ratio, or its reciprocal debt–equity ratio, indicates the extent of unencumbered capital available to a business, which not only provides a cushion against future losses, but also indicates the capacity of an enterprise to borrow additional funds, should such a necessity arise in the future to stave off an impending

[7] For detailed research findings on this phenomenon, see Bhattacharya, Hrishikes, *Total Management by Ratios—An Analytic Approach to Management Control and Stock Market Valuations,* (2nd edition), Sage Publications, New Delhi, 2007, Chapter 12.

[8] Robinson, Ronald. I., *The Management of Bank Funds,* (2nd edition), McGraw-Hill, New York, 1962.

liquidity crisis. Borrowing is a much better way of handling liquidity crises than selling of assets, as the latter sends panic signals to the market that has the snowballing effect of pushing a business faster to bankruptcy. A downward trend of the equity–debt ratio suggests that an enterprise is becoming more and more vulnerable to shocks.

Condition

As a banker deals with various businesses, he has first-hand information of the changing economic and financial environment in which a borrower operates. This enables him to judge the present and future condition of a business unit and take pre-emptive steps, which include advising a borrower to cut down or increase production well ahead of time. Earlier, we have provided a methodology to estimate the industry risk of a borrower in terms of volatility of sales, profitability, and productivity. Although it is true that these variables together ultimately reflect the condition of a business, some further elaboration is necessary.

Almost every industry suffers from some amount of cyclical fluctuations. At the downturn of a cycle, credits may be frozen, while in its upswing, there may be excessive fluctuations in loan volumes. It is important for a banker to know on which side of the cycle a borrowing unit is operating to enable him to adjust between the credit needs of the borrowers and the riskiness of the bank's fund.

There is also the problem of price fluctuations or rigidity, which are not necessarily related to cyclical fluctuations experienced by different industries. For example, industries that produce raw materials like metals and fuels, and durable goods like machine tools, automobiles, and farm equipment suffer from substantial cyclical demand fluctuations, but their prices are fairly stable. On the other hand, industries

in 'necessity' goods, food products, tobacco, and so on enjoy a high amount of stability during a cycle, but the prices of these products are often highly volatile.

Price fluctuations do not always exhibit symmetric behaviour at both ends of the market. For some industries, prices of raw materials may be highly unstable, while the prices of the finished products are relatively stable. These industries feel the greatest pinch when raw material prices go up. Their bottom line is affected because a hike in material costs cannot be passed on to the market. On the other hand, for some industries, the materials market may be stable, but the product market may suffer from instability. Thus, a decline in prices of the product hits the bottom line.

Obsolescence is another problem that industries suffer from. This is the highest in high growth industries. Product obsolescence, (for example, jute) may make an industry stagnant, while technological obsolescence increases the capital intensity of an industry, rendering many a marginal units to fall sick for want of capital needed for replacement of machines or software platforms.

Consideration of the competitive structure of a business has been receiving increased attention of credit analysts in recent times owing to liberalisation and globalisation of national economies. The competitive structure rests on three pillars: product, price, and cost. A borrower may be either a leader, or a follower in all or any of these pillars. An analysis of the competitive strength or weakness of an enterprise in any aspect of the competitive structure reveals the vulnerability of the business to the swings of the market.

Industries enjoying protection tend to be inefficient over a period of time. They are also highly vulnerable to foreign competition in a liberalised regime. Automobile and soft beverages industries of India are two such examples.

Collaterals

Before we discuss collaterals, a note of caution is necessary: collaterals should not drive lending decisions. *The best security of a lender is a thriving business. A credit appraiser should focus on the business more than the collaterals.*

The demand for collaterals as a condition for a loan is an indication that a borrower lacks the required level of creditworthiness. In fact, collaterals, whether as third party guarantees, or real estate mortgage, or a pledge of other financial or non-financial assets are meant to enhance the creditworthiness of the principal borrower.

The test of good collateral lies in its 'shiftability', which in other words, means saleability of assets: the higher the shiftability, the better the collaterals. From this point of view, real estate mortgages are the worst kind of collateral, while government or other gilt-edged securities are the best. The experience of banks all over the world since the mid-1970s negates the traditional belief of the lending community that real estate mortgage was the best form of security. It has been clearly demonstrated that the value of real estate falls drastically during a period of economic downturn. Immovables turn out to be really immovable in the market. This is not the case with dated government securities because with the fall in market interest rate during a cyclical downturn the value of these securities goes up.

In conclusion, we should point out that though collaterals do enhance the creditworthiness of a borrower, there should be a limit to its application. Credit enhancement should not be permitted for a borrower below a certain risk category.

LENDING DECISIONS BASED ON Cs

Out of these five Cs, character, capacity, and capital are the three most important variables for judging the creditworthiness of a borrower. 'Condition' is largely taken care of by the risk parameters developed earlier from an industry analysis, while 'collateral' is regarded predominantly as a means for credit-enhancement after determining a particular level of creditworthiness of a borrower.

Many researchers have developed decision trees based on the three major Cs, character, capacity, and capital in various combinations of which character occupies the first place, followed by the other two.[9] An eclectic presentation of these combinations to fit into our risk category scale is presented in Table 20.20.

COMPREHENSIVE BORROWER RISK ANALYSIS

In Appendix 20.2 we have presented a comprehensive questionnaire for assessing borrower risk. The questionnaire is self-explanatory. It incorporates an evaluation of the following four major aspects of a borrower and her/his business.

1. Evaluation of promoters and management.
2. Assessment of operational risks.
3. Evaluation of future prospects.
4. Financial evaluation.

The first draft of the questionnaire was developed by one of my PGP students working on a project under my supervision. Subsequently, the questions and the form of their presentation under different sections underwent changes to establish their veracity and determine the relative weights through intensive statistical tests. The questionnaire was perfected later by conducting both controlled and uncontrolled tests amongst 350 samples of respondents, divided equally between groups of business executives and loan managers.

---

[9] See for example, Smith, K.V., *Guide to Working Capital Management*, McGraw-Hill, New York, 1978.

TABLE 20.20   Decision Table for Lending Decisions Based on Character, Capacity, and Capital

Risk Category	Risk Character	Variables Capacity	Variables Capital	Converted Risk Index	Decision
0. Excellent	Strong	Strong	Strong	100–91	Accept-minimum control
1. Very good	Strong	Strong	Weak	90–81	Accept-moderate control
2. Good	Strong	Weak	Strong	80–71	Accept-tight control
3. Fair	Weak	Strong	Strong	70–61	Accept as the last option— tighter control and monitoring
4. Doubtful	Weak	Strong	Weak	60–51	Can be accepted under exceptional circumstances— continuous control and monitoring
5. Poor	Weak	Weak	Weak	50 and below	Reject

Administration of the Questionnaire

1. It is not necessary that the respondent must be well versed about the borrowing unit and its business. It is sufficient if he has a working knowledge of the borrower's business, has gone through some of the latest annual reports of the unit, and has some knowledge about the promoters and the managerial structure of the enterprise (which need not necessarily be personal knowledge—secondary sources will be sufficient for this purpose).

2. The questionnaire should be served on at least five randomly selected persons. It is unimportant whether any one or all of them belong to the borrowing organisation. In the latter case, objectivity will be ensured if the exercise is carried out confidentially, and the respondents are not required to sign the questionnaire.

3. Selected respondents should be asked not to consult each other while filling up the questionnaire.

4. The weighted scores so obtained from the respondents should be added and then averaged to determine the risk category of the prospective borrower.

DETERMINATION OF FINAL RISK CATEGORY

All the risk components of a business discussed so far are now summarised in Table 20.21.

It may be seen from Table 20.21 that all the risk indices, except industry risk, have ultimately been expressed along a 100 point scale by index conversion as explained while developing individual risk indices. The industry risk profile has not been so converted, firstly because it is already a product of quite a few such conversions, and secondly because a unit belonging to a particular industry group directly attracts the risk associated with the industry. Hence, while determining the final risk category of a borrowing unit, the risk profile score of the industry to which it belongs is added directly. As all the risk components are of equal importance to a lender in determining the credit risk of an enterprise, no additional weights are attached to them. Let us now explain the methodology of determining the final credit risk of a business with the example of a hypothetical

TABLE 20.21   Risk Components and Categorisation of Risks

| Risk Type | Risk Category | | | | | |
	0 Excellent	1 Very Good	2 Good	3 Fair	4 Doubtful	5 Poor
Sales Risk (Table 20.6)						
Risk Index	1–10	11–20	21–30	31–40	41–50	Below 50
Converted Risk Index	100–91	90–81	80–71	70–61	60–51	50 and below
Operating Risk (Table 20.7)						
Risk Index	1.00–1.45	1.50–1.95	2.00–2.45	2.50–2.95	3.00–3.45	More than 3.45
Converted Risk Index	100–91	90–81	80–71	70–61	60–51	50 and below
Financial Risk (Table 20.7)						
Risk Index	1.00–1.45	1.50–1.95	2.00–2.45	2.50–2.95	3.00–3.45	More than 3.45
Converted Risk Index	100–91	90–81	80–71	70–61	60–51	50 and below
Borrower Risk						
(a) *Based on 3 Cs (Table 20.20)*						
Direct Index	100–91	90–81	80–71	70–61	60–51	50 and below
(b) *Based on Questionnaire (Table 20.23)*						
Direct Index	100–91	90–81	80–71	70–61	60–51	50 and below

Industry Risk (Table 20.18) No separate Risk categorisation is made. Industry-Group's risk-profile score will be directly added with other scores.

enterprise belonging to the machinery manufacturing industry group, which has obtained index values for different types of risk as shown in Table 20.22.

The average risk index for our hypothetical firm being 75, we can place it under risk category 2, that is, 'good risk'.

INTEREST RATE DETERMINATION AND MARGIN REQUIREMENT

The magnitude of the riskiness of a business has a direct bearing on the rate of interest chargeable to a borrowing unit of a particular risk category. We have discussed earlier that a lender is entitled to charge a higher rate of interest for a riskier borrower. We have also explained that the rate of interest (risk premium) increases more than proportionately with the rise in risk. Based on these premises, we have developed the following model for interest rate determination of a risk borrower:

$$I_{Ri} = I_o \left[1 + \frac{10R_i}{95.5 - 10R_i} \right]$$

where,

I_{Ri} = Interest rate for i category of risk
I_o = Interest rate for lowest risk-category
R_i = Risk category of a borrower
i = 0, 1, 2, 3, 4, 5

Our hypothetical firm belongs to risk category 2. Assuming the best rate to be 11 per cent per annum, the risk adjusted interest rate (I_{Ri}) for the firm will be:

$$I_{Ri} = 11 \left(1 + \frac{10 \times 2}{95.5 - 10 \times 2} \right) = 13.91 \text{ say, } 14\%$$

TABLE 20.22 Determination of Final Risk-Category

Risk Type	Index Value of the Enterprise	Converted Index	Calculation of Converted Index
1. Sales risk	12	089	100 – (12–1)
2. Operating risk	2.75	065	100 – 20 (2.75–1)
3. Financial risk	1.35	093	100 – 20 (1.35–1)
Borrower Risk			
4. Based on 3Cs	—	075	No conversion required.
5. Based on questionnaire	—	070	–do–
6. Industry risk (machinery manufacturing) (see Table 20.18)	—	0<u>58</u>	–do–
Total		<u>450</u>	
Average Risk-Index = 450/6 = 75			

This model can also be modified to determine the margin requirements for a particular risk category of borrower. The same principle, as applicable to interest rate determination, will apply here also. That is, the margin requirement for a loan increases more than proportionately with the rise in the risk category of a borrower. The model for margin requirement can be put as:

$$M_{Ri} = M_o \left[1 + \frac{10R_i}{95.5 - 10R_i} \right]$$

where, M_{Ri} denotes margin requirement for i category of risk and M_o denotes minimum margin requirement for the lowest risk category borrower (risk category 0). If we take M_o as 25 per cent (which is a policy decision) the margin requirement for our hypothetical firm belonging to risk category 2 will be:

$$M_{Ri} = 25 \left[\left(1 + \frac{10 \times 2}{95.5 - 10 \times 2} \right) \right]$$

= 31.62, say 30%

When similar calculations are made to determine the risk-adjusted interest rates and margin requirements for other risk categories, it will be observed that the rates are more than proportionate among various risk categories to compensate for more-than-proportionate risk variations among them. In Table 20.23 we have presented by way of illustration, interest rates and margin requirements for different risk categories of borrowers.

TABLE 20.23 Interest Rates and Margin Requirements for Different Risk-Categories of Borrowers

(in percentage)

Risk Category	Interest Rate	Margin Requirement
0	11.00	25.00
1	12.28	27.92
3	16.03	36.45
4	18.93	43.01
5	23.10	52.47

Note: Both the interest rate and margin requirement can be approximated suitably in the appraisal note.

CONCLUDING REMARKS

It may be recalled that for demonstrating the methodology of measuring industry risk, we have analysed ten broad industry groups by way of illustration only. There are other industry groups, and within a group there are finer classifications. Finer classification of industry groups and the relevant data are available at http://mospi.nic.in/asi. A credit analyst is expected to extend his coverage by including some other groups, or all the groups of industries, depending upon the need of his organisation. He may also reconstruct the industry groupings by inducting or deleting any member industry in order to make his analysis more focused to the portfolio of industries that his organisation intends to concentrate on.

The weights assigned to various variables developed in this study are based on a conceptual understanding of the relative impact of these variables on the riskiness of an enterprise or an industry to which it belongs. The weights may change if the external economic environment undergoes substantial changes. It is not possible here to claim full objectivity in assigning different weights, which requires empirical testing of success and failure experiences of a lending organisation over a period. Although experience of failure is not a welcome experience for a lender, it helps a statistician to develop a model from past data by identifying discriminating variables that contribute to the riskiness of a business or an industry. In fact, if there are, say nine rating categories, there must be a sufficient number of default observations within *each* rating category—approximately 100 observations—to yield empirical estimates of the loss distributions that may be used with a high degree of confidence.[10] However, a credit manager cannot wait long for a model to develop from historical data. He must have a workable model at hand, though based on a conceptual understanding, which may be perfected later through a rigorous statistical investigation of the historical performance of various attributes. It must be pointed out that every lending organisation must develop its own model for risk measurement, be it conceptual or empirical. Many generalised empirical models have been developed by a number of researchers, but unfortunately these are yet to exhibit consistent behaviour in subsequent applications.

The last important point is that whatever weights are assigned to different risk variables, they should be held constant for a given period across all borrowers. During this period the weights should not be varied for subjective considerations, for example, to favour a particular borrower. If this consistency is upheld zealously, then even the subjective weights would gain objectivity in application.

---

[10] McAllister, Patrick, H. and John J. Mingo, 'Commercial Loan Risk Management, Credit-Scoring and Pricing: The Need for a Database', *The Journal of Commercial Lending*, May 1994.

Appendix 20.1

CHARACTERISTICS OF SMALL ENTERPRISES

While sufficient information can be had to assess a corporate borrower, little information is available for judging the ability of a small borrower. A banker faces the biggest problem in this area, which is still largely dark. The prospective borrower has no track record; probably no wealth tax or income tax return; no family history of any importance to his present venture, or any business connection of significance. He may be new in the business, probably a first-generation entrepreneur, or not at all an entrepreneur but has come to the business because he could not do anything else. He may not even know how to prepare a project proposal or fill up a bank's standard application form. On top of it, he may even be a cheat, out to have a nice time with the bank's money. It is natural for a bank manager to be stupefied while facing such prospective borrowers. And they are now coming in large numbers.

Prior to nationalisation, banks did not have any store of experience which could be handed down to the new batch of managers to handle this type of borrowers because banks hardly lent to small borrowers. Managers learnt by mistake, by trial and error and often at the cost of their careers. Some experience is gained in the process, which needs systematic collation for the benefit of the credit appraiser.

For this purpose the author undertook a research study some time back. Some of the findings of this research study as laid down below will enable the banker to assess and identify a potential entrepreneur.

An entrepreneur is a queer animal—a complex person who is not often understood by ordinary standards. Operating levels of entrepreneurs vary depending upon their need for achievement. Some are very successful in small ventures; some go for the medium scale, while a few end up creating industrial empires. A number of researches done in India and abroad reveal certain behavioural characteristics of entrepreneurs. In the course of his own research, the author verified some of these characteristics which are given below:[11]

1. An entrepreneur acts out of desire, and not out of necessity. He must be distinguished from an employment-seeker, who, being unable to obtain employment, is forced to enter business, particularly because bank finance is available.
2. He is a marathon runner, and does not settle for a hundred-metre race. This is the reason why he is often found to operate from a high-risk position. His business proposals may often appear to be unusual to the banker, who may shy away from advancing. A thorough scrutiny may, however, reveal the ingenuity of the proposal.
3. He is very active professionally, but lazy in his personal behaviour. This will be reflected by his casual dress, unkempt hair, and unpolished shoes. This casualness enables him to work even with minimal physical facilities and amidst many worldly constraints.
4. He is not a complaining child, but often a brooder. He seeks opportunity in crisis, hence does not complain.
5. He has a tendency to approach the top man of an organisation to get his job done, because he suffers from a feeling that intermediary levels will create obstructions for him. And alas, how true he often is!
6. He has a tendency to take up more than one job at a time to avoid the feeling of being in a void. We often find him talking of multiple products even before one product is successfully launched. It may be necessary for a banker to restrain him sometimes.

[11] Bhattacharya, Hrishikes, *Entrepreneur, Banker and Small-Scale Industry*, Deep and Deep Publishers, New Delhi, 1984.

7.   He acts and learns. The learning process may appear to be costly, particularly for a banker. But while financing an entrepreneurial project, the banker must be prepared to provide for this cost of learning.

8.   Normally, he may have requisite educational and technical qualifications, but he may not have a brilliant academic career. Being a marathon runner, brilliant academic attainments were never his objectives. In fact, the study has shown that brilliant persons hardly become successful entrepreneurs.

9.   He is hopeful about the future, and accepts responsibility for his failure without passing it on to others.

The characteristics stated above are general in nature. Not all the characteristics may be present in one individual entrepreneur. A combination of some of these characteristics may identify an entrepreneur. These general indications will help a banker to differentiate an entrepreneur from the swarm of borrowers.

Managerial Ability

The characteristics mentioned above create problems for the entrepreneur at the time of take-off. The first problem is that entrepreneurs, by their very nature, lack managerial ability by themselves. As mentioned while discussing corporate borrowers, they must have a tier of management below them in order to be successful in their ventures. This may not always be possible for a small entrepreneur with not much of capital to withstand general overheads to start with. In some cases of purely artisan entrepreneurs, the problem is more acute. Even if they have resources to carry initial managerial overheads, they would not like to appoint managers because of the fear of losing control—the worst mental fixation which destroys many entrepreneurial ventures. Bankers often face such entrepreneurs who would neither take on partners nor appoint managers, not even recruit an accountant, claiming that they themselves will be able to manage the 'tit-bits'! Bankers will do well to cut him to size *ab initio* and counsel him properly towards the necessity of taking on managerial hands or partners.

This is all the more important for a technologist entrepreneur and people of a 'scientific' type. Technologists generally have one-track mind. They are good at production. That is their area. In any discussion with the banker, it is observed that they go on talking endlessly about the products they can manufacture and often at the 'cheapest cost'. When the banker points out the marketing aspect, most of them will claim that 'because of the high quality of their product and the cheapest price, marketing will be no problem'! They will try to create an impression that buyers are waiting at their doorsteps with bags full of cash for their products to roll out of the factory, and pity the bank manager for giving such undue importance to such an unimportant aspect of the scheme! Having one-track minds, they do not know, alas that the market is not that benevolent, and their 'cheapest cost' often does not include growing overheads, incidence of excise duty and sales tax. Our research has revealed that the big majority of these entrepreneurs do not have any knowledge about the laws and rules relating to excise duty and sales tax. Most of them have not heard of the Factory Act and similar other legislations relating to management of labour and factories. Many of them do not know what are the licenses to be obtained from various statutory authorities that govern the establishment of factories producing various categories of goods.

Appendix 20.2

CREDIT RISK ANALYSIS QUESTIONNAIRE

Name of Segment Questions/Variables	Response and Score Value		
	1	2	3
I. Evaluation of promoters and management			
1. Experience of the promoters/ directors as businessmen	Not experienced at all	Not well experienced	Well experienced
2. Relationship among the promoters/directors	Bad	Moderately good	Good
3. Willingness of the promoters/ directors to bring in additional funds in case of necessity	Unwilling/unable	Not very sure	Willing and able
4. Attitude of the management	Not at all aggressive	Highly aggressive	Moderately aggressive
5. Meetings of the board of directors	Rarely held	Moderately regular	Regular
6. Composition of the board of directors	Promoters and their relatives only	Dominantly promoters and their relatives	Dominantly professionals and experts
7. Timely submission of data/ information to bank/ lending institutions	Irregular	Occasionally irregular	Regular
8. Audit qualifications of accounting reports	Serious qualifications	Minor qualifications	None qualifications
9. Loss of working hours	Too many	Moderate	Too few
10. Litigation cases pending against the promoters of the company	Too many	A few	None
II. Assessment of operational risk			
1. Present health of the enterprise	Already closed	On the verge of closure	Comfortable position
2. Raw materials supply	Irregular/interrupted	Moderately regular	Regular
3. Customers and market	Few customers and unsteady market	Few customers and steady market	Many customers and steady market
4. Competition	Tough	Moderate	Near-monopoly
5. Product viability	Becoming obsolete	No particular change	Becoming popular
6. Timely assessment of contingent liabilities	Not assessed regularly	Occasional assessment only	Regular assessment
7. Environmental status	Unsafe/unstable condition	Moderately safe and stable	Safe and stable

| Name of Segment | Response and Score Value | | |
Questions/Variables	1	2	3
8. Creditors—Are they thinking of stopping/calling up credits?	Many	A few	None
9. Chances of passing over of control	Exist	Exist moderately	Does not exist
10. Liquidity or working capital problems	Serious	Exist, but not out of control	Not so serous
11. Price of the product	Going against the company	Neutral to the company	Favouring the company
12. Repayment of loans	Already defaulted	May default	No default
13. Relationship with lending bankers	Poor	Moderately good	Good
III. *Evaluation of future prospects*			
1. Product development	Not keeping up well	Some attempts made	Keeping up well
2. Market and market share	No captive market; share low/falling	No captive market, but share high/increasing	Captive market
3. Selling and distribution network	Poor	Moderately good	Good
4. Customer confidence	Losing	No particular change	Gaining
5. Order book position	Insufficient orders	Moderately sufficient orders	Sufficient orders
6. Technology status	Obsolescent/not updated	Some attempts in updation	Modern/updated technology
7. Economic environment of the product(s) of the business	Recession	Normal demand	Boom
8. Expected change in govt policy affecting the business	Unfavourable change	No particular change	Favourable change
9. Possibility of any upward spurt in demand, say by exports	No possibility	May be possible	Just possible

IV. *Financial evaluation*

Trend of the following variables form the basis of financial evaluation of the business for determining the credit risks:

1. Sales
2. Net cash accruals (PAT + depreciation + all other non-cash expenditure)
3. Earnings per share (PAT – preference dividend/number of equity shares)
4. Net worth (share capital + reserves and surpluses – accumulated losses – fictitious assets)
5. Capacity utilisation (in percentage)
6. Turnover of assets (gross sales/total assets)
7. Equity to debt ratio (equity/debt)
8. Debt–service coverage ratio
9. Net profit ratio (PAT/gross sales)

Determining the character of the trend

Take the values of each variable in a time series and call them $X_1, X_2, X_3.........X_n$. Then calculate a ratio in the following manner:

$$\frac{x_1 + 2x_2 + 3x_3 + 4x_4 + 5x_5 \,.......... \, nx_n}{x_1 + x_2 + x_3 + x_4 + x_5 \,.......... \, x_n}$$

If the above ratio is less than $(n+1)/2$, then the trend is downward (decreasing); if it is more than $(n+1)/2$, then the trend is upward (increasing); if it is equal to $(n+1)/2$ then the trend is level. The score for each of the nine variables may be given now according to the following scheme.

Trend of the Financial Variables

	Downward	Level	Upward
Score	1	2	3

For example, let us assume that the sales of an organisation for the last 5 years were 150, 160, 147, 170, and 175 (the last one being the most current year).

The ratio works out to:

$$\frac{150 + (2 \times 160) + (3 \times 147) + (4 \times 170) + (5 \times 175)}{150 + 160 + 147 + 170 + 175} =$$ 2466/802 = 3.07 which is more than $(5+1)/2 = 3$, implying that the trend is upward, and hence it has a score of 3.

CREDIT RATING METHODOLOGY

Step 1

The score of each variable, as determined before, is now weighted according to the importance assigned to such variable, and a weighted score is obtained for each variable and the segment as below.

Weighting scheme and weighted scores

Name of Evaluation Segment	Question/ Variable No. (a)	Score Obtained (b)	Weight Assigned (c)	Weighted Score (col. b × col. c) (d)
I. Evaluation of promoters and management	1		5	
	2		6	
	3		6	
	4		5	
	5		3	
	6		4	
	7		3	
	8		1	
	9		4	
	10		2	
			39	A. Sub-total

Name of Evaluation Segment	Question/ Variable No. (a)	Score Obtained (b)	Weight Assigned (c)	Weighted Score (col. b × col. c) (d)
II. Assessment of operational risk	1		3	
	2		5	
	3		3	
	4		3	
	5		2	
	6		2	
	7		2	
	8		5	
	9		6	
	10		6	
	11		1	
	12		4	
	13		5	
			47	B. Sub-total
III. Evaluation of future prospects	1		4	
	2		2	
	3		4	
	4		4	
	5		6	
	6		5	
	7		2	
	8		2	
	9		5	
			34	C. Sub-total
IV. Financial evaluation	1		5	
	2		6	
	3		2	
	4		4	
	5		4	
	6		4	
	7		3	
	8		6	
	9		4	
			38	D. Sub-total
	Grand Total (A+B+C+D)		158	

Step II

Now add all the weighted scores of all the variables and obtain the total weighted score of the business (Grand Total, as above). Multiply the weighted score with the factor 0.2110 (see note1 below Table 20.24) to get the final score in percentage form. The business can now be graded in terms of credit risk as below (Table 20.24).

TABLE **20.24**   Borrower-Risk Categorisation

Final Score	Rating	Risk Category
100–91	Excellent	0
090–81	Very Good	1
080–71	Good	2
070–61	Fair	3
060–51	Doubtful	4
050 and below	Poor	5

Notes:

1. Derivation of the factor.

| | No. of Questions/ | Maximum Weighted Scores under Each Score Value | | |
| | | SCORE VALUE | | |
Weight Category	Variables	1	2	3
1	2	3	4	5
1	2	2	4	6
2	8	16	32	48
3	6	18	36	54
4	10	40	80	120
5	8	40	80	120
6	7	42	84	126
	41	158	316	474

The number of questions/variables as used in the questionnaire is counted against each weight category (1 to 6) and put in column 2. The maximum scores under each score value (1, 2, and 3) are calculated for each score value category column by multiplying the respective score value with the corresponding figures in columns 1 and 2. For example, maximum weighted score for weight category 5 against score value 3 will be, $5 * 8 * 3 = 120$.

It may be seen that the maximum score a business can obtain is 474 and the lowest is 158. Let 474 be 100. Hence, the multiplicative factor will $100/474 = 0.2110$.

2. This questionnaire can also be used for separate evaluation of each of the four evaluation segments by deriving a separate multiplicative factor for each such segment. One such is worked out below.

Evaluation of Promoters and Management

| | No. of Questions/ | Maximum Weighted Scores under Each Score Value | | |
| | | SCORE VALUE | | |
Weight Category	Variables	1	2	3
1	2	3	4	5
1	1	1	2	3
2	1	2	4	6
3	2	6	12	18
4	2	8	16	24
5	2	10	20	30
6	2	12	24	36
–	10	39	78	117

Hence, the multiplicative factor for this segment will be $100/117 = 0.8547$, which should be multiplied with the weighted scores obtained under this evaluation segment (sub-total A) to determine the rating for this evaluation segment.

Old ideas are prejudices, and new ones caprices.

—Dondan

Bibliography

Abiad, Abdul and Ashoka Mody, 'Financial Reform: What Shakes It? What Shapes It?', *American Economic Review*, March 2005, 95(1): 66–88.

Ahluwalia, L.J., *Productivity and Growth in Indian Manufacturing*, Oxford University Press, New Delhi, 1991.

Akerlof, George, 'The Market for Lemons: Qualitative Uncertainty and the Market Mechanism', *Quarterly Journal of Economics*, 1970, 84: 488–500.

Allen, F. and A.M. Santomero, 'The Theory of Financial Intermediation', *Journal of Banking & Finance*, 1997, 21: 1461–85.

Bank Administration Institute Foundation, *The Bank Director's Handbook*, Chicago, 1981.

Bank for International Settlements, *The Management of Banks' Off-balance Sheet Exposures: A Supervisory Perspective*, Basle, March 1986.

Barrios, Victor E. and Juan M. Blanco, 'The Effectiveness of Bank Capital Adequacy Regulation: A Theoretical and Empirical Approach', *Journal of Banking & Finance*, 2003, 27: 1935–58.

Basel Committee on Banking Supervision, 'New Capital Adequacy Framework', Basel, Switzerland, 1999.

Berger, Allen N., Richard J. Herring and Giorgio P. Szego, 'The Role of Capital in Financial Institutions', *Journal of Banking & Finance*, 1995, 19: 393–430.

Besanko, David and George Kanatas, 'The Regulation of Bank Capital: Do Capital Standards Promote Safety?', *Journal of Financial Intermediation*, 1996, 5: 160–83.

Bhattacharya, Sudipto and Anjan V. Thakor, 'Contemporary Banking Theory', *Journal of Financial Intermediation*, 1993, 3: 2–50.

Bhattacharya, Hrishikes, *Entrepreneur, Banker and Small-Scale Industry*, Deep and Deep Publishers, New Delhi, 1984.

———, 'Towards a Theory of the Value of Capital Goods—A Techno-Economic Approach', *Economic and Political Weekly*, 26 November 1988, pp. M134–9.

———, *Total Management by Ratios—An Analytic Approach to Management Control and Stock Market Valuations*, (2nd edition), Sage Publications, New Delhi, 2007.

———, *Working Capital Management: Strategies and Techniques*, (2nd edition), PHI Learning (P) Limited, New Delhi, 2009.

Blum, Jürg. 'Do Capital Adequacy Requirements Reduce Risks in Banking?', *Journal of Banking & Finance*, 1999, 23: 755–77.

Buser, Stephen A., Andrew H. Chen and Edward J. Kane, 'Federal Deposit Insurance, Regulatory Policy, and Optimal Bank Capital', *Journal of Finance*, March 1981, 35(1): 51–60.

Calomiris, Charles W. and Berry Wilson, 'Bank Capital and Portfolio Management: The 1930s "Capital Crunch" and the Scramble to Shed Risk', *Journal of Business*, 2004, 77(3): 421–55.

Cebenoyan, Sinan A. and Philip E. Strahan, 'Risk Management, Capital Structure and Lending at Banks', *Journal of Banking & Finance*, 2004, 28: 19–43.

Centre for Monitoring Indian Economy, *Corporate Finance: Industry Aggregates*, Bombay, November 1994.

Chakraborty, S.K., 'Management of Working Capital and Working Capital Concept', *Economic and Political Weekly*, 25 August 1973, Chapter 6.

Charles, J. Jacklin and Sudipto Bhattacharya, 'Distinguishing Panics and Information-Based Bank-Runs: Welfare and Policy Implications', *Journal of Political Economy*, 1988, 96: 568–92.

Chick, Victoria, 'Source of Finance, Recent Changes in Bank Behaviour and the Theory of Investment and Interests', in Philip Arestis (ed.), *Contemporary Issues in Money and Banking*, Macmillan Press, London, 1988.

Cooke, Peter, 'International Convergence of Capital Adequacy Measurement and Standards', in Edward P. M. Gardener (ed.), *The Future of Financial Systems and Services*, The Macmillan Press, London, 1990. Chapter 1.

Cooper, Russel and Thomas Ross, 'Bank Runs, Deposit Insurance, and Capital Requirements', *International Economic Review*, 2002, 43: 55–71

Crockett, A., 'Marrying the Micro- and Macro-Prudential Dimensions of Financial Stability', Speech Delivered at the Eleventh International Conference of Banking Supervisors, Basel, 2000.

Crosse, Howard D., *Management Policies for Commercial Banks*, Prentice-Hall, Englewood, New Jersey, 1962.

Daniel, W. Wayne and James C. Terrel, *Business Statistics for Management and Economics*, Miffin Company, Boston, MA, 1992.

Demirgüuc-Kund, Asli and Enrica Detragiache, 'Cross-country Empirical Studies of Systemic Bank Distress: A Survey', International Monetary Fund, Washington DC, IMF Working Paper, 05/96, 2005.

Diamond, Douglas W. and Philip H. Dybvig, 'Bank Runs, Deposit Insurance and Liquidity', *Journal of Political Economy*, 1983, 91(3): 401–19.

Diamond, Douglas W. and Raghuram G. Rajan, 'A Theory of Bank Capital', *Journal of Finance*, 2000, 55 (6): 2431–65.

Donahoo, K.K. and S. Shaffer, 'Capital Requirements and the Securitization Decision', *Quarterly Review of Economics and Business*, 1991, 31(4): 12–23.

Dowd, Kevin, 'Bank Capital Adequacy Versus Deposit Insurance', *Journal of Financial Services Research*, 2000, (17): 7–15.

Drabu, Haseeb, 'State Secrets', *The Money Manager*, *Business Standard*, 6 May 1996.

Economic Research Foundation, 'Economic Reforms and Rate of Saving', *Economic and Political Weekly*, 6–13 May 1995, pp. 1021–41.

Edwards, Ben, 'Let's Shuffle Those Loans', *Euromoney*, August 1995, pp. 22–6.

Estrella, Arturo, 'The Cyclical Behaviour of Optimal Bank Capita', *Journal of Banking & Finance*, 2004, 28: 1469–98.

Fahlenbrach, Rüdigar and Rene M. Stulz, 'Bank CEO Incentives and the Credit Crisis', National Bureau of Economic Research, Working Paper 15212, July 2009. Available at http://www.nber.org/papers/w15212.

Fama, Eugene F. and James D. Macbeth, 'Risk, Return and Equilibrium: Empirical Tests', *Journal of Political Economy*, 1973, (81): 607–36.

Federal Deposit Insurance Corporation (FDIC), 'Basel and the Evolution of Capital Regulation: Moving Forward, Looking Back', Federal Deposit Insurance Corporation, 2003. Available at http://www.fdic.gov/bank/analytical/fyi/2003.

Federal Reserve Bank of Cleveland, US, *Monthly Business Review*, September 1956.

Federal Reserve System, Board of Governors, 'The Supervisory Capital Assessment Program: Overview of Results', 2009. Available at http://www.federalreserve.govt.

Fisher, Donald E., and Ronald J. Jordan, *Security Analysis and Portfolio Management*, Prentice-Hall of India, New Delhi, 1994.

Flannery, Mark J. and Kasturi P. Rangan, 'What Caused the Bank Capital Build-up of the 1990?', FDIC Center for Financial Research, Working Paper, 2004-03, 2004.

Foulke, Roy A., *Financial Statement Analysis*, Prentice-Hall Inc., Englewood Cliffs, New Jersey, 1978.

Furlong, F.T. and M.C. Keeley, 'Capital Regulation and Bank Risk Taking: A Note', *Journal of Banking & Finance*, 1989, 13: 883–91.

——————, 'Reexamination of the Mean-Variance Analysis of Bank Capital Regulation', *Journal of Banking & Finance*, 1990, 14: 69–84.

Gardener, E.P.M. 'Innovation and New Structural Frontiers in Banking', in Philip Arêtes (ed.), *Contemporary Issues in Money and Banking: Essays in Honour of Stephen Frowen*, The Macmillan Press Ltd., London, 1988, pp. 7–27.

Gardner, V. F., *Profit Measurement and Control*, Macdonald and Co., UK, 1971.

Gennotte, G. and D. Pyle, 'Capital Controls and Bank Risk', *Journal of Banking & Finance*, 1991, 15: 805–24.

Gorton, Gary and George Pennacchi, 'Financial Intermediaries and Liquidity Creation', *Journal of Finance*, March 1990, 65 (1): 49–71.

Gorton, Gary and Richard Rosen, 'Corporate Control, Portfolio Choice, and the Decline of Banking', *Journal of Finance*, December 1995, 50 (5): 1377–1420.

Government of the United Kingdom, *Report of the Committee of Company Law Amendment (Cohen Report)*, London, June 1945. Available at *www.takeovers.gov.au*.

Greenworld, Bruce and Joseph Stiglitz, 'Information, Finance and Markets: The Architecture of Allocative Mechanism', Working Paper No. 3652, National Bureau of Economic Research, Cambridge, Mass, 1992.

Gurley, John and Edward Shaw, 'Financial Aspects of Economic Development', *American Economic Review*, September 1955, pp. 515–38.

Hakenes, Hendrick, 'Banks as Delegated Risk Managers', *Journal of Banking & Finance*, 2004, 28: 2399–2426.

Harris, Milton and Artur Raviv, 'Capital Structure and the Informational Role of Debt', *Journal of Finance*, June 1990, 65(2): 321–49.

——————, 'The Theory of Capital Structure', *Journal of Finance*, 1991, 66(1): 297–355.

Hector, Gary, *Breaking the Bank: The Decline of Bank America*, Little Brown & Company, New York, 1988.

Heinkel, Robert, 'A Theory of Capital Structure Relevance under Imperfect Information', *Journal of Finance*, 1982, 37(5): 1141–50.

Hellman, Thomas, Kevin C. Murdock and Joseph E. Stiglitz, 'Liberalization, Moral Hazard in Banking and Prudential Regulation: Are Capital Requirements Enough?', *American Economic Review*, 2000, 90: 147–65.

Hirshleifer, David and Anjan V. Thakor, 'Managerial Reputation, Project Choice and Debt', Anderson Graduate School of Management at UCLA, Working Paper, 1989, pp. 14–89.

Hoggarth, Glenn, Patricia Jackson and Erland Nier, 'Banking Crisis and the Design of Safety Nets', *Journal of Banking & Finance*, 2005, 29: 143–59.

Hovakimian, Armen and Edward J. Kane, 'Effectiveness of Capital Regulation at U.S. Commercial Banks, 1985–94', *Journal of Finance*, 2000, 55: 451–68.

Industrial Credit & Investment Corporation of India Ltd., *Productivity in Indian Manufacturing*, Bombay, 1994.

International Monetary Fund, *World Economic Outlook*, Washington, October 1994.

Jacoby, N.H. and R.J. Saulnier, *Business Finance and Banking*, National Bureau of Economic Research Study, Princeton University Press, Princeton, 1947.

Jones, David, 'Emerging Problems with the Basel Capital Accord: Regulatory Capital Arbitrage and Related Issues', *Journal of Banking & Finance*, 2000, 24: 35–58.

Kane, Edward J., 'Good Intentions and Unintended Evil: The Case against Selective Credit Allocation', *Journal of Money, Credit and Banking*, February 1977, 9: 55–69.

——————, 'Three Paradigms for the Role of Capitalization Requirements in Insured Financial Institutions', *Journal of Banking & Finance*, 1995, (19): 431–59.

Kashyap, Anil K., Raghuram G. Rajan and J.C. Stein, 'Banks as Liquidity Providers: An Explanation for the Coexistence of Lending and Deposit Taking', *Journal of Finance*, 2002, 57(1): 33–73.

Kerkhof, Joroen and Bertrand Melenberg, 'Backtesting for Risk-based Regulatory Capital', *Journal of Banking & Finance*, 2004, 28: 1845–65.

Kim, Wi Saeng and Eric H. Sorensen, 'Evidence on the Impact of the Agency Costs of Debt in Corporate Debt Policy', *Journal of Financial and Quantitative Analysis*, 1986, 21: 131–44.

Kim, D. and A.M. Santomero, 'Risk in Banking and Capital Regulation', *Journal of Finance*, 1988, 43: 1219–33.

Koch, Timothy W. and Scott S. Macdonald, *Bank Management*, Thomson Asia Pvt. Ltd., Singapore, 2004.

Kopecky, Kenneth J. and David VanHoose, 'A Model of the Monetary Sector with and without Binding Capital Requirements', *Journal of Banking & Finance*, 2004, 28: 633–46.

Kuhn, R.L. (ed.), *Mortgage and Asset Securitisation*, Dow-Jones, Irwin, Homewood, Illinois, 1990.

Levin, R.I., C. A. Kirkpatric, and D.S. Rubin, Quantitative Approaches to Management (5th edition), McGraw-Hill International, Tokyo, 1982.

Lindquist, Kjersti-Gro, 'Banks' Buffer Capital: How Important is Risk', *Journal of International Money and Finance*, 23: 495–513, 2004.

Matten, Chris, *Managing Bank Capital: Capital Allocation and Performance Measurement* (2nd edition), John Wiley & Sons Ltd., West Sussex, UK, 2001.

McAllister, Patrick H. and John J. Mingo, 'Commercial Loan Risk Management, Credit-Scoring and Pricing: The Need for a Database', *The Journal of Commercial Lending*, May 1994, pp. 6–21.

Merton, R.C., 'Financial Innovation and the Management and Regulation of Financial Institutions', *Journal of Banking & Finance*, 19: 161 81, 1995.

————, 'An Analytic Derivation of the Cost of Deposit Insurance Loan Guarantees', *Journal of Banking & Finance*, 1977, 2: 3–11.

Miller, Merton H., 'Do the M&M Propositions Apply to Banks?', *Journal of Banking & Finance*, 1995, 19: 483–89.

Morrison, Allan D. and Lucy White, 'Crisis and Capital Requirements in Banking', *American Economic Review*, 2005, 95(5): 1548–72.

Myers, Stewart C. and Nicholas S. Majluf, 'Corporate Financing and Investment Decisions when Firms have Information that Investors Do Not Have', *Journal of Financial Economics*, 1984, 13: 187–221.

Norman, Draper R. and Harry Smith, *Applied Regression Analysis* (2nd edition), John Wiley & Sons Inc., New York, 1981.

Ostry, J.D., and C.M. Reinhart, 'Savings and Real Interest Rates in Developing Countries', *Finance & Development*, December 1995, pp. 16–19.

Park, C. and J.W. Gladson, *Working Capital*, The Macmillan Co., New York, 1963.

Park, Sangkyun and Stavros Peristiani, 'Are Bank Shareholders Enemies of Regulators or a Potential Source of Market Discipline?', *Journal of Banking & Finance*, 2007, 31: 2493–2515.

Pauls, Calem and Michael Lacour-Little, 'Risk-based Capital Requirements for Mortgage Loans', *Journal of Banking & Finance*, 2004, 28: 647–72.

Ramamurthy, V. E., *Working Capital Management*, Institute for Financial Management and Research, Chennai, 1976.

Ravid, S. Abraham and Oded H. Sarig, 'Financial Signalling by Precommitting to Cash Flows', The State University of New Jersey, Rutgers, Working Paper, 1989.

Reed, W. Edward and Edward K. Gill, *Commercial Banking* (4th edition), Prentice-Hall International, Englewood Cliffs, New Jersey, 1989.

Reichert, Alan. K., 'A Comparison of Commercial Bank, Thrift and Mortgage Bank Real Estate Lending Activity', *Journal of Business Finance and Accounting*, June 1991, 593–607.

Reserve Bank of India, *Report of the Study Group to Frame Guidelines for Follow-Up of Bank Credit*, Bombay, 1975.

————, *Report of the Committee on the Financial System*, November, 1991.

————, *Report of the Working Group on Cash Credit System*, Bombay, 1993.

————, 'Indian Financial System: The Emerging Horizon', *RBI Bulletin*, May 1994.

————, *Report of the Expert Group on Credit-Deposit Ratio of Banks*, 2005. Available at www.rbidocs.org.in.

Robinson, Ronald, I., *The Management of Bank Funds* (2nd edition), McGraw-Hill, New York, 1962.

Rochet, Jean-Charles, 'Capital Requirements and Behavior of Banks', *European Economic Review*, 1992, 36(5): 1137–78.

Rodkey, Robert G., *Sound Policies for Bank Management*, The Ronald Press, New York, 1944.

Ross, Stephen, 'The Determination of Financial Structure: The Incentive Signaling Approach', *Bell Journal of Economics*, 1977, 8: 23–40.

Saidenberg, M.R. and P.E. Strahan, 'Are Banks Important for Financing Large Businesses?', *Current Issues in Economics and Finance*, 1999, 5(12): 1–6.

Santomero, Anthony M. and Ronald D. Watson, 'Determining an Optimal Capital Standard for the Banking Industry', *Journal of Finance*, September 1977, 32(4): 1267–82.

Santos, João, 'Bank Capital and Equity Investment Regulations', *Journal of Banking & Finance*, 1999, 23: 1095–1120.

Sarig, Oded H., 'Bargaining with a Corporation and the Capital Structure of the Bargaining Firm', Tel Aviv University, Working Paper, 1988.

Saunders, A. *Financial Institutions Management*, McGraw-Hill, New York, 2000.

Schaeck, Kalus, Cihak Martin and Simon Wolfe, 'Are Competitive Banking Systems More Stable?', *Journal of Money, Credit and Banking*, 2009, 41(4): 711–34.

Schmidt, R.H., A. Hackethal, and M. Tyrell, 'Disintermediation and the Role of Banks in Europe: An International Comparison', *Journal of Financial Intermediation*, 1999, 8: 36–67.

Scholtens, Bert and Dic van Wensveen, 'A Critique on the Theory of Financial Intermediation', *Journal of Banking & Finance*, 2000, 24: 1243–51.

Securities and Exchange Board of India, *Substantial Acquisition of Shares and Takeovers Regulations*, Bombay, 1996.

Sengupta, Arjun, 'Financial Sector and Economic Reforms in India', *Economic and Political Weekly*, 7 January 1995, pp. 39–44.

Smith, K.V., *Guide to Working Capital Management*, McGraw-Hill, New York, 1978.

Stancill, J.M., 'When is the Cash in Cashflow?', *Harvard Business Review*, March–April 1987, pp. 38–52.

Stigilitz, Joseph and Andrew Weiss, 'Credit Rationing in Markets with Imperfect Information', *American Economic Review*, June 1981, pp. 393–410.

Thomson, J.B., 'Predicting Bank Failures in 1980s', *Federal Reserve Bank of Cleveland Economic Review*, 1991, 27(1): 9–20.

VanHoose, David, 'Theories of Bank Behavior under Capital Regulation', *Journal of Banking & Finance*, 2007, 31: 3680–97.

Vietor, R.H.K., 'Bank of America and Deregulation: The Great Turnaround', in S.L. Hayes III (ed.), *Financial Services*, Harvard Business School Press, Boston, Massachusetts, 1993, pp. 1–34.

Wood, J.H., *Commercial Bank Loan and Investment Behaviour*, John Wiley & Sons, London, 1975.

World Bank, *Adjustment Policy Research Report*. Oxford University Press, New York, 1994.

Index